GARLAND MEDIEVAL BIBLIOGRAPHIES
VOL. 14

BEOWULF SCHOLARSHIP

GARLAND REFERENCE LIBRARY
OF THE HUMANITIES
(VOL. 1422)

GARLAND MEDIEVAL BIBLIOGRAPHIES

EUROPE IN TRANSITION
A Select, Annotated Bibliography of the Twelfth-Century Renaissance
Chris D. Ferguson

FRANÇOIS VILLON
A Bibliography
Robert D. Peckham

MEDIEVAL SEXUALITY
A Research Guide
Joyce E. Salisbury

WAR IN THE MIDDLE AGES
A Bibliographic Guide
Everett U. Crosby

THE MEDIEVAL CONSOLATION OF PHILOSOPHY
An Annotated Bibliography
Noel Harold Kaylor, Jr.

THE ROMAN DE LA ROSE
An Annotated Bibliography
Heather M. Arden

GIOVANNI BOCCACCIO
An Annotated Bibliography
Joseph P. Consoli

ROGER BACON
An Annotated Bibliography
Jeremiah Hackett

MEDIEVAL VISIONS OF HEAVEN AND HELL
A Sourcebook
Eileen Gardiner

SPORTS AND GAMES OF THE MIDDLE AGES
John Marshall Carter

SIR GAWAIN AND THE GREEN KNIGHT
An Annotated Bibliography 1978–1989
Meg Stainsby

BEOWULF SCHOLARSHIP
An Annotated Bibliography 1979-1990
Robert J. Hasenfratz

THE MEDIEVAL CHARLEMAGNE LEGEND
An Annotated Bibliography
Susan E. Farrier. Dutch materials treated by Geert H. M. Claassens

PILGRIMAGE IN THE MIDDLE AGES
A Research Guide
Linda Kay Davidson and Maryjane Dunn-Wood

BEOWULF SCHOLARSHIP

An Annotated Bibliography, 1979–1990

Robert J. Hasenfratz

GARLAND PUBLISHING, INC.
New York & London / 1993

Copyright © 1993 Robert J. Hasenfratz
All rights reserved

Library of Congress Cataloging-in-Publication Data

Hasenfratz, Robert J., 1957–
 Beowulf scholarship : an annotated bibliography, 1979–1990 / Robert J. Hasenfratz.
  p. cm. — (Garland medieval bibliographies ; vol. 14) (Garland reference library of the humanities ; vol. 1422)
 A continuation of Douglas D. Short's Beowulf scholarship.
 Includes indexes.
 ISBN 0–8153–0084–0 (acid-free paper)
 1. Beowulf—Bibliography. 2. Epic poetry, English (Old)—History and criticism—Bibliography. I. Short, Douglas D. Beowulf scholarship. II. Title. III. Series. IV. Series: Garland reference library of the humanities ; vol. 1422.
Z2012.H23 1993
[PR1585]
016.829'3—dc20   93-17683
                                         CIP

Printed on acid-free, 250-year-life paper
Manufactured in the United States of America

CONTENTS

Preface vii
   Acknowledgments ix
   Abbreviations xi

Beowulf Scholarship
   Pre-1979 3
   1979 9
   1980 39
   1981 71
   1982 109
   1983 148
   1984 177
   1985 207
   1986 233
   1987 267
   1988 295
   1989 317
   1990 347

Indexes
   Author Index 373
   Subject Index 383
   Word Index 403
   Line Index 409

PREFACE

This volume is a continuation of Douglas D. Short's *'Beowulf' Scholarship: An Annotated Bibliography* (a selective listing of scholarship from 1705 through 1949 and an exhaustive one for the years 1950 through 1978).

Coverage. The present bibliography covers the years 1979 through 1990 as exhaustively as possible, providing detailed summaries along with author, subject, word, and line indices. Dissertations on *Beowulf* are not included, for which *Dissertation Abstracts International* and Philip Pulsiano's *An Annotated Bibliography of North American Doctoral Dissertations on Old English Language and Literature* should be consulted.

Purpose. The intent of this volume remains much the same as Short's, to assist students and scholars in searching through a considerable body of scholarship by providing convenient summaries of a decade's worth of books and articles on *Beowulf* and offering a number of detailed indices to accommodate various research strategies.

Format and Arrangement. As in Short's bibliography, entries are arranged chronologically by year and listed alphabetically by authors' names within each year.

Authors' names have been regularized as far as possible.

Abbreviations have been held to a minimum in order to make the volume easier to use; a list of them for periodicals and book collections follows this preface. The entries for book collections now include a list of contents (by their corresponding item numbers) as well as book reviews. Abbreviations contained in book review references follow the standard *MLA* format.

Vowel length is marked within the summaries, though not in titles.

Cross references appear in square brackets, with a preceding *S* indicating an item in Short and an *F* indicating an item in Donald K. Fry's bibliography, *Beowulf and the Fight at Finnsburh: A Bibliography* [S704]. Routine references to previous scholarship are not cross-referenced, though attacks, replies, and corroborating arguments are.

Summaries followed by initials are based on abstracts provided by various Japanese scholars, an effort coordinated by Tadao Kubouchi.

For *translations* of the poem a short sample passage (usually lines 4-11) is reproduced. This section was chosen because of its accessibility as well as for the problems it presents to the translator: emendations (l. 6a), kennings (l. 10a), and various formulas (ll. 8a, 11b, etc.). Users of this bibliography should be able to form some preliminary judgments about the nature of a particular translation from these uniform sample passages.

Book reviews are listed as comprehensively as possible, though reviews for book collections may be less complete. Authors of book reviews appear in the author index with an *(r)* following the item number of the work reviewed. Users may also wish to consult the excellent reviews of articles and books in the *Old English Newsletter* (OEN) and the *Year's Work in English Studies* (YWES), though these are not listed here.

The subject index retains the general shape and terminology of Short's index, though for convenience some headings have been altered and redistributed. References to individual words are now collected in a separate *word index* which follows the subject listing.

The line index refers users to discussions of particular lines and sections. In general, items included in this index offer either suggestions for textual emendation or interpretations of grammar and syntax. Items covered to a lesser extent include those focusing on literary and stylistic analysis. In most cases, the indexing is more complete for articles than for books, although line indices from individual books have been incorporated into this index, which also covers all items in Short. Thus, the present line index includes comprehensive coverage from 1950 through 1990. Fry's line index [S704] should be consulted for complete references before 1950.

Acknowledgments. I am grateful for the labors of a number of dedicated bibliographers, especially Carl T. Berkhout and the reviewers for the *Year's Work in Old English Studies* (in the *OEN*), without whose efforts my task would have been much more complicated and less complete. My thanks go to Professor Berkhout for having provided advance versions of the *OEN* bibliography as well as to William Schipper for help in arranging abstracts for Japanese materials, an effort graciously coordinated by Tadao Kubouchi of the University of Tokyo, as well as to Haruko Momma for providing copies of Japanese articles. Special thanks to Robert Vrekenac and his staff at the interlibrary loan department of the University of Connecticut's Homer Babbidge Library for their inexhaustible patience, professionalism, and good humor in the face of my avalanche of interlibrary loan requests for *Beowulf* materials. The University of Connecticut's Research Foundation provided consistent and generous support for the project. To my many helpers--Steve Guglielmi, Lisa Houlihan, Eric Schwab, Chris Fee, Kim Freeman--thanks, it's all over now, guys. You can rest. Finally, my heart-felt gratitude goes to friends (Randy, Allison, Brian, Donna, Billy and Lila) and family (Wayne, Nancy, Sally, and Ann) for keeping me sane throughout this project.

Bob Hasenfratz

University of Connecticut
Storrs, Connecticut

ABBREVIATIONS

PERIODICALS

ABR	*American Benedictine Review*
AIUON	*Annali dell'Istituto Universitario Orientali (Napoli)*
AN&Q	*American Notes and Queries*
Archiv	*Archiv für das Studium der neueren Sprachen und Literaturen (Halle)*
ASE	*Anglo-Saxon England*
ChauR	*Chaucer Review*
ELN	*English Language Notes*
ES	*English Studies*
ESC	*English Studies in Canada*
JEGP	*Journal of English and Germanic Philology*
MÆ	*Medium Ævum*
MLQ	*Modern Language Quarterly*

MLR	*Modern Language Review*
MP	*Modern Philology*
N&Q	*Notes and Queries*
Neophil	*Neophilologus*
NM	*Neuphilologische Mitteilungen*
NMS	*Nottingham Mediaeval Studies*
OEN	*Old English Newsletter*
PLL	*Papers on Language and Literature*
PMLA	*Publications of the Modern Language Association*
PQ	*Philological Quarterly*
REAL	*Yearbook of Research in English and American Literature*
RES	*Review of English Studies*
SN	*Studia Neophilologia*
SP	*Studies in Philology*
TSLL	*Texas Studies in Literature and Language*
YWES	*Year's Work in English Studies*
YWOES	*Year's Work in Old English Studies*
ZDA	*Zeitschrift für deutsches Altertum und deutsche Literatur*

Abbreviations   xiii

ZDP   *Zeitschrift für deutsche Philologie*

COLLECTIONS

Beowulfian Scansion   *Approaches to Beowulfian Scansion.* Ed. Alain Renoir and Ann Hernández. Old English Colloquium Series, 1. Berkeley: Dept. of English, U of California, 1982. Contains Creed [1305], Foley [1311], Frese [1314], Hernández [1327], Lehmann [1343], and Renoir [1357].

Reviews: D.C. Baker, *ELN* 21 (1984): 60-63; J.C. Pope, *Speculum* 59 (1984): 433-37.

Clemoes   *Literature and Learning in Anglo-Saxon England: Studies Presented to Peter Clemoes on the Occasion of his Sixty-Fifth Birthday.* Ed. Michael Lapidge and Helmut Gneuss. Cambridge: Cambridge UP, 1985. Contains Bately [1476] and Greenfield [1488].

Reviews: D. Corner, *EHR* 101 (1986): 927-30; P. Godman, *TLS* 10 Jan., 1986: 46; P. Lendinara, *Schede medievali* 10 (1986): 205-09; B. Mitchell, *RES* 37 (1986): 550-51; P. V[erbraken], *RB* 96 (1986): 195-96; M. Budny, *History Today*, Feb. 1987: 57-58; R. Frank, *U of Toronto Quarterly* 56 (1987): 461-63; H. Mayr-Harting, *JTS* 38 (1987): 548-49; A. Bammesberger, *Anglia* 106 (1988): 198-200; T. Reuter, *DAEM* 44 (1988): 196-97; J.B. Trahern, Jr. *JEGP* 87 (1988): 433-37; H. Sauer, *BGDSL* 112 (1990): 461-64.

Dating of Beowulf	*The Dating of 'Beowulf.'* Ed. Colin Chase. Toronto Old English Series, no. 6. Toronto: U of Toronto Press in association with the Center for Medieval Studies, U of Toronto, 1981. Contains Chase [1233], Kiernan [1262], Boyle [1228], Cameron, et al. [1232], Cable [1230], Goffart [1251], Murray [1268], Page [1274], Frank [1249], McTurk [1266], Chase [1233], Clemoes [1237], Pope [1275], and Stanley [1285].
Reviews: T.M. Andersson, *U of Toronto Quarterly* 52 (1983): 288-301; H. Fujiwara, *Studies in English Literature* (Tokyo) 60 (1983): 189-92; Fulk [1315]; A.A. Lee, *English Studies in Canada* 9 (1983): 307-08. G.P. Braccini, *AIUON, filologia germanica* 25 (1984): 251-58; N. Jacobs, *MÆ* 53 (1984): 117-20; E. Stieg, *Canadian Book Review Annual, 1981*; 202-03; Joseph B. Trahern, Jr., *JEGP* 83 (1984): 107-12.
Donaldson	*Acts of Interpretation: The Text in Its Contexts, 700-1600: Essays on Medieval and Renaissance Literature in Honor of E. Talbot Donaldson.* Ed. Mary J. Carruthers and Elizabeth D. Kirk. Norman, OK: Pilgrim, 1982. Contains Irving [1332], Pope [1354], and Stanley [1363].
Greenfield	*Modes of Interpretation in Old English Literature: Studies in Honour of Stanley B. Greenfield.* Ed. Phyllis Rugg Brown, Georgia Ronan Crampton, and Fred C. Robinson. Toronto: U of Toronto P, 1986. Contains Calder [1534], Clemoes [1537], Frank [1548], and Pope [1575].

Reviews: K. Schoening, *Comitatus* 18 (1987): 103-05; P.A. Thompson, *U of Toronto Quarterly* 57 (1987): 100-01; J. Roberts, *N&Q* 35 (1988): 202-03; D.G. Scragg, *RES* 39 (1988): 277-78; N.F. Blake, *MLR* 84 (1989): 912-13; J. Hill, *Anglia* 107 (1989): 512-13; M.A.L. Locherbie-Cameron, *MÆ* 58 (1989): 139-40.

Hero and Exile   Stanley B. Greenfield, *Hero and Exile: The Art of Old English Poetry.* Ed. George H. Brown. London: Hambledon P, 1989. Reprints Greenfield [S470, S493, S581, S914, S994, 1125, 1319, and 1488].

Reviews: H. O'Donoghue, *RES* 42 (1991): 240-41; E.G. Stanley, *N&Q* 38 (1991): 141-42.

Jones   *Saints, Scholars and Heroes: Studies in Medieval Culture in Honour of Charles W. Jones.* Ed. Margot H. King and Wesley M. Stevens. 2 Vols. Collegeville, MN: Hill Monastic Manuscript Library, St. John's Abbey and U, 1979. Contains: Bolton [1108], Crépin [1115], Greenfield [1125], and Ogilvy [1144].

Reviews: B. de Gaiffier, *AB* 99(1981): 187-88; P. Godman, *JEH* 32 (1981): 552-53; D. Pezzini, *Aevum* 56 (1982): 282-84; N.P. Brooks, *EHR* 98 (1983): 181-82; M.R. Godden, *RES* 34 (1983): 321-23.

Kaske   *Magister Regis: Studies in Honor of Robert Earl Kaske.* Ed. Arthur Groos. New York: Fordham UP, 1986. Contains: Bloomfield [1532] and Hill [1560].

	Reviews: H. Sauer, *Anglia* 107 (1989): 134-35.
Literary Perspectives	*Literary and Historical Perspectives of the Middle Ages.* Ed. Patricia W. Cummins, Patrick W. Connor, and Charles W. Connell. Morgantown: West Virginia UP, 1982. Contains Allen [1296] and Bohrer [1301].
Lord	*Oral Traditional Literature: A Festschrift for Albert Bates Lord.* Ed. John Miles Foley. Preface by Robert P. Creed. Columbus, OH: Slavica, 1981. Contains Foley [1247], Clark [1236], Creed [1239], Foley [1245], Foley [1248], Niles [1270], and Renoir [1279].
Modern Critical	*Beowulf.* Ed. Harold Bloom. Modern Critical Interpretations. New York: Chelsea House, 1987. Contains Tolkien [S130], a chapter from Shippey [S1093], Frank [1312], a chapter from Tripp [1414], a chapter from Robinson [1513], and Duncan [1063].
New Readings	*New Readings on Women in Old English Literature.* Ed. Helen Damico and Alexandra Hennessey Olsen. Bloomington: Indiana UP, 1990. Contains Damico and Olsen [1734a], Meaney [1141], Damico [1175], Sklute [S776], Hill [1745], Taylor [1770a], and Chance [1170].
	Reviews: A. Finlay, *English* 40 (1991): 259-64; J. Jochens, *Scandinavian Studies* 63 (1991): 542-44.

OE Poetry	*Old English Poetry: Essays on Style.* Ed. Daniel G. Calder. Contributions of the UCLA Center for Medieval & Renaissance Studies, 10. Berkeley: U of California P, 1979. Contains Clemoes [1113], Greenfield [1124], Robinson [1149], and Stanley [1155].
	Reviews: A.J. Frantzen, *Cithara* 20 (1980): 60-64; D.K. Fry, *Library Journal* 105 (1980): 510; T. Yoshino, *Studies in English Literature* (Tokyo) (English Number, 1982): 117-23.
OEL in Context	*Old English Literature in Context: Ten Essays.* Ed. John D. Niles. Cambridge: D.S. Brewer and Rowman & Littlefield, 1980. Contains Opland [1202], Andersson [1164], Damon [1176], Foley [1180], Lord [1190], and Nagler [1195].
	Reviews: B. Cottle, *British Book News*, 1980: 761-62; T.A. Shippey, *TLS* 13 March, 1981: 291; A. Bammesberger, *Literaturwissenschaftliches Jahrbuch* 23 (1982): 319-20; J. Roberts, *N&Q* 29 (1982): 154-56; H. Gneuss, *Anglia* 107 (1989): 155-57.
On Old English	*On Old English: Selected Papers.* Oxford: Basil Blackwell, 1988. Contains Mitchell [S501, S661, S680, 1348, and 1663].
	Reviews: K.S. Kiernan, *Envoi* 2.1 (1990); 121-24; M. Ogura, *Studies in English Literature* (Tokyo) (English No.) 1990: 164-69; D.G. Scragg, *RES* 41 (1990): 378-79; A. Bravo, *SELIM: Jnl of the Spanish Soc. for Medieval Engl. Lang. and Lit.* 1

	(1991): 158-61; D. Donoghue, *ANQ*, n.s. 4 (1991): 28-31.
Teresawa	*Philologia Anglia: Essays Presented to Professor Yoshio Teresawa on the Occasion of his Sixtieth Birthday.* Ed. Kinshiro Oshitari, Yoshihiko Ikegami,, Eiichi Suzuki,, Shuji Sato,, Tadao Kubouchi, Yasuhiro Yano, and Shigeaki Karakida. Tokyo: Kenkyusha, 1988. Contains Fujiwara [1646], Karibe [1656], Mitchell [1664], Noguchi [1667], and Oshitari [1668].
Tolkien	*J.R.R. Tolkien, Scholar and Storyteller: Essays in Memoria.* Ed. Mary Salu and Robert T. Farrell. Ithaca: Cornell UP, 1979. Contains Bliss [1107] and Stanley [1154].
	Reviews: J.R. Hall, *JEGP* 79 (1980): 148-50; M. Godden, *RES* 32 (1981): 488-93; H. Ilsemann, *Anglia* 101 (1983): 538-45.
Vikings	*The Vikings.* Ed. Robert T. Farrell. London and Chichester: Phillimore, 1982. Contains Farrell [1310] and Hill [1330].
	Reviews: E. Christiansen, *EHR* 100 (1985): 656; H. O'Donoghue, *RES* 36 (1985): 397-98; H. Mytum, *BIAL* 21-22 (1985): 137-38; R.I. Page, *SBVS* 21 (1985): 308-11.

BEOWULF **SCHOLARSHIP**

Pre-1979

807a Mikami, Toshio. "On the Expression of 'King' in Old English Poetry, with Reference to *Beowulf.*" *Bulletin of the Faculty of Literature of Tokai U* 15 (1971): 261-68. In Japanese.

    Discusses thirty-two words meaning "king" in *Beowulf,* dividing them into the following categories: friend of the people, protector of the people, protector of warriors, ruler of a country or people, guardian of a treasure, a giver of treasure, and one who gives joy to the people. (TM)

881a _____. "Studies in the Language of *Beowulf.*" *Bulletin of the Faculty of Literature of Tokai Univ.* 20 (1973): 89-120; 23 (1975): 42-52; 24 (1975): 55-66; 25 (1976): 146-56; 26 (1976): 77-88.

    This series covers the noun, verb, pronoun, conjunction, and prepositional systems in *Beowulf.* (TM)

995b Hasegawa, Hiroshi. "*Wyrd* in *Beowulf.*" *Central Education Review (Nihon Univ.)* 12 (1976): 50-8. In Japanese.

    Deals with the different meanings of *wyrd* 'fate' in *Beowulf,* suggesting that the term ranges in meaning from "events of life," "one's lot as ordained by God," *Metod* 'Ruler,' "death," to "fate," etc. Reprinted in Hiroshi Hasegawa's *Studies in 'Beowulf'* (Tokyo: Seibido, 1988). (HH)

1008a Porsia, Franco. *Liber Monstrorum.* Bari: Dedalo Libri, 1976. Pp. 307; 16 leaves of plates; ill.

    An edition of the *Liber Monstrorum* which suggests in the introduction that the work was composed in Anglo-Saxon England and that it may be directly influenced by *Beowulf* or legends about Beowulf in at least two places. Porsia detects the influence of *Beowulf* in the *Liber Monstrorum*'s reference to Hyglacus, the king of the Geti, an obvious parallel to Hygelac the Dane in *Beowulf,* with certain details making *Beowulfian* influence likely. The second passage in the prologue to Book I of the *Liber* speaks about the destruction of monsters in water: "quia nunc, humano genere multiplicato et terrarum orbe repleto, sub astris minus producuntur monstra, quae ab ipsis per plurimos terrae angulos eradicata funditus et subversa legimus et nunc revulsa litoribus prona torquentur ad undas" ("because now the human race having multiplied and filled the face of the earth, fewer monsters are brought forth under the stars, monsters which have been rooted out completely throughout all corners of the world by these same [humans] and, we read, beaten back and destroyed, prone on the shores, they are driven into the waves"). The image of the monsters killed violently and now abandoned to the mockery of waves and winds may refer to Beowulf's account of his battle with the sea-monsters in his youthful contest with Breca, where the monsters lie dead on the shore (ll. 565-67a). Also contains a more general discussion of monsters in medieval literature.

1022a Bologna, Corrado. *Liber Monstrorum de Diversis Generibus*. Nuova Corona, 5. Milan: Bompiani, 1977.

An edition of the Latin text with a translation into Italian. In the introduction, Bologna speculates that the *Liber Monstrorum* (which contains a reference to Hygelac) is probably of English origin since its author draws on traditions surrounding *Beowulf*.

1037a Jonk, J. *'Beowulf': een prozavertaling*. [Beowulf: A Prose Translation]. Amsterdam, 1977.

Not seen.

1040aa Miyazaki, Tadakatsu. "Pair-Word Expressions and their Contexts in *Beowulf*." *Bulletin of the Section of Cultural Sciences, Yokohama City Univ.* 28 (1977): 121-47. In Japanese.

Not seen.

1063a Bruce-Mitford, Rupert, with contributions by Paul Ashbee. *The Sutton Hoo Ship-Burial. Volume II, Arms, Armour and Regalia. Volume III, Late Roman and Byzantine Silver, Hanging-bowls, Drinking Vessels, Cauldrons, and Other Containers, Textiles, the Lyre, Pottery Bottle and Other Items.* London: British Museum Publications, 1978 to 1983.

Continues Bruce-Mitford [S944], the official study of the Sutton Hoo find. Volume two, *Arms, Armour and Regalia*, offers new reconstructions of the helmet, shield, and scepter, also making some specific suggestions for interpreting lines

in *Beowulf*. The helmet given to Beowulf has a *wala* 'ridge?' *wīrum bewunden* 'wound with wires' (l. 1031), and Bruce-Mitford points out that the Sutton Hoo helmet "alone among Scandinavian helmets, shows a crest or projecting ridge inlaid with wires" (158). The Sutton Hoo helmet had an exterior with the look of silver, implying that the *hwīta helm* (l. 1448a) may best be translated as simply 'the white helmet' not as the more general 'shining helmet.' Also discusses the textual evidence for mail shirts in *Beowulf*. Volume three completes the series: plans for a fourth volume, which was to have included a discussion of Sutton Hoo and *Beowulf*, have been canceled (see III: xlii).
Reviews: J. Graham-Campbell, *TLS* 1 June 1984: 60; R.T. Farrell, *Speculum* 60 (1985): 126-30; C.M. Hills, *Antiquity* 59 (1985): 60-61; J.N.L. Myres, *EHR* 100 (1985): 120-21.

1064a Creed, Robert P. (reader), John Miles Foley (script consultant), Bruce Rosenberg (commentator), and Donald K. Fry (commentator). *The O/Aural Tradition, Parts I and II. Part I: Beowulf and the Grendel Kind. Part II: Beowulf and the Dragon*. New York: Radio Arts, 1978.

Major selections of the poem in Old English read by Robert P. Creed from Magoun's edition [S391]. Also includes translations by Raffel [S504] and spoken commentary by John Miles Foley, Bruce Rosenberg, and Donald K. Fry. See Betsy Bowden's *Listeners' Guide to Medieval English: A Discography* (New York: Garland, 1988) for descriptions of this and earlier recordings.
Reviews: *OEN* 16.1 (1982): 69-70.

1065a Davidson, Hilda R. Ellis. "The Ship of the Dead." In *The Journey to the Other World*. Ed. H. R. Ellis Davidson. Mistletoe Series. Brewer: Cambridge and Totowa, NJ, 1978. Pp. 73-89.

Surveys archaeological and literary evidence for ship burial particularly in Sweden, Norway, and East Anglia from the sixth century, finding in *Beowulf*'s account of Scyld Scefing's funeral (ll. 38-52) the only detailed account of a ship funeral in the early literature of Northwestern Europe. Davidson maintains that "*Beowulf* is a Christian poem, but contains much traditional symbolism which belongs to the pre-Christian period" (86). Scyld's funeral might have been invented to explain funeral practices mythically: after Scyld, who came and left in a ship, all dynastic leaders were to be laid to rest in ships. On the other hand, Scyld's funeral might be an "imaginative reconstruction of the poet, who knew of the wonderful funeral ceremonies once held in pagan East Anglia" (86).

1076a Liberman, Anatoly. "Germanic *sendan* 'To Make a Sacrifice'." *JEGP* 77 (1978): 473-88.

On the basis of Old Norse evidence (primarily the *Atlakviða*), argues that a problematic verb describing Grendel's attacks, MS. *sendeþ* (l. 600), may mean "to make a sacrifice" and that the devouring of Hondscio (ll. 740-45) may represent "an anti-feast leading to what looks like a half-remembered echo of a human sacrifice" (484). Liberman reviews various editorial and lexicographical solutions for the puzzling MS. form *sendeþ* (emended by Klaeber [S67] to *snēdeð* 'cuts') and speculates about the fate of Hondscio, whose death Beowulf seems unwilling to prevent. Though some would try to explain away this contradiction with an appeal to artistic unity, "It is reasonable to suppose that the *Beowulf* poet knew a formulaic theme, something like 'The Hero Kills a Monster,' and it had as its initial component the death of the hero's comrade. Hondscio's death is then artistically justified in that it forms a part of the recognizable formulaic pattern, and at the level of content it is a redeeming sacrifice. Hondscio is 'sent' before the hero is allowed to win, and Beowulf's *(swefeð ond) sendeþ*, used about Grendel's previous onslaughts, can belong to such situations as a verbal relic, a word habitually applied to a monster's victims in the hall" (483).

1076b Locherbie-Cameron, Margaret A.L. "Structure, Mood and Meaning in *Beowulf.*" *Poetica* (Tokyo) 10 (1978): 1-11.

Suggests that the structure and meaning of the poem revolve around the relationship between heroic and elegiac moods, the former dominating the first part of the poem and the latter the second part. "The heroic mood reflects Beowulf's youthful success, the elegiac his defeat in old age" (2). However, elegiac passages occur in the predominately heroic section while heroic passages occur in the elegiac section. Grendel sounds a note of elegy in the retelling of Beowulf's heroic exploits, since he is an isolated outcast, though one portrayed ironically in heroic terms as an anti-thane. Locherbie-Cameron finds further elegiac characteristics in Hrothgar's first lament (ll. 480-88), in the Finnsburh episode, and Hrothgar's sermon, each of which dwells on figures of isolation like Hengest and Heremod. These elegiac passages in the heroic section all stress the need for human courage, a quality lacking in the elegiac mood of the second part of the poem, where "emphatic retrospection" dominates the elegies of the Last Survivor, the Father's Lament, and the Messenger (ll. 2247-66, 2444-59, 3008-37). Wiglaf brings a heroic element to the elegiac mood of the second part, showing what a retainer should be, though the ambivalent symbol of his sword (pointing to fame but also the cycle of revenge) qualifies this heroism and suggests "the central tragic weakness of the Anglo-Saxon heroic code" (8). Locherbie-Cameron concludes that every heroic action necessarily ends in an elegiac conclusion, and thus the intertwining of the two moods becomes not only a structural device but also "the poem's final meaning" (11).

1078a Mann, Betty Tucker. "Water Imagery and the Baptism in *Beowulf*." *Olifant* 5 (1978): 381-83.

A summary of a 1977 dissertation with the same title, arguing that "Beowulf's three water adventures develop the triple immersion motif present in Anglo-Saxon baptism ritual" (381).

1079a Mertens-Fonck, Paule. "Structure des passages introduisant le discours direct dans *Beowulf*." [Structure of Passages Introducing Direct Discourse in *Beowulf*]. In *Mélanges de philologie et de littératures romanes offerts à Jeanne Wathelet-Willem*. Marche Romane, 20. Liège: Marche romane, 1978. Pp. 433-445.

Analyzes forty-five passages which introduce direct discourse in *Beowulf*, dividing them into four categories and identifying a number of recurring motifs. The first category is the most traditional and probably the most ancient, a type represented by line 529 (*Bēowulf maþelode, bearn Ecgþēowes*, "Beowulf spoke, the son of Ecgtheow"). The other three categories are increasingly less traditional and formulaic. Mertens-Fonk examines the syntax of the introductions to see if the speaker (as subject) occurs with verbs of speaking in the same half-line or whether they are separated, and if so, where they occur. Introductions in the first category consist of one full line, whereas categories two through three range from a single half-line to thirteen full lines, with an average length of three to four lines. Other motifs which can appear optionally are a) a more precise definition or qualification of the speaker (either a subject or adjective), b) the position or location occupied by the speaker or the actions and gestures made before speaking, c) the psychological state of the speaker, d) mention of an addressee, and e) indication of the contents of the following speech. Mertens-Fonk concludes that these conventions do not so much limit the poet's freedom as provide occasions for supple workmanship. The indications of psychological states are sometimes particularly subtle. Includes a summary table of results (434-35), listing all the introductions, their categories and motifs. This list of references has been incorporated into the line-index of this volume.

1092a Shimose, Michiro. "A Variety of Expressions for 'Death' used in *Beowulf*—Chiefly on their Figurative Use." *Journal of Kumamoto Junior College* 59 (1978): 25-50. In Japanese.

Explores figurative expressions for death in *Beowulf*, the most typical being kennings or periphrases like "separation of the soul from body," "a man's deprivation from joy," and formulaic sentences whose subject is a personified inanimate noun like "war," "fate," or "sword" (for example, "war took him away"). Also discusses euphemisms for death such as *sīðian* 'go, travel,' *gewītan* 'depart,' and *swefan* 'sleep' for 'die.' (MS)

1979

1106 Amsler, Mark E. "Literary Onomastics and the Descent of Nations: The Example of Isidore and Vico." *Names* 27 (1979): 106-16.

Contains a brief mention of *Beowulf*, proposing that the poet associates the words *grædig* 'greedy' and *gīfre* 'ravenous' almost exclusively with the race of Cain (monsters and kin slayers) and that the association is based on Jerome and Isidore's onomastic analysis of the name Cain. Both Jerome and Isidore gloss the name *Cain* as *possessio* 'seizing, taking possession of,' Jerome adding that the name "prophesied greed and envy for Cain's descendants" (109). The *Beowulf* poet, displaying his onomastic artistry, uses *grædig* and *gīfre* with a knowledge of this tradition, forming a network of connections centering on monsters and kin slayers, which underlines the moral structure of the poem.

1107 Bliss, Alan J. "*Beowulf*, Lines 3074-3075." In *J.R.R. Tolkien, Scholar and Storyteller: Essays In Memoriam*. Ed. Mary Salu and Robert T. Farrell. Ithaca: Cornell UP, 1979. Pp. 41-63.

After examining the individual words (*goldhwæte, gearwor, est, sceawian*), syntax (the functions of *þonne, ær*, etc.), and literary context of lines 3074-75, proposes that they refer to Beowulf's last, dim awareness of God's sole power to grant treasure. They may be translated as follows: "In the past he [Beowulf] had seen and understood the gold-bestowing favour of God much less clearly than he did now" (57). The chiastic patterns in this section of the poem indicate that the lines 3074-75 refer to Beowulf's relationship to the curse, matching the theme of lines 3054b-3057. Bliss sees the curse as a symbol for the corrupting power of gold and Beowulf's susceptibility to it as a sign of his avarice. Beowulf insists improperly on seeing the gold, but just before his death recognizes that God alone has the power to bestow gold (ll. 2794-96). Thus, the statement in ll. 3074-75 refers his belated realization and his earlier ignorance. Beowulf nevertheless dies for his pride and suffers damnation for his avarice, the two vices which Hroðgar warned the hero against in the sermon. Though lines 2819b-20 may seem to indicate Beowulf's salvation, Bliss (after examining the individual words and syntax of the passage in some detail) argues that it must mean "his life-spirit departed from his breast, hoping for the esteem of the true-judging" (50). The *sōðfæstra dōm* 'esteem of the true-judging' is, in short, worldy esteem. Thus, in his death, Beowulf mistakenly believes "that he has done well, and that posterity will judge him as favourably as his own retainers do" (50), while he is in fact heading toward the damnation brought on him by his own avarice. Bliss provides an extensive commentary and translation for lines 3051-3075, commenting on a number of words (*benemdon* 'declare,' among others) and constructions. See Mitchell's response [1348].

1108 Bolton, Whitney F. "Boethius and a Topos in *Beowulf*." In *Jones*, 1:15-43.

Views Beowulf's statements (ll. 632-38, 1490b-91, and 2535b-37)—that he will achieve victory or die—in the context of duality in Boethius' *Consolation of Philosophy*, finding that the Old English poem is a radical "transcultural paraphrase" of the *Consolation* (39). Bolton surveys either-or statements in a number of Old English, Old Norse, and Latin texts and provides an extensive commentary on the topos in Alfred's translation of Boethius. Either-or statements are classified into three categories: cognitive/mental (either one understands or does not), normative/natural (something is either this or that), and optative/moral (where one may choose between the alternatives). Old English texts show a fondness for the optative/moral statement which finds its way into very few Old Norse texts. Bolton sketches a number of similarities between *Beowulf* and the *Consolation*, duality being the most prominent ("adversity and prosperity, glory and ignominy, wisdom and ignorance, youth and age, *sapientia* and *fortitudo*, Providence and Fortune, loyalty and disloyalty, even life and death," 37-38).

1109 Brady, Caroline. "Weapons in *Beowulf*: An Analysis of the Nominal Compounds and an Evaluation of the Poet's Use of Them." *ASE* 8 (1979): 79-141.

A study of the sixty-seven nominal compounds for weapons in *Beowulf*. "The purpose is two-fold: (1) to determine, so far as possible, the exact meaning of each of the sixty-nine terms; and (2) to discern, if we can, the primary use—whether informative, traditional, stylistic or artistic—to which the poet put these formations which he drew from the common stock or created to his own need" (79). Brady discusses words for helmets (*helm*, *heregrīma*, *grīmhelm*, *beadugrīma, gūðhelm, entisc helm,* and *wīgheafola*), swords (*sweord, heoru, bil(l), mēce, hæftmēce, seax, secg, brond, wægsweord, maðþumsweord, gūðsweord, wællseax, hildelēoma, beadolēoma, gūðwine, Hūnlāfing, hildegicel, grægmæl, lāf, yrfelāf, maþðum, geweorc, scūrheard,* etc.), byrnies and arms generally (*-byrne, syrce, searo, hrægl, hringīren, hringnet, brēostnet, herenet, searonet, hringed, locen, hondlocen, broden, gewæde, gūð-gewædo, brēostgewædu, scrūd, herepād, geatwa, rēaf,* etc.), shields (*lind, bord, sīd, rand, regnheard, beorht, geolo, hilderand, bordrand, hildebord, wīgbord,* etc.), spears (*gār, wudu, æscholt, eofersprēot, heorohōcyht, bongār, gārholt, -sceaft, wælsteng, mægenwudu, þrecwudu,* etc.). Brady divides the compounds into six categories based on the differing relationships between the first and second elements: designating-specifying (in which the first component either limits the second, or adds no express lexical meaning) delineating (which adds some detail or dimension), descriptive (in which the first component describes the second), metaphorical bipartite appellatives (of which there are only three, *hildegicel, bongar,* and *guðwine*), and literal and metaphorical circumlocutions. Brady praises several compounds for weapons such as *gārholt* 'spear-wood or forest of spears' (l. 1834b), *hildelēoma* 'battle light' (l. 1143b), and *hildegicel* 'battle-icicle' (l. 1606b) for their "rare and striking beauty" (140) and insists that *Hūnlāfing* is the name of Hnæf's sword: "I believe it to have been the sword which in accordance with custom Hnæf had placed across his own knees when Hengest swore his oath of allegiance upon its hilt" (99).

1110   Bridges, Richard M. "Teaching Leadership through *Beowulf.*" *Massachusetts Studies in English* 7 (1979): 1-6.

Describes a literature course (taught at West Point) which raises issues of leadership, using *Beowulf* as the starting point. Bridges proceeds by analyzing the leadership methods of Hrothgar and Beowulf, seeing Hrothgar, in his patient delegation of power, as an ideal leader, while viewing Beowulf as a flawed and impatient ruler who refuses to delegate "responsibility for mission accomplishment to a member or members of the group" (2). In addition, Hrothgar knows how to distribute treasure, while after his death, Beowulf's desire to see the treasure belies "a misunderstanding of the real purpose behind its procurement in the ring-giving system" (5).

1111 Cassidy, Frederic G. "Under the Hill." In *Linguistic and Literary Studies in Honor of Archibald A. Hill; IV: Linguistics and Literature, Sociolinguistics and Applied Linguistics.* Ed. Mohammad Ali Jazayery, Edgar C. Polomé, and Werner Winter. 4 Vols. Trends in Linguistics: Studies & Monographs, 7-10. The Hague: Mouton, 1979. 4:209-215.

Explores various folkloristic beliefs about barrows, caves, and hills as the underground dwelling place of otherworldly creatures or the dead. The dragon in *Beowulf* is kin to such creatures. After the coming of Christianity, such creatures of popular belief (gods, giants, elves, fairies, and other monsters) were reinterpreted as minions of hell, a development seen in the character of Grendel: "Grendel is an ambivalent figure, a monster at once manlike and diabolical, an underground dweller, hence one of the *hellware* [inhabitants of hell]" (211). In this Christian transformation, "the hill under which figures of pagan belief had dwelt, with the earth as roof, have now become the covering of Hell, the abode of Satan and his crew, the old figures in a new form" (212).

1112 Chase, Colin. "*Beowulf.*" In *A Glance Backward: A Series of Evaluations of the Scholarship on OE Language, Literature, and Civilization Written between 1967 and 1977.* Ed. Colin Chase and Rowland L. Collins. Old English Newsletter, Subsidia Series, 2. Binghamton: CEMERS at SUNY Binghamton, 1979. Pp. 12-15.

Reviews a decade of *Beowulf* scholarship, from 1967 to 1977, identifying four trends: the advent of computer technology and the emphasis on quantifiable entities within the poem; the waning of the Christian-pagan debate, with the interest in oral-formulaics rising to take its place; the overall but not universal decline in the hero's reputation; and finally, continuing textual, metrical, and philological work.

1113 Clemoes, Peter. "Action in *Beowulf* and Our Perception of It." In *OE Poetry*, pp. 147-68.

Argues that Old English poems in general and *Beowulf* specifically treat action differently than modern fiction does. In recounting Beowulf's embarking for Denmark, the poet does not set the scene in such a way that the audience can imagine itself localized in the landscape but instead ignores the point of view of the reader in order to focus on the inner forces and principles of things: Beowulf's heroic intention, the nature of boats on the sea, etc. Clemoes finds that "no Old English narrator ever explicitly invites us, the audience, in our imagination to see and hear happenings for ourselves, to be on the spot and have our own spectators' relationship to events" (150). On the contrary, "[m]ovement in *Beowulf* is not portrayed as a detachable outward concept: it merely identifies action as part of the doer; action belongs to him as an innate, inherent attribute—it is what philosophers call 'immanent'" (155). The poet explores these inner forces in traditional language, one which has a generalizing effect. Thinking about action this way leads the poet to prefer active verbs to passive, nouns and adjectives to finite verbs. Connectives describe "the inner nature of action" (157) rather than external sequence of plot events. Action becomes a tool of characterization not an end in itself: "The poet's predominant interest is how a person's actions successively characterize him and how these actions relate to the forces within him" (160). This concern makes narrative action "psychological," and for this reason the poet sometimes prefers speech rather than immediate action.

1114 Crépin, André. "Les Expéditions de *Beowulf.*" [Quests in *Beowulf*]. In *Voyage, quête, pélerinage dans la littérature et la civilisation médiévals.* Actes du Colloque Organisé par le Centre Univ. d'Études et de Recherches Médiévals d'Aix-en-Provence les 5,6,7 mars 1976 (Senefiance 2). Aix-en-Provence: Centre Univ. d'Études et de Recherches Médiévals, 1979. Pp. 155-66.

Makes several observations about journeys and voyages in *Beowulf*, noting similarities between sea journeys in *Beowulf* and those in other works in the Nowell codex (*Alexander's Letter*, for example), exploring the technique of oral composition in the voyages of Beowulf (ll. 217-224, 1903-1912), rejecting a strictly allegorical interpretation of the monsters, appreciating the interlace of action and meditation, and identifying the voyage of life as a major theme in Old English poetry. Crepín analyzes the word *sīþ* 'journey' and points out that the Anglo-Saxon idea of a comrade (*gesīþ*) is one who 'journeys along.' In summary, for the Germanic hero, life is a military expedition which leads to death but which can and should lead to glory ("la vie, pour l'héros germanique, est une expédition guerrière qui mène à la mort, mais peut et doit mener à la glorie," 165). Also discusses certain problems of translating *Beowulf* into French.

1115 _____. "Wealhtheow's Offering of the Cup to Beowulf: A Study in Literary Structure." In *Jones*, 1:45-58.

Provides a translation of and extensive commentary on lines 607-45, Wealhtheow's presentation of the cup and sees it as part of a larger narrative unit, the description of a banquet, with six other occurrences in *Beowulf*: ll. 491-661, 2009b-69a, 991-1250, 2101-17a, 1785-93, and 1975-2199. The typical banquet scene contains the following elements: getting the hall ready, settling down (either an invitation by the king or a simple sitting down to the banquet), distribution of the drink (by a thane, queen, queen's daughter, *byrelas* 'cupbearers,' or unspecified people), distribution of gifts (by the king or queen), speeches and songs (by a scop or other people). "The offering of drink does not stand by itself: it is part and parcel of the theme of the banquet.... in a given theme motifs can be omitted or expressed in different formulas or altered" (53). He also provides a chart analyzing the various motifs in the six banqueting scenes in *Beowulf*, and traces rhetorical devices (hypozeuxis, dialyton, hirmos) described by Bede and Byrhtferth.

1116 Davidson, Hilda R. Ellis, ed.. *Saxo Grammaticus: 'The History of the Danes'*. Trans. Peter Fisher. 2 vols. Cambridge: D.S. Brewer, 1979-1980.

Provides a translation of (vol. 1) and commentary on (vol. 2) Saxo Grammaticus' *The History of the Danes*, with scattered references to *Beowulf* in the notes and commentary.

1117 De Roo, Harvey. "Two Old English Fatal Feast Metaphors: *Ealuscerwen* and *Meoduscerwen*." *ESC* 5 (1979): 249-61.

Believes that the notoriously difficult word *ealuscerwen* (l. 769a), describing the terror of the Danes as they hear Grendel and Beowulf fight within Heorot, "is part of fatal feast language used to convey an anti-social and monstrous behavior inherent in Grendel" (257). Many of Grendel's actions here become parodies of normal feasting behavior in the Germanic hall. Grendel acts ironically as a kind of hall entertainer, when he sings a "song of sorrow" (ll. 783b-88a) for the Danes. Likewise, the tumult that Beowulf and Grendel produce mimics the uproar of feasting in the hall. Grendel and Beowulf, as ironic *renweardas* 'hall attendants' (l. 770a), dispense "ale." "The receivers of the ale are either one another or an imagined *comitatus* within the hall. . . . On the level of actuality, the noise which the Danes hear is the crashings and smashings of Beowulf and Grendel as they struggle in the hall. These audible signs of struggle are called, in the ironical metonymic metaphor, 'ale-dispensing.' A translation which would clarify the figurative with the literal meaning . . . would be therefore: 'there came to the Danes the noise of an 'ale-dispensing'" (257). De Roo finds a similar, though differently developed, pattern of fatal feast imagery in *Andreas*, line 1526b, containing the parallel construction *meoduscerwen*.

1118 Earl, James W. "Beowulf's Rowing-Match." *Neophil* 63 (1979): 285-90.

Argues that the so-called swimming contest (lasting seven days and nights) between Beowulf and Breca (ll. 506-581) as well as other feats of incredible strength have been misinterpreted, and that Breca and Beowulf engage in a rowing match, not a swimming contest. As opposed to Irish heroes the Germanic hero "is not expected to display grotesque or superhuman powers" (285), and Earl casts doubt on the superhuman feats assigned to Beowulf. The language of the episode suggests that Beowulf and Breca were actually engaged in a rowing, not a swimming contest. Unferth says that the two *on sund rēon* (l. 512b), which has usually been interpreted to mean, 'they swam.' After surveying uses of the word in Old English and Old Icelandic, Earl points out that *sund* can mean 'sea' as well as 'swimming,' and thus the line could be read 'they rowed on the sea.' Beowulf also uses the same phrase in his description of the contest (l. 539b). In addition, the manuscript reading *wudu weallendu* ('tossing ships' or perhaps 'tossing ship,' l. 581a) has been consistently emended to *wadu weallendu* 'tossing seas,' on the assumption that the contest was a swimming match, though the unemended form would fit the context of a rowing contest. Earl also examines two other episodes: Beowulf's swim from Frisia (ll. 2354 ff.) and his dive into Grendel's mere (ll. 1492 ff.), concluding that they too may have been misread as superhuman feats. Finally, he reviews possible analogues to the rowing match in Northern literature. Though no exact parallel is extant, an expression from the sagas, *róa vík á e-n* 'to row against someone,' meaning "to get the better of someone," implies that rowing contests were close to the conceptions of the northern Germanic peoples. [See *fabulous elements* in the subject index.]

1119 _____. "The Necessity of Evil in *Beowulf*." *South Atlantic Bulletin* 44 (1979): 81-98.

Suggests that the monsters are a "purposeful and a necessary evil" (87), one which provides a moral corrective to Hrothgar precisely when he has come to believe that his power might be unchallengeable, and that Hrothgar recognizes the lesson and passes it on to Beowulf in his "sermon" (ll. 1761b-78a). To bolster the argument that evil is necessary, Earl traces compounds for fate and calamity containing the elements *sceaft* 'creation or fate' and *nȳd* 'need, necessity,' pointing out that "Evil in the world, like death, is 'fated of old' and is a necessary part of man's lot" (89). *Nȳd* always has negative connotations and is often used as a synonym for death, though both words have often been misunderstood and mistranslated. Earl points out that Augustine (in the *City of God*) shares this view of evil—that God uses evil for his own purposes. "So Hrothgar's analysis of his own persecution at the end of his sermon, though it may still strike some as trivial moralizing, is actually an attempt to understand history" (93). This interpretation can clear up several troublesome aspects of the poem's moral vision: Hrothgar finally is not weak but wise since he is able, like Augustine, to learn from calamity sent by God—a great Christian theme found also in *Job*; passages which declare that God could stop the monsters' ravages if He wanted no longer seem inconsistent, since God is using Grendel as an instrument; the connection between Hrothgar's analysis of his own plight and his prophecy of Beowulf's death becomes clearer. What he teaches Beowulf about the transience of the world (seen also in the Lay of the Last Survivor) he has learned himself—his life becomes an exemplum for Beowulf. Beowulf faces his own death with strength and piety, showing that he has benefitted from "Hrothgar's hard-earned wisdom" (94). Includes an appendix on the meaning of the word-element *wan/wann* 'lacking' or 'dark.'

1120 Eliason, Norman E. "Beowulf's Inglorious Youth." *SP* 76 (1979): 101-08.

Suggests that lines 2177-89 refer to the "inglorious youth" of Hygelac, not of Beowulf, and that Beowulf had no inglorious youth, in part since lines 2428-34 state that Beowulf was a promising boy at age seven. Eliason believes that the lines immediately preceding the "inglorious youth" passage (ll. 2183b-89) can be reconstrued so that Hygelac is the subject of two verbs which have been traditionally thought to apply to Beowulf and that Beowulf is instead the receiver of the action. He provides the following paraphrase of lines 2177-84: "So he (Hygelac), known for his courage and courteous deeds, supported the son of Ecgtheow (Beowulf), strove after honor.... But he sustained the battle-brave man (Beowulf) because of his power supreme among men, the bountiful gift which God gave him. He (Hygelac) had long been scorned, when the sons of the Geats accounted him worthless" (105). While admitting that some aspects of his reading may seem forced, Eliason points out that the traditional readings are also awkward. He finds that a later passage on Hrethel's sorrow over his sons may also include a reference to Hygelac's inglorious youth (ll. 2451b-53a).

1121 Erben, Johannes. "Die Herausforderung der *ur-hettun* im althochdeutschen *Hildebrandslied.*" [The Challenge of the *ur-hettun* in the Old High German *Hildebrandslied*]. *ZDP* 98 (1979): 4-9.

In order to explain the term *urhettun* in the *Hildebrandslied* (l. 2), surveys possible relatives of the word in a number of Germanic dialects, including the word *ōretta* 'warrior,' which occurs in *Beowulf*, concluding that the words must have originally designated someone who made and was to fulfill an *ur-heiz* 'bold promise' or *biheiz* 'actual defeat of an enemy'—the latter term being cognate to Old English *bēot* (*bi-hāt*) 'boast.'

1122 Feldman, Thalia Phillies. "The Taunter in Ancient Epic: The *Iliad, Odyssey, Aeneid,* and *Beowulf.*" *PLL* 15 (1979): 3-16.

Compares the social roles of taunters in various classical and medieval epics: the poet-taunters of the *Táin Bó Cuailgne*, Unferth in *Beowulf*, Thersites in the *Iliad*, Antinous in the *Odyssey*, and Drances in the *Aeneid*, finding that such figures are officially sanctioned to provoke their heroes to political and social action and thus are much more than the social misfits they first seem to be. In typical epics, such figures usually have names denoting their function (*Unferth* = 'marpeace' or 'folly'), are set off from others usually by a deformity or crime (Unferth's slaying of his kin), test the hero with his words, and taunt him into action. As a comparison reveals, Unferth is less motivated by personal bitterness than some of the other taunters and "Of all the provocateurs Unferth knows and serves his own courtly function best" (16). His crime of fratricide "is the shield for his role as provocateur in that it assures an inviolability by reason of his having committed . . . the ultimate taboo" (7-8). His performance represents no offense to the court and indeed is sanctioned by it.

1123 Goldman, Stephen H. "The Use of Christian Belief in Old English Poems of Exile." *Res Publica Litterarum* 2 (1979): 69-80.

Analyzes two elegiac passages in *Beowulf*—the Lay of the Last Survivor (ll. 2247-70a) and Hrethel's lament along with the Father's Lament (ll. 2425-71)—in a larger study of Old English elegy and its Germanic background, emphasizing that an insistently Christian reading of such elegies overlooks the importance of Germanic ideas of exile. The last survivor's sorrow does not come from spiritual desolation or feelings of loss for his dead race. On the contrary, he mourns his life as an exile. Similarly, the laments of Hrethel and the father (for his hanged son) mourn not the dead but the living: "They are for people in this world who have, given the structure of Germanic society, no real existence and yet are cursed with having to continue to live" (74). Includes readings of the "Seafarer" and "Wanderer," where Goldman argues that Christian elements are adapted to Germanic traditions, not the other way around.

1124 Greenfield, Stanley B. "Esthetics and Meaning and the Translation of Old English Poetry." In *OE Poetry,* pp. 91-110.

After analyzing the translations of *Beowulf* by Morgan [S243], Raffel [S504], and Garmonsway [S669], Greenfield proposes several guidelines for poetic translation which preserve both the esthetics and meaning of the original and which he has employed in his own translation. 1) "the translation must not only be attractive to the reader who knows no Old English, but also appeal to anyone familiar with both the poem and the Anglo-Saxon poetic sensibility."

2) "the translator must not limit himself to a verse-by-verse or even line-by-line translation but, with King Alfred, proceed sometimes word-by-word, more often sense-by-sense *within the syntactic or rhetorical unit* and with some sense of the poem's total configuration." 3) "the metrical system must be equivalent to, but not the same as, the Old English alliterative verse: it must be flexible enough to reflect the freedom of our modern poetry yet have a fixity that suggests, but does not ape, the restraint of the four-stress heavily-caesuraed Anglo-Saxon line." 4) "the poetic translator should utilize not only modern stylistic devices and locutions, but also, where appropriate, stylistic, syntactic, and phonological patterns and features found in Old English poems." 5) the translator "should—indeed must—try to unlock the meaning hidden in Old English images, but not at the expense of falsifying the meaning and esthetic contour of the original" (100). Greenfield goes on to discuss the nature of his own translation and argues against Stanley [1214] that lines 419-26 are not so obscure as to prevent successful translation.

1125 _____. "The Extremities of the *Beowulf*ian Body Politic." In *Jones*, 1:1-14.

Makes two proposals: "1) that references to the literal physical extremities of hands and feet in *Beowulf* resonate with the concept of thaneship, a concept central to the poem's meaning; and 2) that Beowulf's three great fights—against Grendel, Grendel's mother, and the dragon—move hierarchically from the literal and emblematic extremities represented by hands and heads to the centers of the body and the body politic respectively, the heart and the king" (2). Greenfield examines a number of references to hands and feet in the poem, concluding that "the hand/arm/shoulder complex in *Beowulf* has a significant resonance for the body politic" but that references to feet (*fōt* and compounds with *feða*-'foot') have "a certain negative resonance" (7), with Unferth sitting at the feet of Hrothgar. On the other hand, both Handscio [hand-shoe = glove] and Æschere, as loyal thanes, are associated with hands, while Wiglaf fights near Beowulf's shoulder (l. 2853b). Speaking to the second proposal, Greenfield points out that words for the hand are prominent in Beowulf's fight with Grendel; for the head in his fight with Grendel's mother; and for the chest or heart in his fight with the dragon. Includes a discussion of the word *hond/hand* and compounds based on it.

1126 Hardy, Adelaide. "Historical Perspective and the *Beowulf*-Poet." *Neophil* 63 (1979): 430-49.

Takes exception to the view of Tolkien [S130] and others that the *Beowulf*-poet had an "instinctive historical sense" and that he wished to give an accurate picture of the pagan past. Drawing on a number of contemporary texts and events, Hardy concludes that "the claim that the hero of *Beowulf* is a pagan who lives without spiritual hope is based entirely on the false premise that the poet wished to keep his story within the historical confines of the continental past" (439). The Sutton Hoo ship burial shows a mixing of pagan and Christian elements similar to that in *Beowulf*. Further, Unferth may be meant to represent the sinister aspects of the Teutonic god Woden. In the end, the *Beowulf*-poet sees a certain continuity between the old and new religions in the custom of the *comitatus*; however, it is precisely the most pagan characters like Unferth who break the sanctity of the *comitatus*, while those allied with the new religion uphold it. [See *history—attitudes toward in 'Beowulf'* in the subject index.]

1127 Harris, Joseph. "The *Senna*: From Description to Literary Theory." *Michigan Germanic Studies* 5 (1979): 65-74.

Basing his analysis on twelve passages from Eddic poetry as well as others in Saxo Grammaticus and Old Norse prose, finds a structural framework for the *senna* or flyting scene found in Germanic literature (including *Beowulf*), arguing that native compositional units such as this one are to be preferred to more broadly-based notions of the type-scene which cross a number of linguistic and cultural boundaries. The basic framework for the *senna* runs as follows: "there is a Preliminary, comprising an Identification and Characterization, and then a Central Exchange, consisting of either Accusation and Denial, Threat and Counter-threat, or Challenge and Reply or a combination; these structural elements are realized through a more or less regular alternation of speakers, first in question and answer, then comment and reply. The content analysis of the elements may be none too precise. . . . No standard pattern emerges for the ending of a senna: most are resolved into a physical fight; in some the antagonists part to prepare a battle; in others they simply part on bad terms" (66). Harris finds that the Beowulf-Unferth exchange follows this pattern closely and that the accusation of fratricide may be a traditional one. Finally, he argues that such *sennur* or flytings emerged from everyday language use, citing Labov's work with African-American flyting or "the dozens."

1128 Hermann, John P. "*Beowulf,* 2802-08." *Explicator* 37 (1979): 24-25.

Points out that in Beowulf's final speech about his barrow the word *feorran* 'from afar' (l. 2808b) is often mistranslated as 'far away,' and when restored to its original meaning implies that, ironically, the barrow will remind ship-goers coming from afar (i.e., the hostile invaders) of Beowulf's death and hence of the defenselessness of the Geats. Provides the following translation of the passage: "Command the battle-renowned men to build a splendid mound at the promontory after the pyre; it shall stand high on Hronesness as a remembrance for my people, so that seafarers might later call it Beowulf's barrow, those who sail ships from afar over the misty seas" (24).

1129 Hill, John M. "*Beowulf,* Value, and the Frame of Time." *MLQ* 40 (1979): 3-16.

Casts doubt on the notion, widely held since Tolkien's famous essay [S130], that the Christian poet conceived the story as unfolding in the pagan past cut off from the present. Instead, Hill asserts, "the poet's temporal schemes strongly imply that we still inhabit the violent world Beowulf inhabited (although somewhat later in time and somewhat reduced in the splendor of our circumstances). If we look closely at the poet's narrative perspective, that world does not seem to end in a pre-Christian past, nor does it merely continue as a mundane world from which we must turn toward God. Along with the continuity through time the poet seems also to express a continuity of value—mainly by sharing ethical and religious piety with his noble characters. That sharing of value and religion seems to indicate that we should orient ourselves toward Beowulf's world . . . and perceive its uncertainties, much as Beowulf did: we should avoid crimes, live generously, thank a generous God who judges the deeds of all men, and embrace *comitatus* values" (4-5). Nor does fate close off the past, since to the characters (Beowulf in particular) the sweep of events unfolds as an unpredictable, indeterminate process, as it does for us.

1130 Hill, Thomas D. "The Return of the Broken Butterfly: *Beowulf,* Line 163, Again." *Mediaevalia* 5 (1979): 271-281.

A response to Greenfield's attack [S1032] on Hill's earlier article [S798], which proposed that a biblical allusion (Psalms 11:9: "the wicked walk in circles") lies behind the phrase *hwyrftum scrīþað* 'move on in circles' in *Beowulf* (l. 163b) and *Christ and Satan.* Greenfield had maintained that the phrase (in context) translates as: "men do not know whither [such] hellish, mysterious ones *dart swiftly and imperceptibly in their courses."* Hill faults Greenfield's lexicography, particularly the latter's refusal to see 'circuit or circle' as a possible meaning for *hwyrft,* and provides a number of passages from Old English texts in which the word has such a meaning, also rejecting Greenfield's definition of *scrīþan* as 'dart swiftly and imperceptibly' on the basis of other examples. Hill denies that he sees *Beowulf* as a strict allegory and reminds that the Psalter was a well-known, central text in medieval education and liturgy and that undeniable patterns of Christian allusion have been established for the poem by Klaeber [S41] and others.

1131 Holloway, Betsy M. "On Translating *Beowulf."* In *Geardagum* 3 (1979): 66-74.

Discusses "a few of the challenges (and pitfalls) facing the translator" of *Beowulf* (68). After discussing translation theory briefly, Holloway examines various translations of lines 320-24 and line 730b, pointing out successes and difficulties with the current translations.

1132 Jorgensen, Peter A. "The Gift of the Useless Weapon in *Beowulf* and the Icelandic Sagas." *Arkiv för Nordisk Filologi* 94 (1979): 82-90.

Finds that Unferth's gift of the useless sword Hrunting to Beowulf is paralleled by a similar motif in a number of Icelandic sagas, including the *Grettis saga,* the *Hrólfs saga kraka,* Saxo Grammaticus' *History of the Danes,* narratives about Böðvarr Bjarki, as well as a number of lesser-known sagas. In the Icelandic examples of the motif, a king whose court is plagued by an ogre makes the gift of the useless sword to a hero, while in *Beowulf,* the poet "protected Hrothgar's reputation by having the tainted present given by Unferth, a less than noble, but much more fitting member of the court. The switch was not accomplished without some discrepancy, for the antagonistic liegeman must undergo a radical personality change from one scene to the next, which obscures Unferth's Germanic prototype, the evil counselor" (89). Jorgensen suggests that the motif may have developed when Germanic story tellers adapted the non-Germanic motifs of the "bear's son folktale," in which a bear's son, famous for his strength, overtaxes at least two swords before finding one strong enough to kill a monster in a cave. This story may have been combined with another famous tale in which a monster can be killed only with its own sword, suggesting that even the last, supposedly invincible, sword must also fail and that the hero must find a sword in the monster's lair. Thus, the poet may have transferred the epithet *hæftmēce* 'hilted sword' (l. 1457a) to Hrunting from the monster's sword.

1133 Kasik, Jon C. "The Use of the Term 'Wyrd' in *Beowulf* and the Conversion of the Anglo-Saxons." *Neophil* 63 (1979): 128-35.

After reviewing the twelve occurrences of the word *wyrd*, 'fate,' in the poem, concludes that "the *Beowulf*-poet used the term *wyrd* in neither a purely pagan nor a purely Christian sense. The variation in usage indicates that the idea of *wyrd* was not static in this period" (132). In its most pagan sense, *wyrd* represents an uncontrollable fate which overpowers even the gods, possibly even the new God. The Christian or Boethian idea of divine providence is not expressed in a fully worked-out fashion. Instead, the poet begins to merge the concepts of *wyrd* and God so that "the Christian God has taken over much of the inscrutability which *wyrd* possessed under the old religion" (131).

1134 Krol, Jelle, R.C. Smilde, and Popke van der Zee. *It gefjocht fan Beowulf mei Grendel*. [Beowulf's Fight with Grendel]. Grins, 1979.

A translation of lines 1-836 of *Beowulf* into modern Frisian verse. Not seen. See Krol [1445].

1135 Kuhn, Sherman. "Old English *Aglæca* — Middle Irish *Oclach*." In *Linguistic Method: Essays in Honor of Herbert Penzl*. Ed. Irmengard Rauch and Gerald F. Carr. The Hague: Mouton, 1979. Pp. 213-30.

Derives the Old English word *āglǣca* (with 19 occurrences in *Beowulf*) from the Irish word *óclach* which meant originally 'young warrior,' postulating that the Irish word was borrowed into the Mercian dialect in the seventh century and that its primary meaning in Old English is 'a fighter, valiant warrior, dangerous opponent, one who struggles fiercely.' After reviewing other solutions to the etymology of *āglǣca*, Kuhn analyzes the context of its thirty-six occurrences in Old English: "The referent may be a monster, a miscreant, a hero, a saint, a devil, God, a soldier, an inanimate object, or a force of nature. The only factor common to all members of this seemingly ill-sorted group is that they are, or have been, or will be, fighting" (218). This accounts for the varying application of the word to monsters (ll. 159a, 425a, 433b, 556a, 739a, 989b, 1000b, 2520a, 2534a, 2557a, 2905a) but also to the heroes Beowulf (l. 2592a) and Sigemund (l. 893a). Also discusses issues surrounding the phonological development of the word from its Mercian form *ōglǣca* to the West Saxon form *ǣglāca*. See Gillam [S434 and S519], Huffines [S919], and Olsen [1351].

1136 Kurylowicz, Jerzy. "Linguistic Fundamentals of the Meter of *Beowulf*." In *Linguistic and Literary Studies in Honor of Archibald A. Hill, IV: Linguistics and Literature; Sociolinguistics and Applied Linguistics*. Ed. Mohammad Ali Jazayery, Edgar C. Polomé, and Werner Winter. 4 Vols. Trends in Linguistics: Studies & Monographs, 7-10. The Hague: Mouton, 1979. 4:111-119.

Undertakes a study of Old English meter focusing on alliteration and compounding, drawing on *Beowulf* for examples. Kurylowicz concludes: "From the rhythmical point of view the Germanic hemistich is a kind of COMPOUND: $''$x plus $'$x, $'$x plus $''$x, $''$x + $''$x, i.e. a rhythmical unit of a higher order than the ordinary compound word ($'$xx, $'$xxx etc.). But there are points of contact between these two levels. A single compound word may function as hemistich, e.g. *þeodcyninga | þrym gefrūnon* (2). In the first hemistich the first and the second arsis ($''$, $'$) are represented by the primary and secondary stress of a compound.... Hierarchy of the arses, borne out by the possibility of using compound words as hemistichs, is isomorphic with word stress and is an intrinsic feature of the Germanic verse line. It seems to be the principal clue to the understanding of both its origin and its history. Among other things, the optional use of compounds as hemistichs may throw light on the development of the metrical device of alliteration from an originally morphological formative (viz. reduplication)" (119).

1137 Lecouteux, Claude. "Der Drache." [The Dragon]. *ZDA* 108 (1979): 13-31.

In a study of dragons and medieval dragon lore, comments briefly on the dragons in *Beowulf*, implying that though the poet knows later legends about flying dragons, his main picture of the dragon revolves around its earth-bound, serpentine characteristics from earlier European lore. Reviewing terms for dragons (mainly in German), Lecouteux concludes that until the end of the twelfth century, *wurm* (OE *wyrm*) predominates, while the term *nater* (OE *nædre*) also occurs, especially in Christian-influenced texts. *Trache* (OE *draca*) is a translation of *draco*, and mainly appears in texts whose sources are in Latin or one of its descendants (19-20). The dragon that Sigemund slays (ll. 884b-97) is not a flying dragon (as we know from other sources) but instead a gigantic serpent. Though the dragon which Beowulf and Wiglaf defeat does fly, the poet nevertheless conceives of it as a non-flying serpent in the battle scenes (ll. 2538-2708a), where its serpentine characteristics stand out. Includes a number of medieval and renaissance illustrations of dragons.

1138 Lehmann, Ruth P.M. "Contrasting Rhythms of Old English and New English." In *Linguistic and Literary Studies in Honor of Archibald A. Hill, IV: Linguistics and Literature; Sociolinguistics and Applied Linguistics.* 4 Vols. Trends in Linguistics: Studies & Monographs, 7-10. The Hague: Mouton, 1979. 4:121-126.

Discusses language change between Old and Modern English that makes translation of Old English poetry into modern verse difficult, discussing two passages translated from *Beowulf* (ll. 2444-62 and 1357-79). Such changes include loss of the distinction between long and short vowels, loss of inflectional endings leading to an increasing reliance on function words and fixed word order, and the shift to isochrony.

1139 Loganbill, Dean. "Time and Monsters in *Beowulf*." In *Geardagum* 3 (1979): 26-35.

Detects in *Beowulf* a conflict between cyclical and linear time as described by Mircea Eliade and believes that the conflict sheds light on the final death of hero and community at the end of the poem. In archaic cultures, cyclical time allows for ideal heroes, because heroes repeat and reflect the archetypal actions of the gods. This is not the case in *Beowulf*, where the onslaught of linear time amounts to a critique of the archaic heroic world. "Once outside cyclical time, the hero . . . loses his archaic power, because linear time allows or even requires alternatives which depend upon choices and different courses of action beyond the simple repetition of archetypal models" (30). Nevertheless, there is a certain nostalgia for the archaic golden age, which in *Beowulf* seems shaky from the beginning since Heorot is "stillborn" in the face of Grendel's ravages. To hold back the tug of linear time requires communal effort: and Beowulf's failure gives way to "the failure of the Geats to fulfill the (now increasingly necessary) obligations of community. Only by meeting such can they achieve even limited success in holding time at bay. For Beowulf, like Hrothgar, must now fight, not only a monster of the old sort, but time as well. Time *and* a monster get him" (31).

1140 Mastrelli, Carlo Alberto. "La formula germanica: 'sotto l'elmo' (a.isl. *und hjálmi*, ags. *under helme*, m.a.ted. *under helme*)." [The Germanic Formula: 'under the helmet' (ON *und hjálmi*, OE *under helme*, MHG *under helme*]. *AIUON, Studi nederlandesi, studi nordici* 22 (1979): 177-93.

Surveys occurrences of the formula *under helme* 'under helmet' and its variations in the Germanic literatures (Old Norse, Old English, Middle High German), concluding that the formula is ancient and that traces of it can be detected in a number of Latin sources, and further that it often has connotations of magical control. In *Beowulf*, the formula often appears with the adjective *heard* 'hardy, strong': *heard under helme* (ll. 342a, 404a, 2539a). A similar formula, *under heregrīman* 'under war-mask,' occurs frequently (ll. 396a, 2049a, 2605a). These formulas are similar to Ovid's phrase (*Trist.* V, 10, 25), *sub galea* 'under, wearing a helmet.' The Norse sources seem to invest the helmet formula with sacral and religious features connected to the Valkyries, and though the Old English usages come from a Christianized culture and seem to have a literary character, they too reflect aspects of this ancient mentality. Mastrelli discusses other

Latin phrases of a similar structure as well as a number of Old English formulas which consist of the preposition *under* + noun, such as formulas for "under the shield."

1141 Meaney, Audrey L. "The *Ides* of the Cotton Gnomic Poem." *MÆ* 48 (1979): 23-39.

In an analysis of a section of the *Cotton Gnomic Poem* makes several remarks on the roles of women in *Beowulf*, giving perspectives on the words *ides* 'lady' and *dyrne* 'secret.' Evidence from the penitentials and other sources confirm Tacitus's observation that the Germanic tribes held women to be sacred and prophetic. These sources discuss the penalties for women who engaged in sorcery to catch the love of men. Thus the phrase *dyrne cræft* 'secret power' (ll. 2168a, 2290a) may imply sorcery and at the least something "morally and socially evil" (29). The word *ides* carries no moral connotations in *Beowulf* but is used of high-born women, regardless of their moral failings. Gnomic poetry in general often stresses the proper place of women, "represented most clearly by the exemplary queens Wealhtheow and Hygd" (35).

1142 Mellinkoff, Ruth. "Cain's Monstrous Progeny in *Beowulf*: Part I, Noachic Tradition." *ASE* 8 (1979): 143-62.

Suggests, following Kaske [S801], that the Beowulf poet drew on a pseudepigraphical tradition related to the Book of Enoch for the depiction of Grendel and his mother as monstrous descendants of Cain. Kaske suggested Enoch as a likely source (since a short Latin fragment of it, once thought to originate in eighth-century England, is preserved), but Mellinkoff believes that a more ancient Book of Noah, or at least a loosely organized Noachic tradition, preserved in its most ancient form among the Dead Sea Scrolls, provided the poet with materials for the monsters. The Noah fragments, containing the most ancient telling of the fallen angels, may be the ultimate source for several details in *Beowulf*: the combination of gigantic size and cannibalism in the monsters, their corporeal (rather than spiritual) natures, the association of the mere with Grendel's mother and the wastelands with Grendel, the wasteland as the location of Cain's and Grendel's exile, as well as the motif of the sword made by giants. Mellinkoff concludes, "I am neither insisting on nor denying the possibility that an ancient Noah book was circulating in the *Beowulf* poet's environment. Nor do I insist that the Noah fragments are the only writings in the I Enoch compilation that may have served as a source. What I want to stress is that the poet seems to have been acquainted with elements of I Enoch that have their closest affinities with the Noah fragments" (161). See Mellinkoff [1267] for a continuation of this article.

1143 Niles, John D. "Ring Composition and the Structure of *Beowulf.*" *PMLA* 94 (1979): 924-35.

Appears, in somewhat altered form, as chapter seven in Niles [1399].

1144 Ogilvy, Jack D.A. "Beowulf, Alfred, and Christianity." In *Jones,* 1:59-66.

Compares views on fate (*wyrd*), earthly glory, worldly goods, and vengeance in *Beowulf* and Alfred's translation of the *Consolation of Philosophy,* concluding that "*Beowulf* and Alfred's translation of Boethius show such surprisingly close agreement that we can scarcely say that views expressed by the Christian Alfred are pagan in *Beowulf*" (59). Alfred's additions to the discussions of fate show that he finds a place in the workings of providence for man to change his fate and delay his death, parallel to a similar idea in *Beowulf,* lines 572-73. Alfred and the character Beowulf would have disagreed most on the topic of vengeance, especially given the latter's statement (ll. 1384-85) that it is better to avenge a friend than mourn too much and Alfred's Christian forbearance in taking revenge on his Danish enemies. "Beowulf's Christianity was strongly tinged by pagan views, but so was that of most Christian Anglo-Saxons. These pagan elements certainly do not prove that Beowulf was a Christian but, when they also appear in indubitably Christian contexts, they should not be construed as evidence of paganism either" (65).

1145 Payne, F. Anne. "The Danes' Prayers to the 'Gastbona' in *Beowulf.*" *NM* 80 (1979): 308-14.

Argues that the "Christian excursus" (ll. 175-88), in which the poet condemns the Danes as heathen backsliders, is central to the meaning of the poem and that it refers less to a Christian poet's attack on idolatry than to "the poet's vision of the heroic imagination" (308). In turning to the soul-slayer, the Danes reject the freedoms which Christian learning and philosophy brought to the Germanic peoples: a new conception of space, choice, and freedom from the fear of death. As such, the word "heathen" (l. 179a) "means not only 'non-Christian,' but also 'dead,' 'confined,' 'uncreative'" (309). "The heathen temple passage, the only direct clue the poet gives us to the nature of his central concerns, provides us with one of the chief symbols of the poem. It is the enclosure in which men, at terrible moments of crisis, surrender their imaginations. It is the symbol of the narrowest limits of human ideas (hence the designation 'heathen'); it is the symbol of the ruts which confine and channel the drive to discover creative alternatives" (313). The *gāstbona* 'soul-slayer' (l. 177a) is an abstract negation of heroic freedom and imagination represented also by Grendel. At the end of the poem, the Geats are very near this state of heathen despair.

1146 Pfeiffer, John R. "But Dragons Have Keen Ears: On Hearing *Earthsea* with Recollections of *Beowulf.*" In *Ursula K. Le Guin: Voyager to Inner Lands and to Outer Space.* Ed. Joe DeBolt. Port Washington, NY: Kennikat, 1979. Pp. 115-27.

Finds thematic and poetic similarities between *Beowulf* and Ursula Le Guin's Earthsea trilogy (*A Wizard of Earthsea, The Tombs of Atuan,* and *The Farthest Shore*).

1147 Pilch, Herbert and Hildegard L.C. Tristram. *Altenglische Literatur.* [Old English Literature]. Heidelberg: Carl Winter, 1979. Pp. 261.

Under the rubric of "biographical epic," provides a general introduction to *Beowulf,* grouping it with the Old English *Guthlac.* Pilch and Tristram define biographical epic as a narrative genre which selects episodes from the life of a hero and tells them in an *ordo artificialis* 'artificial order'; that is, the plot does not proceed chronologically. The hero struggles against superhuman adversaries and fights for his own glory (*dōm*) and at the same time for the glory of God. The biographical epic as well as Old English epic in general is characterized by a marked Christian ethos (44-45). *Beowulf,* however, contains almost all the other genres of Old English literature within itself. It does not center on suspense-filled narration but on artistic structure and formulation (54). Includes discussions of the digressions, dialogue, foreshadowing, and narrative structure and also mentions *Beowulf* frequently in sections on more general topics: metrics, Old English stylistics (including vocabulary, syntax,

and rhetoric), audience, literary history, and the state of research.
Reviews: Stanley B. Greenfield, *Anglia* 99 (1981): 487-90.

1148 Puhvel, Martin. *'Beowulf' and the Celtic Tradition.* Waterloo, Ont.: Wilfrid Laurier UP, 1979. Pp. ix + 142.

Suggests that "the mosaic of the poem shows enough marks of Celtic influence not only to render some of the puzzling elements explicable . . . but also to explain how the essential plot of the major part of the epic, the struggle against Grendel and his mother, could have grown out of Celtic folktale" (viii). Chapter one, "Review of the Case for Celtic Influence on *Beowulf*," gives an overview of earlier scholarship in this field, with some criticisms and also some endorsements, particularly of the work of Dehmer [F450], Murphy, and Carney [S299].

The following chapters identify various Celtic analogues for specific motifs: "The Might of Grendel's Mother" (paralleled by demonic hags in Irish folktales about Finn mac Cumaill); "The Light-Phenomenon in Grendel's Dwelling" (similar to the slaying of a solar deity with its own light-weapon as told in the *Táin* and other Irish and Scottish texts and the ultimate source of the myth of Excalibur); "The Melting of the Giant-Wrought Sword" (with Irish beliefs in the fantastic heat or destructiveness of blood, particularly that of Cúchulainn); "Beowulf and Irish Battle Rage" (finding that Beowulf's rage takes place well before the heat of battle, as is true for Irish heroes, but not for Germanic berserkers); "The Swimming Prowess of Beowulf" (paralleled by miraculous swimming feats of Dubhdiadh the Druid and Cúchulainn but not that similar to tales of swimming prowess in Northern literature); "Beowulf's Fights with Water-Monsters" (pointing out that Finn mac Cumaill, Cúchulainn, and St. Columba fight semi-demonic water beasts which do not appear in continental Germanic lore); "*Beowulf* and Irish Underwater Adventure" (arguing that Beowulf's ability to survive under water is paralleled by Irish tales in which the hero visits the underworld); and "Beowulf's Slaying of Dæghrefn" (which finds an analogue to Beowulf's deadly bear-hug in Cúchulainn's deadly grip in the *Táin*, a brute force seldom used by Germanic heroes even in the *Grettis Saga*). In each case, Puhvel examines and dismisses the direct relevance of Germanic, particularly Northern sources.

The last chapter, "The Question of the Origin of the Grendel Story," suggests that the fight with Grendel in *Beowulf* is based ultimately on a Celtic folktale called "The Hand and the Child" and that the Germanic folktale of the Bear's Son or "The Three Stolen Princesses" shows parallels "on the whole far less striking than those inherent in the Celtic tale" (87). In the story of "The Hand and the Child," "a long demonic arm reaches in the chimney or smoke-hole to abduct a prince's newborn children. A hero, generally with some comrades, watches over one such infant and he or a companion tears or hews off the intruding arm, but the other arm normally catches the hero off guard and abducts the child, who is subsequently, together with the previously kidnapped children, recovered from the haunt, mostly in a water setting, of the wounded monster, to which this creature is tracked and where he is slain" (2n). In *Beowulf*, as in a subset of the Celtic tales, the hero grapples with the clutching arm and tears it off; thus, Beowulf's strange mode of attacking Grendel (without a weapon) may have its origin in the Celtic tale. In a Scottish Tale of Finn based on this story, Finn's companions fall asleep through magic, while in another version the demon carries a bag into which victims are enticed, details paralleled in *Beowulf*. Puhvel finds that the story helps to explain a number of other puzzling features of *Beowulf*. Though some Scandinavian influence cannot be totally dismissed, "there seems, to me, no need for any such assumption" (137).

Reviews: J. Simpson, *Folklore* 91 (1980): 250; *OEN* 15.1 (1981): 96; G.W. Dunleavey, *JEGP* 80 (1981): 402-03; R.E. Finnegan, *Stud. in Religion/ Sciences Religieuses* 10 (1981): 254; D.N. Klausner, *U of Toronto Quarterly* 50.4 (103-04); A.H. Olsen, *ELN* 18 (1981): 209-11; N. Jacobs, *MÆ* 51 (1982): 112-14; A.A. Lee, *ESC* 9 (1983): 363-71; B. Lindström, *SN* 55 (1983): 204-05; R.W. McTurk, *YES* 13 (1983): 294-95.

1149 Robinson, Fred C. "Two Aspects of Variation in Old English Poetry." In *OE Poetry*, pp. 127-45.

Modifying the definition of Walter Paetzel [F1613], examines two types of variation in Old English poetry: clarifying variation (where the second term explains more literally the metaphorical meaning of the first) and repetitious variation (in which a major word is repeated—usually thought to be defective and in need of emendation). Robinson cites several examples of the first kind of variation in *Beowulf* (ll. 1368-69, 1745-47, 1143-44, 1522-24, 1121-24, 1829-35), arguing that the word *hilde-lēoma* 'battle light' (i.e., sword) is not a dead metaphor in line 1143b since it requires a clarifying variation. Similarly, he makes the case that *gār-holt* 'spear-wood' of line 1834b should be interpreted metaphorically as "forest of spears" since it requires the clarifying variation in line 1835. Robinson rejects the claim of the oral-formulaicists that the poet does not have time to notice the literal meaning of his formulas and defends the apparent mixed metaphor *beadolēoma bītan nolde* 'the battle-light (i.e., sword) did not want to bite' (l. 1523), as consistent with a highly-developed system of fire imagery. He suggests that the second type of variation, in which a word is repeated, need not necessarily be viewed as defective since Old English poets use repetition of word elements to good effect in a number of ways including in envelope patterns. From this point of view, it may be best to let stand ll. 2283-84, where the word *hord* is repeated in the variation.

1150   Sasabe, Hideo. "*Medudrēam* in *Beowulf*." *Review of English Literature* (Kyoto Univ.) 40 (1979): 1-18. In Japanese.

Argues that the word *medudrēam* 'joy of feasting' (l. 2016a) contrasts vividly with the sorrow caused by Grendel and his mother. Just as *medudrēam* was the cause of Grendel's anger, so the dragon was angered by the theft of the *drincfæt dȳre* 'a precious drinking vessel' (l. 2306a), a word suggestive of *medudrēam*, a key word in the poem. (HS)

1151   Schabram, Hans. "Stonc, *Beowulf* 2288." In *Festgabe für Hans Pinsker zum 70. Geburtstag*. Ed. Richild Acobian. Vienna: Verband der wissenschaftlichen Gesellschaften Österreichs, 1979. Pp. 144-156.

Provides previously overlooked evidence that the verb *stincan* (l. 2288a) means 'to sniff, smell' not 'to move suddenly, glide' as the majority opinion now holds. Schabram points out that *gestincan* appears as a verb meaning 'to smell' (transitive) in glosses to *Psalm* 113:14 in the Junius, Lambeth, Cambridge, Stowe, and Salisbury Psalters. Further, the simplex *stincan* (without the *ge-* prefix) also carries the same meaning in the Vespasian and Junius Psalters' gloss of *Psalm* 134:17 (which translate *odorabunt* as *stincad* and *stincað* respectively). The verb *tō-stincan*, used by Ælfric, also means "to smell," as do some OHG and MHG cognates, one in *Ortnit* describing a dragon's sniffing out of a man.

1152   Schubel, Friedrich. *Probleme der 'Beowulf'-Forschung.* [Problems of 'Beowulf' Research]. Erträge der Forschung, Bd. 122. Darmstadt: Wissenschaftliche Buchgesellschaft, 1979. Pp. xiv + 188.

Provides a general overview of issues in *Beowulf* research with special attention to summarizing scholarship between 1960 and 1975. Chapter one, "*Beowulf* as a Work of Art," discusses matters of diction (formulas, irony, contrasts, style in general) and structure (oppositions, interlace, "tectonics," folktale structure, and miscellaneous approaches). Subsequent chapters deal with the author/narrator, sources, themes, characterization (of Beowulf, Unferth, Grendel, Hygd, Hrothulf and Hrothgar, guards and messengers, as well as the figure of the *scop*), the Geats and their identity, the monsters, and the manuscript. Contains an author-title index of works cited as well as a selected bibliography of editions and translations. References to Schubel's commentary on individual passages have been incorporated into the line index of this volume.
Reviews: *OEN* 15.1 (1981): 102; M. Lehnert, *ZAA* 29 (1981): 70-1.

1153   Smith, Sarah Stanbury. "*Folce to Frofre*: The Theme of Consolation in *Beowulf*." *ABR* 30 (1979): 191-204.

Claims that Beowulf as a character embodies "in thought, word and deed commonplaces of Latin consolation literature" (198), but that the consolation he offers as a Germanic king is "shown to be limited by his paganism" (201). Beowulf is "presented as an ideal hero, noble and mighty, the strongest of men. Throughout the Danish section of the poem, Beowulf appears as the answer to consolation in this life, with the accompanying implication that whatever comfort he brings will be no more substantial or lasting than his purged mead hall of Heorot, doomed to fire" (197-98). Themes of consolation are clustered in the first part of the poem but absent from the second half, thus inverting the normal order of the *consolatio*, which moves "from lament through praise for the dead to *solacia* for grief" (203). The poem ends in mourning and dirge, offering "a final refutation of the efficacy of consolation in this life" (204).

1154 Stanley, Eric G. "*Geoweorþa*: 'Once Held in High Esteem'." In *Tolkien*, pp. 99-119.

In explaining the odd form *Geoweorþa* (the Old English rendering of the Latin name *Iugurtha*, the king of the Numidians), discusses patterns of kingship in *Beowulf* and other Old English texts. Stanley believes that Iugurtha's name in Old English may be a pun, meaning "once worthy," from *geō-* 'once' and *weorþa* 'worthy.' As such, it may reflect Anglo-Saxon attitudes towards kingship present in *Beowulf*, where youthful glory gives way to crime (in the case of Heremod), the pattern of Iugurtha's life as told in Sallust's *De bello Iugurthino*. Beowulf's career illustrates the opposite movement, from an inglorious youth to responsible kingship. Hrothulf resembles Iugurtha in his usurpation of his cousins' throne. Stanley concludes: "It seems to me that one of the patterns of kingship, best seen by us now in Old English literature by exemplification and contrast in the many lives of kings which form a single theme of much that is various and digressive in *Beowulf*, has affected the spelling of Iugurtha, king of the Numidians" (119).

1155 _____. "Two Old English Poetic Phrases Insufficiently Understood for Literary Criticism: *Þing Gehegan* and *Seonoþ Gehegan*." In *OE Poetry*, pp. 67-90.

Undertakes to show that our understanding of Old English texts at the level of words and phrases is often shaky by emphasizing a number of obscure and difficult points in *Beowulf*, lines 419-26 and *Phoenix* 491-94, particularly the two phrases in the title. "Exact understanding of words in their context is a prerequisite of literary criticism; and often we lack that understanding for Old English" (90). After pointing out obscurities surrounding *of searwum* (l. 419b), *fāh* (l. 413a), *eotena cyn* (l. 421a), *niceras* (l. 422a), *wēan ā hsodon* (l. 423b), *āglǣcan* (l. 425a) and *þyrse* (l. 426a), Stanley goes on to explore the obscure phrase *gehēgan ðing* 'settle the case? hold a meeting?' (ll. 425b-26a), rejecting Klaeber's claim that it is a legal term in Old English since it occurs in no Old English legal texts and since the verb *gehē gan* is confined to poetry. After reviewing analogues to the phrase in the early Kentish Laws, the *Sigrdrífumál*, Old Icelandic, and Old Frisian legal texts, he concludes that the phrase "goes back to the inherited diction of the Germanic tribes and was not in origin poetic only" (87). Though the

1156 Talentino, Arnold V. "Fitting 'Guðgewæde': Use of Compounds in *Beowulf.*" *Neophil* 63 (1979): 592-96.

Suggests that the *Beowulf*-poet repeats compounds when the contexts in which they occur overlap in some way. The compound *gūðgewǣde* 'war garment' is unusual in that it occurs six times—more than any other compound—once at the beginning of the poem (l. 227a) and then several times in the last section (ll. 2617b, 2623b, 2730a, 2851a, and 2871b). To test the hypothesis, Talentino examines other compounds for armor which occur more than once as well as other repeating compounds and finds that their contexts do overlap. The poet first uses *gūðgewǣde* to describe the armor of Geats as they approach Heorot but uses it again only in the last section to describe the armor of the craven Geats at Beowulf's death and the armor Beowulf would pass on to a son, if he had one. The repetition near the end of the poem shows a close contextual overlap in that all the occurrences emphasize the close bond between a lord and his retainers. Such repetitions produce an ironic effect: the word used to describe the armor of the heroic Geats at the beginning now describes that of the cowardly ones at the end.

1157 Tejera, Dionisia. "Date and Provenance of *Beowulf.*" *Letras de Duesto* 9 (1979): 165-76.

Accepts a date in the mid to late eighth century (mainly because of the reference to Offa I) and generally argues against the notion that *Beowulf* is a poem composed in a pre-Christian period dominated by Germanic paganism, suggesting that the poem's northern lore was brought to England at the time of the invasions of the Angles, Saxons, and Jutes. Neither burial customs nor the treasures described in the poem can suggest convincingly that *Beowulf* was written before the coming of Christianity to England. Instead, "it is a very credible assumption that the [Christian] poet chose to depict for his audience the very vivid contemporary pagan customs *abroad*" (172). Tejera discusses archaeological evidence, including that of the Sutton Hoo find and argues point by point against the conclusions of Clark Hall [S45].

term may have been a legal one originally, by the time it reaches Old English, it has become an exclusively poetic turn of phrase. Also discusses the similar phrase *seonoð gehēgan* 'hold a synod?' from *Phoenix* (l. 493b).

Further, the "Geatas" are to be identified with the "Götar" of southern Sweden and thus cannot be considered the ancestors of the "Jutes." Thus, Beowulf cannot be considered an "English" hero. Tejera points out, however, that Germanic singers often praised heroes outside their own tribes. The northern lore in the poem, Tejera believes, cannot support the idea that *Beowulf* is a translation of a Scandinavian original. "The obvious conclusion is that these Scandinavian traditions were brought to England by the settlers in the sixth century" (175).

1158 Tripp, Raymond P., Jr. "On 'Post-Editorial' Editions of *Beowulf.*" *In Geardagum* 3 (1979): 18-25.

Critiques student editions of *Beowulf* with minimal notes and facing translation (Nickel [S1003], Chickering [S1023], and Swanton [S1097]) because they fail "to provide truly new editions in the sense of resolving the many long-standing difficulties which still burden the poem" and "they fail to advance 'editing' into the literary process it now must become if we are ever to arrive at the poet's meaning" (24). Tripp analyzes each edition's treatment of line 2564a, *ecgum ungleaw*, often emended to *ecgum unslāw* 'with sharp edges,' finding the scanty editorial notes insufficient. He goes on to suggest wordplay in the phrase between 'with very sharp edges' (modifying the sword) and 'unknowledgeable about swords' (modifying Beowulf). Tripp reviews Beowulf's knowledge of swords and finds it inaccurate in a number of places. The phrase *gomele lāfe* 'old heirloom' (l. 2563b) might also apply to Beowulf as "the grand old warrior of his nation" (21) as well as to the sword. These student or "post-editorial" editions of *Beowulf* cannot reveal such a level of meaning, given their Spartan notes and commentary.

1159 Viswanathan, S. "On the Melting of the Sword: *wæl-rāpas* and the Engraving on the Sword-Hilt in *Beowulf.*" *PQ* 58 (1979): 360-63.

Explores the thematic importance of lines 1607b-11, in which the poet describes how the giant-sword melts from the blood of Grendel. The poet compares the melting of the sword to God's loosing the frozen bonds of winter. Viswanathan considers that whether the compound *wæl-rāpas* (l. 1610a) means 'pool-ropes' or 'slaughter-ropes,' "[t]he suggestion underlying the simile in *Beowulf* is that of God's control and release of his subjects through and from the bondage of 'wyrd'" (362). Viswanathan sees this theme of divine control as central to the poem and particularly to Hrothgar's sermon and suggests a parallel between the bladeless sword-hilt and Grendel's bodiless head.

1160 Warren, Lee A. "Real Monsters, Please: The Importance of Undergraduate Teaching." *Journal of General Education* 31 (1979): 23-33.

In a plea to take undergraduate teaching more seriously, compares *Beowulf* and Camus' *The Plague* as a way of stimulating undergraduates' interest in books: "A discussion of *Beowulf* and *The Plague*, deriving from a Freshman English course I taught several years ago, shows how books from different periods and different cultures can be used in undergraduate courses to provoke thought about issues that are at once contemporary and ancient. They work together conveniently for several reasons. The first is that they concern themselves with common issues: they wrestle with the problems of evil and death; they define heroism, dignity, nobility; they discuss both what is the best way to live and how to think of oneself. The similarities and differences in their perceptions of these problems provide room for debate about the issues. Secondly, these issues are of particular concern to young people" (24). Both *Beowulf* and *The Plague*, Warren argues, take strikingly similar (though not identical) stances toward evil and death.

1161 Whitman, F. H. "Constraints on the Use of the Relative Pronoun Forms in *Beowulf*." *TSLL* 21 (1979): 1-16.

Finds rules governing the use of three principal forms of the relative pronoun in *Beowulf*, forms which might otherwise seem to have been selected arbitrarily: 1) the various forms of *sē / sēo / þæt* standing by themselves, 2) the indeclinable particle *þē*, and 3) a combination of the first two, as in *sē þe*. Whitman draws two conclusions from the evidence: "(1) that the use of the relative pronoun forms from categories 1 and 2 was contingent on whether the verse structure was able to support the inclusion of an unstressed syllable between the initial relative pronoun and the first stress; and (2) that when the verse was able to do so, the poet could resort to the combined form (category 3) in order to avoid a metrically deviant verse" (4). With some exceptions, dependent clauses headed by monosyllabic conjunctions reflect the same phenomenon as the relative clauses. Also discusses structures which block the inclusion of unstressed syllables in key positions.

1162 Wilts, Ommo. "Die Friesen im *Beowulf*—Rezeption und epische Grundlage." [The Frisians in *Beowulf*—Reception and Epic Foundation]. *Nordfriesisches Jahrbuch* n.s. 15 (1979): 131-44.

Not seen.

1980

1163 Anderson, Earl R. "Formulaic Typescene Survival: Finn, Ingeld, and the *Nibelungenlied.*" *ES* 61 (1980): 293-301.

Using the terminology of Fry [S667], proposes a Germanic "type-scene" called "the tragic court flyting," arguing that it lies behind two scenes in *Beowulf* (the Finnsburh episode, ll. 1071-1159, and Beowulf's speculations on the Danish-Heathobard feud, involving Ingeld, ll. 2020-31) as well as a scene in the *Nibelungenlied*. The type-scene contains the following sequence of events: "(1) A tense situation is created by the presence or arrival of strangers in the hall—potential enemies.... (2) Hostility comes to the surface with an exchange of threats or insults, (3) accompanied by the appearance of a particularly provocative weapon or weapons. The provocative weapon is a detail essential to the typescene, for it brings to mind an old feud and is instrumental in the renewal of hostility. (4) The provocation results in a battle which takes place in the hall and ends with the destruction of court and hall" (293-94). On the basis of this conventional chain of events, Anderson suggests that ll. 1142-59a need not be broken into two or three parts, as they frequently have been by other critics, but can remain as a unified scene.

1164 Andersson, Theodore M. "Tradition and Design in *Beowulf.*" In *OEL in Context*, pp. 90-106.

Modifying Buchloh [S575], argues that the *Beowulf* poet inherits traditional type-scenes from the Germanic lay but alters them to form a new genre, "a quasi-epic narrative illustrating the mutability of the heroic life" (105). Andersson identifies ten characteristic narrative situations in the Germanic lays (*Fight at Finnsburg*, the *Hildebrandslied*, *Atlakviða*, *Atlamál*, *Hamðismál*, *Hlǫðsviða*, the Sigurd and Walter materials, etc.) also present in Beowulf: (1) battle scenes (Hygelac's raid, Ravenswood, the dragon), (2) hall scenes of conviviality (mostly at Heorot), (3) hall battles (in Heorot and in the underwater hall), (4) journeys in quest of heroic confrontation (to Denmark and back, to the mere and back), (5) sentinel scenes (the coastguard and Wulfgar), (6) welcoming scenes, (7) the use of intermediaries, (8) the consultation of heroes with kings or queens (Beowulf with Hygelac, Hrothgar, or Wealhtheow), (9) incitations or flytings

(Unferth), (10) leave-taking scenes (92). The *Beowulf* poet arranges these inherited scenes, not to achieve narrative simplicity, but to construct mood and atmosphere. Andersson finds a consistent pattern of dramatic reversals in the narrative movement of the poem: sorrow gives way to relief, joy to disaster. The constant ups and downs underline the message of futility: "The traditional episodes of heroic poetry are organized according to the notion that life is unstable and is lent stability only by trust in the hereafter" (105). The main narrative flow follows a pattern of reversals that ends in Beowulf's ambiguous triumph over the dragon. Andersson outlines this and other narrative reversals in a series of diagrams.

1165 Bammesberger, Alfred. "Altenglische Komposita mit *hild(e)*." [Old English Compounds with *hild(e)*-]. *Münchener Studien zur Sprachwissenschaft* 39 (1980): 5-10.

Takes issue with Nickel's thesis [S1003] that compounds with the first element *hilde-* (such as *hilderæs*, l. 300a) are not compounds but separate words (*hilde ræs*). Nickel denies that *hild* ever had a regular connecting morpheme (*Fugenmorphem*) -e-, but does accept compounds based on *hild-* (without -e-) + substantive. Bammesberger refutes this argument by pointing out that Nickel's parallel between *gūð* and *hild* ultimately fails since the two nouns come from different stem classes (*ō* and *ijð* respectively). Further, the connecting morpheme -e- is not irregular or sporadic, but (behaving as an a-stem) *hildijō-* first became *hildija-* in compounds, then the *j* and *a* disappeared and the -*i*- weakened to -*e*-, thus providing for a regular connecting morpheme, as found in the name *Hildeburh*. Further, the disappearance of the -*e*- in some *hild-* compounds is to be explained by syllable structure: *hild-* appears without -*e*- when the second element of the compound contains a short root-vowel but retains the -*e*- when the root-vowel of the following element is long. Thus, the connecting vowel -*e*- (from -*i*-) is syncopated before a light root-syllable. Not all combinations of *hild-e-* + substantive must be compounds, but, according to Bammesberger, Nickel's view that none of them can be is surely wrong (*sicherlich falsch*, 9).

1166 ——————. "Three *Beowulf* Notes." *ES* 61 (1980): 481-84.

On the principle that "emendations should be avoided unless absolutely necessary" (481), Bammesberger proposes solutions to three difficult passages, allowing the manuscript readings to stand by repunctuating and reanalyzing the text. 1) The clause in lines 2297b-2299a lacks a predicate, and several emendations have been proposed. However, "the manuscript seems to allow one further reading if we omit any mark of punctuation in between 2298a and 2298b and consider the four half-lines 2297b-2299a as one main clause. The subject of the whole clause is *ænig mon*, the predicate *gefeh*; it can be translated as 'nobody in the desert, however, rejoiced in fighting, in the battle deed'" (482). 2) In lines 2844a-2845a, the manuscript reading *æghwæðre* has been traditionally emended to *æghwæðer* in order to supply a subject for the clause. Since the manuscript reading is probably an instrumental singular, it cannot function as the subject. It is therefore preferable to take the subject of the preceding clause, *dryhtmāðma dæl* as the subject of this clause and repunctuate accordingly. The new reading yields the following sense: "the treasure had through (the action of) each brought about the end of the transient life" (483). 3) There is some confusion about whether *orwearde* (l. 3127a) is an adjective or an adverb. Bammesberger sides with Klaeber [S67] that it is an adjective but maintains that it is not a *ja*-stem, which would have undergone i-mutation. Instead, he proposes the base form *orweard* 'without a guardian' on the model of words like *ormod* 'without courage,' a form which would be "totally regular within the Germanic morphological pattern" (483). Merging this passage with the following clause, placing a full stop after line 3127a, and interpreting *læne* as an adverb belonging to *licgan*, allows the manuscript reading to stand. The lines can now be translated as follows: "There was no lot-casting as to who should rob the treasure, (which was) from then on without a guardian. The men saw a certain amount (of the treasure) remaining in the hall, lying in a perishable way" (484).

1167 Bjork, Robert E. "Unferth in the Hermeneutic Circle: A Reappraisal of James L. Rosier's 'Design for Treachery: The Unferth Intrigue'." *PLL* 16 (1980): 133-41.

Seeks to refute Rosier's contention [S478] that the word *þyle*, applied to Unferth in lines 1165b and 1456b, carries a clearly pejorative meaning. Bjork finds several logical inconsistencies in Rosier's argument: his equating of *þyle* with the compound *fœ-þele* 'wicked jester' and his assumption that *glēoman* 'singer', sometimes glossing the same word as *þyle*, is also pejorative, as well as his interpretation of the Old Norse evidence (from the *Hávamál* and *Fáfnismál*). Bjork concludes: "The meaning of *þyle* remains enigmatic, and the question of Unferth's role in *Beowulf* remains vexed" (141).

1168   Bremmer, Rolf H., Jr. "The Importance of Kinship: Uncle and Nephew in *Beowulf*." *Amsterdamer Beiträge zur älteren Germanistik* 15 (1980): 21-38.

Argues that the relationship between the mother's brother and the sister's son plays a significant role in *Beowulf*, describing an ideal kinship pair, while the relationships between the father's brother and the brother's son are often troubled. After surveying a number of historical, legal, and literary examples of the mother's brother-sister's son relationship in Anglo-Saxon sources, Bremmer turns to *Beowulf*, showing that the poet idealizes this relationship between Beowulf and Hygelac as well as between Fitela and Sigemund. He identifies certain characters who are identified through their maternal uncles, not through their fathers: Heardred as the nephew of Hereric (l. 2206b) and Hygelac as the nephew of Swerting (l. 1203a), his mother's brother (or father), Eomer as the nephew of Garmund through his sister Modthryth. Since mother's brother and sister's son generally fight together, it seems likely that in the Finnsburh episode Hildeburh's brother Hnæf and her unnamed son fought not on opposite sides of the battle but on the same side. Such an assumption increases the sense of pathos—the uncle and nephew, the ideal pair, placed together on the same funeral pyre and consumed by flames. Finally, Bremmer argues that Wiglaf was Beowulf's nephew by an unnamed sister, the wife of Weohstan, and that the poet holds up Beowulf and Wiglaf as the ideal uncle-nephew pair. While the mother's brother and sister's son always appear in a positive relationship, the father's brother and brother's son are usually in conflict (as with Hrothgar and Hrothulf, Onela and Eanmund and Eadgils).

1169   Brown, Alan K. "The Firedrake in *Beowulf*." *Neophil* 64 (1980): 439-60.

A wide-ranging review of dragon lore from patristic, Biblical, historical, folkloristic, and "scientific" sources, accounting for various details of the dragon in *Beowulf*: its fiery breath, flying ability, venom, etc. Brown maintains that the poet first invokes the dragon as a "great meteor-dragon who brings alive the whole spectrum of popular and even heathen beliefs implied in the term *fyrdraca*" (453). As the story advances, however, the poet appeals to the learned and religious sides of his audience as well by drawing on various bits of dragon lore, from the fiery Leviathan of Job and commentaries by Jerome, Gregory the Great, and Phillipus the Priest (fifth century) to lore derived from an early *Life of Samson* and Pliny. This connection to Job implies that Beowulf ultimately fails and is damned. His burning on the funeral pyre may reflect the burning of the God's enemies as depicted in a commentary by Jerome. With this, "we are to be reminded, terribly, of the fire brought forth out of the midst of Leviathan and those like him in order to consume [the damned], and of the inextinguishable flame which is to burn his deeds, and their souls, like straw" (456). The praise and ritual accorded to Beowulf at the end of the poem, though it appeals to our feelings about Beowulf's worthiness, shows that human judgment is "totally irrelevant" in the face of "apparent figurations of damnation" (456).

1169a Chance (Nitzsche), Jane. "The Anglo-Saxon Woman as Hero: The Chaste Queen and the Masculine Woman Saint." *Allegorica* 5 (1980): 139-148.

Considers evidence from wills, charters, writs, chronicles, saints' lives, and other historical and legendary accounts to document the role of women in Anglo-Saxon society, finding that "What is clear from these accounts is an identification of the sexes with complementary traits—the masculine with reason and determination, leading to active and heroic social and political role, and the feminine with passion and passivity, leading to a reduction of political activity unless a queen disassociates herself from her sex by maintaining exceptional chastity and spirituality, like the woman saint" (144).

1170 _____. "The Structural Unity in *Beowulf*: The Problem of Grendel's Mother." *TSLL* 22 (1980): 287-303.

Though other accounts of the poem's structure would see the episode involving Grendel's mother as "largely extraneous," argues that images of women cluster around the middle of the poem and provide structural links to the other parts. The poet is concerned to show Grendel's mother as a perversion of the ideal roles which women like Wealhtheow and Hygd play as mother and queen. "The role of mother highlights the first half of the middle section with the scop's mention of Hildeburh (1071 ff.) and the entrance of Wealhtheow, both of whom preface the first appearance of Grendel's dam (1258) in her role as avenging mother. Then the introduction of Hygd, Thryth (Modthryth), and Freawaru after the female monster's death (1590) stresses the role of queen as peace-weaver and cup-passer" (290). Mothers, as the story of Hildeburh shows, can only passively mourn their lost sons, not avenge them as a father would do. Thus, Grendel's mother acts as a monstrously masculine female, the poet often applying masculine epithets to her. As anti-queen, she perverts and parodies the hospitality code which women in particular (through their passing of the mead-cup and their role as advisors and peaceweavers) should uphold. Chance traces several inversions of the hospitality code in Beowulf's fight with Grendel's dam (ll. 1501-69), a scene which operates as a mock hall visit and notes a sexual undercurrent in the mutual grapplings and stabbings: "the poet exploits the basic resemblance between sexual intercourse and battle to emphasize the inversion of the feminine role of the queen or hall-ruler by Grendel's mother" (293-94). Grendel's mere itself, with its blood and intricate passages "almost projects the mystery and danger of female sexuality run rampant" (295). The women who appear outside the middle section (such as Freawaru and the unnamed Geatish mourner) show that women cannot ensure peace. Finally, "Despite the poet's realization that these roles cannot be fulfilled in this world, this Germanic ideal [of womanhood] provides structural and thematic unity for *Beowulf*" (299). Reprinted in Damico and Olsen.

1171 Clover, Carol J. "The Germanic Context of the Unferth Episode." *Speculum* 55 (1980): 444-68.

Argues that a detailed understanding of Norse flyting scenes is important for understanding the verbal duel between Beowulf and Unferth over the swimming contest with Breca. Since no systematic treatment of Norse flytings has been undertaken, Clover attempts a morphology of this "readily identifiable compositional unit" (444), showing the inadequacy of such traditional terminology as *senna* 'quarrel,' *mannjafnaðr* 'man-comparison,' and *nið* 'sexual defamation.' A typical flyting scene "consists of an exchange of verbal provocations between hostile speakers in a predictable setting.

The boast and insults are traditional, and their arrangement and rhetorical form is highly stylized" (446). To establish the commonplaces of these flyting scenes, Clover examines a catalogue of nearly forty flytings—including examples from the Edda (*Lokasenna, Skírnismál,* the *Helgakviður, Guðrúnarkviða,* etc.), Saxo Grammaticus, classical sagas (*Njáls saga, Bandamanna saga, Egils saga, Eyrbyggja saga, Gunnlaugs saga,* etc.) and legendary sagas (*Hjálmþés saga, Ketils saga hængs, Gríms saga loðinkinna, Örvar-Odds saga,* etc.)—in terms of setting, contenders, dramatic situation, content, and outcome. Several parallels emerge between the reconstructed paradigm for Norse flytings and the Unferth episode in *Beowulf,* "both with respect to situation (the hostile investigation into the reputation of a newcomer by a man who stands in a delegate relation to the king and is explicitly known as a man of words) and the nature of the speeches themselves: in form (Claim, Defense, and Counterclaim); in tone (the blend of insult, competitive boasting, and curse); in the use of sarcasm (most characteristically in concessive clauses); in the emphatic I/you contrast and the use of names in direct address; in the combat metaphor; in the matching of personal histories and the exposure of dubious or shameful deeds (and their sarcastic reconstruction); in the telltale preoccupation with the moral negotiability of past events; in the use of familiar oppositions and paradigms; and in such correspondences of detail as the charges of drunkenness and fratricide and the Hel curse. The only conspicuous incongruity is the absence of a sexual element" (466). [For further references, see *flyting* in the subject index.]

1172 Corso, Louise. "Some Considerations of the Concept of 'nīð' in *Beowulf.*" *Neophil* 64 (1980): 121-26.

Studies forty occurrences of the word *nīð* as a single word and as an element in poetic compounds in *Beowulf,* questioning Klaeber's narrow definition [S67] of the word as external 'violence' or 'strife,' and pointing out that it often seems to refer to the internal emotion of hatred, spite, or jealousy merging into a sense of malice or wickedness. Corso studies *nīð* as a word or word-element in four contexts: 1) in gnomic passages, 2) in references to the monsters, 3) in reference to feuds, and 4) in miscellaneous contexts, usually revolving around a historical legendary figure. In the Biblical translations, *nīð* is used to indicate evil, malice, and wickedness, a meaning which would strengthen the image of Grendel and the monsters as wicked beings, not just violent ones. Reading the word this way, however, would force an ironic reading on certain passages like line 2417b, where Beowulf is referred to as *nīðheard cyning* 'battle-strong king' or 'king strong in hatred.' Corso does not attempt to solve this dilemma but suggests that Klaeber's definition defines away ambiguity and nuance.

1173 Creed, Robert P. "Is There an Ancient Gnome in *Beowulf* Line 4?" *Folklore Forum* 13 (1980): 109-126.

Finds traces of an ancient gnome in the triplet *scyld scēfing sceaþe[na]* (l. 4), words associated by alliteration and which may preserve, through the medium of oral verse, an ancient memory of "the Neolithic Revolution," when human groups learned about agriculture. Essentially, the idea behind this gnome is that "Sheaves beget scathers and need shields," that is, crops must be defended from outsiders who would steal them. Creed examines the Indo-European roots of the three words. Alliteration holds the three words together as does their semantic content, especially as it relates to agriculture. Further, Scyld cannot really be the son of Scef, if we remember that Scyld arrives as an orphan and that Scef, in the other West Saxon genealogies, appears generations before Scyld. Creed also discusses the mnemonic function of traditional verse and how for the sake of memory concepts are often turned into characters, a shield becomes King Scyld, and a sheaf becomes Scef. Finally, he lists three criteria for identifying an ancient gnome of this sort: 1) the gnome must be recorded in the earliest form of a language, 2) the syllables of the passage must be linked as the traditional verse-dialect requires, and 3) the cluster or capsule of words must have a significance as a group.

1174 Dahood, Roger. "A Note on *Beowulf* 1104-8a." *MÆ* 49 (1980): 1-4.

Argues on paleographical grounds that one or more letters are missing at the end of verse 1106, allowing for a short infinitive to complete the faulty sense of the lines, perhaps *fōn* 'seize, grasp,' or *þȳn* (from *þeōwan*, 'urge on or pierce, stab'), though these solutions cannot be advanced with certainty given the paleographical evidence and the metrical environment of line 1106. "If *fon* were inserted, the line could be translated, 'Then the sword's edge must thereupon take it', it referring to the implied quarrel between the Frisians and the Half-Danes. If *þȳn*, a variant of *þeōwan*, were inserted, the line could be translated, 'Then the sword's edge must afterwards urge it on'" (3).

1175 Damico, Helen. "The Valkyrie Reflex in Old English Literature." *Allegorica* 5 (1980): 149-167.

Traces the manifestations of valkyrie figures in Old English and Old Norse literature, showing that aspects of the dual nature of the valkyrie type as fierce battle-demon as well as benevolent guardian can be detected in *Beowulf*, particularly in the figures of Grendel's mother and Modthryth. The Old Norse *dísir* (OE *ides*), semi-divine beings related to the valkyries, were powerful, priestly, and armed, receiving sacrifices at a shrine or altar (ON *hörgr*). Damico detects a resonance of this myth in the heathen sacrifice of the Danes at the hærg-trafum 'heathen temple' (l. 175b) after the attack of Grendel, who associated with female demons (i.e., his mother) by the word *helrunan* 'demons, sorceresses' (l. 163). The picture of the valkyrie as deadly battle-demon is seen in the figure of Grendel's mother, whom the poet twice identifies as an *ides* 'divine lady.' Like the valkyrie figures in the *Gísla saga*, she is also ambisexual—having a woman's likeness (l. 1351) but referred to with masculine pronouns. Modthryth, on the other hand, shows both sides of the valkyrie tradition as fierce ravager and benevolent guardian, her weaving of slaughter bonds (l. 1936) connects her to the *dísir*, as does her designation as an *ides*. After her transformation under the authority of Offa, she becomes a benevolent battle-maid. Damico also discusses conventions for portraying women in Old Norse literature—conventions based on the valkyrie tradition—and goes on to analyze Old English warrior-saints (Elene, Judith, and Juliana) from this point of view.

1176 Damon, Phillip. "The Middle of Things: Narrative Patterns in the *Iliad*, *Roland*, and *Beowulf*." In *OEL in Context*, pp. 107-16.

Analyzes *Beowulf* from the point of view of its paired opposites, particularly the theme of *sapientia et fortitudo* (see Kaske [S361, S676]), taking an approach based loosely on Lévi-Strauss's work on myth. Lévi-Strauss had identified "polarities or binary oppositions which have a thematically proportional relation to each other and in this relation bear meanings of fundamental cultural significance" (107). In a Shimsian Indian myth, the hero tries to mediate between the binary oppositions like earth and heaven, land and water, matrilocal and patrilocal residence but fails each time. Damon finds similar balanced, contrasting, or interacting pairs in the *Iliad*, the *Chanson de Roland*, and *Beowulf*, regarding their paired incidents as sets of ratios and showing that they constitute a thematic statement. The contrasts have the effect of complicating our judgment of their heroes: Beowulf possesses both *sapientia* and *fortitudo*, while Hrothgar and Hygelac have only one or the other. In death, Beowulf seems to have committed an act of pure fortitude, with little regard for wisdom (in taking on the dragon alone). But in the end, Beowulf seems to have served the mysterious workings of God's providence, attaining heaven and thus complicating and qualifying our view of his rash act, "an extravagant feat of pure fortitude" (116).

1177 Earnest, James David. "Spanish Translation of *Beowulf*: Or Pains of the Danes in Spain." *Revista/Review Interamericana* 10 (1980): 195-199.

Discusses the difficulties of translating *Beowulf* into Spanish and reviews the relative merits of translations by Vincente García Diego and Orestes Vera Pérez [see S25], offering suggestions for future translation.

1178 Edwards, Paul. "Art and Alcoholism in *Beowulf*." *Durham U Journal* 72 (1980): 127-31.

A light-hearted look at drink and drinking in *Beowulf*. Among Edwards' more memorable proposals are that the opening word of the poem, *hwæt*, represents in onomatopoeia a preparation for hawking, that an inter-vocalic "r" may have been lost from Beowulf's name, which originally was *Beorwulf* 'the Beer-Wolf,' that Grendel's dam becomes a figure of pathos when it is realized that she is condemned "to make her home in, nay, to drink nothing but water" (129). Concerning Wiglaf's splashing of water on his dying lord (ll. 2853-55), Edwards comments: "Quite apart from the painful absurdity of Wiglaf's effort to give water to the mighty beer-swiller, lifelong enemy of water and its dismal occupants, there is the witty play on the verbs *spōwan*, to succeed, and *spīwan*, to spew. In consequence, the sense is not that 'He (Wiglaf) did not succeed', but also that 'He (Beowulf) did not spew'" (130). Contains other suggestions in a similar vein. See also Edwards [1545].

1179 Eliason, Norman E. "The Burning of Heorot." *Speculum* 55 (1980): 75-83.

Rejects the widely-held notion that lines 81b-85 refer to the burning of Heorot in the Danish-Heathobard feud and offers an alternative reconstruction and reading. Most modern editors emend the MS reading at line 84, *þ[æt] se secg hete aþum swerian* to *þæt se ecghete āþum-swēoran* in order to restore alliteration. Wrenn's translation [S276] of the reconstructed line (in its context) runs as follows: "it [Heorot] awaited the surgings of hateful fire. Nor was the time yet nigh at hand that the deadly enmity between son-in-law and father-in-law was to be roused up because of a mortal and violent deed." Eliason points out that the current reading of these lines provides a poor transition to the attack of Grendel which follows. It involves other difficulties: a doubtful use of the dative to mean "between" in *āþumswēorum* and a strained sense for *lenge* (l. 83b). Further, the burning of Heorot is not mentioned either in *Beowulf* in connection with the Danish-Heathobard feud (ll. 2024-69) or in *Widsith* (ll. 45-49), which describes the feud between Ingeld and Hrothgar. Eliason offers a different emendation line 84, *þæt se [þe] secghete [oþ]swerian [dorste]*, which may be translated as "'It was by no means a long time until one who dared to abjure sword-hostility was to rouse to murderous onslaught,' or—to bring out the sense of the line more clearly—paraphrased as '... until one [i.e., Grendel] who dared to fight without a sword ...'" (80). This reading restores the alliteration and provides a better transition to the attack of Grendel which follows.

1180 Foley, John Miles. "*Beowulf* and Traditional Narrative Song: The Potential and Limits of Comparison." In *OEL in Context*, pp. 117-36.

Argues that those who compare the oral style of *Beowulf* to that of the Serbo-Croatian singers or the Homeric epics must remain aware of significant differences in these traditions. Foley looks at three areas in which the traditions diverge: metrical constraints on formulas, construction of "multiform" type-scenes, and larger patterns of narrative structure. About meter, Foley concludes that "the Old English alliterative line, specifically the meter of *Beowulf*, depends much less on syllabicity and internal structure than do its [Greek and Serbo-Croatian] counterparts. On this basis, Foley offers a definition of formula specific to Old English as a "recurrent substitutable phrase one half-line in length which results from the intersection of two compositional parameters—a morphemic focus at positions of metrical stress and a limited number of metrical formulas" (122). Comparing a type-scene from the Serbo-Croatian tradition ("Shouting in Prison") to the sea-voyages in *Beowulf* (ll. 205-303a and 1880b-1919), he finds that the motif structure is similar in both scenes but that verbal correspondences peculiar to the Serbo-Croatian metrical situation are difficult to find in *Beowulf*, since the metrical demands are different. *Beowulf* repeats individual morphs and occasionally a half-line formula (of which Foley provides a list) while the Serbo-Croatian type-scene repeats entire lines and cola. Finally, in larger narrative patterns, Foley finds evidence of "song amalgam" or the stitching together of separate poems in Serbo-Croatian return songs, suggesting that a similar process may be going on in *Beowulf*.

1181 _____. "Epic and Charm in Old English and Serbo-Croatian Oral Tradition." *Comparative Criticism* 2 (1980): 71-92.

In a broader article on Old English and Serbo-Croatian charms, uses two passages from *Beowulf* (ll. 1-2, 833b-52), the former to illustrate the alliterative requirements of Old English verse and the latter to illustrate "responsion," or the repetition of key root words or morphemes. Also provides an overview of scholarship on oral-formulaic theory.

1182 _____. "The Viability of the Comparative Method in Oral Literature Research." *Comparatist* 4 (1980): 47-56.

Cautions that comparing oral poetry from different traditions (Homeric, Serbo-Croatian, and Old English) and from different genres is often reductive and suggests that valid work in the area will distinguish carefully the native elements of each tradition and will be careful to compare poetry which shares the same genre. Foley points out that the Old English verse of *Beowulf* differs significantly from the Homeric and Serbo-Croatian traditions in "metrical formulas and systems, verbal formulas and systems, morphemic responsion, themes, and story patterns." Further, "a careful attention to congruency in genre will make possible new insights of much greater fidelity" (53). Includes a brief comparison of the charm genre in Old English and Serbo-

Croatian and analyzes features of the Old English poetic tradition in *Beowulf*, lines 833b-852.

1183 Garmonsway, George N., Jacqueline Simpson, and Hilda R. Ellis Davidson. *'Beowulf' and Its Analogues*. Revised ed. London: Dent, 1980. Pp. xi + 368.

A revised edition of Garmonsway [S669], including an updated essay, "Archaeology and *Beowulf*," by Hilda Ellis Davidson as well as a number of corrections to the text and an updated select bibliography by Jacqueline Simpson. Davidson's essay takes into account the revised reconstructions of Sutton Hoo artifacts, more recent finds such as those at Yeavering, and more recent scholarship on Germanic artifacts from the Continent and Scandinavia. Archaeology, more than linguistic and literary approaches, can teach us about "the life and ideals of the heroic society which this poem presents" (351). Davidson goes on to identify archaeological parallels for objects and practices in the poem: the royal hall, the Hart symbol, drinking customs, harp playing, treasure gifts, weapons, ships and seafaring, and cremation. Lines 4-11 of Garmonsway's prose translation of *Beowulf*: "Many a time did Scyld Scefing with troops of warriors deprive his foes among many races of their mead-benches, and strike terror into the Heruli, after that time when he first was found destitute. He lived to know consolation for that; beneath the skies he throve and prospered in every honour, so that all neighbouring nations across the whale-ridden seas were forced to obey him and pay him tribute. A fine king was he!"

Reviews: R.W. McConchie, *AUMLA* 55 (1981): 105-07; A. C[répin], *EA* 36 (1983): 108.

1184 Greenfield, Stanley B., and Fred C. Robinson. *A Bibliography of Publications on Old English Literature to the End of 1972*. Toronto: U of Toronto P, 1980. Pp. 125-97.

An exhaustive bibliography of scholarship on Old English literature through 1972. The section on *Beowulf* is divided into the following sub-categories: bibliographies; concordances; editions; translations; cultural and historical studies and questions of authorship and date; textual criticism; literary interpretations; style, language and grammar; prosodic studies; and studies of scholars and

scholarship. The entries are lightly annotated, and the volume includes author and subject indexes.
Reviews: *OEN* 15.1 (1981): 101; Anon., *British Book News*, 1981: 462; A. Bliss, *N&Q* 29 (1982): 353-54; V. Fenster, *American Reference Books Annual* 13 (1982): 664-65; Helmut Gneuss, *Anglia* 100 (1982): 487-93; C.T. Berkhout, *Speculum* 57 (1983): 897-99; J.D. Burnley, *Lore and Language* 3.6 (1983): 134; Roberta Frank, *U of Toronto Quarterly* 52 (1983): 302-03; D.K. Fry, *Analytical and Enumerative Bibliog.* 6 (1983): 183-86; M.R. Godden, *MÆ* 52 (1983): 311-12; B. Mitchell, *RES* 34 (1983): 320-21; M. Rissanen, *NM* 84 (1983): 271-73; M.L. Samuels, *Library Review* 31 (1983): 298-99; E.P. Sheehy, *College & Research Libraries* 42 (1983): 351; R.H. Bremmer, *ES* 65 (1984): 38; J.E. Cross, *MLR* 79 (1984): 412-14; P. Lendinara, *Schede medievali* 5 (1984): 491-92; K. Bitterling, *Mittellateinisches Jahrbuch* 21 (1987): 257-58.

1185 Hart, Thomas Elwood. "Tectonic Methodology and an Application to *Beowulf*." In *Essays in the Numerical Criticism of Medieval Literature.* Ed. Caroline D. Eckhardt. Lewisburg, PA: Bucknell UP, 1980. Pp. 185-210.

Argues that the structure of *Beowulf* is "tectonic" (based on numerical positionings of both verbal and structural units) and provides a critique of the methodology of earlier tectonic studies. Hart points out that much earlier work relied on selective and partial data and suggests that future work integrate several kinds of evidence: "(1) graphic, such as manuscript punctuation marking relevant divisions; (2) formal or textual, such as numerically controlled patterns of wording, rhyme, or other textual features within structural divisions; (3) numerical, especially precision and consistency among parts and whole . . . ; and (4) thematic, such as change of person, place, time, or action, coincident with numerical junctures and parallels among resulting structural units" (188-89). Applying this new methodology to *Beowulf*, Hart finds an intricate chiastic patterning within and between four passages in *Beowulf* and argues that the implications of symmetries and proportions such as these "have an aesthetic as well as a historical dimension" (264). Includes diagrams. [See *numerical structure* in the subject index.]

1186 Hasegawa, Hiroshi. "The Sutton Hoo Ship-Burial and *Beowulf*." *Annual Review of Science (Nihon Univ.)* 26 (1980): 131-6. In Japanese.

The finds from Sutton Hoo appear to be closely related to the precious things and arms described in *Beowulf*. Judging from archaeology, it would seem to be a logical conclusion that the date for the composition of the poem was not earlier than 610 and most probably A.D. 680-700. Reprinted in Hiroshi Hasegawa's *Studies in 'Beowulf'* (Tokyo: Seibido, 1988). (HH)

1187 Hume, Kathryn. "From Saga to Romance: the Use of Monsters in Old Norse Literature." *SP* 77 (1980): 1-25.

Makes some brief remarks about *Beowulf* in a study devoted to monsters in Old Norse literature, tracing four functions of monsters (giant, dwarf, dragon, and *draugr*): "(1) The monster exists to test the protagonist and to affirm his status as professional hero. (2) The monster preys upon society, thus letting the hero put his strength to the service of others. (3) The supernatural being serves as a comic or ironic device for reducing exaggerated heroes to more human stature. (4) The monster forms part of a deliberate comment on the nature of heroism" (3).

1188 Kabell, Aage. "Unferð und die dänischen Biersitten." [Unferð and Danish Beer Customs]. *Arkiv för Nordisk Filologi* (1980): 31-41.

Noting the parallels between the *Grettissaga* and *Beowulf*, Kabell believes that the Unferth episode must have been added to the poem at some later stage in its development. The incidents surrounding Unferth are not fully digested, suggesting the hand of a later adapter or interpolator. The much-discussed word *þyle*, as applied to Unferth, as well as its Old Norse cognate *þulr*, may be related to Latin *tulo* "to bear or bring"), which may be used as an abstract way of denoting a beginning. Thus, the word *þyle* can be defined as "initiator of the verbal act" ("Urheber der mündlichen Handlung," 39). Kabell agrees that the *þyle* was a court figure whose function was to initiate a flyting test and compares the Unferth-Beowulf exchange to the King Frotho Frithgothus-Ericus Disertus flyting as told by Saxo. The last adapter of *Beowulf* must have failed to understand the conventional, Germanic context of the flyting scene, mistaking it for outright verbal aggression. That leads him to exaggerate an accusation (made by Beowulf) that Unferth killed his own brothers (l. 587). Kabell thinks that the original account contained not an accusation of fratricide, but an ironic remark that Unferth came to his brothers' aid too late or that they fell because they came to him for help. Thus, Unferth may not originally have been a disreputable fratricide but merely an honorable *þyle*. Kabell also discusses the words *scop* and *skald* in their etymological meaning as "scold, scolder" and suggests that it is in this sense that Unferth's name may be a play on *unfrið* 'mar-peace.' (40-41).

1189 Koike, Kazuo. "The Sword in *Beowulf.*" *Obirin Studies in English Literature (Obirin Univ.)* 20 (1980): 125-48. In Japanese.

Considers various words and phrases for "sword" in *Beowulf*, analyzing ten simple words, thirty-seven compounds, and three combination words from the viewpoint of lexical and contextual meaning. (KK)

1190 Lord, Albert B. "Interlocking Mythic Patterns in *Beowulf.*" In *OEL in Context*, pp. 137-42.

Finds that two narrative patterns occurring in oral epics (the Homeric epics and *Gilgamesh*) also occur in *Beowulf*. The first pattern involves the following three stages: "(a) A powerful figure is not present or, for various reasons, is powerless in a situation of danger to his people. (b) During the period of his absence, or of his inability or unwillingness to act effectively, things go very badly for those around him, and many of his friends are killed. Finally, (c) the powerful figure returns or his power is restored, whereupon he puts things to right again" (137). Lord locates this pattern in the *Iliad* (with Achilles as the absent hero) and the *Odyssey* (Odysseus's absence also following the three stages outlined above). The three-stage pattern manifests itself in *Beowulf* in (a) the powerlessness of Hrothgar against Grendel, (b) the long reign of Grendel and the deaths of Æschere and Handscio, and (c) Beowulf (as Hrothgar's surrogate) defeats the monsters and re-establishes peace and joy. The second pattern involves "the encounter of the hero and a companion, or companions, with first a male monster, which he overcomes, and then a female monster, or divine temptress who wants to keep him in the 'other' world. His escape from the one and his rejection of the offers of the other involve breaking a taboo and/or insulting a deity, and as a result one or more of his companions is killed" (139). Lord finds examples of this pattern in the *Odyssey* and *Gilgamesh*, noting the obvious parallel in the story of Grendel and Grendel's mother in *Beowulf,* though noting that the Germanic epic does not involve a breaking of taboo.

1191 Mirarchi, Giovanni. "Il duale ellittico nella poesa anglosassone. I. *Widsith* 103; II. *Cristo e Satana* 409; III. *Genesi* 387; IV. *Beowulf* 2002; V. *La Dicesa all'Inferno* 135." [The Elliptical Dual in Anglo-Saxon Poetry]. *AIUON, filologia germanica* 23 (1980 for 1979): 27-39.

Reinterprets the genitives in line 2002b, *uncer Grendles*, arguing that *Grendles* modifies *wange* (l. 2003a) while the dual pronoun *uncer* modifies *gemēting* (l. 2001a), and translating the passage (in context) as follows: "Beowulf, son of Ecgtheow, answered: 'Many men know, O Lord Hygelac, of our [*uncer*: Beowulf's and Grendel's] encounter in the abode of Grendel, where he inflicted an overwhelming number of afflictions, of continuing sufferings, on the Danish people." ("Beowulf, figlio Ecgtheow, rispose: 'Molti uomini sanno, o principe Hygelac, quale fu il nostro (*uncer*, let.: di noi due ...) scontro nel luogo di Grendel, dove egli inflisse un numero stragrande di afflizioni, di continue sofferenze ai Danesi,'" 238). Also discusses occurrences of the dual in four other Old English poems.

1192 Mooney, Thomas J. "Is Bigfoot the Star of *Beowulf?*" *Fate* 33 (1980): 72.

Poses the question, "Is the Anglo-Saxon epic poem *Beowulf* an ancient tale of an encounter between human beings and Bigfoot?" (72). Though Grendel has many physical similarities to Bigfoot, he actively seeks out Hrothgar's hall to kill warriors while Bigfoot avoids human beings. Encroachment of the human community may have driven Bigfoot creatures to attack.

1193 Moore, Bruce. "The Thryth-Offa Digression in *Beowulf.*" *Neophil* 64 (1980): 127-33.

Attempts to explain the thematic relevance of the so-called Thryth-Offa digression (ll. 1925-62), finding that the contrast between the good Hygd and the evil Thryth (or Modthryth) parallels a number of other striking contrasts:

"Sigemund and Heremod, Hama and Hygelac, the creation of Heorot and the prediction of its destruction, Heorot and Grendel, Heorot and the world of the haunted mere" (128). Moore shows that the diction of the episode tends to connect Thryth with the negative forces of Grendel and the monsters, while at the same time allying her with forces of human social chaos. Thus, the digression takes part of the general reversal from order to disorder in the poem. However, the appearance of Offa seems to offer hope that a hero can reverse the course of decay. Thryth journeys over the sea to marry Offa where she is transformed into a good and noble woman. The sea journey is significant because the sea "is associated with other acts of re-ordering" (130). The digression appears at "a point when the hope that all may be turned to good is paramount. Offa is presented as a glorious king who is able to bring about good. . . . The poem begins in praise of Scyld Scefing, and it ends in praise of Beowulf. Midway through the poem there is this passage in praise of Offa. These glorious kings stand in contrast to the failed king Heremod, and also to the qualified images of kingship in Hrothgar and Hygelac" (131).

1194 Morrison, Stephen. "*Beowulf* 698a, 1273a: 'Frōfor ond fultum'." *N&Q* 27 (1980): 193-96.

Believes that the phrase *frōfor ond fultum* 'comfort and help' in lines 698a and 1273a derives from a Biblical context, proposing several possible Psalter texts (Ps. 85:17, 32:20, 39:18, 93:22, 113b:11) as well as a Latin hymn as possible sources and noting a parallel to Blickling Homily XVII, "To Sanctae Michaheles Mæssan," where the phrase describes divine intervention in a Christian-pagan battle. Morrison concludes, "bearing in mind that the collocation of *frōfor* and *fultum* in Old English writings is wholly confined to firm religious contexts, it seems certain that the *Beowulf* poet, through his conscious repetition of the phrase, intended to convey that Beowulf's victory over Grendel was as unambiguously spiritual in nature as was that of the Christian forces in the *Blickling* homily" (194). Surveys appearances of the phrase in several glossed psalters.

1195 Nagler, Michael N. "*Beowulf* in the Context of Myth." In *OEL in Context*, pp. 143-56.

Explores the mythic aspect of *Beowulf*, in particular its relation to the "widespread Indo-European and Near-Eastern combat myth" (143) studied by Fontenrose [S381]. Nagler outlines the myth, which also underlies Odysseus's fight with Polyphemus, as follows: "when the hero descends from the realm of the sky-god to do battle with the demon of darkness, whatever (relatively) ordinary, earthly weapons he brings with him are of no avail. Reduced to desperation, he must have recourse to the demon's own weapon—or rather . . . to a weapon [of the sky-god] in the demon's possession" (145). Nagler sees this myth as central to an understanding of Beowulf's fight with Grendel's dam, the failure of Hrunting, and the meaning of the giants' sword. He also maps out several correspondences to the *Odyssey* and the ancient Indian *Rāmayāṇa*. The giants' sword "is the weapon of the sky-god, which the chaos-demon has stolen" (146). Light breaks out at the defeat of Grendel and his mother, symbolizing the victory of the sky god. Unferth, in lending Hrunting to Beowulf, is a proxy of the chaos-demon, and thus the failure of Hrunting "is an expected and a positive development" (152). Finally, Nagler explores the workings of the myth at a psychological level: the giants' sword symbolizes a great power of creativity and light which can overcome forces of chaos and disorder. It is hidden in the depths of a cave—the depths of the unconscious—where a demonic enemy guards it. The hero, the waking will, must liberate it to destroy the chaos-demons. Given this movement, "the pessimism of *Beowulf* has been exaggerated" (156).

1196 Nicholson, Lewis E. "The Art of Interlace in *Beowulf*." *SN* 52 (1980): 237-49.

Investigates the "microstructure" of interlace patterning in *Beowulf* treated on the macro-level by Leyerle [S634]. Nicholson traces single and double strand motifs in the poem: a) the motif of weaving, from the hand-woven slaughter-bonds prepared by Hygd (or Modthryth) (l. 1937), the woven snare or *inwitnet* (l. 2167a), to the woven neck-ring passed from the Danes to Beowulf to Hygd; b) the intertwined and parallel actions of men and monsters—seen, for example, in the fact that the kin of Scyld and the kin of Cain each have their own genealogies, that Grendel slays thirty sleeping warriors while Beowulf (in Frisia) takes thirty suits of armor back to Geatland, that both Geats and the dragon guard a hall broken into while they sleep, etc.; c) the metaphor of the body as a house, seen in the way that the wrecking of Heorot parallels the dismemberment of Grendel, that the shining of Heorot parallels the shining of Beowulf's armor, implying in both a "beauty tinged with pride" (242), that Heorot like a human body has a mouth (l. 724a), that Beowulf, like a hall, contains a hoard (*brēosthord*, l. 2792a), that Hrethel's sorrow is paralleled by his empty and desolate house (ll. 2455-59), and that sorrow is connected with the burning of Heorot and the destruction of Beowulf's hall; d) an arrow motif, starting with the arrows with which the Geats kill the monsters in Grendel's mere, through the arrow of pride spoken of in Hrothgar's sermon, to the arrow which kills Herebeald, to the final storm of arrows that Beowulf had survived (ll. 3114-19)—all contrasting inner versus external battles.

1197 Niles, John D. "*Beowulf* 431-2 and the Hero's Civility in Denmark." *N&Q* 27 (1980): 99-100.

Finds the current editorial solution to the strained sense of lines 431-32 dissatisfying since it makes Beowulf seem an awkward and ungracious guest. Niles proposes a new reading, one in which Beowulf instead makes a "gesture of civility" (100). In the current editions, Beowulf remarks that he alone—and his troop—will cleanse the hall. This solution depends on transposing an *ond* (represented by the symbol 7) from the beginning of line 432a to the beginning of line 431b. Such a reading makes Beowulf seem boastful, one who thinks of his own troop in an afterthought and ignores the presence of the Danes. Niles instead proposes that *ond* is in its correct place and that the scribe has omitted by hapology a leading *mid* in line 431b, reading the lines as follows: *þæt ic mōte āna [mid] mīnra eorla gedryht/ ond þes heardra hēap Heorot fælsian*, "that I alone, with my band of retainers [the Geats] and this brave troop [the Danes], might cleanse Heorot" (99). Such a reading portrays Beowulf as a gracious guest who fittingly pays respect to the Danes as well as to his own men.

1198 No Item.

1199 Nolan, Barbara and Morton W. Bloomfield. "*Bēotword, Gilpcwidas*, and the *Gilphlæden* Scop of *Beowulf*." *JEGP* 79 (1980): 499-516.

In an analysis of boast speeches in *Beowulf*, suggests that "these public announcements of strength and fearlessness cannot be construed as 'boasting' in our modern sense of that word. The hero's speech as it is matched by subsequent deeds appears to serve a ritual function not unlike that of incantation, bolstering the sense of his own ability and fortifying his will to fulfill the tribal definition of heroism by facing death for the community's sake" (503). After investigating the etymologies of two words for boasting, *gilp* and *bēot*, Nolan and Bloomfield distinguish them as follows: *bēot* refers promises of future deeds of valor, while *gilp* "emphasizes the manner of presentation and perhaps also the ritual" (504). Next, they sketch an eight-part pattern for a *gilp* speech containing a *bēot* (ll. 407-55) and show that this pattern operates in Beowulf's other boast speeches. Finally, Nolan and Bloomfield show how an understanding of boasting and its function sheds light on two difficult passages. The first, lines 868-70a, describe the scop who sings Beowulf's deeds: he is *gilphlæden* 'laden with *gilp*' (l. 868a), mindful of songs, knowing all sorts of old stories. As analysis of the passage shows, the scop or official story-teller's role is to remember former boasts and their fulfillment and to judge the hero's present performance against the pattern stored in heroic tradition. In this sense, the poet is *gilphlæden*, that is, a rememberer and judger of boasts. The second passage, lines 2527b-28, seems to indicate that Beowulf will forgo (*ofersitte*) boasting about his fight with the dragon. Given the function of boasting in the poem, this meaning seems highly unlikely. As Nolan and Bloomfield show from uses of the word in glosses, however, that the word *ofersittan* may have the meaning of 'take up' or 'employ,' strongly suggesting that Beowulf is precisely engaging in a *bēot* at this point, a boast which gives him the final impetus to defeat the dragon (with the aid of Wiglaf).

1200   Nucciarelli, Franco Ivan. "La formula dell'allitterazione in inglese antico." [The Form of Alliteration in Old English.] In *Problemi di analisi linguistica.* Ed. Pierangiolo Berrettoni. Rome: Cadmo editore, 1980. Pp. 167-79.

Uses *Beowulf* to illustrate a general linguistic analysis of alliteration in Old English, formulating rules of syllable structure. Nucciarelli formulates the following rules of alliteration, where x is the alliterating element of the second half-line, y the alliterating element of the first half-line, C a consonant, S a sonorant, acc. the principal tonic accent, V a vowel, Z subsequent sounds, and # the beginning of a word or morpheme: x: # C (S') V'acc Z'; y: # C (S") V"acc. Z" (177).

1201   Opland, Jeff. *Anglo-Saxon Oral Poetry.* New Haven: Yale UP, 1980. Pp. xi + 289.

Treats *Beowulf* in a larger study of Old English oral poetry, arguing that the tradition indicates two distinct types of singers—the tribal poet or *scop* in service of a sacral king and the wandering harper or *glēoman*. Opland finds the distinction maintained in those passages in *Beowulf* describing poets and poetic activity. The tribal poet, enjoying high status as a servant to the king and singing without accompaniment of the harp, "would tend to produce elliptical, allusive eulogies susceptible of immediate interpretation [only] by an audience that was familiar with the events and personalities referred to" (191), while the harper, an entertainer on a par with itinerant jugglers and actors and enjoying a much lower status, purveyed simpler and more popular narrative songs for pure entertainment to the accompaniment of the harp, sometimes playing melodies without words. By the eighth century, "it is likely that the tradition of the scop underwent a radical alteration as a result of the development of a Christian theology of kingship and of a monastic ideal among the royal families in the seventh century" (197). After this period the distinction between the scop and the harper seems to grow fuzzier.

In a chapter entitled "The Evidence of the Poetry," Opland finds indications in *Beowulf* for the separation between scop and harper and argues that that scop did not sing his songs to the accompaniment of the harp. When the poet tells of the joy in Heorot before the first attack of Grendel, he mentions the sound of the harp and the clear song of the scop (ll. 89b-90a). Opland believes that the passage may refer to two separate performances, the first by a harper and the second by the scop and that the two are not synonymous. In introducing the Finnsburh episode, the poet may seem to imply that the scop accompanies his narrative to the harp, but the punctuation of the line makes this conclusion at least ambiguous; by placing a period at the end of line 1065, one could conclude that a harper sang first and then the scop, in a separate unaccompanied performance, related the story contained in the Finnsburh episode. The fact that this performance is referred to as the *glēomannes gyd* 'harper's song' (l. 1160a) may be an indication that by the eighth century the functions of the scop and harper had fallen together. Concerning the scop's song about Sigemund and Heremod after Beowulf's defeat of Grendel, the scop sings a eulogy for Beowulf, not separate exploits of Sigemund or Heremod, in the typically allusive eulogistic style of the court poet. Though Hrothgar seems to sing a song accompanied by

the harp (ll. 2105-17), Opland points out that again the punctuation makes such a conclusion problematic, arguing that the old Scylding who strokes the harp may not be the same person as Hrothgar. Finally, the laments at the end of the poem seem to be eulogistic songs, though not sung by the scop, indicating a tradition of eulogistic poetry in which all Anglo-Saxons could participate.
Reviews: *OEN* 15.1 (1981): 72-77; Donald K. Fry, *ELN* 19 (1981): 53-55 and *Library Journal* 105 (1981): 2413; D.G. Calder, *Speculum* 57 (1982): 401-04; J.J. Campbell, *JEGP* 81 (1982): 249-51; Roberta Frank, *N&Q* 29 (1982): 153-54; S.B. Greenfield, *Comparative Lit.* 34 (1982): 67-70; T. Ikegami, *Eigo-Seinen* 127 (1982): 583-84; M.Y. Miller, *Lit. in Performance* 2.1 (1982): 100-01; R.J. Reddick, *Allegorica* 6.1 (1982): 192-95; J. Turville-Petre, *MÆ* 51 (1982): 237-39; B. Mitchell, *RES* 34 (1983): 200-01; P.B. Taylor, *ES* 64 (1983): 567-68; R.F. Leslie, *MP* 81 (1984): 298-300; A.H. Olsen, *Pacific Quarterly Moana* 8.4 (1984): 70-73; K. Reichl, *Anglia* 103 (1985): 172-78.

1202 _____. "From Horseback to Monastic Cell: The Impact on English Literature of the Introduction of Writing." In *OEL in Context*, pp. 30-43.

Contrasts the performance of the Danish scop (ll. 853-77, 898-904a) in praise of Beowulf—"a typical Anglo-Saxon oral performance"—to the epilogues of Cynewulf—an "Anglo-Saxon literate poet," (33)—in order to elucidate some of the changes made in the Anglo-Saxon oral poetic tradition by the introduction of writing. The physical contexts of the two productions differ: the Danish thane's performance is unique to a certain locality (on the path back from the mere) and audience (Danish retainers) while Cynewulf's production is not limited to time or locality, achieving a certain universality from the fact that it is written down and can outlive its author. Cynewulf's runic signature must be perceived visually to be understood and thus assumes literacy. In Cynewulf's written text, the words alone command all our attention, whereas in the thane's production, the words are only part of the performance. The thane's poem is deeply social in that it speaks to the shared values and assumptions of a tight-knit group. Cynewulf's poems are, in contrast, asocial since the poet in his cell is not influenced by the audience. The thane's performance is ephemeral and immediate while Cynewulf's is permanent and reflective—revision and careful criticism are possible. Taking the example of Caedmon as well as African oral performances, Opland suggests that the epic tradition as we see it in *Beowulf* is not a native Anglo-Saxon or even Germanic development but the result of a fusion between traditional Germanic oral techniques and literate Christian traditions in Latin (42-43).

1203 _____. "Southeastern Bantu Eulogy and Early Indo-European Poetry." *Research in African Literatures* 11 (1980): 295-307.

In a discussion of African folklore genres and methodological approaches to them, includes a passing reference to *Beowulf*, noting similarities between Bantu eulogy and the importance of fame in the Indo-European tradition, particularly Beowulf's famous statement that fame is a worthy object (ll. 1386-89).

1204 Puhvel, Martin. "A Scottish Analogue to the Grendel Story." *NM* 81 (1980): 395-398.

Provides the following summary: "This article considers a Scottish variant of the folktale known as 'The Hand and the Child' as an analogue to the story of Beowulf's struggle with Grendel. *Am Prìomh Sgeul* ('The Chief Story') recounts the carrying off of a queen's newborn children by a 'Great Claw-like Hand' that enters through the roof. A prince transformed by magic into a wolf tears it with his teeth from the shoulder but, as usual in this folktale, the other arm then carries off the infant, who is, together with the previously abducted children, recovered the next day from the giant's island dwelling, where the latter is decapitated with his own 'sword of light'; this weapon, as well as the head of the giant, is brought back as booty. The parallelism with *Beowulf* is compounded by the fact that the sword is also employed, albeit later, to decapitate the offspring of the monster. In all, one may well conceive an impression of a connection, if a distant one between folktale and epic" (395).

1205 Riley, Samuel M. "The Contrast between Beowulf and Hygelac." *Journal of Narrative Technique* 10 (1980): 186-97.

Examines the structure and themes of fitts xxviii-xxx, finding that the poet manipulates the voices of Hygelac, Beowulf, and the narrator/commentator to praise Beowulf's fitness to rule, especially by contrast to the rash Hygelac. Riley identifies three overlapping passages important for this theme: lines 1968-2176 (containing Hygelac's speech and Beowulf's reply as well as narration and commentary), lines 2166b-83a, and lines 2177-99 (the last two passages alternating between narration and commentary). In the first passage, Hygelac expresses his former doubts about Beowulf's expedition, and Riley notes a compressed doubling of Beowulf's entry into the Danish court: Hygelac's "challenge" parallels Unferth's attack, perhaps to "increase the hero's glory at his uncle's court once he answers the charges" (188). Beowulf's answering speech "is a masterful blend of tact and boast, the utterance of a man loyal to his lord.... The report's deferential tone continues throughout, creating an heroic glory in whose reflection Hygelac and the Geatish court may bask" (191). In the first passages and the two that follow, the narrator/commentator contrasts Beowulf to Hygelac by mentioning Hygelac as the (rash) slayer of Ongentheow (l. 1968) and by reminding us of Hygelac's ignominious death. By praising Beowulf as a thane, the narrator builds up to praising him as a potential king, noting the contrast to Beowulf's own inglorious youth.

1206 Roberts, Jane. "Old English *Un*- 'Very' and Unferth." *ES* 61 (1980): 289-92.

Reviews evidence for the theory that *un*- serves as an intensifier rather than a negator in a select number of Old English words, including *unforht* (very afraid) in *Dream of the Rood* and the name *Unferth* in *Beowulf*. Roberts finds six unambiguous examples of this intensifying *un*-, and goes on to suggest that the *un*- element in the name *Unferth* may be an intensifier rather than a negator. "A reinterpretation of the name Unferth, following Robinson's [S932] identification of the element *-ferhð* rather than *-frið* but suggesting an intensifying *un*-, would give this important Danish warrior a commendatory name; wisdom and greatness of heart are traits he displays both in his generosity with Hrunting and in his praise for Beowulf's achievement. Perhaps at some point in the transmission of the poem a scribe was, as critics have been, dissatisfied with what had all the appearances of an antithetical or at least pejorative prefix in this name and therefore substituted a prefix [*Hun*-] more familiar in proper names" (291).

1207 Sato, Noboru. "*Beowulf* and Sophocles' *Oedipus Tyrannus*." *The Ronso [Bulletin of the Faculty of Letters of Tamagawa Univ.]* 20 (1980): 353-71.

Compares Beowulf to Oedipus, finding that both heroes earn their reputations by killing monsters, marry a queen, are overthrown, and meet tragic deaths. (NS)

1208 ──────────. "A Play on Some Runic Letters in *Beowulf* and the Ruthwell Cross Inscription." *Otsuka Review* 16 (1980): 1-9.

Not seen.

1209 Schrader, Richard J. "Caedmon and the Monks, the Beowulf-Poet and Literary Continuity in the Early Middle Ages." *ABR* 31 (1980): 39-69.

Argues that *Beowulf* shows extensive influence of the classical literary tradition. Schrader reviews the extent to which pagan literature influenced and was allowed by Gregory the Great, Bede, Aldhelm, Boniface, and Alcuin, concluding that the "age of Bede faithfully preserved a rhetorical tradition that encouraged emulation of whatever could be made to serve Christian ends. The monasteries . . . were not beehives of classicism, but their masters taught and their scribes helped to save classical literature" (56). The *Beowulf*-poet himself was undoubtedly a monk and probably received rhetorical training of the sort suggested by Bede's treatise on schemes and tropes. Schrader hypothesizes that "A student in the early Middle Ages, rightly disposed and properly equipped, would have deemed *Beowulf* a true classic. It would have appeared to him to be part of the poetic (and rhetorical) continuum extending from Virgil to Statius to such Christian epic writers as Arator and Corippus, now undeservedly forgotten, and from them to Aldhelm and Bede" (69).

1210 Short, Douglas D. "*Beowulf* and Modern Critical Tradition." In *A Fair Day in the Affections: Literary Essays in Honor of Robert B. White, Jr.* Ed. Jack D. Durrant and M. Thomas Hester. Raleigh: Winston Press, 1980. Pp. 1-23.

Attempts "to sort out some of the major trends in *Beowulf* scholarship and occasionally to offer some strictures and suggestions for future directions" (1). After calling for a new scholarly edition of the poem and discussing bibliographic resources, Short identifies and critiques several schools of criticism: the aesthetic approach (which attempts to find beauty and unity in the poem), the structural approach (including theories about fitt structure and interlace patterning), folktale morphology, thematic criticism (revolving around the question of Beowulf's failure or triumph), Christian or "neo-exegetical" readings, and oral-formulaic studies.

1211 _____. *'Beowulf'* Scholarship: An Annotated Bibliography. New York: Garland, 1980. Pp. xvi + 353.

An annotated bibliography of *Beowulf* scholarship, covering the years 1705-1949 selectively and 1950-1978 exhaustively. The entries are arranged by year and alphabetized by the author's name within each year. Includes an author and subject index. The present volume is a continuation of Short.
Reviews: *OEN* 15.1 (1981): 101.

1212 Silber, Patricia. "Unferth: Another Look at the Emendation." *Names* 28 (1980): 101-111.

Endorses Nicholson's suggestion [S970] that the MS. name *Hunferð* should be retained and that it means 'Hun-hearted,' or 'uncivilized,' rejecting the widely-accepted etymology *Unferth* 'Un-peace' on thematic grounds since Hunferth is not depicted as a figure of discord. Silber refutes or casts doubt on four common assumptions about Hunferth: that "he is a privileged counselor to Hroðgar; jealous of Beowulf's heroic exploits, he attempts in the flyting to discredit the Geat; he is a warrior of the *comitatus*; he will play a role in Hroþulf's treacherous attack on Heorot" (102). She counters that he is a) a court entertainer of minor standing, b) that he is jealous of Beowulf's story-telling abilities, not his heroic exploits, c) that he is not a warrior, but a story-teller, and d) that there is no evidence to link him to the future treachery of Hrothulf or to any significant breach of the peace. Summing up what we can know with certainty about the character, she writes, "he is mean-tempered, grudging, and very likely prone to the petty deceits and pranks that usually accompany such a nature. All of this amounts to excellent reason to believe that the poet's references to Unferð are heavily cloaked in an irony that would be immediately evident to the audience of *Beowulf*" (108). Silber concludes with a discussion of alternate etymologies, including *hune* 'horehound, or bitter herb', *hunu* or *hunel* 'diseased, leprous', *hun* 'bear cub.'

1213 Smirnickaja, O. A. "Sinonimiceskie sistemy v *Beovul'fe*." *Vestnik Moskovskogo Universiteta* ser. 9, filologiia 5 (1980): 44-57.

Not seen.

1214 Stanley, Eric G. "The Narrative Art of *Beowulf*." In *Medieval Narrative: A Symposium*. Ed. Hans Bekker-Nielsen, Peter Foote, Andreas Haander, and Preben Meulen Gracht Sørensen. Odense: Odense UP, 1980. Pp. 58-81.

Following Klaeber [S67] and Chadwick [S42], points out some faults in the poem's narrative structure and suggests that the poet retards action in order to reflect on universal truths. "Though we may like the poem, we can see deficiencies in its narrative art: lack of steady advance; lack of narrative turning-point demanding resolution; lack of the critical point of the action" (66). The poet often values reflection over vigorous narration. "The plot of *Beowulf* seems not much of a vehicle to me: barely a chassis, a base-frame, a mere convenience for linking story-matter and reflection. The poet has let reflection nobble action" (70). However, it is "one of the patterns of narrative in *Beowulf* to build a structure of action out of a universalizing statement" (77). Stanley also discusses narrative and thematic contraposition (contrast), fitt structure, and poetic chronology.

1215 Tajima, Matsuji. "Gnomic Statements in *Beowulf*." *Studies in English Language and Literature (Kyushu Univ.)* 30 (1980): 83-94.

Following J.E. Price's unpublished doctoral dissertation (*Some Aspects of the Gnomic Elements in Anglo-Saxon Poetry*), classifies the gnomes of *Beowulf* into three categories: "Gnomes about God, Pagan Gods, Fate and Christ" (total of eight), "Gnomes about Mankind in General or Specific Groups of Men" (total of twenty-eight), and "Gnomes about Natural or Cultural Phenomena" (total of four). The gnomes seem to indicate, on the whole, that human beings have little control over the outcome of events. Finally, Tajima classifies the gnomic statements according to speaker, finding that the narrator-poet speaks twenty-three gnomes,

Beowulf ten, Hrothgar four, Wiglaf two, and Hrothgar's coast-guard one. Those not spoken by the poet, thus, come from the mouths of "three men of highest or comparable rank," indicating the didactic weight of the poem (92). Includes an appendix tabulating all the gnomes in *Beowulf* from the lists of Williams [S49], Klaeber [S67], Malone [S420], and Price.

1216 Toda, Shizuo. "Grendel's Arm and Goblin's Arm: Notes." *ESELL* 71 (1980): 85-100.

Not seen.

1217 Tripp, Raymond P., Jr. "Hate and Heat in the Restoration of *Beowulf* 84: *Þæt se Secg Hete Aþum Swerian*." *ELN* 18 (1980): 81-86.

Agrees with Eliason [1179] that the traditional emendation of l. 84 (*þæt se ecghete āþumswēoran*, MS. *þæt se secg hete aþum swerian*) is unsatisfactory but rejects Eliason's own emendation as unwarranted. According to Tripp, the line is not metrically faulty if one assumes that *h* may alliterate with vowels; thus, the manuscript reading should be retained. "The poet's meaning may be, then, not that Heorot waited for actual flames to destroy it, but that Heorot endured (and survived) the immediate flame-like surges of Grendel's hatred" (84). Tripp proposes the following translation of ll. 81-85: "The hall rose high, high and horn-lofty; it endured battle-surges, the flame of hate; nor was it very long then, that that man [Grendel] hate with oaths should swear, on account of a murderous tide of hate, should wake" (85).

1218 ———. "The Restoration of *Beowulf* 2781a: *Hāt ne forhogode* ('Did Not Despise Heat')." *MP* 78 (1980): 153-58.

On stylistic, metrical, and paleographical grounds, argues that line 2781a should restore *-hogode*, a reading which a scribe had mistakenly corrected to *horde* and that the remaining elements of the half-line should be reconfigured to read, *hāt ne forhogode* 'he did not despise the heat.' This form of the half-line, referring litotically to the dragon's lack of concern about heat, is in line with the poet's use of litotes elsewhere.

1219   Tuso, Joseph F., James R. Aubrey, Ann Hernández, and John J. Pollock. "The Teaching of *Beowulf*." *OEN* 13.1 (1980): 23-27.

Contains a progress report by Joseph F. Tuso on the revised edition of the Norton Critical Edition of *Beowulf* and prints three reports on approaches to teaching the poem. James R. Aubrey, "Taming Beowulf's Monsters," discusses the symbolic roles of the monsters and how to teach them. Ann Hernández, "*Beowulf* Lives," describes the teaching of *Beowulf* at the University of California, Berkeley. Finally, John J. Pollock, "*Beowulf* in Jungian Perspectives," outlines a Jungian reading of *Beowulf* with advice for teaching.

1220   Vaught, Jacqueline. "*Beowulf*: The Fight at the Center." *Allegorica* 5 (1980): 125-137.

Maintains that Beowulf's fight with Grendel's dam is the decisive event both of Beowulf's early life and of part one of the poem because there, alone, he stands "with unflinching resolve in the face of inevitable death" (127). In earlier fights, Beowulf's development was not yet complete: in the contest with Breca, "His 'heroic' actions . . . are more accidental than willed" (130). In the fight with Grendel, Beowulf fights a clearly weaker enemy and gathers strength by standing in the center of society. But in order to "save society, the potential hero must leave the necessarily restrictive bounds of society and confront . . . the destructive force directly. He must, paradoxically, become like the monsters, alienated from society" (131). Vaught goes on to discuss the cosmological, social, and psychological implications of Beowulf's victory, drawing on Joseph Campbell's *A Hero of a Thousand Faces* to explain why Beowulf must "enter the unconscious, a symbolic landscape of the irrational and the unknown that can be entered only willingly and alone" (134).

1221   Wright, Louise E. "*Merewioingas* and the Dating of *Beowulf*: A Reconsideration." *Nottingham Mediaeval Studies* 24 (1980): 1-6.

Assembles evidence that the word *merewīoingas* (l. 2921a) is a compound formed on the name *Merovech* and the patronymic *-ing*, not (as previously believed) an Old English approximation of *Merovingi* or 'Merovingian' and that this fact can be used to date the poem "possibly as late as the early ninth century" (5). The *Beowulf* poet would probably have heard of Merovech from the chronicle of Fredgar, written in the seventh century but not widely circulated until the rise of the Carolingians, who used the story of a legendary founder, Merovech, complete with a genealogy including a minotaur, to legitimize themselves.

1981

1222 Ackland, Michael. "Blakean Sources in John Gardner's *Grendel.*" *Critique* 23 (1981): 57-66.

Traces the influence of William Blake's poetry on John Gardner's *Grendel*, with a few remarks on *Beowulf*: "While *Beowulf* provides Gardner with the basic outline and characters of his story, Blake's highly pictorial imagination affords a wealth of related images" (65).

1223 Amos, Ashley Crandell. *Linguistic Means of Determining the Dates of Old English Literary Texts*. Medieval Academy Books, No. 90. Cambridge, MA: Medieval Academy of America, 1981. Pp. xiii + 210.

Reviews and evaluates several techniques for dating Old English literary texts—phonological-metrical tests, syntactic and grammatical tests, lexical tests, and stylistic tests—concluding that most single tests are at present unreliable. "The linguistic tests are far from unambiguous; none is completely reliable, all must be qualified in one respect or another. The tests that are the least subject to mistaking scribal variants for original forms, the metrical and stylistic tests, are each vulnerable in other ways: the metrical tests because our understanding of meter is still uncertain, the stylistic tests because they are less objective than the others. Nevertheless, when taken together the tests will sometimes provide suggestive indications of date that, while not unassailable, are yet far more reliable than any subjective gauging of the Christian spirit or cultural ambience" (166). With regard to *Beowulf*, few of the tests applied so far (for example, the Lichtenheld tests, Bliss's test [S353] for short and long vocalic endings, or Girvan's work with *bahuvrihi* compounds [S119], or any of the various stylistic tests) has produced any undisputable results. However, knowledge of the chronological development of individual words holds promise, since the word *mōdig* (in the pejorative sense), with a very few exceptions, can be shown to appear only in the tenth century and after. Further, "Alliterative practice with respect to palatal and velar *g* is by far the most reliable of the purely metrical tests" (168). In general, though individual metrical styles could make a final judgment difficult, poems in which palatal and velar *g* alliterate are earlier than those in which they do not.

Reviews: P. Herzog, *Die Sprache* 28 (1982): 106; M. Rissanen, *Speculum* 57 (1982): 112-14; G. Cillufo, *Schede medievali* 4 (1983): 171-73; T. Karibe, *Studies in English Lit.* (Tokyo) 59.2 (1983): 352-58; H. Ogawa, *Poetica* (Tokyo) 14 (1983): 99-109; C. Sisam, *MÆ* 52 (1983): 138-39; C. Wetzel, *Anglia* 101 (1983): 487-96; M.R. Godden, *RES* 35 (1984): 346-47; J. Roberts, *YES* 15 (1985): 268-69; T. Cable, *JEGP* 85 (1986): 93-95; K. Toth, *ASNSL* 223 (1986): 155-57.

1224 Anderson, Earl R. "Beowulf's Retreat from Frisia: Analogues from the Fifth and Eighth Centuries." *ELN* 19 (1981): 89-93.

Proposes several analogues from Greek and Armenian sources to show that the mixture of historical and fabulous elements in *Beowulf*, particularly Beowulf's superhuman swim from Frisia to Geatland, are not without precedent, though Robinson [S932] finds the feat implausible and lacking textual support. On the basis of similarly incredible feats by Greek and Armenian heroes, Anderson concludes "that it is unwise to assume, given two alternative readings of a text, one fabulous and one realistic, that the realistic one must be the right one" (93). [See *fabulous elements* in the subject index.]

1225 Andrew, Malcolm. "Grendel in Hell." *ES* 62 (1981): 401-410.

Summarizes various proposed translations and explanations of the seemingly difficult line in which Grendel is described as a *fēond on helle,* 'fiend or enemy in hell' (l. 101b), though he is not at that moment in hell. Many translate the phrase simply with "hellish fiend," "fiend from hell," or some equivalent epithet, while other commentators suggest emendation. Andrew finds these arguments unconvincing and proposes that "this half-line carries an embedded allusion to conceptions of hell and sin well-known in the writings of the Church Fathers, and that once this is recognised, the difficulties of interpretation disappear" (403). Drawing on the writings of Augustine and Gregory, he sees Grendel as a type of sinful man, distorted and deformed by evil, one who carries hell and hell-fire with him wherever he goes.

1226 Beard, D. J. "*þá Bitu Engi Járn*: A Brief Note on the Concept of Invulnerability in the Old Norse Sagas." *Occasional*

Papers in Linguistics and Language Learning 8 (1981): 13-31.

Reviews evidence from Old Norse literature for an earlier Germanic belief that iron weapons cannot harm berserkers or semi-troll men, though wood can, and relates these beliefs to a similar invulnerability to weapons displayed by Grendel and his mother (ll. 1522-25, 801-05). Beard notes invulnerability to iron weapons in a number of sagas (*Gunnlaugs Saga, Njáls saga, Grettis saga, Egils saga, Ynglinga saga*, the *Hávamál*, and others) as well as in Tacitus' *De Germania* and Saxo's *History of the Danes*.

1227 Bliss, Alan J. "Auxiliary and Verbal in *Beowulf*." *ASE* 9 (1981): 157-182.

A study of the syntactic positions of auxiliaries and verbals in *Beowulf* with an eye to understanding the constraints under which Old English poetry was composed. Building on Hans Kuhn's work on word order, Bliss examines "the word order in the clauses in *Beowulf* which contain an auxiliary, which I define as a finite verb used with a dependent infinitive or past participle" (159). He proposes that the position of auxiliaries is affected by their metrical value and distinguishes between the placement of mono- and disyllabic auxiliaries. However, the placement of verbals in a clause is apparently not dependent on its metrical value. In an appendix, Bliss argues that the appearance of the *ge-* prefix is metrically conditioned.

1228 Boyle, O.P. "The Nowell Codex and the Poem of *Beowulf*." In *Dating of 'Beowulf'*, pp. 23-32.

On the basis of a detailed codicological examination, describes how the Nowell codex was produced, also providing a reconstruction of the foliation of the copy text (the predecessor of the Nowell codex). Some of Boyle's conclusions are as follows: 1) Scribe B was called on to take over from Scribe A after the former had already completed the last three quires of the codex (containing the ending of *Beowulf* and the text of *Judith*). 2) This explains why Scribe B attempted to squeeze in more lines before the end of quire 11. 3) "Scribe B knew exactly where he was in relation to the end of that quire because this quire 11 into which he had to copy this part of *Beowulf* was exactly of the same size, text-frame, and ruling as those of his 'copy-quire'" (25-26). 4) The

Copy-*Beowulf* "clearly was part of a composite codex, just as *Beowulf* is today in the Nowell Codex" (29). 5) "[O]ne might not be too far off the mark in suggesting that the codex of which the Copy-*Beowulf* was simply a part contained all that comes before *Beowulf* in the Nowell Codex—*Christopher, Wonders [of the East], Alexander's Letter [to Aristotle]*—and that, further, *Beowulf* was the last item in that copy-codex.... Probably what the patron wanted ... was simply a copy of these four 'monster' tracts in prose and verse which were cheek-by-jowl in one unbound set of quires, and then threw in *Judith* as well from another or a separate codex" (30). Boyle provides a table listing the reconstructed foliation of the postulated Copy-*Beowulf* as well as the present text in the Nowell codex.

1229   Busse, Wilhelm G. and R. Holtei. "*Beowulf* and the Tenth Century." *Bulletin of the John Rylands U Library* 63 (1981): 285-329.

Examines *Beowulf* from the point of view of reception theory and text-pragmatics in order to discover the poem's relation to its social and historical background. Although the poem may be much earlier, the tenth century produced the unique copy of the poem, and it seems unlikely that a secular text like *Beowulf* would have been untouched by changing social conditions during its transmission. The poem, especially as a secular text, must have participated in a "dynamic text tradition" (288) in which it was dynamically "altered or adapted to changed social conditions" (287). Thus, despite the demands of earlier social contexts, *Beowulf* must have fit into and been adapted for the tenth century communicative context in which it is preserved. Text-pragmatic signals reveal several important social preoccupations in the poem: the obligations of kings and their followers as well as the pursuit of renown as a model for social rise. These themes were the urgent concerns of tenth-century English society, particularly in the reign of Ethelred II. Busse and Holtei examine several historical and cultural parallels from this period, concluding that "it is self-evident after all we have said about Ethelred's reign that we have to regard primarily the class of thegns as the addressees of *Beowulf*" (328).

1230   Cable, Thomas. "Metrical Style as Evidence for the Date of *Beowulf*." In *Dating of 'Beowulf'*, pp. 77-82.

Attempts to date *Beowulf* by quantifying the metrical style (taking the percentages of Sievers' metrical types C, D, and E) of various datable poems and comparing it to that of *Beowulf,* concluding that there is no metrical reason to exclude a ninth century date for *Beowulf.* Cable finds a consistent decline in percentages of lines with three levels of ictus (i.e., Sievers' types C, D, and E) over time. *Beowulf*'s percentage (38 percent) seems to place it with poems of the middle period (eighth to ninth centuries): *Daniel* (33.6 percent), *Exodus* (40.8 percent), *Elene* (35.8 percent), *Fates of the Apostles* (34 percent), *Juliana* (34.5 percent), *Andreas* (36.8 percent), *Preface* and *Epilogue* to *The Pastoral Care* (33.7 percent), and the *Meters of Boethius* (34.5 percent). Cable presents a table of percentages as well as several detailed conclusions about the historical development of Old English meter.

1231 Camargo, Martin. "The Finn Episode and the Tragedy of Revenge in *Beowulf.*" *SP* 78 (1981): 120-134.

Maintains that "The function of the Finn episode . . . is to cast doubt on the revenge ethic at the very point in the narrative where such a code appears most glorious" (132). Camargo suggests that the episode is designed to engage the emotions by contrasting dark tragedy with the joyous celebrations after Beowulf's defeat of Grendel. The poet focuses on the tragic victim, Hildeburh, who has no recourse in a system of revenge which demands retribution against slayers of kin: "the inadequacy of the revenge ethic is displayed in a way that must arouse pity and fear" (130). Beowulf, though he abhors the killing of kin, nevertheless displays "the limitation of his knowledge" (131) when he tells Hrothgar that it is better to avenge a friend than to mourn too much (ll. 1384b-85). Hengest (and Beowulf) both fall short of Christian compassion and cannot break the cycle of revenge. "The only hope for sure peace, the poet clearly implies, lies in the love and compassion which Christianity offers as its ideal and which the women in *Beowulf* seem to symbolize" (133).

1232 Cameron, Angus, Ashley Crandell Amos and Gregory Waite. "A Reconsideration of the Language of *Beowulf.*" In *Dating of 'Beowulf'*, pp. 33-76.

Provides an extensive "catalog of linguistic forms in the poem, arranged on the levels of orthography/phonology, morphology, syntax, and vocabulary" (35) as a preliminary step in determining dating and localization of both the manuscript and the poem. Cameron et al. believe "that careful comparison of the language of *Beowulf* on various levels with that of other Old English texts will allow us to place the manuscript and possibly the text in the context of the surviving Old English literary remains" (36). They suggest comparing the language of *Beowulf* to that of a) other texts in BL MS. Cotton Vitellius A.XV., b) other texts contained in the poetic codices, c) texts in contemporary manuscripts, and d) texts known to be earlier than the *Beowulf* manuscript. One preliminary conclusion is that "the mixed spellings in *Beowulf* are not necessarily to be explained by a long or complicated textual transmission, but may represent copying conventions or tolerances in a number of late tenth-century scriptoria" (37). Further, "The vocabulary of *Beowulf* has most in common with *Andreas*, but shares a surprisingly high number of forms with *Judith*" (36).

1233   Chase, Colin. "Opinions on the Date of *Beowulf*, 1815-1980." In *Dating of 'Beowulf'*, pp. 3-8.

Provides a survey of scholarly opinion on the date of *Beowulf*, including summaries of the work of Thorkelin [S5], Grundtvig [S6, S11] Müllenhof [S13], ten Brink [F223], Barnouw [F62], Morsbach [S30], Schücking [S56], Girvan [S119], Whitelock [231], Wrenn [S276], Sisam [S274], and others. Though proponents of later dates have become more numerous after Whitelock, some scholars (Wormald [S1105], Bolton [S1063], and John [S921]) assume a date in the age of Bede.

1234   _____ "Saints' Lives, Royal Lives, and the Date of *Beowulf*." In *Dating of 'Beowulf'*, pp. 161-72.

Proposes to date *Beowulf* on the basis of the poet's attitude toward the heroic world, which is neither "romantic idealizing nor puritan rejection, but a delicate balance of empathy and detachment" (162), finding that the ninth century would best support such an attitude. Early saints' lives tend to exclude the heroic, while later ones integrate the heroic tradition more confidently. Standing between these two poles, *Beowulf* "is likely to have been written neither early, in the eighth century, nor late, in the tenth, but in the rapidly changing and chaotic ninth" (163). Chase points out that until Asser's *Life of Alfred*, no literary life of a king had been written in Anglo-Saxon England. Royal saints receive more frequent attention from later hagiographers but are not the subject of formal lives in the earlier period. Ælfric's adaptations of Bede, particularly in the *Life of Oswald*, betray this shift in emphasis. Ælfric develops heroic motifs which Bede seems consciously to have avoided. The post-conquest *Life of Oswine* goes even further in investing Bede's account with the full emotional machinery of the heroic tradition, an argument Chase develops in a later article [1481]. He reviews other saints' lives (Cuthbert, Guthlac, Martin, and Wilfrid) for their relative avoidance or acceptance of heroic life, concluding that *Beowulf*'s particular blend of piety and heroic values belongs to the ninth century, exhibiting many parallels in this regard to Asser's *Life of Alfred*.

1235 Chickering, Howell D. "Correction Sheet for Howell D. Chickering, ed., *Beowulf: A Dual-Language Edition*." *OEN* 15.1 (1981): 12.

Lists forty-four corrections to the Old English text of his dual-language edition [S1023], with one correction to the translation. See Chickering [1687] for the corrected edition.

1236 Clark, Francelia. "Flyting in *Beowulf* and Rebuke in *The Song of Bagdad*: The Question of Theme." In *Lord*, pp. 164-193.

Modifies and partially refutes Lord's thesis [S416, S925] that *Beowulf* shows the same kinds of repeated themes (or type-scenes) as the oral Yugoslavian epic, *The Song of Bagdad*, and that both derive this structure from oral traditions. After analyzing possible type-scenes from each epic, with tabulations of repeated elements, Clark concludes that the speeches of Beowulf and Unferth (ll. 506-48, 580-606), though rhetorically similar in structure (with an address, an insult, a story, and an application to the present situation), do not qualify as a theme (or type-scene) because the repetitions of words and half-lines result in a number of changes and contradictions, while such repetitions in *The Song of Bagdad* are used to construct a consistent and recognizable theme.

1237 Clemoes, Peter. "Style as the Criterion for Dating the Composition of *Beowulf*." In *Dating of 'Beowulf,'* pp. 173-86.

Postulates a general shift in Old English poetic style roughly around the ninth century, placing *Beowulf* in this transitional period. In the primitive verbal style, traditional language is integral to a shared social meaning whereas the later, "modern" style of Wulfstan and Ælfric becomes more rhetorical since it is applied from without to ornament abstract thought. Preaching probably gave rise to this modern style. Compares the word order, imagery, and point of view of *Beowulf* to that of several other Old English poems such as the Cynewulfian *Andreas, Elene,* and *Guthlac B*, finding that *Beowulf*'s style remains more internal and intregal than the more rhetorically-charged Christian poems. The *Beowulf* poet, however, lies between the primitive and modern styles and may very well have composed the poem during a transitional period, most probably in the late eighth or early ninth centuries. To place the poem at a later date would require that we view the poem as an "antiquarian exercise" (179) since it would no longer be part of a living social tradition, one which did not survive in the written culture of the later period. "The latest stylistic component in *Beowulf* seems . . . to be Hrothgar's moralizing 'sermon' (1700-84)," which exhibits several characteristics of the modern style and was probably influenced by vernacular preaching of a type common to the eighth and ninth centuries (180). Clemoes concludes that "the poem's characteristic, organic blend of social constraint and active imagination . . . must have belonged to a still living aristocratic tradition. It could not have come about in the society that produced Ælfric's articulate and articulated prose for laymen. . . . But in the second half of the eighth century or the early ninth conditions would have been right for the origination of *Beowulf*" (185). Discusses the style of lines 2319b-23 and 2333-36, along with various literary and historical parallels to objects and events in *Beowulf*.

1238   Conquergood, Dwight. "Boasting in Anglo-Saxon England: Performance and the Heroic Ethos." *Literature in Performance* 1 (1981): 24-35.

Provides an analysis of boasting as social performance rather than mere egotistical display and discusses its function in *Beowulf, The Battle of Maldon*, the Old English Orosius, and *The Wanderer*. Though easily misunderstood, "Throughout Old English heroic poetry, boasting is associated consistently with the best and most noble parts of life" (26). Boasts often begin with the hero's lineage, recount past deeds of glory, then move to a prediction of future prowess. "Past deeds function within a boast as both signposts and springboards for ever more daring feats of valor" (28). Though boasting may seem egotistical, "Few types of utterance are more essentially communal than the boast" (29). The community itself decides what kinds of heroic action to celebrate, and the boaster must choose from and arrange past exploits which fit into this social matrix. The boast is, in terms of speech-act theory, "constative" or "performative" in that instead of describing something else, a boast *does* something. It is a pledge for heroic action, witnessed by the audience. Many boasting scenes occur in a "theatrical" context, with brandishing of spears, raising of shields, taking of center stage. In fact, "the public nature of boasting is an expression of sociability" (32). The boast can give meaning even to acts that end in defeat. Examines several boasts in *Beowulf* (ll. 407b-55 and others).

1239 Creed, Robert P. "The *Beowulf*-Poet: Master of Sound-Patterning." In *Lord*, pp. 194-216.

On the assumption that *Beowulf* was originally composed in an oral environment dependent "in no way upon the use of writing" (194) and only later committed to vellum, applies Berkley Peabody's work on oral compositional techniques in Homer and Hesiod (*The Winged Word*, 1975) to the poem, finding that *Beowulf* contains intricate sound-patterning as well as other features identified by Peabody. Specifically, Creed applies five tests for oral composition: the phonemic test (high redundancy in sound patterning), the formulaic test (the presence of formulas), the enjambment test (the absence of syntactic periods which extend beyond metrical lines), the thematic test (the repetitious clustering of words—"lexical clumps"—when treating a particular theme), and the song test (consistency in larger narrative patterns). In the course of the argument, Creed provides a detailed analysis of the *æþeling* formula system (formulaic test) as well as the frequent clustering of the words *feor* 'far' and *cuman* 'to come' as in ll. 361, 825, and 1805-06 (thematic test). Finally, Christian elements do not require a literate composition for *Beowulf* since oral tradition was "an adaptive mechanism" which was able to incorporate Christian ideas (207). Includes a close analysis of sound patterns in lines 1803-25 as well as a list of *æþeling* formulas.

1240 Crépin, André. *Poèmes héroïques viel-anglais: Beowulf, Judith, Maldon, Plainte de l'exilée, Exaltation de la Croix*. [Old English Heroic Poems: *Beowulf, Judith, Maldon, The Wanderer, Dream of the Rood*]. Bibliothèque médiévale, v. 1460. Paris: Union générale d'éditions, 1981.

Includes a French prose translation of *Beowulf* in a collection of other translations of Old English poems, including a brief introduction (24-28). Lines 4-14: "Souvent Scyld, de la lignée de Scef, à nombre d'ennemis, à maintes tribus arracha les trônes du festin: fit trembler le guerrier après s'être jadis trouvé fort démuni. Il connut revirement et salut, vit sa puissance croître sous les nues, s'affirmer son prestige au point que chaque peuple installé alentour, riverain des mers frayées par la baleine, dut lui obéir, lui verser tribut. Ce fut un noble roi!"
Reviews: J. De Caluwé-Dor, *Le Moyen Age* 91 (1985): 281-82.

1241 Doig, J. F. "*Beowulf* 3096b: Curse or Consequence?" *ELN* 19 (1981): 3-6.

Disputes the efficacy of the pagan curse laid on the dragon's hoard. Translators have tended to render the word *benemndon* (l. 3069b) as "cursed," though there is no justification for this reading. Doig suggests that the misfortunes which are to befall any plunderer of the hoard come from the consequences of meddling with heathen treasure rather than from the chanted "curse" of the heathen princes. To any Christian, such a hoard would be contaminated and dangerous, bringing defilement on anyone who touched it. In any case, the spell cannot affect Beowulf since he enjoys the favor of God, and God has the power to negate the spell. The following translation of ll. 3069-73a incorporates this new view: "The renowned princes who had placed that treasure there had spoken solemn words over it, to last till the Day of Doom, with the consequence that whatever man might rifle that place would be guilty of sin, kept captive in the shrines of false gods, held fast in hell's bonds, tormented with plagues" (4).

1242 Dumville, David N. "*Beowulf* and the Celtic World: The Uses of Evidence." *Traditio* 37 (1981): 109-60.

In a wide-ranging essay suggests that future work on the language, dating, and localization of *Beowulf* consider the methods and evidence of scholarship on Celtic literature, coming as it does from a culture "which both had direct links with that of Anglo-Saxon England and also shared many points of development with it" (159). With respect to the direct influence of Irish culture on *Beowulf*, Dumville doubts that Irish heroic literature provides a useful context and instead suggests that more work be done on the possible influence of Irish Christianity on Old English religious vocabulary and on the general Christian culture of Anglo-Saxon England, endorsing in part Donahue's work [S216, S540]. Though linguistic and metrical tests for dating and localizing texts have been abandoned for the most part by twentieth-century *Beowulf* scholars, their use on Celtic texts has shown them to be more promising than unreliable studies of general historical context, and Dumville calls for more work in this area, particularly that the text of *Beowulf* be reconstructed into various period dialects in order to judge the relative merits of their claims. With respect to the poem's anachronistic view of the pagan past, he suggests that scholars of Irish literature (particularly of the "King-tales") have understood such anachronisms better and that their insights should be applied to *Beowulf*. He calls for more work on reconstructing the text-history of *Beowulf* with insights from the better-known transmission of Celtic texts such as the Welsh heroic poem, the *Gododdin*, and the poems in the Ulster-Cycle, which show a complicated intertwining of oral and written transmission. Finally, Dumville casts doubt on Whitelock's argument [S231] for a secular context for the poem and instead places it within a monastic context, given the fact that Irish monasticism could nurture heroic literature.

1243 Farina, Peter. "The Christian Color in *Beowulf*: Fact or Fiction." *U of Southern Florida Language Quarterly* 20 (1981): 21-26.

Claims that it is unnecessary to see any Christian coloring at all in *Beowulf* and that apparent references to Christian or Old Testament ideas could have been absorbed by the Germanic tribes from a number of non-Christian sources in the time of the migrations. Farina points out that "the biblical legends mentioned in *Beowulf* have existed among pagan nations from time immemorial and may have survived among the Germanic races side by side with, but independently of, Jewish and Christian tradition" (22). The explicit reference to Cain can be explained if the Genesis account itself derives from a pagan source and was filtered down independently or by direct influence of the Hebrew tradition to the Germanic tribes. Farina, using Blackburn's classification of the assumed Christian passages [S22], shows how each has its parallel in non-Christian traditions such as Iranian-Zorastrian mythology as well as Babylonian and Hindu myth.

1244 Feldman, Thalia Phillies. "Grendel and Cain's Descendants." *Literary Onomastics Studies* 8 (1981): 71-87.

Reviewing several words applied to Grendel, concludes that "As revealed in the onomastic terminology of *Beowulf*, it seems that the nature of Cain's Germanic descendants, the *fifelcyn* including Grendel, derived from the broadest range of pagan antecedents" (83). Feldman denies a strong Christian background for the monsters, finding pagan associations for a majority of the names applied to Grendel: *fifelcyn* (l. 104b, related to ON *fifl*, 'fool, clown, madman'), *untȳdras* (l. 111, meaning 'frail, weak' or 'unskilled, ignorant'), *eoten* (l. 112a, derived from *etan*, 'to eat' and implying cannibalism), *gī gantas* (l. 113a, associated with Germanic giants or the classical Titans), *orcnēas* (l. 112b, associated by glossators with the Roman god of death, Orcus), *thyrs* (l. 426a, related to an ON term meaning 'giant' or 'surly, stupid' and perhaps to *thyrstan*, 'to thirst' indicating Grendel's blood-lust). Feldman argues that *fēond* 'enemy' and *syn* 'crime' do not carry moralistic connotations in the poem and retain their pre-Christian meanings. Nevertheless, the Old Testament story of Cain influenced the depiction of Grendel as a "vicious, feral" man rather than a deformed monster.

1245 Foley, Joanne De Lavan. "Feasts and Anti-Feasts in *Beowulf* and the *Odyssey*." In *Lord*, pp. 235-261.

Taking Fry's definition of the formula as a starting point [S623], finds that Old English poets often combine formula systems into a larger unified group of related systems that form oral themes, one of the most prominent of which is the frequent combination of formulas for feasting (built around *symble*, 'feast') and sleeping (built around *swefan*, 'to sleep'). These themes are related on the mythic level and constitute "essential ideas" built into the oral system (238). Foley analyzes the thematic and mythic implications of several individual *symble* and *swefan/swebban* formulae, finding that they establish a thematic pattern of order (ritual) moving to disorder (anti-ritual) and finally back to order (ritual). Feasts establish rhythm and order, but this order is disturbed in sleep (as in the attacks of Grendel and his mother), requiring a ritual to re-establish order. Foley finds similar combinations of formulas in the *Odyssey*. Foley analyzes and lists *symble* (ll. 81a, 119a, 489a, 564a, 619a, 1008a, 1010b, 1782b, 2104a, 2431a) and *swefan* formulas (ll. 600a, 679, 703b, 729a, 1280a, 1672a, 1741b, 1800b, 2060b, 2256b, 2457b, and 2746a).

1246   Foley, John Miles. "Narrativity in *Beowulf, The Odyssey* and the Serbo-Croatian 'Return Song.'" In *Classical Models in Literature.* Ed. Zoran Konstantinovic, Warren Anderson, and Walter Dietze. Innsbrucker Beiträge zur Kulturwissenschaft, Sonderheft 49. Innsbruck: Institut für Sprachwissenschaft der U Innsbruck, 1981. Pp. 296-301.

Looks at "mistakes" in orally-composed Serbo-Croatian return songs in order to shed light on an important structural problem in *Beowulf*: the awkward transition from Beowulf's youthful exploits to his last adventure against the dragon (ll. 2199-2200)—a flaw which implies lack of unity. After reviewing a mistake by the oral singer (or *guslar*) Mujo Kukuruzovic, who mixes plot elements from two similar story lines, Foley concludes that such "song amalgams" may provide "a potential model for considering traditional epic structure and narrativity in other literatures, for understanding how combinations of tales need be neither editorial redaction nor *Liedertheorie*, but a thoroughly traditional process." *Beowulf* may lack the kind of unity we expect from literate, non-traditional narratives; however, "with the Yugoslav analogy in mind, we can, in effect, have it both ways: the *Beowulf* text is concurrently a whole and a combination of tales, an amalgam which can be explained as the product of a traditional process" (299). The *Odyssey*, Foley suggests, may also provide evidence for the process of song amalgamation, a phenomenon linked to oral performance.

1247   _____ "The Oral Theory in Context." In *Lord*, pp. 27-122.

Contains an introductory section on "The Oral Theory and Old English Poetry," which summarizes and discusses a wide range of books and articles (from 1878-1978) concerning formula and oral composition in *Beowulf* and other Old English poems. The overview is divided into two sections, "Formulaic Structure and the Text (1878-48)" and "Oral Tradition Theory (1949-1978)," the second section commencing with a discussion of the seminal work of Parry and Lord [S416].

1248 _____ "Tradition-Dependent and -Independent Features in Oral Literature: A Comparative View of the Formula." In *Lord*, pp. 262-281.

Cautions that any understanding of the concept of formula must recognize the different constraints on each oral tradition, contrasting the nature of formula in Homeric Greek, Serbo-Croatian, and the Old English of *Beowulf.* "The metrical foundation of Old English poetry, so different from that of Homeric Greek and Serbo-Croatian, demands a conception of formula which de-emphasizes the roles of syllabicity and internal structure in favor of the tradition-dependent parameters of stressed position and metrical formula" (275). Foley elaborates these ideas in [1737].

1249 Frank, Roberta. "Skaldic Verse and the Date of *Beowulf.*" In *Dating of 'Beowulf'*, pp. 123-40.

Suggests a date for *Beowulf* in the late ninth century or the first half of the tenth century on the basis of similarities between *Beowulf* and tenth-century skaldic verse. The points of contact are most clearly seen in the use of dynastic terms (Geat and Scylding, ON *Gautr* and *skjöldungr*), the use of political catchwords (*Beowulf*'s *þēod-cyning* 'tribal king' and the skaldic term *þjóðkonungr*), the depiction of heroes (the shape of the Sigemund-Fitela story in Beowulf and in *Ragnarsdrápa* and the *Eiríksmál*; the connection between Sigemund and Heremod in *Beowulf* and in the *Eiríksmál* and *Hákonarmál*), echoes of Scandinavian turns of phrase in *Beowulf* (though Beowulf acts unlike the Odinic, pagan champions of the skalds), the familiarity with the skaldic memorial ode in *Beowulf* (the eulogy for *Beowulf* and the skaldic memorial ode or *erfidrápr*, one of which uses the word *lofgjarn*—c.f. *Beowulf*'s *lofgeornost* 'most eager for praise,' l. 3182—to praise the dead hero Sigurthr), and shared technical vocabulary (words for benches, burial rituals, and standards). Frank detects the closest similarity in style and feeling between Beowulf and the poetry of the skald Sighvatr.

Frank suggests that if the *Beowulf* poet reacted to the traditions "of the Danelaw skalds and storytellers . . . , it is easy to imagine that he was composing not long after, or far from, the Danish skalds he was outdoing" (138). Finally, Frank suggests several archaeological and art-historical facts which would also support a Viking age date for the poem.

1250 Fry, Donald K. "Launching Ships in *Beowulf* 210-216 and *Brunanburh* 32b-36." *MP* 79 (1981): 61-66.

Offers a new explanation for several confusing elements in the ship launching scene (ll. 210b-16), reinterpreting the phrase *on stefn stigon* 'climbed on the stem' (l. 212a). The sequence of events surrounding the launching of Beowulf's boat have confused a number of readers. D.R. Evans [S489] explains the difficulties by positing two vessels: the ship (*flota*, l. 210b), which was anchored in a fjord, and a dinghy (*bāt*, l. 211a), by which Beowulf and his men reached the ship and brought it to shore for loading. Fry argues against this view, examining other launchings in the poem (ll. 32b-36) and one in the *Battle of Brunanburh*. The evidence shows that the ships were grounded in the sand and then anchored. To launch such a ship, the crew had to free it from the sand. Thus, the following reinterpretation of the events in lines 210b-216 seems more plausible: "the ship sits in the surf, with its bow grounded in the sand. . . . [T]he crewmen climb up on the stem, that part of the stern farthest outboard from the shore, and press down their weight (211b-212a), freeing the ship; the water swirls around (*wundon*) the vessel and against the now empty sand (212b-213a); the crew loads the ship, and off they go (213b-215), shoving away from the shore" (65).

1251 Goffart, Walter. "*Hetware* and *Hugas*: Datable Anachronisms in *Beowulf*." In *Dating of 'Beowulf'*, pp. 83-100.

Examines the terms which the *Beowulf* poet applies to the peoples whom Hygelac attacked in his disastrous raid on the Franks (the *Hetware* and *Hūgas*) in order to shed light on the dating of the poem, concluding that the poem could not have been written earlier than the second quarter of the tenth century. Many scholars (including Klaeber [S67]) have assumed that these names are ancient ones transmitted to the poet through an oral tradition and that the Heteware are to be identified as the ancient Chatti and Chattuarii while the

Hūgas are to be connected with the Chauci. Goffart casts doubt on these assumptions, showing that the connection between the Heteware and Hygelac's raid is a detail added to Gregory of Tours' account by the author of the eighth-century *Liber Historiae Francorum*, who tends to add geographical embellishments. Goffart argues against the idea that the author of this eighth-century history had more information about the raid than Gregory and suggests that the former added the detail that the raid took place at the village of the "Attoarii" because it had been the site of a recent raid by the Saxons in 715. The *Beowulf* poet could only have gleaned this detail from the *Liber Historiae Francorum* itself, setting the *terminus a quo* for *Beowulf* "no earlier than the latter half of the eighth century" (100). The name "Hugas" provides a different set of problems. Discounting the idea that the name is an ancient one transmitted by oral tradition, Goffart believes that it is connected with the proper name *Hugh*, attested in Frankish territories only in the ninth and tenth centuries, "when men named Hugh controlled a Frankish *regnum*" (100), as attested by Widukind and the *Annals of Quedlinburg*. "The implications of this argument for the date of *Beowulf* seem to be that the poem was written no earlier than the second quarter of the tenth century" (100).

1252 Harada, Yoshio. "Some Observations on the Epic Formula in *The Phoenix* and *Beowulf*." *Kitasato Journal of Liberal Arts and Sciences* (Kitasato Univ.) 15 (1981): 33-40.

Not seen.

1253 Hart, Thomas Elwood. "Calculated Casualties in *Beowulf*: Geometrical Scaffolding and Verbal Symbolism." *SN* 53 (1981): 3-35.

Taking Howlett's article [S918] as a starting point, examines the placement of number words in *Beowulf*, particularly those used to describe the decreasing strength of Beowulf's troop (15-14-13-12), concluding that the poet consciously placed these number words at proportionate intervals in the poem. Hart summarizes his conclusions: "(1) the poet intended the number-word design to be proportional; (2) the number-words themselves to imply regular polygons as structural (and in part, at least, symbolic) moduli; and (3) the proportionality of the design to reflect as many possible ratios involving these polygons as could be coordinated consistently and with precision" (27). The total number of lines (3182) is the diameter of a circle with a circumference of 10,000. Discusses various proportionalities within the poem and includes diagrams of poetic-numerical structure. [See *numerical structure* in the subject index.]

1254 Hasegawa, Hiroshi. "The *Beowulf* Manuscript." *General Education Review* (College of Agriculture and Veterinary Medicine, Nihon Univ.) 17 (1981): 43-69. In Japanese.

Deals with the state of the manuscript, its forms, and the sectional divisions in the poem. Reprinted in Hiroshi Hasegawa's *Studies in 'Beowulf'* (Tokyo: Seibido, 1988). (HH)

1255 Henry, P. L. "Furor Heroicus." *Occasional Papers in Linguistics and Language Learning* 8 (1981): 53-61.

Finds evidence for a West-European tradition of "an inordinately grim, magic form of martial action," involving physical distortions of the hero in time of battle (55) in the *Táin*, *Beowulf*, and the Old Norse sagas. In *Beowulf*, the physical distortions revolve around the word *-bolgen* 'enraged' which derives from a verb originally meaning 'to swell.' Thus *gebolgen* (l. 723b) might mean 'distended in spirit' as well as 'enraged.' Similarly, the element *collen-* of *collen-ferhð* (ll. 1806a, 2785a) may derive from an Indo-European word meaning 'to swell.' Such terms as these (as well as the word ēacen 'huge, mighty') "express martial fury as a swelling, welling up or expansion" (56). Another common form of the *furor heroicus* has the hero turn into bear or wolf, a theme attested frequently in the Old Norse sagas.

1256 Horowitz, Sylvia Huntley. "The Ravens in *Beowulf*." *JEGP* 80 (1981): 502-11.

Investigates literary and theological backgrounds for ravens in the poem, arguing that three different incarnations of the raven signal the life-to-death cycle of the pagan hero Beowulf, a view of history derived ultimately from Augustine's *City of God*. "The Anglo-Saxons, sharing Augustine's notion of the City of Man . . . , were certain that whole pagan societies, as well as individual pagan heroes, went through a life cycle from an innocent goodness that was rewarded by God with power and glory, to a fratricidal middle age, to death" (507). The ravens signal this progression in the life of Beowulf and his entire tribe as well. The rejoicing raven of lines 1801-02a announces the glorious morning after the defeat of Grendel's mother. This raven, though a harbinger of joy, has disturbing connections to the carrion-loving raven in commentaries on the Noah story, which connect the release of the raven from the ark into the sunshine with the death of Cain's descendants in the flood. This raven thus signals the initial glory granted to Beowulf by God but contains disturbing hints of future corruption. Next, the ravens which linger near the gallows along with Beowulf's slaying of Dæghrefn, the 'day raven,' signal Beowulf's entry into fratricidal middle age just as the Geats' battle at Ravenswood begins their implication in the City of Man and loss of innocence. The last raven, which will pick at the bodies of the dead Geats (ll. 3024b-27), points to the moral death of Beowulf and the Geats.

1257 Jacobs, Nicolas. "The Old English Heroic Tradition in the Light of Welsh Evidence." *Cambridge Medieval Celtic Studies* 2 (1981): 9-20.

Investigates the social role of the Old English poet by contrast and comparison with the bards Aneirin and Taliesin in the Welsh poetry, finding that there is little pure heroic poetry in Old English. Jacobs sees *Beowulf*, with its meditation on the values of the pagan past from a Christian present, as "a secondary development of heroic poetry, [which] cannot be compared with the work of Taliesin" (10). If heroic poetry celebrates in its purest form the values of heroic society, however, the Ravenswood and Finnsburh episodes from *Beowulf* (as well as the Finn Fragment, *Waldere, Deor*, and *Widsið*) do qualify as heroic poems. After examining each of these in some detail, Jacobs concludes: "it is possible to define a number of common or comparable elements in the two traditions concerning the social function of the poet in early Wales and England" (20). When *Beowulf* was composed, there was still a living poetic tradition with two missions: to sing the exploits of past heroes and to celebrate the glory of heroes actually present. These functions are similar to the differing missions of the Welsh *pencerdd* or court poet and the *bardd teulu* or comitatus poet. As time went on, Old English heroic poetry came to focus on the retelling of ancient lays, though the tradition of praising or lamenting a contemporary hero is demonstrated in *Beowulf* and probably existed beyond the eighth century. The Welsh and English traditions also share certain motifs, in particular the idea of the comitatus and the taking of oaths over mead.

1258 Kavros, Harry E. "*Swefan æfter symble*: the Feast-Sleep Theme in *Beowulf*." *Neophil* 65 (1981): 120-28.

After discussing and defining oral-formulaic themes, goes on to propose that the motifs of feasting and sleeping, when joined, form a theme unit in *Beowulf* and that it appears in ironic or apparently inappropriate contexts for poetic effect. Sleep naturally follows feasting in *Beowulf*, and the poet uses the theme on the literal level of the plot at least twice, when warriors go to rest after celebrating in feast the defeats of Grendel (ll. 1232-37a) and Grendel's mother (ll. 1787-93). But the theme of sleep after feasting is used for other purposes: "it can synecdochically refer to the entire cycle of life; it can be used to parody an unheroic life; it can be used as a conceptual analogue and hence become a metaphor for another human action" (123). The theme highlights unheroic behavior in lines 128-40a, where the Danes after feasting seek beds in the outbuildings to avoid the terror of Grendel. In lines 1735-42a, the theme becomes a figure for spiritual death, when the watchful guardian of the soul sleeps (as it should not) after feasting. The theme appears in its most elaborate form in Grendel's fight with Beowulf. There, Grendel sees the sleeping warriors and has an expectation of feasting (ll. 728-34a), but the theme is unresolved here since not all the warriors are sleeping nor does Grendel finish his feast.

1259 Keller, Thomas L. "The Dragon in *Beowulf* Reconsidered." *Aevum* 55 (1981): 218-28.

Examines northern lore about dragons in order to place the dragon in *Beowulf* in critical perspective, concluding that "The significance of the dragon in *Beowulf* is that it is the appropriate adversary for an heroic king" (228). Keller shows that in the northern analogues (the story of Sigurd in the *Völsung saga* and the *Fáfnismál*, as well as narratives about Frotho and Fridlevus in Saxo Grammaticus' *Danish History*) a single hero combats a fierce serpent-like dragon with invulnerable scales on his back but with a soft underbelly. The account in *Beowulf* differs by having two heroes attack: Wiglaf is present to report first-hand about the battle and harangue the cowardly thanes who abandoned their lord. Keller also finds that Beowulf's age, not his ignorance about dragons, demands that Wiglaf come to his aid: "The answer seems to lie in Beowulf's age. When he undertakes the adventure, he is no longer the warrior he once was. Fridelvus knew nothing of the anatomy of dragons, but through trial and error found the vulnerable spot. Beowulf, on the other hand, had to rely on the agility of Wiglaf to find the soft belly, himself not being able to maneuver sufficiently to hit the mark. This does not detract from Beowulf's courage but enhances it" (225). Keller rejects Goldsmith's allegorical reading [S759] and discusses other Norse analogues as well as the physical attributes of dragons.

1260 *Key-Word Studies in 'Beowulf' and Chaucer, 1.* Tokyo: Centre for Mediaeval English Studies, 1981.

Not seen.

1261 Kiernan, Kevin S. *'Beowulf' and the 'Beowulf' Manuscript.* New Brunswick, NJ: Rutgers UP, 1981. Pp. xvi + 303; 1 leaf of plates; ill.

Makes a case for an eleventh-century date for the poem in three stages: 1) examines historical and linguistic evidence for an eleventh-century date, 2) undertakes an extensive physical description and analysis of the Cotton Vitellius A.xv, finding evidence that *Beowulf* was copied as a separate codex, and 3) assembles a variety of paleographical and codicological evidence indicating that the poem underwent substantial correction and revision, implying a text far more reliable than has been assumed. The following abstract is based in part on Kiernan's detailed summary (4-12).

Part one, "The Poem's Eleventh-Century Provenance," begins with the suggestion that the reign of Cnut the Dane (1016-1035) would have "provided an excellent environment for the creation of the poem" (4). The manuscript has been dated on paleographical grounds to between 975 and 1025. The Danish raids by Swein Forkbeard (Cnut's father) against Æthelred Unræd (978-1016) would have made an English poem in praise of the Danes unlikely, but with a Dane on the throne, such a poem becomes much more likely. Kiernan doubts the value of linguistic tests which support an early date: "the syntactical tests magnify the occurrence in *Beowulf* of some acknowledged archaisms found in unquestionably late verse; the phonetic-metrical tests are based on subjective interpretations of the meter that require sweeping, yet inconsistently selective emendations to unrecorded, early, linguistic forms; and the lonely phonetic-morphological-orthographical test is based on a MS 'ghost'" (5), that is, the form *wundini*, (l. 1392a) which Kiernan reconstructs as *wundun*, a leveled form of *wunden*. The dialect of the poem does require some explanations, having a mixture of Late West Saxon and other forms, mainly Mercian. But this does not necessarily indicate that the poem had gone through a long and complicated transmission. The same data could be explained by supposing that the *Beowulf* manuscript was copied outside West-Saxon territory, probably in the area around the old Danelaw boundary or in Danish Mercia itself, thus accounting for the non-West-Saxon forms.

Part two, "The History and Construction of the Composite Codex," points out problems with the present foliation of the manuscript, proposing that the foliation written in the manuscript (after correcting it in a few places where it is wrong) be preferred to the "official" foliation of 1884. The flyleaves reveal important information about foliation and suggest "two distinct foliations before the fire," a discovery which "provides startling proof that the *Beowulf* MS was missing a folio at the time. A study of the various foliations (six different ones are documented and dated) shows precisely how three different folios from *Beowulf* were shifted from place to place from the early 17th century to the late 18th century" (7). The remainder of this section "is devoted to describing the physical makeup of the various MSS, and to defining their relation to the codex as a unit" (7). Kiernan examines both the Southwick and Nowell codices, reconstructing gatherings by comparing flesh and hair sides of the now-separated folios. Though earlier studies see *Beowulf* as the fourth part of the Nowell codex and believe that the text starts in the middle of a gathering, Kiernan, comparing hair and flesh sides, postulates that *Beowulf* began a new gathering and further that it once existed as a separate codex. "It now seems that the Nowell Codex became a composite codex in two stages: first, the *Beowulf* MS was combined with the prose codex, probably soon after *Beowulf* was copied; then, undoubtedly, the *Judith* fragment was added on in early modern times" (8). Patterns of scribal correction confirm this view, since the *Beowulf* text was carefully corrected by both scribes and the prose texts were not. "More important, it is eloquent testimony that the scribes were neither lazy nor inattentive in copying the poem" (9).

Part three, "The *Beowulf* Codex and the Making of the Poem," begins by arguing for the authority of the manuscript text as a late, carefully corrected text and pointing out that even texts with long transmission histories are more accurate than have been believed. "Until now, it has been impossible to see the MS as anything other than a very late transcript of an early poem, and this limited view has ... justified many scores of needless emendations" (9). Since Kiernan postulates no long and complicated transmission for the poem, he believes that a "rigorous textual conservatism" is in order, urging scholars to re-examine manuscript readings. "Only by rejecting those emendations and interpolations based solely on an arid application of [metrical and alliterative] 'rules' can the individual style of a late, traditional poet be studied" (10). Kiernan defends a number of manuscript readings (in l. 389-90, 401b, 403b, 499a, 589b, 965a, 1073b, 1128b-29a, 1163-68, 1488a, 1541b, 1960b, 1981, 1261b, 2094b, 2929b, 2972b). To show the authority of the text, he undertakes a study of scribal proofreading in the manuscript and examines all erasures under ultraviolet light. Next, Kiernan finds paleographical evidence that the manuscript remained in the hands of the second scribe, who continued to correct and maintain it long after copying it, proposing that the second scribe made a palimpsest of the folio containing lines 2207-2252 by scraping and washing it down after the binding of the manuscript. Instead of a freshening of the page, the text was scraped off and replaced, in the hand of the second scribe, but at a much later stage of development, perhaps many years later. "An objective transcription of the new text on the folio discloses a number of anomalous linguistic forms, which can be interpreted as signs of later attrition in the standard literary dialect, a process that accelerated as the 11th century advanced. A closer look at the badly damaged condition of the text, particularly at the textual lacunas, shows that parts of the revised text were erased for some reason, and that a full restoration *of the revised text* was never carried out" (11).

This leads to the possibility that the *Beowulf* MS "is in effect an unfinished draft of the poem" and "actually preserves the last formative stages in the creation of the epic" (11). Kiernan theorizes that the second scribe, at this juncture, may have united two originally separate texts, artificially appending the second to the first. "If so, the revised text on the palimpsest may have been written to provide a smoother, more natural transition between the two, originally distinct, and perhaps even totally unrelated MSS" (12). The palimpsest occurs on the first folio of the dragon episode, and fitt numberings and patterns of rulings offer proof that the gathering immediately preceding the palimpsest, which holds the text of Beowulf's homecoming, was copied by the second scribe *after* he had copied the last two gatherings of the MS. The obvious conclusion is that the Danish and Geatish exploits of Beowulf were first brought together in the extant MS by the second scribe" (12). Finally, Kiernan examines the historical context for the poem afresh: the lament on the fall of the Geats may reflect sorrow for the passing of the Anglo-Saxon dynasty into the Danish empire. "If the last poet of *Beowulf* was the second scribe, as the paleographical and codicological evidence encourages one to believe, he increased, and continued to polish, an Anglo-Saxon treasure during the reign of the Danish Scylding lord" (278).

Reviews: *OEN* 16.1 (1982): 73-76; D.K. Fry, *Library Journal* 107 (1982): 260-61; N.F. Blake, *ES* 64 (1983): 72-75; Fulk [1315]; J.D. Niles, *Speculum* 58 (1983): 765-77; R.W. Clement [1426]; S. Sato, *Studies in English Lit.* (Tokyo) 61 (1984): 167-70; E.G. Stanley, *MÆ* 53 (1984): 112-17; J.B. Trahern, Jr., *JEGP* 83 (1984): 107-12; D. Yerkes, *Germanic Review* 59 (1984): 110-115.

1262 _____ "The Eleventh-Century Origin of *Beowulf* and the *Beowulf* Manuscript." In *Dating of 'Beowulf,'* pp. 9-22.

Investigates "the possibility that *Beowulf* was composed at the time of its only surviving manuscript" (9). Given the poem's special homage to the Danes, a date sometime after 1016, the year that Cnut ascended the English throne, seems "an eminently appropriate time for the composition of *Beowulf*" (10). Hrothgar could have been modelled on Cnut, and the genealogy with which the poem begins seems best suited to flatter the Danes rather than the English. Kiernan draws on paleographical and codicological studies of the manuscript to support an eleventh-century date, warning that the available facsimiles can be misleading. The main conclusions are that "the *Beowulf* manuscript was contemporary with the poem: apparently it was copied as a separate codex; without doubt it was thoroughly, repeatedly, and intelligently proofread by the scribes; it was dutifully repaired by the second scribe as time and use damaged it; and most importantly, a wide range of evidence persistently suggests that it was revised by both scribes in one specific, and seemingly relevant, section of the manuscript, between folios 163 and 180, and especially between folios 171 and 179. The evidence of revision implies as well that the

Beowulf manuscript is an unfinished draft of the poem, and that it preserves for us the artistic fusion of two originally distinct *Beowulf* narratives" (20). Folio 179v is a palimpsest: the second scribe scraped off the original text in order to make a smoother transition for the dragon episode, originally a separate narrative in a separate manuscript. In fact, the second scribe may have himself composed the dragon episode. See also Kiernan [1261].

1263 Kindrick, Robert L. "Germanic Sapientia and the Heroic Ethos of *Beowulf*." *Medievalia et Humanistica* 10 (1981): 1-17.

Finds that references to wisdom in *Beowulf* reveal a pattern of political concerns more traceable to Germanic traditions than to the Christian-Latin tradition of *sapientia* mapped out by Kaske [S361] and that similar attitudes are found in Tacitus' *De Germania* and the Old Norse *Hávamál*. Hrothgar's sermon (ll. 1700-1768) in particular shows more interest in political themes (with positive and negative models of kingship) than in a Christian sense of wisdom, while many of the "digressions" can be explained in terms of their political themes. The Germanic model of wisdom prized above all political acumen, restraint of physical violence, rhetorical ability, and strategic or tactical talent. Beowulf's rhetorical ability comes out most clearly in his debate with Unferth (ll. 535-39, 607-10).

1263a Koike, Kazuo. "The Spear in *Beowulf*." *Obirin Review (Obirin U)* 5 (1981): 19-22. In Japanese.

Considers the various words and phrases signifying "spear" in *Beowulf*. Four simple words and nine compound words are considered from the viewpoint of lexical and contextual meaning. (KK)

1264 Liggins, Elizabeth. "Irony and Understatement in *Beowulf*." *Parergon* 29 (1981): 3-7.

Identifies and traces two kinds of irony in the poem: contrast and understatement. Liggins finds that understatement occurs in the descriptions of characters and their actions and often has an epigrammatic or gnomic force. Contrast highlights the difference between characters' expectations and the actual outcome of events. Liggins concludes that the "presentation of contrasts between the hopes and plans of men and women (and even of monsters) and the actual course of events, together with the constant use of understatement both in narrative and in dialogue frequently give the poem a duality of perspective which in modern critical terms is surely ironic" (6). Also discusses narrative and verbal irony.

1265 Matsui, Noriko. "Old English Alliterative Verse vs. Middle English Alliterative Verse—the Case of *Beowulf* and *Morte Arthure.*" In *The History and Structure of the English Language: Presented to Kikuo Miyabe on the Occasion of his Sixtieth Birthday.* Ed. Yoshio Terasawa. Tokyo: Kenkyusha, 1981. Pp. 165-98.

Compares several passages in *Beowulf* to those in the alliterative *Morte Arthure*, concluding that the poetic style of the latter seems to reflect the rationalized treatment of human experiences in the later Middle Ages. (NM)

1266 McTurk, Rory. "Variation in *Beowulf* and the Poetic *Edda*: A Chronological Experiment." In *Dating of 'Beowulf'*, pp. 141-60.

Building on Paetzel's [F1613] and Campbell's [S460] work on parallelism and variation in Old English poetry, proposes to explore "the assumption that the more variation there is in an Old English or eddic poem, the later the poem is likely to be" (143). McTurk concludes that "the amount of variation does not differ sufficiently between the groups to show a chronological development; and that information about the distribution of the different types of variation in both groups can only be approximate and slight. The negative result of this paper, then, is that, if the Old Norse-Icelandic evidence is anything to go by, variation is unlikely to serve as a guide to the chronological interrelationship of Old English poems. The positive result, however, is that Old English and eddic poetry show a number of striking similarities in their use of variation, that deserve further study" (160). Provides a summary table of results, listing for each Old Norse text its predominant metrical form, the number of variations recorded by Paetzel, and the number of *vísorð* in a poem or group.

1267 Mellinkoff, Ruth. "Cain's Monstrous Progeny in *Beowulf*: Part II: Post-Diluvian Survival." *ASE* 9 (1981): 183-197.

In a continuation of Mellinkoff [1142], explores what knowledge the poet is likely to have had about a cannibalistic race of Cain that survived the Flood. After examining lore contained in a number of pseudepigraphical and rabbinical traditions, Mellinkoff conlcudes that "The source from which the *Beowulf* poet derived his belief that some of Cain's monstrous progeny survived the Flood . . . rested on rejecting or misunderstanding or ignoring or forgetting or not knowing traditional exegesis and favoring an interpretation more extravagantly fanciful. The widespread capacity for such a preference has been demonstrated in the belief that the Flood was not universal; by the story of the survival of the giant, Og; by the fabulous survival of Cain's kin described in the Zohar—giants, Jethro, evil spirits, demons, necromancers and goblins; by the view that Naamah the Cainite was Noah's wife; by the Muslim tradition that the daughters-in-law of Noah were all descended from Cain; by the wild karl of Cain's kin in the Middle English *Ywain and Gawain*; by the confused and murky mix-ups of Ham and Cain; and by the Mormon doctrine that Cain's descendants were literally perpetuated through Ham's wife. But, on present knowledge, we cannot explain the poet's belief in terms of influence from a specific tradition, let alone a specific text" (196-97).

1268 Murray, Alexander Callander. "*Beowulf*, the Danish Invasions, and Royal Genealogy." In *Dating of 'Beowulf'*, pp. 101-112.

Examines the long-held notion, formulated most memorably by Whitelock [S231], that *Beowulf* could not have been composed after the late eighth century, because no Englishman would honor the ancestors of the invading Danes, suggesting a West-Saxon context for the poem. Building on the work of Sisam [S272], points out that West Saxon genealogies—composed after the arrival of the Scandinavian invaders—show an interest in fusing Danish and English lore in order to consolidate dynastic power in the descendants of Alfred. There is evidence from the reigns of Æthelstan, Edgar, and Alfred himself that West Saxon kingdoms were "not built upon the kind of inveterate hostility which would preclude the composition and appreciation of a poem like *Beowulf*" (110). In fact, the genealogy of the Danes which opens *Beowulf* has close ties to the West Saxon genealogies. The reference to Offa the Angle, cited by Whitelock as evidence for a late eighth-century date and Mercian origin, may also have a connection with the West

Saxons, for Alfred's wife Ealhswith was a Mercian and descendant of Offa of Mercia. Thus, all of Alfred's descendants could claim Mercian ancestry. "The genealogical allusion suggests . . . that the poem was intended for a patron connected with the West-Saxon dynasty, but he need not have been a king nor an immediate member of the royal family; he may have been a cleric or layman and his poet could have come from any part of England that the language of the poem will allow" (110).

1269 Niles, John D. "Compound Diction and the Style of *Beowulf.*" *ES* 62 (1981): 489-503.

Appears, in somewhat altered form, as chapter six in Niles [1399].

1270 _____. "Formula and Formulaic System in *Beowulf.*" In *Lord*, pp. 394-415.

Appears, somewhat altered, as chapter five in Niles [1399].

1271 Ohba, Keizo. "The Dangers of Emendation and Modern Punctuation in *Beowulf.*" *Annual Reports of Studies (Doshisha Women's College)* 32.1 (1981): 1-27. In Japanese.

Not seen.

1272 O'Keefe, Katherine O'Brian. "*Beowulf,* Lines 702b-836: Transformations and the Limits of the Human." *TSLL* 23 (1981): 484-494.

Argues that Grendel, far from being a mere demonic spirit, gains human characteristics as he approaches the hall and that the poet explores the limits of the human in both Grendel and Beowulf. Though editorial emendations and slanted translations obscure the fact, Grendel's essential nature is deeply ambiguous: epithets applied to him identify him as a spirit, a man, and a recognizable monster. (O'Keefe rejects an emendation in line 707a that would make Grendel demonic.) The word *æglæca* 'monster, hero,' applied to both the monsters (Grendel and the dragon) and heroes (Beowulf and Sigemund) emphasizes this ambiguity. As Grendel approaches the human community, he himself becomes more human, an aspect highlighted by repeated references to his mental states. O'Keefe suggests "that this ambiguity is intentional, unresolvable, and designed to prepare us for the merging of hero and hostile one" (489). Beowulf, by contrast, must become more "monstrous" by stripping himself of human armor and weaponry, and in the middle of the fight scene, the poet stresses through ambiguous syntax the synonymy of the two fighters. Beowulf succeeds in defeating Grendel without succumbing to the taint of Grendel's monstrousness. As it emerges, the humanity the poet values "lies in the need for order within the group: to be human is to live in community.... Grendel's threat to the human is obvious. An unwelcome hall-thane, he renders Heorot useless, and, by extension, prevents the conduct of civilized life" (491). Also discusses Heremod as a monster.

1273 Owen, Gale R. *Rites and Religions of the Anglo-Saxons*. Newton Abbot: David & Charles, 1981.

In a larger study of Anglo-Saxon paganism, makes some remarks on Germanic pagan customs *Beowulf*. Owen suggests that the hanged son mourned in the Father's Lament may be connected to the cult of Woden, who was associated with hanging. Further, in the cremation funerals of Hnæf and Beowulf, the poet dwells on the gruesome details of ritual burning, and "uses the practice, which Christians would condemn as barbaric, to point out the awfulness of disloyalty among kindred [in the Finnsburh episode] and of the perversion of the heroic ideal, and the wastefulness of war" (85). Owen also considers the roles of women in funeral rituals and in the life of the hall, reflections of the story of Balder, the significance of boar images (as connected to Freyr and Freyja), superstitions about monsters, etc.
Reviews: P.S. Baker, *Albion* 13 (1981): 393; P.M. Bassett *Religious Studies Review* 8 (1982): 287; W.A. Chaney, *AHR* 87 (1982): 1068; H.D. Chickering, *Speculum* 58 (1983): 267; C. Hills, *Antiquity* 57 (1983): 65-66; D.A. Hinton, *ArchJ* 139 (1983): 465; H.R. Loyn, *AntJ* 62 (1983): 427-28; D.W. Rollason, *History* 68 (1983): 135; H.R. Ellis Davidson, *Folklore* 95 (1984): 130; I.N. Wood, *NH* 20 (1984): 233-36.

1274 Page, R.I. "The Audience of *Beowulf* and the Vikings." In *Dating of 'Beowulf'*, pp. 113-122.

Takes issue with Whitelock's argument [S231] that *Beowulf* could not have been composed after the Viking age due to the presumed animosity of the Anglo-Saxons against their invaders. Page sums up his rebuttal: "(1) the Anglo-

Saxon reaction to the viking invaders was often, perhaps overwhelmingly, expressed in religious rather than racial terms. (2) there were influential Anglo-Saxons who could distinguish, even in the midst of the viking raids, between the villains who attacked England and their more virtuous compatriots who stayed at home. (3) at various times and places there were important Anglo-Saxons who were on friendly terms with the Danes, even with those taking over parts of England" (122). Page does not insist that *Beowulf* is a late poem, but "[i]f there is other reason for placing Beowulf after, say, 835, there is nothing in the political situation to preclude it" (122).

1275 Pope, John C. "On the Date of Composition of *Beowulf*." In *Dating of 'Beowulf'*, pp. 187-96.

Mainly on the basis of linguistic and metrical tests, accepts "a date for the composition of *Beowulf*, more or less as we have it, at almost any time in the eighth century.... [A] seventh-century date is unlikely, though of course not unacceptable if strong reasons for it could be discovered" (195). Pope believes that linguistic tests can, if used carefully and with due allowance for exceptions, help to date the poem: the Lichtenheld test [F1244](depending on the use of the weak adjective and the definite article), a metrical test (developed by Carl Richter and others), and the early disappearance of the second 'h' in *hēah* 'high' if the following inflection begins with a vowel. The apparent exceptions to some of these tests in the *Gloria I*, *The Meters of Boethius*, *Genesis B*, and *The Battle of Maldon*, can be explained historically. Pope finds the form *wundini* (l. 1382) rather weak as evidence for an early date.

1276 Poussa, Patricia. "The Date of *Beowulf* Reconsidered: The Tenth Century?" *NM* 82 (1981): 276-88.

Provides the following summary: "The writer argues the case for a tenth-century dating of *Beowulf*. Historical evidence for the number of Scandinavian immigrants to England in the ninth and tenth centuries, and their political significance is reviewed. It is proposed that the *Beowulf*-poet may be an Anglo-Dane, in touch with both the oral literature brought over by Scandinavian settlers, and, by education, the literary culture of Anglo-Saxon England. The model for the society of *Beowulf* may be found in the tenth-century Viking trading towns of the Baltic. The Norman Conquest, with its anti-

Danish policy in history-writing and destruction of the OE literary language, is responsible for the misunderstanding of *Beowulf* in later centuries" (276). Poussa compares four likely periods for the composition of *Beowulf* (the ages of Bede, Offa, Alfred, as well as the tenth century) in terms of four requirements: a) high literary culture, b) a familiar and positive attitude to Danes, c) Christianity long established, and d) access to sources of Scandinavian history. The tenth century alone meets all four. She endorses some of Schücking's suggestions [S56] about the Danelaw and its possible cultural associations with *Beowulf*, suggesting that like the Homeric poems, *Beowulf* was written down when members of an oral culture (the Danish settlers in the Danelaw) made a sudden transition to literacy. The folktales of the Danelaw could have provided the Scandinavian motifs in the poem. Includes a brief analysis of linguistic evidence.

1277 Queval, Jean. *'Beowulf': L'Épopée fondamentale de la littérature anglaise.* Paris: Gallimard, 1981. Pp. 193.

Translates the poem into modern French using rhythmical prose and also providing a general introduction, notes to the text, and a brief bibliography. The introduction discusses issues of style, literary history, date, historical setting, and translation. Lines 4-11: "C'est souvent que Scyld Shefing d'haute lutte avait le meilleur des bataillons ennemis et des tribus. Même il était l'effroi de quiconque empiétait sur ses terres—lui l'enfant trouvé nu comme un ver, grandissant sous les cieux en force et en stature. Oh, de son dénuement il eut consolation. Et un jour, les clans voisinent en paix le long des côtes. Sur la route de la baleine ils lui font obédience et lui rendent hommage. Il fut un bon roi!" (63)
Reviews: T.A. Shippey, *TLS* 1 Jan. 1982: 9; *OEN* 17.1 (1983): 85.

1278 _____. "Beowulf." *La nouvelle revue française* 339 (1981): 179-92.

Provides a general introduction to the genesis, date, transmission, editing, and scholarship of *Beowulf*, including a detailed plot summary in French (184-92).

1279 Renoir, Alain. "Oral-Formulaic Context: Implications for the Comparative Criticism of Mediaeval Texts." In *Lord*, pp. 416-439.

Proposes that an understanding of type-scenes from an oral-formulaic tradition may provide a counterbalance to the loss of literary context which current trends of criticism, including deconstruction, promote. Renoir illustrates this point by analyzing a type-scene for "telling a tale" (adapted from Creed [S462]) in the *Odyssey, Beowulf,* and the *Hildebrandslied,* showing how a type-scene affects literary expectations and provides a context for poems like *Beowulf,* "whose immediate chronological context happens to be poverty-stricken" (423). He identifies the flyting between Beowulf and Unferth (ll. 499a-529b) as a type-scene conforming to the content and sequence of motifs identified by Creed and compares it to analogous scenes in the *Odyssey* and the *Hildebrandslied.* There are two advantages to this method: "The first is that it provides a flexible but *specific* context whose integrity is readily ascertainable and against which we may in turn measure the integrity of a given text, about which we are thus enabled to make reasonably objective statements. The second is that it provides us with the means for understanding certain aspects of ancient texts through legitimate comparison with more modern texts" (432).

1280 Sato, Noboru. "A Sound Symbolism in the Alliterative Thorn in *Beowulf.*" *Tamagawa Review* 6 (1981): 82-93.

Suggests that patterns of alliteration based on thorn (þ) symbolize the devilishness of the monsters, the monsters' massacre of warriors, their noble fights, and their sublime deaths. (NS)

1281 Schabram, Hans. "*Andreas,* 303a und 360B-362b: Bemerkungen zur Zählebigkeit philologischer Fehlurteile." [Remarks on the Persistence of Philological Misjudgments]. In *Geschichtlichkeit und Neuanfang im sprachlichen Kunstwerk: Studien zur englischen Philologie zu Ehren von Fritz W. Schulze.* Ed. Peter Erlebach, Wolfgang G. Muller, and Klaus Reuter. Tübingen: Narr, 1981. Pp. 39-47.

Takes issue with the assumption that the *Andreas* poet echoed the lines from *Beowulf* awkwardly without understanding their context, and reiterates his doubts, expressed in Schabram [S562], that the *Andreas* poet knew *Beowulf* directly. Schabram concludes that no one will be able to decide with absolute certainty concerning the proposed echoes of *Beowulf* in *Andreas* whether they are imitations, allusions, or reminiscences from *Beowulf*, or whether they should be seen as conventional formulas rooted in the common poetic tradition, which were just as available to the *Andreas* poet as to the *Beowulf* poet (46-47). He shows that two supposed infelicities of style and grammar in *Andreas* (l. 303a and 360b-362a) have been misunderstood. Discusses the possible echoes of *Beowulf*, lines 2991-2995a and 36b-42, in *Andreas*.

1282 Shaheen, Abdel-Rahman. "The Style of *Beowulf*: A Study of Diction and Rhetorical Devices." *Studia Anglica Posnaniensia* 13 (1981): 149-162.

Undertakes a general stylistic study of the poem, concentrating on the rhetorical devices such as variation, enumeration, kenning, *kent heiti*, antithesis, etc., and concluding that "the professional scop of *Beowulf* (who certainly had had no academic degree in classical rhetoric) was a lettered poet familiar with past and present literary traditions is more than a reasonable hypothesis" (161).

1283 Silber, Patricia. "Rhetoric as Prowess in the Unferð Episode." *TSLL* 23 (1981): 471-483.

Maintains that the Beowulf-Unferth flyting scene (ll. 499-606) is a contention "not over physical valor, but rather over ready wit, eloquent speech, and telling allusions" (473) and goes on to analyze the rhetorical devices used in the passage in order to support this thesis. Silber identifies devices described by Adeline Courtney Bartlett [S117] as well as examples of classical rhetoric, including parallelism, chiasmus, rhetorical description, envelope patterns, metaphor, incremental lists, gnomes, etc. She agrees with Bartlett that the rhetoric of the poem represents a mixture of Germanic and classical elements and goes on to point out similarities in method between the flyting speeches of Beowulf and Unferth and Cicero's techniques (in the *De Inventione*) for refuting an opponent's arguments.

1284 Spamer, James B. "*Beowulf* 1-2: An Argument for a New Reading." *ES* 62 (1981): 210-214.

Questions the two current explanations of the genitive plural *Gar-dena* (l. 1) and proposes an alternate way of construing the syntax. Most translators analyze *Gār-dena* as either depending on *þēodcyninga* ('tribal-kings of the spear Danes') or as forming a variation on it ('We have heard of... the glory of the spear Danes, of the tribal kings'). Neither of these structures has any parallel in *Beowulf*. Countering the first analysis, Spamer shows that in Beowulf "a genitive cannot be separated from its head noun by a prepositional phrase" (210). Examining the second, he finds that in all cases in *Beowulf* in which two genitives stand in variation, only the second instance can be placed freely—the opposite of the situation in lines 1-2. Spamer goes on to propose a syntactic pattern attested in the poem to explain *Gār-dena*. Constructions like *sigorēs tō lēane* 'as a reward of victory' (l. 1021b) and *līfes æt ende* 'at the end of life' (l. 2823) have a genitive (preceding the preposition) modifying the object of the preposition and *Gār-dena in gēardagum* can be construed in the same way. Spamer offers the following translation of ll. 1-2: "Lo! We have heard of the courage of the tribal kings, / in the bygone days of the Spear-Danes" (214).

1285 Stanley, Eric G. "The Date of *Beowulf*: Some Doubts and No Conclusions." In *Dating of 'Beowulf'*, pp. 197-211.

On the basis of a broad range of evidence, Stanley considers "a date of composition in the earlier tenth century more rather than less likely than a date in the ninth century, and origin in some part of the Danelaw is not impossible, though I still incline on the whole to origin of the poem 'among the English'" (201). Stanley believes that "the onus of proof of a date so much earlier than the date of the manuscript is on those who assume such an early date" (200) and doubts that the reference to Offa the Angle or the presence of the strange forms *merewīoinges* (l. 2921) and *wundini* (l. 1382) can provide a firm basis for an early date. Nor can the connection to Sutton Hoo be made too specific since the dating of the coin hoard and thus the entire find is tricky. He also argues that the absence of Scandinavian or Scandinavian-influenced proper names in the poem does not necessarily argue for a date before the Viking Age. Other philological facts (the metrical treatment of i-stem nouns and uncontracted forms) seem to undermine the argument for an early date.

1286 Stephenson, Edward A. "Hopkins' 'Sprung Rhythm' and the Rhythm of *Beowulf*." *Victorian Poetry* 19 (1981): 97-116.

Finds remarkable similarities between Gerard Manley Hopkins' "sprung rhythm" and the meter of *Beowulf* and Old English poetry but admits that "Old English poetry cannot have provided the *direct* source of Hopkins' sprung rhythm; for the poet-priest was not acquainted with Old English until the latter part of 1882" (103). Stephenson notes Hopkins' admiration for Anglo-Saxon verse and points out that "Dipodic rhythm is the essential link between the Old English alliterative meters and Hopkins' sprung rhythm, although the old poetry exhibits nearly all the points of sprung rhythm as well" (116).

1287   Taylor, Paul Beekman. "*Beowulf* 1130, 1875, and 2006: In Defence of the Manuscript." *NM* 82 (1981): 357-359.

Argues that in three cases where editors insert negative particles into difficult lines (ll. 1130a, 1875b, 2006a) the emendations are unnecessary and the manuscript readings should be restored. Inserting the particles implies that "in the Finnsburh episode, Hengest can*not* leave; in Hrothgar's farewell to Beowulf, he expects *not* to see him again; and, in Beowulf's account to Hygelac he says that Grendel's kin need *not* boast of that fight. Each of these negative particles can be removed to restore a pertinent and acceptable reading" (357). Hengest *could* leave despite the season, but chose to remain. Hrothgar, like Grendel, has the mistaken *wēn* 'expectation' that he will see Beowulf again. And, taking *begylpan* to mean 'full, or carry out, a boast, Grendel's kin need to fulfill their boast.

1288   Tilling, P. M. "William Morris's Translation of *Beowulf*: Studies in His Vocabulary." *Occasional Papers in Linguistics and Language Learning* 8 (1981): 163-175.

Analyzes William Morris' 1895 translation of *Beowulf* [F1482], often criticized as unreadable, insisting that Morris' project was a serious one and that "once the principles of his method are grasped, many of the apparent obscurities will become clear. At the same time, it has to be admitted that the glossary is inadequate and should have been expanded" (164).

1289   Tripp, Raymond P., Jr. "A Reconsideration of the Textual Evidence for the Existence of a Thief in *Beowulf*." *Bulletin of the Medieval English Literature Discussion Group, Tokyo* 19 (1981): 14-27.

Denies that the text of *Beowulf* contains references to a thief, reinterpreting four key passages and suggesting that the last survivor, the thief, and the animal dragon are really two characters: "an ancient *race*, not an individual [last survivor], and an evil *king*, who, driven from society, takes refuge in a barrow, utters a bitter complaint, and dies, to become a mandragon who later steals a cup from Beowulf. The desperate human thief and the animal dragon turn out to be but a single character, a man who became a dragon, editorially divided into two" (14). Tripp re-analyzes and re-punctuates four crucial passages (ll. 2210b-20, 2221-25, 2278-93a, 2401-24), discarding a number of traditional emendations and suggesting many new readings. See Tripp [1368, 1414] for a continuation of this argument.

1290 Trnka, Bohumil. "The *Beowulf* Poem and Virgil's *Aeneid*." *Poetica* (Tokyo) 12 (1981): 150-56.

Considers the possible influences of Virgil's *Aeneid* on *Beowulf*, concluding that the *Beowulf*-poet "had evidently the plan of an extensive epic poem and Virgil's *Aeneid* was most probably his chief model," though it is difficult to judge the extent of indebtedness (156). Trnka dismisses the idea that Germanic and early Roman poetry (the alliterative Saturnian verse) stemmed from the same tradition by pointing out that the stress-based Germanic alliterative tradition could only have taken place after the completion of Verner's Law. *Beowulf* is like the *Aeneid* in its use of two principal settings (Denmark and Geatland, corresponding to Carthage and Italy) but lacks the political nature of the hero's mission and the human adversaries found in the *Aeneid*. The most convincing area of influence is the handling of episodes: "the skillful manner how to introduce and subordinate them to the main narrative was undoubtedly a heritage of Latin heroic poetry and especially Virgil's *Aeneid*" (155). Trnka goes on to compare Beowulf's recounting of his contest with Breca to Aeneas' retelling of his adventures in the opening books of the *Aeneid*. Thus, the "Romanic contribution to the structural features of the oldest Germanic epic of *Beowulf* cannot be doubted" (156).

1291 Tuso, Joseph F., Samuel M. Riley, Bruce V. Roach, Melvin Storm, and W. Ken Zellefrow. "The Teaching of *Beowulf*." *OEN* 14.2 (1981): 17-22.

Contains brief contributions on the teaching of *Beowulf.* Samuel M. Riley, "Germanic Ethic and Poetic Craft in *Beowulf,*" discusses how to teach the concept of fate as it occurs in the poem by focusing on voice and context. Bruce V. Roach, "One Flew over the Mere," argues that comparing *Beowulf* to the film version of *One Flew over the Cuckoo's Nest* can tap into issues pertinent for teaching the poem. Melvin Storm, "Genealogy in *Beowulf,*" suggests distributing and discussing genealogical charts for the Danish, Geatish, and Swedish royal lines as "an effective way of initiating discussion of the poem as a whole" (19). W. Ken Zellefrow, "*Beowulf* Enhanced by Comparison with Primary Epics," suggests teaching the poem with other early epics: *The Song of Roland, The Nibelungenlied,* and *The Poem of the Cid.*

1292 Watanabe, Shoichi, and Peter Milward. *Monogatori Eibungakushi: Beowulf Kara Virginia Woolf made.* [Folktale in English Literature: from Beowulf to Virginia Woolf]. Tokyo: Taishukan, 1981. Pp. 424.

Not seen.

1293 Wentersdorf, Karl P. "*Beowulf*: The Paganism of Hrothgar's Danes." *SP* 78 (1981): 91-119.

Denies as unlikely the notion that the *Beowulf*-poet sought to reconstruct faithfully the pagan culture of his pre-Christian characters; instead, like Chaucer and Shakespeare, the *Beowulf*-poet conceived of his characters "in the social idiom of his own day" (92) and depicted the backsliding Danes in terms of contemporary (eighth-century) Anglo-Saxon struggles with paganism. After an extensive review of criticism on the so-called "Christian excursus" (ll. 170-88), Wentersdorf draws upon a number of historical documents (ecclesiastical records, law texts, and homilies) to show that pagan practices persisted in Anglo-Saxon England from the seventh through the eleventh centuries. Though pagan burial practices had been outlawed, they would have been known to an eighth-century audience. "What is said in 180b-2b about the idolatry of the Danes is what an eighth-century homilist might have said about those Anglo-Saxons who from time to time lapsed into apostasy and returned more or less openly to the worship of their ancient gods" (111). The verbs *cūpon* and *wiston* 'they knew' (ll. 180b, 181b) at first appear to deny that the Danes had any knowledge of God, but evidence from key Biblical passages and their Old English translations suggest that both can mean 'to acknowledge,' thus leaving the possibility that the Danes, like eighth-century Anglo-Saxons, were Christians, knowing of God, but not acknowledging his authority. Hrothgar and Wealhtheow "remained steadfast in their faith" (119) in contrast to those among the Danes who turned to idolatry. (See *history—attitudes toward in 'Beowulf'* in the subject index.)

1294 Yada, Hiroshi. "'A and B' Construction in *Beowulf.*" *Descriptive and Applied Linguistics* (International Christian U, Tokyo) 14 (1981): 173-84.

Provides evidence that 83 out of 190 pairs of words connected by *ond* are used as "oral formulas" (182). Yada accepts Fry's definition of "formula" [S623] and classifies "A *ond* B" constructions as formulaic when they meet the following criteria: 1) they alliterate, 2) they fit into a half-line, the basic unit of the formula, 3) they recur elsewhere in *Beowulf* or the Old English poetic corpus, 4) they are employed as "space fillers." When such a construction meets these criteria, it can be "considered as a direct product from a system something like 'X *ond* Y'" (175).

1982

1295 Albrecht, Roberta Adams. "*Beowulf.*" *Explicator* 40 (1982): 4-6.

Examines several images and words in the last fitt of the poem (ll. 3137-3182), finding an overriding sense of fatalism, despite the Christian overtones of some of the imagery and noting a number of plays on words. Albrecht finds sea imagery in several words used to describe Beowulf's funeral and notes a play on two senses of *beorg*: 'barrow or burial place' and 'protection or refuge' (l. 3143). She suggests that *rēc* 'smoke, vapor' (l. 3155b) rising from the pyre may refer to Beowulf's evanescent spirit and that the last word of the poem, *lofgeornost*, may also mean 'a song of praise or hymn,' implying that Beowulf becomes a song.

1296 Allen, David G. "The Coercive Ideal of *Beowulf.*" In *Literary Perspectives*, pp. 120-132.

Argues that *Beowulf* reflects a shift from the Germanic concept of kingship (based on the ideas of loyalty, kinship, and free choice) to the more coercive ideal of Christian monarchism (claimed from divine authority). The poet suggests the possibility for disaster when Beowulf and Wiglaf make heroic choices associated with the older *comitatus* model and shows that both Beowulf's decision to aid the Danes and Wiglaf's unwillingness to become a tribal leader involve inherent contradictions "within a social order that relies too heavily on human freedom" (125). Allen sees in the Modthryth episode an allegorical representation of this political theme: Modthryth finds happiness only after Offa restricts her free choice and coerces her into proper behavior—a theme reflected in the common exegetical figure of Christ as the royal bridegroom as explicated by Augustine. "The poet's presentation of the range of conflicting choices and responsibilities, bearable just barely to the exceptional man and dangerous even for him, could push the Anglo-Saxon auditor to long for the system of ecclesial kingship that would, in theory, minimize human choice in reliance upon a certainty firmer than human freedom" (126).

1297 Amos, Ashley Crandell. "An Eleventh-Century *Beowulf?*" *Review* 4 (1982): 335-345.

An extended refutation of Kiernan's thesis [1261], finding fault with Kiernan's selective summaries of previous scholarship, his use of linguistic and paleographical evidence, and with a number of his conclusions. Amos sees Kiernan's description of the codex and its history as "interesting and useful" but denies that the manuscript has been ignored.

1298 Anderson, Earl R. "Grendel's *Glof* (*Beowulf* 2085b-88) and Various Latin Analogues." *Mediaevalia* 8 (1982): 1-8.

Finds in Grendel's glove (described in ll. 2085b-88) a possible allusion to the Roman practice of executing parricides by enclosing them in a leather bag or *culleus*, with an ape, cock, and snakes, and throwing them into the ocean, a practice described in a number of classical and medieval Latin sources, including Cicero's *De Inventione Rhetorica*, Prudentius' *Peristephanos*, the *Codex Theodosianus*, and Isidore's *Etymologiae*—texts known in Anglo-Saxon England. Anderson suggests that "the *Beowulf* poet, when composing the glove passage, had in mind not only the folklore motif of the troll's glove, but also the Latin tradition of the *culleus* as an instrument of punishment" (7). Such an allusion would help to explain why Beowulf says that Grendel wanted to put him (Beowulf), though *unsynnigne* 'guiltless,' into the glove (l. 2089).

1299 Bammesberger, Alfred. "A Note on *Beowulf* 83b." *NM* 83 (1982): 24-25.

Provides the following summary: "On syntactic grounds *lenge* in *Beowulf* 83b cannot be interpreted as the comparative of the adverb *lange*; *lenge* must be an adjective, its meaning can most probably be given as 'suitable, fitting, proper'" (24).

1300 Bauschatz, Paul C. *The Well and the Tree: World and Time in Early Germanic Culture.* Amherst: U of Massachusetts P, 1982. Pp. xx + 256; ill.

Includes a chapter on *Beowulf* that reconstructs how early Germanic peoples with thought about time (as seen in the cosmic iconography of Yggdrasil the world tree and Urth's Well). Bauschatz explores this central myth, identifying the well of Urth (cognate with OE *wyrd* 'fate'), which waters Yggdrasil, as a symbol of the "past" and its effect on the present. The two other Norns, Verðandi (present) and Skula (future, fate), are not nearly as important to this myth. The relationship between the world tree and the well "implies a continual, supportive intrusion of past upon present existence. Events, conditions, and predicaments of present life are, therefore, influenced by the realm of Urth" (16). Many cultures depict time as a flowing fluid, but the Germanic myth is unique in depicting a well (OE *burna*), which is paradoxically contained (by its surrounding wall) yet free flowing and contributes to the growth of the cosmic structure (Yggdrasil).

The *Beowulf*-poet, informed by the iconography of Urth's well, does not see time as a series of causally-connected events: in Beowulf's battle with Grendel's mother or his fight with the dragon, for instance, the events come out of order. Actions become separable objects, and the poem associates material objects (weapons, gifts, treasure) with actions, frequently lavishing more detail on a sword or gift than on human action. An ancient sword, like the one which Beowulf brings back from Grendel's mere, embodies a past which intersects with and feeds the present events of the poem. Various gifts and treasures partake of this relationship between past and present. Bauschatz also detects the iconography of Urth's well in the ship funeral of Scyld (enclosure, water, and tree or mast) as well as in Beowulf's approach to the dragon's barrow (an enclosure from which fire flows in waves). Finally, he notes that speech also provides a link between actions and objects. A *bēot* 'boast' or vow links "foreseeable events with the words representative of them" (110), and such vows are usually made at a ritual feast or *symbel*, several of which Bauschatz analyzes.

Chapter four, "Action, Space, and Time," contains further observations on *Beowulf* and time, postulating several types of actions (horizontal and vertical) according to their direction and orientation in a diagram of the Germanic cosmos. Bauschatz finds significance in narrative linking words such as *þā* 'then' and *þæt* 'that' in a number of passages in *Beowulf*, including ll. 1537-46, depicting the fight with Grendel's mother. The most important events in this narrative sequence become object-like and are marked by *þæt*, while *þā* is reserved for depicting on-going processes. Bauschatz then turns to the ways in which Christianity altered the Germanic view of time. The last chapter makes a number of observations about time in language, focusing on the tense system of the Germanic languages. Throughout, Bauschatz illustrates temporal and spatial relationships with diagrams.

Reviews: *OEN* 18.1 (1984): 97-98; E.S. Dick, *Speculum* 59 (1984): 616-19.

1301 Bohrer, Randall. "*Beowulf* and the Bog People." In *Literary Perspectives*, pp. 133-147.

Endorses a suggestion by Robert Bly that *Beowulf*, particularly in its depiction of Grendel and his mother, reflects the rejection of an earlier Germanic mother cult in favor of a strongly patriarchal system and that one of the poem's major themes is "the celebration of the triumph of patriarchal values" (142). Bohrer reviews anthropological and archeological evidence for a matriarchal culture in southern Scandia before the fifth century and its subsequent replacement by the patriarchal Odinic cult. The poet draws on certain aspects of the mother cult—human sacrifice in a lake, lunar connections, and offerings of weapons—in the depiction of Grendel's mere but omits and denies the regenerative power of such fertility cults. "If the monsters were originally vegetation-chthonic figures they would, like the Green Knight and other fertility demons, possess the magical power of invulnerability to human weapons because of a mastery of the secrets of regeneration" (141). The poem, however, puts the power of regeneration squarely in the hands of the patriarchal God (ll. 1605-11). The Modthryth episode also reflects the triumph of the patriarchal over the matriarchal.

1302 Bradley, S.A.J. *Anglo-Saxon Poetry*. London: Dent, 1982. Pp. xxvi + 559.

Includes a prose translation of *Beowulf* in a volume which translates most of the poetry in the four major codices and in other sources. Bradley provides introductions to the manuscript and bases his introduction to the poem itself on the largely-ignored reading of N.F.S. Grundtvig [S6, S11]. For *Beowulf*, Bradley adopts a "slightly more expansive manner of translation" (411). Lines 4-14: "Many a time Scyld Scefing dispossessed the throngs of his enemies, many nations, of their seats of feasting and struck awe into men of stature, after he had first been found, scantly provided. For that, he was to meet with consolation: here below the skies he flourished and prospered in the estimations of his worth until each one of his neighbours across the whale-traversed ocean had to obey him and yield him tribute. He was a good king."

Reviews: G.L. Brook, *British Book News* Dec. 1982: 769; *OEN* 17.1 (1983): 85; J. Gillingham, *London Review of Books* 17-30 Nov., 1983: 19; M. Godden, *TLS* 8 July, 1983: 736; G.R. Owen, *Critical Quarterly* 25.1 (1983): 85-86; A. Crépin, *EA* 37 (1984): 318; T.F. Hoad, *N&Q* 31 (1984): 436; M. Alexander, *MÆ* 54 (1985): 287-88; P. Lendinara, *Schede medievali* 6-7 (1985): 206; N.F. Blake, *MLR* 81 (1986): 440-41.

1303 Brynteson, William E. "*Beowulf*, Monsters, and Manuscripts: Classical Associations." *Res Publica Litterarum* 5 (1982): 41-57.

Examines in some detail the transmission history of other texts appearing in or associated with the *Beowulf* codex (*Marvels of the East*, *The Letter of Alexander to Aristotle*, *The Letter of Fermes*, *The Letter of Premo to the Emperor Trajan*, and the *Liber Monstrorum*), concluding that the monsters in *Beowulf* "have an association with the Alexandrian and Apocryphal monsters found in the other items of this codex and other codices" (42). Brynteson seeks to demonstrate that encyclopedic monster books like the *Beowulf* codex circulated throughout Western Europe and that such codices, particularly those organized around the figure of Alexander, provide a literary context for the monsters of *Beowulf*.

1304 Cassidy, Frederic G. "Knowledge of *Beowulf* in Its Own Time." *REAL* 1 (1982): 1-12.

Suggests that *Beowulf* was not well known in its own time because the poet fashioned a poem so intricate in structure (using *Zahlenkomposition* and other learned techniques) as to baffle popular audiences. Cassidy believes "that the *Beowulf*-poet . . . , a poet of high order who wished to emulate Latin poets through writing in his own English, produced a poem so unconventional—so monumental in length, so unusual in subject-matter, that it was little understood. . . . I assume he was a monastic, and that he could count on a monastic audience, perhaps captive, but the poem as it stands, essentially a literary work, could hardly have had a popular audience" (10). It further seems unlikely that the work was ever performed. Includes a discussion of the papers delivered at the Toronto conference (see Chase, *The Dating of Beowulf*), a summary of Hart's work on tectonic structures in Beowulf [1253], as well as a brief history of the modern popularity of the poem. See Weinstock's response [1371].

1305 Creed, Robert P. "The Basis of the Meter of *Beowulf*." In *Beowulfian Scansion*, pp. 27-35.

Endorsing Heusler [F798] and Pope's [S170] theory of isochrony in Old English meter, maintains that "we can demonstrate that every line of *Beowulf* realizes the same underlying configuration. In a sense, there is only *one* type of measure in *Beowulf*, one that begins with a HEAVIER stress and continues and concludes with a lighter stress" (30). Such a system, which Creed developed with John Miles Foley, eliminates the need for anacrusis. However, this single, underlying "measure" is open to complicated variations. Creed bases much of his theory on rules for lineating Old English verse and describes a computer program which scans and lineates *Beowulf* according to a few simple principles. "Lineating teaches one lesson very clearly: the first alliterating syllable of an alliteration marks the beginning of the verse-line *unless* its place is co-opted by a clause boundary or proclitic. But even when co-option takes place, the first alliterating syllable is the only clear signal among the data that a new line is forming" (29-30). On this basis, he criticizes Sievers' "Five Type" theory as "disastrous" (29). Includes a chart of lines 210-28, lineated by the computer, as well as a metrical analysis of these lines, including Foley's *eta* measure.

1306 Dane, Joseph A. "Finnsburh and *Iliad* IX: a Greek Survival of the Medieval Germanic Oral-Formulaic Theme, the Hero on the Beach." *Neophil* 66 (1982): 443-49.

Questions the validity of the "Hero on the Beach" theme, proposed by David Crowne [S408] and elaborated by Fry [S911], arguing that the "Hero on the Beach" is a misleading and arbitrary concept since the motifs (a flashing light, retainers, a hero, and an imminent journey) are part of a larger and more significant narrative structure, not "merely fixed components of an autonomous theme in the baggage of an oral poet" (444). Dane examines the Meleager episode from the *Iliad*, the Phoenix's stories of its youth from the Old English *Phoenix*, and the Finnsburh Episode and Fragment, finding a larger narrative structure "involving explicit or implied conflict, temporary resolution, passing time, and crisis and flight" (444). The individual units or motifs are arranged as follows: introduction (l. 1063), beseeching (ll. 1142-44), motifs related to the theme of enclosure (by sea, ll. 1130-33 and by oaths or curse, ll. 1085 ff.), curse by kin (not in *Beowulf*), sterility (implied in ll. 1131-33), lament (various exclamations by Hildeburh), passing time (ll. 1031-36), and flight (ll. 1145 ff.). In each of the works under discussion, this unit generally ties in with themes in the main narrative. Thus, this larger theme is part of a common narrative technique, not a type-scene restricted to oral Germanic poets.

1307 De Roo, Harvey. "*Beowulf* 2223b: A Thief by Any Other Name?" *MP* 79 (1982): 297-304.

Argues against the reading *þēow* 'slave,' now accepted in standard editions of the poem, for the illegible word in l. 2223b (fol. 182r). The initial thorn is clear, but the following letters—there is room for three—were illegible from the time of Thorkelin and probably earlier. Instead, he supports W.W. Lawrence's suggestion [S58]: *þegn* 'retainer.' Though others have used general context to support the "slave"-reading, De Roo contends that lexical context, which "involves those words in the immediate passage the meanings of which might shed light on the missing word" (299), supports *þegn* better. An examination of words applied to the thief's lord (*mandryhten*, l. 2281b; *hlāford*, l. 2283a; *frēa*, l. 2285b; and *āgend*, l. 3075a) shows that they do not support the meaning "slave." The thief is a noble retainer of an aristocratic lord—in short a *þegn*. See also Andersson [1420].

1308 Earl, James W. "Apocalyptism and Mourning in *Beowulf*." *Thought* 57 (1982): 362-370.

Sees *Beowulf* as an act of "cultural mourning" which blends native, pre-Christian notions of the apocalypse with those of Christianity. Germanic eschatological myth "is first of all historicized, according to the demands of the new religion, and is then used to depict the death of the old heroic world, thereby clarifying the culture's renunciations of its own pagan past. The past is internalized and transformed in a strong Anglo-Saxon Christian culture—all the stronger because it has been mourned properly, respectfully, and lovingly, not just discarded" (370). Earl finds in Freud's psychology of mourning a useful model for the celebration and loss of heroic culture in *Beowulf*. For a further elaboration of these ideas, see Earl [1385].

1309 Ellis, Helen B. and Warren U. Ober. "Grendel and Blake: The Contraries of Existence." In *John Gardner: Critical Perspectives.* Ed. Robert A. Morace and Kathryn VanSpanckeren. Carbondale: Southern Illinois UP, 1982. Pp. 46-61.

Comments briefly on John Gardner's use of *Beowulf* in his 1971 novel *Grendel* [S793] in an article mainly concerned with the influence of Blake.

1310 Farrell, Robert T. "*Beowulf* and the Northern Heroic Age." In *Vikings,* pp. 180-216.

Surveys "current opinion on Scandinavian contact with England during the period 400-1000, as a basis for a better understanding of the literary text, and to show in turn how *Beowulf* is at least in part a predictable outcome of this contact" (180). Farrell begins by pointing out that *Beowulf* has an unusual tolerance for Scandinavians and their history, a tolerance not shared by Wulfstan, Ælfric, or the poet of the *Battle of Maldon.* As a heroic poem, *Beowulf* takes the northern heroic age for its topic and often lavishes more admiration on the heroes of the north than the corresponding Scandinavian versions. "It is extremely significant that the *Beowulf* poet has little interest in general Germanic heroes" (188), with scant references to such general Germanic figures as Weland the Smith, Offa, and Eormenric. Instead, *Beowulf* shares an interest in the north with other English works of art like the Franks Casket, *Deor,* and *Widsith.* In the following discussion, Farrell covers the range of Scandinavian-English contacts between 400 and 1000, turning to such topics as the nature of warfare in early Germanic and Scandinavian society, Scandinavian contact with the classical world, East Anglia and Sutton Hoo with their Swedish connections, the seventh and eighth centuries, 793-878, the Vikings as town builders, evidence of Viking contact from English place names, Scandinavian effects on the English language, the evidence of sculpture, and of English-Scandinavian assimilation in general. Farrell concludes that an East Anglian origin is more likely for *Beowulf* than a Northumbrian one, though the kingdom of Offa (757-796) provides a possible context. In any case, *Beowulf* seems "designed to serve as an almost perfect instrument for bringing Scandinavian and Anglo-Saxon together, on the basis of a glorious shared past." *Beowulf* itself shows evidence of "the sustained and fruitful contact" between England and Scandia for over five hundred years (206).

1311 Foley, John Miles. "The Scansion of *Beowulf* in Its Indo-European Context." In *Beowulfian Scansion*, pp. 7-17.

Notes differences in meter and formula between *Beowulf* and the reconstructed Indo-European system and argues that comparative work should more fully recognize idiosyncratic or "tradition-dependent" features of individual literatures and aim at a diachronic understanding of the roots of poetic traditions. Meter and formula in *Beowulf* differ synchronically as well as diachronically from the Indo-European model (based on the Greek hexameter and the Serbo-Croation *deseterac*) in three crucial features: 1) consistent syllable count, 2) colon structure, and 3) right justification. Foley argues "that the meter of *Beowulf* has from a comparative point of view received rather shoddy treatment, and has in particular suffered greatly from overzealous and reductive assumptions made by those who would study the Old-English formula through Homer's 'rosy-colored' glasses" (13).

1312 Frank, Roberta. "The *Beowulf* Poet's Sense of History." In *The Wisdom of Poetry: Essays in Early English Literature in Honor of Morton W. Bloomfield.* Ed. Larry D. Benson and Siegfried Wenzel. Kalamazoo: Medieval Institute Publications, Western Michigan U, 1982. Pp. 53-65.

Argues that the "*Beowulf* poet's reconstruction of a northern heroic age is chronologically sophisticated, rich in local color and fitting speeches. The poet avoids obvious anachronisms and presents ... an internally consistent picture of Scandinavian society around A.D. 500" (54). This generous celebration of the pagan past would have been very unlikely in the early Anglo-Saxon period when Bede and Alcuin condemned heathen practices with severity. A more positive attitude toward paganism, though, is perceptible in the translations of Alfred and his circle. The Old English Orosius celebrates noble Romans, while Alfred's version of Boethius' *Consolation of Philosophy* employs pagan myths as analogies for Christian concepts. Other sources for such positive views of pagans are Widukind's history of the Saxons, Remigius of Auxerre's commentary on Boethius, Odo of Cluny's Life of St. Gerald of Aurillac, Hrotsvitha's

Gongolfus, and Ruotger's *Life of Bruno*—Carolingian texts. "Like these works, the Old English poems that we can date to the tenth century set up no unresolvable contradictions between piety and the heroic life" (63). This synthesis between heroic and religious ideals seems not to have occurred in the age of Bede and Alcuin. Finally, the poem's concern with a national king ruling over many tribes "fits nicely with the efforts of Alfred and his successors to promote an Anglo-Danish brotherhood" (64). [See *history—attitudes toward in 'Beowulf'* in the subject index.]

1313 _____. "Old Norse Memorial Eulogies and the Ending of *Beowulf*." *The Early Middle Ages, Acta* 6 (1982): 1-19.

Argues that "the sequence of laments that concludes *Beowulf* may have been put together with a Norse poetic genre in mind, the *erfidrápa* or memorial eulogy" (3) and that the poem contains various Nordicisms which may belie an origin in the late ninth or tenth century, a time when "two vernacular literary cultures—Old Norse and Old English—were in constant interaction" (13). Frank points out that the burial customs in *Beowulf*, particularly the rite of cremation, are associated with Oðinn—who demands that warriors destined for Valhöll be burnt with the treasures they wish to accompany them. The poet, though he transmutes these customs, may have known of them not through dim memories from the continent but from the traditions and verse of the late ninth or tenth-century Danelaw. Old Norse memorial eulogies, several with strong English connections, may have contributed to the ending of *Beowulf*, for their structure is strikingly similar: they move "from a detailed narrative of the king's death, through lament, to triumphant praise; at the moment of closure, all attention is riveted on the fallen king" (7). In addition, they predict an impending catastrophe for the survivors, a theme taken up in *Beowulf* as well, where the Geats will perish without Beowulf to protect them from the Swedes and other enemies. Frank considers four such eulogies in detail: the *Eiríksmál* for Erik Bloodaxe, the *Hákonarmál* for King Hákon the Good of Norway, Hallfeðr's lament for Olaf Tryggvason, and a condensed eulogy by Þorkell Skallason for Eal Walþeof of Northumbria. Finally, Frank suggests that *Beowulf* contains several Nordicisms in its vocabulary and syntax, oddities which have been overlooked or misinterpreted: in particular, the controversial word *lofgeornost* (l. 3182b) may be a

"Scandinavianism," for while the word has negative implications in English prose where it often means 'ostentatious, boastful,' the Norse word *lofgjarn* appears in an unambiguously good sense as applied to heroes like Siguðr. All this evidence would suggest "that the *Beowulf* poet had more than a passing acquaintance with the poetry and myths of the Danelaw" (13).

1314 Frese, Dolores Warwick. "The Scansion of *Beowulf*: Critical Implications." In *Beowulfian Scansion*, pp. 37-46.

Reviews the other contributions to the volume and suggests that scholarship on the meter of *Beowulf* (and Old English verse in general) find a common vocabulary, take into account how the various theories account for modern live performances, and make use of computer technology to discover possible bridges between divergent theories.

1315 Fulk, R.D. "Dating *Beowulf* to the Viking Age." *PQ* 61 (1982): 341-357.

An extended review and critique of papers in *The Dating of Beowulf* (edited by Colin Chase, 1981), rejecting a Viking age dating for *Beowulf* because the proper names in the poem show no influence of Old Norse forms and undertaking an extensive refutation of Kiernan's paleographical and codicological arguments [1261]. Fulk offers an alternative explanation for the condition of folio 179v (a palimpsest according to Kiernan): fol. 179v (containing ll. 2208-39) was originally the front cover of a unit and thus became soiled and worn. The scribe may have decided to immerse and scour it. Since he seems to have written on wet vellum, something an experienced scribe would know not to do, the best explanation is that "a scribe who had committed his irrecoverable exemplar to memory might write on wet vellum, being afraid he would forget the verses before the parchment dried. The same haste would also account for the carelessness that produced the long dittograph" (355).

1316 Greene, Jesse Laurence. "Object-Verb and Verb-Object Sequences in *Beowulf*." *Journal of Indo-European Studies* 10 (1982): 71-115.

Places *Beowulf* in the middle of a shift in Old English syntax from O-V structure (Object-Verb) to S-V-O (Subject-Verb-Object)—a change which took place, according to

Greene, after the death of Bede but before the ascension of Alfred. *Beowulf* contains a mixture of both systems, but is "predominantly, but not consistently, O-V in syntax" (78). Greene compares O-V and S-V-O systems in other Indo-European languages and speculates on the causes of the shift in English.

1317 Greenfield, Stanley B. *A Readable 'Beowulf': The Old English Epic Newly Translated.* Intro. by Alain Renoir. Carbondale: Southern Illinois UP, 1982. Pp. x + 161; ill.

Translates *Beowulf* into modern English using a nine-syllable line (with occasional shortening or lengthening) and freely-placed alliteration. Greenfield discusses the difficulties of translating *Beowulf* (27-34) and states his aim to remain faithful to the text while producing readable poetry. The introduction by Alain Renoir contains the following sections: "Outline of Contents," "Organization," "Traditional and Oral-Formulaic Features," "Pagan and Christian Elements," "The Characters," and "Narrative Technique." Lines 4-11: "Often Scyld Scefing shattered the hosts,/ unsettled many a nation's mead-hall,/ terrorized tribes, since first he was found/ abandoned; comfort and abundance/ later came his way, and worldly fame,/ until neighboring nations, near or/ far over whale-big seas, obeyed him,/ gave tribute: a good king indeed!" Also included are footnotes, a glossary, list of poetic translators, and a short bibliography.

Reviews: *OEN* 17.1 (1983): 82; A.H. Olsen, *Denver Quarterly* 18.1 (1983): 119-21; B. Raffel, *In Geardagum*, 5 (1983): 91-96; D.C. Baker, *ELN* 21 (1984): 58-60; D.K. Fry, *Comparative Literature* 36 (1984): 177-80; C. Rizzo, *Schede medievali* 6-7 (1985): 238-39.

1318 _____. "Of Words and Deeds: The Coastguard's Maxim Once More." In *The Wisdom of Poetry: Essays in Early English Literature in Honor of Morton W. Bloomfield.* Ed. Larry D. Benson and Siegfried Wenzel. Kalamazoo: Medieval Institute Publications, Western Michigan U, 1982. Pp. 45-51.

Argues that the Coastwarden's maxim (ll. 287b-89), notoriously difficult to construe, refers to the coastguard's recognition that Beowulf's words are likely to be backed up by deeds, criticizing "the leap from the literal meaning of the words" (48) made by Kaske [S361] and Shippey [S1093], though endorsing Shippey's observations about tautology and illogicality in gnomic statements. Greenfield finds that the phrase *gescād witan* means 'to separate' or 'distinguish' in a parallel construction in Bede's *Historia Ecclesiastica*, and paraphrases the maxim as follows: "the sharp shield-warrior must learn to tell the difference between 'empty' words and words which have the resolution and capability of deeds behind them" (51). See Kaske's reply [1440].

1319 _____. "A Touch of the Monstrous in the Hero, or Beowulf Re-Marvellized." *ES* 63 (1982): 294-300.

Responds to the view of Robinson [S932] that Beowulf's feats of superhuman strength have been imposed on the text out of a desire to see folktale and mythic dimensions rather than the more basic epic quality. Greenfield re-examines Beowulf's three aquatic feats: the swimming contest with Breca, the descent into Grendel's mere, and the swim home from Frisia. Greenfield defends the notion that Beowulf's descent into the mere takes the better part of a day, *hwīl dæges* (l.1492b-93), by correlating other narrative events and pointing out other elements of the marvellous in the story: the magical sword, the bright light when Grendel's head is cut off, and the immediate cleansing of the waters. In Beowulf's return from Frisia and his swimming contest with Breca, Greenfield argues against Robinson's thesis that Beowulf actually rowed in a boat on both occasions, a reading which Robinson supports in part by arguing that the word *swimman* can mean 'to float or sail.' Greenfield rejects this meaning in line 2367a, since other uses of the word as 'sail' specify the vessel. Similarly, he points out several details in the swimming contest with Breca that demand that Beowulf be in the water. Greenfield concludes that "a good case can still be made for the hero's superhuman, and epic, qualities in the three aquatic episodes. At the least, I feel, Robinson's de-marvellizing of the received interpretation of Beowulf's character and deeds is 'not proven'" (300). [See *fabulous elements* in the subject index.]

1320 Guerrieri, Anna Maria. "La congiunzione *ond* nel *Beowulf*: problemi di dizione, di sintassi e di stile." [The Conjunction *ond* in *Beowulf*: Problems of Diction, Syntax, and Style]. *AIUON, filologia germanica* 25 (1982): 7-55.

Examines the use of the conjunction *ond* in *Beowulf*, noting that the poem employs more *ond*'s than any other Old

English poem and concluding that the poet employs them creatively to regulate narrative pacing and emphasize parallels between characters and events. At times, *ond* does not appear at all for extended intervals (ll. 1338-1417) suggesting that the poet deploys the conjunction consciously. Guerrieri goes on to examine the etymology of *ond*, its cognates, as well as its semantic and syntactic functions. Though the overwhelming majority of its occurrences are copulative, *ond* can have a concessive function (l. 1604a), but even at the level of coordinate conjunctions, the word can oscillate in meaning. Guerrieri also examines "split constructions," in which an intervening noun or verb separates the *ond* from its coordinate elements: *Onelan modor ond Ohteres* 'Onela's mother and Ohtere's' (l. 2932) and *discas lāgon ond dȳre swyrd* 'plates lay about and precious swords' (l. 3048), showing that in a number of instances the poet employs this construction for poetic effect. Includes discussions of a great many specific passages as well as the functions of other conjunctions such as *oððe* 'or.'

1321 Hansen, Elaine Tuttle. "Hrothgar's 'Sermon' in *Beowulf* as Parental Wisdom." *ASE* 10 (1982): 53-67.

Maintains that Hrothgar's "sermon" (ll. 1700-84) is meant "to be recognized as the conventional admonitory address of a wise king and father to a young prince, a 'set-piece' of wisdom literature" (61), which parallels the Exeter Book *Precepts*, and that the poet uses conventions of wisdom literature, such as gnomes, to render the sermon a pivotal and unifying event in the poem. Concerning the structure of the "sermon," Hansen argues that "Hrothgar uses each of the three kinds of narrative example or illustration commonly used by wise speakers in OE poetry—one from legend or 'history' [Heremod, ll. 1709b-22a], one from hypothetical or fictional material [the arrogant man, ll. 1728-57] and one from personal experience [ll. 1758-68]. The illustrations are held together by transitional passages combining the two kinds of instructional devices found in a less complex parental instruction poem like *Precepts*: admonitory, imperative sentences and longer gnomic observations" (62). Hansen also analyzes the conventional structure and narrative function of gnomes in the poem as a whole, in particular the four gnomes on fame, concluding that "gnomic formulations in *Beowulf* typically function both as integral parts of their immediate contexts and as a generalized and unifying commentary" (56). Appears in somewhat altered form as a chapter in Hansen [1653].

1322 Harada, Yoshio. "Didactic Expression in *Beowulf.*" *Kitasato Journal of Liberal Arts and Sciences* 16 (1982): 66-71.

Not seen.

1323 Harris, Anne Leslie. "Hands, Helms, and Heroes: The Role of Proper Names in *Beowulf.*" *NM* 83 (1982): 414-421.

Finds patterns of wordplay surrounding the names and characters of Grendel's two victims (Æschere and Hondscio) as well as characters involved in the dynastic struggles of part two of the poem (Wulf, Eofor, and Dæghrefn). In the first instance, the wordplay highlights Beowulf's heroic qualities: as "references to hands and arms informing the accounts of Hondscio's death emphasize the strength necessary to a hero, so the reiteration of the head-motif with Æschere points up the second quality Hrothgar praises—sagacity" (417). Secondly, Wulf 'wolf,' Eofor, 'boar,' and Dæghrefn 'day-raven' suggest the traditional beasts of battle (with the substitution of a boar for the eagle), which "stress the ongoing violence of the Geatish wars and the historical inevitability of their destruction" (420).

1324 _____. "Techniques of Pacing in *Beowulf.*" *ES* 63 (1982): 97-108.

Examines techniques of narrative pacing in *Beowulf*, focusing on variation, parallelism, and verb progression, as well as "often-slighted transitional features" (97). Accepting Robinson's definiton of variation [F1725], Harris stresses the need to distinguish between variation and parallelism. "Generally, variation contributes to retarding the tempo, making transitions, marking structural divisions, amplifying, repeating, or emphasizing a point, and indicating emotion.... Thus, we can naturally expect denser concentration of variations to be well suited to long conversational or reflective passages" (101). In action sequences, by contrast, variation appears less frequently, and the poet prefers to compress the narrative and increase its pace by using "non-variational effects" like parallelisms and verb progressions (103). Harris analyzes the Ravenswood battle scene (ll. 2941-81) and the Finnsburh episode in detail, finding that parallelism and verb-progression drive the narratives forward at a quick pace. Finally, she examines the narrative functions of *swā* 'so, thus' and *þā* 'then, when.' *Swā* "rarely occurs in action sequences and appears most often in reflective sections of the poem" (108), while *þā* appears most densely immediately before the battles with the monsters and less so in reflective or conversational passages.

1325 Harris, Joseph. "*Beowulf* in Literary History." *Pacific Coast Philology* 17 (1982): 16-23.

Proposes that *Beowulf*, like the *Canterbury Tales* and the *Waste Land*, is a poem which combines a number of genres "summarizing the literary past and seeming either to generate no direct progeny or to devour their own by overshadowing them" (16), and that the best hope of understanding such culminating works (*summae litterarum*) is to investigate their constituent genres. "Beowulf criticism . . . has overlooked the poem's anthology-like characteristics and therefore its place in literary history. The *Beowulf*ian *summa* includes genealogical verse, a creation hymn, elegies, a lament, a heroic lay, a praise poem, historical poems, a flyting, heroic boasts, gnomic verse, a sermon, and perhaps less formal oral genres. In addition, a number of other genres are alluded to" (17). After dividing the genres of *Beowulf* into two groups: the "marked" (those formally introduced) and the "unmarked" (included silently), Harris goes on to examine in more detail two genres not much studied in connection with the poem: genealogical verse and panegyric. The skaldic genealogical poem *Ynglingatal*, among others, provides some insight into the genealogical materials in *Beowulf*, since the *Ynglingatal* also emphasizes the details of death and burial place, as well as the role of fate. Harris finds Old Norse praise poems useful for understanding whether or not the Heremod-Sigemund references are part of the scop's song in praise of Beowulf's victory: the *Eiríksmál* and *Hákonarmál* "can be cited to support the traditional appearance of Sigemund, Fitela, and Heremod within a *Preislied*" (20). These and other praise songs contain similar narrative exempla. Finally, Harris suggests that the inspiration for *Beowulf*'s "multi-generic originality" may be found in a genre not obviously represented in the poem: mnemonic verse (or *thula*), which has perhaps "been absorbed into the very frame of Beowulf" (20-21).

1326 Hashimoto, Shuichi. "On Norman E. Eliason's 'The Thryth-Offa Digression in *Beowulf*.'" *Sophia English Studies* 7 (1982): 1-10.

Not seen.

1327 Hernández, Ann. "Selective Bibliography and Suggestions for Further Reading." In *Beowulfian Scansion*, pp. 47-58.

Provides a selected bibliography for the volume.

1328 Hieatt, Constance B., trans. *'Beowulf' and Other Old English Poems*. Intro. by Kent A. Hieatt. 2nd ed. Bantam: Toronto and New York, 1982. Pp. xxxviii + 149.

A revised and enlarged second edition of Hieatt's prose translation of *Beowulf* [S627]. This edition recasts the chapters of the first edition to correspond with the fitt divisions in the manuscript and undertakes a number of revisions in order to "improve the rhythmic effect of the prose" (ix). Kent Hieatt's introduction, also revised, provides a general account of the poem, with sections on prosody, structure, style, Christianity and Paganism, and dating. Lines 4-11: "Scyld Scefing often drove troops of enemies from their mead-hall seats; he terrified the lords of many tribes, although he had once been a destitute foundling. He found consolation for that: he prospered under the heavens, and grew in glory, until every one of his neighbors over the sea had to obey him and pay him tribute. That was a good king."
Reviews: *OEN* 17.1 (1983): 64.

1329 Hill, John M. "Beowulf and the Danish Succession: Gift Giving as an Occasion for Complex Gesture." *Medievalia et Humanistica* 11 (1982): 177-97.

Believes that gift-giving in the poem goes beyond mere reward and extends to complex political gestures: when Hrothgar offers Beowulf dynastic treasures, he offers him, implicitly, the succession to the Danish throne; Wealhtheow, with her gifts to Beowulf, makes a counter-offer that the hero should remain a retainer in vertical relationship to Hrothgar; finally, Beowulf, on his return to Geatland, makes sure to retell these gift-givings in such a way to emphasize his utter loyalty to Hygelac—i.e., that he has not accepted Hrothgar's offer of kinship and kingship. Hill suggests that references to friends and friendliness (ll. 1017-18, 1027-29) may carry legal meanings related to the responsibilities being offered to Beowulf, while the phrase, "use [these gifts] well" (l. 1045b) may have an almost ritualistic use here and later in the poem. Also contains an analysis of Wealhtheow's speech (ll. 1169-87).

1330   Hill, Thomas D. "The Confession of Beowulf and the Structure of *Volsunga Saga.*" In *Vikings*, pp. 165-79.

Suggests that Beowulf and the *Beowulf*-poet consciously reject the type of heroism portrayed in the Volsung cycle and that "Beowulf is, in effect, defining himself as an anti-Volsung, as a hero and king who has avoided the heroic faults which are so large a part of the story of the Volsungs" (172). Hill begins with an analysis of Beowulf's remarkably modest death speech (ll. 2732b-43a), which claims only that Beowulf ruled well, without violence, and without slaying his kin. This confession stands in stark contrast to the story of the Volsungs (alluded to in *Beowulf* in the Sigemund digression), the major themes of which Hill identifies as their refusal to accept limitations (Old Norse *ofrkapp*) and their violation of kinship ties. Beowulf specifically acts according to limits (primogeniture) and refuses to slay his kin. The *searonīð* '(l. 2738a) which Beowulf (but not the Volsungs) avoids may refer to chosen, intentional violence, since the word *searo* means 'craft, skill, art,' and Hill translates it as 'conflict which a man has devised.' Further, the larger structure and thematic development of *Beowulf* show the importance of the Volsung themes of *ofrkapp* and kinship violation. Also discusses the function of kinship in Germanic social structure as well as Volsung themes in the *Nibelungenlied*.

1331   Huppé, Bernard F. "Nature in *Beowulf* and *Roland.*" In *Approaches to Nature in the Middle Ages.* Ed. George D. Economou. Medieval & Renaissance Texts & Studies. Binghamton: Center for Medieval & Early Renaissance Studies, 1982. Pp. 4-46.

Finds that descriptions of nature in *Beowulf* parallel in spirit those in the *Book of Kells*, which depicts nature as hostile and dangerous, with its monsters, intertwining serpents, and menacing animals, and that in both books the artists are concerned to show postlapsarian nature. Nature as hostile enemy to fallen man can be seen in the major descriptions of nature in *Beowulf*: in that of (1) Grendel's mere, (2) of the sea, (3) of the dragon, (4) of sea journeys, and (5) in metaphors of light and dark. Before proceeding to examine each of these descriptions in detail, Huppé looks at the song of creation (ll. 87-114), showing that embedded in it is a reference to the Fall, with the phrases *drihtguman* 'lordly men' (l. 98a) and *fēond on helle* 'enemy in hell' (l. 101b) referring both to the Danes and Grendel (respectively) but also to the freshly created human race and Satan. "Creation and Fall are interlocked as primordial cause and model of man's beleaguered estate, of his finding himself in hostile environment" (8). In the depiction of Grendel's mere (ll. 847-52, 1402b-41a, etc.), post-lapsarian nature is hostile to man except when providential design intervenes, allowing Beowulf to cleanse its waters. The sea as the abode of monsters in the Breca story emphasizes the theme of menace (ll. 539-67). Again, Beowulf is able to triumph against this menace through God's grace, showing how "through God, man may overcome the horror of evil" (14). In the description of the dragon and his barrow, the subject of an elaborate nature description (ll. 2542-59, etc.) the relation of the hero to nature has changed. In his adventures in Denmark, Beowulf overcame evil (begotten by humanity at the Fall) through God, but in battling the dragon, he seems to have offended God, suggesting "that man, estranged from God, is profoundly involved in the hostility of nature" (17). In sea journeys, nature may at first appear to be friendly, but on closer inspection Beowulf's journeys to and from Denmark show the menace of nature subdued by divine protection. Thus, nature here shows a lack of menace rather than abundance of joy. Finally, Huppé traces the menace of nature in a number of metaphors: "These center on the opposition between sunlight and dark, warmth and cold or fierce flame; there are, in addition, two intertwined examples of animal imagery" (21). Also discusses the role of nature in the *Chanson de Roland* as well as the concepts of literary interlace. See G. Economou's response (pp. 42-46) for an opposing view.

1332 Irving, Edward B., Jr. "Beowulf Comes Home: Close Reading in Epic Context." In *Donaldson*, pp. 129-143.

Defends lines 1651-2199 (Beowulf's retelling of his adventures to Hygelac) against the frequent charge that they are irrelevant and repetitious, by proposing that Beowulf is proving himself against the skepticism of Hygelac and the Geats. It becomes clear from his speech (ll. 1987-98) that Hygelac regards Beowulf's journey to Denmark as ill-conceived and unnecessarily dangerous. Irving believes that Hygelac has undervalued Beowulf as a hero, thus Beowulf's undeserved reputation as a slack youth (ll. 2177-84, 2183-89). "We can then see much of [Beowulf's] report as answering charges either explicit or implicit in Hygelac's speech: it is a genuine reply" (137). Irving also sees a series of contrasts between Denmark and Geatland in this section: Hrothgar is old, Hygelac young; Beowulf, as a foreigner, is challenged many times before entering Heorot, but here at home he gains speedy entrance to Hygelac's hall; Denmark has a long history and ancient lineage, Geatland is younger. The Thryth (or Modthryth) episode (ll. 1931-62) may be tied to this theme of youth: "We may tentatively conclude then that the Thryth episode is chiefly intended to show us both negatively . . . as well as positively . . . what a good court Hygelac and Hygd have, young as they are" (133).

1333 Jackson, W.T.H. *The Hero and the King: An Epic Theme.* New York: Columbia UP, 1982. Pp. viii + 141.

In a book-length study of major European epics, considers *Beowulf* (along with the *Iliad, Odyssey, Aeneid,* the *Nibelungenlied, El Cid,* and others) especially in light of the common epic theme of conflict between a hero-intruder and king. In part one, "The Conflict between Hero and King," Jackson explores how the hero-king confrontation effects the structure of epics like *Beowulf*: "It produces, almost enforces, an 'inside-outside' structure, a central passive court surrounded by a moving and not very predictable hero" (132). Hrothgar's court is passive, civilized, but wrecked since Hrothgar has abdicated his first duty, to protect his people. Beowulf arrives as an intruder-hero, and his reception is paralleled in many epics. Wulfgar, as herald, protects the king from any physical danger and preserves the dignity of his kingship. "The greatness of Beowulf lies in the fact that he acts in precisely the opposite fashion to that to be expected of an intruder-hero who has demonstrated unmistakably the weakness of a king and his failure as shepherd of his people. Beowulf could easily have taken over but he has too much sense of nobility" (31). Beowulf has an unusual attitude about the legitimacy of succession, but there is much evidence that as a policy it is ineffective. In part two, instead of playing the role of the intruder-hero, Beowulf plays the part of king.

Here, there is no real intruder-hero, since the challenge comes from inside the kingdom. The poet alters the normal pattern perhaps to suggest some solutions to longstanding problems of kingship and succession, showing that strength and courage, not weapons, defeat the dragon. He also may imply a solution to the problem of succession: Wiglaf (no intruder-hero) will succeed Beowulf (not the typical passive king) because he shows himself worthy in the fight. "There is no question here of an incompetent ruler's being replaced by an intruder-hero. The solution is attractive, but the conclusion of the poem hardly seems to demonstrate that the author believed it would work" (35).

Part two, "The Conflict and the Nature of Epic," argues that in most Western epics, the position of the ruler is rarely stable, but the source of instability varies from epic to epic. In *Beowulf*, old age seems to be one of the main causes of instability. Hrothgar, after glorious accomplishments as a young man, succumbs to a passive old age: "He has allowed himself to think that there is no further need for warlike preparations and acts—or for a ruler to sacrifice himself for his people" (112). Beowulf as king breaks this pattern. First, he does not need to deal with the typical intruder-hero, and he does not succumb to the ravages of age in the same way that Hrothgar does, but he does die. Here, "The instability of rule seems to lie in the instability of life itself" (113). Beowulf's behavior towards Hygelac and the succession of the Geats is very uncharacteristic of the intruder-hero in other epics. "It is difficult to escape the conclusion that the normal self-centered nature of the hero has been modified because the author wishes to prepare the audience for Beowulf the king" (124).

Reviews: *OEN* 17.1 (1983): 84; P.H. Stäblein, *Speculum* 58 (1984): 1057-60.

1334   Jiang, Zeiju. "Some Woman Figures in the Heroic Epic Poem *Beowulf.*" *Waiguoyu* 5 (1982): 35-39.

Not seen.

1335   Johansen, J. G. "Grendel the Brave? *Beowulf*, Line 834." *ES* 63 (1982): 193-197.

Suggests that line 834, *syþðan hilde-dēor hond āledge*, refers not to Beowulf's placing Grendel's arm on the wall (as commonly supposed), but that *hilde-dēor* 'battle-brave one' refers to Grendel, who "lays down" or loses his arm in Heorot. Johansen proposes the following translation of the lines and those immediately following: "after the one brave in battle [Grendel] laid the/ hand down, arm and shoulder—/ there altogether was Grendel's grasp—/ under the vaulting roof" (195). This interpretation solves certain problems with the older reading: for later, in lines 982-84, the arm appears to be on the outside of the hall, and even more troubling, the word *alegde* usually means to 'lay down,' not 'hang up.' Johansen shows that it is not improbable that Grendel should be described as *hilde-dēor*, for Beowulf himself describes Grendel to Hygelac as a *dīor dǣd-fruma* 'brave performer of deeds' (l. 2090a).

1336 Joseph, Brian D. "Using Indo-European Comparative Mythology to Solve Literary Problems: The Case of Old English Hengest." *Papers in Comparative Studies* 2 (1982-1983): 177-86.

Believes that the Hengest of the Finnsburh episode is to be identified with the legendary, quasi-historical Hengest and his brother Horsa, who share the characteristics of a number of Indo-European twins, and that Hengest in *Beowulf* combines the traits of both, since Horsa does not appear. Joseph begins by sketching Hengest's unheroic behavior: He does not immediately avenge Hnæf's death but instead makes peace with Finn. He stays with Finn apparently to take revenge later on but then must be urged on by Hunlafing. "In terms of the functions of the Indo-European twins, Hengest actually displays traits of *both* twins, being both a warrior and a more passive type embodied in one figure. Thus, if Hengest in *Beowulf* is taken to be the reflection in one character of a set of Indo-European twin-heroes, then the ambivalence he displays in the Finnesburg episode becomes understandable, for he continues both the war-like Hengest and the passive Horsa" (182). Also discusses a number of twins from Indo-European folklore, arguing that comparative mythology offers a stimulating methodology for understanding literary figures in various traditions. See Joseph [1389].

1337 Kendall, Calvin B. "The Prefix *un*- and the Metrical Grammar of *Beowulf*." *ASE* 10 (1982): 39-52.

Investigates the metrical position of the *un*- prefix as well as more general principles of the alliteration of compounds. Kendall formulates two rules, part of the "metrical grammar of the *Beowulf* poet, which apply to both halves of the line: (1) The stressed prefix *un*- alliterates. If the prefix does not alliterate, it is not stressed. (2) An initially stressed compound in which the second element is semantically significant is marked for alliteration. That is to say, the first element of every such compound normally alliterates in *Beowulf.* It follows from (2) and from the fundamental alliterative principle that any *a* verse which contains such a compound in second position (that is, following a metrically stressed word) displays double alliteration. It also follows that these compounds are normally excluded from the second position in the *b* verse" (52). Includes a discussion of "metrical grammar," the set of rules or regularities governing Old English poetry. "Each Anglo-Saxon scop absorbed such a grammar during the course of long immersion in the poetic tradition of his culture. No two scops' metrical grammars could have been exactly alike; in addition to individual differences, there must have been regional and dialectal variations" (39).

1338 Knapp, Fritz Peter. "Lebens und Ausdrucksformen des germanischen und romanischen Heldenepos des Mittelalters." [Patterns of Behavior and Expression in Germanic and Romance Heroic Epic of the Middle Ages]. In *La représentation de l'antiquité au moyen âge.* Ed. Danielle Buschinger and André Crépin. Wiener Arbeiten zur germanischen Altertumskunde und Philologie, 20. Vienna: Verlag Karl M. Halosar, 1982. Pp. 375-98.

Takes issue with the thesis of Curtius (in *European Literature and Latin Middle Ages*), who finds that classical Latin traditions taught in European schools were decisive for vernacular epics. Knapp argues instead that oral traditions cannot be overlooked: they provided the materials and poetic traditions for a wide range of Germanic and Romance epics, including *Beowulf.* However, Knapp makes the case that *Beowulf* is a transitional work, that its contents and style derive mainly from the Germanic oral tradition, but that its references to the Christian God and the Cain materials indicate the influence of the Latin manuscript culture. The *Nibelungenlied,* by contrast, shows Christian elements in only a passingly practical way and may lie much closer in spirit to the earlier Germanic materials. *Beowulf* is the product of a learned written culture which adapted the heroic in order to reach the warrior class. Discusses a wide range of Germanic and Romance texts.

1339 Koike, Kazuo. "'Shield' in *Beowulf.*" *Obirin Studies in English Language and Literature* 22 (1982): 103-15. In Japanese.

Considers Old English synonyms or synonymous expressions for "shield" found in *Beowulf* from the viewpoint of lexical and contextual meaning. There are ten words signifying "shield" in *Beowulf*, and if we count *scildweall* 'shield-wall' among this number, we can identify eleven words. Four out of the ten words are simple ones and the rest compounds. (KK)

1340 Krishna, Valerie. "Parataxis, Formulaic Density, and Thrift in the *Alliterative Morte Arthure.*" *Speculum* 57 (1982): 63-83.

Finds that *Beowulf* has fewer characteristics of oral-composed verse (as described by Milman Parry) than does the *Alliterative Morte Arthure*: Parry identifies parataxis, formulaic density, and thrift as key indicators of oral composition. Necessary enjambment, a feature associated with hypotaxis, occurs in 41% of *Beowulf*'s verses but in only 12% of the *Morte Arthure*'s lines, indicating a far more paratactic style for the *Morte*. After arguing for Parry's more narrow definition of the formula, Krishna cites studies which indicate high repetition of exact formulas in the *Alliterative Morte* but lower repetition in *Beowulf*. With respect to thrift (where one formula and one formula only fits a particular metrical niche), Krishna points out that "in *Beowulf* variability or duplication of function within one alliterative niche seems to be the rule, standardization the exception. In the *Morte Arthure*, the opposite is true" (79). This evidence does not necessarily indicate that *Beowulf* is a lettered poem, or that the *Morte Arthure* is an oral one, but perhaps that the former "represents an early, the other a late phase in the evolution of an oral composition" (82-83). Krishna argues that scholars should return to the methods worked out by Parry. Also provides tabulation of statistical evidence.

1341 Landiss, Morris P. "Wealhtheow and the Wife: Limits of Anglo-Saxon Femininity." *Tennessee Philological Bulletin* 19 (1982): 13.

Provides an abstract of a conference paper which contrasts Wealhtheow and the wife of the *Wife's Lament* as two "limits of Anglo-Saxon womanhood.": "Wealhtheow is a charming and lively picture of mature, queenly wifehood and motherhood; the wife presents only disillusioned and egotistic womanhood" (13).

1342 Lapidge, Michael. "'Beowulf,' Aldhelm, the 'Liber Monstrorum' and Wessex." *Studi Medievali* 3rd Ser., 23 (1982): 151-92.

Reexamines the notion that a late seventh- or early eighth-century date for *Beowulf* must locate the poem in the cultural flowering of Bede's Northumbria and instead argues that the poem exhibits several connections, both indirect and direct, to Aldhelm's Wessex, though no absolutely certain date or localization is yet possible. Lapidge outlines the following connections: 1) Aldhelm was arguably familiar with Old English verse concerning dragon fights, since according to Asser he was an accomplished singer of native verses and since the dragons added to accounts in the *De Virginitate* bear certain resemblances to the dragon of *Beowulf*. 2) The *Liber Monstrorum*, which evidence suggests was compiled in England using Aldhelm's library, contains a reference to Hyglac (the Hygelac of *Beowulf*) and identifies him as a Geat, not a Dane as the continental sources do, implying a common English tradition about Hygelac. 3) Place-names with the element *Grendel* (and one with *Beowa*) are clustered around Malmesbury in the western half of Wessex and Western Mercia. 4) Alfred extended his genealogy beyond Geat to include the names Sceaf, Scyld, Heremod, and Beow, possibly having heard these names from *Beowulf* or some form of it. "This evidence suggests, though it does not prove once and forever, that some of the characters and possibly the story recorded in *Beowulf* were known in Wessex by the late ninth century at latest, and may well have been known there two centuries earlier" (188-89).

1343 Lehmann, Winfred P. "Drink Deep!" In *Beowulfian Scansion*, pp. 18-26.

Insists that any account of Germanic meter in general or that of *Beowulf* in particular must begin with an understanding of principles laid down by Snorri Sturlason in his thirteenth-century metrical handbook, the *Háttatal*. After translating and examining the relevant passages from Snorri, Lehmann identifies two essential criteria applicable to all Germanic verse: placement of staves (alliterating syllables) and observation of syllabic quantity (the fact that only stressed syllables alliterate). More specifically, stave-placement (ON *stafnasetning*) demands that "the principal stave is the first of the off-verse and the on-verse commonly has two matching staves, though one is adequate" (20). Such principles rule out the possibility of isochrony (equal measures). Finally, Lehmann maintains that "Any treatment of metrics which disregards this fact [of stave placement] is groundless" (20).

1344 Logan, Darlene. "Battle Strategy in *Perelandra*: *Beowulf* Revisited." *Mythlore* 9 (1982): 19, 21.

Argues that C.S. Lewis borrowed materials from *Beowulf* to construct the character Ransom in *Perelandra*.

1345 Loikala, Paula. "Funeral Rites in *Beowulf*." *Quaderni di Filologia Germanica* (Bologna) 2 (1982): 279-292.

Discusses the burial rites surrounding three characters in the poem (Scyld, Hnæf, and Beowulf) in terms of archaeological, historical, and literary evidence. Loikala discusses several details in the funeral of Beowulf (ll. 3137-82), speculating on the identity of the mourning woman (l. 3150b) as either Beowulf's widow, Hygd, or just a Geatish woman. She concludes that the "funeral rites described in the *Beowulf* text are rich and varied, including as they do both ship funeral and cremation. Many details of the burial customs can be confirmed on the basis of archaeology, even if there is some confusion and overlapping with the older traditions. Mythological, literary, and folklore elements are mingled with actual practices" (288).

1346 Magennis, Hugh. "*Beowulf*, 1008a: *Swefeth Æfter Symle*." *N&Q* 29 (1982): 391-392.

Finds that in lines 1004-08, the poet uses the image of feasting in an unusual way, "unlikely to have derived from his knowledge of the traditions of Christian Latin literature" (391). According to Magennis, the phrase *swefeþ æfter symble* '[everyone] sleeps after feasting' (l. 1008a), refers to the joy of secular life and the inevitability of death. In this image, "Life is seen as the feast, as the brightness of revelry in the hall, surrounded by the darkness of death" (391) whereas elsewhere in Old English Christian poetry, feasting refers negatively to unreliable temporal happiness or positively to heavenly bliss. The closest parallel to the image in lines 1004-08 comes from the famous story of the conversion of King Edwin, employing the image of a sparrow flying through a hall in winter, "although the sweep of the lines in the *Beowulf* passage and the quality of the imagery suggest the naturalness of death rather than—as in the Bede passage—the dread of death. Death brings rest" (391).

1347 McConchie, R. W. "Grettir Asmundarson's Fight with Karr the Old: A Neglected *Beowulf* Analogue." *ES* 63 (1982): 481-486.

Ultimately rejects Chambers' position [S63] that *Beowulf* is constructed out of various folk-tale motifs, by comparing and contrasting Grettir's fight with the Old Kárr in the *Grettis saga* to Beowulf's fight with Grendel's mother. Though there are many external similarities (a solitary descent into a lair, close hand-to-hand combat, the discovery of a sword, the abandonment of the hero by his helper(s), the appearance of treasure and light), McConchie finds the differences between the two narratives significant and concludes that "Beowulf's battle with Grendel's mother is more profoundly conceived poetically and more subtly worked" than the Sandhaugar episode. "Further, the coherence of *Beowulf* weighs against the suggestion that it is merely constructed out of folktales; it seems more reasonable to suggest that *Beowulf* is closer than these analogues to an older myth, and that this dovetailed neatly with the interests of a Christian re-interpreter of the story" (485).

1348 Mitchell, Bruce. "*Beowulf*, Lines 3074-3075: the Damnation of Beowulf?" *Poetica* (Tokyo) 13 (1982): 15-26. Rpt. in *On Old English*, pp. 30-40.

A detailed refutation of Bliss's interpretation [1107] of lines 3074-75, arguing that they do not indicate the damnation of Beowulf as Bliss claims. Mitchell accepts the emendation of *næs* to *næfne* (rejected by Bliss) also disputing Bliss's account of the syntax and temporal relationships in the passage. Mitchell's literal translation of the lines runs as follows: "In the past he had not at all seen and understood the gold-bestowing favour of God more clearly [than he did when he went to meet the guardian of the barrow and his subtle emnity]" (24). Mitchell also discusses the interpretation of lines 2819b-20, arguing against Bliss's proposed translation ("his spirit departed from his breast, hoping for the esteem of the true-judging") and for the "standard" reading ("his spirit departed . . . to seek the glory that belongs to the just"), providing evidence that *sōδfæstra* may be an objective genitive, and examining the range of meanings of the words *dōm* and *sōδfæst* (20-21). However, Mitchell endorses Bliss's reading of lines 3066-73 as "the most satisfying I have yet encountered and believe it to be basically right" (23-24).

1349 Nakagawa, Ryoichi. *A Study of 'Beowulf': Metre and Syntactic Structure*. Tokyo, 1982.

Not seen.

1350 Nickel, Gerhard, ed. *'Beowulf' und die kleineren Denkmäler der altenglischen Heldensage* 'Waldere' und 'Finnsburg': Teil 3, Konkordanz und Glossar. [*Beowulf* and the Smaller Monuments of Old English Heroic Poetry . . . : Part 3, Concordance and Glossary]. Compiled by Jürgen Strauss. Heidelberg: Carl Winter, 1982. Pp. ix + 190.

The third and final volume of Nickel's edition [S1003], containing a glossary/concordance compiled and edited by Jürgen Strauss. To ensure accuracy, the initial word list was generated by computer from the *Beowulf* text edited in volume one. Each entry is lemmatized and defined (in German), with complete line references, grammatical information, and occasional notes on etymology and cognates. For the most part, the entries exclude critical interpretations of compounds, referring the reader to the appropriate section in the commentary (vol. 2), unless such interpretations prove necessary for the immediate understanding of the text or translation ("für das unmittelbare Verständnis von Text oder Übersetzung," vii).

Reviews: C. Lecouteux, *Études germaniques* 36 (1981): 228; Ruth P.M. Lehmann, *Speculum* 56 (1981): 157-59; J.D. Pheifer, *MÆ* 50 (1981): 118-20; C. Wetzel, *BGDSL* 104 (1982): 324-32; C. Lecouteux, *Études germaniques* 38 (1983): 240-41; R. Sch[ützeichel], *BN* 18 (1983): 322; K.R. Grinda, *IF* 87 (1984): 328-37; P. Lendinara, *Schede medievali* 5 (1984): 506-08.

1351 Olsen, Alexandra Hennessey. "The *Aglæca* and the Law." *AN&Q* 20 (1982): 66-68.

Endorsing Kuhn's suggestion [1135] that the difficult word *āglǣca* is a borrowing from Old Irish *óclach* 'young warrior,' suggests that by folk-etymology the word took on the added connotation of 'law breaker.' The second element, -*lǣca* is most easily connected to *lācan* 'to play, fight', while the first element *āg*- may be a folk etymology for *ǣ* 'law', assuming that the *g* in *āg*- would be palatalized after *ā* or *ǣ*, thus rendering the meaning "a person who plays or fights with the law" (67). After examining occurrences of the word in the poem, Olsen argues that the poet uses it "to manipulate our sympathies for his characters" and that the word hints at the unlawful actions of Sigemund, Grendel's mother, Beowulf himself, and the dragon (67).

1352 Ozeki, Yasuhiro. "The Roles of the Compound 'sea' in *Beowulf.*" *Takachiho Ronso* (1982 for 1980-81): 1-31.

Not seen.

1353 Pàroli, Teresa. *La morte di Beowulf.* [The Death of Beowulf]. Testi e studi di filologia, 4. Rome: Istituto di Glottologia, U di Roma, 1982. Pp. 132; 8 pages of plates.

Provides an edition, translation, commentary, analysis, and glossary for lines 2711a-2820, concerning the death of the hero. Chapter one provides a basic account of the *Beowulf* manuscript, its history and transcriptions, while chapter two concerns the variety of thematic elements, the historical elements, the structure of *Beowulf,* its digressions, also providing a summary in Italian of the main events of the poem and going on to trace the complex genesis of the poem from its Germanic-Scandinavian sources (in the sixth century) through its probable first written draft (in the eighth century) through successive copies dating from the Alfredian to the late West Saxon period. Such a transmission would account for the mixture of linguistic forms as well as the complex relationship between the Christian and pagan elements. Chapter three contains the edition and translation of lines 2711b-2820, also providing a number of notes to the text (mainly explanations of compounds and rare forms). Chapter four discusses themes and compositional techniques, dividing lines 2711a-2820 into three sections. The first section (ll. 2722b-23) functions as a prologue, introducing basic themes in three descriptive passages which echo events and themes in the later sections. The second section begins with the solemn speech of Beowulf (ll. 2724-2751) which is based on a single *leitmotiv*, the intertwining of the future (an heirless future), past (his fifty-year reign), and present (the

treasure). The third section revolves around Beowulf's viewing of the hoard and his subsequent death. Pàroli denies that Beowulf is a Christ figure in his death and stresses that Beowulf's actions are judged on the basis of natural ethics, not Christian morality. The ideals of Beowulf seem to be inspired by ideals exclusively heroic and Germanic, while the Christian element reveals itself as a later insertion which gives the text only a superficial religious coloring ("mentre l'elemento cristiano si rivela come un più tardo inserimento che dona al testo solo una superficiale coloritura religiosa," 76). Beowulf's death is negative then by contrast to the positive, heroic nature of his life. Death renders him simply an "old one," a hero preserved only in poetic memory. Chapters five and six provide a basic account of the meter and style of the section.
Reviews: T.H. Leinbaugh, *Speculum* 59 (1984): 935-37.
See Pàroli's rejoinder [1629].

1354 Pope, John C. "The Existential Mysteries as Treated in Certain Passages of Our Older Poets." In *Donaldson*, pp. 345-56.

Argues that the elegiac mood in the second part of *Beowulf* is limited to rhetorically self-contained laments, like that of the Last Survivor, and that several elements in the story resist the prevailing mood of mutability. Beowulf himself, though he laments several losses, believes that the treasure will last as a help for his people and that his barrow will stand as a bulwark against time. The treasure itself, though decayed, resists the principle of mutability by lasting throughout time, and this is perhaps the meaning of the controversial lines 2764b-66, where *oferhīgian* may mean 'outlast' or 'overtake' rather than 'overcome.' "Beowulf feels something of this long life of treasure—and is perhaps in some way reconciled by it to his own death" (352). The dragon's barrow, whose construction is admired by the poet in ll. 2715-19, also stands firm and strong, resisting mutability." Beowulf shares with the poet a wonder at something that pulls his mind away from his pain and his impending death, to admire the skill that made it and its power to endure" (354). Also discusses Chaucer's *Troilus*, the *Wanderer*, *Seafarer*, *Ruin*, among others.

1355 Pound, Ezra. "The Music of *Beowulf*." *Yale Literary Magazine* 150 (1982): 88-91.

An essay, written in 1928, but published here for the first time, in which Pound writes about a performance of Hebridean music he heard in December of that year and the ways in which it reminds him of Anglo-Saxon meter. Pound thanks "the twelve gods of Latium" that Anglo-Saxon songs cannot be sung to the *Wearing of the Green* or *Tipperary* but finds that two lines of *Beowulf* can be fitted into the opening of the *Aillte*. "This traditional music is the 'heroic chant' of the Gael. It is, I think fairly safe to suppose, the sort of rhythm to which the Saxons chanted epos" (90).

1356 Redwine, Bruce. "'Ofost is selest': The Pragmatics of Haste in *Beowulf*." *SN* 54 (1982): 209-216.

Examining 147 words for swiftness in *Beowulf*, concludes that "haste in *Beowulf* . . . serves as a signalling device, a method of demonstrating the sincerity of one's intentions and showing a willingness to act in a forthright manner" (210). Thus, references to slowness (only six occurrences) have negative connotations of cowardice or laxity. Swiftness on the other hand is associated with the heroic life, the efficient use of time in the face of the transitory world. Haste is also a part of ritualized ceremonies, which usually consist of two parts: "the events begin with a flurry of activity during which the participants rush through a series of ritualized movements, and then follows a period of rest which enables serious communication to take place" (215). Redwine finds this pattern in Beowulf's first reception in Heorot (ll. 354-402), Beowulf's return to the Geatish court (ll. 1967-1975), and preparations for Beowulf's funeral (ll. 3001-07).

1357 Renoir, Alain. "Introduction." In *Beowulfian Scansion*, pp. 1-6.

Introduces the volume (a collection of papers read at the 1979 MLA convention in San Francisco), which aims to present accessible outlines of various theories of scansion. Renoir gives a brief reprisal of the work of the contributors, Winfred P. Lehmann [1343], Robert P. Creed [1305], John Miles Foley [1311], and Dolores Warwick Frese [1314].

1358 Rigg, A.G. "*Beowulf* 1368-72: An Analogue." *N&Q* 29 (1982): 101-102.

Finds a parallel in Alexander Neckham's *De laudibus divinae sapientiae* (written before 1211) for the statement in *Beowulf* that Grendel's mere is so terrible that a hart would rather give up its life on the shore rather than plunge into it. Neckham describes a lake so terrifying that "no wild animal will trust itself to its waters. Though the powerful stench of hounds press[es] on, though bitter death presses on, nevertheless the animal, disturbed will not enter the place" (102). Some of Neckham's marvels have parallels in Pseudo-Nennius, but others, like the one under discussion, may follow local traditions.

1359 Riley, Samuel M. "*Beowulf*, Lines 3180-82." *Explicator* 40 (1982): 2-3.

Finds little tension in the last two lines between Christian and Germanic virtue: "The shared meaning of the three adjectives *mildust* ['mildest'], *monðwærust* ['gentlest'], and *līðost* ['most generous'] suggests that they may be consciously employed synonyms. Rather than revealing Beowulf as a paradigm of Christian excellence, or being 'poised in gentle tension' with *lofgeornost*, they may instead work in harmony with it to complete a portrait of a hero who exemplifies the two best traits of an ideal Germanic ruler—generosity and bravery" (3).

1360 Romano, Timothy. "*Beowulf* 1. 1331b: A Restoration of MS *hwæþer*." *Neophil* 66 (1982): 609-613.

Defends the manuscript reading *hwæþer* 'whether' in line 1331b over the now-standard emendation to *hwæder* 'whither,' first suggested by Grein. In this passage, Hrothgar grieves for the missing Æschere: *ic ne wāt hwæþer/ atol æse wlanc eftsīðas tēah/ fylle gefægnod* (ll. 1331-33). With the restored reading, it may be translated, "I know not *whether* [rather than *whither*] the horrible one, exulting in carrion, took return routes, gladdened by feasting" (609). "Confronted with the possibility that Æschere has met an ignominious end unbefitting his dignity, Hrothgar descends to the level of distracted cynicism and speaks of his *eaxlgestealla* as though he were no more than a morsel eaten up as at a feast. He calls Grendel's dam a *wælgāst* 'slaughter-guest' (l. 1331), playing the role of concerned host as he wonders whether she 'went home exulting in her bellyful, happy for having feasted here'" (610). Surveys the use of *hwæþer* in other Old English poems.

1361 Sato, Noboru. "*Beowulf* and Gregorian Chant." *Otsuka Review* 18 (1982): 85-100.

A comparison of the structure of Old English poems with that of contemporary Gregorian chant, showing that the extant *Beowulf* manuscript was completed around 1000. (NS)

1362 _____. "Beowulfian Aesthetic Suggested in the Assonance and the Rhyme." *Tamagawa Review* 22 (1982): 285-302.

Argues that the irregular rhyme in the poem suggests the irregularity of its structure as well as persons uncertain in religion. (NS)

1363 Stanley, Eric G. "Translation from Old English: 'The Garbaging War-Hawk,' or, The Literal Materials from Which the Reader Can Re-Create the Poem." In *Donaldson*, pp. 67-101.

Surveys and comments on most of the English verse translations and some prose translations of *Beowulf*, providing a short, typical passage from each. Stanley believes that the most successful verse translations are the ones closest to prose (68). "Unadorned, muted prose, as far from *Kunstprosa* as it is possible to go, as far from archaism as modernity ensures, seems best for literary success. The alternative is poetry, but poetry invites comparison with the original. No poet has really succeeded with translating Anglo-Saxon verse; Longfellow [F1261], Tennyson, William Morris [F1482]—they have not done as well as have less famous poets, Edwin Morgan [S243] especially" (101).

1364 Swanton, Michael J. *Crisis and Development in Germanic Society 700-800: Beowulf and the Burden of Kingship*. Goppinger Arbeiten zur Germanistik, Nr. 333. Goppingen: Kummerle Verlag, 1982. Pp. 160.

A historical study of Germanic and Roman concepts of kingship, finding that *Beowulf* shows a mixture of the two systems and suggesting that it was composed during a time of political transition, most likely in the later eighth century. Chapter one, "Vox Populi," argues that the Anglo-Saxons in general retained the continental Germanic concept of kingship in which the power to govern was derived from the people and guided by councils, in contrast to the Roman model of vertical power exercised from above. Swanton reviews evidence from Tacitus and from Germanic history on the continent, stressing that a Germanic "king" was selected by the people from a pool of worthy fighters and leaders (not by blood descent), that he could be deposed or slain by the people, that treason was an offense against common law and the community, not the king's person, that certain royal properties belonged to the community, not to the king personally (see the compound *þēod-gestrēon*, 'people-treasure', *Beowulf*, ll. 44, 1218). These concepts are mirrored in Germanic names for rulers, *dryhten* (from *dryht*, 'troop') and *þēoden* (from *þēod*, 'people'). An extensive review of English history reveals a similar pattern. In *Beowulf* Swanton notes the influence of the vertical Roman idea of kingship, mediated principally by the Church. He studies the use of the words denoting social relationships: *wine* 'friend', *trēow* 'good faith, fidelity', and *hyldo* 'friendship, loyalty', finding "a complex semantic situation, apparently caught in a process of transition" (29).

Chapters two and three, "Vox Dei" and "Vicarius Dei," document the shift from the old Germanic system of kingship to the vertical Roman model in which the king is seen as a divinely-sanctioned ruler. Central to the process was the church's intervention in crowning Pippin I in 750, described in detail. Anglo-Saxon kings of this period (principally Æthelbald and Offa) quickly made use of the titles and ceremonies of divine sanction used to establish the legitimacy of Pippin. Accompanying the shift came a loss of communal rights and the development of new ideas of treason against the king's sacred person as well as the idea that a good king must be mild and merciful to his inferiors, a trait echoed in the last lines of *Beowulf*.

Chapters four through six, "Beowulf and the Scyldings," "Beowulf's Mighty Grip," and "King Beowulf" present a reading of the poem which finds various mixtures of the two ideas of kingship. In the end, Hrothgar is seen as a type of the older, purely Germanic ideal (inadequate to cope with dire calamities like the attacks of Grendel and his mother), while Beowulf fuses ideas from both worlds, tending however to the Roman model of vertical power and primogeniture. Unferth, an empty talker, represents the decline of Hrothgar's court. Swanton believes that Beowulf finally succumbs to *oferhygd* 'pride' and avarice, forgetting to rely on God as the ultimate source of vertical power. [See *succession—questions of* in the subject index.]

Reviews: *OEN* 18.1 (1984):91.

1365 Taylor, Paul Beekman, and P.H. Salus. "Old English *Alf Walda*." *Neophil* 66 (1982): 440-442.

Argues that editors should allow the manuscript reading at l. 1314a, *alf walda* 'elf-ruler?' to remain "in the text as a crux" (441) rather than accept the standard emendation to *alwalda* 'ruler of all things.' In the poetic corpus, *alwalda* always occurs with another term, making it clear that God is the referent (e.g., *fæder alwalda, ealwalda god, alwalda engelcynna*, etc.). Though *alf* is not an attested Old English form, it does occur in Early Middle English, and the simplex *Ælf* is a component of Anglo-Saxon names like *Ælfred* and *Ælfhere*. In the North Germanic context, the ruler of the elves would be an appropriate epithet for Freyr, and if Freyr is considered as a form of Old English *frēa* 'lord,' *alfwalda* may be "an oblique reference to God in kenning form" (441). Though this explanation may not be completely satisfactory, the burden of proof is on those who would emend the text.

1366 _____, and R. Evan Davis. "Some Alliterative Misfits in the *Beowulf* MS." *Neophil* 66 (1982): 614-621.

Disputes a number of editorial emendations whose primary aim is to restore alliteration in lines whose sense is not lacking. Recent work by Sebastino Timpanaro suggests that scribal error rarely produces nonsense forms. Further, rhythm may be just as important as alliteration in certain contexts. "If this is so, whatever the text renders should normally be defendable" (615). The authors go on to support manuscript readings in ll. 454, 461, 976, 1960, 1981, 2341, and 2882. Emendations which drop an initial *h* to restore alliteration may also be mistaken if *h* plus vowel in a stressed syllable could alliterate with the initial vowel of a stressed syllable in the remaining half-line, an idea explored by Bliss [S353] and Greenfield [S834]. The authors then defend the manuscript rendering *Hunferð* against the usual emendation to *Unferð* even in lines where it does not alliterate. Similarly unnecessary emendations occur at ll. 332, 1541, 2523, and 2929.

1367 Tolkien, J.R.R.. *Finn and Hengest: The Fragment and the Episode*. Ed. Alan J. Bliss. London: G. Allen & Unwin, 1982. Pp. xii + 180.

An edition and translation of the Finn Episode (ll. 1063-1159a) and the Finn Fragment, with an introduction, textual commentary, glossary of names, and an extensive reconstruction of the story—edited by Alan Bliss from Tolkien's unpublished lectures and other materials. Among a number of emendations, Tolkien inserts a line after 1067 to supply the missing sense and provides a detailed discussion of other emendations and textual matters in the commentary. Tolkien suggests that Hildeburh's son by Finn may have been fostered by Hnaef, that Finn encouraged Jutes in exile to settle in Frisia, that Frisians were drawn into the fight, that the word describing the sword, *hildelēoma* 'battle light' (l. 1143b), may be its name, that Hunlafing is the name of the warrior who places Hnaef's sword into Hengest's lap, that the Danes departed in the spring, leaving Hengest behind, and that Hengest may have left for Kent after the episode. Includes appendices on the dating of events in the lives of Healfdene and Hengest and a brief essay by Bliss on the nationality of Hengest, who, he suggests, may have been an Angle of royal stock.

Reviews: G.L. Brook, *British Book News* July (1983): 455; M. Godden, *TLS* 8 July, 1983: 736; E. Jackson, Unisa English Studies 21.2 (1983): 31.

1368 Tripp, Raymond P., Jr. "Third Thoughts on Some *Beowulf* Readings." *In Geardagum* 4 (1982): 56-67.

Modifies some readings (ll. 2216b, 2217b-18a, 2221, 2226a, and 2409) given in Tripp [1289] but still supports the notion that the thief of conventional interpretations does not exist. See also Tripp [1414].

1369 Ushigaki, Hiroto. "The Image of 'God Cyning' in *Beowulf*: A Philological Study." *Studies in English Literature (Tokyo)* 58 (English No.) (1982): 63-78.

Examines the epithets (characterizing adjectives) applied to the three principal kings of the poem: Hrothgar, Hygelac, and Beowulf, finding that on the whole the poet sees Hrothgar as wise and kingly, Hygelac as heroic and perhaps somewhat reckless, but Beowulf as combining the positive characteristics of both in a picture of the ideal Germanic king. "Epithets of generosity, wisdom and age, and renown are applied most often to Hrothgar, in contrast to those of endearment and prowess most abundantly used in reference to

Beowulf. The only epithet of noble birth is used of Hrothgar, whilst those rare epithets of pride or noble spirit are limited to Beowulf and Hygelac. Young Hygelac is characterized mainly by epithets of prowess, showing, quite reasonably, his lack of other essential kingly virtues, such as wisdom. And it deserves special mention that the sole epithet of honour, in the superlative form, is used of Beowulf. More importantly, superlative epithets show a marked tendency to be reserved only for Beowulf" (68). Includes an appendix listing the epithets (divided by category).

1370 Verdonck, J. *"Beowulf vertalen."* [Translating *Beowulf*]. *Handelingen der Koninklijke Zuidnederlandse Maatschappij voor Taal- en Letterkunde en Geschiedenis* 36 (1982): 239-58.

Not seen. According to the report in *YWOES, OEN* 18.1 (1984): 94, Verdonck "deals with the problems of translating ancient texts in general ... [and] mentions many familiar problems, e.g., the translator making explicit what the text only suggests or the imposition of punctuation on poetry that was originally delivered orally."

1371 Weinstock, Horst. "Comment on 'Knowledge of *Beowulf* in Its Own Time' by Professor Frederic G. Cassidy." *REAL* 1 (1982): 13-25.

A response to and an endorsement of F.G. Cassidy's essay [1304]. Weinstock believes that the poet was a monk (rather than a *scop*) and that the audience for the poem was monastic rather than courtly—otherwise, it would have achieved a wider reputation. "Onomastic echoes, the cautious handling of historical sources, the homogenized presentation of different periods and cultures in art, literature, and translation as well as the Anglo-Saxon dynastic interest in their Continental Germanic origin all harmonize with a late(r) date" (23). Weinstock suggests that the poem may have been composed for Anglo-Saxon missionaries converting the Continental Saxons and read out in the refectory.

1372 Williams, David. *Cain and Beowulf: A Study in Secular Allegory.* Toronto: U of Toronto P, 1982. Pp. 118; ill.

Surveys the patristic lore concerning Cain and its relation to the themes of *Beowulf*, arguing (in chapter one) that the poem is a non-theological or secular allegory and that it employs Cain lore as a metaphor for social struggles in post-coversion England. Chapter two, "The Cain Tradition," examines the various sources of Cain lore from patristic and rabbinical traditions, with particular emphasis on Augustine's treatment in *The City of God*. There, Cain (as a founder of cities) becomes a type of the worldly, carnal life as well as an explanation of evil in human history. Williams discusses other attributes of Cain and his kin from the exegetical tradition: violence toward kin, stinginess, animal appetite (including the drinking of blood), permanent exile, abode in a watery region (related to the Flood), production of giants and monsters. Further, Ham was seen as a type of Cain since Ham revived Cain's evil after the flood had cleansed the earth. The reference to *champ* in line 1261b, often emended to *Cain*, may plausibly refer to Ham as the continuer of Cain's tradition of murder and worldliness.

Chapter three, "The Poetic Present and the Fabulous Mode," argues that the poet unites the historical elements (the history of Beowulf, the Danes, and the Geatish wars) with the fabulous elements (the monsters) by means of the Cain materials, which informs the theme of the entire poem. Cain inspires human crimes throughout the poem, producing a "society threatened by internecine wars and the human vices of greed, ambition, blood-thirstiness, and kin hate." The dragon in his hoarding of treasure resembles the niggardly Cain especially "as the particular force that negates civilization" (59). In Chapter four, "Past through Allusion, Future through Prophecy," the historical episodes or "digressions" are seen to be intimately connected to the moral and social significance of the Cain materials. The poem's historical digressions show that all human history (past, present, and future) is plagued by the spirit of Cain in an unbroken history of evil and social discord. Williams further agrees with Kaske [S631] that the word *eoten* refers to giants rather than Jutes. Though Kaske argued that "giant" was a word meaning "enemy" in a generalized sense, the giants of *Beowulf* could be understood as the strife-bearing progeny of Cain. The feuds with the Swedes and Heathobards have a similar origin in Cain-centered strife.

Williams concludes that the "pagan institutions of kinship, comitatus, wergeld, and peace-bond marriage are seen in every instance as inadequate to the menace of ambition and blood-lust that threaten civilization. The vision is ideological, and while it presents the pagan past with a certain admiration and recognition that the struggle for good existed then, too, it is uncompromisingly Christian in

perceiving the failure of pagan society as inevitable and complete" (96). Beowulf, though he himself participates in the chief evil of the poem, vengeance, is a force for good. He comes to recognize by the end of the poem the dynamics of human history contained in the Cain legend and illustrated in the historical digressions.
Reviews: C.T. Berkhout, *Allegorica* 6.2 (1982): 155-57; *OEN* 17.1 (1983): 82; D.G. Calder, *Speculum* 58 (1983): 838-40; J.E. Cross, *N&Q* 30 (1983): 446-47; S.B. Greenfield, *MP* 81 (1983): 191-94; M.E. Goldsmith, *MÆ* 54 (1985): 134-35.

1373 Yada, Hiroshi. "Coordinated Words used as Variation in *Beowulf*." *Studies in English Literature* (Baiko Jogakuin College) 18 (1982): 141-63.

Not seen.

1374 Zyngier, Sonia. "A Forca Mitica de Beowulf." [The Mythic Power of Beowulf.] *Ilha do Desterro* 3 (1982): 77-88.

Sees Beowulf as a mythic hero battling forces of social and political disintegration. Zyngier draws a number of parallels to other mythic heroes in Germanic and European literature.

1983

1375   Alexander, Michael *Old English Literature*. Macmillan History of Literature. London: Macmillan, 1983. Pp. xv + 248; ill.; 16 pp. of plates.

In a general account of Old English literature, includes a discussion of the poem in a chapter entitled "Heroic Poetry Including *Beowulf*" (58-71). After briefly recounting the history of *Beowulf* scholarship, Alexander goes on to discuss the poem's major themes, with particular attention to the meaning of the monsters. He notes a number of Christian elements but argues that "*Beowulf* is not, however, a theological work, still less a pigeon-holing one, nor an allegory, though it can be read allegorically. Its significance resides on the single level of its own story, the story of a superhuman deliverer—such as Perseus or Theseus, or St Michael—yet subject to mortality, who made of mortality as fine a thing as could be made" (71).
Reviews: N.F. Blake, *ES* 65 (1984): 172-73; P. Lendinara, *Schede medievali* 5 (1984): 466-67; E.G. Stanley, *N&Q* 31 (1984): 99-100; S.A.J. Bradley, *MÆ* 54 (1985): 284-86; D. Baker-Smith, *Downside Review* 104 (1986): 57-58; J. Roberts, *MLR* 82 (1987): 434-35.

1376   Anderson, J. J. "The 'Cuþe Folme' in *Beowulf*." *Neophil* 67 (1983): 126-130.

Proposes that the phrase *cūþe folme* (l. 1303a) describes Æschere rather than Grendel's arm, as is usually assumed: as she flees the hall, Grendel's mother takes this *cūþe folme* 'renowned hand,' covered in blood. Anderson offers the following translation of ll. 1302-4: "There was an uproar in Heorot; she took the famous hand (of Æschere) covered in blood; grief was renewed, came to pass in the dwellings" (127), and points out that Grendel's mother does not sever Æschere's hand but that *cūþe folme* is a metaphorical way of referring to Æschere. Several considerations support this conclusion. There is no reference to Grendel's mother having taken Grendel's arm, except the disputed passage here. Hrothgar's lament for Æschere refers to him (metaphorically) as a *hand* (ll. 1343-44). Further, the word *hand* is used elsewhere in the poem to denote the whole person. Understanding *cūþe folme* as Æschere also explains lines 1304-6 more clearly: "That was not a good exchange, which they on both sides had to pay for with the lives of loved ones."

Æschere's hand is traded for Grendel's hand, and each side loses a loved one. This interpretation also makes more sense thematically: "all parties are now caught up in a futile cycle of retribution in which moral issues become confused and in which all suffer" (128).

1377 Barksdale, E. C. "The Fragile Cathedral: Harmony and Chaos in the *Igor Tale*." In *Festschrift für Nikola R. Pribić*. Ed. Josip Matešić and Erwin Wedel. Selecta Slavica, 9. Neuried: Hieronymus Verlag, 1983. Pp. 19-26.

Briefly compares the sense of chaos in *Beowulf* to that in the medieval Russian *Igor Tale* (*Slovo o polku Igoreve*), finding that in *Beowulf* chaos is personified in the monsters whereas in the *Igor Tale*, the source of chaos comes from the human community, from the Polovtsians and from within man himself.

1378 Björnsson, Halldóra B. *Bjólfskviða*. [Beowulf]. Ed. Pétur Knútsson Ridgewell. Illus. by Alfreð Flóki. Reykjavík: Fjövaútgáfan, 1983. Pp. 141; ill.

Translates the poem into modern Icelandic verse, approximating the meter and alliteration of the Old English original. Lines 4-14: "Oft Skjöldur Skefingur skæður féndum/ bægði mörgum frá bekki mjaðar,/ hann sem áður var allslaus fundinn/ ægði herskáum sér til hugarléttis./ Óx hróður hans und himinskautum/ uns einn og sérhver umhverfis sátu/ handan hvalvega hlýða urðu,/ gjöld guldu. Það var góður konungur!" Includes a name index and illustrations by Alfreð Flóki.
Reviews: *OEN* 21.1 (1987): 83.

1379 Brady, Caroline. "Warriors in *Beowulf*: An Analysis of the Nominal Compounds and an Evaluation of the Poet's Use of Them." *ASE* 11 (1983 for 1982): 199-246.

Undertakes a detailed study of nominal compounds for "warrior" in *Beowulf*, 88 nominal compounds and 13 genitive combinations. Brady breaks down her discussion into several categories: compounds applied to the Danes up to the slaying of Grendel, to the Geats up to the slaying of Grendel, to Danes and Geats up to the departure of the Geats, to individual Danes, to individual Geats, to the Geats at their return home; compounds in part II of the poem, and compounds applied to Beowulf in part I. Brady makes the following conclusions: Only 55 of the 101 terms actually refer to warriors, while the rest refer to men as retainers. The poet, in describing the Danes, carefully mixes compounds for warriors, for retainers, and for other occupations in order to give a "well-fleshed portrait of a royal court worthy of Hrothgar" (240). Compounds used of the Geats, on the other hand, stress their warrior rather than retainer attributes. Genitive combinations denoting a warrior are rare, and the poet seems to use them as a characterizing device, emphasizing a unique quality in an exceptional warrior (for example, Dæghrefn, Offa, and Beowulf). Eight such genitive combinations are applied to Beowulf. The index of compounds compiled by Jonathan Wilcox (245-46) has been incorporated into the word index of this volume.

1380 Cavill, Paul. "A Note on *Beowulf*: Lines 2490-2509." *Neophil* 67 (1983): 599-604.

Disputes the assumption that Dæghrefn was Hygelac's slayer, that Beowulf's motivation in killing him was revenge, that Hygelac was dead when Beowulf slew Dæghrefn, or that the *brēostweorðung* 'breast ornament' (l. 2504) is to be identified with the *healsbēag* 'neck ring' (l. 2172) which Wealhtheow gave to Beowulf and which he supposedly retrieved from the dead Hygelac. Cavill conjectures that Dæghrefn is the foremost Frank, not necessarily Hygelac's slayer. In fact, the slaying of Dæghrefn may have occurred while Hygelac was still alive. The conjectural reconstruction of the scene runs as follows: "Dæghrefn as standardbearer of the Franks leads them into battle; Beowulf as champion of the Geats seeks him out, either before the opposing armies meet, or as battle is joined. They fight, and Beowulf's sword fails him at some point. . . . Dæghrefn presses his advantage and Beowulf falls; Dæghrefn tries to plunder his valuables, collar, helmet, byrnie. . . . Beowulf crushes Dæghrefn in a bear-hug as he comes within reach" (603). Includes a discussion, with archaeological evidence, of the function of the *healsbēag*.

1381 Collins, Rowland L. "Blickling Homily XVI and the Dating of *Beowulf*." In *Medieval Studies Conference Aachen 1983: Language and Literature*. Ed. Wolf-Dietrich Bald and Horst Weinstock. Frankfurt a.M.: Peter Lang, 1983. Pp. 61-69.

Examines the relationship between *Beowulf* and Blickling homily XVI (XVII in the old numbering), concluding that the *Beowulf* poet probably borrowed from the homilist, not the homilist from *Beowulf*. It has been recognized that poet's description of Grendel's mere (ll. 1357b-1366a, 1411, 1414-1417a) is related in some way to the description of hell in the Blickling homily, the ultimate source of which is the *Visio Sancti Pauli*. Collins reviews previous opinion on this matter which generally assumes that the Blickling homilist echoes *Beowulf*. However, much of the wording in the *Beowulf* passage seems peculiar to the homiletic idiom, suggesting that the *Beowulf* poet borrowed from the Blickling homily, not the other way around. Such a suggestion does not necessarily demand a late date for *Beowulf* since the Blickling material could have been interpolated into the poem by later scribes or redactors. "The language of the two passages points toward an influence on *Beowulf* from Homily XVI and that influence is historically possible and entirely plausible in terms of the extant literature" (69).

1382 Crépin, André. "La Conscience de soi héroïque: L'exemple de Beowulf." [Consciousness of the Heroic Self: The Example of Beowulf]. In *Genèse de la conscience moderne: Études sur le développement de la conscience de soi dans les littératures du monde occidental*. Ed. Robert Ellrodt. Publications de la Sorbonne, Série Littérature, no. 14. Paris: Presses universitaires de France, 1983. Pp. 51-60.

Undertakes to explore the consciousness of self in *Beowulf*, a characteristic usually denied to literature from the early Middle Ages, and suggests an allegorical reading of the poem in which Beowulf's adventures against the monsters represent the odyssey of the conscious mind against the forces of the unconscious. Crépin finds evidence in the poem of a consciousness guiding Beowulf's actions, particularly in Hrothgar's statement about vigilance (i.e., consciousness): when vigilance, the "guardian of the spirit," sleeps, the soul is open to the attacks of evil (ll. 1739-57). This idea of a consciousness controlling both body and spirit parallels Alcuin's concept of reason in the *De anima ratione*. The monsters may represent allegorically the dangerous forces of the unconscious, with Grendel symbolizing bestial appetite or hunger, Grendel's mother, dangerous sexual appetites, and the dragon, egotistical and anti-social avarice. See also Hanning [S1033].

1383 Damico, Helen. "*Sörlaþáttr* and the Hama Episode in *Beowulf.*" *Scandinavian Studies* 55 (1983): 222-35.

Argues that the Old Norse myth of Loki's theft of Freya's necklace, as told in the *Sörlaþáttr*, may lie behind the story of Hama and the Brosings' necklace in *Beowulf* (ll. 1197-1201) but that Germanic legends of Heimir and Eormenric do not prove useful as analogues. Damico points out a number of problems with proposed reconstructions of the story and goes on to suggest that mythic rather than legendary materials are in operation in the Beowulf passage. In the myth of the *Brísinga men* 'Brosings' necklace,' Loki, the retainer of Oðinn, steals Freyja's necklace by transforming himself into a flea, entering Freyja's bower through a hole, biting her, and stealing the necklace. He takes the ring back to Oðinn to win back his lord's favor. Damico compares this theft with the theft of the cup later in *Beowulf* (ll. 2214-26), noting a number of similarities. The problem with identifying the Hama passage with the theft of Freyja's necklace revolves around the proper names Hama and Eormenric, both legendary characters with no original connection to Freyja's necklace. "This difficulty can be overcome, however, if one renders *hāma* and *eormenrīc* as common terms rather than as personal names. Old English *hāma* 'cricket, house cricket,' is—like Loki's fly-personality—an insect small enough to slip into a bower through a hole.... Translating *eormenrīc* as 'universal power' likewise accords with mythological interpretation. The word evokes the cosmic authority of Oðinn and is an appropriate epithet for the war-god" (231).

1383a Davis, Victor, and Betty Jane Wylie. *'Beowulf': A Musical Epic*. Toronto: Lilly Pad Productions, 1983.

A recording of a musical adaptation of *Beowulf*, with music by Victor Davis and lyrics by Betty Jane Wylie.

1384 Dieterich, Lana Stone. "Syntactic Analysis of Beowulf's Fight with Grendel." *Comitatus* 14 (1983): 5-17.

Analyzes the syntax of Beowulf's fight with Grendel (ll. 703b-828a) in detail, highlighting the way in which it intertwines Beowulf and Grendel and noting the effects of this process, particularly on Beowulf. Dieterich shows how the poet melds the two fighters by obscuring the subject of several clauses and linking the two with alliteration, common phraseology, and plurals. Finally, though Grendel gains some humanity through this melding, "Beowulf has not emerged untainted. Hero or no, he is a man just like the taintable Danes and men live in a world that changes them" (16). This deflation of the hero "prefigures the change in Beowulf at the end of the poem—an old man bereft of innocence and the faith in the power of God he had initially, who finally eschews God's help for his own shrewdness and ends up losing his life to the dragon" (17).

1385 Earl, James W. "The Role of the Men's Hall in the Development of the Anglo-Saxon Superego." *Psychiatry* 46 (1983): 139-60.

Using Freud's *Civilization and Its Discontents* as a starting point, examines the psychological development of Anglo-Saxon culture "from primitive tribe to civilized state," from its early stages in which the lordship system of the male warrior class (symbolized by the hall) and the feminized system of kinship-revenge (symbolized by the domestic hut) formed competing institutions of social control, to a stage after the migration in which the male culture of the hall dominated that of the hut, to a final stage in which the Christianized Anglo-Saxons reject but mourn the culture of the hall in ways similar to an individual's renunciation and internalization of the Oedipal conflict, producing guilt, and in the case of culture, a higher level of civilization. *Beowulf*, Earl argues, shows traces of this cultural evolution. The poem's world is exclusively the world of the hall (with its male, warrior values), and the feminine-dominated hut (agriculture, kinship, domesticity) is all but suppressed, though it does surface in a threatening form in Grendel's mother and her demands of revenge for kin. "Grendel's avenging mother . . . represents among other things the threat that women and the ancient claims of kindred pose to the civilizing work of men" (153). But finally, the Christian poem (showing the highest civilized state) mourns and more deeply internalizes the superseded culture of the hall, producing a super-ego on the cultural level. In light of this evolution, "The tone of the poem is not confused and does not reflect a partial or even ambivalent Christianity; rather, it is devoted to mourning for that past, which demands both a full acknowledgment of the love that has been withdrawn, and a clean detachment from it by accepting its death as absolute" (158). Includes a discussion of anthropological theory.

1386 Hanning, Robert W. "*Beowulf* and Anglo-Saxon Poetry." In *The Middle Ages and the Renaissance: Prudentius to Medieval Drama*. Ed. William T.H. Jackson and George Stade. European Writers. New York: Scribner's, 1983. 1:51-87.

Provides a general introduction to the poem, including sections on Germanic society, oral culture, folk-tale structure, the heroic ideal, cultural synthesis, the Old English poetic corpus, poetic technique, the manuscript and its date, a summary of critical approaches, and finally a reading of the poem. Also includes an extensive bibliography.

1387 Heinemann, Fredrik J. "*Ealuscerwen-Meoduscerwen*, the Cup of Death, and *Baldrs Draumar*." *SN* 55 (1983): 3-10.

Suggests that the terms *ealuscerwen* (*Beowulf*, l. 769) and *meoduscerwen* (*Andreas*, l. 1526) may be explained by a Germanic rite in which a "pagan ritual libation predicts, commemorates, and even causes death" (8); such cups of death appear in *Baldrs Draumar*, the *Niebelungenlied*, and the *Hákonarmál* and may reflect a belief that warriors arriving in Valhalla received a welcoming drink. An alternate explanation is that the half-line refers to the Christian Cup of Death (*poculum mortis*). In either case, in *Beowulf*, the Danes fear this ominous drink as a foreshadowing of disaster: "we cannot be certain of the intended recipient of the drink, Beowulf or the Danes. The phrase could mean that the Danes feared they would be drinking Beowulf's *minne* ['libation'] or that he would be forced to drink his own libation on entering the afterworld. But whichever of the two is to be imagined as partaking of the drink, *ealuscerwen* predicts disaster that fails to materialize" (8).

1388 Hollis, Stephanie J. "*Beowulf* and the Succession." *Parergon* n.s., 1 (1983): 39-54.

Argues that by giving the corslet of Heorogar to Beowulf (described in lines 2155-62), Hrothgar reveals a complex strategy for making Beowulf a contender for the Danish throne but that Beowulf adheres strictly to the rule of primogeniture. The corslet is a significant gift in that earlier it went from Heorogar to his brother Hrothgar, not to Heorogar's son, Heoroweard, indicating that possession of such prized armor is connected in some way to the succession. Hrothgar uses the gift also as a diplomatic signal to Hygelac that Beowulf is worthy of succession to the Geatish throne. Hollis analyzes Wealhtheow's nervous speech on the succession as well as Beowulf's report to Hygelac (ll. 1836-39) in terms of this implication. Hrothgar, true to the ancient Germanic practice, sets up a number of claimants for his throne—Hrothulf, Beowulf, and his sons—using "complex calculations and stratagems.... Beowulf, on the other hand, is a staunch adherent of primogeniture, for simple loyalty to kinsmen, whatever the politics" (48). Hrothgar's method "reflects an older, tribal mode of operation" (49), while primogeniture was comparatively recent among the Anglo-Saxons. The poet, however, seems to endorse primogeniture, revealing the possibility for conflict and tragedy in the old system as well as indicating through the Danish genealogy that primogeniture is actually more ancient. [See *succession—questions of* in the subject index.]

1389 Joseph, Brian D. "Old English Hengest as an Indo-European Twin Hero." *Mankind Quarterly* 24 (1983): 105-115.

Applying Indo-European comparative mythology to the Finnsburh episode, proposes that Hengest's ambivalence about fighting with Finn can be explained in light of myths about Indo-European twins, one of which is passive and the other fierce, and that the Hengest of the poem represents an amalgamation of the quasi-historical twins Hengest and Horsa. "In terms of the functions of the Indo-European twins, Hengest [of the poem] actually displays traits of *both* twins, being both a warrior and a more passive type embodied in one figure. Thus if Hengest in *Beowulf* is taken to be the reflection in one character of a set of Indo-European twin-heroes, then the ambivalence he displays in the Finnsburh episode becomes understandable, for he continues both the war-like Hengest and the passive Horsa" (112). Joseph also notes that Indo-European twins are often associated with horses and swans, a connection which holds for Hengest and Horsa, whose names mean "horse" and whose sister is said to be named "Swana." Cf. Joseph [1336].

1390 Kelly, Birte. "The Formative Stages of Beowulf Textual Scholarship: Part I." *ASE* 11 (1983 for 1982): 247-274.

Together with Kelly [1391], seeks to "establish as comprehensive a picture as possible of the early contribution to modern textual criticism" by such pioneering *Beowulf* editors as Grundtvig [S11], Kemble [S8], Thorpe [S10], and Grein [F675]. In this installment, Kelly lists all textual emendations "proposed by 1857 and accepted in at least one edition published from 1950 onwards" (247). Kelly breaks the list into several categories, reflecting the reasons for emendation and the extent of acceptance of the reading in modern editions. "It emerges from the analysis of the various categories that the more consensus there is among the present-day editors the higher chance there is that the proposed emendation had its origin in the formative stages: thus more than three-quarters of the readings agreed by all editors from 1950 onwards originated in the period up to 1857, and, even where only some of the editors from 1950 onwards accept a need to emend, an agreed solution is more likely than not to have been proposed by 1857. Conversely where editors from 1950 onwards adopt various solutions, these are more likely to have been first proposed by 1857. To some extent, doubtless, these correlations are connected with the probability that the early emenders dealt with simpler and more obvious matters. . . . But, even with this reservation, the contribution of the [early editors] remains considerable in quality as well as quantity, and it is hoped that this article will serve to remind modern critics of both these facts" (250-51).

1391 _____. "The Formative Stages of *Beowulf* Textual Scholarship: Part II." *ASE* 12 (1983): 239-275.

Continues Kelly [1390] by providing a comprehensive list of "all conjectures and emendations accepted in at least one edition of *Beowulf* from 1950 onwards. It thus adds to part I the readings which have been proposed since 1857. The list is intended as a survey only. No context is given for readings proposed by 1857, since that was done in part I, at pp. 253-74. For readings proposed since 1857 the immediate context is given where necessary, but it is assumed that an edition of *Beowulf* will be used in conjunction with the list" (239). Kelly provides the statistical results derived from these lists on pages 270-72 as well as an appendix containing a list of "conjectures or emendations which were proposed by 1857 but which have not been accepted by any editor from 1950 onwards although a majority of such editors believe that there have been scribal errors or omissions at the places concerned"

(273). Another appendix lists addenda and corrigenda to part I.

1392 Kendall, Calvin B. "The Metrical Grammar of *Beowulf*: Displacement." *Speculum* 58 (1983): 1-30.

Undertakes a detailed study of metrical "displacement" in *Beowulf* (when certain word classes are moved from "normal" position to a more stressed position), concluding that the rapidity of oral composition caused the *Beowulf*-poet to mark each half-line as initial (I), noninitial (II), or unrestricted (III) in his metrical grammar. "So long as he began with an initial or unrestricted half-line and subsequently used only noninitial, unrestricted, or displaceable (Ib) half-lines until he concluded his verse clause, he would necessarily conform to the rules of the metrical grammar" (26). This analysis confirms Kuhn's laws, and establishes a principle of linear integrity: "If the half-line behaved in different ways in different contexts it would have been of no use under the conditions of oral composition. Therefore it is possible to formulate a principle of linear integrity: the metrical-grammatical shape of the half-line is invariable. Wherever the half-line appears and however it is used it will have the same internal metrical and grammatical properties" (26).

1393 Kiernan, Kevin S. "Thorkelin's Trip to Great Britain and Ireland, 1786-1791." *The Library* 6th ser., 5 (1983): 1-21.

A study of Grímur Jónsson Thorkelin's research activities, concluding that "All combined, the evidence on Thorkelin's trip to Great Britain and Ireland between 1786 and 1791 strongly suggests that Thorkelin copied the *Beowulf* MS sometime between 1788 and 1791. While he may well have done basic research at the British Museum prior to 1788, the extant records rather suggest that he had not yet made any transcripts" (20). Appears in expanded form in Kiernan [1566].

1394 Koike, Kazuo. "Armour in *Beowulf*." *Obirin Studies in English Language and Literature* 32 (1983): 169-91. In Japanese.

Considers Old English synonyms or synonymous expressions for "armor" in *Beowulf*. Eight simple words, thirty compounds, and two genitive collocations signifying such defensive items as "armor," "byrnie," and "coat of mail" are considered from the viewpoint of lexical and contextual meaning. (KK)

1395 Larsen, Elizabeth. "The Creative Act: An Analysis of Systems in *Grendel*." In *John Gardner: True Art, Moral Art*. Ed. Beatrice Mendez-Egle. Edinburg, TX: Pan American U, School of Humanities, 1983. Pp. 36-51.

Analyzes John Gardner's transformation of the *Beowulf* story in his 1971 novel *Grendel* [S793].

1396 Luecke, Jane-Marie. "*Wulf* and *Eadwacer*: Hints for Reading from *Beowulf* and Anthropology." In *The Old English Elegies: New Essays in Criticism and Research*. Ed. Martin Green. Rutherford, NJ: Fairleigh Dickinson UP: 1983. Pp. 190-203.

Suggests that *Beowulf* may show traces of an earlier matrilineal culture among the Germanic peoples and that such traces can suggest new ways of interpreting the enigmatic lyric, "Wulf and Eadwacer." Luecke points out that though the culture of the Danes is more fully patriarchal, the social arrangements of the Geats "seem less advanced toward patriarchy" (192) and resemble in several details matrilocal or matriclan societies studied by modern anthropologists. Particularly associated with matrilocal or matriclan societies are a) the importance of the sister's brother, b) the relative instability of marriage ties, and c) the prevalence of exogamy (where a woman marries outside of her clan). Several of these features are traceable in *Beowulf*, especially in the story of Hildeburh. Since the oral tradition is conservative, "even if Anglo-Saxon society was thoroughly patriarchal in practice by the time *Beowulf* was written down, the poem could still reflect earlier cultural values" (194).
Reviews of Green: S.A.J. Bradley, *MLR* 82 (1987): 697-98; H. Sauer, *BGDSL* (Tübingen) 110 (1988): 303-06.

1397 Miller, William Ian. "Choosing the Avenger: Some Aspects of the Bloodfeud in Medieval England and Iceland." *Law and History Review* 1 (1983): 159-203.

Finds evidence of a ceremony connected with the bloodfeud—a ceremony which legally charges one of its participants to pursue vengeance—and connects episodes in *Beowulf* and in a number of Icelandic sagas to this ceremony.

In a general discussion of blood-feud in Germanic culture, Miller argues that it often kept the peace in the absence of a centralized authority but that conflicting loyalties and complex kinship patterns often made the obligation to take vengeance an ambiguous one. A "charging" ceremony was one way of resolving this ambiguity. In *Beowulf*, the ceremony involves swords, and Miller identifies two episodes in which a "charging" occurs: in the Finnsburh episode, when Hunlafing places a sword (probably belonging to the slain Hnæf) into the lap of Hengest. Hengest does not refuse the *woroldrædenne* 'universal law' (l. 1142b) to avenge one's lord—here Miller retains the manuscript reading. Hunlafing, Miller believes, is joined by his uncles Guðlaf and Oslaf, "to play the grievant's role in the ceremony" (198). As in the Icelandic analogues, the ceremony is used "to clarify conflicting obligations" (199) which Hengest has to his kin and to the dishonorable *āð* 'oath' he swore Finn. The second charging ceremony is more subtly drawn. Weohstan, Wiglaf's father, kills Eanmund and returns his armor and sword to Eanmund's uncle Onela. In presenting the sword to Onela, Weohstan must have been aware of the conflicting loyalties which Onela has as Eanmund's enemy but also his uncle. Miller argues that Onela accepts the sword but "forgives" the feud (l. 2616b) by returning the sword to Weohstan in a public gesture (thus explaining how the sword comes into Wiglaf's hands). "What could be neater than to ask Onela to reconfirm their prior understanding by 1) enacting the ceremony that obliges Onela to pursue the feud so that 2) the lord can formally and publicly release his claim against his ideal retainer" (202). Though the Icelandic and English ceremonies have a similar function, their symbolism is different. Also discusses the practices of wergild and heriot.

1398 Mitchell, Bruce. "A Note on Negative Sentences in *Beowulf*." *Poetica* (Tokyo) 15-16 (1983): 9-12.

Taking Miyabe [S927] as a point of departure, observes that in Old English poetry there is a reluctance to multiply negatives—a reluctance not found in prose—and thus the emendation proposed for line 949b, where *ænigre* is emended to *nænigre* to supply alliteration, is suspect. Mitchell points out that *næfre* 'never' stands without *ne* in seven out of the eight occurrences in *Beowulf*, while *ænig* 'any' occurs in twenty-four negative clauses, carrying the alliteration in eighteen. *Nænig* does occur eight times with other negation, but these are either in subordinate clauses or in clauses not negated by *ne*. Thus, "there is no syntactical parallel in *Beowulf* to support the emendation of *ǣnigre* to *nǣnigre* (or some other form of *nǣnig*)" though such a construction would be quite acceptable in prose and would supply the missing alliteration (12).

1399 Niles, John D. *'Beowulf': The Poem and Its Tradition.* Cambridge: Harvard UP, 1983. Pp. vi + 310; ill.

A book-length study of the poem divided into three sections: context (chapters one through four), style and structure (chapters five through eight), and interpretation (chapters nine through fourteen).

Chapter one, "The Marvelous," examines approaches to the monsters and the marvelous, agreeing with Tolkien [S130] that the monsters are at the center of the poem and stressing the poet's use of ambiguity in portraying them. Niles rejects several attempts to explain away the marvelous which a) interpret Beowulf's heroic feats in realistic terms (Earl [1118] and Robinson [S932]), b) see the monsters as fairy-tale elements (Panzer [S36]), or c) interpret the monsters allegorically. Rather, "the poet takes pains to account realistically for their origins in the world in which we ourselves live" (12). Thus, Grendel is both a demon and a human. "The poet leaves us in doubt by calling him both a man (*wer*, 105a) and a spirit or demon (*gǣst*, 86a and 102a). We are left free to choose" (8). Not only is Grendel ambiguously human or monstrous, but the mere itself is both a physical mere and perhaps also the entrance to hell.

Chapter two, "The Art of the Germanic Scop," offers "a brief sketch of the native development of Old English poetry" (50). Niles re-emphasizes the Germanic background of *Beowulf*'s poetics, reminding us that we cannot assume the author to have been a learned ecclesiastic. Includes discussions of the function of poetry in Germanic society (to assign praise or blame), memory and memorization in oral poetry, meter and formula, apposition, metaphoric diction, and poetic compounds. Niles distinguishes between the lay (of proto-Germanic origin) and the epic (an Anglo-Saxon development): the first is a short episode, the latter a more elaborate narrative, "ample, involuted, and richly allusive and digressive" (63). *Beowulf* is a part of this native Anglo-Saxon epic tradition, which also includes the fragmentary *Waldere*.

Chapter three, "Latin Christian Letters," rejects direct influence of patristic writings on *Beowulf*, instead tracing the poet's Christian learning to the vernacular Christian writings fostered by Alfred's educational reform. Similarly, Niles rejects the direct influence of Latin epics like the *Thebaid* and the *Aeneid*: arguing that almost all the proposed parallels are vague and that *Beowulf* has none of the epic machinery of classical epics. Niles also rejects the direct influence of Christian Latin writers like Lactantius, Prudentius, Boethius, Gregory, Augustine, Bede, and Alcuin. "The few possible instances of direct influence are counterbalanced by many examples of critics' strained efforts to pursue comparisons that prove weightless" (91). The Cain materials and the "Christian excursus" (ll. 183b-88), where the poet condemns the Danes' return to pagan sacrifice, can be more easily traced to vernacular sources in the saints' lives and homilies. "The poet was a pious author, not a zealot, who was able to articulate some of the basic concepts of Christianity in a work whose primary appeal was secular rather than religious" (92).

Chapter four, "The Danes and the Date," argues that the poem can best be dated to the period after the initial Danish raids (approximately the second quarter of the tenth century), when "Englishmen and Norsemen were at peace and viewed one another with mutual respect" (116). Niles rejects several methods of linguistic dating, most of which have been used to suggest an early date for the poem, as well as Whitelock's *terminus ad quem* [S231] of the Viking invasions. The poet's ambiguous attitude toward the Danes, both lauding and undercutting their prowess, "reflects interests and attitudes that would have been prevalent among aristocratic Englishmen of the early or middle years of the tenth century, but not earlier" (111). Modifying Schücking's proposal [S56], Niles suggests that "the poem was composed for an English patron and, in all probability, for a mixed Anglo-Scandinavian audience. Such a mixed audience would have been the norm in practically any great court held during the reign of Athelstan or his successors" (112). Niles places the origin of the poem and perhaps other Old English secular literature in the "secular" monasteries of the Danelaw before the Benedictine reform.

Chapter five, "Formula and Formulaic System," outlines the functioning of formula systems which the *Beowulf*-poet inherited from the oral poets of the Germanic tradition. While Parry saw thrift as the key principle of the Homeric formulaic style (with fixed formulas appearing in certain metrical environments), Niles points out that variation is at the center of Old English verse. The *Beowulf*-poet does not rely on fixed formulas or tags but works with flexible formulaic systems which allow a variety of substitutions and interlocking patterns. Modifying the approach of Magoun [S265], who looks for fixed formulas in the first twenty-five lines of the poem, Niles re-examines these same lines for evidence of *flexible* formulaic systems, providing an appendix which lists other representatives of the system and provides diagrams of their internal structure. On the basis of this and a larger study of the first five hundred lines, Niles concludes that "[c]lose to two out of three verses in the poem are members of an identifiable formulaic system" (128).

Chapter six, "Compound Diction," examines compounds in *Beowulf* as part of a flexible formulaic system developed by Germanic poets. Again, Parry's principle of thrift fails to account for the function of compounds in Germanic verse. In Homer, formulas (epithets for Achilles, for example) are used with considerable thrift, with few or no variants for each metrical environment. In *Beowulf*, by contrast, epithets for Hrothgar proliferate, suggesting that formulas in Old English operate on the principle of variety. The compound, as the Germanic singers developed it, became the heart of the *Beowulf*-poet's verse-making techniques. Seeing compounds in this way—as part of an established formulaic system—implies that poets, disregarding thematic overtones, sometimes used compounds in large part for their utility in a certain metrical environment and that studies which claim to find sophisticated patterns of meaning in substituting compounds thus may be misguided. After comparing *Beowulf*'s style to that of the *Meters of Boethius*—countering Benson [S537]—Niles concludes that the *Beowulf*-poet took part in the living system of formulaic verse-making while the translator of Boethius relies on fixed formulaic tags.

Chapter seven, "Ring Composition," examines the three main episodes of the poem—Beowulf's fights with Grendel (ll. 702b-836), Grendel's mother (ll. 1279-1802a), and the firedrake (ll. 2200-3136), finding that they are composed in ring-like patterns often found in oral narrative poetry. Ring composition accounts for many structures in the poem from verbal echoes (envelope patterns) to the shape of episodes and even of the entire poem. Niles sees the overall design of the poem fitting into a ring pattern, with the fight with Grendel's mother at the center: "(A) introduction, (B) fight with Grendel, (C) celebrations, (D) fight with Grendel's mother, (C) celebrations, (B) fight with dragon, (A) close" (158). Such patterning may have been a mnemonic device useful to an oral poet. He also explores the aesthetic implications of such a structure: joy and sorrow, success and failure, creation and dissolution are knitted together in ring patterns, creating a mood which some find fatalistic, but which Niles sees as "an innate part of the heroic view of life" (162).

Chapter eight, "Barbaric Style," attempts to describe some of the conventions of Old English verse and the aesthetic principles upon which they operate. The poem's style is often abstract, non-naturalistic, and non-representational, unlike the styles associated with classical literature. Such a style is "barbaric," to borrow the non-pejorative term art historians use to describe the abstract designs of Germanic and Celtic tribes. Niles identifies and exemplifies several conventions which tend to confuse or irritate readers expecting a realistic or naturalistic narrative: "the occasional use of a word or phrase without regard to its narrative context; an occasional disregard for the ordinary relations of time and space; a lack of psychological depth in the characterization of lesser figures, and the consistent subordination of such figures to the principle of contrast; the relative independence of each scene from the others, and the consequent presence of narrative inconsistencies; and the introduction of motifs that lead nowhere" (175).

Chapter nine, "The Dimensions of Time," examines how the poem (as an epic) handles time differently than folk tale and the shorter heroic lays. The poem places the hero into "a complex net of temporal interdependencies" (179), ranging from the "mythic past (Creation, Cain and Abel, Flood), the legendary past ('timeless' heroes, such as Sigemund, Weland), historical past: narrative past (Hrethel, Ongentheow, and so on), narrative present (Beowulf's adventures), narrative future (fate of the Geats, and so on), the present of the poem's performance (real or imagined), the present of reading the text, mythic future (Doomsday)" (181). "Rather than compose events in accord with strict chronology, the poet allows them to unfold in a slow, considered growth, as a hero's responses to three separate threats are examined in the light of sacred history, profane history, and the constant values that transcend such distinctions" (195).

Chapter ten, "The Narrator's Voice," contends that in oral narrative, "[t]he narrator speaks with an impersonal voice that assumes some important experience shared within the group. His tone is rarely ironic or confessional, for he utters his words as a spokesman for all rather than as a person sharing private perceptions" (197-98). Such shared experience is often contained in the narrator's use of gnomes, which is more flexible and impersonal than that of individual characters, who use gnomes in a highly individualized way. For the most part, the narrator's assignment of praise or blame is straightforward, often in the form of superlative (best or worst), and is restricted "to matters pertaining to the proper behavior of a lord or thane" (203).

Chapter eleven, "The Listening Audience," admits that a satisfying reconstruction of the poem's original audience may not be possible, and explores instead "the more fruitful question of the nature of the audience *in* the poem" (206). The poet assumed a sophisticated knowledge of Germanic lore from his audience, as well as a less-detailed knowledge of Christian concepts: Cain and Abel, the Creation, the Flood, Doomsday, heaven and hell, and salvation. "The audience needs no more detailed religious knowledge than any layman of the time possessed" (207). The audiences within the poem—such as the Danes who witness Beowulf's first fight with Grendel—help to direct emotional reactions: "a complex interplay is established between the audience *in* the poem—the chorus, as it were—and the audience *of* the poem, which sometimes sees what the chorus sees and sometimes has superior knowledge" (212). Discusses several internal audiences in the poem.

Chapter twelve, "Reciprocity," suggests that the critical controversy over the "useless" treasure buried with Beowulf can be better understood in the context of Anglo-Saxon social institutions in which "material objects functioned as part of a complex system of exchange that was at the heart of the social order" (213). The principle governing such exchange is reciprocity: gifts secure loyal service. Reciprocity also governs the nature of feuding and its monetary settlement, *wergild*. When a lord fitted a thane with war gear (the institution of heriot), the thane was expected to provide military service in return. When the ten Geatish warriors abandon Beowulf and Wiglaf, they fail in their obligations to their lord and gift-giver and thus do not deserve the dragon's treasure. In turn, these treasures are buried with Beowulf as a sign of his glory: "They are Beowulf's price. In their refulgent splendor, they are the material equivalent to the life he sacrificed for his people" (222). Thus, the fate of the treasure is not a biting irony but remains true to the principle of reciprocity.

Rejecting Kaske's formulation of *sapientia et fortitudo* [S361 and S676] as too broad and Hume's idea of "threats to social order" [S962] as somewhat one-sided, Chapter thirteen, "The Controlling Theme," proposes that "The poem's controlling theme is *community*: its nature, its occasional breakdown, and the qualities that are necessary to maintain it" (226). If such an idea is accepted, the "digressive" structure of the poem "can be seen to have a certain rationale, for the digressions are always directed to an elucidation of the social context of the action and away from a simple narrative of 'what happens next'" (228). Further, "[s]uch a concept of the controlling theme . . . accounts fairly well for the way in which the three great fights that constitute the plot are narrated" (229). The non-narrative portions of the poem, particularly the elegiac sections, are also tied to the theme of community and its impending loss. "Throughout *Beowulf*, interest centers not on man as solitary hero but on people and what holds them together" (233).

Chapter fourteen, "The Fatal Contradiction," rejects readings, principally Leyerle [S550], that believe that the poem undercuts and criticizes its hero and that there is "a fatal contradiction at the core of heroic society," to use Leyerle's famous phrase. "In my own view, *Beowulf* expresses an essentially conservative impulse. First and foremost, it praises a life lived in accord with ideals that help perpetuate the best features of the kind of society it depicts. The ideals deserve the name 'heroic,' but they are of Christian and well-nigh universal significance as well" (236). Niles goes on to answer three key questions in the negative: 1) Is Beowulf's decision to fight the dragon imprudent? 2) Should the hero have accepted help? and 3) Does the hero act for his own glory, out of pride? He shows that the section of Wiglaf's speech often construed as criticism of the hero (ll. 3077-84a), does not support this meaning linguistically or dramatically. The Geats' own cowardice, not Beowulf's arrogant pride brings about the destruction of the Geatish nation.

In an afterword, "The Excellence of *Beowulf*," Niles argues that *Beowulf* is superior, as a poetic creation, to most other roughly contemporaneous works of Old English and Old Saxon origin: "Particularly when one imagines the poem in its primary context, as a performance shared among a singer and the members of a listening audience, its appeal is persuasive even over a gap of many centuries." (249). The poem and its hero are neither blood-thirsty nor pacifistic but combine the best of Christian and pagan ideals.

Reviews: *OEN* 19.1 (1984): 89; J.E. Milosh, Jr., *Cithara* 24.1 (1984): 73-74; D.C. Baker, *ELN* 23 (1985): 67-69; D.G. Calder, *MLQ* 45 (1985 for 1984): 191-93; T.D. Hill, *JEGP* 84 (1985): 540-43; H. Chickering, *Speculum* 61 (1986): 186-89; M.E. Goldsmith, *MÆ* 55 (1986): 266-67; S.B. Greenfield, *Comparative Literature* 38 (1986): 98-100; E.G. Stanley, *RES* 37 (1986): 70-73; S.A.J. Bradley, *MLR* 82 (1987): 697-98; B. Schik, *Anglia* 105 (1987): 178-81.

1400 Nobumori, Hiromitsu. "Observation on Noun Polysemes in *Beowulf.*" *Bulletin of the Fukuyama City Junior College for Women* 9 (1983): 1-8.

Not seen. *OEN* report: "surveys several examples of polysemantic nouns: *nīð, mǣrðu, ār, sǣl, weorc, duguð, mægen.* These are used both with abstract and with concrete senses; so, for example, *mǣrðu* can mean 'glory' and 'glorious deed'" (*OEN* 19.1 [1985]: 88).

1401 Ogilvy, Jack D.A., Donald C. Baker, with Illustrations by Keith Baker. *Reading 'Beowulf': An Introduction to the Poem, Its Background, and Its Style.* Norman: U of Oklahoma P, 1983. Pp. xvii + 221; ill.

A general introduction to and reading of the poem, including chapters on the manuscript, Germanic poetry, dating and authorship, the nature of Anglo-Saxon Christianity, relevant cultural backgrounds for the monsters as well as the comitatus group, the problems of versification, formula and formulaic style, and in a chapter entitled "Interpretations and Criticism of *Beowulf* in Our Own Time," a summary of the major interpretive approaches to the poem (stylistic studies, the role of Christian themes, and the oral-formulaic approach). Includes an extensive summary and analysis of the poem as well as a bibliography with brief annotations.

Reviews: *OEN* 18.1 (1984): 90; E.B. Irving, Jr., *Speculum* 60 (1985): 487; J. Roberts, *N&Q* 32 (1985): 387-88; T.A. Shippey, *ES* 66 (1985): 272-76; W. Obst, *Anglia* 104 (1986): 466-68.

1402 Pàroli, Teresa. "L'alternativa tra iniziazione e conversione nella cultura germanica medievale." [The Alternative between Initiation and Conversion in Medieval Germanic Culture]. In *Sigfrido nel nuovo mondo: Studi sulla narrativa d'iniziazione.* Ed. Paolo Cibibbo. Rome: Goliardica, 1983. Pp. 53-87.

Not seen.

1403 Puhvel, Martin. "The Ride around Beowulf's Barrow." *Folklore* 94 (1983): 108-112.

Examines the suggestion made by Klaeber [S81] that the depiction of Beowulf's funeral may be related to either

Jordanes' account of Attila's funeral or funerals in Homer and Virgil. Surveys many recent and ancient funeral rites which involve circumambulation of the grave by the mourners, concluding that "the parallelism in question between the funeral rites of Beowulf and Attila does not, on careful scrutiny, seem particularly close. The circumambulatory rite in *Beowulf* shows a strong enough affinity with popular rituals, such as the circling of the filled-in grave and the wailing and lamenting of mourners moving around the corpse, to preclude any need to assume influence from Jordanes—or other report of Attila's funeral—or, indeed, classical epic" (110).

1404 Riley, Samuel M. "A Reading of *Beowulf* 168-69." *In Geardagum* 5 (1983): 47-56.

Presents a new reading of the *gifstōl* crux (ll. 168-69) by examining the probable context for the troublesome word *metode*, 'measurer' (l. 169); the proposed translation runs, "he [Hrothgar] could not come near the gift-throne,/ the treasure, because of Fate; he knew not its favor" (52). Riley attempts to show that concepts applied to God, fate, and Grendel reveal a Christian poet revising an earlier oral work, often adapting pagan concepts to Christian meanings. "[L]ines 168 and 169 may be deliberately unaltered remnants from an earlier oral version, thus lending probability to *metode*'s meaning 'Measurer' (Fate) rather than 'Creator' (God)" (52). In other instances, ll. 178b-183a, for example, the Christian meaning of *metod* prevails, suggesting that the poet deliberately left the meaning of *metod* unaltered.

1405 Rudanko, Martti Juhani. *Towards Classifying Verbs and Adjectives Governing the Genitive in 'Beowulf'*. Publications of the Department of English and German, Series A, No. 6. Tampere, Finland: U of Tampere, 1983. Pp. v + 111.

Classifies verbs and adjectives governing the genitive into three categories: where noun phrases (NPs) governed by verbs or adjectives are 1) unambiguously in the genitive, 2) ambiguously genitive, and 3) unambiguously in a case other than the genitive (though they occur in the genitive elsewhere in the poem). Rudanko analyzes each class in some detail, dividing them into subcategories on the basis of the meaning of the verb and the semantic role of the NP and attempting to classify the ambiguous cases systematically. He concludes that "the majority of verbs and adjectives governing genitives in *Beowulf* do not govern any unambiguous nongenitives in *Beowulf*.... On the other hand, with verbs and adjectives that govern unambiguously nongenitival NPs in addition to genitival NPs in *Beowulf,* the incidence of the former is quite sizable" (102).

1406 Schrader, Richard J. *God's Handiwork: Images of Women in Early Germanic Literature.* Contributions in Women's Studies, No. 41. Westport, CT: Greenwood Press, 1983. Pp. x + 129.

In a larger survey of women in earlier Germanic literature, considers the women of *Beowulf* in a chapter on England, with ensuing chapters on Germany and Scandinavia. Schrader examines in turn the major scenes in which the principal women of the poem appear: Wealhtheow, Hildeburh, Grendel's mother, Freawaru, and the grieving woman at Beowulf's funeral, stressing their roles as peaceweavers (or in the case of Grendel's mother and the young Modthryth) their inversion of this ideal. Cycles of revenge generally thwart these women in their roles as peaceweavers. By their gift-giving and attention to proper ceremony, the ideal women try to hold together a fragile peace. Concerning Wealhtheow, for instance, "[o]ne senses that the poet is contrasting the 'correctness' of her postures with a larger reality that makes her postures inadequate" (39). Hygd, similarly, "suffers from the dead-end heroism of her husband" (43). Schrader derives the stereotyped roles for these women from the models of Eve and Mary.

1407 _____. "Sacred Groves, Marvelous Waters, and Grendel's Abode." *Florilegium* 5 (1983): 76-84.

Identifies several parallels to details of Grendel's mere (ll. 837-56, 1345-76, and 1408-36) in classical and medieval Latin literature, concluding that the classical topos of the sacred grove, not Germanic tradition (such as the analogue in the *Grettis saga*), underlies the account in *Beowulf.* Schrader reviews the topoi of the sacred grove in Virgil, Lucan, Claudian, Silius, Statius, Tacitus, Isidore of Seville, and the *Visio Pauli.* An educated Anglo-Saxon poet would have recognized such groves as the site of ancient pagan worship, and "the haunted grove and mere in *Beowulf,* rich in literary, historical, and religious overtones, would have had many hellish associations" (81).

1408 Stanley, Eric G. "The Continental Contribution to the Study of Anglo-Saxon Writings up to and Including That of the Grimms." In *Towards a History of English Studies in Europe*. Augsburger Schriften, 21. Augsburg: U Augsburg, 1983. Pp. 9-39.

Reviews Wilhelm and Jacob Grimm's work on Anglo-Saxon texts, documenting their knowledge of particular texts and editions and pointing out that they used *Beowulf* most often to "illustrate Germanic story, customs or ways of expression" (19). In general, Stanley concludes that "Wilhelm used Anglo-Saxon evidence but did not advance the understanding of Anglo-Saxon writings," while "Jacob Grimm's use of Anglo-Saxon evidence was more extensive and more profound, and his contributions to the subject are similarly more extensive and profound" (23). Includes a bibliography of early continental scholarship on Anglo-Saxon topics.

1409 Talbot, Annelise. "Sigemund the Dragon-Slayer." *Folklore* 94 (1983): 153-162.

Suggests that the story of Sigemund, as related in ll. 875-97, may be based on authentic historical materials. After reviewing his appearance in other Germanic sources like the *Niebelungenlied*, *Völsunga saga*, and a variety of Norse sources as well as Gregory of Tour's *History of the Franks*, Talbot maps out a number of similarities between the account of Sigemund in *Beowulf* and Tacitus' description (in the *Histories*) of the Batvian king Civilis, who led a raid against the Romans in 69 A.D. "Although one cannot claim to prove the identity of Civilis with Sigemund, there are a surprising number of features in his history which tally with the description of the deeds of Sigemund in *Beowulf*" (160).

1410 Taylor, Paul Beekman. "Searoniðas: Old Norse Magic and Old English Verse." *SP* 80 (1983): 109-125.

Studying the etymologies of the words *searo* 'artifice' and *nīð* 'enmity' as well as compounds containing them, suggests that the word *seoronīðas*, unique to *Beowulf* (ll. 582a, 1200b, 2738a, 3067a), may refer to a Germanic tradition about "a myth of a magically endowed treasure, used as a fertility token, and associated with the concept of *searo*" (120), and that *searonið* and other *searo* compounds carry "an aura of magic" (123). Taylor argues that the *Beowulf* poet derived the idea from legends about Eormenric and his conflict with Hama over the Brosing necklace (retold in ll. 1192-1201), a story partly reflected in the Old Norse *Hamðismál*, in which the brother of Hama (ON Hamðir) appears as *Sörli*, a name related etymologically to the OE word *searo*, and who may (in legends now lost) have carried the necklace to the court of Eormenric (ON Jörmunrek). Some relatives of the words *searo* and *nīð* designate sexual union, reinforcing the connection to the Brosing necklace, a symbol of fertility. "*Searonīð* is a malice which spoils nature and art alike. It is accomplished magic, achieved sorcery. If *searo* alone is a binding power or craft, *searonīð* is an undoing, an unraveling of life threads which shifts creative spirit away from nature and kinship towards spoil and death" (124). Taylor reviews a number of cognates and native relatives of the words *searo* and *nīð*.

1411 Thundy, Zacharias P. "*Beowulf*: Geats, Jutes, and Asiatic Huns." *Littcrit* 9 (1983): 1-8.

Believes that the Geats were originally Scythians (Goths and Huns) who came to Europe from Asia and became Germanized and that this fact helps to explain certain similarities between Germanic customs and beliefs and those of the Jats (descendants of the Scythian Goths/Geats) in India. Thundy advances the story of Vidushaka (who cuts off the arm of a marauding ogre) as a possible analogue to the story of Beowulf and argues that "we must not necessarily rule out a common Getic/Scythian source for the Indian story and *Beowulf*" (7). He traces a number of parallels between the two stories and mentions parallels between events in *Beowulf* and those surrounding the Asiatic Huns, particularly Attila. Also includes a discussion of the tribal names *goti* (Goths), *iuti* (Jutes), *geti*, and *geatas*—implying that these different forms are dialectical variations of the same name.

1412 ———. "*Beowulf*: Meaning, Method, and Monsters." *Greyfriar: Siena Studies in Literature* 24 (1983): 5-34.

Finds that the main subject of *Beowulf* is Germania, "its rise, decline, and possible fall" (19), in which the monsters represent adversaries that the Germanic peoples had to face: Imperial Rome, represented by Grendel (the Roman legions) and his mother (Rome itself), and Celtic peoples, represented by the dragon. Thundy surveys Roman attitudes about the Germanic peoples. The Danes, under attack from Grendel, suffer three weaknesses also common to the Germanic peoples under attack from Rome: a) they used the wrong weapons; b) they suffered from a life-style of affluence and godlessness; c) they were isolated from other Germanic tribes and thus, alone, were vulnerable. "As the poet extols the virtue of unity or *comitatus*, he condemns the vice of disunity prevalent among the Germanic tribes. The purpose of many of the digressions in the poem is to throw into full relief the intertribal blood-feuds among the Germanic nations" (22). The dragon "represents British power in general the Welsh in particular," resembling as it does the red dragon of Wales (30). As such, the dragon represents an indigenous Welsh threat to Anglo-Saxon government. The ending of the poem, with Beowulf's death, is "a tragic chapter from which lessons have to be learned" (33) about how the Germanic Anglo-Saxons should deal with future threats from abroad. Includes the suggestion that the name *Wealhþēow* means 'Welsh princess or goddess.'

1413   Tripp, Raymond P., Jr. "Like It or Lump It: Thematic Remarks toward an Accurate Translation of *Beowulf*." *In Geardagum* 5 (1983): 13-28.

Believes that an understanding of word play, based not only on coincidence of sound pattern but also on historic semantic developments, is crucial for a sensitive translation of *Beowulf*, illustrating these points with a discussion of ll. 733b-734a. "Word play, of many varieties, is triggered, not only by similar sounds, but also by apprehension of undifferentiated root meanings. The Old English poet can pun on *hell*, 'hell,' and *heall*, 'hall,' not only because the central phonemes have become allophones, so that each word evokes the other, but also because both words in fact derive from the same root **kel*, 'to conceal, cover'" (15). These developments are not just the invention of modern philology but are part of the collective, poetic memory which motivated them. Tripp goes on to note the multiple meanings of key words in ll. 733b-734a and to suggest a number of puns on them, providing the following translation: "within him [Grendel] swelled an ugly hope/ Of lumping down a lively fill of food" (20). The translation depends on the punning associations of three key words: *wēn* 'hope' (punning on words for 'struggle,' 'joy,' and a 'swelling or tumor') *ālumpen* 'to befall' (on words for 'lump or swelling'), and *wistfylle* 'fill of food' (on words for 'life' and 'cruel or foul').

1414 _____. *More About the Fight with the Dragon: 'Beowulf' 2208b-3182, Commentary, Edition and Translation.* New York: UP of America, 1983. Pp. x + 480.

Edits, translates, and provides an extensive commentary for lines 2208b-3182 (part two of the poem), insisting that emendation be held to an absolute minimum and revising radically a number of traditional critical and editorial assumptions. Tripp points out that *Beowulf* scholars have applied emendation to the text as a way of rationalizing their interpretative difficulties: editors have emended "Instead of checking to see if the supposed contradictions [requiring emendation] have been created out of misreading—or even a refusal to read" (7). Tripp asserts that even damaged portions of the text like those on folios 179r and 179v can be read and interpreted if one pays strict attention to what can be seen and applies good literary sense to it. The commentary in the nine chapters that follow discusses textual and literary questions in detail. Tripp summarizes his main conclusions: "If we restore the poet's language and let it speak for itself, an entirely different story emerges. Then there is no thief, no *animal* dragon, and no last survivor. These all return to their original identity in the form of a single evil king, most likely Heremod himself, who became a dragon and later, for reasons of hateful greed, like Grendel before him, attacks a good king. If we thus restore the poet's language, there is also no ancient curse, but in its place a contemporary prohibition placed by the Geats themselves upon any further abuse of treasures as a means to survive against God's will. The poet's language even allows a waterfall to break from the mountainside to supply a key link to Scandinavian analogues. Beowulf too emerges as the ideal king he really is, and once and for all the picture of a prideful primitive vanishes. Such are but a few of the numerous 'subtractive rectifications' the poet's language allows" (ix). Includes textual notes, a bibliography, and an index.

Reviews: *OEN* 18.1 (1984): 90; D.G. Calder, *Speculum* 60 (1985): 755-56; H. Schabram, *Anglia* 103 (1985): 445-52; R.H. Bremmer, Jr., *ES* 67 (1986): 364-66; H. Ushigaki, *Poetica* (Tokyo) 25-26 (1987): 193-200.

1415 Waterhouse, Ruth, and John Stephens. "The Backward Look: Retrospectivity in Medieval Literature." *Southern Review* 16 (1983): 356-373.

Identifies "retrospectivity"—how great poets "force us to reassess what we already know in the light of new information" (357)—as a device used particularly by medieval writers, the *Beowulf*-poet among them. Waterhouse and Stephens identify and discuss three types of retrospectivity: the simple type ("in which unexpected information revealed at the end of a work demands a radical shift in our broad interpretation of the whole"), complex (in which we may be forced to re-consider a minor element as major), and cumulative ("in which the methods of small scale retrospectivity are extended over the whole work") (360). *Beowulf* shows cumulative retrospectivity especially in the depiction of Unferth, where our first negative impressions are modified by later positive ones without necessarily being "resolved into a state of unity, but are rather left to jostle with one another and leave us in a state of uncertainty" (369). Similarly, the two re-tellings of Beowulf's fight with Grendel's mother do not allow us to reconstruct the narrative events more accurately. The original listening audience "heard each narration at its given place and in its given context, so that each would have had some modifying effect on the previous one and would add new details which might not cohere with previous ones" (369). The authors also discuss retrospectivity in *Troilus and Criseyde*, the *Canterbury Tales*, *Gawain and the Green Knight*, the *Confessio Amantis*, and Shakespeare's *Antony and Cleopatra*.

1416 Webber, Philip E. "Preliterate Formulaic Patterns Suggested by Old English *Earfoðe*." *Michigan Germanic Studies* 9 (1983): 109-112.

In an article on the development of the word *earfoðe* 'hardship' in Old English poetic formulas, discusses briefly five half-lines in *Beowulf* (ll. 463b, 623b, 783b, 1584b, and 2779b) which seem at first glance to be very rare Sievers' type E verses with a half-lift on a short syllable, a structure which seems to operate in a number of *earfoðe* formulas. "Upon closer examination, however, we note that in four of these instances the half-lift falls on the second element in a nominal compound.... The remaining example (1584b) involves secondary stress on the derivation suffix *-līc-*, a syllable whose vowel is frequently long in Old English" (109-10).

1417 Wellman, Don. "So for then also the Dragon: A Working of the Funeral Passages from the Old English *Beowulf*." In *Translations: Experiments in Reading*. Ed. Don Wellman. Cambridge, MA: O.Ars, 1983. Pp. 57-59.

Translates lines 3038-3182 into modern English free verse. Lines 3137-48: "Then for him the gates people prepared a ritual pile on the earth/ no small one/ adorned with helmets shields gleaming mail as he wished then they laid the famous prince in the middle bewailing the man the loved lord/ warriors began then to waken an intense funeral fire in the barrow/ woodsmoke rose swart over the flames/ soughing fire twisted in weeping/ the whirling wind abated/ until it had crushed the bonehouse/ hot in the heart."

1418 Whallon, William. "When in *Beowulf* is beer drunk, or mead, when ale or wine?" In *Inconsistencies: Studies in the New Testament, the 'Inferno,' 'Othello,' and 'Beowulf'*. Totowa, NJ: Biblio, 1983. Pp. 82-97.

Surveys the use of the words for beer, ale, mead, and wine in *Beowulf* (43 occurrences of simplexes and compounds based on *bēor*, *ealu*, *meodo*, and *wīn*) and concludes that the poet uses them interchangeably for the sake of achieving alliteration, though at times they retain their specific meaning. Whallon notes a similar phenomenon in the Homeric poems (in the metrical uses of *woinos* 'wine' and *methu* 'sweet drink') and goes on to discuss the metrical constraints of Old English, Homeric Greek, and Old Testament Hebrew verse. Homeric formulae tend to be very specific and unchanging whereas those in Old English are generic and variable. For this reason, he doubts that verbal echoes play a great part in the meaning of the poem, since the formulas are generic and traditional.
Reviews: J. Simpson, *N&Q* 31 (1984): 413-15; A. Crépin, *EA* 38 (1985): 73; R. Gleissner, *Literaturwissenschaftliches Jahrbuch* 26 (1985): 394-96.

1419 Wilmont, Barry. *'Bjowulf': Et heltedigt fra Danmarks sagntid*. [Beowulf: A Heroic Poem from Denmark's Legendary Period]. Copenhagen: Nordiske Landes Bogforlag, 1983.

A translation of *Beowulf* into Danish. Not seen.

1984

1420 Andersson, Theodore M. "The Thief in *Beowulf*." *Speculum* 59 (1984): 493-508.

Reviews Germanic lore concerning theft and thieves in order to illuminate the thief episode in *Beowulf* and proposes a new reconstruction of line 2223b, in which the thief's situation is described. "The key problem in all of this is the reading of 'þ(. . .)' in v. 2223b. The competing proposals are 'þ(egn)' [warrior] and 'þ(ēow),' [servant] one implying high status and the other low. But a third conjecture is possible, namely 'þ(ēof)' [thief]" (495). The line, in context, can then be translated as follows: "the thief of some object fled the hostile blows of the children of men." Andersson points out that "The advantage of this reading is that it explains why the individual is an outcast and must flee the 'hateful blows' of his people; he is already a known thief and seizes the dragon's cup in order to make good a previous theft" (495). He then turns to Old Norse literature for parallels to the situation of the thief in *Beowulf*. He begins with a look at the Icelandic lawbook *Grágás*, which distinguishes between open robbery (seizure) and secret stealing (theft). The sagas show that seizure or open robbery is not stigmatized but that to accuse a man of theft (concealed stealing) was a grave insult. Andersson reviews scenes in several sagas (*Egils saga, Heiðarvíga saga, Laxdoela saga, Eyrbyggja saga, Grettis saga, Fóstbroeðra saga, Vatnsdoela saga, Brennu-Njáls saga*), concluding that the thief was characteristically lowborn, often a foreigner or otherwise estranged from the community. Theft was not infrequently connected with sorcery, another crime regarded as particularly contemptible. The thief in *Beowulf*, like the thieves in the sagas, is lowborn, defective (*synbysig* 'guilty,' l. 2226a), and conceals his theft. Nevertheless, Andersson points out the ways in which he is not like the thieves of the sagas: he is a figure of pathos, an unwilling thief who "longs for reintegration" into society (507). The thief's appearance may herald "some slippage toward the end of Beowulf's fifty-year rule" (507).

1421 Atkinson, Stephen C. B. "Beowulf and the Grendel-Kin: Thane, Avenger, King." *Publications of the Missouri Philological Association* 9 (1984): 58-66.

Sees the monsters as distorted parodies of the social roles which Beowulf is called upon to play—Grendel as thane and

Grendel's mother as avenger. Grendel, as a perverted thane, rules (not follows), remains solitary (not within the community of the hall), and goes without a lord, feasting by himself, an exile. The story of Cain explains Grendel the thane's basic relationship to his lord. Thus, he fails as both a human thane and as God's thane, helping to explain the notorious *gifstol* crux (ll. 168-69), where the throne is both Hrothgar's and God's. Grendel's mother, on the other hand, seems to represent unalloyed revenge. "The perversion of her revenge ... is due less to her motive than her nature: it is not that she avenges the death of her only son, but that the killing of Æschere continues her race's feud with mankind and with the Creator" (62). Digressions show that the duty of revenge imposes new responsibilities on the avenger, responsibilities which Beowulf accepts, drawing him more thoroughly into a social and political sphere, and giving him a confidence and wisdom which is revealed in his report to Hygelac. "Beowulf emerges as a heroic exemplar but also as a figure drawn increasingly into demanding social responsibilities and complex political situations with which no degree of personal heroism, no strength of hand or will, can ultimately deal" (61). Continued in Atkinson [1527].

1422 Bessinger, Jess B., Jr., and Robert F. Yeager, eds. *Approaches to Teaching 'Beowulf'*. New York: Modern Language Association, 1984. Pp. xvii + 214.

A volume covering many aspects of the teaching of *Beowulf*, including a number of short articles by a variety of contributors. In part one, "Materials," Bessinger and Yeager discuss the editions of the poem, audio-visual resources, modern adaptations, as well as the possible contents of the instructor's library (listing useful reference works, background studies, critical and stylistic studies, and manuscript studies and facsimiles). Also included is Douglas D. Short's survey of prose and verse translations.

The bulk of the volume is devoted to part two, "Approaches." Joseph F. Tuso discusses the results of an international survey on the teaching of *Beowulf*. Howell D. Chickering, Elizabeth Greene, George Clark, Paul Beekman Taylor, and Robert F. Yeager present methods of teaching *Beowulf* in Old English to undergraduates, while Elaine Tuttle Hansen, Bernice W. Kliman, Edward J. Rielly, and Diana M. DeLuca discuss ways to teach the poem in translation to the same audience. Other contributors offer approaches to teaching the poem in Old English to mixed undergraduate and graduate classes as well as to graduate students (Michael D. Cherniss, Mary Elizabeth Meek, Alain Renoir, Victor L. Strite, Stanley J. Kahrl, John C. McGalliard, Marijane Osborn, and Harry Jay Solo). A section entitled "Teaching the Backgrounds" includes three more extended essays. Fred C. Robinson's "History, Religion, and Culture" outlines historical elements in the poem's action, the relation between Christian and pagan ideals, and the social features of the text (including concepts of gift-giving and fate) as well as the relevance of Germanic, Latin, and Irish analogues. Constance B. Hieatt's "Parallels, Useful Analogues, and Elusive Sources" surveys Old English, Norse, Latin, and folkloristic analogues, while John Miles Foley's "*Beowulf*: Oral Tradition Behind the Manuscript" argues for the importance of oral composition in *Beowulf*, covering such topics as the *scop*, oral traditional theory, the formula, type scenes, and the pedagogical implications of oral traditional theory.

The final section, "Special Approaches," contains the following essays: "The New Rhetoric: Writing as an Instrument for Teaching *Beowulf*" (Myra Berman), "Visual Materials for Teaching *Beowulf*" (Donald K. Fry), "Women in *Beowulf*" (Alexandra Hennessey Olsen), "Teaching *Beowulf* as Performance" (John D. Niles), "Forgeries and Facsimiles: Paleography without Tears" (Jess B. Bessinger, Jr.), "The Words" (Stephen A. Barney), and "Old English Prosody" (Thomas Cable). Also included is a list of survey participants along with a bibliography, index, and discography.

Reviews: *OEN* 19.1 (1985): 82-83; P.J. Lucas, *N&Q* 33 (1986): 94. See also Frantzen [1738].

1423 Bethel, Patricia. "On the Combination of A-Types into Lines in *Beowulf*." *N&Q* 31 (1984): 292-293.

Pursuing Bliss's observation [S353] that the *Beowulf* poet avoids putting two A-verses together in a single line, notes that when two such verses do occur, the poet avoids identical cadences and thus the proportion of rare subtypes increases, "dictated by the predominance of 1A1a-, 1A*1a-, and 2A1a-Types, accounting as these three do, for 2075 of the 2549 A-Types of the poem" (293).

1424 Black, Vaughan, and Brian Bethune. "Beowulf and the Rites of Holy Week." *Scintilla* 1 (1984): 5-23.

Accepting Cabaniss's suggestion [S298] that Beowulf's descent into Grendel's mere reflects elements of the baptismal liturgy of Holy Saturday, goes on to argue that "[t]here are a number of liturgical ceremonies immediately preceding and following the baptismal ceremony, which find a parallel in events in *Beowulf* that precede and follow the fight with Grendel's mother" (6). Black and Bethune find a number of reflections of the liturgy of Holy Week in *Beowulf* and claim that they occur in the same order and often at the same time of day. Beowulf's descent into the mere (as a reflection of Baptism) takes place on Holy Saturday, placing his arrival in Heorot on Holy Thursday. The Lenten-like sadness in Heorot before Beowulf's arrival mirrors the sad *Tenebrae* service on Holy Thursday when candles were extinguished. The first feast after Beowulf's arrival parallels the celebration of the Lord's Supper. Next, the experiences of Beowulf during his first night recall Christ's sufferings in the Garden of Gethsemane, for Christ's disciples fall asleep in the same way that Beowulf's retainers do, and only after the struggle is over do they awake and attempt to rescue their leader: Simon Peter uses a sword in the same ineffectual way as Beowulf's men (ll. 794-805). Black and Bethune find in the joyous viewing of Grendel's arm a reflection of the Adoration of the Cross on Good Friday, where both the cross and the arm are trophies of victory. The arm, like the cross, is elevated (after Hrothgar's sermon). The Deposition of the Cross, where the crucifix was buried, is paralleled when Grendel's mother removes the arm from the hall. Similarly, the Burial of the Host (signifying Christ's absence at this hour) is reflected in Beowulf's absence from the hall at the same point. The mournful lamentations of Hrothgar and the Danes on the morning after Grendel's mother attacks mirror the *Tenebrae* service, when a *Miserere* chant began at Lauds (the dawn service). After the central baptismal imagery in the mere episode (sketched by Cabaniss), two further services are of interest: the *Elevatio* and the *Visitatio Sepulchri*: in Beowulf these events are paralleled by the viewing of Grendel's head (which substitutes for his arm) and the raising of the cruciform sword hilt. The *Visitatio Sepulchri*, in which the catechumens gaze upon and bless the clean water of the baptismal font, purified by Christ's victory, is echoed in *Beowulf* when the bloody waters of the mere are purified. In conclusion, "The preservation of the time scheme of the liturgy of the Easter cycle in the central portion of *Beowulf* should refute those who claim that the Christian allusions in the poem are mere later additions or that there are no elements from the New Testament in *Beowulf* (21).

1425 Caie, Graham D. *Notes on 'Beowulf'*. York Notes, 225. Harlow, Essex: Longman / York Press, 1984. Pp. 96.

A general introduction to and study guide for *Beowulf*. Caie's introduction includes discussions of the manuscript, other Old English manuscripts, the date and location of *Beowulf*, the Anglo-Saxons and their language, and a note on the text. The next section provides both general and detailed summaries, with several notes on Old English phrases and words. The commentary (part three) discusses Germanic society (the comitatus, the hall, revenge, reputation and glory, weird or fate), the major characters (Beowulf, Hrothgar, the female characters, the monsters, Wiglaf), as well as significant themes and episodes (the Swedish wars, Hrothgar's "sermon," the theme of gold and treasure, Sutton Hoo and *Beowulf*, funeral customs, and the "Finnsburh Fragment"). Part four, "Hints for Study," gives a general account of the prosody, diction, style, formulas, and structure of the poem, suggesting several essay questions and possible answers. The guide concludes with a brief annotated bibliography for further reading.
Reviews: *OEN* 20.1 (1986): 76.

1426 Clement, R.W. "Codicological Consideration in the *Beowulf* Manuscript." In *Proceedings of the Illinois Medieval Association, 1984*. Ed. Roberta Bux Bosse. Macomb, IL: Western Illinois U, 1984. Pp. 13-27.

Takes issue with Kiernan's collation of the Nowell Codex [1261], which assumes that *Beowulf* formed an originally separate codex and that *Judith* was not originally part of the codex, instead endorsing the collation as described by Kemp Malone [S499]: "In summary, the collation of the Nowell Codex is as Kemp Malone described it in his facsimile: 1^{10}, 2^6, $3-11^8$, $12-13^{10}$, 148. *Christopher, Marvels of the East, Alexander's Letter, Beowulf,* and *Judith* make up a single, unified, composite manuscript—the Nowell Codex" (25). Includes detailed discussions of Kiernan's proposed foliation.

1427 Damico, Helen. *Beowulf's Wealhtheow and the Valkyrie Tradition*. Madison: U of Wisconsin P, 1984. Pp. xiii + 270.

A study of Wealhtheow and her possible connections to the valkyrie-figures in Germanic literature. Chapter one, "Wealhtheow and Contextual Problems," undertakes a formal analysis of Wealhtheow's place in *Beowulf*, examining closely the 95 lines devoted to her (the two principal scenes, ll. 611-41, 1159b-1232a, as well as briefer references: 664-65a, 923b-24, 1649b-50, 2016b-19, 2172-76). Damico finds that the poet develops Wealhtheow as a major figure by staging two elaborate entrances for her and by employing techniques of antithesis and parallelism, formula, strategic repetition, complex syntax and metrics in the dialogue and narrative surrounding her appearance, and provocative structural relationships with other characters. "Within a single personage, then, one finds compressed traces of female character types peculiar to various aristocratic heroic epics: the queen-mother prophetess, the exemplary hostess, the queen politician, the erotic bride, the warrior-woman" (6). The depiction of Wealhtheow may, Damico suggests, derive from existing lays about the house of the Scyldings and suggests parallels between Wealhtheow and the valkyrie-brides Sigrun and Svava as well as Hrolf's mother-sister, Yrsa.

Chapter two, "Wealhtheow and the Heroic Tradition," sketches out a number of verbal and thematic similarities between Wealhtheow, the title Christian female warriors of *Elene, Judith*, and *Juliana*, the queen in *Maxims I*, and the valkyries of the northern tradition, the shining maidens of Odin. Damico goes on to identify several martial characteristics of Wealhtheow and the Anglo-Saxon warrior queens (Elene, Judith, and Juliana): they are described with words (like *gūð-cwēn* 'war queen' and *folc-cwēn*) mirroring those used of male warriors (*gūð-cyning* 'war king' and *folc-cyning*); they are bright and gold adorned (a characteristic associated with the armor and weapons of heroes); they are *bēaghroden* 'ring adorned' or possibly 'shield-adorned' (on the evidence of ON *baugr* 'ring, shield'). Both Wealhtheow and Elene speak in identical formulaic language, implying a common formulaic system for depicting women.

Chapter three, "The Valkyrie-Figure in Anglo-Saxon and Old-Norse," examines evidence of the valkyrie tradition in the Old English and Old Norse materials, surveying a number of prose and poetic texts. In the Norse tradition, the valkyries appear in two guises. An earlier tradition depicts them as elemental forces and fierce battle demons who bind and fetter hapless warriors, while later texts show them as shining, dignified women who ride horses in full armor or welcome warriors into Valhalla with a cup or outstretched drinking horn. The valkyries in the Eddic lays (Sigrun, Svava, and Brynhild) become much more individualized, possessing erotic potential as brides to the hero and becoming enmeshed in human warrior societies. Damico traces these two pictures of the radiant, courtly valkyrie and the fierce battle demon through a number of Old Norse texts. In Old English, the valkyrie (OE *wælcyrge* 'chooser of the slain') appear in charms and homilies as dangerous sorceresses, indicating the primacy of the second tradition. She identifies both Grendel's mother and Modthryth as types of the fierce valkyrie and draws parallels between Wealhtheow's passing of the cup (OE *ful*) to the passing of the cup (ON *full*) at sacrificial feasts, where warriors make binding oaths. Similarly, Wealhtheow passes the cup and incites the warriors to take oaths.

Chapter four, "Wealhtheow and the Valkyrie-Figure," undertakes a detailed study of Wealhtheow's connection to the valkyrie tradition, focusing on the lexical evidence of her name as well as the epithets applied to her. After discussing a number of etymological explanations for the name Wealhtheow, Damico suggests that it may mean the servant (*þēow*) of the (chosen) slain (*wealh*, identified with *wæl-*'slaughter'). Like the valkyries, Wealhtheow "chooses" Beowulf as the purger of Heorot, readies him for and incites him to battle, and like Odin's maids "she has a religious significance" (67). A further connection between Wealhtheow and valkyries is made through the word *ides* 'lady,' applied to Wealhtheow and probably related etymologically to ON *dísir* and OHG *idisi*, female figures with a number of connections to the valkyries. Damico also points out that Wealhtheow shares a number of traits with Freyja (for example, in the role of peace weaver) and wears a necklace which resembles Freyja's necklace, the *Brísinga men.*

Chapters five through seven, "Wealhtheow and Helgi's Valkyrie-Brides," "Wealhtheow and the Scylding Queens of the Sagas," and "Wealhtheow and Yrsa," explore in detail the "affinities that the queen shared with Helgi's valkyrie-brides in descriptive epithet (physical splendor, mental agility, southern origin); in motif (the bondmaid raised to the status of a queen); in authority (the task of charging the hero with his heroic identity); in the formal organization and thematic content of their narrative sequences; in their speech and action; and in the identifying epithets *ides Helminga* : *man Ylfinga* and *ides Scyldinga* : *dís Skjöldunga*—all cumulatively serve to transform Heorot's enigmatic queen into a generally recognizable rendering of the traditional female figure exemplified by the Scylding king Helgi's wife, Sigrun-Svava in the lays, and Yrsa in the sagas. The plethora of correspondences that are discernible between the Scylding-Scylfing queen of *Hrólfs saga kraka* in particular and the Scylding-Helming queen of *Beowulf* strongly supports (to use Malone's words) 'Yrsa, and Yrsa alone' as the appropriate legendary personage from whom Wealhtheow derives, even though the identification must properly remain provisional" (180).

Reviews: *OEN* 19.1 (1985): 83-84; E. S. Dick, *Res Publica Litterarum* 8 (1985): 293-97; M. C. Ross, *Scandinavian Studies* 57 (1985): 465-66; J. Harris, *Speculum* 61 (1986): 400-03; J. Hines, *N&Q* 33 (1986): 94-96; D.G. Calder, *JEGP* 85 (1986): 441-43.

1428 de Looze, Laurence N. "Frame Narratives and Fictionalization: Beowulf as Narrator." *TSLL* 26 (1984): 145-156.

Makes the case that Beowulf prepares himself for the fight with the dragon by contemplating several historical and one fictional analogue to his situation and that he is the only character in the poem who uses fictionalization in this way, the other characters drawing solely on Germanic history. De Looze summarizes: "When Beowulf marches to his final battle, he does so after having carefully determined his course of action within the framework of two polar strategies of response, active and passive. Illustrative of the active response are (1) the cycle of vengeance in the Swedish-Geatish wars and (2) the hasty action of Hygelac in his Frisian raid [ll. 2349b-99a]. The passive alternative is represented by (1) the impossibility of effective action in the Haethcyn-Herebeald episode [ll. 2462b-71] and (2) the choice not to act in the fantasy of the father's lament [ll. 2444-62a]. Through these events Beowulf is able to examine his own situation with increasing objectivity before deciding his course of action—a middle course of considered action" (155). Beowulf fictionalizes the father's lament, exploring and finally rejecting the frozen helplessness of the mourner. De Looze sees a nesting of episodes here with the father's lament at the middle and the dragon fight (ll. 2287-349a, 2508b ff.) at both ends.

1429 Diller, Hans-Jürgen. "Contiguity and Similarity in the *Beowulf* Digressions." In *Medieval Studies Conference Aachen 1983: Language and Literature.* Ed. Wolf-

Dietrich Bald and Horst Weinstock. Beiträge zur englischen Sprachwissenschaft, 15. Frankfurt a.M.: Peter Lang, 1984. Pp. 71-83.

Applies Roman Jakobson's theories of speech pathology and style psychology to the digressions in *Beowulf*. The digressions are not pathological, but Jakobson's categories provide a useful framework for examining narrative structure. Jakobson identifies two types of "aphasic" disorders: "contiguity disorders" and "similarity disorders." "A patient suffering from a similarity disorder, on whose linguistic behaviour Jakobson reports, was unable to classify objects according to such criteria as colour, shape, or size, but arranged them 'on the basis of their spatial contiguity as home things, office materials, etc.' Conversely, aphasics suffering from a contiguity disorder are unable to distinguish between semantically contiguous terms, such as *grant-grantor-grantee*. When faced with word-finding difficulties, the 'contiguity aphasic' will resort to metaphor, say for instance *spy-glass* for microscope, while the 'similarity aphasic' will resort to a word designating a spatially contiguous object, and will perhaps say *knife* instead of *fork*" (74). Diller classifies the digressions according to these two types, concluding that double authorship proposed by Kiernan [1261] seems likely given the distribution of contiguity and similarity digressions. Includes a summary appendix of the digressions and their classification.

1430 Engberg, Norma J. "*Mod-Maegen* Balance in *Elene*, *The Battle of Maldon*, and *The Wanderer*." NM 85 (1984): 212-26.

Provides the following summary: "*Mōd* with its synonyms and *mægen* with its synonyms form contrasting lexical collocations. One refers to mental ability; the other, to physical ability. Passages in *Elene* describing the Jewish converts and in *Beowulf* describing the youthful hero establish the premise that a healthy man is one who is both mentally and physically able. This is *mōd-mægen* balance" (212). Engberg goes on to examine the balance or imbalance of these two virtues in other texts, endorsing but seeking to further the work of Kaske [S361] on the *sapientia et fortitudo* theme. Though the youthful Beowulf is first referred to purely in terms of *mægen* 'strength,' two later statements, balanced syntactically, emphasize that he possesses both *mægen* and *mod* 'mind' (ll. 1705b-1706a and 1844). Also discusses the *mōd-mægen* balance in *The Battle of Maldon* and *The Wanderer*.

1431 Haarder, Andreas. *Sangen om Bjovulf.* [Beowulf]. Copenhagen: G.E.C. Gad, 1984. Pp. 166.

A translation of *Beowulf* into Danish verse, including a discussion of other Danish translations. Also features prose arguments for each fitt, genealogical charts, a list of names, a brief bibliography, and illustrations. Lines 4-11: "Skjold Skefing bemægtigede sig mjødsæder nok/ fra fjenders mængder, fra mange stammer,/ indgød frygt, siden først han blev opdaget/ lille og ene; alt fik han trøst for,/ han voksede under himlen og vandt sig ære,/ indtil alle de folk, som fandtes omkring ham,/ over hvalens vey måtte være ham lydig,/ give ham skat; han var en god konge!"
Reviews: B. Morris, *TLS* 6 Feb., 1987: 140.

1432 Hanning, Robert W. "Poetic Emblems in Medieval Narrative Texts." In *Vernacular Poetics in the Middle Ages.* Ed. Lois Ebin. Studies in Medieval Culture, 16. Kalamazoo: Medieval Institute Publications, Western Michigan U, 1984. Pp. 1-32.

Explores poetic "emblems" in *Beowulf* (as well as in *Cligès, Partonopeu de Blois,* and *Sir Gawain and the Green Knight*), focusing in *Beowulf* on the concept and function of *lāf* 'survivor, heirloom'. In Hanning's terminology, an emblem is "a symbolic artifact or character within a narrative that transcends its role as element of the fiction in which it appears and becomes a powerful comment on the artistic enterprise of its creator" (1). Artifacts such as the necklace which Wealhtheow gives to Beowulf and the sword hilt that Beowulf brings back from Grendel's mere function emblematically as "mnemonic devices, prompting the characters who see them and the poet who describes them to recall and link together various stages of the Germanic past" (3). The poet uses the ambivalent word *lāf* to describe poetic emblems: on the one hand, a *lāf* is a glorious heirloom or inheritance but on the other a pathetic survivor. This dual meaning of *lāf* lays bare the contradictions in heroic society, which is itself both glorious and fragile. Hanning provides a commentary on two important emblems in the poem: the sword ("a metaphorical time-bomb," 8) whose memory is fated to rekindle the feud between the Danes and the Heathobards (ll. 2024b-69a) and the human emblem, Wiglaf, whose name means 'battle-*lāf*,' suggesting that he is both a treasure and a pathetic survivor. Both emblems show "the burden of the past in a heroic culture" and possess power because they are organized "around an heirloom-artifact that embodies and stimulates memories crucial not just to individuals but to societies within which they live" (8).

1433 Haudry, Jean. "*Beowulf* dans la tradition indo-européenne (I): Structure et signification du poèm." [*Beowulf* in the Indo-European Tradition (I): Structure and Meaning of the Poem]. *Études Indo-Européennes* 9 (1984): 1-56.

Finds in the structure of *Beowulf* an echo of a widespread Indo-European myth about cycles of creation (and destruction), pointing out similarities in this regard between *Beowulf* and a number of texts in the Indo-European tradition, including the Vedas, the poetic *Edda*, several Norse sagas, and Armenian folk-epic. In simple terms, this cycle runs as follows: preceded by a period of chaos, a golden age of heroism takes root (associated with water), followed by a "historical" period associated with crimes and sin. When the forces of decadence have overcome the traditions of the golden age, the final disaster, "catastrophe ultime," comes (associated with fire). The cycle appears to derive from an Indo-European cosmogonical myth (seen in the Vedas, Hesiod, and northern Germanic myth) about the daytime world and the nocturnal world, in which the day is associated with life and the night with death and which pits the forces of day (usually a pantheon of gods) against those of darkness (demons and monsters) in order to restore spring after the night of winter, thus incorporating the cycle of the year as well as that of day and night. The golden age is the age of the day, while the time of decadence represents twilight, with the final disaster bringing night. Haudry sees this structure in *Beowulf*: Grendel is a spirit of twilight while Grendel's mother is a spirit of absolute night. The light which breaks forth in Grendel's cave after the beheading of Grendel's corpse signifies the triumph of the forces of light. Beowulf, along with Scyld, represents, in turn, the force of day and daylight, paralleling depictions of Indra. Hrothgar attempts to protect the traditions of this "golden age" or daytime world.

The structure of *Beowulf* reflects this myth: the prologue and the part one (ll. 1-2199) are dominated by a cosmological tonality, "tonalité cosmogonique," that is, the golden age of the Danes, which has its culmination in the building of Heorot. Grendel's entry announces a period of decadence, the counter-offensive of the nocturnal world, which again reveals the cosmogonical theme. Water crossings dominate this section because in the original myth, crossing of dangerous winter waters symbolizes the fact that winter is a dangerous period that man must traverse: Scyld arrives by and returns on the sea as does Beowulf, who also recounts his exploits in battling water monsters. Further, Beowulf plunges into the water of Grendel's mere, and the sword hilt tells of the Flood. Part two (ll. 2220 to the end) has an eschatological tonality, indicating the final victory of the forces of night (the final disaster) and echoing the major themes of the Northern eschatological myth of Ragnarök. Here, fire dominates. Finally, the digressions about "contemporary history" are inserted into both parts in order to illustrate the progress of decadence, the breaking of the social, natural, and contractual ties leading to the final catastrophe.

Thus, the poem expresses a philosophy of history in showing the twilight of the Danes and then of the Geats: history as in the Vedas and in Hesiod tends ultimately towards decay, but as in those traditions, *Beowulf* valorizes the golden past, particularly by valuing heritage, tradition, and lineage (often represented by swords). Haudry discusses a great many secondary issues relating to Indo-European myth, and discusses the derivations of several names as they connect to this myth: those of Beowulf, Heorot, Hrothgar, Heorogar, Halga, Herebeald, Hæthcyn, etc., and compares various elements in *Beowulf* to related Indo-European myths (for example, the killing of Herebeald with the death of Balder). Continued in Haudry [1558].

1434 Heinrichs, Heinrich Matthias. "'Beowulf' und andere altenglische Heldendichtung." ['Beowulf' and other Old English Heroic Poems]. In *Epische Stoffe des Mittelalters*. Kröners Taschenausgabe, Bd. 483. Stuttgart: A. Kröner, 1984. Pp. 156-164.

Surveys Anglo-Saxon knowledge of heroic legends (*Heldensagen*) in *Beowulf* as well as in *Widsið*, *Waldere*, and *Deor* and concludes that such legends were well-known to the Anglo-Saxons but that in *Beowulf,* they are alluded to darkly and suggestively, often for their emotional impact, and not retold precisely ("Mehr andeutend als präzise erzählend, werden Inhalte von Heldensagen oder Heldenliedern wiedergegeben," 159). Heinrichs discusses briefly the *Beowulf* poet's treatment of the legends of Sigemund, the fight at Finnsburh, Offa, and Ingeld.

1435 Hieatt, Constance B. "Modþryðo and Heremod: Intertwined Threads in the *Beowulf*-Poet's Web of Words." *JEGP* 83 (1984): 173-182.

Asserts that the poet's method of characterization by contrast is more complex than usually allowed. Though Beowulf is contrasted with both Heremod and Sigemund, verbal links show that Heremod's and Sigemund's lives are compared and contrasted to each other as well, while Hrothgar is compared to both Beowulf and Heremod. Assuming that *Mōdþrȳðo* (l. 1931b) is indeed a name and not an epithet for Hygd, Hieatt suggests that certain verbal echoes in the characterizations of Heremod and Modthrytho show that the two characters are linked in the poet's mind. The poet may have altered the traditional names *Thryth*, *Cynethryth* or *Eormenthryth* to *Modthrytho* in order to make a thematic point and perhaps to link her name to Heremod's, for the etymologies of the two names are strikingly similar: *Heremōd* 'army-mind,' *Mōdþrȳðo* 'mind-strength.' "The two names are, then, more-or-less anagrams of each other, with the elements in reverse order, just as the significant events of the characters' careers occurred in reverse order" (179). Hieatt accepts the name *Mōdþrȳðo* as it stands in the manuscript.

1436 Horowitz, Sylvia Huntley. "The Interrupted Battles in *Beowulf*." *NM* 85 (1984): 295-304.

Provides the following summary: "Nine fitt divisions in *Beowulf* interrupt descriptions of battles, but their placement appears to be artistically purposeful, pointing up two general patterns of structure, each with four examples. In the first pattern the hero suffers an unexpected loss of power and is in grave danger at the end of the first fitt, while a new, greater power is introduced at the beginning of the second (Breca incident, mere battle, twice in the dragon battle). In the other pattern the antagonists are locked in stasis at the end of the first fitt; then the stasis continues, time passes, and a killing revenge occurs (Grendel, Finnsburh episode, Heathobards, Onela-Heardred). The ninth interrupted battle (in the messenger's speech) relates to both patterns" (295). Horowitz discusses the narrative effect of the two patterns: the first makes for cliff-hanger suspense, while the second resists easy closure. The nine interrupting fitt divisions occur at the following lines: 559 (fitt IX), 791 (fitt XII), 1125 (fitt XVII), 1557 (fitt XXIII), 2039 (fit [XXVIIII-XXX]), 2391 (fitt

XXXIIII), 2602 (fitt XXXVI), 2694 (fitt XXXVII), and 2946 (fitt XLI).

1437 Huppé, Bernard F. *The Hero in the Earthly City: A Reading of* 'Beowulf'. Medieval & Renaissance Texts & Studies, 33. Binghamton: MRTS, State U of New York at Binghamton, 1984. Pp. 201.

Provides a translation and extensive interpretation of *Beowulf*, including explanatory notes as well as a detailed summary and outline of the argument of the poem (98-102). Chapter two, "Thematic Polarity," contrasts the heroic careers of Beowulf and Byrhthnoth (of the *Battle of Maldon*): "Byrhthnoth is a hero who follows Christ and in so doing redeems that which is merely heroic within him. Beowulf is a hero who lacks Christ and reveals that the heroic in itself is an empty ideal" (40).

Chapter three, "Narrative Polarities," argues that the "poem juxtaposes the unity and clarity of Christian life against the unresolved polarities of pagan life" (58). The juxtaposition is seen in "lexical polarities" (where the Christian and pagan meanings of words like *fāh* 'hostile,' *fæþm* 'embrace,' and *bearm* 'lap, bosom,' play off one another). Next, though the heroic values of the poem seem to contrast the good of Sigemund to the evil of Heremod, this apparent polarity is not actual (since both are motivated by pride), while the true polarity of heavenly versus Christian rewards reveals itself. Polarities in the depiction of nature take up the rest of the chapter. "God's creation, nature, is everywhere beautiful, like Eden, but the Fall has caused the perversity of human life at war with itself and nature. . . . [T]he threatening monsters . . . overcome the false Eden of worldly prosperity, except as they may be overcome by redeeming grace or providential design" (51). Huppé finds evidence of the perversity of fallen nature in Grendel's tarn, the sea, the dragon, and metaphors of light and dark.

Chapter four, "Structure," argues that fitt divisions are functional, and not, as Klaeber thought, merely decorative or rhetorical. Examining fitt structure in detail, Huppé finds that formulas introducing fitts offer clues to the overall design of the poem and discusses a variety of restrictions on fitt structure. He argues that fitt 31, which makes an abrupt shift from Beowulf's adventures in Denmark to his old age as king of the Geats, cannot be arbitrarily divided at line 2200 because the fitt itself develops the theme of reversal or *edwenden*, rendering an abrupt narrative shift appropriate. He then provides an overview of the poem's structure based on fitt groupings along with a detailed analysis of each section. The prologue (fitts 1-3) introduces the "earthly city" of the Danes. Part one concerns youth and consists of three episodes of eight fitts each: the prelude to battle (fitts 4-11), the fight with Grendel (fitts 12-19), and the fight with Grendel's dam (fitts 20-27). Part two concerns age and also consists of three episodes: Beowulf's homecoming (fitts 28-31), the battle with the dragon (fitts 32-39), and the aftermath (fitts 40-43). Also considered are the number of days in each episode along with possible number symbolism based on "the counterpointing of two and three" (89).

The verse translation rests on Huppé's reading of the poem in its "inescapable Augustinian frame of reference" (ix) and suggests the alliterative system of Old English verse without aiming at a strict reconstruction of Old English meter. Each line consists of two half-lines with a caesura, both connected by alliteration. Huppé uses modern punctuation but warns that it can be misleading, given the way the poem uses clusters of phrases and clauses. Lines 4-11: "Oft Scyld Scefing in shock of battle/ took the meadhalls of many nations/ from the terrified foe; a poor foundling/ he appeared in Denmark and there prospered,/ growing to greatness, gaining much honor,/ until every nation neighboring his/ paid him tribute over the seapaths,/ gave him obedience —he was a good king." Includes notes to the translation.

Reviews: *OEN* 19.1 (1985): 85-86; E.B. Irving, Jr., *Speculum* 61 (1986): 668-70; J. Hill, *Anglia* 105 (1987): 465-68.

1438 Imaizumi, Youko. "The Women in *Beowulf*." *Studies in Language and Culture (Nagoya Univ.)* 5.2 (1984): 1-9.

Not seen.

1439 Irving, Edward B. Jr. "The Nature of Christianity in *Beowulf*." *ASE* 13 (1984): 7-21.

Undertakes to "look at the Christian dimension in *Beowulf* as it exists in the poem ... without going on to clarify or order the poem by some external system" (8), particularly patristic writings, finding the poet to be a Christian but no strict theologian. Irving tabulates the number of Christian references in the poem, finding that "the narrator makes one Christian reference every sixteen lines; Hrothgar makes one every eight lines or twice as often; Beowulf makes one every twenty-four lines or only one-third as often as Hrothgar. The remaining speakers as a group, with 12% of the lines, are the least Christian of all: they make only 5% of the Christian references, or one every forty-three lines. . . . These figures confirm our sense that we have in *Beowulf* a poem narrated by an unquestionably Christian poet who has created one outstandingly pious character in King Hrothgar, but nevertheless a poem about actions and characters much less closely involved with Christianity" (9). Irving argues against Williams [1372], that the Cain materials have a limited scope of importance and that neither Grendel's dam nor the dragon can be seen as enemies of God since they are never named as such, as Grendel is. Further, names for God in *Beowulf* represent a distinct and limited subset of those available to an Old English poet. "We see only those aspects of him visible to our heroic world, principally his rôles as loyal master and just lord" (17). Finally, Christian references drop off dramatically in the last third of the poem where the poet focuses on the enduring values of the heroic world. "If no victory is possible, God is remote indeed. Man's only reward then is the chance epic offers to know his fate, to live *in* it with peculiar vitality, to make articulate his acceptance of it, to speak those 'few words' that give us humanity" (20). Beowulf is not damned, but God has taken him to some safe place where heroes go.

1440 Kaske, Robert E. "The Coastwarden's Maxim in *Beowulf*: A Clarification." *N&Q* 31 (1984): 16-18.

A rejoinder to Greenfield's critique [1318], which doubts Kaske's interpretation [S361] of the Coastwarden's maxim (ll. 287b-89) as an expression of the *sapientia et fortitudo* theme. Kaske argues that the phrase *gescād witan* (l. 288), interpreted by Greenfield as 'distinguish between,' need not carry so strong or unequivocal a meaning. Since the anthologized version of Kaske's article [S361] contains an editorial translation at odds with Kaske's reading, he provides a fresh paraphrase of the lines: "The keen shield-warrior who thinks effectively must be aware of the differing conclusions that can be drawn from observing words and works." Kaske adds, "the maxim is a gnomic generalization about human conduct, applied by the Coastwarden with, I suspect, a certain wry note of self-correction—to himself" (18), not primarily to Beowulf as Greenfield assumed.

1441 *Key-Word Studies in 'Beowulf,'* 1. Yoshio Terasawa, ed. Tokyo: Centre for Mediaeval English Studies, 1984.

The first of a continuing series of word studies generally listing etymologies, forms, compounds, alliteration, collocations, variations on, Latin equivalents, etc. Hiroshi Fujiwara studies the word *sweord* 'sword' and its relatives, concluding that the word describes weapons of attack rather than those of defense. Tadao Kubouchi examines *middangeard* 'middle earth,' surveying occurrences of different forms in the poetic corpus and also analyzing two synonyms, *eorþe* 'earth,' and *worold* 'world,' suggesting that the terms may be interchangeable. Shigeru Ono's entry on words meaning "wise" (*frōd, gewittig, snotor, wīs,* and *wītig*) charts how frequently these words are used of the main characters, proposing that *frōd* may have two separate meanings, 'old' and 'wise.' The words *snotor* and *wīs* are used irrespective of age, while *wītig* is used only of God. Words meaning 'wise' describe Hrothgar most often, then Beowulf. Kinshiro Oshitari provides an overview of words describing the dragon (*draca* and *wyrm*) as well as of epithets applied to him. Shuji Sato's "A Note on *God* and *Cyning*" provides the standard information on these two words as well as listing the verbs they are associated with and surveying the epithets applied to kings. Yoshihiko Ikegami's "The Semological Structure of the English Verbs of Motion: Old and Middle English" treats a number of verbs of motion, some of which occur in *Beowulf*. "From a semological point of view, verbs of motion are distinguished from each other (1) by their tactical properties and (2) by their componential properties" (47).

1442 Kiernan, Kevin S. "Grendel's Heroic Mother." *In Geardagum* 6 (1984): 13-33.

Finds that though no one will mourn her death, "one cannot help noticing that Grendel's mother, living and dying by the sword, was memorably heroic in defeat. For some reason we are meant to see her actions in a persistently 'monstro-heroic' light" (24). Unlike the more inhuman Grendel, she accepts the modes of heroic society, including a hall with monster retainers and weapons worthy of a hero. Further, she has the fighting skills of a warrior, particularly as described in lines 1547-56 and accepts and adheres to the heroic demands of blood feud. Thus the monstrous slaying of Æschere may be seen as a compensation for the dismemberment of Grendel. Grendel's mother has, in fact, "both legal and textual precedent for her attack on Heorot" (27), especially in the pattern of revenge described in the Finnsburh episode, where the plight of Hildeburh is essentially that of Grendel's mother. In her revenge-taking, she resembles Hengest as well. "Because she is a monster, however, her case turns out to be an indictment of the kind of heroism she represents" (31). Kiernan illustrates this analysis with a number of quotations from his edition in progress, "an ultraconservative text that preserves and defends the scribes' already edited manuscript" (14).

1443 Kjellmer, Göran. "On a New Reading of *Beowulf* 1-2." *NM* 85 (1984): 192-193.

Finds syntactical problems with Spamer's suggestion [1284] that the word *Gār-Dena* 'spear-Danes' (l. 1a) modifies *gēardagum* 'ancient days' (l. 1b). Kjellmer shows that the most common structure or syntagm is preposition + genitive + headword or perhaps preposition + headword + genitive and that unusual patterns (six in all) like Spamer's proposed reading (genitive + preposition + headword) are all confined to single half-lines in *Beowulf*, probably to avoid ambiguity, though Spamer's reading spans two half-lines. "It can therefore be argued that the caesural break in the proposed syntagm would make it less recognizable as a syntagm" (193). Nevertheless, Kjellmer finds all of the alternate readings problematic and urges caution in accepting any interpretation until more conclusive evidence is advanced.

1444 Krämer, Peter. "Neuenglisch *to die*—ein skandinavisches Lehnwort? Überlegungen zu *Beowulf* 850a." [Modern English *to die*—a Scandinavian Loanword? Thoughts on *Beowulf* 850a]. In *Linguisitica et Philologica: Gedenkschrift für Björn Collinder (1894-1983)*. Ed. Otto Gschwantler, Károly Rédei, and Hermann Reichert. Philologica Germanica, 6. Vienna: Wilhelm Braumüller, Universitäts-Verlagsbuchhandlung, 1984. Pp. 279-86.

Believes that the word *dēog* (l. 850a) derives not from *dēagan* 'to hide or be hidden' but from OE **dēgan* 'to die' (Anglian form) and that the Modern English verb *die* comes not from the Old Norse *deyja*, as assumed by most modern reference works, but from this native English word. Krämer bases his suggestion on the form of the verb, which he takes to be originally strong, reduplicating verb class, giving the

West Saxon forms *dīegan-*dēo(w)-*dēowum-*dawan but the Anglian forms *dēgan-*dēo(w)-*dēowum-*dawan. He identifies the dēog of line 850a as an Anglian form of the third person indicative preterite of the verb, with -g instead of -w by analogy to the present forms. He would translate the half-line as follows "Es starb der Totgeweihte" (the doomed one died, 283). The fact that *die* appears in Middle English only around 1200 is explained by the fact that the form was preserved in the Anglian, not the West Saxon, dialect.

1445 Krol, Jelle, and Popke van der Zee. *'Beowulf' in proazaoersetting út it Aldingelsk.* ['Beowulf' in a Prose Translation from the Old English]. Koperative Utjowerij: Boalsert, 1984. Pp. 151; ill.

Translates the poem into modern Frisian prose, including introductory material covering the manuscript, date and authorship, contents, themes and structure, prosody, as well as an essay on the Frisians in *Beowulf*, notes to the translation, genealogical charts, a list of names, and a bibliography. Lines 4-11: "Gauris berôve Scyld Scefing binden fijannen, hiele folksstammen fan meabanken, jage de Herulen de strik op it liif. Nei't er eartiids yn earmoed fûn wie, is him dêr yn syn libben fertreasting foar jûn: hy waard grut ûnder de himel, hy wûn safolle oansjen dat alle oanbuorjende folken, dy't oarekant de walfiskwei wennen, him hearrich wêze en skatten betelje moasten. Dat wie in grut kening!" See also Krol [1134].

1446 Lock, Richard. *Aspects of Time in Medieval Literature.* Garland Publications in Comparative Literature. New York: Garland, 1984. Pp. iii + 270; ill.

Studies several patterns of time in *Beowulf*, concluding that "In *Beowulf* there is a very strong feeling of linear time both within the poem itself and in the way the audience is distanced in time by the narrator. Nearly all the 'digressions' involve shifts in time, some of which are in the poem's future but in the audience's past" (ii-iii). Lock argues that an essentially cyclical view of time belongs to oral cultures while a linear sense of time indicates a lettered tradition. Though the evidence of *Beowulf* is somewhat mixed, he places the poem among literate works because of the way it contrasts past, present, and future events to give "a feeling of the inevitability and linearity of the passage of time" (253). Lock also provides graphs and tables analyzing the main time line

and its various digressions (whether future or past). He finds that almost every narrative block is modified or qualified by various elaborations or digressions. Further, the day-night cycle in *Beowulf* becomes prominent when we realize that most of the fights take place at night. Lock discusses various words for the concepts of year, day, night, and time, frequently contrasting the handling of time in *Beowulf* with that in *La Chanson de Roland* and also analyzing the time patterns in the *Yvain* of Chrétien, the *Atlakviða*, *Gunnlaugs saga*, and *Sir Gawain and the Green Knight*.
Reviews: *OEN* 20.1 (1986):79.

1447 Nicholson, Lewis E. "The Literary Implications of Initial Unstable *h* in *Beowulf*." *Classica et Mediaevalia* 35 (1984): 265-83.

Points out that the distribution of mistaken *h*'s in *Beowulf* is highly unusual and proposes that the *Beowulf* poet deliberately uses a feature of Latin orthography (the intrusive *h*) in order to make thematic puns and that, further, the crux at line 62 can be solved by assuming a missing *h*. In the latter case, Nicholson believes that the problematic line 62 refers not to Healfdene's daughter but to a fourth son and his queen. The proposed reading is *hȳrde ic þæt [wæs] (H)elan cwēn* ... , translated (with the next line) as follows: "I heard that the bedfellow (wife) of Hela [was] the queen of the Battle-Scilfing" (269). Sound patterning, which Nicholson finds in the opening lines of the poem (ll. 1-8), reinforces the notion that line 62 should alliterate on *h*. The Battle-Scilfing of line 63 would then be Ongentheow, his wife having been taken in a raid and forced to serve as the bond-woman of *Hela*, the youngest son of Healfdene. Next, Nicholson examines thirteen cases of intrusive *h*, noting that all instances, except perhaps one, create deliberate puns: *hondlean* 'hand-reward' (ll. 1541b, 2094b) and *hondslyht* 'hand-blow' (ll. 2929b, 2972b) pun on the *h*-less forms *ondlean* 'repayment' and *ondslyht* 'counter blow'; the form *Hunferth* allows at least two meanings, 'with the spirit of a Hun' and 'mar-peace' or 'unintelligence' (in its *h*-less form); *hroden* (l. 1151b) when applied to blood in the hall can either mean 'decorated' (with the *h*) or 'reddened' (without); the remaining instances reveal similar punning: *gehnægdon* and *hnægde* for *nægan* (ll. 2916b, 1318b), *hæleþum* for *æleþum* (l. 332b), and *hattres* for *attres* (l. 2523a). Also proposes that the term *Hetware* 'Jutes' (l. 2363, 2916) may represent a similar pun on an *h*-less form, *etware* or *eotware* (from *eoten-* 'giant'), confirming Kaske's idea that *eoten* means 'enemy' in the poem [S631].

1448 Nishide, Kimiyuki. "Notes on *Beowulf* (I)." *Research Bulletin of Obihiro Univ.* II, 6.3 (1984): 1-18. In Japanese.

Provides word-by-word glosses (in Japanese) to lines 53-63, 90b-101, 111-14, and 159-93. (KN)

1449 Olsen, Alexandra Hennessey. "'Þurs' and 'Þyrs': Giants and the Date of *Beowulf*." *In Geardagum* 6 (1984): 35-42.

In a response to Beekman Taylor [1465], suggests that the word *þyrs* in line 426a may not mean 'powerful giant' (as does its relative *þurs* in Old Norse mythological poems) but that it may carry the same meaning as later uses of *þurs* in the sagas, particularly *Egil's saga*, where it indicates a large, formidable man, using this and other terms for monsters with a humorous undertone. Such an interpretation is all the more likely if one dates *Beowulf* to the tenth or eleventh centuries. Olsen suggests "that the *Beowulf* poet expects us to be cognizant of the humorous connotations of the word, especially since its only use occurs in the cocky speech in which Beowulf tells Hrothgar that he has come to slay the monster.... As a result, when he says 'āna gehēgan / ðing wið þyrse' (ll. 425b-426a), he may be saying, 'By myself, I'll take on this big fellow'" (39). In thus underrating Grendel as an adversary, Beowulf shows a lack of *sapientia*.

1450 Oresnik, Janez. "The Origin of the Cliticness of the West Germanic Definite Article: The Case of Beowulf." *Linguistica* 24 (1984): 383-389.

Not seen.

1451 Osborn, Marijane. *'Beowulf': a Verse Translation with Treasures of the Ancient North*. Intro. by Fred C. Robinson. Berkeley: U of California P, 1984. Pp. xix + 141; ill.

A translation of the poem into free verse which includes an introduction by Fred C. Robinson, several pages of explanatory notes, and numerous illustrations of contemporary artifacts and manuscript illustration. The introduction contains sections on "The Language of *Beowulf*" (with a discussion of poetic compounds), "The Narrative Method in *Beowulf*," and "The Thought-World of the *Beowulf* Poet" (a discussion of Christian and pagan elements). Lines 4-11: "Often Shield Shefing shattered the courage/ of troops of marauders by taking their mead-seats./ He terrified those nobles—long after the time/ he appeared as a foundling. Comfort for that fate/ came when he grew and prospered in glory/ until those who lived in the neighboring lands/ over the whale's road had to obey him,/ yield him tribute. Yes—a good king!"

Reviews: R.E. Bjork, *Albion* 16 (1984): 404-05; R. Tripp, *In Geardagum* 6 (1984): 71-85; *OEN* 19.1 (1985): 90; N. Jacobs, *Essays in Criticism* 35 (1985): 260-64.

1452 Oshitari, Kinshiro. "A Note on *Beowulf* and Hagiography." In *Studies in English Philology and Linguistics in Honour of Dr. Tamotsu Matsunami*. Tokyo: Shubun International, 1984. Pp. 221-32.

Sketches out a number of parallels between *Beowulf* and early saints' lives, suggesting that the description of Beowulf's mission bears a strong resemblance to Felix's *Life of Guthlac* in particular and that the poet was most probably familiar with hagiographic materials. Like a number of saints, Beowulf travels by sea to bring salvation to an afflicted people, and sea imagery plays an important role in both the poem and the saints' lives. The central portion of the *Life of Guthlac* like that of *Beowulf* is taken up with an account of the protagonists' battle against demonic enemies who live in fens. Beowulf produces no miracles, but like Guthlac, he does battle evil creatures at night. Both texts treat the death of their heroes with similar panegyrics. Oshitari finds a number of more specific parallels between the two stories and concludes that though the influence may not be direct, saints' lives may have played a role in the development of the poem.

1453 Princi Braccini, Giovanna. "Recupero di un lemma germanico e connesse questioni etimologiche (*wala-paus* in Rotari, *wala* nel *Beowulf*, fracese *galon*, italiano *gala*, e tedesco *posse*)." [Recovery of a Germanic Lemma and Related Etymological Questions . . .]. *AIUON, filologia germanica* 27 (1984): 135-205.

Explains the difficult word *wala* (used to describe part of a helmet given to Beowulf, l. 1031b) as a strip used to cover and protect the eyes, providing a reconstruction and diagram of this sort of helmet (205) and connecting the word to other Germanic and Romance words which describe strips of material, some of which can be worn as masks for disguises or ornament. Princi Braccini finds an etymological connection between the words *wala-paus* 'a disguising mask' (a Langobardic word contained in the *Edictus Rothari*), Old English *wala* (*Beowulf*, l. 1031b), Old High German *wala*, the French *galon* 'band, decorative strip' and Italian *gala* 'decorative strip made of lace,' the Romance words deriving from a Germanic source. Klaeber [S67] defined the word as a "rounded projection on the helmet, rim, roll," the precise nature of which is unknown and connected it to the verb *weallan* 'to roll' and the *-wale* in *gunwale*. With the alternate etymological explanation given above, Princi Braccini reinterprets line 1031b, *wala ūtan hēold*, to mean "on the outside the helmet had a 'visor'" ("esternamente una visiera aveva," 165). Also discusses other phrases describing the helmet (ll. 1030-31), the synonymous word *here-grīm* 'battle mask,' the etymology of the second element of *wala-paus*, as well as phonological considerations supporting the idea that *gala* comes from *wala*.

1454 _____. "Tra folclore germanico e latinità insulare: presenze del *Liber monstrorum* e della *Cosmographia* dello Pseudo-Etico nel *Beowulf* e nel cod. Nowell." [Between Germanic Folklore and Insular Latinity: the Presence of the *Liber monstrorum* and the *Cosmographia* of Pseudo-Aethicus in *Beowulf*]. *Studi Medievali* 3rd ser., 25 (1984): 681-720.

Following Whitbread [942], finds a number of correspondences between the *Liber Monstrorum* and *Beowulf*, suggesting that it and the *Cosmographia* of Pseudo-Aethicus (both works of Insular Latinity) may be related to Beowulf in some way, especially in the motif of the sword melting in blood (ll. 1605b-1608), the cannibalism of the monsters, and the description of grand objects. Though Whitelock [S231] argued that the monsters come from popular folk legends, Princi Braccini finds that these two Insular Latin treatises contain a similar learned transformation of popular legend. Includes two appendices, one supporting the Insular origin of the *Liber Monstrorum* and one concerning the theme of blood which injures or invigorates.

1455 Roberts, Gildas. *'Beowulf': A New Translation into Modern English Verse.* St. John's, Nfld.: Breakwater, 1984. Pp. xii + 99.

A translation of *Beowulf* into free verse, "using alliteration wherever it seemed natural, unforced, and pleasing to do so" (xi) and preserving kennings wherever possible. Roberts aims "to produce a poem that has the liveliness and vigour of Burton Raffel's poetic reworking of *Beowulf* [S504] and the fidelity of John R. Clark Hall's [S24] literal 'translation into modern English prose'" (xi). The short introduction doubts a late date for the poem and views Beowulf as a Christ-figure, also providing a discussion of the main themes of the poem (mutability, the fragile nature of civilization, and the heroic code). Lines 4-11: "Often did Scyld-Scefing tear away the mead-benches/ From many nations, from the armies of his enemies,/ Put terror into warriors, after he was first found/ Destitute. He lived to see consolation for that—/ Increased under the heavens, grew with glorious deeds,/ Until each and every neighbour across the whale-road/ Had to obey him, had to yield tribute./ That was a good king!" Includes a brief bibliography, list of unusual words, notes, name index, a map, and genealogical charts.

Reviews: *OEN* 20.1 (1986): 84; C.-D. Wetzel, *Anglia* 106 (1988): 200-03; M.C. Seymour, *ES* 67 (1986): 364; E.G. Stanley, *N&Q* 33 (1986): 96.

1456 Rogers, H.L. "*Beowulf*, Line 804." *N&Q* 31 (1984): 289-292.

Argues that line 804 applies to Beowulf's refusal to bear arms against Grendel, not to Grendel's having cursed the warriors' swords, as Klaeber thought [S67]. Rogers shows that the word *forswerian* cannot mean 'curse,' a meaning carried by OE *wergan* (Lat. *devotare, maledicere*) and that the meaning 'renounce' was extant far earlier than Klaeber thought. If the word is reinterpreted in this way, the subject of the verb *forswerian* must be Beowulf, not Grendel, giving an abrupt shift in pronoun reference, though one paralleled in other passages in *Beowulf*. Finally, no curse is needed to account for Grendel's resistance to swords—his monster's hide is armor-like as is that of his mother.

1457   Sakemi, Kisei. "Toward the Textual Criticism of *Beowulf* (2)." *Research Bulletin* (Hiroshima Institute of Technology) 18.22 (1984): 33-43. In Japanese.

Surveys the textual problems (various conjecture, emendations, and interpretations) of lines 189-370, using Dobbie's edition [S256]. Continued in Sakemi [1577]. (KS)

1458   Sato, Noboru. "The Semantics of *Beowulf* I: the Polysemy of *æt*- 'Scribal Errors', Prefix *un*-, and Homonymic Clashes." *Otsuka Review* 20 (1984): 35-41.

Explores the polysemy of the word element *æt*- 'to or from,' analyzing scribal "errors" connected with it as well as how it and its homonyms are distinguished from one another. (SN)

1459   Sato, Shuji. "A Note on *dryhten, frea, helm,* and *hyrde* in *Beowulf*." *Journal of the Faculty of Literature* (Chuo Univ.) 110/111 (1984): 39-59.

Not seen.

1460   Schmid-Cadalbert, Christian. "Mündliche Traditionen und Schrifttum in europäischen Mittelalter." [Oral Traditions and Literacy in the European Middle Ages]. *Amsterdamer Beiträge zur älteren Germanistik* 21 (1984): 85-114.

In a broader study of oral traditions and how they interact with and merge into written traditions, finds that the scop's song about Beowulf's exploit with Grendel (ll. 867-915) betrays many characteristics associated with oral narrative. That is, his deed becomes meaningful only when it is fitted into a traditional narrative pattern through the comparison with Sigemund. Oral tradition, Schmid-Cadalbert emphasizes, serves a mnemonic function and relies on devices such as narrative patterns, formulas, meter, fixed motifs and themes, etc. Thus, lived experience must be transformed into oral songs in order to be remembered. However, the form remains vital since features which no longer fit into present social conditions are forgotten. Schmid-Cadalbert also observes that the reception of oral narrative belongs to a group while the model of the individual reader arrives only after the Enlightenment. Further, fact and fiction cannot be separated in oral narrative, a separation made possible by the arrival of literacy. Though few pure examples of oral narrative are preserved in writing, it is possible, through ethnology, anthropology, and narrative studies, to gain some sense of oral narrative and its conversion to written modes (113-14).

1461 Schmidt, Gary D. "Unity and Contrasting Kingships in *Beowulf.*" *Concerning Poetry* 17 (1984): 1-11.

Warning of some pitfalls inherent in a search for unity in *Beowulf,* suggests that issues of kingship unite the two parts: "Taken from the perspective of kingship, *Beowulf* is the same story told twice, although Part II has a different focus and a different ending" (4). In such a reading, Beowulf and Hrothgar are compared and contrasted as kings: both are old, both undergo the attacks of monsters, and both have young helpers (Hrothgar has Beowulf, while Beowulf has Wiglaf). Hrothgar, perhaps prudently, chooses not to fight Grendel while Beowulf decides to attack the dragon himself. "The poem, then, presents two aged kings with similar situations and similar options. Each chooses a different course, one perishes, and neither guarantees the continued prosperity of the kingdom" (5). Though Hrothgar's despair prevents him from acting, the poet never criticizes him for putting the welfare of his nation above his own fame as a hero. Beowulf, by contrast, seems more heroic, but neither can save his kingdom from dark destruction. Schmidt briefly analyzes other characters, themes, and digressions in light of this two-part structure. Finally, a dark vision rules both parts: "There is the strong sense here that Wyrd has doomed these two kingdoms, and the decisions by mortals, whether wise or foolish, are, in the end, unimportant" (11).

1462 Schrader, Richard J. "The Deserted Chamber: An Unnoticed Topos in the 'Father's Lament' of *Beowulf.*" *Journal of the Rocky Mountain Medieval and Renaissance Association* 5 (1984): 1-5.

Suggests that a topos from classical literature lies behind the epic simile in *Beowulf,* lines 2444-62, where the father laments his hanged son in an empty, ruined house. Similar scenes, where mourning figures linger in the rooms and over the personal objects of their beloved dead occur in Valerius Flaccus, Statius, and Claudian. The poet need not have drawn the topos directly from the authors mentioned but may have absorbed it through *florilegia* or grammatical treatises.

Includes a brief discussion of the *ubi sunt* motif in the Old English elegies.

1463 Sullivan, C.W. III. "Names and Lineage Patterns: Aragorn and Beowulf." *Extrapolation* 25 (1984): 239-46.

Compares the name and disclosure of lineage of Aragorn (a character in J.R.R. Tolkien's *Lord of the Rings*) to similar patterns in *Beowulf*, finding that Tolkien's trilogy betrays a broad knowledge of naming practices and genealogies in Heroic Age literature, including *Beowulf*.

1464 Tandy, David W. "Evidence for Editing in *Beowulf*." *NM* 85 (1984): 291-294.

Provides the following summary: "Two patterns of diction suggest that the *Beowulf*-poet edited his poem. The subtle distribution, with carefully chosen adjectives, of the formulaic *þæt* (or *þa*) *wæs . . . cyning* [ll. 11b, 863b, 1306b, 1885b, 2209b, and 2390b] unifies the poem by linguistically buttressing the broadly articulated parallels between Scyld, Hrothgar and Beowulf (especially the later two). Similarly, the coincidence of language in the account of the first celebration in Heorot [ll. 1170-76, 1219-20, and 1228-30] and in the final tristich of the poem unifies the epic by establishing guidelines of behavior for Beowulf and by articulating the hero's adherence to them. With this evidence for editing, an argument is then advanced that *Beowulf* is in fact a 'transitional' text, one composed orally, but edited (for a specific segment of the audience) and thus bearing characteristics of both oral and written techniques" (291).

1465 Taylor, Paul Beekman. "Grendel's Monstrous Arts." In *Geardagum* 6 (1984): 1-12.

Believes that the poet uses Germanic lore concerning giants in his depiction of Grendel, who like the giants in Norse myth, possesses "skills and science that far surpass normal human capacities" (3). Taylor suggests that Grendel may have the power to forge weapons, weave cloth, speak charms, and read runes. Beowulf calls Grendel a *þyrs*, 'giant, demon, wizard' (l. 426a), linking him to the Old Norse *þurs* or "kin to the gods, creator and artificer" (2). Evidence for such powers may be found in a) the swords and armor in Grendel's lair, b) his magical "glove," c) his use of charms (putting the hall-men to sleep and unhinging Heorot's door), and his possible knowledge of runes (explaining the terms *helrūne*, literally 'hell-rune' [l. 163a] and *forsworen* [l. 804b], which Klaeber interprets as 'lay a spell on' but which Taylor claims to mean 'abandon or abjure an oath,' an act which requires speech).

1466 Tripp, Raymond P., Jr. "Grendel Polytropos." *In Geardagum* 6 (1984): 43-69.

Lists 163 names and designations for Grendel in the poem, sorting them alphabetically and by frequency of occurrence. Tripp comments on Grendel's human nature and speculates that "His many names point to a composite and, most likely, psychologized creature, one who, like Zeus among the Greeks, has absorbed the characteristics of a number of formerly specific and solid denizens of the pluralistic pagan world behind him. Nonhuman creatures, it seems, have found something of their humanity as complexes within Grendel's mental make-up.... Perhaps the only incontrovertible conclusion one might reach would be that Grendel is indeed a creature of *many names*, no matter how we select or arrange them" (46).

1467 Vidal Tibbits, Mercedes. "El Cid, hombre heroico, y Beowulf, heroe sobrehumano." [The Cid, Heroic Man, and Beowulf, Superhuman Hero]. In *Josep Maria Solà-Solé: Homage, homenaje, homenatge: Miscelanea de estudios de amigos y discipulos.* Ed. Victorio Aguera and Nathaniel B. Smith. Barcelona: Puvill Libros, 1984. Pp. 267-273.

Compares the heroes of the twelfth-century *Poema de Mio Cid* and *Beowulf,* finding that the Cid remains a human character who struggles with human enemies with human capacities, while Beowulf is a superhuman character fighting supernatural monsters with extraordinary strength. For this reason the *Poema de Mio Cid* today remains more of a living symbol of an entire era and community, while the meaning of *Beowulf* has come to appear rather blurred. Tibbits points out that the Cid uses swords with natural human strength, requiring enormous courage, while Beowulf requires no weapons against Grendel and uses an enormous sword against Grendel's mother, a sword inappropriate for a human being. The Cid is at all times prudent and astute, knowing that victory is never certain, while Beowulf is rarely prudent or astute: in fact he shows absolute certainty about his powers.

1468 Warsh, Lewis. *Beowulf.* Barron's Book Notes. Woodbury, NY: Barron Educational Series, 1984. Pp. vii + 99.

A general introduction to and study guide for *Beowulf,* including an introductory section on "the author and his times," as well as on plot, characters, themes, style, language, point of view, structure, and sources. The bulk of the book is taken up by a detailed summary of the plot (based on Burton Raffel's translation [S504]) along with interpretative notes. Also included are multiple choice and essay questions, a list of term paper ideas, a brief bibliography, a glossary of names, and short excerpts from the major critics.
Reviews: *OEN* 20.1 (1986): 75.

1469 Yamada, Jiro. "A Study of 'Variation' of *Beowulf* (1)." *Journal of Commerce and Economics (Humanities Special Number)* 33 (1984): 1-17. In Japanese.

Not seen.

1470 Yamanouchi, Kazuyoshi. "Some Notes on Alliteration and Non-Alliteration of Adverbs in *Beowulf.*" *Studies in Humanities (Shizuoka Univ.)* 34 (1984): 25-45. In Japanese.

Divides the 127 adverbs in *Beowulf* into four groups according to metrical stress and alliteration, making some comments on the relationship between the use of adverbs and alliterative structure. (KY)

1471 _____. "Some Notes on Non-Alliterating Finite Verbs in *Beowulf.*" In *Studies in English Philology and Linguistics in Honour of Dr. Tamotsu Matsunami.* Tokyo: Shubun International, 1984. Pp. 65-78.

Explores the characteristics of non-alliterating finite verbs in the first lift of the *a*-verse from the point of view of their lexicality and usage. (KY)

1472 Yoshida, Kiyoshi. "Some Notes on Time, and Life and Death in *Beowulf.*" *Bulletin of Linguistics and Literature* (Kyushu Women's U) 14 (1984): 45-47. In Japanese.

Not seen.

1473 Yoshimi, Akinori. "Hamlet to Beowulf no Aida o Musubu mono: Hamlet, Amleth, Onela ni kansuru oboegaki." [Connections between Hamlet and *Beowulf*: Hamlet, Amleth, Onela]. In *Shakespeare no Shiki*. Tokyo: Shinzaki, 1984. Pp. 32-42.

Not seen.

1474 _____. "On 'Hȳrde ic þæt [. . . On]elan cwēn' in *Beowulf* (l. 62)." *Meiji Gakuin Review* (English Language and Literature, 57-9) 358-60 (1984): 11-19.

Not seen.

1985

1475 Andersson, Theodore M. "Heathen Sacrifice in *Beowulf* and Rimbert's *Life of Ansgar*." *Medievalia et Humanistica* 13 (1985): 65-74.

Believes "that the apparent contradiction between the pagan sacrifice of the Danes and the Christianity of Hrothgar's court can be resolved by the assumption of a divided community. King, queen, and noblemen are Christians, but the Danish people have not yet been won over to the new faith. . . . This situation is readily comprehensible in terms of northern conversion history" (72-73), with particular parallels to an episode contained in Rimbert's *Life of Ansgar*, which describes a ninth-century court whose leader (Herigarius) is Christian but the majority of whose people are pagan. As in *Beowulf*, the people (the inhabitants of Birka) resort to pagan sacrifice in time of trouble. Thus, a similar conversion rhetoric can be seen in both works: "*Beowulf*, no less than the *Life of Ansgar*, dramatizes the defeat of the gods and the victory of God" (72).

1476 Bately, Janet. "Linguistic Evidence as a Guide to the Authorship of Old English Verse: A Reappraisal, with Special Reference to *Beowulf*." In *Clemoes*, pp. 409-32.

Reviews theories by Schücking [S28] and Kiernan [1261], and others that *Beowulf* is a composite poem, suggesting that linguistic evidence may provide useful clues to determining authorship. Before proceeding, Bately examines Kiernan's claim that the poem was assembled in the reign of Cnut. After surveying several typically early spelling patterns (particularly the West Saxon *ie* graph) in *Beowulf* and the rest of the corpus, she concludes that any date in or after the late tenth century seems unlikely (415). The best hope for determining authorship is to compare the distribution patterns of one small (but significant) area of linguistic usage not only in the three major sections of *Beowulf* but also in a body of work whose authorship seems assured (the Cynewulf canon) and in other works whose unity has been challenged (*Christ I, II* and *III, Guthlac A* and *B*, and *Genesis A* and *B*). Different distribution patterns may not necessarily suggest different authorship, since certain kinds of variation in the distribution of nouns and adjectives, for example, may be conditioned by subject matter or meter. Verbs and adverbs, though less bound to a traditional poetic style than nouns and adjectives, offer little help in that sample variations in verb and adverb patterns have no statistical significance (418). Even less dependent on stress patterns are "sentence words," notably conjunctions. In the remainder of the study, Bately examines the distribution of *siþþan* as a conjunction as well as the type, position, and semantic content of the subordinate clauses which it governs, finding that *Beowulf* often employs the word differently than the rest of the poetic corpus. Some uses of *siþþan* are unique to all three sections of *Beowulf*. "Proof of a single authorship for *Beowulf* as we have it cannot be founded on a limited analysis of selected linguistic details. However, a study of the handling of *siþþan* . . . provides no evidence against the theory that one man was responsible for all three parts" (431).

1477 Bolton, Whitney F. "A Poetic Formula in *Beowulf* and Seven Other Old English Poems: A Computer Study." *Computers and the Humanities* 19 (1985): 167-173.

Proposes the existence of a hitherto unstudied formula. "The formula is the three-word a-verse (XYZ) in which the first and last words (X, Z) are alliterating content words and the second word (Y) is a preposition" (167). Typical examples would be half-lines like *wēox under wolcnum* (l. 8a) and *folce tō frōfre* (l. 14a). *Beowulf* contains 248 such constructions, though computer-assisted analysis reveals that they are distributed in such a way as to suggest that the first and second parts of the poem were originally separate. Many b-verses have this XYZ structure, but none of them has the alliterative pattern characteristic of the formula. The Z word tends to be the most "content rich" part of the formula and often dictates the X word. The conception of formula which emerges here is based less on meaning and lexical items and more on part of speech and syntactic form. Includes tables of examples from *Beowulf* and a number of other Old English poems.

1478 Bragg, Lois. "Color Words in *Beowulf*." *Proceedings of the PMR Conference* 7 (1985 for 1982): 47-55.

Reviews words for color in *Beowulf*, attempting "to discover whether or not color is [actually] intended by each instance, and once color meaning is established, will seek to specify hue whenever possible" (47). Bragg, citing a number of previous word studies, examines *brūn, fealu, gēolo, græg, hār, gamol-, blonden-, gold, blōd, blanca, hwīt, blāc, blæc, sweart*, and *wan(n)*. A few of the more important conclusions are that a) *brūn* 'brown' as applied to metal objects most likely refers "to the dark brown color of browned metal" though the meaning "glossy" should not be disregarded. b) *fealu* may "refer to a color that we would call 'dun,' or more prosaically, 'mud,'" while *æppelfealuwe* (l. 2165a) may indicate apple-shaped markings. c) *grǣg* 'gray' is never applied to human hair, but to animals and metals, while the word *hār* seems to indicate age rather than greyness. d) colors for black often indicate lack of light or color. "The brief survey of color words in *Beowulf* has demonstrated that, although the spectrum is limited—there is no blue, no green, no purple, orange or red—the colors used . . . are used with considerable specificity as to hue—dark warm brown, dark blackish brown, yellow, grey, salt and pepper, silver, and three synonymous blacks" (53).

1479 Bravo García, Antonio. "Las fórmulas verbales en la épica anglosajona y castellana: un estudio contrastivo." [Oral Formulas in the Anglo-Saxon and Castilian Epic: a Comparative Study]. In *Homenaje a Álvaro Galmés de Fuentes*. Ed. Ana M. Cano Gonzáles. 2 Vols. Madrid: Editorial Gredos, 1985 to 1987. 2:39-47.

Compares the formulaic styles of *Beowulf* and the *Poema de Mio Cid*. Bravo García maps out both the differences and similarities in formulaic styles between the two poems. Differing metrical constraints as well as different sources of traditional language (Germanic and Romance/Arabic) account for the most important differences. On the other hand, the verse line in both poems is constructed of two hemistichs and the formula is associated with the hemistich. The two poems also have high proportions of formulas employing proper names, introducing speeches, expressing religious sentiments, and describing attributes of heroes (epithets). In both poems, some formulas appear over and over again. Bravo García also notes that while *Beowulf* contains legendary and fabulous materials, the *Mio Cid* is more historical and realistic, more down-to-earth and human ("más histórico y realista . . . , más doméstico y humano," 39).

1480 Brennan, Malcolm M. "Hrothgar's Government." *JEGP* 84 (1985): 3-15.

Examines the official governmental roles of the Coastguard, Wulfgar, Hrothgar, Unferth, and Wealhtheow, concluding that "Each of these Danes is first of all an official of the realm, and each one attempts, in accord with the functions of his office, to induce Beowulf to accept the political *status quo* while in their kingdom. At first they require him to defer to appointed officials and established customs; then they impose a stipulation on his proposal to fight the monster; finally they extract from him a promise that he will not use his victory over Grendel as a claim against the Danish kingdom" (3). In meeting Beowulf, the Coastguard identifies his authority and instructs the Geats in established procedure which they have violated, and finally makes a quick judgment about the petition of the Geats. Wulfgar, on the other hand, is more punctilious, proceeding in "typically bureaucratic fashion" (5). He points out established protocol to the Geats: they must leave their weapons outside and wait for Hrothgar's judgment. Hrothgar himself hears Beowulf's rather brash petition and immediately reminds Beowulf of his obligations to the Scyldings through his father. Here Beowulf shows a lack of seasoning in making so insulting a request. Hrothgar accepts his petition again, but omits to render a formal judgment. Unferth, functioning like "a public prosecutor" (10), challenges Beowulf not out of personal animosity but in order to challenge the petitioner officially. Wealhtheow uses her official function as cup-bearer to enlist Beowulf's aid for her two sons: she adapts the ceremony to her own purpose. In his reception into the Danish court, Beowulf receives an education in diplomacy. He enters as an inexperienced negotiator but receives an apprenticeship in governmental operation.

1481 Chase, Colin. "*Beowulf,* Bede, and St. Oswine: The Hero's Pride in Old English Hagiography." In *The Anglo-Saxons: Synthesis and Achievement.* Ed. J. Douglas Woods and David A.E. Pelteret. Waterloo: Wilfrid Laurier UP, 1985. Pp. 37-48.

Compares the heroism of Beowulf to that of Oswine (as told by Bede and the anonymous writer of the Norman *Vita Oswini*). While Bede restricts to one phrase the Anglo-Saxon horror at the betrayal of a king by his own thane, the anonymous *Life* fills in such sentiments plentifully, showing a much more living link with the world of *Beowulf,* where the subject of loyalty to one's lord is an urgent concern. The anonymous *Life* shows Oswine struggling between honor and love of his men when he backs down from a battle with his rival Oswy. In this, Chase sees a parallel to Beowulf's decision to fight the dragon alone. Though Leyerle [S550] finds a fatal contradiction between personal honor and responsible kingship, Chase argues that the *Life* reveres both, refusing to resolve the conflict in one way or the other. He disagrees with Goldsmith [S759] and Leyerle, who accuse Beowulf of pride in taking on the dragon alone. Beowulf does not succumb to the pride against which Hrothgar warned in his sermon, though his decision does lead to a profound tragedy.

Reviews of Woods and Pelteret: R.H.C. Davis, *Albion* 19 (1987): 45-46; J.F. Futhey, *ESC* 13 (1987) 323-25; A. Bammesberger, *Literaturwissenschaftliches Jahrbuch* 30 (1989): 327-28; F. Barlow, *EHR* 104 (1989): 449-50; P. Lendinara, *Schede medievali* 14-15 (1989): 113-14.

1482 Conner, Patrick W. "The Section Numbers in the *Beowulf* Manuscript." *AN&Q* 24 (1985): 33-38.

Proposes that the out-of-sequence section number XXIIII (fol. 166r) does not indicate a lost section or a misnumbering but that a change in the method of numbering the fitts has taken place. Conner argues that "the first twenty-four sections of *Beowulf* were enumerated after the section the numeral is intended to label and that sections twenty-five to forty-three were enumerated ahead of the section" (34). Conner surveys sectional numbers in the other vernacular poems, showing that they never appear at the beginning of a poem but that the beginning section is counted in the series. Thus, it seems unlikely that the first fifty-two lines of *Beowulf* are an unnumbered proem. The *Vercelli* codex, he argues, supports the possibility that section numbers could appear after the material they identify. Paleographical evidence suggests that scribe one altered his method of writing section numbers, since the numbers up to section twenty-three are small and written with a different pen than the rest of the poem but starting with twenty-five become much larger and are written with the same pen as the text.

1483 Dahlberg, Charles R. "*Beowulf* and the Land of Unlikeness." In *CUNY English Forum, 16*. Ed. Saul N. Brody and Harold Schechter. New York: AMS Press, 1985. Pp. 105-127.

Suggests that "the elegiac motif is central to the poem and that it may have developed, indirectly, from the Augustinian concept of earth as a land of unlikeness" (105). After tracing the concept of "unlikeness" from Augustine to Pseudo-Dionysius and Bede, Dahlberg detects it in three areas in *Beowulf*: in the poem's unusual chronology, its use of increasingly artificial direct discourse, and the ambiguities surrounding issues of kingship and treasure. Each of these unlikenesses (or contrasts) reinforces the idea of the mutability of earthly existence. The distorted chronology of the poem emphasizes the transitory nature of the legendary past as contrasted to the permanence of the *ēce rǣdas* 'eternal counsels' (l. 1760a) of Christian revelation. Digressions concerning Geatish history and the Swedish wars distort the chronological sequence. The poet moves away from "relatively verisimilar" direct discourse "toward longer, more complex, and allusive monologue" in order "to reinforce the elegiac emphasis in both content and form" (110). Finally, the poet exploits the ambiguous melding of Christian and Germanic concepts of kingship, an ambiguity realized most fully in the treasure hoard at the end of the poem. For Dahlberg it represents both transitory, earthly treasure and bright, heavenly treasure. Provides two detailed appendices: the first an outline of the chronology of the poem, the second, a list of twenty-three passages containing direct discourse.

1484   Deratzian, David L. "Runic Mysticism and the Names in *Beowulf*." *Literary Onomastics Studies* 12 (1985): 119-136.

Proposes a new method for interpreting names in *Beowulf* which replaces individual letters of a name with the original runic equivalents and then analyzes "the mystical meanings assigned to them [the runes] by the original users of the alphabet" (120). After sketching the history of runic writing and listing the word equivalents of runic symbols (on the basis of the *Rune Poem*), Deratzian analyzes the names *Beowulf*, *Heremod*, *Grendel*, *Hygd*, and *Modthrytho*. "The name 'Beowulf' is composed of the runes *beorc*, the rune of the birch tree, a symbol of fertility; *eh*, the horse, associated with the course of the sun; *ōs*, the rivermouth, a source of divine utterance; *wynn*, the rune of joy; *ur* rune of manly strength; *lagu*, rune of fertility and transition; and *feoh*, rune of possessions and wealth. Reading from right to left, we find Beowulf's life painted" (129). Deratzian also analyzes the names *Heremod*, *Grendel*, *Hygd*, and *Modthrytho*, finding that the runes for *Heremod* mirror negatively the runes for Beowulf. "There might be those who would criticize this method as too unscientific a method of literary or philological analysis, but it does tend to shed new light on old names, perhaps the very light that the writers of old wanted to reveal" (134).

1485 Evans, Jonathan D. "Semiotics and Traditional Lore: the Medieval Dragon Tradition." *Journal of Folklore Research* 22 (1985): 85-112.

Treats *Beowulf* briefly in an article on the semiotic "code" which underlies medieval dragon folk tales, finding that the dragon fight in *Beowulf* accentuates "tragic aspects of the heroic code . . . to mount a critique of the heroic ethic" (107). After discussing the utility of joining semiotics with folk tale research, Evans examines a number of dragon-slaying episodes from Old Norse sources, among them the *Egils saga* and *Sigurðar saga*. "Two fundamental semic systems are deployed simultaneously in dragon-slayer episodes: the opposition human/monster and its implied contradictories, and the opposition hero/villain and its contradictories. The medieval heroic code promotes a correlation between these two systems by which *human* and *hero* are seen as equivalents; likewise, *monster* and *villain* are correlated" (99). Generally, the dragon dies at the hands of the hero, and thus the story generally "affirms the heroic ethos" (100). *Beowulf*, however, blurs these oppositions by describing the dragon and Beowulf in remarkably similar terms, often representing the ambiguity grammatically in clauses where either Beowulf or the dragon could be the subject. In this sense, *Beowulf* represents a critique of the heroic life and "bears traces of the mediation between dragon and human, traces that are not fully realized or perhaps consciously suppressed" (108).

1486 Gould, Kent. "*Beowulf* and Folktale Morphology: God as Magical Donor." *Folklore* 96 (1985): 98-103.

Modifies the folktale morphology of Vladimir Propp and applies it to the Beowulf-Unferth exchange, showing how the poet blends pagan and Christian ideas. Gould sees Unferth as Propp's "magical donor" (in the reconstructed bear's son folktale), a figure who has two functions: testing and donating. Unferth tests Beowulf in the flyting match but later donates the sword Hrunting to him. This sword fails, however, and Beowulf wins the battle with Grendel's mother by means of a magical sword which he finds in her hall. The poet makes it clear that God directs Beowulf to the magic sword (ll. 1161-64). "God is now the magical donor to Beowulf because He replaces Unferth's failed sword with an unfailing one, supplanting any heathen donors" (100). This is "Christian magic" of a type found in Norse literature. By splitting the donor's functions (testing and donating) into two characters, Unferth and God, the poet "is demonstrating to his audience that an impeccable pagan in pre-Christian times could still merit divine assistance in spite of his religious ignorance" (101).

1487 Green, Eugene. "Power, Commitment, and the Right to a Name in *Beowulf.*" In *Persons in Groups: Social Behavior as Identity Formation in Medieval and Renaissance Europe.* Ed. Richard C. Trexler. Medieval & Renaissance Texts & Studies. Binghamton, NY: Medieval & Renaissance Texts & Studies, 1985. Pp. 133-140.

Surveys personal names in *Beowulf,* concluding that the poet has no interest in stressing the individuality of a character by naming him or her but that he names them to call attention to "matters of communal responsibility and power, to the possibilities of mutual assistance as well as to those of threat and challenge" (134). Green finds that poem names members of the royal family (Hrethel, Hrothgar, Hygelac, etc.), royal uncles and nephews (Hygelac/Beowulf, Sigemund/Fitela, Swerting/Hygelac, Heardred/Hereric), retainers close to a king or leader (Handscio, Æschere, Wiglaf), and members of intertribal conflict (Dæghrefn, Ingeld, Guthlaf, Oslaf, Grendel). Understanding that naming in *Beowulf* has to do with power relationships of this sort helps to explain why certain characters are not named. Women are not named unless they are married to kings and are themselves royal (Yrse[?], Hildeburh, Freawaru). Thus, Beowulf's mother, Ecgtheow's wife, is not named. Hildeburh's son (the member of a royal family) is not named because he dies uncrowned. Grendel is named because he is "a usurper, a mock king" (138) who has a number of human characteristics which his dam and the dragon, who are not named, lack.

1488 Greenfield, Stanley B. "Beowulf and the Judgment of the Righteous." In *Clemoes,* pp. 393-408.

Explores "the poet's attitude towards hero and heroic world" (395), arguing against a number of interpretations which see Beowulf either as blameworthy or suspect, particularly Leyerle [S550], Goldsmith [S759], Short [1210], and Shippey [S1093]. Instead, Greenfield argues, "the poet has presented both the hero and his world with more *humanitas* than *Christianitas*" (396). Strict Christian interpretations see the men and women in *Beowulf* as flawed because they lack Christian salvation, arguing *ex silentio*: the poem makes no overt mention of Christian redemption. However, the poet clearly approves of the heroic ideals of loyalty and generosity, particularly in the normative gnomic passages, and seems far from condemning the heroic ideal of revenge: he approves of Beowulf's revenge against the Swedes, for example, and God himself takes revenge on the kin of Cain. Concerning criticism of the hero, Greenfield makes the case that "Hrothgar's sermon is no touchstone for a negatively portrayed Beowulf" (401). Hrothgar's warning about failing strength, for example, does not apply to old Beowulf, who is still mighty enough to break Nægling. Instead of marking him as a sinner, Beowulf's mistake in judgment (in attacking the dragon single-handedly) humanizes the almost monstrously strong Beowulf. Wiglaf's supposed criticism of Beowulf's last act as foolhardy (*dǣda dollīcra*, l. 2646) is less negative than it seems since this phrase stands in variation with two other terms of clear approbation: *mǣst mǣrða* 'the greatest of glorious deeds' (l. 2645) and *ellenweorc* 'noble work' (l. 2643a). In the end, "[l]ife has its limits, not heroism or the heroic world" (407).

1489 Haudry, Jean. "Saint Christophe, Saint Julien L'Hospitalier et la 'Traversée de l'eau de la ténèbre hivernale'." [Saint Christopher, Saint Julian the Hospitaler, and the 'Crossing of Water in Winter Darkness']. *Études Indo-Européennes* 14 (1985): 25-31.

Believes that a formulaic Indo-European type-scene involving the crossing of water in winter darkness underlies Beowulf's swimming contest with Breca as well as certain details in the story of St. Christopher and St. Julian as well as an adventure of Grettir in the *Grettis Saga*. First and foremost, the crossing of water in the difficulties of winter is a qualifying ordeal ("épreuve qualifiante") for each of the heroes. Having withstood this arduous test, both Christopher and Beowulf go on to their main adventures (28). Christopher carries the Christ-child across a river while Grettir carries a farmer and his daughter across a rising river. Haudry argues that Christopher, at this stage, is essentially a pagan hero in search of the greatest martial power and that the heroic nature of his story contributed to its extraordinary popularity in Germanic countries of the late Middle Ages. The eastern versions of this scene have a transformed monster making the crossing, while the western versions depict the hero as gigantic and superhumanly powerful (as in the case of Beowulf, Grettir, and Chistopher).

1490 Hieatt, Constance B. "Cædmon in Context: Transforming the Formula." *JEGP* 84 (1985): 485-497.

Examines a number of creation scenes in Old Norse and Old English literature in order to determine whether a formulaic "type-scene" (see Fry [S667]) underlies these accounts. The creation hymn in *Beowulf* (ll. 90-98) follows the Germanic type-scene, reconstructed by Lönnroth, in many respects: it contains a list of created items, a reference to adornment, a possible allusion to greenness (l. 93a), and is elicited by a kind of challenge. However, it lacks the most common feature of such type scenes, an alliterative formula contrasting *eorðe* (earth) and *upheofon* (high heaven). Hieatt speculates that this formula "may have been suppressed because of the poet's consciousness that the *scop* and his audience within the poem were pagan and thus not fully aware of the implications of the Christian concept of heaven." Though the poet has the Biblical account in mind, "there is no good reason to suppose that the Bible is the immediate or primary source" (495).

1491 Hirabayashi, Mikio. "On the Uses of Oblique Cases of Noun in *Beowulf*." *Bulletin of Daito Bunka Univ.: Humanities* 23 (1985): 19-31.

According to Edward Sapir, the decay of the noun inflection system of English is considered to be part of the drift of language. This short paper discusses how noun cases preserve their original function. (MH)

1492 Hock, Hans Henrich. "Pronoun Fronting and the Notion 'Verb-Second' Position in *Beowulf*." In *Germanic Linguistics: Papers from a Symposium at the University of Chicago, April 24, 1985.* Ed. Jan Terje Faarlund. Bloomington: Indiana U Linguistics Club, 1985. Pp. 70-86.

Examines pronoun fronting in *Beowulf*, concluding that the poem does not take the "smart" solution of other Indo-European languages by placing the finite verb (shifted by fronting) directly after the first word or noun phrase; instead, "in this text, the WHOLE initial string, however long or complex, ordinarily counts as occupying the first position, and is followed by the shifted verb" (77). From this, Hock draws two conclusions: "Beowulfian syntax operates with initial strings," and "'clause-second' position of the verb is defined as post-initial string" (79). The initial string hypothesis may help to explain other aspects of Beowulfian word order and may help clarify some developments in later West Germanic texts.

1493 Kaske, Robert E. "The Gifstol Crux in *Beowulf.*" *Leeds Studies in English* n.s., 16 (1985): 142-151.

Reviews the various solutions to the *gifstōl* crux (164-69) and proposes a new interpretation. Kaske argues that the half-line *nē his myne wisse* (l. 169b) refers to God's not knowing the mind of Grendel. Gregory, in his *Moralia on Job*, develops a similar motif in explaining Job 1:7, where God does not know where Satan has come from. Light knows no shadow and God knows no evil. *Gifstōl* is probably to be construed as God's throne (as in *Christ* 571-73) and the *þone* preceding it is emphatic, "THAT gift-throne." "If these various conjectures can be entertained, lines 166b-69 may be paraphrased somewhat as follows: 'Heorot he [i.e., Grendel] held, the treasure-adorned hall [including, of course, its gift-throne], in the dark nights; but never could he have approached that other gift-throne, that treasure before God—nor did God even know him'" (147).

1494 Kiernan, Kevin S. "The State of the *Beowulf* Manuscript 1882-1983." *ASE* .13 (1985): 23-42.

Disputes the idea that the *Beowulf* manuscript has deteriorated since 1882, when Julius Zupitza undertook his transcription, and offers a list of readings invisible to Zupitza because of the obscuring paper frames and binding tape but visible today with the aid of fiber-optic lighting. "Apart from readings that have crumbled away from fire-damage, neither [Thorkelin] A nor B provides any reading that we cannot see as well or better today. Moreover, ultra-violet light allows us to read some words not visible to eighteenth- and nineteenth-century readers, and continuing technological advances, in particular electronic photography and digital image-processing, give us some legitimate hope for future discoveries in this manuscript" (24). "Fibre-optic light reveals forty-nine whole letters and ten virtually whole letters where Zupitza saw nothing, 118 whole letters where he saw only part of a letter, and 171 parts of letters where he saw either nothing at all or considerably less than what actually remains in the manuscript" (25). Kiernan also discusses a number of methods by which the manuscript might be rebound, making letters obscured by the paper frames and tape more visible and avoiding damage from buckling.

1495 Kinney, Clare. "The Needs of the Moment: Poetic Foregrounding as a Narrative Device in *Beowulf*." *SP* 82 (1985): 295-314.

Sees the "digressions" as important individual events in *Beowulf*, not just as parts of an integrated whole (a corrective to the views of Bonjour [S202], Brodeur [S373], and Leyerle [S634]). The digressions achieve "however briefly, a kind of dynamic autonomy, a self-sufficiency which draws its audience in to share *this* particular experience at *this* particular time for its own sake" (298). In these individual moments, the poet employs a number of genres: elegiac, homiletic, and heroic modes. Gnomic utterances are particularly interesting in this regard because they shift from the past tense of the narrative into the present tense of the proverb (ll. 991-1009). Occasionally the poet switches to the present tense to achieve a greater immediacy, a technique particularly prominent in lines 159-63, 2270b-75a, 1921b-24, and 2484-86. Examines passages like the father's lament for his hanged son which make extended use of the present tense amidst narrative set in the past. Skillful manipulation of point of view is another technique by which the poet focuses on the aesthetic needs of the moment. Kinney concludes that such individual poetic moments become "spontaneous alternative realities, near-autonomous parts which temporarily take over the narrative foreground and can only be ordered, retrospectively and synchronically, after the hero has died and his story been closed" (314).

1496 Magennis, Hugh. "The Beowulf Poet and his *druncne dryhtguman*." *NM* 86 (1985): 159-164.

Believes that the *Beowulf*-poet does not condemn intoxication from a moral point of view but sees it as part of the good life of warriors feasting in the hall, condemning it only when it leads to social disruption. Thus, when Wealhtheow says that her *druncne dryhtguman* 'drunken troop-men' (l. 1231a) do her bidding, she offers no insult to her men but "sees this intoxication as perfectly unexceptionable" (160). Though reckless drunkenness is mentioned in the Unferth episode, it seems to be a commonplace of the flyting ritual: Unferth himself cannot be portrayed unproblematically as a drunken fratricide. Finally, lines 2179b-80a, where the poet praises Beowulf for not having slain his hearth companions, have often been mistranslated: the phrase *nealles druncne slōg heorðgenēatas* must mean "he did not at all slay his hearth-companions when they had been drinking," though the adjective *druncne* is often misapplied to Beowulf: "never did he, drunk, slay his hearth-companions." Magennis concludes that for "this society the participle *druncen* need bear no sense of disapproval" (159).

1497 Mastrelli, Carlo Alberto. "Motivi indraici nel *Beowulf* e nella *Grettis Saga* (ags. *hæftmēce* e a.isl. *heptisax*)." [Indric Motifs in *Beowulf* and in the *Grettis Saga*]. *AIUON, filologia germanica* 28-29 (1985 to 1986): 405-20.

Proposes a new interpretation of the word *hæftmēce* 'hilted sword' (l. 1457a) along with its Old Norse relative *heptisax* (which appears in the *Grettis Saga*), arguing that the elements *hæft-* and *hept-* originally implied 'divine or demonic power' and that the two words may represent the degraded remains of an Indo-Iranian cosmological myth about Indra. The original story, Mastrelli suggests, must have revolved around a marvelous sword, though the characteristics of the sword are distributed among three weapons in *Beowulf*: Beowulf's sword (Hrunting, the *hæftmēce*), Grendel's Mother's dagger, and the magical giant sword hanging on the wall—each having its counterpart in the *Grettis Saga*. The myth of Indra's victory over the demon Valla and the snake Vrtra, symbolizing the establishment of cosmic order over chaos, has a number of features in common with the stories in *Beowulf* and the *Grettis Saga*, and Mastrelli suggests the possible traces of this Indo-Iranian myth among the early Germanic peoples. With the gradual passage of paganism to Christianity, the pagan meaning of the *heptisax* (the weapon of divine or demonic powers, locked in the handle) degraded to the banal and unjustified meaning "weapon with a handle" (415-16).

1498 Mazzuoli Porru, Giulia. "*Beowulf*, v. 33: īsig ond ūtfus." In *Studi linguistici e filologici per Carlo Alberto Mastrelli*. Pisa: Pacini, 1985. Pp. 263-74.

Suggests that the description of Scyld's funeral ship as *īsig ond ūtfus* 'covered with ice and ready to depart' (l. 33a) may preserve a faded memory of a burial practice (common to cultures on the Baltic sea) where the corpse was frozen to preserve it. The principal evidence for this custom comes from the Old English *Orosius* (a translation of Orosius' *Historiarum adversum Paganos*), where in an added episode Ohtere and Wulfstan describe their journey to the Baltic sea, including a story about a tribe, the Estas, who freeze dead bodies as well as vessels of ale or water, either in summer or winter. Mazzuoli Porru suggests that the corpse, or perhaps the deck of the ship is covered with ice so that the body could be preserved longer for its voyage into the unknown ("perché la salma possa conservarsi più a lungo nel suo viaggio verso l'ignoto," 266). She examines Latin, Old Norse, and Old English texts to identify the Estas and shows that they are known to several Baltic cultures and that the story of Scyld and his line also has Baltic ties (in Old Norse and possibly Finnish). Reviews other explanations of the word *īsig*, such as 'shining like ice,' etc.

1499 McAlister, Caroline. "Beowulf Confronts Death." *Mind & Nature (Emory Univ.)* 5 (1985): 13-17.

Not seen.

1500 Mikawa, Kiyoshi. "The Use of the Prepositional 'on' in *Beowulf* (2)." *English Literature (Waseda Univ.)* 61 (1985): 110-21.

Not seen.

1501 Mitchell, Bruce. *Old English Syntax*. 2 vols. Oxford: Clarendon Press, 1985.

A detailed account of Old English syntax containing numerous analyses of lines from *Beowulf*. Mitchell's "Index of Passages Particularly Discussed" for *Beowulf* (II:1070-1071) has been incorporated into the line index for this

volume. Addenda and corrigenda for this study appear in Mitchell [1756a].
Reviews: A. Oizumi, *Gakuto* 81.11 (1984): 64-65; T. Kubouchi, *The Rising Generation* (Tokyo) 131 (1985): 124-25; T.A. Shippey, *TLS* June 28, 1985: 716; S. Ono, *SEL* (Tokyo), English # 1986: 99-104; Anon., *OEN* 18.2 (1985): 15-16; E.G. Stanley *RES* 37 (1986): 234-37; A. Bammesberger, *Die Sprache* 31 (1985): 198; N.F. Blake, *Lore and Language* 4 (1985): 113; K. Koerner, *Diachronica* 2 (1985): 293-94; MM and KT, *OEN* 20.1 (1986): 51; W. Koopman, *Neophil* 71 (1987): 460-66; H.H. Meier, *Fuse Quarterly* 23 (1985): 12; S.B. Greenfield, *JEGP* 86 (1987): 392-99; P. Lendinara, *Schede medievali* 11 (1986): 396-98; R.J. Reddick, *OEN* 20.2 (1987): A 29-30; R.D. Fulk, *PQ* 66 (1987): 279-83; F.C. Robinson, *Speculum* 63 (1988): 700-02; U. Fries, *BGdSL* (Tübingen) 110 (1988): 243-47; V. Adams, *Journal of English Linguistics* 21.1 (1989): 88-96.

1502 Murphy, Michael. "Vows, Boasts and Taunts, and the Role of Women in Some Medieval Literature." *ES* 66 (1985): 105-112.

Distinguishes between two closely related phenomena known to the heroic world: boasting and vowing. A boast refers to past accomplishments while a vow promises future accomplishments. The two have different functions: the boast "established [the hero's] credentials for a given task, and it served . . . to remind him and others that he had something to live up to" (105-6). The vow, on the other hand, "was meant to keep at a premium the loyalty and pride in martial prowess essential to the survival of a tribe or nation. . . . When the time to fight came, men remembered (or were reminded of) their brave words spoken in the beer hall which had now to be matched with equally brave deeds" (106). Beowulf's boasts about his earlier exploits establish his credentials for the fight with Grendel. Murphy reviews the appearance of boasting and vowing in a number of later works including the *Alliterative Morte Arthure*, Malory's *Morte D'Arthur*, the *Pelerinage de Charlemagne*, *Sir Thopas*, the *Tournament of Tottenham*, *Sir Gawain and the Green Knight*, and others, concluding that writers of romance took such heroic conventions less seriously and would often burlesque them. Finally, Murphy examines women who act as taunters. Such women are strong-willed and forceful in the sagas, but only traces of such figures appear in *Beowulf*. Though

Wealhtheow is not an official "taunter," she does elicit a vow from Beowulf in lines 636-38.

1503 Nagucka, Ruta. "Remarks on Complementation in Old English." In *Papers from the Fourth International Conference on English Historical Linguistics, Amsterdam, 10-13 April, 1985.* Ed. Roger Eaton, Olga Fischer, Willem Koopman, and Frederike van der Leek. Amsterdam Studies in the Theory and History of the Language Sciences. Series IV, Current Issues in Linguistic Theory, 41. Amsterdam: Benjamins, 1985. Pp. 195-204.

Opposes the thesis of Anthony Warner that accusative and infinitive constructions in Middle English come about through the influence of Latin syntax; instead, by comparing such constructions in both Latin-influenced (Ælfric's prose) and Latin-free Old English (*Beowulf*), Nagucka shows that Latin cannot have served as a model for this construction, since both groups show statistically similar distributions of the constructions. A discussion of statistical method follows.

1504 Nagy, Joseph F. "Beowulf and Fergus: Heroes of Their Tribes?" In *Connections between Old English and Medieval Celtic Literature.* Old English Colloquium Series, 2. Lanham, MD: U Presses of America, 1985. Pp. 31-44.

Following a suggestion by Carney [S299], explores "the structural and thematic parallels between the story of Beowulf ... and the story of Fergus mac Léti from Irish narrative" (31) and suggests that the similarities may be due to a shared Indo-European kingship myth. Both Beowulf and Fergus are "heroes of the tribe," that is, "a figure who is marked by extraordinary power and therefore functions as a mediator between the categories of human and divine." Both stand in contrast to the "hero outside the tribe," who has tremendous strength but whose energies do not serve the community (34). In terms of Indo-European mythology, both Fergus and Beowulf combine elements of the Vayu and Indra types. Nagy sketches a three-part pattern which describes the mixed natures of the two warrior kings: 1) they prove their kingliness in an exploit which protects the tribe or expands its territories (Beowulf in defeating Grendel; Fergus in his avenging of the death of the befriended exile), 2) first, the hero wins a beautiful object or quality but almost dies in the process (Beowulf in the fight with Grendel's mother; Fergus in his gaining the power of existing underwater) and next violates some kind of interdiction or prohibition (Beowulf in the thief's breaching of the cursed hoard; Fergus in disobeying the leprechaun's condition), and 3) they fight with a symbolic monster and die, forfeiting their kingship but gaining praise as warriors (Beowulf in his fight with dragon; Fergus in his encounter with the bellows-monster). Nagy agrees with Leyerle [S550] that Beowulf (as well as Fergus) suffers the tragic contradiction between kingship and heroism.

1505 Nelson, Marie. "*Beowulf,* II.2824b-2845a." *Explicator* 43 (1985): 4-7.

Following Niles [1399], suggests that the poet is concerned to show the dragon as a worthy adversary to Beowulf rather than as a representation of spiritual or social evil, finding several stylistic features in lines 2824b-2845a to support this idea. The poet stresses not only the dragon's strength and readiness to fight but often pairs him with Beowulf in such a way as to elevate him as an enemy. Beowulf is the guardian of his people, while the dragon is guardian of the barrow, etc. The description of the dragon's death "suggests a human experience of deprivation. . . . The dragon who formerly flew in the air displaying his magnificence now lies dead on the ground, unable to defend his treasure" (6). Thus, the poet defines the heroic character of Beowulf by contrast to this worthy opponent.

1506 Onega, Susana. "Poesía épica anglosajona: *Beowulf.*" [Anglo-Saxon Epic Poetry: *Beowulf*]. In *Estudios literarios inglesés: Edad Media.* Ed. J.F. Galvan Reula. Madrid: Catedra, 1985. Pp. 17-41.

Provides a general account of the poem, including a discussion of structure and theme, as well as an introduction into Anglo-Saxon meter, alliteration, diction, and style. Onega emphasizes the interlocking narrative structure of the three main episodes and discusses theories of structural unity. She points out that the *Beowulf*-poet uses negative constructions to define concepts: often showing what they are not instead of showing what they are: Beowulf is not a Heremod, while Grendel does not pay wergild. These negative expressions show that the contrast between good and evil, between the heroic and the anti-heroic, exists at a grammatical level and constitutes the thematic center of the poem. In terms of structure, the use of negation creates the repeating sequence "something good followed by something bad" and points to the fatalism of the entire poem.

1507 Orton, P.R. "Verbal Apposition, Coordination and Metrical Stress in Old English." *NM* 86 (1985): 145-158.

Seeks "to reconsider the meaning of *Beowulf* 1117b-20a and defend an alternative to Klaeber's punctuation of the passage; to examine the distribution of a species of apposition between finite verbs in Old English verse and to comment on its significance as an element of style; to assemble evidence of a connection between verbal apposition in a-verses and verbal stress in b-verses, and to suggest an explanation for this connection; and finally to reconsider some of the questions raised by b-verses with alliterating verb in Old English verse, and to suggest a classification of these" (145). In light of a pattern in which an a-verse beginning with a finite verb stands in opposition to the preceding b-verse, Orton would take *wand tō wolcnum* 'wound to the clouds' (l. 1119a) as an apposition to *gūðrinc āstāh* 'the battle warrior ascended' (l. 1118b) and begin a new sentence with *wælfȳra mǣst* 'the greatest of slaughter-fires' (l. 1119b). He finds and analyzes thirty-nine instances of this structure, which the poet uses stylistically in order to attribute a range of traits, usually heroic ones, to a character or action, a phenomenon that Orton finds in the Unferth-Beowulf exchange (ll. 506-81). Also includes a discussion of line 2717b, a b-verse with an alliterating verb.

1508 Pintzuk, Susan, and Anthony S. Kroch. "Reconciling an Exceptional Feature of Old English Clause Structure." In *Germanic Linguistics: Papers from a Symposium at the University of Chicago, April 24, 1985.* Ed. Jan Terje Faarlund. Bloomington: Indiana U Linguistics Club, 1985. Pp. 87-111.

Maintains that the syntax of *Beowulf* (and early Old English) was verb-final and that apparent exceptions can be explained by an optional "verb-second constraint." Pintzuk and Kroch map "syntactic units onto metrical ones" in order to provide information about intonation (87).

1509 Potter, Joyce Elizabeth. "Eternal Relic: A Study of Setting in Rosemary Sutcliff's *Dragon Slayer*." *Children's Literature Association Quarterly* 10 (1985): 108-112.

Analyzes Rosemary Sutcliff's *Dragon Slayer* [S856], an adaptation of *Beowulf* for children.

1510 Pulsiano, Phillip. "'Cames Cynne': Confusion or Craft?" *Proceedings of the PMR Conference* 7 (1985 for 1982): 33-38.

Argues that the scribal correction of MS. *cames* to *caines* in line 107a (where Grendel is cursed "in the race of Cain") indicates a knowledge of "a widespread exegetical tradition linking Cham [Ham] with Cain" (36) and that the uncorrected reading be considered equally valid as the corrected. Pulsiano reviews exegetical evidence from Alcuin, Cassian, and Tertullian, which tells of Ham as the reviver of Cain's evil and as the progenitor of a race of monsters. This tradition helps to explain lines 1687-93, where the "*Beowulf*-poet clearly had in mind a conflated Cham/Cain tradition through which he was able to explain the re-entry of monsters into the world" (36). Pulsiano concludes, "I suggest then that the original manuscript reading of *cames* be given equal consideration in favor of choosing *caines* and thereby ignoring the related Cham tradition" (37).

1511 Rausing, G. "*Beowulf, Ynglingatal* and the *Ynglinga Saga*: Fiction or History?" *Forväannen* 80 (1985): 163-78.

Not seen.

1512 Riedinger, Anita. "The Old English Formula in Context." *Speculum* 60 (1985): 294-317.

In a study of formulaic style, redefines three key terms: formula, system, and set. Riedinger points out that a number of formulas, *niht-lagne fyrst* (l. 528a) 'night-long period' and *ofer cald wæter* 'over cold water' (for example) are consistently associated with certain themes: the former with a terrifying period of time before a battle and the latter with scene of impending carnage. However, these themes are not contained in the formulas themselves. Riedinger redefines formula to take these extra-semantic themes into account: a formula must have one general concept or theme, belong to one substitution system, and perform one metrical function.

She introduces the concept of a "set" to clarify these relationships: a substitution system such as "*x hrēmig*" may have several sets, each of which has its own general theme and function. "A system may contain several different sets, each of which is a different formula.... By making a distinction between verses that are members of the same system, but of different sets, one can identify word groups that are the equivalent of the 'same formula,' even though they contain variables" (306). Riedinger analyzes several systems, identifying a number of sets (each with its recognizable theme) for each: *X X fyrst*, *X reorde*, *x X wæter*, "the greatest of x buildings," and others, with many examples from *Beowulf*.

1513 Robinson, Fred C. *'Beowulf' and the Appositive Style*. The Hodges Lectures. Knoxville: U of Tennessee P, 1985. Pp. 106.

Examines appositions—juxtaposed elements—in *Beowulf*: from "the smallest element of microstructure—the compounds, the grammatical appositions, the metrical line with its apposed hemistichs—to the comprehensive arc of macrostructure, the poem seems built on apposed segments. And the collocation of the segments usually implies a tactic meaning" (25).

Chapter one shows how meaning arises from these apposed elements and how meaning is uniquely related to the theme of the poem. With respect to theme, *Beowulf* is a "profoundly retrospective narrative" (7), meditating on the meaning of the pagan past. Robinson surveys a number of contemporary attitudes about paganism from Tertullian, Pope Zacharias, to Alcuin, Dante, and the *Legenda Aurea*, concluding that an Anglo-Saxon audience would have recognized that *Beowulf* and his pagan companions could not achieve salvation. The poet, then, sought to "acknowledge his heroes' damnation while insisting on their dignity" (13). Such a perspective requires readers or listeners to entertain two different points of view at the same time. Apposed elements—from the structure of compounds, juxtaposed clauses and sentences, to retold and juxtaposed narrative episodes—contribute to a complex paratactic style which the poet presses into service for his dual vision of the poem's damned but noble characters. Modern editorial practices often obscure the openness of such appositions.

Chapter two, "Apposed Word Meanings and Religious Perspectives," argues that the poetic vocabulary available to a

Christian Anglo-Saxon poet already contained the possibility for a dual vision of the pagan past. Caedmon was one of the first poets to renovate the old heroic vocabulary for a distinctly Christian context. Words like *dryhten*, which once applied to the lord of a comitatus, now could be applied to the Christian God. The *Beowulf* poet carefully manipulates the pre- and post-Caedmonian meanings of his words—epithets for God (*se ælmihtiga, waldend, metod, alwalda, god*, etc.), fate (*wyrd, metodsceaft*), sin, etc.—to draw a picture of noble pagans who unwittingly refer to Christian concepts through the dark lens of their pagan conceptions. Such characters are admirable in that they attain a limited insight into the spiritual realm. However, "when the poet says that Beowulf and his men 'gode þancedon,' the Christian audience knows that on the level of the characters in the poem, with their limited perception and their pre-Cædmonian diction, the noun could only refer to whatever god they knew—Thunor or Woden. . . . But on the level of the poet and his audience, it is commonly known who the supreme being really was at the time when the Geatas were addressing their thanks to whatever god they perceived" (41). This device allows the poet to add "to his celebration of ancestral valor a compassionate tone of Christian regret" (59). The epithets for the monsters contain a similar duality as names for pagan divinities which in a Christian context came to signify demonic powers. Words like *dōm* 'glory' or 'judgment,' *mægen* 'strength' or 'virtue,' and *synn* 'crime' or 'sin' have a similar dual perspective. Robinson points out that the editorial capitalization of names for the deity eliminates the essential ambiguity of such words as *metod*.

Chapter three, "Grammatical Apposition and Some Beowulfian Themes," returns to a consideration of grammatical appositions or variations and how they relate to a particular theme or sub-theme. The poet often uses appositives in such a way as "freshen the sense of poetic formulas in various ways" (64). "Other appositions . . . exercise the audience's mind in noticing elemental meanings of words or in recalling etymological origins" (66). A sub-theme developed through apposition is that human artifacts are allies in the fight against chaos and that patterned artifacts parallel patterned behavior of man. The mutual loyalties between thanes and their lord is another such sub-theme. The poet treats drinking rituals especially carefully, implying that drinking beer is a confirmation of a vow or boast to one's lord. When Beowulf says that Unferth is *bēore druncen* (l. 531a), he may be saying that "'Having drunk your lord's mead, Unferth, you do not make the expected *gilpcwide* [boast]'" (79). Finally, the word *lofgeornost* 'most eager for [heroic] fame' or 'vainglorious' (l. 3182b) is emblematic of the poet's dual perspective: it represents a pagan virtue but a Christian vice. "In *lofgeornost* [the Christian audience] could only have seen that the hero lived and died in ignorance of Christian truth" (81-2). (Robinson's "index of verses from *Beowulf* individually discussed" has been incorporated into the line index of this volume.)

Reviews: *OEN* 20.1 (1986): 77; Roberta Frank, *Speculum* 61 (1986): 922-24; J. Hill, *N&Q* 33 (1986): 530-31; M.C. Seymour, *ES* 67 (1985): 363-64; W.G. Busse, *Anglia* 106 (1988): 203-10.

1514 Rosenberg, Bruce A. "Reconstructed Folktales as Literary Sources." In *Historical Studies and Literary Criticism.* Ed. Jerome J. McGann. Madison: U of Wisconsin P, 1985. Pp. 76-89.

Discusses the applicability of folklore methodology to *Beowulf*, particularly the Finnish or historic-geographic method. Folklorists have argued for some time that the Beowulf story corresponds to a folktale type catalogued by Aarne and Thompson as "The Three Stolen Princesses" (Type 301). *Beowulf* incorporates four out of six of the elements in type 301, and a knowledge of the common pattern helps to explain otherwise inexplicable details in the poem. Nevertheless, the pioneering folkloristic approach to *Beowulf* made by Panzer [S36] has methodological weaknesses. The historic-geographic method offers perhaps a more promising way to explain the folklore elements in *Beowulf* since it accounts for the geographical distribution and thematic variation in folktale types in statistical terms, allowing the folklorist to determine the original shape of the type and locate variants and sub-types in a geographical region. Such an examination of the Scandinavian folktale analogues to *Beowulf* shows that *Beowulf* deviates from the statistical norm in not depicting the childhood of the hero first but referring to it in flashbacks. Such a structure may result from the traditions of the Germanic epic. Rosenberg also discusses the issue of monogenesis vs. polygenesis and oicotyping.

1515 Sato, Noboru. "*Beowulf* and Music." *The New Perspective (Kantogakuin Univ.)* 16 (1985): 17-21. In Japanese.

Finds similarities between the structure of *Beowulf* and that of polyphonic music composed in the early eleventh century, indicating a date for the poem of around 1000. The historical elements in *Beowulf* relate to the unhistorical elements as do the melodic lines in contemporary polyphony. (NS)

1516 Taylor, Paul Beekman. "Beowulfs Second Grendel Fight." *NM* 86 (1985): 62-69.

Explains the two masculine personal pronouns in lines 1392b and 1394b as references to Grendel, not (as has been assumed) to the masculine properties of Grendel's mother. "Nothing in the text makes it clear that the hero knows that Grendel is dead" (66). In the second fight, "Beowulf ventures against the unknown and the mysterious. The rhetoric of his reply to Hrothgar's plea for help abstracts the unknown into *hē* perhaps for no other reason than Beowulfs awareness that Grendel's power is at the source of all the ills Hrothgar can expose. His fight in the underwater cavern is a second fight against Grendel himself" (69).

1517 No Item.

1518 Tripp, Raymond P., Jr. "Lifting the Curse on *Beowulf.*" *ELN* 23 (1985): 1-8.

Supports Doig [1241] in the premise that the spell on the dragon's hoard is not actually a curse but a prohibition against entry into the hoard. Repunctuating lines 3050-51, Tripp goes on to claim that this spell is not ancient but rather was made by the Geats after Beowulfs death: "It is the abuse of treasure which has brought them [the Geats] to their present plight; and they do the logical—if not necessarily effective—thing: they attempt to 'ban' treasure by laying a spell, a prohibition, upon it, so that it will never be abused again" (6).

1519 Tuso, Joseph F. "Beowulfs Dialectal Vocabulary and the Kiernan Theory." *South Central Review* 2 (1985): 1-9.

Compares the type and percentage of dialect forms in *Beowulf* to those in the late tenth-century *Lindisfarne*, *Rushworth*, and *Corpus* gospels in order to test the theory of Kiernan [1261] that archaic and dialect forms in *Beowulf* "can be accounted for by its use of a general OE poetic dialect, [and that] one need not postulate with Klaeber and others, earlier dialectically diverse manuscripts of the poem to account for these mixed forms" (1). Tuso's study ultimately endorses Kiernan's view of the mixed poetic dialect, finding that the poem shares 101 dialectical forms with the tenth-century gospels (each from a different dialect area), that of the shared words "the majority, or 67% are Anglian; however, in the 1,223 occurrences of these words in *Beowulf,* 57% are West Saxon," that excluding certain prepositions, "59% of the remaining dialectical word occurrences in *Beowulf* are Anglian, that "*Beowulf*'s 101 dialectal words appear rather consistently in all three parts of the poem," that "Anglian words appear 18% more often in Parts I and II than in Part III," that the "highest concentration of Anglian words is in Part II, ll. 1888-2199, ... which Kiernan believes to be a scribal collaboration," and that this evidence "tends to support Kiernan's view that the poem is written in general OE poetic dialect, since *Beowulf* freely uses throughout words from all three historical dialects—Northumbrian, Mercian, and West Saxon" (2-3). Tuso provides charts and tabulations of dialect forms.

1520   Ushigaki, Hiroto. "The Image of Beowulf as King and Hero: Some Interpretative and Critical Problems." *Studies in English Literature* (Tokyo) English No. (1985): 13-20.

Not seen. The report in *YWOES, OEN* 20.1 (1986): 81, describes the argument as follows: "Ushigaki ... mounts a sturdy defense of Beowulf as king, arguing that the demands of heroism and kingship are not at odds, as some have claimed, but the same: to become a king at all one must display heroic conduct. Hrothgar's sermon, whose precepts some have seen Beowulf as violating, is 'practical and philosophical rather than exclusively Christian' (p. 7). So are Beowulf's concerns at the end of his life: like Hrothgar, he speaks of specific practices, not of principles. Ushigaki remarks on the poem's 'general tone of praise,' noting for example that in Beowulf's final eulogy he is given 'the greatest praise that a language is capable of' (p. 12). Yet, he says, the characters themselves seem to have mixed feelings about the heroic enterprise—most notably Wiglaf, but also the messenger who elaborates the consequences of Beowulf's death and the 'Geatish woman' who appears (perhaps) in the poem's closing lines. In the 'noble aspiration' of heroism, Ushigaki says, 'lurks ... a dark brutal impetus driving man to the tragic, if glorious destruction of his own self and those around him' (p. 18)."

1521 Wachsler, Arthur A. "Grettir's Fight with a Bear: Another Neglected Analogue of *Beowulf* in the *Grettis Saga Asmundarsonar.*" *ES* 66 (1985): 381-390.

Following the procedure of McConchie [1347], finds a neglected analogue for Beowulf's fight with Grendel and his mother in chapter twenty-one of the *Grettis saga*: Grettir's contest with an enormous bear. Wachsler sees a number of parallels between the two contests: "1) identical provocation for the monster's attacks; 2) dismemberment of the monster by the hero in the initial fight; 3) use of the monster's severed limb as a trophy; 4) the adversarial relationship of the hero [Beowulf/Grettir] with one of the retainers [Unferth/Bjorn] of the host [Hrothgar/Thorkel]; 5) the foreign origin of the hero; and 6) the desertion of the hero by his companions" (383). He provides a detailed summary of the bear-fight scene and argues that the bear can be seen as a revenant since in Norse mythology the bear is thought to be the spirit (ON *fylgja*) of a great leader. Wachsler uses the analogue to explain the detail in *Beowulf* in which the hero severs the head of the already-dead Grendel. In the *Grettis saga*, Grettir needs the paw as proof of his deed. "In both stories, the trophy serves as conclusive proof of the monster's death" (387).

1522 Watanabe, Hideki. "*Beowulf* 1020: *brand Healfdenes.*" *Linguistic Research (Tokyo Univ.)* 3 (1985): 121-31.

Supports Kuhn's view [F1168] that the MS. reading *brand Healfdenes* 'sword of Healfdene' (l. 1020b) should stand, though it is often emended to *bearn Healfdenes* 'son of Healfdene' in order to supply a human subject for the preceding verb *forgeaf*. Watanabe provides corroborating evidence that *brand Healfdenes* refers literally to Healfdene's sword. (HW) Mitchell [1756] describes the arguments of this article.

1523 Wetzel, Claus-Dieter. "Die Datierung des *Beowulf*: Bemerkungen zur jüngsten Forschungsentwicklung." [The Dating of *Beowulf*: Remarks on the Latest Research Developments]. *Anglia* 103 (1985): 371-400.

Reviews and critiques several recent proposals for dating the poem, including metrical, linguistic, historical, and paleographical approaches. Particular attention is paid to the papers delivered at the Toronto Conference (edited by Chase) as well as to a refutation of Kevin Kiernan's book-length study [1261]. Wetzel concludes that the possible range of dates has been plausibly extended into the tenth century but rejects an eleventh-century date. The key to this apparently insoluble problem is not to be found in the poem's historical context but in its language. It is to be hoped that ninth- and tenth-century dating, so much more prominent in recent scholarship, will not become a silent assumption. Even if the ninth century has won out generally, it is not so easy to dismiss the eighth; the tenth century, not likely on linguistic grounds, appears possible from a historical point of view, while the eleventh century drops out of consideration on linguistic grounds. In the end, the dating of *Beowulf* remains (and should remain) an open question (400).

1524 Yada, Hiroshi. "Functional Classification of the Use of Word- and Phrase-Binding *Ond* in *Beowulf.*" *Studies in English Literature* (Baiko Jogakuin U) 20 (1985): 91-113.

Not seen.

1525 Yamada, Jiro. "Study of 'Variation' in *Beowulf* (2)." *The Meijo Shogaku (The Journal of Commerce and Economics)* 34 (1985): 1-17. In Japanese.

Not seen.

1526 Yoshida, Kiyoshi. "A Study of *Beowulf*: Time, Life and Death." *Bulletin of Linguistics and Literature (Kyushu Women's College)* 15 (1985): 87-93. In Japanese.

Not seen.

1986

1527 Atkinson, Stephen C. B. "'Oð ðæt ān ongan . . . draca rīcsian': Beowulf, the Dragon, and Kingship." *Publications of the Missouri Philological Association* 11 (1986): 1-10.

In a continuation of an earlier article [1421], argues that "the monsters represent perversions of the social roles Beowulf is called upon to play at each stage of his career—thane, avenger, and king" (1), concentrating here on the role of the dragon as a perverted image of a king and examining a number of digressions which incorporate this theme. A number of verbal and thematic echoes connect Beowulf to the dragon (particularly ll. 2210b-11). The dragon, like Heremod, perverts the values of kingship by hoarding treasure and living alone, without followers. Digressions about the dragon and his hoard underscore "the fragile quality of peace and the ultimate futility of achievement" (4), while digressions on the Swedish-Geatish wars raise "doubts about the compatibility of personal heroism and successful kingship" (6). Finally, "Beowulf's conduct can be measured by his conquest of the monsters who represent perversion of his own legitimate roles, and in this regard his career is exemplary. At the same time, he is incapable of altering the fundamental nature of his world and we see him in the last third of the poem as a victim" (9).

1528 Bammesberger, Alfred. "On Old English *gefrægnod* in *Beowulf* 1333 a." In *Linguistics Across Historical and Linguistic Boundaries: In Honour of Jacek Fisiak on the Occasion of His Fiftieth Birthday.* Ed. Dieter Kastovsky and Aleksander Szwedek. 2 Vols. Trends in Linguistics: Studies and Monographs, 32. Berlin: Mouton de Gruyter, 1986. I:193-197.

Proposes that the manuscript form *gefrægnod* (l. 1333a), emended by Klaeber [S67] and others to *gefægnod* 'made happy,' be retained and that it be construed as a reinterpretation (by analogy) of the rare form *gefregen* or *gefrigen*, the participle of *fregnan/frignan*, 'to ask.' An earlier form of the text could have read *fylle gefregen*, 'having asked for a glut.' "In the course of the textual transmission the form *gefregen*, which had become rare or even obsolete, had an originally explanatory gloss *gefrægnad* substituted for it. *gefrægnad* corresponds to the tenth-century preterital form *gefrægnade.... gefrægnad* was finally transposed into West-Saxon as *gefrægnod*" (195).

1529 Berkhout, Carl T., and Renée Medine. "*Beowulf* 770a: *rēþe renweardas.*" *N&Q* 33 (1986): 433-434.

Suggests that the phrase *rēþe renweardas* (l. 770a), describing Grendel and Beowulf while they struggle in the hall, may be a poetic compound meaning 'ferocious watchdogs.' Berkhout and Medine marshall evidence from Old Norse and Old Saxon sources which use the element *-weard* 'guardian' to describe dogs as house guardians and point out that *ren-* may mean 'house.' Such an interpretation would help to explain the thirteenth-century form *renhund*. "The metaphor is a good one, applying equally well to both Beowulf and Grendel and conveying at once the full fury of their scrambling fight about the hall" (433).

1530 Berlin, Gail Ivy. "Grendel's Advance on Heorot: The Functions of Anticipation." *Proceedings of the PMR Conference* 11 (1986): 19-26.

The poet's frequent anticipation of the outcome of narrative events, though viewed by many critics as clumsy and unappealing, allows for several sophisticated effects, as a detailed analysis of Grendel's approach to Heorot (ll. 702b-736) shows. Berlin argues that in this section the poet repeats the event of Grendel's approach several times, following each repetition with an anticipation of the monster's ultimate failure and death. She assigns several functions to this device of anticipation: it establishes a sense of community between author and audience, "provides a basis for contrast, for comparison of action and outcome, and thus for an irony based on knowledge shared by both narrator and audience," and "increases understanding of the 'true' significance of the events" (23-24). "Explanation would thus seem to be more valued than suspense, and action, not so much of interest in itself, but as a demonstration or proof of the point" (24).

1531 Bhattacharya, Prodosh. "Hrothgar's 'Sermon' in *Beowulf.*" *Journal of the Department of English (Univ. of Calcutta)* 22 (1986 to 1987): 148-160.

Following Klaeber [S41], compares passages from Hrothgar's "sermon" (ll. 1700-1768) to analogous passages in various Old English homilies (including the *Catholic*

Homilies of Ælfric and those in the Blickling collection), concluding that Germanic references are Christianized while at the same time, Christian references are often fleshed out by references to heroic life. "It is interesting how, while Germanic legends such as Heremod's are given a Christian interpretation in the poem, the specifically Christian allusion to the arrows of the devil is expanded in terms of a regular Heroic battle" (155). In the end, "The effect is not only that Beowulf's present achievements are seen in Christian terms, but he is also seen as belonging to a society in which the older Heroic values seem to have been fused with the new Christian ones" (157).

1532 Bloomfield, Morton W. "'Interlace' as a Medieval Narrative Technique, with Special Reference to *Beowulf*." In *Kaske*, pp. 49-59.

Points out the dangers of using the concept of interlace from the plastic arts to refer to narrative features of texts like *Beowulf* and finds that a better explanation is that part two of the poem may reduplicate the thinking patterns of old age, where the increasing intrusion of the past (in back references) mimics the thinking patterns of the aged. Bloomfield points out that "[u]nlike art, the very nature of narration demands one line of action at a time. This fact of verbal art makes interlace based on simultaneous events impossible" (51). Narrative lines, when they are not being told, simply disappear until the narration returns to them. However, the "thread or line in art, if it disappears, disappears only slightly to let another line pass over it. It is still clearly 'there'" (55). Thus, Bloomfield prefers Carol Clover's term "stranding" (*The Medieval Saga*, 1982) for narratives that move back and forth between various story lines. Part two in particular "seems to be more broken and interrupted in style than the earlier part, although both parts share similar back-curlings of reference" (57). Here there are many longer and shorter digressions referring to the real and mythic past but very few referring to the future. "This procedure blurs the clean and sharp effect of the main story line and thus reduplicates as far as is possible by structural means the mode of aged thinking. . . . It is an atmosphere suitable to the story of an old and worn-out hero" (58).

1533 Braeger, Peter C. "Connotations of *(earm)sceapen*: *Beowulf* ll. 2228-2229 and the Shape-Shifting Dragon." *Essays in Literature* (Western Illinois U) 13 (1986): 327-30.

Bolsters Tripp's suggestion [1414] that the dragon of *Beowulf* may actually be a man transformed into a dragon for his wickedness, arguing that Tripp's reconstructed reading *earm-sceapen* (ll. 2229b) may be associated with the verb *forscippan* 'to transform.' Elsewhere, the word *earm-sceapen* describes transformed demons and, in *Daniel*, the transformed Nebuchadnezzar. Braeger seconds Tripp's suggestion that the text is damaged on fol. 179 (182 in the official foliation) because a pious scribe recognized this word as a "description of an old-fashioned pagan metamorphosis from man into dragon" and did not wish good Christians to read of such things (329).

1534 Calder, Daniel G. "Figurative Language and Its Contexts in *Andreas*: A Study in Medieval Expressionism." In *Greenfield*, pp. 115-136.

Maintains that though the style of *Andreas* is often linked to that of *Beowulf*, the two poems approach their narratives in radically different ways, suggesting that their styles, despite their surface similarities, are also different. Calder's main concern is to analyze *Andreas* as a purposefully anti-mimetic, expressionistic poem, but he also contrasts *Andreas* and *Beowulf*. Essentially, "*Beowulf* takes place in something which strongly resembles a world we know, a world where chance and human error too frequently triumph; it is mimetic. *Andreas* plays out its action on a cosmic stage where the end is known even as the narrative unfolds under the protective eye of providence; it is abstract, ritualistic, and symbolic" (119-21).

1535 Canitz, A.E.C. "Kingship in *Beowulf* and the *Nibelungenlied*." *Mankind Quarterly* 27 (1986): 97-119.

Examines qualities of kingship (liberality, sound judgment, power, inherited "luckforce," and personal prowess) in *Beowulf* and the *Nibelungenlied*, finding that all but the last quality remain constant: "What has, however, altered is the degree of emphasis placed on the personal prowess of the king—and this change is crucial." In *Beowulf* every king must have a high degree of personal prowess while in the *Nibelungenlied*, kings, though they still need to be strong, can act by proxy through deputies, showing the transition "towards the king as head of state rather than the king as personal, heroic guardian of the people" (117). Thus, one can trace ideas of kingship from their prefeudal state in the time of the migrations (in *Beowulf*) through a transitional period in which personal prowess is still important but not decisive (as with Siegfried), and finally to the fully institutionalized feudal state (seen in Gunther) in which deputies enforce the will of the head of state. Canitz traces the importance of the above-named virtues in several passages in *Beowulf,* showing that Hrothgar solidifies his power base by giving gifts, but also wins *dōm* 'fame'. Both Hrothgar and Beowulf have enough personal prowess to win lands and to prevent the incursions of neighboring tribes. Hrothgar shows more sound judgment than Beowulf in avoiding Grendel while Beowulf, somewhat lacking in foresight, takes on the dragon single-handedly. Hygelac lacks this quality in taking on the foolish attack in Frisia.

1536 Chance, Jane. *Woman as Hero in Old English Literature.* Syracuse, NY: Syracuse UP, 1986. Pp. xvii + 156; ill.

Proposes the Virgin Mary and Eve as types for understanding the Anglo-Saxons' image of women. The Virgin, passive and peace-bringing, embodied all the proper roles for an Anglo-Saxon woman as peacemaker and mother. Eve, on the other hand, represented an anti-type, decidedly non-passive and masculine. Wealhtheow represents the Germanic ideal of a noble woman (*ides*), a passive peace-weaver, who through marriage, child-bearing, and ritual passing of the mead-cup cements the social order. Thryth, on the other hand, is only ironically called a peace-weaver since she is an active agent against peace. Includes a chapter on Grendel's mother as an inversion of the Anglo-Saxon image of a woman. "Grendel's mother monstrously inverts the image of the Anglo-Saxon queen because she behaves in a heroic and masculine way. She thus serves as a foil for other failed women, like Thryth, and contrasts with more positive images of women, like Wealhtheow and Freawaru, all of whom appear primarily in the middle section of the poem dominated by the female monster. She also resembles the politically active but socially and morally castigated queens of the chronicles and legendary histories discussed in the second chapter, exceptions to the ideal of the conventional peacemaker" (xvi).

Reviews: M. Hallissy, *Library Journal* 110 (1985): 110; A.J. Frantzen, *AN&Q* 24 (1986): 124-26; *OEN* 21.1 (1987): 62; L.S. Robinson, *Women's Review of Books,* June 1987: 14;

C. Brewer, *RES* 39 (1988): 280-81; H. O'Donoghue, *MÆ* 57 (1988): 299-300; H. Weissman, *Speculum* 63 (1988): 134-36; J.W. Nicholls, *MLR* 84 (1989): 114-15; H. Watanabe, *Studies in English Literature* (Tokyo) 66 (1989): 111-16 [in Japanese].

1537   Clemoes, Peter. "'Symbolic' Language in Old English Poetry." In *Greenfield*, pp. 3-14.

Finds that action in *Beowulf* proceeds from ideas about the inner nature of characters and objects and that the traditional language of Old English poetry (including formulas) preserves a socially cohesive and culturally established set of such natures as linguistic symbols. For example, the poet describes Beowulf as the *eorla hlēo* 'protector of noble warriors' when he fights Grendel the *cwealmcuma* 'slaughter-comer' (ll. 791-92): "By activating the expression 'eorla hleo' mentally and emotionally in his story-telling [the *Beowulf*-poet] releases in his audience some of the imaginative potential of it as a token of experience which has been endorsed by society time out of mind. A new event takes place in the cultural tradition of which the linguistic symbol is a part" (9). Through these linguistic symbols, Beowulf becomes a social force pitted against the anti-social *cwealmcuma*. The narrative in *Beowulf* is about the interaction of basic essences symbolized in traditional epithets and phrases: Beowulf shows himself as the *Wedra helm* 'protector of the Weders' (l. 2705a) precisely when he dispatches the dragon; Wiglaf fights alongside Beowulf because of his innate nobility and strength (*ellen cȳðan* 'showed his courage,' l. 2695b); to the Danes, Grendel's attacks symbolized (*gebēacnod*) his inner nature of hate (ll. 140b-42a). Material symbols, not just linguistic ones, operate in a similar fashion, and Clemoes discusses Grendel's arm and Beowulf's funeral barrow in their symbolic function. Whereas the native tradition tended to store narrative kernels in its traditional language (preserving past social experience), later Christian poets and prose writers such as Cynewulf and Ælfric exploit the binary structure of Old English verse more rhetorically to service world-wide Christian symbolism. Also includes a discussion of the name and characterization of Hygelac.

1538   Cox, Rosemary D. "*Bronwen*: Dickey and the Making of a Myth." *Dekalb Literary Arts Journal* 19 (1986): 2-5.

Compares James Dickey's mythologization of his granddaughter in *Bronwen* to the mythic scope of Beowulf's heroism, particularly in their courage, their slaying of monsters, and their rescuing of their communities, suggesting that both can conquer because they "represent the conquest of Christian values over the dark, obscure forces of evil" (4).

1539 Creed, Robert P. "The Remaking of *Beowulf*." In *Oral Tradition in Literature: Interpretation in Context*. Ed. John Miles Foley. Columbia: U of Missouri P, 1986. Pp. 136-146.

Explores the possibility that the *Beowulf*-poet was "a virtuoso traditional poet who may have radically reshaped the tradition in order to preserve it" (136). Creed contends that the "*Beowulf*-poet preserved something important from the heathen past by making parts of that past acceptable to his own newly adopted Christianity. At the same time, he also—and very subtly—reshaped for himself and his people Christian ways of thinking" (136). Creed argues that the poet preserves an ancient story of an old god (Beowulf) by changing him into a human, almost superhuman hero. "Beowulf the god seems always to have come from afar, probably at the request of suppliants" (145). The poet, in adapting this pagan story, now makes the human Beowulf come from a distant country (Geatland). In so doing, he rescues from the pagan past what is worth saving: "Beowulf's bravery, his generosity, his willingness to travel distances to help those in dire distress" (145). Creed also provides an extended discussion of alliteration, how it defines the verse line, and how it may be connected to the structure of memory itself.

1540 Cronan, Dennis. "Alliterative Rank in Old English Poetry." *SN* 58 (1986): 145-158.

Maintains that certain synonyms alliterate more frequently than others because they have more "poetic worth," that is, they satisfy the need for alliteration but also possess poetic qualities. Cronan studies a corpus of 151 words, all simplexes, 91 of which are poetic, 60 non-poetic, including terms for man/warrior, lord/king, sword, shield, spear, boat, sea, battle, treasure, hall, fire, woman, horse, earth, hand, death, and blood. He draws the following general conclusions: "a) A word found only in poetry is likely to alliterate more frequently than one that is found in prose as well. b) A word that is descended from the common Germanic poetic tradition is likely to alliterate more frequently than one that is not. c) When a word is used in a figurative sense, it will probably alliterate more often than when it is used in its literal sense" (150). Alliterative frequency, however, is not an absolute guide to poetic worth: two other factors are the placement of the word in complex phrases and in the poetic line.

1541 Daldorph, Brian. "Mar-Peace, Ally: Hunferð in *Beowulf*." *Massachusetts Studies in English* 10 (1986): 143-160.

Rejects negative, allegorical readings of Hunferth (retaining the manuscript reading of the name) as a figure of discord by Bloomfield [S211] and a treacherous *þyle* by Rosier [S478], finding instead that the character serves as a complex human foil for Beowulf's heroism. Daldorph doubts that *Hunferth* means 'mar-peace' and that the word *þyle* can be confidently connected with its appearances in Old Norse and in Old English glosses. Further, Hunferth's supposed fratricide need not brand him as a figure of evil, especially since other Germanic warriors (including Sigemund, Gunnar, Hrothulf, Hnæf, Hæthcyn, and Weohstan) committed fratricide in their dealings with the comitatus. Other charges against Hunferth—that he conspired with Hrothulf to overthrow Hrothgar or that he treacherously loaned a weak sword to Beowulf—are seen to lack merit. Instead, according to Daldorph, "the poet uses Hunferð as a 'final test' in a series of encounters; one which confirms and amplifies Beowulf's qualities, and leaves him recognized, at least provisionally, as the new Danish champion" (146).

1542 D'Aronco, Maria Amalia. "Per una rilettura del *Beowulf* fra rito e fiaba." [Toward a Rereading of *Beowulf* between Rite and Fable]. *Revista di cultura classica e mediovale* 28 (1986): 139-59.

Considers the parallels between Beowulf's fight with Grendel's mother and the reconstructed "bear's son folktale," also comparing the Sandhaugar episode from the *Grettis saga*. D'Aronco concludes that it is not possible to sustain the hypothesis according to which *Beowulf* would be but a version of the so-called "bear's son folktale," or more correctly, Aarne-Thompson 301, from which would be eliminated the elements inapplicable to Germanic culture. In the final analysis, both *Beowulf* and the *Grettis saga* go back to an initiation cycle. But the differences between the two stories and the "bear's son folktale" can only be accounted for by postulating two distinct branches of this cycle. The first, more ancient type, found in *Beowulf* and the *Grettis saga*, depicts a hero who victoriously confronts a devouring figure of death ("la morte divoratrice," 150), while the second, more recent type, from which the "bear's son folktale" derives, concerns a hero who descends into the realm of death to liberate someone snatched away by him in order to restore him to the society of the living.

1543 Damico, Helen. "Þrymskviða and Beowulf's Second Fight: The Dressing of the Hero in Parody." *Scandinavian Studies* 58 (1986): 407-428.

Explores a number of parallels between Beowulf's fight with Grendel's mother and the theft and recovery of Thor's hammer Mjöllnir in the *Þrymskviða*, concluding that the *Beowulf*-poet treats the battle with high seriousness while the Eddic lay is parodic. Just as Þrym steals Thor's hammer, Grendel's mother steals Grendel's arm. Later, the image is doubled in the *ealdsweord eotenisc* 'ancient sword of the giants' (l. 1558a) which also bears a striking similarity to Thor's hammer. Damico then focuses on the arming scenes in both poems, drawing parallels to similar scenes in the Homeric and Virgilian epics. In the *Þrymskviða*, Thor is "armed" elaborately as a woman in a send-up of heroic values, while Beowulf's arming (ll. 1441-72), following a four-step sequence both here and in other arming scenes in the poem, stresses his high heroism. Damico also discusses "undressing" scenes in Germanic literature and in *Beowulf*, where warriors disdain weapons and armor and strip them off.

1544 Derolez, René. "Focus on *Beowulf*: Variation or Meaning." In *Essays in Honour of Kristian Smidt*. Ed. Peter Bilton, Lars Hartveit, Stig Johansson, Arthur O. Sandved, and Bjørn Tysdahl. Oslo: U of Oslo, Institute of English Studies, 1986. Pp. 9-16.

Examines the poetic device of variation, making the case that, in many passages, terms and phrases which seem to stand in apposition to one another may actually contain mutually-exclusive information, and that we should pay careful attention to semantic distinctions. Brodeur [S373] found variation in lines 1-3 between the terms *þēodcyninga* þrym and hū ðā æþelingas ellen fremedon, but Derolez points out that the words cyning 'king' and æþeling 'retainer' cannot be forced into apposition since they are mutually exclusive: kings have þrym 'power, host of troops' while æþelingas must rely on their ellen 'strength, deeds of valor.' The passage may announce the two main figures: Hrothgar (the king) and Beowulf (the æþeling). Derolez examines some other passages in which æþeling seems to stand in variation to a word for lord or king and finds that the poet maintains the distinction. In lines 50-52, the terms for men (who don't know who will receive the cargo of Scyld's treasure ship) describe two distinct groups: selerædende 'hall-councilors' and hæleþ under heofenum 'widely-traveled warriors'—the terms, Derolez argues, cannot stand in variation to each other. Finally, a description of Æschere (ll. 1325-28a) seems to appose a number of terms, but Derolez argues that each refers to a distinct stage in Æschere's career: he starts out as an eaxlgestealla 'shoulder-companion or comrade-in-arms,' next becomes a rǣdbora 'one of many advisors to the king' and finally ascends to rūnwita 'privy councilor.' In cases such as these, instead of the flattened meanings demanded by variation, "a more literal interpretation produces a richer sense, which can hardly diminish the poet's artistic stature" (13).

1544a Donoghue, Daniel. "Word Order and the Poetic Style: Auxiliary and Verbal in *The Metres of Boethius*." *ASE* 15 (1986): 167-96.

In an examination of the syntax of verbals and auxiliaries in *The Meters of Boethius*, uses *Beowulf* as a point of comparison, theorizing that a number of differences between the syntax of the two poems may be accounted for by positing two conventional styles, that of the earlier lay (*Meters of Boethius*) and that of the more developed epic style (*Beowulf*). The epic style normally does not allow "a finite verb to alliterate in a half-line containing a noun, especially in the second half-line" (192). This structure is common in *The Meters of Boethius* but occurs only once in *Beowulf*. Other characteristics of the epic style are "strict adherence to Kuhn's First Law and the practice of alliteration only on the first stressed word of a half-line" (192), characteristics more loosely observed in the *Meters*. Includes a discussion of the work of Kendall [1392] and Lehmann.

1545 Edwards, Paul. "Alcohol into Art: Drink and Poetry in Old Icelandic and Anglo-Saxon." In *Sagnaskemmtun: Studies in Honour of Hermann Pálsson on his 65th Birthday*. Ed. Rudolf Simek, Jónas Kristjánsson, and Hans Bekker-Nielsen. Philologica Germanica, 8. Vienna: Hermann Böhlaus, 1986. Pp. 85-97.

Surveys the connections between drinking and poetry in Northern literature, including some suggestions made about *Beowulf* in an earlier article [1178].

1546 Evans, Angela Care. *The Sutton Hoo Ship Burial*. London: British Museum Publications, 1986.

Includes a brief essay "Sutton Hoo: Poetry and Style," which notes some similarities and differences between the funerals of Scyld and Beowulf and details of the Sutton Hoo ship burial, also tracing Swedish elements in the Sutton Hoo materials.
Reviews: J. Graham-Campbell, *TLS* 12 Sept., 1986: 1008; G. Arwidsson, *Forvännen* 83 (1989): 121-24; R. Bruce-Mitford, *AntJ* 68 (1989): 356-57; M.Welch, *ArchJ* 145 (1989): 432-33; M.G. Welch, *Bulletin of the Inst. of Archaeology* (London) 25 (1990): 115.

1547 Farrell, Eleanor. "The Epic Hero and Society: Cuchulainn, Beowulf and Roland." *Mythlore* 13 (1986): 25-28, 50.

Compares the heroes Cuchulainn, Beowulf, and Roland, finding that their relationship to the supernatural, their sense of honor, and the nature of their deaths provide a way of comparing "the values of the respective cultures the heroes represent" (27). Compared to the other two epic heroes, Beowulf has an unusual mixture of supernatural and human powers, a communal sense of honor, and does not die young as the other two heroes do. Thus, "the Anglo-Saxon epic fits somewhere between the Celtic and Norman ideas of fate and death; it has some Christian elements but hasn't incorporated these in any cohesive form" (27).

1548 Frank, Roberta. "'Mere' and 'Sund': Two Sea-Changes in *Beowulf*." In *Greenfield*, pp. 153-72.

Provides evidence that the *Beowulf* poet exploits the differing poetic and prosaic meanings of two words *mere* (meaning 'sea' in poetry, 'lake or pond' in prose) and *sund* ('sea' in poetry, 'swimming' in prose). In describing Grendel's abode as a *mere*, the poet forced his hearers to use "their own knowledge to abstract from the physical 'mere' ('unbounded sea') of poetry and its polar opposite, the metaphysical 'mere' ('confined and confining water') of prose. If Grendel himself was a riddle, a crosser of categories, no less could be expected of his dwelling place" (157). With regard to *sund*, Frank connects the ambiguity of the poetic 'sea' and prose 'swimming' senses to Unferth's skill in flyting: he is intentionally ambiguous about whether Beowulf and Breca *on sund rēon* (ll. 512b, 539b), whether they 'rowed [their arms] in swimming' or 'rowed on the sea,' whether they had a swimming or a rowing contest. "The Old Norse skald was skilled in this kind of duplicity, turning praise into blame and vice versa. On a more elementary level, Unferth seems to be playing the same game of disguises, riddling in such a way as to make his meaning clear to the initiated and misleading to the naïve" (161).

1549 Frey, Leonard. "Comitatus as a Rhetorical-Structural Norm for Two Germanic Epics." *Recovering Literature* 14 (1986): 51-70.

Argues that the concept of the *comitatus* helps to explain the fifty-year time gap in the poem between Beowulf's youth and old age. Frey makes the case that the poem is structured not so much by plot-unity as by a focus on the *comitatus*: "The ideals of *comitatus* involve reciprocity, loyalty for generosity and the reverse. The youthful and aged Beowulf enacts first the one then the other dimension of the bond, first showing up Hrothgar's ineffectual thanes (the king's nominal *comitatus*) then his own ineffectual followers (who nominally stay within the letter of the *comitatus*-law in 'obeying orders'). . . . [T]he youth and age dichotomy is effectively underscored in the roles of Hrothgar and Wiglaf, who like Beowulf himself properly fulfill the terms and conditions of *comitatus*-behavior" (69). Also includes a discussion of the *comitatus* in *Waltharius*.

1550 Fujiwara, Hiroshi. "eald sweord . . . ecgum þȳhtig." *Annual Report of the Faculty of Letters (Gakushuin Univ.)* 32 (1986): 25-35. In Japanese.

Provides evidence that in *Beowulf* and other heroic epics, the adjective *eald* 'old' is an epithet generally associated with the noun *sweord* 'sword' but not with other weapon names.

The low production of iron in the Germanic world may be the reason for this pattern. (HF)

1551 _____. "The Relative Clauses in *Beowulf*." In *Linguistics Across Historical and Geographical Boundaries: In Honour of Jacek Fisiak on the Occasion of His Fiftieth Birthday*. Ed. Dieter Kastovsky and Aleksander Szwedek. 2 Vols. Trends in Linguistics: Studies and Monographs, 32. Berlin: Mouton de Gruyter, 1986. I:311-316.

Examines the syntax of relative clauses in *Beowulf* preceded by the particle *þe*, concluding in part that *þe* has a function similar to that of *ond* 'and.' "As far as the relative clause and the *ond*-clause are concerned, we have no difference in word order between *Judith*, *The Battle of Maldon*, and *Beowulf*" (315).

1552 Gabbard, G.N. "Film Clip from an Epic." *Literary Review* 30 (1986): 84-86.

A free translation of lines 1-53. Lines 4-11 (approximately): "To the Danes—kicked,/ clipped, elbowed and killed/ by neighbors—world-nagged, fearful after years/ hungry of leaders/ a king came:/ a gift from the blue, adrift on the sea and/ boated through surf in a rawhide shield/ cushioned with wheatstraw, a baby, so named/ Shyld Sheaflock.// Fated to know that/ Kings do not plant, cultivate, garner/ the grain,/ but they own it—/ he rose from orphan to emperor,/ a binder of tribes,/ chiefs trembled before him./ His right arm laid waste whole armies./ His sword scythed gold to fill up bins;/ his gleaners, peeling the gold leaf, left/ royal bench and bedstead bare./ His world echoed overseas. Over seas/ bright ships brought tribute money/ and words of submission from each/ race within his reach./ O he was a king of kings."

1553 Gahrn, Lars. "The Geatas of *Beowulf*." *Scandinavian Journal of History* 11 (1986): 95-113.

Surveys in detail various theories about the identity of the Geats in *Beowulf*, urging caution in accepting any one theory but favoring the idea that they were Danes or Gautar, and concludes that *Beowulf* cannot serve as a reliable source of information about early Swedish history. Gahrn surveys the following theories about the identity of the Geats: the Danes theory, the Gautar theory, the Jutes theory, the combined Jutes and Gautar theory, and the Getes (Goths) theory. "Beyond doubt, the Danes theory and the Gautar theory are the best ones. The former is based on the oldest source—Gregory of Tours—and the latter on the source which tells us most about the North—the Beowulf epos itself. The Jutes theory rests on shaky grounds, but it cannot be disregarded. The Getes theory is based on no grounds at all, but it cannot yet be excluded" (107). Going on the assumption that the Geats were the Gautar, Gahrn shows the danger of locating the sixth-century Gautar (and thus the Geats) in the same region occupied by the eleventh-century Gautar in Västergötland. Place names in the poem provide no conclusive hints. Attempts to locate the homeland of the sixth-century Gautar are "all weak and some are rather curious" (109). Finally, Gahrn points out that the poem does not speak unequivocally about any final victory of the Swedes over the Geats, though the poet does seem anxious to spare the Geats from shame. "Unfortunately, we have no contemporary sources to check the epos against, and we do not know who the Geatas really were. It is most daring and useless to attempt to draw conclusions under such circumstances, and we must abandon the idea of doing so" (112).

1554 Glosecki, Stephen O. "Men among Monsters: Germanic Animal Art as Evidence of Oral Literature." *Mankind Quarterly* 27 (1986): 207-14.

Advances evidence that "Germanic animal art reflects the themes of preliterary songs," particularly in its depiction of man against monsters, usually wolves, bears, or serpents (207). The Torslunda dies show evidence of a bear hero: "the bear was once a creature of power; traces of his importance remain in Bjarki's overt and Beowulf's obscure ursine associations" (208). Other interlace subjects show snake shapes, suggesting "the *wyrm* subdued by Beowulf or Sigurð" (213). Glosecki concludes: "Produced in the Germanic milieu well before writing took root, the earliest figural artifacts—the Sutton Hoo plaques, the Torslunda dies—are the most important evidence of an associated oral tradition. Rarely, the men among monsters illustrate actual episodes from stories we know. But even in the absence of any obvious link between a certain carving and a particular legend, these men among monsters all by themselves practically sing their own song" (214).

1555 Greenfield, Stanley B., and Daniel G. Calder. *A New Critical History of Old English Literature*. New York: New York UP, 1986. Pp. x + 370; 2 pages of plates; ill.

Provides a general introduction to the poem in a chapter entitled "Secular Heroic Poetry." Greenfield and Calder review the history of the manuscript and its transmission and give a detailed plot outline of the poem. They identify contrast as *Beowulf*'s controlling aesthetic principle: "Contrasts and parallels, interfacing in the poem, unify the larger structural elements, character presentations, themes, and even the most detailed stylistic matters. This unifying technique allows the poet to introduce the many apparent digressions.... And it permits the Christian and pagan elements to coexist meaningfully within the poem's framework" (139-40). Thematically and structurally, the poem focuses on the contrasts between youth and age, success and failure, and the rise and fall of nations. The heroic dominates Part I, while the elegiac dominates part two. Though some think the Christian poet criticizes Beowulf or his heroic society, Greenfield and Calder argue that "the poem's perspective seems more universal than specifically Christian, suggesting it is *life* which has its limits rather than heroism or the heroic world" (142). The Finn Episode is shown to fit into the overall structure of the poem.

Reviews: M.-M. Dubois, *EA* 40 (1987): 345-46; D.K. Fry, *Envoi* 1.1 (1988): 127-29; M. McC. Gatch, *CH* 57 (1988): 80-81; J.C. Pope, *MLR* 83 (1988): 660-62; H. Sauer, *N&Q* 35 (1988): 506-07; E.G. Stanley, *Comparative Literature* 50 (1988): 286-89; H. Gneuss, *Anglia* 107 (1989): 149-51; P.E. Szarmach, *Speculum* 64 (1989): 173-74.

1556 Griffin, Henry William. "Beer, *Beowulf*, and the English Literature Syllabus, 1936." *Bulletin of the New York C. S. Lewis Society* 17 (1986): 1-3.

A brief account of C.S. Lewis's approach to teaching *Beowulf* as well as Tolkien's participation in Lewis's "beer and Beowulf" evenings.

1557 Haruta, Setsuko. "The Women in *Beowulf*." *Poetica (Tokyo)* 23 (1986): 1-15.

Argues that "the women in *Beowulf* are by no means a collection of colorless types" and divides the eleven women in the poem into three basic categories: "women who play merely passive roles, women who are aware of the danger and who try their best to avert it, and women who do not hesitate to step out of their assigned roles by acting violently. The poet keeps offstage all women of the first type [Hildeburh, Freawaru, Ongentheow's queen, Onela's wife, Beowulf's mother, and Hygelac's daughter], except the old mourner. Since the last 'violent' type [Grendel's mother and Modthryth] is clearly regarded as undesirable, the greatest interest falls naturally on the second 'wise type' [Wealhtheow and Hygd]" (14). The introduction of Hildeburh and Freawaru as passive peace-weavers allows the poet to appeal to the audience's emotions and to invite them to see the events from a woman's point of view. The other failed peace-weavers appear only in passing. Wealhtheow and Hygd, however, play much more prominent roles as clever manipulators. Wealhtheow is a complex and dramatic character who attempts to protect her sons using verbal persuasions (ll. 1175-87, 1228-31) and the gift of the precious neckring. This ring links Wealhtheow to Hygd, who receives the treasure next. Hygd's role is different and more daring in that she offers Beowulf the crown itself in order to protect her son, "an extraordinary decision for a queen-mother" (10). Grendel's mother and Modthryth (ll. 1931b-1962) represent yet a different type of woman. Grendel's mother contrasts and interacts with Wealhtheow's role, while Modthryth sets off Hygd. Grendel's mother displays a type of violence elsewhere praised in women saints, and Haruta notes a parallel between Judith's beheading of Holofernes and Grendel's mother's beheading of Æschere. Interestingly, the three types of women are introduced in contrastive pairs: Onela's queen/Hrethel's daughter, Ongentheow's queen/Hygelac's daughter, Wealhtheow/Hygd, Grendel's mother/Modthryth. Finally, the nameless old woman who mourns at Beowulf's funeral comes to represent all the women in *Beowulf*: just as the heroic men have failed, the women have also failed and now can only mourn.

1558 Haudry, Jean. "*Beowulf* dans la tradition indo-européenne (II)—L'héritage littéraire traditionnel: forme et contenu." [*Beowulf* in the Indo-European Tradition (II)—Traditional Literary Heritage: Form and Content]. *Études Indo-Européennes* 19 (1986): 1-51.

Continues Haudry [1433], here elaborating on the idea of the Indo-European tradition, what it is, how it was transmitted, what some of its principal themes are, and its importance to *Beowulf*. Haudry defines the Indo-European tradition as a literary heritage, constituted essentially by formulas and notional themes (*schèmes notionnels*), which covertly express and transmit a conception of the world which guides the behavior of the individual and can coalesce into social institutions (2). The language of formula and theme are bound up in a traditional style with recognizable formal traits (see 4-5), including syntactical and semantic cues, and serve primarily as mnemonic devices, insuring the transmission of the tradition. In *Beowulf*, the preservation of this tradition leads to the hero's successes over the Grendel-kin while its abandonment leads to the final catastrophe and Beowulf's death. The central content of the tradition revolves around three such notional themes: 1) the myth of the three heavens, a cosmogonical theme (see Haudry [1433]) which pits the forces of day/spring (life) against those of twilight/autumn (decadence), and full night/winter (defeat and death), associating each stage with a color—white, red, and black respectively; 2) the theme of "crossing of water in winter darkness" (see Haudry [1489]); and 3) the triadic theme of thought, speech, and action. Haudry traces each of these themes in *Beowulf*, finding parallels in a number of Indo-European traditions.

Concentrating on the last theme listed above, Haudry shows that formulas and notional themes preserve the triad in the Vedas, Homerian epic, Hittite materials, and the *Hávamál*. Haudry shows that the three ideas (thought, speech, and action) are represented by Indo-European roots which are preserved in the later traditions: Old English *weorc* for 'action' and *mon* for 'thought' have equivalents in Greek, Old Indic, and other languages. In *Beowulf*, the theme is clear in the Coastguard's statement (ll. 287b-89) and the poet's statement about Wiglaf (ll. 2600b-01): thinking well, leads to speaking well and acting well, while evil thought leads to bad speech and bad deeds, as in the case of Heremod. Haudry traces some of the formal features of Indo-European traditional language in *Beowulf*: grammatical archaisms, the reinforcement of an affirmation by the negation of the contrary, chiasmus, kennings, pleonasm, the concept of "peace-weaver," amplification through a double dative, variation, etc. He also shows that the cosmogonical theme of the three heavens and three colors (white, black, and red) exists on three interrelated levels: the cosmic (daytime sky, twilight sky, nighttime sky), the social (superior caste, intermediate caste, and the inferior caste), and the individual (the good or truth, eagerness, and the inertia of spiritual darkness). Throughout, Haudry discusses a number of secondary issues, often dealing with the linguistic evidence or that of other Indo-European myths.

1559 Higley, Sarah Lynn. "*Aldor on Ofre*; Or, The Reluctant Hart: A Study of Liminality in *Beowulf.*" *NM* 87 (1986): 342-53.

Finds in the image of the hart which would rather die on the shore than plunge into Grendel's mere (ll. 1368-72) an ironic inversion of a type-scene known as the "hero on the beach" (see Crowne [S408])—where a hero triumphantly crosses a border with a band of warriors—finding that the poem is much concerned with borders or "liminality." As a symbol for Hrothgar and the Danes and a probable pun on the name of their hall *Heorot*, the hart represents the passivity and fear of ordinary human beings as they try to cross a border from the natural to the unnatural, while powerful beings like Grendel, Beowulf, and heroes of the hero-on-the-beach type-scene cross them without fear. Higley argues that the passage (ll. 1368-72) is intricately structured on the principle of chiasm and that at its center is the phrase *aldor on ōfre* 'life on the shore' or perhaps 'prince on the shore'—the ambiguity providing the link to the hero-on-the-beach motif. The hart thus symbolizes "the general predicament of humanity—caught in Middangeard between salvation and damnation" (342).

1560 Hill, Thomas D. "Scyld Scefing and the 'Stirps Regia': Pagan Myth and Christian Kingship in *Beowulf.*" In *Kaske*, pp. 37-47.

Finds that the prologue concerning the arrival of Scyld Scefing shows the poet's interest in kingship and orderly royal succession and that in constructing it he adapted a pagan Germanic myth to Christian circumstances. As a myth, the story of Scyld Scefing explains why legitimate kingship requires divine sanction and sets "the *stirps regia* apart from other great families who might aspire to kingship" (41). Hill suggests that the name *Scyld Scefing* may contain a hint about the kind of kingship which the story endorses: Scyld Scefing "brought the protection of the shield (*pax*) and the prosperity of the sheaf (*abundantia*)," an idea echoed in the Anglo-Saxon coronation formula, *pax et habundantia salutatis* (40-41). Beow (Beowulf I), as the only son of Scyld, is the unquestioned successor, though orderly succession—the poet hints—breaks down when Hrothulf challenges Hrothgar's sons or Hrothgar himself for the throne. Beowulf, by contrast, does not deviate from orderly succession even when offered the throne by Hygd: he serves as regent under Hygelac's son Heardred. In short, "the *Beowulf*-poet emerges as an unhesitating and zealous exponent of the new Christian patrilineal rules of royal succession" (45). Hill speculates that the poet may have constructed his narrative to establish the aristocratic credentials of a contemporary Anglo-Saxon family that claimed the Geats as descendants: "This history—whether true or fictional—would provide an appropriately aristocratic heritage for the social group in question" (47). [See *succession—questions of* in the subject index.]

1561 Jorgensen, Peter A. "Additional Icelandic Analogues to *Beowulf*." In *Sagnaskemmtun: Studies in Honour of Hermann Pálsson on his 65th Birthday*. Ed. Rudolf Simek, Jónas Kristjánsson, and Hans Bekker-Nielsen. Philologica Germanica, 8. Vienna: Hermann Böhlaus, 1986. Pp. 201-08.

Identifies several previously unrecognized Icelandic analogues to *Beowulf*, all related to the "bear's son folktale," which seems to lie behind Beowulf's fight with Grendel and Grendel's mother. Jorgensen briefly summarizes the reconstructed bear's son folktale as follows: "Life in a dwelling was made miserable by a creature with supernatural powers, who kills or carries off the inhabitants. A stranger with superhuman prowess, often with an unpromising youth behind him and descended from a bear, wrestles with the monster and tears off its arm. Although the creature escapes, it is followed to a cave near a body of water, and some difficulty must be overcome before entrance can be gained. A bright fire or light is usually mentioned. The hero encounters two assailants (originally the first opponent either dead or dying) and an ogress. After the failure of the sword given him by a king, the hero is virtually helpless until some external aid enables him to draw a specially hafted sword on the wall. The hero is usually thought to be slain and his companions waiting outside leave, only to be surprised at his return with treasure from the cave" (202). Several Icelandic sagas besides the *Grettis saga* contain elements of this story, often transmuted in some way: *Ólafs Saga Tryggvasonar, Þórodds þáttr Snorrasonar* (embedded in *Ólafs saga helga*), *Gunnars saga Keldugnúpsfífls, Hálfdanar saga Eysteinssonar, Egils* saga, *Göngu-Hrólfs saga, Hrana saga hrings*, and the *Ála flekks saga*. Jorgensen finds the most striking analogue to *Beowulf* in *Þórodds þáttr Snorrasonar*, where the superhuman hero Arnljótr encounters an ogress and slays her with a golden spear. Before that battle, however, twelve merchants enter the hall, make a loud and merry feast, and fall asleep. The ogress snatches up the closest of the sleeping men and "tears him asunder as does Grendel" (207). "In this episode the attack on an inhabited hall by a monster is preserved in a form closer than any other saga to Grendel's assault on Heorot" (206).

1562 *Key-Word Studies in 'Beowulf' and Chaucer, 2*. Tokyo: Centre for Mediaeval English Studies, 1986.

Not seen.

1563 Kiernan, Kevin S. "The Legacy of Wiglaf: Saving a Wounded *Beowulf*." *The Kentucky Review* 6 (1986): 27-44.

The text of a lecture in which Kiernan details his interest in and work on the *Beowulf* manuscript, summarizing many of the conclusions which he reached in his book-length study [1261]. Kiernan's first motive was to read the text stripped of modern editorial emendations, and in the process he found linguistic and codicological evidence contradicting an early date for the poem. He goes on to discuss the foliation of the manuscript, the evidence for scribal correction, and the dangers of using metrical/alliterative theory as the basis for emendations. His major conclusions are: that the text of the poem is far more reliable than modern editors assume, that the poem is contemporaneous with its manuscript (i.e., composed after 1015), that it consists of two originally separate poems which the second scribe attempted to unite, that the same scribe may have been responsible for copying the *Blickling Homilies*, that the text of *Beowulf* began a separate manuscript, with the first and last pages showing signs of wear from serving as covers.

1564 _____. "The Lost Letters of *Beowulf* 2253a." *Neophil* 70 (1986): 633-635.

Claims on paleographical grounds that the standard reconstruction at l. 2253a, *feormie* 'polish,' is incorrect and proposes *fægnige* 'to welcome, receive with pleasure' as a possible restoration. Modern artificial lighting reveals that the downstroke which Zupitza [S14] took as the descender of an *r* is actually the angular loop of a *g*. That being the case, the space between the *f* and the *g* is not large enough to admit two large letters like *eo*, but too small for a single letter, thus making the letter ash (*æ*) a likely possibility. Kiernan translates lines 2252b-53 as follows: there is no one "who might wear the sword or joyfully receive the ornamented cup" (634). See Gerritsen's counter-proposal [1694].

1565 _____. "Madden, Thorkelin, and MS Vitellius/Vespasian A XV." *The Library* 6th ser., 8 (1986): 127-32.

Discovers through the diaries of Sir Frederic Madden that the *Beowulf* codex, Cotton Vitellius A.XV, had been misshelved as Cotton Vespasian A.XV by the early nineteenth century, a fact which aids Kiernan in dating Grímur Jónsson Thorkelin's work on the manuscript. The *Reading Room Register* for the British Library shows that Thorkelin used Cotton Vespasian (for Vitellius!) A.XV in 1789. Also includes an overview of Madden's work on the manuscript. See Kiernan [1566].

1566 _____. *The Thorkelin Transcripts of 'Beowulf'*. Anglistica, Vol. 25. Copenhagen: Rosenkilde and Bagger, 1986. Pp. xiii + 155 p; ill.

Casts doubt on the independence and reliability of Thorkelin B, the transcript of *Beowulf* prepared by Grímur Jónsson Thorkelin, several years later, according to Kiernan, than the commonly accepted date of 1787. Kiernan provides the following summary of his study: "In Part One, 'Thorkelin's Discovery of *Beowulf*,' neglected archival documents from Great Britain and Denmark reveal that Thorkelin found out about the poem only after he began researching Danish antiquities at the British Museum. They suggest that in 1787 he hired a member of the Museum staff, most likely a man by the name of James Matthews, to make the facsimile of the manuscript we now call Thorkelin A, while Thorkelin himself sojourned in Scotland. They further indicate that he did not make his own copy, Thorkelin B, in 1787, but considerably later . . . no earlier than 1789, probably in 1790 or 1791.

"Part Two, 'Restorations and Collations,' attempts to present in a usable form the results of three new collations—A with the manuscript text, B with the manuscript text, and A with B. The collations ... [are] supplemented by descriptive notes for letters not visible in photographs and not fully described in either of the facsimile editions. For each page of the manuscript there is a tally of the number of letters restored by the transcripts, followed by a list of words dependent on those restored letters. Then follow the collations, a list of A's mistakes and a list of B's.

"Part Three, 'The Reliability of the Transcripts,' uses the data from Part Two to show that Thorkelin A is far more reliable than Thorkelin B. Thorkelin's scribe, although ignorant of Old English and insular script, was nonetheless an accomplished facsimilist. He made a few mistakes many times over, but these mistakes are in fact so predictable that they can be corrected without recourse to the manuscript.... Thorkelin's unreliability in B has many facets. The overall problem is that Thorkelin B is an edition-in-progress, not an objective or even an independent transcript of the poem. The coincidence of error in A and B reveals that Thorkelin sometimes copied A instead of the manuscript for crucial readings, probably because the damage to the manuscript was more advanced when he copied it than it was for A. Most of Thorkelin's later proofreading of his transcript was done with A rather than with the manuscript. In addition to producing a conflation of A and the manuscript, Thorkelin in B made many emendations and conjectural restorations of lost readings, both in the course of copy and in the course of later proofreading, when he no longer had access to the manuscript.

"The possible implications of this study for conservative textual criticism are manifold. It now appears that agreement between A and B on a lost reading need not carry conviction, since we have no way of knowing whether Thorkelin depended on A or the manuscript for his reading. For letters in B unconfirmed by A, we have reason to suspect a conjectural restoration of a lost reading. In short, we cannot rely on Thorkelin's edition-in-progress as an authoritative textual tool, but only as the first editor's attempt to reconstruct a damaged text" (ix-xi).

Reviews: *OEN* 21.1 (1987):83-84; R.P. Creed, *ELN* 26.1 (1988): 75-77; M. Griffith, *MÆ* 57 (1988): 296-97; B. Lindström, *SN* 60 (1988): 264-67; J. Wilcox, *PQ* 67 (1988): 267-69; R.H. Bremmer, Jr., *ES* 70 (1989): 172-73; T.A. Shippey, *Speculum* 64 (1989): 727-29; E.G. Stanley, *N&Q* 37 (1990): 323-24.

1567 Kroll, Norma. "Beowulf: The Hero as Keeper of Human Polity." *MP* 84 (1986): 117-129.

Sees the conflicts in *Beowulf* as more political and temporal than spiritual and eternal. The *Beowulf* poet reshapes the concept of sin: ignoring the fall of Adam and Eve, he defines it in terms of Cain's murder of his brother, a failure of loyalty and civility. This theme—the possibility of Cain- or Heremod-like uncivility—controls the interplay between the digressions and the main plot. "The primacy of political over spiritual needs in the moral design of the poem is made clear in Hrothgar's 'sermon,' the most Christian part of the poem.... Hrothgar does not warn Beowulf against satanic pride but against repeating the wickedness of Heremod, against the earthly pride, anger, and selfishness that lead to the destruction of the human community" (120). Kroll argues that the poet refuses to see his characters in black and white terms: Human beings (and monsters) both have the potentials for Cain-like violence against social harmony. Modthryth is evil because of her violence against the community, but she contains the possibility of good. Similarly, Beowulf and Grendel are not diametrically opposed as representatives of good and evil, but are actually doubles: they both play out the drama of Cain. "In political terms, Grendel's and Beowulf's feelings and positions are identical as well as opposite" (124). Unferth is also far from a patently evil character. He contains the possibilities of uncivility (murdering his brother) but also of sustaining brotherhood (by lending Hrunting). Kroll also detects doubling between Beowulf and the dragon—they strive for the same treasure.

1568 Lester, G. A. "*Earme on eaxle (Beowulf* 1117a)." *SN* 58 (1986): 159-163.

Proposes a new reading of *Beowulf* 1117a, taking *earme* as an adverb meaning 'wretchedly' (following Fry [S911]), interpreting the phrase *on eaxle* as a reference to Hildeburh's own shoulder, and translating the line as follows: "wretchedly the woman lamented upon her shoulder" (162). Such a posture of grief appears in a number of Anglo-Saxon manuscript illustrations. Lester undertakes an extensive review of other occurrences of *eaxl, sculdor,* and *earm* in the corpus of Old English texts to shed light on the line, rejecting the solution of Wrenn/Bolton [S276], who read *earme* 'wretched' as a weak feminine adjective referring to

Hildeburh, as well as that of Klaeber [S67], who emends *earme* to *eāme* 'uncle'.

1569 Liberman, Anatoly. "Beowulf-Grettir." In *Germanic Dialects: Linguistic and Philological Investigations.* Ed. Bela Brogyany and Thomas Krömmelbein. Current Issues in Linguistic Theory, 38. Amsterdam : John Benjamins Pub. Co., 1986. Pp. 353-401.

A nearly exhaustive survey of one hundred and ten years of scholarship on the connections between the Grendel episode in *Beowulf* and the Sandhaugar episode in the *Grettis Saga*, concluding that both stories rely on a distantly-shared Germanic myth of a magic hilted sword. Liberman summarizes the similarities which scholars have found between the two stories, discussing the verbal coincidence between *Beowulf*'s *hæftmēce* 'hilted sword' (l. 1457a) and the *Grettis saga*'s *heptisax*, the similarity in locales, in the behavior of the heroes' helpers, etc. He finds most of the parallels unconvincing: "All the narrative similarities between *Beowulf* and other sagas, poems, legends, fairy tales, etc. can be explained away as either *loci communes* or universally known formulaic themes" (366-67). The *hæftmēce/heptisax* correspondence, however, is a key to the relation between the two epics, and Liberman believes that neither word is used casually but that both go back to a common Germanic ritual involving a magic hilted sword. He reconstructs this folkloristic episode, in which the hero fights a female monster at the bottom of a sea or lake. "He is attacked by the female monster but is unable to injure her, because she fights with her own magic sword, the only one that can bring her death; the magic is contained in the haft. The hero wrests the *hæftmēce/heptisax* from the monster and kills her with it. (But this sword can only be used once: when the hero wants to take it as a trophy, it melts, and nothing remains but the magic haft)" (380). This reconstructed tale explains details in both *Beowulf* and the *Grettis saga*. Thus, the two narratives are connected by a common Germanic myth about a magic hilted sword: the question of direct influence of the one story on the other is implausible. Liberman also reviews the history of the sword Hrunting and dismisses the supposed etymological connections between the names *Grendel* and *Grettir*.

1570 Macrae-Gibson, O.D. "The Metrical Entities of Old English." *NM* 87 (1986): 59-91.

Provides the following summary: "The system of analysis set out by A.J. Bliss in *The Metre of Beowulf* [S353] has proved a valuable refinement of that of Sievers, but his use of the proportion of the occurrences of any metrical type which appear in the a-verse, and the proportion of these which have double alliteration, as evidence of which types form significant groups requires extensive methodological correction before its conclusions can be accepted. In particular it is essential to consider what syntactic structures create the types, not merely the types themselves. When this is done a very different picture emerges from that displayed by Bliss" (59). Provides detailed diagrams for the distribution of the various metrical types.

1571 Nicholson, Lewis E. "*Beowulf* and the Pagan Cult of the Stag." *Studi Medievali* 3rd ser., 27 (1986): 637-69.

Argues that the poet connects the Danes and Heorot (hart) hall to a pagan cult of the stag-god Cernunnos, whose rites were celebrated at New Year by Germanic and Celtic peoples. Nicholson, after reviewing Christian interpretations of the hart from scripture (Psalm 41:2) and exegesis (Ambrose, Augustine, and others), collects evidence for a stag cult from a broad range of homilies, penitentials, and other documents (collected in an appendix) as well as from archaeological artifacts and modern folk practices. The documents speak of a New Year fertility rite in which men "played the stag" (*cervulum facere*) by putting on antlers and animal skins and mounting carts, practices which may have originated in the cult of the stag god Herne, whose Latinized name is Cernunnos. Augustine specifically descried the joyous revelry of the pagans in a series of New Year's sermons. In *Beowulf,* "Noble and shining though the Danish hall may be, by providing Heorot with projecting antlers, the poet takes the first subtle, irreversible step towards transforming the residents of Heorot into the horned worshippers of the pagan stag god" (656). In this light, the poet's condemnation of the Danes' pagan sacrifices (ll. 175-88) makes much more sense: they drink, feast, and give gifts "in their bright but unclean, shrine-like palace dedicated to the pagan stag god, Cernunnos" (660). Further, Grendel and his mother do not so much attack Heorot as inhabit it, symbolizing the spirit of Cain which has dominated Danish history from the beginning. Nicholson argues that the word *bānfāg* 'bone decorated' (l. 780a) may describe Grendel's horns (if the MS. reading of the preceding word *hetelīc* 'hateful' is retained) and also connects the regnal scepter (crowned with a stag image) from the Sutton Hoo find with this pagan cult, discussing Rædwald's attachment to pagan beliefs. He notes that dragons and stags are associated in both the Christian and pagan versions of myth, a resonance also found in *Beowulf*.

1572 Osborn, Marijane. *'Beowulf': A Guide to Study*. Los Angeles: Pentagle, 1986. Pp. ix + 115.

Not seen.

1573 Overing, Gillian R. "The Object as Index: a Peircean Approach to *Beowulf*." In *Semiotics 1985*. Ed. John Deely. Lanham, MD: UP of America, 1986. Pp. 569-83.

Appears, in expanded form, as chapter two in Overing [1761].

1574 Parks, Ward. "Flyting and Fighting: Pathways in the Realization of the Epic Contest." *Neophil* 70 (1986): 292-306.

On the assumption that flyting is a phenomenon common to many oral cultures, not just Germanic culture, Parks compares examples from Old English and ancient Greek poems to construct a broader account of the phenomenon, defining epic flyting as a situation in which the participants do not merely quarrel: they negotiate in a contractual way the terms under which personal honor will be decided, usually by martial contest. In the Unferth-Beowulf flyting episode (ll. 499-610), though they fight verbally, Beowulf and Unferth agree that Beowulf's battle with Grendel will decide the issue at hand—Beowulf's courage. Their flyting amounts to a contract for such a test. Since flyting generally requires two groups, the nature of the groups determines the type of contest that will be negotiated. If the two groups are hostile ones, the outcome is usually hand-to-hand combat between the contestants, as in the *Battle of Maldon*. If they are in a host-guest relationship (as in the Unferth episode), the outcome excludes mortal combat between the contestants themselves but must be decided some other way. The encounter with the Coastguard (ll. 229-319) fits at first into the battlefield paradigm, but an actual combat is unnecessary, once the identities of the Geatish strangers are made known.

Flyting within a single social group seems to violate its purpose and structure. Appears in altered form as a chapter in Parks [1762].

1575 Pope, John C. "*Beowulf* 505, 'Gehedde,' and the Pretensions of Unferth." In *Greenfield*, pp. 173-187.

Offers a reconsideration of the word *gehedde* (l. 505a), finally siding with the view of Robinson [S774, S932] that MS. *gehedde* is the preterite subjunctive of *gehēdan* 'to heed, care for' not—as Klaeber and other editors have surmised—a defective present subjunctive of *gehēgan* 'to perform' which must be emended to *gehēde*. Pope provides an extensive review of the word's editorial history, pointing out the two main difficulties with the *gehēde* emendation: 1) the definition 'perform' for *gehēgan* is problematic in light of the other occurrences of the word, 2) *gehēgan* does not take a genitive object (though *gehēdan* often does). He disagrees, however, with Robinson's view that the line means, roughly, "Unferth did not care for glorious deeds and could not grant that any other man could care for them either." Pope translates lines 503-505 as follows: "for he would not grant that any other man on earth could ever, under the heavens, care more for glorious deeds than he himself did" (180). Unferth thus emerges as a character who "is mainly, and expertly, used as a foil to Beowulf, helping primarily to allow Beowulf, in the flyting, to reveal his astonishing powers in anticipation of his defeat of Grendel, and secondarily, in the lending and failure of the sword Hrunting, to allow a tacit acknowledgment on Unferth's part of Beowulf's superiority" (182).

1576 Purdy, Strother. "Beowulf and Hrothgar's Dream." *ChauR* 21 (1986): 257-273.

Suggests that one way out of the insoluble difficulties of interpreting the poem is to imagine it as the dream of Hrothgar: such a reading provides a different sense of underlying unity, placing Beowulf and the monsters on the same plane as dream emanations of Hrothgar's psyche. Having displaced his nephew on the throne, Hrothgar, who may in turn be displaced by his nephew Hrothulf, appears by day to be a wise king, but at night "his deep-seated fears take over, and he dreams of a foul monster, the spirit of fratricide," a monster which embodies the murders he must commit to gain power (268). Hrothgar dreams a hero to release him from his nightmare, a hero which reminds him of his grandfather, Beowulf I (Beow). Since, however, Hrothgar "has come to enjoy these night sessions with Grendel . . . he will make the fight hard, make Beowulf really prove himself" (269). Grendel's mother appears so suddenly because she is dreamed. Part II of the poem—though Hrothgar is now dead—is still linked to Hrothgar, "here too the old king's hall is attacked by a monster that comes in the night while the king sleeps elsewhere" (270). The problems of succession are central here too, the dragon "is the dream of the dead," and the uselessness of the treasure suggests that gaining power by taking it from the dead must fail. Purdy also provides a commentary for a number of sections and individual lines.

1577 Sakemi, Kisei. "Toward the Textual Criticism of *Beowulf* (3)." *Research Bulletin of the Hiroshima Institute of Technology* 20.24 (1986). In Japanese.

Surveys textual problems in lines 371-558, using some editions and notes, especially Dobbie's [S256]. A continuation of Sakemi [1457]. (KS)

1578 Sato, Suhi. "A Note on *(e)aldor, (-)fruma, lēod, þēoden, (-)wine*, etc. in *Beowulf.*" *Journal of the Faculty of Literature (Chuo Univ.)* 119.58 (1986): 29-69. In Japanese.

Not seen.

1579 Schichler, Robert Lawrence. "Heorot and Dragon-Slaying in *Beowulf.*" *Proceedings of the PMR Conference* 11 (1986): 159-175.

Reviews allegorical representations of the rivalry between harts and dragons from the bestiary tradition (Isidore and the *Physiologus*) and from patristic exegesis (Jerome, Rabanus Maurus, and Augustine), suggesting that such lore has been incorporated into the characterization and structure of the poem. The *Physiologus* represents the hart as a mortal enemy of the dragon. The hart lures hidden dragons and serpents with its sweet breath, tears them apart, and purges itself of their venom by drinking from a pure fountain. Jerome and others interpret the serpents as vices and the hart as the good Christian who overcomes them and arrives at redemption. "Structurally, *Beowulf* is divided into two main parts, each with its representative animal: the hart and the dragon—two great symbols poised in balanced rivalry" (159). Schichler discusses how this material is reflected in the depiction of Hart hall, in the characters of Hrothgar and Beowulf, the giant's sword, and the dragon, also suggesting some parallels between Hrothgar and Wealhtheow and the generous couple of Psalm 111. He believes that "Beowulf valiantly performs the functions of a hart to the end" (in his struggle against the dragon) and that the poet intends no criticism of the hero (169). The symbols of hart and dragon establish a system of imagery between good and evil, light and darkness, community and isolation, Christianity and paganism. Schichler traces this imagery in lines 723-27, 1368-72, etc.

1580 Schneider, Karl. *Sophia Lectures on 'Beowulf'*. Ed. Shoichi Watanabe, and Norio Tsuchiya. Tokyo: Taishukan for the Japan Science Society, 1986. Pp. xviii + 308.

Based on a series of lectures delivered at Sophia University in Tokyo in 1981 and in Tokyo and Kyoto in 1981 and 1984, this study proceeds from the thesis that *Beowulf* shows signs of "camouflaged paganism" and finds a number of connections to the Germanic myths of the gods Ing and Frea, making many suggestions about genealogical, textual, philological, archaeological, and other matters. Schneider defines camouflaged paganism as "the survival of pagano-religious concepts under deliberate disguise in an intolerant Christian society. Therewith I give to understand that camouflaged paganism is a manifestation of the intellectual creativity that belongs to the period of transition from paganism to Christianity" (199). For this and other reasons, Schneider dates the poem to the seventh century (between 640 and 650), and places it in the court of Penda the Mercian, finding several connections between the genealogies in *Beowulf* and those of the Mercian royal line.

Schneider reconstructs the pagan background of the poem, particularly the functions of the "primary god" (Frea or Ing in the genealogies) as dispenser of *hælu* 'prosperity and thus victory.' Words which seem to apply to the Christian God in fact often apply to the primary God of the Old Germanic religion. Thus, Christian references in the poem are, Schneider argues, fewer than have been previously seen. He finds overt Christian elements (the mention of Cain and Abel, the concept of God as judge, the allusion to the day of judgment, and the concept of the devil) rather sparsely scattered in the text and discusses the more central role of the primary Germanic god (the giver of all gifts, the protector of mankind, the lord of life and death, the giver of *hǣlu*, the lord of time and seasons, the creator of the world, the all-knowing and omnipotent one), going on to argue that the song of creation (ll. 90b-98) reveals a number of pagan elements and that scholars have mistakenly posited the influence of Genesis.

Besides these central issues, Schneider discusses a great many others, including funeral customs, the Modthryth episode, the beast of battle, runic lore, the importance of fame in the pagan world, the nature of *Beowulf* as a work of art (its structure, characterization, and digressions), among others. Throughout, he supplements his discussion with etymological, philological, and archaeological information, proposing a number of emendations to the text of *Beowulf*, and drawing on runic lore. The volume includes transcriptions of question-and-answer sessions on a wide range of topics, as well as the following appendices: "On Camouflaged Paganism in Anglo-Saxon England," "On the Conversion of the Anglo-Saxons to Christianity," "The OE Names of the Months," "The OE *æcerbōt*—an Analysis."

Reviews: Roberta Frank, *Colloquia Germanica* 22 (1990): 302-03.

1581 Smits, Kathryn. "Die 'Stimmen' des schweigenden Königs: ein Erzählmotiv im *Beowulf*, im *Nibelungenlied* und im *Parzival*." [The 'Voices' of the Silent King: a Narrative Motif in *Beowulf*, the *Nibelungenlied*, and *Parzifal*]. *Literaturwissenschaftliches Jahrbuch* 27 (1986): 23-45.

Identifies a type-scene revolving around the reception of a foreign hero into court in *Beowulf*, the *Nibelungenlied*, and *Parzifal*. The scene has the following structure: a host, usually a king, receives a stranger to whom he reacts with mixed feelings. Since the dignity of the host prevents him from expressing this reaction spontaneously, two characters, a man and a woman, represent these feelings for him. The man expresses the aggressive feelings of the lord while the woman represents the peaceful, conciliatory aspect of his reaction. This tripartite configuration of silent King and his two opposed "voices" appears to rest on a narrative motif preserved in the oral tradition (24). In *Beowulf*, Unferth and Wealhtheow act as the "voices" of Hrothgar in dealing with the newcomer Beowulf. Clearly, Unferth represents Hrothgar's fears about the possible rival Beowulf while Wealhtheow acts as welcomer immediately following Unferth's performance. Seen in this way, Unferth bears no responsibility for what he says as Hrothgar's representative, allowing him to appear as a positive character later on. He bears no personal grudge against Beowulf and can act as an independent character after he plays the role assigned to him in the type-scene. For the contemporary audience familiar with such a scene, the suspense and curiosity would revolve less around what is to happen and more around how the familiar elements would be deployed.

1582 Stanley, Eric G. "Rudolf von Raumer: Long Sentences in *Beowulf* and the Influence of Christianity on Germanic Style." *N&Q* 33 (1986): 434-438.

Examines the controversy between Rudolf von Raumer and an anonymous reviewer of his *Die Einwirkung des Christenthums auf die Althochdeutsche Sprache* [The Influence of Christianity on the Old High German Language] (Stuttgart, 1845). While the reviewer believes that "pagan" syntax consists of short sentences placed side by side and Christian-influenced literature exhibits longer periods, Raumer doubts that the situation can be accounted for so easily and points out that *Beowulf*, as an ancient epic, has long sentences, going on to make a distinction between periods and long sentences. *Beowulf*'s longer sentences do not contain Latinate subordination and coordination typical of the Latinate period; thus, the poem contains longer sentence structures but not periods.

1583 Taylor, Paul Beekman. "*Beowulf* 4-6a: Scyld's *Scaþan*." *In Geardagum* 7 (1986): 37-43.

Proposes that the phrases *sceaþena þreatum* 'troops of warriors' and *monegum mægþum* 'many tribes' (ll. 4b, 5a) may not be parallel dative constructions but that *sceaþena þreatum* could have an instrumental sense and further that *scaþan* can mean "warrior" (as it does in ll. 1803b, 1895a). Thus, the lines might be translated "Scyld Scefing with his troop of warriors deprived many tribes of mead-benches." Taylor also examines syntactic parallels in a number of Old English poetic and prose texts.

1584 _____. "The Traditional Language of Treasure in *Beowulf*." *JEGP* 85 (1986): 191-205.

Believes that words for treasure in *Beowulf* show a primitive belief in the fetishistic power of treasure as a way of bringing forth and preserving a life-force. The etymologies of such words bring out this connection: *gestrȳnan* 'to win, or beget a child' plays against the word *gestrēon* 'treasure, something brought forth' in lines 2794-98, where Beowulf consoles himself "with the notion that a treasure won is a benefit to a people comparable to, if not equal to, a son" (191). Taylor also examines the etymological connections between such pairs as *searo-seorðan, frætwe-frætwian*, and *lāf-lifian*. He concludes that "there is a conventional stock of etymological associations between treasure goods and the lifeforces believed to reside in them, and that these associations are discernible in the poetic style of Old English traditional poetry" (197). These associations, vestiges of Germanic beliefs and practices, are also found in Nordic literature such as the *Ynglinga saga, Egils saga, Grettis saga*, the *Hervarga saga*, and the "Lay of Fafnir" in the *Edda*. The *Beowulf*-poet minimizes the treasure's pagan, fetish value but does not suppress all tribal burial conventions. Divides words relating to treasure into seven categories: words for general goods or possessions (*ar, ǣht, ēad, feoh, gōd, ingesteald, wela, weorð*, and *wist*), for gifts and offerings (*ēst, gafol gif, gift, giftu, gifu, gombe, lāc, lēan, mēd*, and *meord*), for booty and plunder (*hūþ* and *rēaf*), for metal goods and coin (*gold, seolfor*, and *sceat*), for precious artifacts (*frætwe, geatwe, geweorc, gleng, hyrst, searo, wrǣt*, and *wundor*), for heirlooms or inherited items (*lāf* and *yrfe*), and for unspecified precious objects (*gersum, gestrēon, hord, māððum*, and *sinc*).

1585 Temple, Mary Kay. "*Beowulf* 1258-1266: Grendel's Lady-Mother." *ELN* 23 (1986): 10-15.

A study of the word *ides* as it applies to Grendel's mother in line 1259a: *ides āglǣcwīf* 'lady monster-wife.' After a survey of the word's use in other Old English texts, Temple concludes that it usually applies to exceptional women, often saints or the mothers of important men but can also describe exceptionally sinful women such as Modþryð or Eve. "The *Beowulf*-poet, then, could expect his audience to respond to *ides* with certain expectations. Its prosaically flattering meaning of 'noble lady' would cause them to take special note of the irony of its application to the discourteous monster-wife." Thus, Grendel's mother appears as "a ghastly caricature of the cup-bearing hostess" (14). The word, consistently associated with Eve and the wives of Cain, also implicates Grendel's mother in the human tragedy of the Fall.

1586   Thundy, Zacharias P. "*Beowulf*: Date and Authorship." *NM* 87 (1986): 102-116.

Dates the poem to the years 927 to 931 on the basis of perceived allusions to events in the reign of King Æthelstan and further identifies the poet as one Wulfgar, who appears in a charter which uses place-names containing the elements *Beowa* and *Grendel*. Thundy finds in the character of Beowulf several references to Edward the Elder and associates the ravages of the dragon with Welsh uprisings of 924 in Chester. Beowulf's death mirrors that of Edward in this battle as Wiglaf's role mirrors that of Edward's son Æthelstan. Thundy finds a number of other parallels between events in the poem and those in the reign of Æthelstan.

1587   Tripp, Raymond P., Jr. "*Beowulf* 1314a: The Hero as *Alfwalda*, 'Ruler of Elves'." *Neophil* 70 (1986): 630-632.

Maintains with Taylor and Salus [1365] that the manuscript reading of l. 1314a, *alf walda* (elf-ruler), usually emended to *alwalda* (ruler of all), should be retained. Tripp argues, however, that the word does not apply to God, but to Beowulf, as the ruler or conqueror of elves, for the poet does not distinguish clearly between *eoten* (giant), *nicor* (monster), or elf. Accepting *alfwalda* as a human referent clears up some confusion. The *eorla sum* 'a certain warrior' (l. 1312a) is not Beowulf himself but one of his men, and the *būr* 'chamber' (l. 1310a) is not Hrothgar's but Beowulf's. The lines can now be translated: "Right away at his chamber was Beowulf fetched,/ That victory charmed man. Just before daybreak/ Went an earl, another noble fighter,/ Himself and his companions, to where the wise warrior [Beowulf] was staying./ To see whether the *ruler of elves* [Beowulf] would continue/ After a story of woe to work a change for the better" (631).

1588   Ushigaki, Hiroto. "On the Backslide of the Danes: *Beowulf*, ll. 175-88." *Cultural Science Review of Kagoshima Univ.* 21.2 (1986): 41-59. In Japanese.

Not seen.

1589   Weise, Judith. "The Meaning of the Name 'Hygd': Onomastic Contrast in *Beowulf*." *Names* 34 (1986): 1-10.

Suggests that the poet consciously exploited Germanic naming conventions as well as learned Christian traditions of name interpretation in creating the name *Hygd* for Hygelac's consort. "Through variation of and alliteration with an inalterable received name, *Hygelāc* ['mindless,' or 'frivolity'], the *Beowulf* poet developed the probably Old English name *Hygd* ['thought'], which, by juxtaposition, underscores the multiple etymologies possible in an historical name" (9). Discusses onomastic lore of the Middle Ages as well as the etymologies of the names *Hygelāc* and *Hygd*.

1987

1590 Barquist, Claudia Russell. "Phonological Patterning in *Beowulf.*" *Literary and Linguistic Computing* 2 (1987): 19-23.

Studies sound patterning in *Beowulf* by analyzing distinctive features of vowels and consonants in stressed morphs, using A. Campbell's reconstruction of eighth-century pronunciation as a guide and making several conclusions about poetic patterns. Using computer graphing, Barquist plots the "percent of shared distinctive features of each pro-vocalic non-initial consonant or consonant cluster, each morph[-]internal vowel or diphthong, and each post-vocalic consonant or consonant cluster in stressed morphs with every other sound in the same position in a variable range of preceding and succeeding verses" (20). She draws the following conclusions: "An obvious lack of a concentration of specific features is used in this poem mainly for verses which help set the mood of a visual atmosphere; they describe darkness, light, brightness, and gold armour and treasure. When there is a high degree of sharing of features we find mention of God, of goodness, of song, of feasting and the re-telling of stories. The emphasis in this group of categories is one of group concord and a benign view of things" (23). Barquist also suggests that the poem intensifies psychological meaning as it proceeds and that this dramatic quality is mirrored in the phonological patterns.

1591 Bloom, Harold. "Introduction." In *Beowulf.* Modern Critical Interpretations. New York: Chelsea House, 1987. Pp. 1-4.

A brief introduction to the *Modern Critical Interpretations* volume on *Beowulf.* Bloom endorses Robinson's [1513] proposal that the poem shows the dual perspective of a Christian poet admiring but judging the pagan past, though he refuses to find the hero wanting: "Rereading *Beowulf* gives one a fierce and somber sense of heroic loss, in a grim world, not wholly unlike the cosmos of Virgil's *Aeneid.* In spirit, the poem does seem to me more Virgilian than Christian. Though addressed to a Christian audience, it seems not to be addressed to them *as* Christians but as descendants of heroic warriors" (4).

1592 Boenig, Robert. "Time Markers and Treachery: The Crux at *Beowulf* 1130." *ELN* 24 (1987): 1-9.

Notes that the *Beowulf* poet occasionally omits time markers and that such missing markers can help to explain a confusing sequence of events in the Finnsburh episode and whether Beowulf's advisors discouraged or encouraged his expedition to Denmark (ll. 202-04). In the first instance, Boenig thinks that Hengest stays in Frisia, not because the winter makes the sea journey impossible, but because he chooses to stay and take revenge. If an elliptical time marker is supplied, the sequence of events would run this way: Hengest decides to stay with Finn although it is still possible for him to sail home. *Then* (the missing time marker) winter makes a sea voyage perilous. Boenig also proposes that the difficult word *unhlitme* (l. 1129a) may be intentionally ambiguous in that the prefix *un-* can be either a negator or an intensifier, and that it would have struck an Anglo-Saxon reader as unusual. In the case of Beowulf's advisors, assuming a missing time marker in l. 204 helps solve the apparent contradiction. Boenig translates, "Then wise men reproached him a little for that exploit, although he was dear; [later] they encouraged the valiant hearted one, [when] they examined omens" (6).

1593 Bosse, Roberta Bux, and Jennifer Lee Wyatt. "Hrothgar and Nebuchadnezzar: Conversion in Old English Verse." *PLL* 23 (1987): 257-271.

Proposes that Hrothgar undergoes a conversion similar to that experienced by other figures in Old English narratives—Edwin in Bede's *Ecclesiastical History*, Constantine and Judas in Cynewulf's *Elene*, and Nebuchadnezzar in the Old English *Daniel*—finding that Hrothgar most nearly resembles Nebuchadnezzar in his pride, chastisement, and ultimate conversion. Like Nebuchadnezzar, Hrothgar is subject to overweening pride. Having aspired "to build the perfect society, his Heorot is a feeble human parody of the court of heaven with himself playing God, doling out treasures to the favored" (267). He must, like Nebuchadnezzar, be humbled—in Hrothgar's case by the ravages of the monsters. Both Hrothgar and Nebuchadnezzar must next acknowledge their need for assistance (salvation) and voice pleas for help. Finally, Hrothgar learns the truth of God's grace through the ministrations of Beowulf and in his parting "sermon" triumphantly confesses his faith as a new convert.

1594 Brinton, Laurel J. "A Linguistic Approach to Certain Old English Stylistic Devices." *SN* 59 (1987): 177-185.

Argues that the structure of metaphor, understood from a linguistic point of view, also underlies a number of Old English stylistic devices usually considered as separate phenomena: the epithet (*uiðkenning*), kenning, variation, compounds, as well as metaphor, simile, metonymy, and synecdoche. Metaphor is less a way of comparing two things as a way to establish identity between them. The other stylistic devices also function as a type of identification, though they do not require as much "reconstruction" as metaphors do. Brinton goes on to analyze several stylistic devices (listed above) in *Beowulf* and other Old English poems, including a consideration of kennings for ships.

1595 Busse, Wilhelm G. *Altenglische Literatur und ihre Geschichte: Zur Kritik des gegenwärtigen Deutungssytems*. [Old English Literature and Its History: Towards a Critique of the Present System of Interpretation]. Studia humaniora, Bd. 7. Düsseldorf: Droste, 1987. Pp. 314.

Challenges the assumption that Old English poetic texts must be much older than the manuscripts in which they are preserved, specifically calling into question the widely-held belief that the poetry went through a period of development (*Entstehung*) before being recorded in the now-extant manuscripts. Busse points out that though the major poetic codices all bear secure dates in or after the middle of the tenth century, literary historians have assumed that the golden age of Old English poetry actually ended before the ninth century when prose texts begin to appear in numbers and that the poetry is clearly older than the prose. *Cædmon's Hymn*, *Bede's Deathsong*, and the *Leiden Riddle* are preserved in a number of earlier manuscripts but comprise a total of only twenty-eight lines of verse—thin evidence for the assumption that all poetic texts were composed in the same rough period from the eighth to ninth centuries. Busse finds no support for this assumption, which has not been challenged since the turn of the century, and attacks it on three counts: 1) it mistakenly uses the Cædmon paradigm as a way to push back the genesis of a text to a period much earlier than its late manuscript; 2) linguistic studies which claim that a heterogeneous poetic language argues for earlier dating have little basis; 3) various historical arguments for early dating are circular. At several points in the following discussion, Busse comments on the dating of *Beowulf*, and ends his study with the suggestion that a tenth-century context for the major poetic codices must be considered.

Reviews: A. Fischer, *ASNSL* 226 (1989): 139-41; J.C. Pope, *Speculum* 64 (1989): 135-43; E.G. Stanley, *N&Q*, 36 (1989): 216-18; U. Schaefer, *Anglia* 107 (1989): 152-55; M. Griffith, *MÆ* 59 (1990): 152-53.

1596 Butts, Richard. "The Analogical Mere: Landscape and Terror in *Beowulf*." *ES* 68 (1987): 113-121.

Explains the apparent inconsistencies in the description of Grendel's mere (ll. 1345-79b) by pointing out that the poet does not aim at describing a particular topography in realistic terms but means to depict, by analogy, the landscape of the reader's mind, his psychological reaction to the terror of Grendel. The description of the mere stresses its remoteness in time and space as well as its unknowable nature, mixes supernatural and natural elements, confuses sea and lake imagery, emphasizes both the human and monstrous qualities of Grendel and his mother. Such contradictions help to create a dream-like landscape in which topographical features correspond by analogy to the psychology of terror.

1597 Creed, Robert P. "*Beowulf* on the Brink: Information Theory as Key to the Origins of the Poem." In *Comparative Research on Oral Traditions*. Ed. John Miles Foley. Columbus, OH: Slavica, 1987. Pp. 139-160.

Applies Claude Shannon's information theory to the meter of *Beowulf*, concluding that the Old English metrical constraints form a generative communication system which provides the redundancy (in alliteration and stress patterns) which Shannon deems necessary for effective communication but also allows for a certain amount of "entropy" (the potential for variability). Creed posits an "ideal structure" for the alliterative line: it contains at least two stressed syllables which alliterate. Such a redundant structure sets up expectations. "This principle lies at the core of information theory. The receiver, that is, the listener, constantly balances expectations against the not-quite-expected" (150). The poet plays on such expectations in the subtle relationship between the alliterative pair *dōm* 'judgment, glory' and *dēaþ* 'death,' by establishing the expectation that they will occur together (thus forming an ideal structure). Creed examines the pattern of relationships between these two words and their relatives in the verse of *Beowulf* and later poets, arguing that the oral system makes the collocation possible. Also describes a computer program which parses Old English verse lines, showing the generative and systematic nature of the meter.

1598 Crépin, André. "L'Espace du texte et l'esprit liturgique dans la civilisation vieil-anglaise." [The Space of the Text and the Liturgical Spirit in Old English Civilization]. In *Liturgie et espace liturgique*. Papers presented at a Colloquium at the University of Paris XII, December 13-14, 1985. Paris: Didier, 1987. Pp. 49-58.

Finds that the effect of Christian liturgy on *Beowulf* reveals itself not so much in individual references or proposed parallels to the baptismal liturgy or the harrowing of hell (McNamee [S423] and Cabniss [S298]) but in the rhythms and organization of the text, what Crépin calls "l'espace du texte" (56). The divine office has its own rhythms, moving from readings, to psalms, antiphons, collects, and responses—with the narrative of scriptural readings giving way to antiphons and responses which direct the attention heavenward in praise of God. The digressions and allusions in *Beowulf* evoke a similar rhythm, with sections of secular praise (the funerals of Scyld and Beowulf) alternating with the larger narrative. The two solemn funerals answer, resemble, and oppose one another in the manner of readings, psalms, or anthems in the divine office: "se répondent, se ressemblent et s'opposent. A la manière des leçons, psaumes ou entiennes de l'office divin" (56). Two passages of secular praise (ll. 12-25 and 3178-82) as well as the allusion to the Danes' pagan rites (ll. 175-88) show evidence of such influence. Further, the poem is filled with references to solemn chanting, while the hall itself, filled with songs of praise accompanied by the passing of the cup, may be compared loosely to liturgy in the church. The organization, rhythm, and composition of the poem recall those of the divine office: "L'organisation, le rythme, la composition du poème rappellent ceux de l'office divin" (58).

1599 Cronan, Dennis. "Old English *Gelad*: 'A Passage across Water'." *Neophil* 71 (1987): 316-319.

Advances evidence that the word *gelād*, contrary to Klaeber's glossary entry [S67], is not a poetic word meaning 'way, course, tract' but a word found commonly in place names and meaning 'passage across water.' Cronan examines the word as it occurs in several place names and points out that it never alliterates in the poetic corpus, thus implying that it is not a poetic word. In line 1410b, the phrase *uncūð gelād* would then refer not to 'unknown paths' but to an 'unknown passage across water' and take part in a formulaic description of unknown territory (as found also in *Exodus*, ll. 56-58). The word *fen-gelād* (l. 1359a), Cronan suggests, should be translated as 'fen-stream.'

1600 Crossley-Holland, Kevin. *Beowulf: The Poetry of Legend*. Woodbridge, Suffolk: Boydell Press, 1987. Pp. 142; ill.

A translation of the poem into English verse (see Crossley-Holland [S661]) with a new introduction and several photographs of contemporary artifacts. The front matter includes sections on the historical, social, and literary backgrounds, as well as a time chart, map, genealogical tables, a list of characters, explanatory notes, and an index. Another essay, "How to Read the Poem," discusses Christian and heroic elements. The large-format book prints the poem in frames on several photographic backgrounds depicting northern landscapes, church architecture, manuscript illustration, or contemporary artifacts. Lines 4-11: "Scyld Scefing often deprived his enemies,/ many tribes of men, of their mead-benches./ He terrified his foes; yet he, as a boy, had been found a waif; fate made amends for that./ He prospered under heaven, won praise and honour/ until the men of every neighbouring tribe,/ across the whale's way, were obliged to obey him/ and pay him tribute. He was a noble king!"

1601 Derolez, René. "Hrothgar King of Denmark." In *Multiple Worlds, Multiple Words: Essays in Honour of Irène Simon*. Ed. Hena Maes-Jelinek, Pierre Michel, and Paulette Michel-Michot. Liège: U de Liège, 1987. Pp. 51-58.

Objecting to the approach of several papers at the Toronto conference (Chase, *The Dating of Beowulf*), points out that the poet's supposed Danophilia is "largely meaningless" for dating *Beowulf* because "the poet's image of the Danes is anything but flawless" (53); thus, there is no need to justify positive reactions to Danes or their ancestors in the Viking age. Derolez goes on to argue that "there is little to recommend Hrothgar as an ideal king" (54) and that the poet portrays him as a feeble and passive: he sleeps in the outbuildings when Grendel attacks the hall, reveals his position of weakness in several speeches, watches passively as the resentful Danes, represented by Unferth, attack the honor of Beowulf, remains silent about royal succession, and is outflanked by Wealhtheow in political astuteness.

1602 Donoghue, Daniel. "On the Classification of B-Verses with Anacrusis in *Beowulf* and *Andreas*." *N&Q* 34 (1987): 1-5.

Accepting Bliss's view of metrical anacrusis [S353] argues that "the first unstressed syllable of b-verses is *not* anacrustic (that is, extrametrical), but that the medial unstressed syllable is" (2). The eight anacrustic b-verses in *Beowulf* (ll. 93b, 666b, 1223b, 1504b, 1773b, 1877b, 2247b, and 2592b) are better explained by this scansion since the medial unstressed syllable is either *ne* or a prefix (a structure dependent on and even inseparable from the following syllable) while the initial unstressed syllables in five cases are separate particles.

1602a _____. *Style in Old English Poetry: The Test of the Auxiliary*. New Haven: Yale UP, 1987.

A book-length study of verbal auxiliaries in Old English poetry which distinguishes the individual styles of Old English poems by the placement and proportion of auxiliaries. "This study tests whether auxiliaries can . . . be used to pinpoint differences in poetic styles and whether those distinctions can be identified as 'lay' and 'epic' or other such broad categories. The picture that has emerged . . . is quite complex, and does not lend confidence to assigning poems to common schools or styles. If anything, the diversity of the results shows that each poet pursued his craft in his own way" (100). Donoghue goes on to characterize the individual style of the *Beowulf*-poet with respect to auxiliaries: relative to the other poems, *Beowulf* has "a moderate overall proportion of auxiliaries, of initial auxiliaries, of bracketing patterns, of principal clauses, and of dependent clauses. Unlike the other poems, however, it allows a great deal of variation in word order and stress in principal clauses" (101). The *Beowulf*-poet uses verbal-auxiliary half-lines with particular deftness but

avoids passive constructions, preferring modals and other auxiliaries. Appendices include detailed statistical information as well as a list of relineations, repunctuations, and emendations to the *Anglo-Saxon Poetic Records*. (Donoghue's index of *Beowulf* passages [231-32] has been incorporated into the line index of this volume.)
Reviews: A.A. MacDonald, *Studies in Language* 13 (1989): 525-27; B. Mitchell, *Speculum* 64 (1989): 407-09; R.L. Thomson, *General Linguistics* 29 (1989): 68-76; R.P. Creed, *ELN* 27 (1990): 73-74; A.S.G. Edwards, *MLR* 85 (1990): 400-01; J. Roberts, *N&Q* 37 (1990): 453-55; E.G. Stanley, *RES* 41 (1990): 233-34; J.W. Earl, *Comparative Lit.* 43 (1991): 185-87; Roberta Frank, *JEGP* 90 (1991): 239-41.

1603 Duncan, Ian. "Epitaphs for Æglæcan: Narrative Strife in *Beowulf*." In *Modern Critical*, pp. 111-30.

Warning against the dangers of reconstructing a monolithic genre for *Beowulf*, finds that the poem is governed by two interacting genres, the mythological and the historical "which represent different (antithetical) epistemological and interpretive modes" (117). The mythological genre takes internal social problems and externalizes them into monsters which can be defeated while the historical genre both criticizes human failures and monumentalizes human achievements. In the first part of the poem, these two genres contest each other in such a way that the final purging of evil which the mythological aims at cannot be achieved. History and men undo the social fabric far more completely than the vanquished Grendel. In the dragon episode, the modes "have collapsed into each other, from a relationship of would-be dialectic to one of mutual deconstruction" (119). The historical mode finally wins out, for "if the contest of narratives has a theme, it is the failure of the mythic and imaginary mode to resolve or contain what turns out to be privileged as the mode of historical reality" (119). Unlike monsters in folktales and in the sagas, the monsters of *Beowulf* are mysterious and unknown. The poem associates evil, both that of the monsters and of men like Heremod, with mystery, while its heroes perform their acts in open view. This is a social rather than a moral vision: the dragon's hoard "is sinister because its stagnant, sepulchral occlusion from proper social exchange and circulation is identified with the rhetoric of secrecy. Secrecy in itself generates malignity, breeds dragons" (123). The poem ends in the genre of epitaph, where Beowulf himself becomes a hero "overwhelmed by the self-canceling strategies of the [mythic] genre that would petrify its lonely *æglæcan* against the dissolving reversals of history: monumentality, the genre of epitaph" (128).

1604 Earl, James W. "Transformation of Chaos: Immanence and Transcendence in Beowulf and Other Old English Poetry." *Ultimate Reality & Meaning* 10 (1987): 164-185.

Identifies pre-Christian elements in Bede's story of the conversion of Edwin (with its parable of the sparrow) and finds traces of similar ideas in the monsters of *Beowulf* as well as in "The Seafarer," "Maxims I," and "Christ I." In the unnamed counselor's parable of the sparrow, "Man's point of view remains inside the hall, and what lies outside is experienced only as the border where the immanent meets chaos and the unknown" (167). The Christian perspective, however, inverts this image: this world is chaotic and dangerous while all meaning is anchored in the afterlife. In accepting Christianity on these terms, the speakers in Bede's story "seek a religion that will fulfill their material expectations and clarify, without really changing, their dark, realistic picture of the universe" (168). Essentially, the world inside the hall (the immanent) remains the safe center while the winter storms outside represent a mysterious chaos (the transcendent). *Beowulf* shows the same attitude toward the transcendent-unknown: the story of Scyld (ll. 26-52) acts as a direct parallel to that of the sparrow: both come from and return to the unknown. Further, the monsters represent this Germanic sense of chaos as balanced against the immanence of the hall. Grendel is not a moral force but an abstraction of the chaos called forth by the very act of creation: "for every order there is an equal and opposite chaos" (182). Grendel's mother "represents the violence Anglo-Saxon kingship was most at pains to control" (182), a violence particularly represented by the claims of women. The dragon is less a symbol of pure evil (in the Christian sense) than a reminder that "man is ultimately powerless to control history, and history itself is as mortal as man" (183). Beowulf himself, like the sparrow, departs into the darkness with only the barest glimpse of his destination. Earl sees the statement of the poem as unique, "so metaphysically secular, so slightly Christianized, its stoic reserve refusing to see beyond the surrounding, threatening borders of the immanent" (184).

1605 Feldman, Thalia Phillies. "A Comparative Study of *Fēond, Dēofol, Syn,* and *Hel* in *Beowulf.*" *NM* 88 (1987): 159-174.

Argues that "Analysis of *fēond, dēofol, syn* and *hel* in *Beowulf* reveals the concept of evil as societal harm, not as moral, personal sin injurious to the individual soul" (159), particularly with respect to Grendel. Though Christian interpretations of *Beowulf* read these words with their modern meanings, Feldman believes that they retain different, preconversion meanings which had not yet disappeared. Grendel is described as a *fēond* 'enemy,' a word which had not yet become 'fiend,' while the word *dēofol,* also applied to Grendel, seems to refer better to the giants of Northern and protohistoric belief than to devils of the Christian system. *Hel* or 'hell' is a homonym with *hél,* 'calumny,' implying the Northern belief that it was a place of punishment for slanderers, while *synn* originally meant 'crime.' Further, Feldman suggests that the word *hel-* be emended to *heall-* 'hall' in three instances: lines 101b, 788a, and 1274a, in each case revealing Grendel as an enemy in the hall (rather than from hell).

1606 Frank, Roberta. "Did Anglo-Saxon Audiences Have a Skaldic Tooth?" *Scandinavian Studies* 59 (1987): 338-355.

Explores the possibility that skaldic poetry may have influenced Old English poetic idiom in *Exodus* and *Beowulf* directly. The *Beowulf* poet uses compounds related to skaldic kennings (*herenet* 'battle-net', *hildegicel* 'battle-icicle,' *beadulēoma* and *hildelēoma* 'battle-light) but almost always clarifies the more obscure ones. "His echoes of skaldic diction seem to be heard at a great distance, from outside the tradition, and recorded to supply a touch of Scandinavian color" (343). Skaldic verse, like *Beowulf,* interchanges words for strong drink somewhat indiscriminately and can also help to illuminate such troublesome words as *lofgeornost* 'eager for praise' (l. 3182b) and *dollīc* 'foolish' (l. 2646a) which in skaldic poetry mean 'most eager for praise' and 'bold, ready to risk' respectively. Skaldic poetry prizes double-sided metaphors, a property found in such words (in Unferth's flyting speech, ll. 506-28) as *sund,* which can mean either 'sea' or 'swimming', and in other expressions—*þehton, mæton, brugdon, glidon*—which are "double-valenced terms appropriate for swimming as well as rowing" (346). In fact,

"Unferth seems to be playing the same skaldic game of disguises, riddling in such a way as to make his meaning clear to the initiated and misleading to the naive" (347). Frank also suggests that the beasts of battle motif may derive from direct skaldic influence rather than from common Germanic inheritance.

1607 Fulk, R.D. "Unferth and His Name." *MP* 85 (1987): 113-27.

Reviewing interpretations and etymologies of the name *Unferth*, Fulk concludes that the name cannot mean 'not-peace' or 'nonsense, folly,' nor does it reflect allegorically on Unferth's character; instead, the name is derived from traditional Germanic sources and is "a normal Germanic hero's name" related to the widely-attested OHG names *Unfrid* and *Hunfrid* (113). Fulk rejects Robinson's [S774] and Greenfield's [S834] preference for *-ferhð* as the etymological form of the second element in the name and derives it from *frið*, "peace," also viewing as unlikely the suggestion that the poet invented the name. He discusses at length the derivation and phonological development of the *un-*, *hun-* element, concluding that it cannot mean 'not' and that it may be related to the name of the Huns, though it is not possible to reconstruct the etymology with any assurance. Fulk supports the emendation of the MS. *Hunferð* to *Unferð* on the grounds that no other Germanic name beginning with 'h' and a vowel alliterates with vowels in *Beowulf*. He rejects allegorical readings of the name and character as unwarranted by both the comparative linguistic evidence as well as the literary evidence.

1608 Gahrn, Lars. "Beowulf och Nordhalland." [Beowulf and Northern Halland]. *Varbergs Museum Årsbok* 38 (1987): 13-26.

Reviews proposed geographical locations for Geatland, pointing out problems with the solutions offered thus far, and suggesting that it may have been located in the district of Skaraborg, not in the valley of the Göta älv (near Gothenburg) as has been more generally assumed. Gahrn focuses on the place names *Hronesnæs* (Cape of the Whales) and *Earnanæs* (Cape of the Eagles). He concludes (in an English summary): "The author points out that the Götar were inlanders. Their royal hall is to be searched for in the plains of the district Skaraborg but not in the valley of the

Göta älv nor in Halland. In Northern Halland the powerful people of Fjäre lived. As a matter of fact not a single parish by the sea belonged to Västergötland before the 13th century. All these coastal areas belonged to Halland. The poetical pictures of the Beowulf epic have accordingly fascinated many historians to the point of overlooking important facts, searching for Götar where no Götar have lived and preferring a late poem to contemporary sources. We have *no* certain knowledge about Beowulf and his Geats. They cannot be placed in a geographical framework" (26). In Swedish with English summary.

1609 Georgianna, Linda. "King Hrethel's Sorrow and the Limits of Heroic Action in *Beowulf.*" *Speculum* 62 (1987): 829-50.

Analyzes Beowulf's last speech (ll. 2425-37), finding that through the sorrow of Hrethel over his dead son the poet distances us from the heroic action and questions "the value and effectiveness of heroic action at precisely the moment when the hero is most relying on it" (831). In this section, "the poet engages in what might nowadays be called a revolt against the narrativity of the poem's first half. He frustrates our desire for narrative progress and logic even as he frustrates his hero's need for clarity of vision and purpose in this speech," displaying an almost "modern or postmodern taste for subversive elements in narratives" (834). At the heart of Beowulf's speech (spoken before his fight with the dragon) is his retelling of Hrethel's sorrow for his son Herebeald, killed inadvertently by his other son Haethcyn. Hrethel is helpless in his sorrow since he cannot avenge one son's death by killing the other. Action becomes impossible for him as it does for the father who grieves for his hanged son. "King Hrethel's confusion and paralysis, instigated by what he views as a mysterious, random act, and resulting in what is imagined as the irrevocable loss of the joys of the hall, serve for us, if not for Beowulf, as an example of a more general confusion and paralysis at the heart of heroic society" (848). Beowulf meditates on these stories to steady himself for his final challenge, though they and the digressions on the Swedish wars point to the irony of heroic action. Georgianna also argues that line 2469b, where the poet says that Hrethel *Godes lēoht gecēas* 'chose God's light,' is a painfully ironic phrase since Hrethel, as a pagan, cannot choose God's light—nor can Beowulf.

1610   Glosecki, Stephen O. "*Beowulf* 769: Grendel's Ale-Share."
        ELN 21 (1987): 1-9.

    Undertakes to explain the difficult word *ealuscerwen* in line 769a, agreeing with Smithers [S246] that the word must mean 'dispensing of ale,' and arguing that the term must be an ironic term for death, but that its reference is to Grendel, not to the Danes. Glosecki proposes that -*scerwen* may be a poetic neologism based on the strong infinitive *sceran* 'to shear, cut' and contaminated by the thematic glide of the feminine noun *scearu* 'share,' in order to make the connection between death and drinking. He goes on to suggest that *ealuscerwen* 'dispensing of ale' is associated with the *poculum mortis* or cup of death motif found in a number of Germanic texts and that a further level of irony is added if one imagines a reference to the Germanic wassail, where one drinks to the health of a friend (a custom described in Lagamon's *Brut*). "The wassail cup, antithetically invoked, becomes the *poculum mortis*—momentarily at least. . . . when the *Beowulf* poet says that ale is shared out for the Danes, he implies, ironically, that a hostile action has been undertaken by a powerful ally *on behalf of* the Danes—that the hero has wreaked vengeance upon the archenemy of the tribe. Here we need to recognize a particular use of the benefactive dative . . . : the ale-share, the *poculum mortis*, is not given *to* the Danish warriors. Rather, the drink of death is given to Grendel by Beowulf *for* (on behalf of) the Danish warriors. Grendel is the one who receives *ealuscerwen*" (9).

1611   Heinemann, Fredrik J. "*Beowulf* 665b-738: a Mock Approach-to-Battle Type Scene." In *Perspectives on Language in Performance: Studies in Linguistics, Literary Criticism, and Language Teaching and Learning to Honour Werner Hüllen on the Occasion of His Sixtieth Birthday*. Ed. Wolfgang Lörscher and Rainer Schulze. Tübingner Beiträge zur Linguistik, Bd. 317. Tübingen: Gunter Narr, 1987. Pp. 677-94.

    Detects in lines 665b-738 an ironic handling of a type-scene, the "approach to battle" and compares the comic treatment of Grendel to the derisive depictions of defeated villains in *Judith* and *Andreas*. Heinemann first reconstructs the elements of the typical approach-to-battle type-scene, listing a number of topoi, including the following: "The Commander Summons the Troops to Battle," "The Troops Assemble," "The Troops Arm Themselves," "The

Commander Directs the Battle Tactics of his Troops," "The Troops Anticipate (or Fear) the Battle," "The Troops Perceive the Enemy from a Distance," "The Commander (or Narrator) Predicts the Outcome of the Battle," "The Commander Orders his Troops to Advance," "The Narrator Relates the Troops' Intentions and Thoughts," and "The Troops Advance." The *Beowulf*-poet employs many of these topoi ironically, particularly the prediction, advance, and intention topoi. Balancing predictions with unconventional elements allows the poet to dampen the terror of Grendel by juxtaposing his horrific qualities with predictions of Beowulf's success. The narrator dwells on Grendel's arrogant intentions (another topos), which are comically distant from his actual success. Even Grendel's advance toward Hrothgar's hall has comic overtones. As a comic figure, Grendel serves as a contrast to Beowulf: the monster is "a parody of the heroic ideal represented by Beowulf" (693).

1612   Helder, William. "The Song of Creation in *Beowulf* and the Interpretation of Heorot." *ESC* 13 (1987): 243-255.

Finds in the Song of Creation (ll. 90-98) a number of allusions to the typology of *ecclesia* as found in the exegetical writings of Bede, Ambrose, and others and supports the idea that Heorot "should not be labeled as a symbol of wickedness if it is not perfect in the full prelapsarian sense.... The allusions in the Song of Creation to the typology of the *ecclesia* strongly suggest that Heorot points to the standard for human action in a fallen world" (253). Helder accounts for a number of elements in the Song which are not found in Genesis by suggesting specific sources in Bible commentaries and the liturgy. He ties the poem's mention of the moon (not in Genesis 1) to Bede's and Ceolfrith's discussions of the Easter controversy.

1613   Huppé, Bernard F. *'Beowulf': A New Translation*. Pegasus Paperbooks. Binghamton, NY: MRTS, State U of New York at Binghamton, 1987.

A revised version of Huppé's 1984 translation [1437] with a condensed version of the introduction. Includes numbered headings and subheadings indicating the structure of the poem, a dynastic chart, a commentary on individual lines and passages, and a select list of key words and their Old English originals. Lines 4-11: "Oft Scyld Scefing   in shock of battle/ took the meadhalls   from many nations,/

made nobles fearful; after he was first found/ alone and destitute he did not lack comfort/ and under the clouds came to be honored/ until every nation neighboring his/ over the seapaths paid him obedience,/ gave him tribute —he was a good king."
Reviews: *OEN* 22.1 (1988):74.

1614 Irving, Edward B., Jr. "What to Do with Old Kings." In *Comparative Research on Oral Traditions: A Memorial for Milman Parry.* Ed. John Miles Foley. Columbus, OH: Slavica, 1987. Pp. 259-268.

Finds in the characterization of Hrothgar a number of inherited conventions for depicting old kings from oral-derived tradition and argues that "Hrothgar must be granted the very maximum of formal dignity, on the one hand, but it must somehow be a dignity fully consonant with his real impotence" (260). A stream of honorific epithets helps to maintain this facade of dignity, as does the poet's use of Unferth as "a projection into a safe area of Hrothgar's real incompetence and failure" (261). In addition, the poet shows Hrothgar undertaking one truly heroic action by leading the Danes and Geats to the terrifying mere, but the heroism of even this act is sharply limited. The poet also masks over Hrothgar's possible weaknesses by assigning blame elsewhere or by keeping him absent during the most ignominious of the Dane's failures. Another of Hrothgar's qualities, his expressiveness and love for Beowulf, cuts both ways, displaying fine sensibility but also "a terrible dependence" (264). Finally, Irving identifies a technique called "zero-grade narration" (the absence of conventional, heroic characteristics), which the poet uses to characterize subliminally Hrothgar's weakness: he is a passive spectator and resigned to God's providence (not an active, heroic doer like Beowulf); he lacks a history of past heroic achievement; except with Beowulf, he has few warm connections to family or retainers. In the end, "Hrothgar seems a thing of empty formulas and patches, a stuffed figure" (266). Irving praises the poet's manipulation of flat conventions for the depiction of old kings. Appears in adapted form in Irving [1702].

1615 *Key-Word Studies in 'Beowulf,' 2.* Ed. Yoshio Terasawa. Tokyo: Centre for Mediaeval English Studies, 1987.

Part of a continuing series of word studies and word lists edited by Yoshio Terasawa. As a rule, each entry provides the following information for the words it covers: etymology, frequency of occurrence in *Beowulf,* inflected forms, definitions, collocations and variation, alliterative environment, as well as derivatives and compounds.

In a study of the word *dōm* 'judgment' or 'glory' (pp. 1-4), Shunichi Noguchi surveys the twenty occurrences of the word in *Beowulf* according to speaker and context, pointing out that it is "in the nature of semantic development that judgement, pronounced by authority, is associated with 'discretion' and 'power', and judgement upon admirable people, with 'repute' and 'glory'" (1). Noguchi highlights the core meaning 'judgment' and speculates on the demise of the positive sense of the word in English.

Hiroshi Ogawa (pp. 5-17) studies words for 'joy' (*drēam, frōfor, gamen, hrōðor,* and *wynn*). He concludes that *drēam* and *wynn* are the most productive 'joy' words in forming compounds and derivatives. *Gamen* carries a concrete sense of festivity and occurs most often in the nominative, while *drēam* is more abstract, a quality which Grendel lacks. *Wynn* fails to receive alliteration in the majority of its occurrences, while *frōfor* always alliterates and almost always appears without a qualifying genitive.

Six nouns concerning death (*cwealm, dēað, fyll, hryre, morðor,* and *swylt*) are the subject of an entry (pp. 19-33) by Shigeru Ono, who likewise considers the etymology, frequency, inflectional forms, collocations, alliteration, and compounds for each word. He lists other words denoting 'death' and observes that *fyll* and *hryre* indicate violent death while *cwealm* and *morðor* involve killing and murder. All the words bear alliteration, with the exception of four instances. The choice of synonyms (in variation) is conditioned by alliteration. Simplexes tend to occur in the b-verse and compounds in the a-verse.

Shuji Sato examines (in a first installment, pp. 35-47) "Words Used in Connection with *God* and *Cyning,*" including the following: (for God) *sē ælmihtiga, alwalda, anwalda, dēmend, fæder, gehyld, kyningwuldor, metod, rædend, scyppend, wealdend,* (for king) *æþeling, frumgār, mundbora, rīca,* and *wīsa.*

"A Note on Adjectives denoting Bravery" by Hiromitsu Yamagata (pp. 49-65), provides a similar treatment of the following: *bald, cēne, collenferhð, dēor, dol, dyrstig, forht, frec, frēcne, from, gōd, grim(m), gūþmōd, heard, hrēoh, hwæt, mōdig, rōf, snell, stearc, stīð, swīð, þrīst,* and *unforht.* Yamagata charts the frequency with which each word is applied to characters in *Beowulf,* observing that the adjective *gōd* combines notions of physical strength and nobility, noting ironic uses of the words, possible confusions between *dēor* 'brave' and *dēore* 'excellent,' and the association of the adjective *hwæt* with the noun *Scyldingas*. The volume ends with "Studies in Beowulf Vocabulary: A Select Bibliography" (pp. 67-82) compiled by Tadao Kubouchi, Yoshihiro Yoshino, and Hiromitsu Yamagata, listing items under the following headings: facsimiles; editions; bibliographies; dictionaries; concordances, glossaries, and commentaries; manuscript, grammatical, prosodic, and background studies; and word studies.

1616 Köberl, Johann. "The Magic Sword in *Beowulf.*" *Neophil* 71 (1987): 120-128.

Proposes that the giantish sword hilt which Beowulf brings back from Grendel's mere and which Hrothgar examines before delivering his "sermon" is inscribed with Heremod's name and that this interpretation clears up textual problems in the passage (ll. 1677-98) and renders the other Heremod references less abrupt. Köberl believes that Heremod goes out to fight the *eotenum* or 'giants' (l. 902b)—not 'Jutes' as Kaske argued [S631]—and dying in this battle, his sword passed into their hands. It remained in the giant's cave, waiting by divine providence, for Beowulf to use in his attack on Grendel's mother.

1617 Koch, Ludovica. *Beowulf.* Turin: Einaudi, 1987. Pp. xxxix + 281.

A translation of *Beowulf* into Italian. Not seen.

1617a Koike, Kazuo. "The Expressions for Death in *Beowulf.*" *Obirin Review* (Obirin U) 11 (1987): 14-18. In Japanese.

Five simple words and twenty-eight compound words are considered from the viewpoint of lexical and contextual meaning. Collocations meaning "death" are also considered. (KK)

1618 Kumazawa, Sukeo. "Verb-Positions of Finite Verbs in Adverb Clauses in *Beowulf.*" *Research Report of Ikutoku Technical Univ.: Part A Humanities and Social Science A* 11 (1987): 31-49. In Japanese.

Examines adverb clauses in *Beowulf*, showing where finite verbs stand in adverb clauses and how many finite verbs stand at the end of adverb clauses. (SK)

1619 Lucas, Peter J. "Some Aspects of the Interaction between Verse Grammar and Metre in Old English Poetry." *SN* 59 (1987): 145-175.

Investigates the interaction between verse grammar (based on Kuhn's Laws) and meter, particularly enclisis and convertibility, and observes that the *Beowulf* poet, more than other Old English versifiers, adheres more successfully to "traditional norms of correctness" (168) than other poets.

1620 Maeth Ch., Russell. "*El cuento de Zhou Chu*: ¿Un precursor sino-tibetano de la Edad Media temprana de *Beowulf?*" [*The Song of Zhou Chu*: A Sino-Tibetan Precursor of the Early Middle Ages of *Beowulf*?]. *Estudios de Asia y Africa* 22 (1987): 535-546.

Compares the events of *Beowulf* to those in the Tibetan poem, *The Song of Zhou Chu*, finding a number of similarities, perhaps indicating that a version of the Chinese folktale could have found its way to the West by Sino-European contacts in the fifth century. The story of Zhou Chu appeared in a collection of poems compiled for Liu Yiqing (403-444) and tells how local inhabitants beg Zhou Chu, a powerful, but feared warrior, to kill two beasts (a tiger and a dragon), in the hopes that Zhou Chu himself (the third "beast") would be killed. After fighting with the dragon for three days, he vanquished it. In the meantime the people believe Zhou Chu to have died and begin rejoicing. When he suddenly appears from the water they flee in terror, and Zhou Chu (seeing the hatred of the villagers) decides to reform. Zhou Chu's brand of heroism is part of the Xiá tradition, a heroic ethos in which warriors train themselves in martial arts and adhere to standards of chivalric behavior. Maeth sketches out a number of specific parallels: both heroes fight under water, both decapitate their adversaries, etc.—motifs which show more than coincidental resemblance to similar motifs in the stories of Cinderella and Odysseus. Such Chinese folk-motifs could have reached the West through martial or commercial contacts between the Chinese and Indians and Western Europeans.

1621 Magnusson, Magnus, Sheila Mackie, and Julian Glover. *'Beowulf': an Adaptation by Julian Glover of the Verse Translations of Michael Alexander and Edwin Morgan.* Gloucester: Alan Sutton, 1987. Pp. 133; ill.

A condensed, free verse translation of *Beowulf*, interspersed with several passages in Old English, based on the translations of Alexander [S858] and Morgan [S243], adapted by Julian Glover for the stage. Glover cuts the historical digressions to achieve a performance of about an hour and a half. Magnus Magnusson's introduction summarizes and comments on the poem, also discussing Sheila Mackie's illustrations. Lines 4-11 (approximately): "Was it not Scyld Sheving that shook the halls,/ Took mead-benches, taught encroaching foes to fear him—/ Who, found in childhood, lacked clothing?/ Yet, he lived and prospered, grew in strength and stature under the heavens. Ðæt wæs god cyning! He was a good king!"

1622 Mc Hugh, Maire. "The Sheaf and the Hound: A Comparative Analysis of the Mythic Structure of *Beowulf* and *Táin Bó Cúalnge.*" In *La narrazione: Temi e techniche dal medioevo al nostri giorni.* Quaderni del dipartimento di lingue e letterature straniere moderne, Università di Genova, v. 1. Abano Terme: Piovan, 1987. Pp. 9-43.

Maintains that a primitive vegetation myth underlies both *Beowulf* and the *Táin Bó Cúalnge*, the former in the central mythic figure of *Scyld Scefing* and the latter in the hero Cúchulainn. In the case of *Beowulf*, Mc Hugh sees Scyld Scefing (connected etymologically to "sheaf") as a manifestation of a cyclical vegetation god whose son is Beow (connected etymologically to "barley"). Both Grendel and the dragon are associated with the dark destructive force of water and the ocean. Thus, Beowulf becomes a representative of the mythic vegetation hero: "The victory of the hero symbolizes the triumph of vegetation in spring and summer over the waters of the northern winter" (24). Though the two epics differ radically in tone and structure, both share a "deep faith in a continuous regeneration of time, and a similar conception of its cyclical nature" (42).

1622a Mizuno, Tomoaki. "You Evil Hero, Beowulf: On the Legendary Association between Strangers and Accidental Murder." *Shiron, Kawauchi* 26 (1987): 1-18.

Not seen. See Mizuno [1709] for a development of the same argument.

1623 Monnin, Pierre E. "Namings of the Hero and the Structure of *Beowulf.*" In *The Structure of Texts.* Ed. Udo Fries. Swiss Papers in English Language and Literature. Narr: Tubingen, 1987. 3:111-121.

Taking Whallon's lists of names and epithets for Beowulf [S735] as a starting point, examines epithets for the hero which are also applied to other characters (including Hrothgar, Hygelac, Sigemund, Wiglaf, Scyld, Grendel, and the dragon). Monnin claims that these repetitions "'ring bells' in rather subtle ways for the appreciative ears of an experienced audience and furthermore develop around the central character patterns that show the structure of the poem" (121). The distributional patterns of epithets give clues to structure: for instance, the majority of epithets which Beowulf shares with Hrothgar are applied to Beowulf only after line 2200, suggesting the validity of Tolkien's division of the poem into two parts [S130]. Other shared names, particularly those in common with Wiglaf, reinforce the contrasts between parts A and B. Namings applied also to the monsters stress "shared fierceness" (120).

1624 Obst, Wolfgang. *Der Rhythmus des 'Beowulf': eine Akzent- und Takttheorie.* [The Rhythm of 'Beowulf': an Accent and Syllable Theory]. Anglistische Forschungen, 187. Heidelberg: Carl Winter, 1987. Pp. 189.

Establishes four verse types for the meter of *Beowulf*: 1) !_!_o, 2) ~!_~!_o, 3) !_(~) !_~~_o, and 4) ~!_o (where ! indicates a lift, *o* a syllable, ~ an unspecified number of syllables, ( ) an optional element; underlining in 2 and 3 denotes that one or both of the two drops must remain unfilled (112). Obst rejects Sievers' waiving of resolution [S20] in certain cases and argues that verses with three lifts are possible, also finding some support for isochrony but rejecting Sievers' foot analysis which uses caesura to establish metrical feet—because it produces too high a number of types to be "aesthetically relevant." Instead, he reduces and regroups Sievers' list of types "to form a more adequate typology" (112). "A statistical survey of all the half-lines permits the formulation of the fundamental principle in the metrical grammar of [*Beowulf*]: All normal half-lines are derived from a single rhythmical structure by a variation device. A half-line consists of two bars with an unspecified number (m) of unstressed beats: /Xxm/Xx. (x indicates a beat, X the option between x and x^X, the double beat caused by resolution. In the second bar the number of unstressed syllables/beats is automatically 1 for linguistic reasons.) This double bar can be prefixed by any kind and number of beats within the limits of one extra bar" (113). Obst also discusses double beat, verses prefixed by an upbeat, verses prefixed by a downbeat, the requirements of alliteration, and the distribution of verse types in first and second half-lines. He also considers the aesthetic rules governing the composition of Beowulfian lines and states a number of preferences and rules observed by the *Beowulf* poet (107-110). Includes a summary in English and several appendices (an inventory of the four main verse types and their subtypes, the frequency of the fill types, conditionally regular verses, verses outside of the schemas of rule one, verses with problematic interpretations, a list of corrupt and emended verses, and a statistical overview).

Reviews: E.G. Stanley, *N&Q* 35 (1988): 1.

1625 Olsen, Alexandra Hennessey. "Literary Artistry and the Oral-Formulaic Tradition: The Case of Gower's *Apollonius of Tyre*." In *Comparative Research on Oral Traditions*. Ed. John Miles Foley. Columbus, OH: Slavica, 1987. Pp. 493-509.

In a defense of his stature as a poet, argues that John Gower uses the sea voyage type-scene and other elements of oral narrative, drawing on the same Old English traditions available to the *Beowulf* poet.

1626 Overing, Gillian R. "Swords and Signs: A Semiotic Perspective on *Beowulf*." *The American Journal of Semiotics* 5 (1987): 35-57.

Appears in somewhat altered form in chapter two of Overing's *Language, Sign and Gender in Beowulf* [1761].

1627 Parker, Mary A. *'Beowulf' and Christianity*. New York: Peter Lang, 1987. Pp. vii + 224.

Takes on the problem of the poem's Christianity from an interdisciplinary point of view. The study is divided into three parts: part one reviews the history of the Anglo-Saxon conversion, the nature of Christian education in Anglo-Saxon

England, and archaeological evidence of burial practices, focusing on the period between 597 and 800 (which Parker accepts as the most probable date for the poem); part two provides an extensive review of criticism on the question of the Christian or pagan/secular nature of the poem; part three examines the language of the poem (including words for fate, God, heaven, hell, grace or ēst, soul, glory/judgment [dōm], etc.). In each case Parker finds that the evidence (historical, religious, archaeological, and linguistic) is difficult and that conversion was a slow, complicated process in which pagan and Christian ideas co-existed. The language of *Beowulf* itself shows little reason to separate totally the sentiments of the characters from that of the poet—he uses many of the same expressions for God, fate, and death as they do. Parker concludes that *Beowulf* presents us with a mixture of secularism and Christianity which captures "a reality that we also see reflected in the history and archaeology of the period, a stage in the process of absorption of Christian culture in England" (201).

Reviews: H. Chickering, *Speculum* 65 (1990): 214; M. Griffith, *MÆ* 59 (1990): 153-54; J. Ruud, *Clio* 20 (1991): 211-12.

1628 Parks, Ward. "The Flyting Speech in Traditional Heroic Narrative." *Neophil* 71 (1987): 285-295.

Identifies and describes five rhetorical principles in typical flyting scenes: the identitive, the retrojective, the projective, the attributive-evaluative, and the comparative, finding that the Unferth-Beowulf exchange, as well as flytings in the Homeric poems, betray these "characteristic mental operations" (287). Identification demands that a flyter name or refer to the identity of his opponent, as Unferth does in line 506 and Beowulf in line 530. When the Coastguard asks for identification, the answer involves a genealogy which allows for a "modulation of flyting into a kind of guest-host friendship bonding" (287). In retrojection, the flyter examines a past exploit as a way of projecting the outcome of the current flyting. Both Beowulf and Unferth use the swimming contest with Breca in this way. Projection involves the predictions of the flyters as to the future outcome of the contract: Unferth predicts that Beowulf will fail, while Beowulf predicts victory. Attribution-Evaluation bring the past and future events together to evaluate the present worthiness of the flyter. In comparison, the flyter must compare his merits with those of his opponent, establishing "the *contestual relevance* of other discursive materials" (291). Appears in altered form in Parks [1762].

1629 Pàroli, Teresa. "The Elusive 'Death of Beowulf.'" *Res Publica Litterarum* 10 (1987): 263-66.

A rejoinder to T.H. Leinbaugh's review of *La morte di Beowulf* [1353].

1630 Reichl, Karl. "Beowulf, Er Töstuk und das Bärensohnmärchen." [Beowulf, *Er Töstuk* and the Bear's Son]. In *Fragen der Mongolischen Heidendichtung, IV.* Asiatische Forschungen: Monographienreihe zur Geschichte, Kultur und Sprache der Volker Ost- und Zentralasiens, 101. Wiesbaden: Harrassowitz, 1987. Pp. 322-50.

Not seen.

1631 Richardson, John. "The Critic on the Beach." *Neophil* 71 (1987): 114-19.

Finds that the so-called "hero on the beach" theme, first proposed by Crowne [S408] and elaborated by a number of scholars, occurs in enough texts outside the alliterative-oral tradition to suggest that it is not an oral type-scene at all but in fact a common heroic situation grounded in the widespread myth of "crossing of the threshold." Thus, Richardson argues, the "hero on the beach" motif is not a literary convention, and the *Beowulf* poet does not play with it in lines 562-70a (Beowulf's landfall after the swimming contest with Breca), where Crowne found an ironic reversal of the theme, with the slain monsters acting as "retainers," and where the arrival is accompanied by the bright light of the sun—both identified as elements of the theme. Instead, Richardson sees the passage in a mythic and literary light: "the journey of the sun becomes linked to the heroic journey, emphasizing the inevitability and dependability of the heroic victory. The description of the dead monsters is an ironic use of the conventional *comitatus* relationship. . . . [Thus,] oral-formulaic theory is not needed to explain the presence of these details. If the oral-formulaic method has any function in the passage, it must be only as a mnemonic device" (116).

1632 Russom, Geoffrey. *Old English Meter and Linguistic Theory.* Cambridge: Cambridge UP, 1987. Pp. x + 178; ill.

Presents a new theory of Old English meter, with special reference to *Beowulf*. Russom summarizes the four fundamental principles of his approach: "Principle I: *Foot patterns* correspond to native Old English word patterns. The foot patterns most easily perceived are those that correspond to the most common word patterns. Principle II: The *verse* consists of two feet. Foot patterns corresponding to unusual word patterns add to the complexity of verses in which they appear. Principle III: *Alliterative patterns* correspond to Old English stress patterns. A metrical rule that mimics the Old English compound stress rule determines the location of alliterating syllables. Principle IV: The *line* consists of two adjacent verses with an acceptable alliterative pattern" (150). After comparing *Beowulf* to other poems, Russom concludes that "[t]he *Beowulf* poet's search for variety manifests itself as a determination to exploit all possible two-foot patterns while allowing for employment of word groups within the foot. The rule system defines the point at which this determination confronts the limits of metrical coherence" (148). (Russom's index, "*Beowulf* Verses of Special Interest" [175-76] has been incorporated into the line index of this volume.)

Reviews: J.A. Burrow, *London Review of Books* 21 Jan., 1988: 19; C.B. McCully, *Lingua* 75 (1988): 379-83; M. Griffith, *MÆ* 58 (1989): 140-41; W. Obst, *Anglia* 107 (1989): 506-10; P.S. Baker, *Speculum* 65 (1990): 490-91; B.R. Hutcheson, *Envoi* 2.1 (1990): 203-05; P.J. Lucas, *SN* 62 (1990): 113-15; S.D. Spangehl, *Language* 66 (1990): 427-28; R.L. Gates, *Poetics Today* 11 (1990): 689-94.

1633 _____. "Verse Translations and the Question of Literacy in *Beowulf*." In *Comparative Research on Oral Traditions*. Ed. John Miles Foley. Columbus, OH: Slavica, 1987. Pp. 567-580.

Finds that too polemical a stand on the literacy (Benson [S573]) or orality (Niles [1270]) of the *Beowulf*-poet's art is unfortunate and misleading and compares the style of *Beowulf* to that of Old English verse translations from Latin sources (*The Meters of Boethius*, *The Paris Psalter*, and *Exodus*), finding that neither show clear-cut orality or literacy in their use of compounds. Examining compounds for war and the sea (based on *gūð-*, *heaðu-*, *hild(e)-*, *medu-*, *beadu-*, *heoru-*, *here-*, *hyge-*, *mægen-*, *sǣ-*, *wæg-*, *wæl-*, *wæter*, and *wīg-*) in *Beowulf* and the verse translations, Russom shows that neither the concept of oral-metrical utility nor of literary sophistication can account fully for the patterns of diction in these poems. Russom argues that the *Beowulf*-poet uses combinatives less often for metrical utility than Niles suggests. "In fact, one can show that the *Beowulf* poet rejects ordinary compounds in favor of poetic compounds no more useful" (575). Paradoxically, the translators, though they deal with written texts, tend to rely on repetitive, useful compounds. Nevertheless, evidence for the literacy of *Beowulf*'s diction is lacking.

1634 _____. "Word and Foot in *Beowulf*." *Style* 21 (1987): 387-398.

Proposes that foot patterns in Old English meter are linked to word patterns. Russom points out that "every reliably attested verse type can be filled by exactly two Old English words" (387). Thus, the key to understanding the Old English metrical foot is to match "actual words in the linguistic material against idealized two-word paradigms" (388). The essentials of the theory may be stated in two parts: "Rule I: Foot patterns correspond to native word patterns. Rule II: Verse patterns consist of two readily identifiable foot patterns" (395). Since metrical feet would, according to this theory, be intimately connected to word structure, the Old English poets would select from patterns which they had internalized as native speakers. Russom analyzes several verses from *Beowulf* and also discusses word boundaries in Old English.

1634a Swanton, Michael J. *English Literature Before Chaucer.* London and New York: Longman, 1987.

Provides a general introduction to *Beowulf* in a history of early English literature, discussing the poem's narrative structure, folk-heroic elements, allusions to Germanic history, the symbol of the hall, the theme of the nature of heroic life, the function of the monsters, etc. Swanton concludes, "Beowulf's three great fights mark a progression in our understanding of the source of the hero's power: from total self-reliance, through closer questioning of the adequacy of his sole strength and the recognition that God provides the necessary resources to the right man; and finally in old age falling into despair thinking that he must have offended God in some way. The figure of Beowulf himself contains the dilemma of heroic society—the need for a strong man, and yet uncertainty as to the source of his authority.... The active ideal of self-reliance is an élitist and isolative one, and ultimately alien to the open society which engenders it" (66). Reviews: T.P. Dolan, *Peritia* 6-7 (1987-88): 358-59; D.K. Fry, *Albion* 19 (1988): 595-97; P.J. Lucas, *N&Q* 36 (1989): 78; B. Millett, *Envoi* 1.1 (1988): 170-76; D.G. Calder, *Speculum* 64 (1989): 769-71; C. von Nolcken, *RES* n.s. 40 (1989): 243-44; ; K. Reichl, *ASNSL* 226 (1989): 144-47; D.G. Scragg, *Anglia* 107 (1989): 510-12; E.G. Stanley, *MÆ* 58 (1989): 143-46.

1635 Tejera, Dionisia. "Theme and Structure of *Beowulf.*" *Letras de Deusto* 17 (1987): 105-114.

Finds Aristotelian unity in the main plot of *Beowulf*, which shows Beowulf's heroic development through three successive battles and justifies the various digressions: "There is not a passage that is really irrelevant; *everything adds meaning to the whole*" (110-11). Also discusses three theories about the theme of *Beowulf*, that it is about "how a hero defeats external evils," that it demonstrates "the role of the Hero-Leader in a warrior society," and that it revolves around the rise and fall of a warrior king, with attendant symbolism: Youth and Age," etc. (105).

1636 No Item.

1637 Tripp, Raymond P., Jr. "*Beowulf* 1834b, *Gārholt*: 'Spear-Wood,' Wordplay and Plowshares." *In Geardagum* 8 (1987): 19-34.

Believes that the word *gārholt* 'spear wood' (l. 1834b)—referring to the Geats' spears—contains a submerged reference to the tanged or spear plow in use in Anglo-Saxon England and finds a general agricultural metaphor operating throughout the passage. Tripp identifies punning agricultural connotations for several words *tilian* 'strive for,' but also 'cultivate' (l. 1823b), *gēoce* 'help,' but also 'yoke' (l. 1834a), *herian* 'to praise' for *erian* 'to plow' (l. 1833b), etc. Hygelac becomes, in this interpretation, a metaphorical plowboy. Tripp translates the passage (ll. 1817-35), bringing out the agricultural puns he sees: "Beowulf made a speech, fierce Harrower's son./ 'Now we tillers of the sea wish to say, from/ Across its furrows come, that we are looking/ To set sail for Higelac. Good harvests have been/ Wheeled our way, so well have you given for gore./ If then in any way on the teaming earth I may cultivate/ More grounds for your love, than I have yet done/ With intestine labors of war, I'll be pointed your way./ If I hear from over the sea's wide fields/ That close-planted men drive you into conflict's thorny field,/ As for awhile shouting enemies did by the wheels of war,/ So I'll produce for you here many seasoned thanes,/ Men harnessed to your aid. I see in Higelac/ A country leader, though to you he's but a boy,/ Herdsman of folk, and know he'll help me/ With voice and arm, to plow your enemies properly under,/ Honor you with aid, and yoked to pointed wood bear/ A harvest of help, where you need power of men" (27-28). Includes diagrams of Anglo-Saxon plowshares.

1637a Watanabe, Hideki. "*Swyrd Gifu—Beowulf* 1020b: *brand Healfdenes* Revisited." *Chiba Review* 9 (1987): 50-63. In Japanese.

Provides an English summary in *Chiba Review* 9 (1987): 64-67. Mitchell [1756] describes much of the argument of this article. Not seen.

1638 Wolff, Hope Nash. *A Study in the Narrative Structure of Three Epic Poems: 'Gilgamesh,' 'The Odyssey,' and 'Beowulf'*. Harvard Dissertations in Comparative Literature. New York: Garland, 1987. Pp. iv + 120.

Finds a common mythic structure in the *Epic of Gilgamesh*, the *Odyssey* and *Beowulf*, a myth which revolves around the affirmation of culture and the negation of the forces of anti-culture (63). After undertaking a general analysis of each epic, Wolff sketches the pattern common to all three: the hero's life cycle begins with an auspicious birth, marked out in some way by a special quality (massive strength in the case of Beowulf). Next, he undergoes a period of initiation in which he matches himself against forces living outside the civilized area (Beowulf slays water monsters during his swimming contest with Breca). After proving himself, the warrior enters the life of the city (culture) and undergoes a period of development or education. Each of the three epics employs a sub-hero to indicate this development: Wiglaf passes from raw experience into mature understanding of the world. In the second main stage, the hero enters into the life of his city and achieves fame as a warrior, often leaving the city for further exploits (Beowulf of course, defends a foreign city, Heorot). In the third stage, the hero returns to his city from having wandered in the underworld (the mere in *Beowulf*) in order to become king, establishing and maintaining order (Beowulf returns to Geatland and becomes king). The city is a crucial symbol of culture, and its isolation against forces of destruction is repeated in each epic. "The threat of anti-culture is the dissolution of the city; it is symbolized by the personal risk of death run by the hero, whose return is a victory for mankind" (63).

1988

1639 Baker, Peter S. "Beowulf the Orator." *Journal of English Linguistics* 21 (1988): 3-23.

Believes that Anglo-Saxon attitudes toward rhetoric and stylistic ornamentation differed from modern ones and more specifically, that in *Beowulf* the power to wield words is synonymous with heroic action, this attitude contrasting with modern skepticism of rhetorical skill. Beowulf's aggressive verbal performance in his exchange with the Coastguard and Unferth shows his potential as an aggressive doer of deeds. Baker analyzes the Coastguard's enigmatic reply to Beowulf (ll. 287b-89), taking the much-discussed word *gescād* to mean 'knowledge, understanding' rather than 'difference' (as some commentators, including Greenfield [1318], have done). He translates the passage as follows: "the intelligent shield-warrior who thinks well must have an understanding of each, [that is] of words and of deeds" (8). "The quality of Beowulf's rhetoric is such that the coast guard has taken his word as virtual equivalents of the feats he is going to perform. Far from asserting a difference between words and deeds, his maxim sets them rhetorically and imaginatively equal to each other" (10). Baker finds a similar tension in the flyting scene between Beowulf and Unferth: "Beowulf has offered to fight Grendel, but before being allowed to do so, he must take on a Danish champion, the weapons being not swords or fingers, but words" (17). He analyzes two passages in detail: Unferth's charge (ll. 510b-518a) and Beowulf's clever reply (ll. 539-548). Though modern readers are trained to be suspicious of "silver-tongued" characters, for Anglo-Saxon audiences "no blame attaches to the elegant speaker" (20), and we should resist the temptation to read Unferth as a corrupt but witty courtier—in fact, Beowulf has bested him linguistically and rhetorically.

1640 Dahlberg, Charles R. *The Literature of Unlikeness.* Hanover: UP of New England, 1988. Pp. xiv + 207.

Contains a chapter on *Beowulf* in a book-length study of Augustine's concept of "unlikeness" of the heavenly and earthly cities and its manifestation in medieval literature. After reviewing concepts of kingship from a number of patristic sources as well as contemporary treatises on kingship, Dahlberg concludes that "during the period when *Beowulf* must have been written, private and public virtue were seen not only as interconnected but as related in a theological, ecclesiological manner" (35). Beowulf acts for the public good against the private evil of the monsters. Though human treachery is apparent in *Beowulf,* it is the monsters that represent most clearly the "dark and violent nature of Augustine's earthly kingdom" (36). The Father's Lament also lays bare these issues with its inverted image of a private act (the son's crime) overturning a public function (his position as heir). Though Beowulf, in his zeal for the public, instead of the private good, becomes a Christ figure, the poet emphasizes his (and all earthly kings') unlikeness to the divine Ruler, a contrast which Dahlberg finds in the poet's increasingly-ironic uses of the phrase, *þæt wæs gōd cyning!* 'that was a good king!' (ll. 11b, 863b, and 2390b). In the end, "Beowulf is the mildest and gentlest king in the world; to the audience, he is, finally, both like Christ in his mildness and gentleness and, as one of the kings of the world, unlike him in his eagerness for praise" (51).

Reviews: J.A. Burrow, *TLS*, Dec. 16, 1988: 1401-02; *OEN* 23.1 (1989): 67; R.W. Hanning, *Speculum* 65 (1990): 963-66; K. Kerby-Fulton, *MLR* 85 (1990): 683-84; R. Psaki, *Comparative Lit.* 44 (1992): 94-97.

1641 Denton, Robert F. "*Beowulf,* the Thorkelin Transcripts, and the Resistance to Reading." *Analytical & Enumerative Bibliography* 2 (1988): 101-106.

Endorsing J. Hillis Miller's "ethics of reading," which emphasizes "our primary ethical obligation to read 'in the original'" (101), points out that the "original" *Beowulf* has been obscured by textual scholars who have been reluctant to read carefully the evidence of the manuscript and the Thorkelin transcripts. Denton uses Kiernan's work on the Thorkelin transcripts [1566] to reveal "a resistance to reading, and to reading in the original, by those upon whom modern editors of the poem have relied for their readings, and upon whom readers, reading 'in the original,' have also relied" (102).

1642 Dumville, David N. "Beowulf Come Lately: Some Notes on the Palaeography of the Nowell Codex." *Archiv* 225 (1988): 49-63.

After reviewing the development of the two scripts contained in the *Beowulf*-manuscript (Scribe A's newer insular minuscule and Scribe B's older square minuscule), concludes that the *Beowulf*-manuscript was written very early in the eleventh century, a date which excludes Kiernan's [1261] thesis that the poem was composed in the reign of Cnut (1016-35). Dumville examines the precise meaning and rationale of Neil Ker's dating of the Nowell Codex to "s. X/XI," considering paleographical evidence from a number of tenth- and eleventh-century manuscripts. He concludes: "The new minuscule was not being employed as a bookhand before the first decade of the eleventh century. Square minuscule is likely to have been in use for only a very few years after A.D. 1000. The few manuscripts, like that containing *Beowulf*, which display contemporaneous writing in these two successive styles of Insular minuscule must therefore have been written in the eleventh century. It is in the highest degree unlikely that the *Beowulf*-manuscript was written later than the death of Æthelred the Unready (1016) or earlier than the mid-point of his reign (which fell in A.D. 997)" (63).

1643 Enright, Michael J. "Lady with a Mead-Cup: Ritual, Group Cohesion and Hierarchy in the Germanic Warband." *Frühmittelalterliche Studien* 22 (1988): 170-203.

Analyzes the roles of Wealhtheow and Hygd by examining the relationship of the Germanic queen to her king and *comitatus*, concluding that Germanic queens played a limited but integral role in establishing rank and succession. In Wealhtheow's presentation of the mead cup after Beowulf's arrival (ll. 607-41), Enright sees a common Germanic ritual in which the queen establishes her lord's superior rank by giving him the cup first and then helps to stipulate the relative ranking of the remaining warriors by the order in which she serves them. She encourages the warriors to make binding oaths, but her role in political matters (the succession of her sons) is limited to pleading and suggestion. Hygd, on the other hand, as a widowed queen, has an important say in the succession of the kingdom, which she offers to Beowulf, implying a marriage which the poet does not mention. This power, however, is dependent on the voice of the deceased lord's *comitatus*. The picture which emerges after an examination of both fictional and historical Germanic queens implies that "the queen's activities are too thoroughly integrated, too nicely interwoven, to consider her any longer as an attending but essentially extraneous character comparable, say, to a steward or groom. Although she does not fight, and while her role is undeniably unique, her ritual and ministrations would seem to be too closely tied to the maintenance and thus existence of the group to view her as a total outsider and too functional during successions to describe her as really extraneous. The mortar that cements the bricks must be regarded as part of the building" (202). In addition, Enright calls into question an overly-idealized picture of the *comitatus*: it was far from a happy society of friends but was based much more on hierarchical ranking and jockeying for position than has been recognized.

1644 Florey, Kenneth. "Grendel, Evil, 'Allegory,' and Dramatic Development in *Beowulf*." *Essays in Arts and Sciences* 17 (1988): 83-95.

Rejecting any specific allegorical interpretation, explores "what it is in the text that appears to encourage an allegorical reading" (83), finding that the poet begins with a mythic world where good and evil are separate entities represented by the Danes and Beowulf on the one hand and the monsters on the other, but gradually shatters this simple illusion by moving to a more realistic mode of depiction in which human institutions and Beowulf himself are implicated in chaos and evil. In the beginning, Scyld and his line culminating with the construction of the splendid hall Heorot represent a kind of mythic state of innocence and primal joy. In such an idealistic, pastoral world evil and chaos can only appear externally in the form of monsters (Grendel and his mother) who become the adversaries of God. Beowulf arrives (as does Scyld) as a divinely directed vanquisher of evil. But in moving to historical materials in the second part of the poem, the poet reveals that evil and chaos are not external agents "and that the simplicity of Denmark was a temporary narrative illusion. Evil and Chaos, far from being isolated in such creatures as Grendel, are, in the poem, embodied in those very institutions of the civilized world upon which one depends for social order" (94). Also discusses the role of suspense in the first attack of Grendel—from the "allegorical" point of view, there can be no suspense, for God must triumph, but from the narrative point of view, suspense is necessary. Florey finds that the poet skillfully balances "the demands of both allegory and dramatic terror" (92).

1645 Fujiwara, Hiroshi. "Struggles between Paganism and Christianity in *Beowulf*: A Lexical Study." *Bulletin of the Language Institute of Gakushuin Univ.* 10 (1988): 108-21. In Japanese.

Suggests that using the names for three animals (dragon, wolf, and boar) as a clue, we can distinguish two strata in *Beowulf*, the Christian and the pagan. In interpreting the poem, it is best not to emphasize only one of these aspects of Anglo-Saxon life. (HF)

1646 _____. "The VSO Construction in *Beowulf*." In *Teresawa*, pp. 60-70.

Examines VSO (verb-subject-object) word order in *Beowulf*, concluding that VSO order may be more ancient than SOV (the order theorized for Indo-European). Fujiwara finds 132 examples of VSO constructions in the a-verse and 77 in the b-verse, with weak-stressed verbs occurring in 103 of the first group and 64 in the second. However, only by circular reasoning can one state that the verb of the VSO construction is generally weak-stressed. Fujiwara concludes: "We have a number of examples of the VSO order in *Beowulf*. But the stress on the verb is not always the cause of the construction. Verbs are sometimes strong-stressed in this construction, but at others they are weak-stressed. This fact seems to hint at the possibility that the VSO order was a relic of the past age when it was normal and unmarked. It is much older than the order SOV, not used even in subordinate clauses. In some cases this order was used to put emphasis on the subject and, conversely, to stress the verb in others. Many seemingly formulaic expressions have this order. This seems to support our hypothesis that the order VSO is a very old type" (66-67). Provides an appendix of weak-stressed verbs in VSO constructions and discusses the work of Kuhn and Campbell.

1647 Gerritsen, Johan. "British Library MS Cotton Vitellius A.xv—a Supplementary Description." *ES* 69 (1988): 293-302.

Undertakes a formal description of the Southwick and Nowell codices (comprising Cotton Vitellius A.xv), dismissing some of the conclusions of Kiernan [1261]. Gerritsen provides a number of details about the contents, condition (buckling, spots, holes, etc.), binding (present binding, flyleaves, frames, sewing thread, etc.), make-up (quire structure, arrangement of hair and flesh sides), scribes, and foliations. Under the latter rubric, he describes the various foliations marked either on the paper frames or the manuscript itself as well as their most likely dates. With the help of ultraviolet lighting he attempts to decipher some of the earliest folio numbers written on the manuscript leaves themselves, suggesting that Wanley's catalogue may accurately identify the leaves on which the various works of the Nowell codex began.

1648 Glosecki, Stephen O. "Wolf of the Bees: Germanic Shamanism and the Bear Hero." *Journal of Ritual Studies* 2 (1988): 31-49.

Maintains that "The hero we know as Beowulf . . . probably owes both his ursine name and bear-hug battle grip to a dim figure from a totemistic past—a primeval were-bear from a tribal tradition, a shamanistic shape-shifter" (40). Glosecki discusses the evidence for shamanism in Germanic culture, linking both Odin and the *berserker* tradition to shamanistic practices and examining Germanic and Amerindian mythology of the bear. He sees the name *Bēo-wulf* 'bee-wolf', a kenning for bear, as a euphemism "coined to prevent overt reference to the tabooed entity" (38), also discussing parallels between *Beowulf* and the *Hrólfs saga*, which features a were-bear and several characters whose names mean 'bear': Bera, Bjorn, and Bjarki. Bjarki, often cited as an analogue of Beowulf himself, uses shaman-like powers during the fight at Leyre. Glosecki sees further evidences of Germanic shamanism in the boar-images (mentioned in *Beowulf* and *Hrólfs saga*) and in Germanic animal imagery from the Torslunda and Sutton Hoo finds. Thus, Beowulf's journey into the mere is best seen as "the typical shaman's descent into the underworld" (48) where he does battle with spiritual forces, not as an allegory of the harrowing of hell, as Augustinian readings maintain. See Weldon's response [1681] and Glosecki's rejoinder [1649].

1649 _____. "Response to James Weldon's Critique of 'Wolf of the Bees: Germanic Shamanism and the Bear Hero' JRS 2/1 Winter, 1988." *Journal of Ritual Studies* 2 (1988): 257-262.

A rejoinder to James Weldon's critique [1681] of Glosecki's earlier article [1648], providing more evidence for survivals of shamanism in Old Norse literature, repeating his rationale for connecting Beowulf to bear-shamans, and reviewing archaeological evidence for shamanism among the Germanic peoples.

1650 Gómez Lara, Manuel José. "The Death of Anglo-Saxon Secular Heroes: A Linguistic Discussion on *Beowulf* and *The Battle of Maldon*." *Revista canaria de estudios ingleses* 17 (1988): 269-80.

Applies speech-act theory to the final speeches of the dying heroes Beowulf (ll. 2788-2816) and Byrhtnoth (*Battle of Maldon*, ll. 166-80), also suggesting that short lines in both passages should be retained rather than emended. In a Christian framework, the death of a hero demands two basic speech performances which are present in the speeches of Beowulf and Byrhtnoth: a) a declarative act of loyalty to God, expressed by the naming of his attributes, and b) expressive illocutionary acts which stress the hero's gratitude toward God by linking previous plot events to God's agency. This situation type (the death speech of the hero) can shed light on "the relationship that the speaker—the hero—establishes between his life and the divinity" (270). Both speeches contain these elements, but afterwards diverge. Beowulf's speech moves on to a sequence of assertions which explains the meaning of the treasure and which makes clear his heroic relationship to death and God. Byrhtnoth, on the other hand, makes a plea for divine aid against demons. Beowulf, in his heroic individualism, is preoccupied with earthly fame, while Byrhtnoth, with his devout plea, concerns himself with everlasting salvation. "[T]he differences in the development of the *auxiliary illocutionary acts* show not only the requirement of two different narrative contexts, but even more, two types of heroic perspective in the characters" (273). Gómez Lara goes on to argue that short lines in both speeches (*Beowulf*, l. 2792, *Maldon*, l. 172), thought by many to be metrically defective, should stand as they are, both on metrical and rhetorical grounds. For both lines, most editors supply an off-verse containing a subject (for the hero) plus a speech act verb. But in both cases, the short lines seem to introduce "rhetorical silences" and dwell on gesture rather than speech.

1651 Haarder, Andreas. "The Seven Beowulf Reviewers: Latest or Last Identifications." *ES* 69 (1988): 289-292.

Identifies the authors of reviews of G.J. Thorkelin's 1815 edition of *Beowulf* [S5] as Abraham Jakob Penzel, Friedrich Bouterwek, William Taylor, G.W. Gumælius, and Peter Erasmus Müller, also discussing briefly the signed reviews by

N.F.S. Grundtvig and Nicolaus Outzen. Haarder outlines the careers of these early *Beowulf*-scholars.

1652 Handelman, Anita F. "Wulfgar at the Door: *Beowulf,* 11. 389b-90a." *Neophil* 72 (1988): 475-77.

Analyzing the poet's handling of direct speech, theorizes that more than two half-lines may be missing after line 389a. Handelman first shows that the poet never ends a speech in the middle of the line, making it likely that the lost line 389b belonged to Hrothgar's speech. Second, the poet elsewhere uses a minimum of one full line to introduce a speech: "Given the poet's usual treatment of speech, two full lines are probably missing—a half-line belonging to Hrothgar's speech and a line and a half belonging to a full two-line introduction of Wulfgar's speech" (476). Handelman speculates briefly as to the more exact contents of the missing lines but stops short of offering a reconstruction.

1653 Hansen, Elaine Tuttle. *The Solomon Complex: Reading Wisdom in Old English Poetry.* Toronto: U of Toronto P, 1988.

Adapts Hansen [1321] for chapter two, "Parental Instruction in Old English Poetry: *Precepts* and Hrothgar's 'Sermon.'"

Reviews: *OEN* 23.1 (1989): 54; C. Larrington, *MÆ* 58 (1989): 319-20; J.M. Ziolkowski, *JEGP* 89 (1990): 210-11; D.G. Scragg, *RES* 42 (1991): 84-85; T.A. Shippey, *Speculum* 66 (1991):886-88.

1654 Harris, Anne Leslie. "Litotes and Superlative in *Beowulf.*" *ES* 69 (1988): 1-11.

Asserts that the poet uses litotes and superlative to elicit "admiration for a long-past world even as he portrays its flaws" (1). Litotes consists of various kinds of understatement, indicated by morphology, syntax, context, or (most commonly) by negation. Superlatives usually appear morphologically with superlative endings on adjectives or adverbs, though in *Beowulf,* superlatives often appear as negative litotes: for example, "I have never seen a greater man." The results of boasts are often expressed in litotes, and "Beowulf's response to Unferth is a public boast of his courage and prowess using extended litotic references" (5). More generally, "Litotes illustrates the customs and beliefs—the value system—of the characters, their expectations of such a system, and the frustration of these expectations. The superlatives not only point out what is admirable in this society and its values but also show its separateness, its distance, from the world of the poet" (1).

1655 Hengen, Shannon. "A Note on the Existential Coloring of *Beowulf*." *NM* 89 (1988): 171-173.

Believes that the poet associates *b* alliteration with the hero Beowulf and *n* alliteration with Grendel and that patterns of alliteration reveal the ultimate victory of Beowulf, since *b*-alliterating lines predominate ultimately. Further, *b* alliteration associates Beowulf with the verb *bēon* 'to be,' while the *n* alliteration associates Grendel with Old English forms of negation and non-being such as *næfre* 'never,' *nænig* 'none,' *næs* 'by no means,' and *niht* 'night,' thus revealing the poet's interest in an "existential conflict" (172). Though the usurping Grendel is described in *b*-alliterating lines, Beowulf finally takes over the *n*-stave. "By having described the hero in an alliterative pattern previously reserved for the villain, the poet suggests that Beowulf has, in fact, redeemed himself, the night, and life along with the *n*-stave" (173).

1656 Karibe, Tsunenori. "On the Glory of Beowulf and the Demise of the Danes." In *Teresawa*, pp. 328-35.

Finds the beginnings of Denmark's decline in Hrothgar's attitude toward Beowulf, one which seeks to preserve royal dignity in the face of turmoil. (TK)

1657 Klegraf, Josef. "Testing Faithful Copying in the *Beowulf* Manuscript." In *Essays on the English Language and Applied Linguistics on the Occasion of Gerhard Nickel's 60th Birthday*. Ed. Josef Klegraf and Dietrich Nehls. Studies in Descriptive Linguistics, 18. Heidelberg: Julius Groos, 1988. Pp. 206-220.

Aims "to develop a quantitatively oriented method for reconstructing a scribe's individual handwriting techniques as they may be deduced from a several-text corpus. Object of demonstration is the letter pair for the dental spirant, i.e., the two variants *þ* vs. *ð*, as they show up in the five texts of the *Nowell Codex*" (207). Klegraf compares how each of the two scribes of the Nowell codex handles this feature, which he charts according to its position (initial, medial, and final) within its glosseme. Also considered are "graphico-mechanical factors," such as the position of þ or ð in the line (initial or final), in clusters of letters (initial, medial, and final). Scribe 1 (who copied *St. Christopher, The Wonders of the East, Alexander's Letter to Aristotle,* and *Beowulf,* to line 1939) has a complex style combining faithful with mechanical copying, while Scribe 2 (responsible for the rest of *Beowulf* and *Judith*) copies mechanically. Scribe 2 employs a simple principle in copying the dental spirant: "He obviously adheres to his own, individual spelling conventions which may be paraphrased by the simple imperative: *Never write thorn in the middle and at the end of words, if however, a word begins with a [dental spirant] and spacing in front of it is feasible you may write the thorn variant as well*" (214). Also considers abbreviations for þām and includes tables of results.

1658 Klein, Thomas. "Vorzeitsage und Heldensage." [Prehistoric Legend and Heroic Legend]. In *Heldensage und Heldendichtung im Germanischen.* Ed. Heinrich Beck. Ergänzungsbände zum Reallexikon der Germanischen Altertumskunde, 2. Berlin and New York: de Gruyter, 1988. Pp. 115-47.

Examines the development of heroic narrative in the Germanic languages, noting a shift from the classic heroic tale (which remains near to the present-day world of reality) to a *Vorzeitsage* or tale set in the misty, prehistoric past (which specifically distances itself from realism in characterization and plotting), and charting this development in a number of Old Norse, German, and Old English texts (including *Beowulf*). Classic heroic tales (the oldest sagas, the oldest portions of the Poetic *Edda,* the *Hildebrandslied,* etc.) depict remarkable heroes, but these heroes remain within the realm of the human, while the "prehistoric" tales (*Beowulf,* the later Old Norse materials, narratives in Saxo Grammaticus, the Dietrich epics, etc.) give their protagonists superhuman strength (like Beowulf's) and often pit them against supernatural beings such as giants, dwarves, and dragons. The "prehistoric" hero needs no particular motivation beyond himself to undertake an adventure (as in Beowulf's decision to aid Hrothgar), while the classic hero is called to action by a specific situation, often the need for revenge. What in the classic tales appears as great inner strength is expressed in the prehistoric ones externally in the huge physical size of the heroes. More than classic tales, the prehistoric tales depend on hyperbole and must justify and legitimize their marvelous elements: in *Beowulf* this takes the form of a Christianized pedigree for the Grendelkin and references to the Flood.

1659 Knapp, Peggy A. "Alienated Majesty: *Grendel* and Its Pretexts." *Centennial Review* 32 (1988): 1-18.

Makes the case that Gardner's "*Grendel* consistently demythifies *Beowulf*'s claims, only to reinstate them from a seemingly alien, seemingly contemporary vantage point" (4). Similarly, when *Grendel* [S793] seems to stabilize the interpretive openness of *Beowulf*, these attempts are "always unraveling, implying their contraries" (14). Also discusses other literary influences on *Grendel*.

1660 Lehmann, Ruth P.M. *'Beowulf': An Imitative Translation*. Austin, TX: U of Texas Press, 1988. Pp. 119; ill.

Translates *Beowulf* into a four-stress alliterative line, "imitative of Germanic alliterative verse. A more exact imitation is compromised by an effort not to distort modern English into something awkward and unintelligible" (16). Given the structure of modern English, the translation shows more anacrusis in Sievers types A, D, and E than the original. The introduction includes brief discussions of the manuscript, the Germanic background, the place of women, the historical background, and the fabulous elements. Lines 4-11: "Oft Scyld Scefing   by the shock of war/ kept both troops and tribes   from treasured meadbench,/ filled foes with dread after first being/ discovered uncared for;   a cure for that followed:/ he grew hale under heaven,   high in honor,/ until no nation   near the borders,/ beyond teeming seas   but was taught to obey,/ giving tribute. He was a good ruler."
Reviews: *OEN* 23.1 (1989): 67; T.F. Hoad, *YES* 21 (1991): 323-25.

1661 _____. "Some Problems in the Translation of *Beowulf*." In *Languages and Cultures: Studies in Honour of Edgar C. Polomé*. Ed. Mohammed Ali Jazayery and Werner Winter. Trends in Linguistics: Studies and Monographs, 36. Berlin: Mouton de Gruyter, 1988. Pp. 365-371.

Discusses three cruxes in the poem and how they may be translated: 1) *ealuscerwen* (l. 769a) probably contains some of the associations of ON *alu* / *ōl* 'ale' with its associations of "beer," "good luck," "magic," and "protection," though the compound itself is best translated with a term meaning "deprivation," rather than "pouring out" or "distribution." 2) the phrase *æþelum dīore* 'beloved for her virtues' (l. 1949a), though clearly feminine and referring to Thryth (Modthryth), is assigned by about twenty-five translators out of thirty to Offa, perhaps due to the fact that an uninflected language like modern English can only use apposition, not gender and case to signal meaning. 3) the word *fealu* (l. 1950a), when applied to the sea, might be rendered "furrowed by winds," "rough," while *æppelfealu* (l. 2165a) could be translated as "dapple bay" or "having large round spots" (370).

1662 Miletich, John S. "Muslim Oral Epic and Medieval Epic." *MLR* 83 (1988): 911-924.

In a broader discussion of oral epic, argues that "thus far no solid case has been made for the oral composition of *Beowulf* in a close comparison of data based on study of the poem and the admittedly scant information available from analysis of Serbo-Croatian oral epic" (918). The hallmark of demonstrably oral epics such as the oral Muslim epics from the former Yugoslavia is a high incidence (33%) of repeated stylistic elements (including formulas) diffused evenly throughout the text, while written texts show a smaller percentage of repeated elements (approximately 20% for *Beowulf*). Miletich believes that "the low 'formula' density of *Beowulf* appears to me to be the result of a learned written-style technique in which variation is sought for its own sake and verbatim metrical repetition, which could have been more prominent, is deliberately restricted" (917). He finds Foley's explanation of the low density of formulas unconvincing [1248].

1663 Mitchell, Bruce. "1987: Postscript on *Beowulf*." In *On Old English*, pp. 41-54.

Argues against the assumption that the audience of *Beowulf* was homogeneous, all possessing the same knowledge (or lack of knowledge) about the Germanic past or the Church Fathers, pleading instead for an appreciation of the poem's "amphibolical" or enigmatic nature as poetry. Mitchell examines various scholarly interpretations of the last word in the poem, *lofgeornost*, arguing against Stanley's definition [S509] 'most vainglorious' on the basis of a reexamination of the word *lofgeorn* as recorded in the *Microfiche Concordance*. The philological evidence shows this meaning to be "at best very flimsy" (49). Robinson's approach [1513], emphasizing the ambiguous nature of *lofgeornost* as both 'vainglorious' and 'most eager for pagan *lof*' seems more suggestive, though Robinson does finally side with Stanley about the Christian implications of the word. Mitchell questions the notion of Stanley (also endorsed by Robinson) that Beowulf, as a pagan (*paganus*), is necessarily lost and damned (*perditus*), a belief which Stanley finds in Alcuin and which Mitchell traces in Biblical texts. He concludes: "I accept that some Anglo-Saxon hearers or readers thought that because *paganus et perditus*, Beowulf was damned. (In fact, I am prepared to concede that most modern interpretations of *Beowulf* might have been felt or thought by one Anglo-Saxon or another.) But I cannot accept that all did; some, I believe, would have found a message of hope, not despair" (53). Also discusses the "Christian excursus" (ll. 170-88) and quotes excerpts from a letter of Tolkien.

1664 _____. "Relative and Personal Pronouns in *Beowulf*: Eight Notes." In *Teresawa*, pp. 3-12.

After reviewing the three combinations of cases in the *sē þe* relative, goes on to examine and reinterpret the grammar of eight passages in *Beowulf* involving various possible confusions between relative and personal pronouns: ll. 841b-43, 1750b-52, 1845b-53a, 2053-56, 2377-79a, 2646b-50a, 2468-70, 2999-3007a.

1665 Müller, Wolfgang G. "Syntaktisch-semasiologische Analyse des Grendel-Kampfes im *Beowulf*." [Syntactic-Semantic Analysis of the Battle with Grendel in *Beowulf*]. *Literaturwissenschaftliches Jahrbuch* 29 (1988): 9-22.

Finds that the *Beowulf*-poet alternates between hypotactic and paratactic styles in order to achieve different artistic effects: hypotaxis is reserved for authorial comment and the description of characters' thought processes, while parataxis dominates when the poet turns to physical action. Parataxis rises to asyndeton at moments of narrative intensity, breaking into asyndetic clauses which fill a series of half-lines at the most extreme dramatic moments. Such passages throw into relief the sharp contrasts between Grendel as terrifying, blood-thirsty attacker and Beowulf as hero. Müller analyzes in detail the hypotactic and paratactic styles employed in Beowulf's fight with Grendel (ll. 710-836).

1666 Navarro Errasti, Maria Pilar. "Traducir Anglosajon." [Translating Anglo-Saxon]. *Revista Canaria de Estudios Ingleses* 16 (1988): 239-245.

Contains a brief mention of *Beowulf* in a discussion of approaches to teaching Old English. Navarro Errasti insists that students should come into contact with authentic Old English texts very early in their language training.

1667 Noguchi, Shunichi. "Beowulf and 'sōthfæstra dōm'." In *Teresawa*, pp. 251-58.

Assembles philological evidence to show that the poet alludes to Beowulf's salvation (either in a Christian or Germanic sense) and discusses the crucial phrase *sōþfæstra dōm* 'judgment of the righteous' (l. 2820b). Noguchi examines the meaning of *sōþfæst* in the *Paris Psalter* and a number of other Old English texts, finding that in the *Psalter* it translates Latin words such as *justi* 'the just,' *recti* 'the upright,' *seniores* 'the elders,' and *innocens* 'innocent.' In the poetry, the *sōþfæste* are keepers of God's law, opponents of God's enemies, and hardy in withstanding the attacks of the enemy. Noguchi agrees with Bliss [1107] that *sōþfæstra* is an objective genitive and refers to the judgers and not the judged, but argues with Bliss's contention that the *sōþfæstra* are earthly judgers and that Beowulf seeks only worldly esteem (and thus is damned). He also counters Bliss's charge that Beowulf succumbs to the curse on the treasure (l. 3069) by reinterpreting the word *swā* (l. 3069a) as an intensifier and repunctuating the passage. If the poet depicted Beowulf's salvation at the hands of Christ, he would have been historically inaccurate (since Beowulf is historically a pagan), but on the other hand, damning the character would damage the poetic truth of Beowulf's self-sacrifice.

1668 Oshitari, Kinshiro. "A Japanese Analogue of *Beowulf*." In *Teresawa*, pp. 259-69.

Translates into English two versions of a Japanese story which contains a number of similarities to Beowulf's fight with Grendel and Grendel's mother. In a version in book 32 of the *Taiheiki*, Watanabe-no-Tsuna is sent to rid a temple of a marauding demon, but the demon, after trying to trick the hero, suddenly seizes him and attempts to carry him off. Tsuna, however, severs the monster's arm with a sword given to him by his lord Yorimitsu and takes the arm as a trophy to him. Later, Yorimitsu's mother comes and wants to see the arm. When she sees it, she turns into a demon with an arm missing, seizes the arm, reattaches it, and attacks Yorimitsu. Before this can happen, Tsuna beheads the monster with his sword. In another version contained in the fifteenth-century Noh play *Rashômon*, Tsuna (at first incredulous about stories of an ogre in Rashômon) goes to defeat the monster for the good of the emperor. When he encounters the ogre, he cuts off its arm, and it escapes into the air, with Tsuna shouting his resolve to track it down and kill it. Mentions other versions as well.

1669 Overing, Gillian R. "Reinventing Beowulf's Voyage to Denmark." *OEN* 21.2 (1988): 30-39.

Recounts an enactment of Beowulf's sea-voyage from Geatland to Denmark made by Gillian Overing and Marijane Osborn in August of 1985. Beginning at the river Göta Älv, probably linked to the tribal name of the *Gautar* (i.e., Geats), the pair considered the possibility that Bohuslän was the starting point for Beowulf's voyage and, thus, the home of the Geats. Along the two-day journey to Gamle Lejre, the proposed site of Heorot, Overing finds that many of the geographical features described in the poem (ll. 210-28) correspond to actual features of their journey. Though theories of oral composition would seem to discount the poet's direct knowledge of Scandinavian topography, it remains possible that he had a practical understanding of the area. Overing concludes: "Our experience at sea gave us a clearer visual sense of the world of the poem and helped us to imagine some of the possible conditions of seafaring in the time of the *Beowulf*-poet. We believe that teachers and students of the poem can benefit greatly from such a direct and realistic attention to the text" (36). Includes a map and photographs.

1670 Parks, Ward. "Ring Structure and Narrative Embedding in Homer and *Beowulf*." *NM* 89 (1988): 237-51.

Argues for ring-structure as an important narrative device in *Beowulf*. Such a structure is a common feature of oral or residually oral literature as it appears in the *Iliad* and the *Odyssey*, both of which exhibit ring patterns. Parks discusses independent research into repetitive patterns in *Beowulf* by Bartlett [S117] and Hieatt [S960] and reviews other studies of ring-structure by Tonsfeldt [S1051] and Niles [1143, 1270]. Parks examines three ring systems revolving around the creation hymn, the family history of Grendel's mother, and the Lay of the Last Survivor, arguing that the insurgencies of the monsters provide a structural focal point for the poem. Includes diagrams.

1671 Pope, John C. "The Irregular Anacrusis in *Beowulf* 9 and 402: Two Hitherto Untried Remedies, with Help from Cynewulf." *Speculum* 63 (1988): 104-113.

Proposes two minor emendations to remove the irregular anacrusis in lines 9 and 402. In line 9, the MS. form *þāra* (the first vowel being long) produces such an anacrusis: *oðþæt him æghwylc þāra ymbsittendra*. Pope, on the basis of lines 32-24 in Elene, suggests that *þāra* be construed not as an article but as a form of the adverb *þǣr*, thus alleviating the anacrusis (109). In line 402, *Snyredon ætsomne, þā secg wīsode*, the anacrusis caused by *þā* is less severe; nevertheless, Pope proposes shifting the *þā* to the a-verse in order to improve the line both metrically and stylistically. (A great many formulas of the "____ wīsode" type lack adverbs. The emended line reads, *Snyredon þā ætsomne —secg wīsode—/ under Heorotes hrōf* (111).

1672 Porter, John. *Beowulf.* Drawings by Nicholas Parry. Tern Press: Market Drayton, 1984. Felinfach: Llanerch Enterprises, 1988.

A translation of the poem into modern English free verse, with a brief introduction and genealogical charts. Lines 4-11: "Though he was found destitute as a child,/ Scyld Scefing lived to make that good;/ he grew in the world, walked in honour,/ he captured mead-seats from enemy clans,/ terrorized the chiefs of many tribes,/ until all neighbouring nations around/ the whale's road must submit to him/ and pay him tribute; this was a good king." Cf. Porter [S971] for an earlier translation by the same author.
Reviews: *OEN* 23.1 (1989): 67; E.G. Stanley, *N&Q* 39 (1992):145-47; M. Griffith, *MÆ* 61 (1992):166.

1673 Potter, Joyce Elizabeth. "'Wylm' and 'weallan' in *Beowulf*: a Tidal Metaphor." *Medieval Perspectives* 3 (1988): 191-99.

Examines the thirty-six uses of *wylm* 'surge' and *weallan* 'to roll, surge' in the poem, finding that repeated uses of the two words "construct a long sustained foundational image and submerged metaphor in *Beowulf*" (192). The two words, though employed most commonly in sea imagery, also describe the surging of fire, emotional upheaval, and the more cosmic process of waxing and waning. Particularly in the narration of Beowulf's fights, the two terms "hover between concreteness and abstractness, between the denotation of actual, deep, troubled waters and flaming fire, and the connotation of Beowulf's emotional upheaval" (193). When used to describe apocalyptic disasters in the poem, they hint at cosmic processes. These intertwining meanings serve to create "a modern-style metaphor" which suggests that the "breaking of the tides, the churning movement of the sea, and its tidal thrust in one direction, are like the throes of the heart as it faces death" (195). Find the image particularly resonant in lines 2267-2293, depicting the death of Beowulf.

1674 Renoir, Alain. *A Key to Old Poems: The Oral-Formulaic Approach to the Interpretation of West-Germanic Verse.* University Park: Pennsylvania State UP, 1988. Pp. xiv + 224.

In a general discussion of oral-formulaic poetry in the Germanic languages, includes a chapter on *Beowulf*, "Oral-Formulaic Context in *Beowulf*: The Hero on the Beach and the Grendel Episode," which finds a number of implementations of the hero-on-the-beach type-scene first proposed by Crowne [S408]. Renoir focuses on the affective function of such type-scenes and finds that the poet, after beginning with a "pure" example (ll. 207b-15a), repeats the scene, with different elements missing, but generally linked by the repeated references to flashing lights, one of the elements of the hero-on-the-beach motif. (The motifs of this theme include the hero's crossing of a border at the beginning of a journey which will lead to violence as well as the presence of retainers and flashing equipment). Listeners attuned to oral-formulaic style would sense tension and suspense at the points where this motif is reinvoked. Renoir argues that "the theme of the hero on the beach is sustained in our mind by strategically located mentions of flashing lights" and by miniature repetitions of the theme (123), several of which he analyzes in detail. Finally, the hero-on-the-beach motif can be seen to reverberate in three other pivotal scenes:

a) in inverted form with Grendel's arrival in the hall (ll. 702-727): he comes as a traveler, crossing a border, and with an ugly gleam of light emanating from his eyes. b) In Beowulf's arrival at the mere, with companions, and accompanied by the flashing of his armor, as well as the flashings of the giant sword and the light which illumines the mere after the slaying of the monsters. And c) in his last fight with the dragon, as he crosses a stream to arrive at the dragon's cave, where there is a flashing of the dragon's fire. The poet's skillful manipulation of an oral-formulaic theme for rhetorical and affective purposes does not necessarily argue for oral composition but that the poet and audience knew such devices.

Reviews: *OEN* 23.1 (1989): 53; R.P. Creed, *MLQ* 50 (1989): 273-75; A.S.G. Edwards, *MLR* 85 (1990): 679-81; P.F. Ganz, *RES* 41 (1990): 613; M. Griffith, *N&Q* 37 (1990): 72-73; E.R. Haymes, *Speculum* 65 (1990): 745-46; R. Kellogg, *JEGP* 89 (1990): 346-48; W.P. Lehmann, *Semiotica* 85 (1991): 163-71; K. Reichl, *ASNSL* 228 (1991): 119-23; H.L.C. Tristram, *Anglia* 109 (1991): 166-69; A.Volfing, *MÆ* 60 (1991): 344; T.M. Andersson, *Comparative Lit* 44 (1992): 86-88.

1675 Tripp, Raymond P., Jr. "Beowulf and Chaucer's Walter: Memory and the Continuity of Compulsion." *In Geardagum* 9 (1988): 59-74.

Compares the compulsive behavior of Walter in Chaucer's *Clerk's Tale* with that of Beowulf, the former in his inexplicable desire to test his wife and the later in his unquenchable desire to fight the dragon alone. Both poets excuse their characters (through the Clerk and Wiglaf, ll. 3076-86) by alluding to their headstrong natures. Tripp explains these only partially-convincing excuses by noting a "movement from external to internal expression of heroism" (69) in the evolution of western consciousness. "From Wiglaf's more internalized point of view actional solutions to life's problems are inadequate. Personal heroism is replaced by political cooperation, in something like the first step toward the current diplomatic pacifism" (69). By Chaucer's time, this process has gone much further.

1676 ——————. "The Restoration of *Beowulf* 1051b: *brimlēade*, 'sea-lead'." *MP* 86 (1988): 191-195.

Argues against the commonly accepted emendation of MS. *brimleade* to *brimlāde* 'sea-path' (l. 1051b). "As a compound, *brimlēade* gives 'sea-lead' and points to plumbing or sounding the depth of the sea as a logical kenning-like metonymy for sailing" (192). Thus, the verb *tēon* could be translated more literally as 'to pull,' giving the translation "who. . . pulled at the sea-lead" (192). The poet intends an ironic comment on Beowulf's companions in that the restored phrase, *brimlēade tēah* could alternately mean "'pulled at the brimming cup,' which is to say, at drinking a 'sea-cup'" (193). Also points out interlocking sound patterns in the passage.

1677 Vickrey, John F. "On *Beowulf* 997-1002." *Archiv* 225 (1988): 339-342.

Supports Nickel's reading [S1003] of *þē* (l. 1000b) as 'because' not 'when' or 'which' but reconstrues and repunctuates the passage. Vickrey sees the entire passage (ll. 997-1002) as a single sentence and removes the usual editorial period or semi-colon after line 999a, taking the phrase *hrōf āna genæs,/ ealles ansund* as a parenthetical statement. Thus understood, the passage translates approximately as follows: "the hall, despite the strength of its iron bands, was much broken up, its hinges sprung apart, *þē* 'because, in that' the *āglǣca* turned in flight" (342). The poet had earlier implied that the main damage sustained by the hall came from Grendel's attempt to escape. In the *þē* clause the elements *āglǣca* 'monster' (1000b), *fyrendǣdum fāg* 'stained with crime-deeds' (l. 1001a), *aldres orwēna* 'despairing of life' (l. 1002a) and *on flēam* 'in flight' (l. 1001b) "imply Grendel's strength, his sense of guilt and despair, and his impulse to flee—all of which amount to the cause, the circumstance by which this damage was incurred" (342).

1678 ──────────. "*Un[h]litme* 'Voluntarily' in *Beowulf* Line 1097." *JEGP* 87 (1988): 315-328.

A rejoinder to Bliss [1367], who believes that the manuscript reading *finnel unhlitme* (l. 1129a) should read *elne unflitme* 'with ill-fated courage' (as in l. 1097a). Vickrey defends his [S1057] and Fry's [S910, S911] earlier position, arguing that "the translation 'ill-fated' is not satisfactory for *unhlitme* and that on contextual as well as philological grounds *unhlitme* 'not by necessity', hence 'willingly', gives very good sense in *Beowulf* at line 1097 as well as 1129"

(315). As such, this reading of 1129a would make Hengest's stay in Frisia voluntary and heroic. For line 1097a, it portrays Finn as unconquered in spirit in making his treaty with Hengest. "The pairing of *unhlitme* 1097 and 1192 emphasizes the contrast between Finn's and Hengest's expectations and so anticipates the outcome" (327). Vickrey finds a parallel to this situation in accounts of the death of Hrolf in Saxo's *Gesta Danorum* and the *Hrólfs saga kraka*.

1679 Vigil, Julián Josué. *'Beowulf': Text Search, A Color Computer Program*. Las Vegas: Published by the Author, 1988. Pp. 33.

The *OEN* review, 23.1 (1989): 64, describes the program as follows: "Written in interpreted BASIC, the program searches through several disk files containing Klaeber's text for a character string typed in by the user" (65).

1680 Watanabe, Hideki. "Monsters Creep?: the Meaning of the Verb *Scriðan* in *Beowulf*." *Studies in Language and Culture* (Osaka Univ.) 14 (1988): 107-20.

Points out that the verb *scrīþan*, which occurs four times in *Beowulf* (ll. 163b, 650b, 703a, and 2569b), always describes the motions of monsters: Grendel, Grendel's mother, and the firedragon. Thus, the poet unites the three antagonists under the category of "the dragon," intending to arouse primeval fear among the audience with a verb which originally meant 'to creep.' (HW)

1681 Weldon, James. "Response to Stephen Glosecki's 'Wolf of the Bees: Germanic Shamanism and the Bear Hero.'" *Journal of Ritual Studies* 2 (1988): 50-57.

A critique of Glosecki's article [1648] which claims that traces of shamanism can be found in *Beowulf*, particularly in the name and depiction of the hero. Weldon finds the evidence from Icelandic sources incomplete, points out that there are no overt references to bears in *Beowulf*, and cites the need for archaeological evidence of shamanism.

1682 Wieland, Gernot. "*Manna mildost*: Moses and Beowulf." *Pacific Coast Philology* 23 (1988): 86-93.

Believes that the *Beowulf*-poet borrows phrases and motifs from the Old English *Exodus* in order to portray

Beowulf (who shares many of the characteristics of Moses) as a type of God. In particular, Numbers 12:3 describes Moses as *vir mitissimus* 'most mild man,' a phrase also used of Moses in the Old English *Exodus*, *manna mildost*, 'mildest of men,' (l. 550), and of Beowulf (l. 3181a). A similar phrase describes God in the Old High German *Wessobrun Prayer*, a poem written under the influence of the Anglo-Saxons. Wieland sketches out a number of similarities between the Moses of the Old English poem and Beowulf: both are rescuers and both battle the evil of Cain in water through the agency of God. Both Grendel's mere and the Red Sea are brimming with blood, and in both accounts the story of the Deluge appears, though some have called it an irrelevant interpolation in the Old English *Exodus*. The story of Noah's flood, the defeat of Pharaoh's men, and the fight against Grendel's mother all depict the death of God's enemies under water and thus put Beowulf on a par with Old Testament figures "in what can only be considered a typological relationship to God" (91).

1683 Wolf, Alois. "Die Verschriftlichung von europäischen Heldensagen als mittelalterliches Kulturproblem." [The 'Writing down' of European Heroic Lays as a Cultural Problem of the Middle Ages]. In *Heldensage und Heldendichtung in Germanischen*. Ed. Heinrich Beck. Ergänzungsbände zum Reallexikon der germanischen Altertumskunde, Bd. 2. Berlin and New York: de Gruyter, 1988. Pp. 305-28.

Studies how oral heroic narratives in the European Middle Ages came to be written down and the transformations which they underwent in this process (*Verschriftlichung*), observing that *Beowulf* seems to be a transitional text in that a number of its features depart from those of traditional heroic songs. Some heroic songs made the transition to writing in a more or less unproblematic way, but *Beowulf* shows the influence of written traditions, particularly that of the great epic, borrowed from Biblical poetry. *Beowulf* does not narrate the typical heroic conflicts of the oral songs (tribal feuds, treachery, killing of kin, problematic offers, and heroic battle against superior forces). Though these themes appear in *Beowulf*, they serve as a foil to less typical themes. The hall, for example, is in *Beowulf* not the typical showplace for heroic action since the challenge comes from the outside and less from human enemies and traitors. Beowulf, again atypically, battles monstrous foes. The heroic past itself becomes an object of dispute and criticism (unlike the admirable heroic age in the oral songs). The *Beowulf*-poet was able to reshape the aesthetic of the vernacular heroic legends into the mold of the grand literary epic (*epische Großform*) only because the heroic tradition must have been a considerable cultural force in Anglo-Saxon England. Wolf analyzes *The Battle of Maldon*, *Waltharius*, the *Ludwigslied*, and the *Song of Roland* from the same perspective.

1684 Wrenn, Charles L., and Whitney F. Bolton. *Beowulf with The Finnesburg Fragment*. Exeter Medieval English Texts and Studies. 3rd ed. Exeter: U of Exeter, 1988. Pp. 303.

A reprint of the 1973 edition. See Wrenn [S276].

1989

1684a Blockley, Mary. "Old English Coordination, Apposition, and the Syntax of English Poetry." *MP* 87 (1989): 115-31.

Argues that Anglo-Saxon poets distinguished between enumerative lists and appositional series by reserving a particular structure for the lists and comments on the subordinating role of the conjunction *ond*. Modern readers often have difficulty telling the difference between a list of separate items and a series of appositions or variations on a single item. For enumerative lists, Blockley argues, the poets reserved the following structure: A/ B ond C (where / indicates a line boundary). Thus, "the line ending can substitute for a conjunction whenever an immediately subsequent half-line is a conjoined pair" (115). She locates and identifies several such structures (ll. 1724b-27a, 2810b-12, 103b-04a, evaluating the relative merits of a number of published translations of the poem. After analyzing various types of coordination in modern English, Blockley argues that Old English *ond* has a semi-subordinating effect so that in line 61, *Heorogār, Hrōðgār, ond Hālga til, Halga* is subordinate to the first pair *Heorogar-Hrothgar*. "Poets add modifiers to the third member to offset the asymmetrical ([A and B] and C) structure of the series. The need to balance the last member syntactically with the sum of the first two motivates the placement of the heaviest phrase at the end of the series" (126). Also discusses coordination in Old English prose syntax.

1685 Bradley, S.A.J. "Grundtvig, Anglo-Saxon Literature and 'Ordets Kamp til Seier'." *Grundtvig-Studier* 41 (1989-1990): 216-45.

Assesses the contribution of N.F.S. Grundtvig not only to *Beowulf* scholarship but to the wider sphere of Anglo-Saxon studies, finding that "in Grundtvig's endeavours to do justice to the status of *Beowulf* as *epos*, in his conviction that the true epic narrative must be a record of 'Ordets Kamp til Seier' ['The word's struggle for victory'], in his wider reflections upon the extensive historical writings of the Anglo-Saxons, and in his evolving concept of a universal history in which the Christian culture of the Anglo-Saxons held a crucial and providential position, it is here that we may observe some of the most fruitful consequences of Grundtvig's encounter with the ancient Christian literature of England, and it is here too,

I think, that some of the most potentially fruitful research remains to be done" (221-22). Includes an extensive review of Grundtvig's activities as translator [S6] and editor [S11] of the poem as well as a discussion of his views of Christian history in *Beowulf*.

1686 Cherniss, Michael D. "Beowulf Was Not There: Compositional Implications of *Beowulf*, Lines 1299b-1301." *Oral Tradition* 4 (1989): 316-29.

In telling of the attack of Grendel's mother and the death of Æschere, the poet mentions that Beowulf is not present (ll. 1299b-1301) only after the attack has begun, an apparently belated detail which may be explained if we assume that the poem was composed using oral techniques. Cherniss identifies a series of ring patterns (associated with oral composition) in the introduction and attack of Grendel and his mother and argues that such ring patterns echo between the two attacks. "In the second attack-passage, the location of the statement about Beowulf's absence suggests that it occupies a particular place in a particular narrative pattern, that its function is not simply informative but compositional as well. The sequence within the description of Grendel's attack is (1) the monster seizes (and eats) a victim (739-45a); (2) the hero reacts and the fight begins (745b-66); (3) a great commotion ensues . . . (767 ff.). Correspondingly, in the later attack on Heorot, the monster seizes (and kills) a victim (1294-99a); the hero fails to react (because he is not there) (1299b-1301); (3) a great commotion ensues . . . (1302a)" (327). Thus, the statement about Beowulf's absence is structurally necessary to maintain the ring patterning.

1687 Chickering, Howell D. *'Beowulf': a Dual-Language Edition*. Corrected ed. Garden City, NY: Anchor Books, 1989.

A corrected edition of Chickering [S1023].

1688 Christensen, Bonniejean. "Tolkien's Creative Technique: *Beowulf* and *The Hobbit*." *Mythlore* 57 (1989): 4-10.

Maintains that J.R.R. Tolkien's *The Hobbit* is "a retelling of *Beowulf*, but from a Christian rather than a pagan point of view, and as a fantasy rather than an elegy" (4).

1689 Creed, Robert P. "*Beowulf* and the Language of Hoarding." In *Medieval Archaeology: Papers of the Seventeenth*

Annual Conference of the Center for Medieval and Renaissance Studies. Ed. Charles L. Redman. Medieval and Renaissance Texts and Studies, 60. Binghamton, NY: SUNY, Binghamton, 1989. Pp. 155-67.

Examines the cursed treasure hoard in *Beowulf* in order to help interpret hoards unearthed by archaeologists in northwestern Europe, defining a "hoarding behavior" (159) on the basis of the poem. Creed argues that "the last third of *Beowulf* can be read as a traditionally preserved account of the appropriate behavior to be followed when a valuable hoard is accidentally discovered. The discoverer should either leave the hoard intact or re-bury it. But it should be re-buried only after it has been seen and examined by the folk acting in concert and only after it has been formally declared useless. If the discoverers behave in this way, they will keep the curse from the people and leave undisturbed the dragon that always finds such treasure and enforces the curse. From the point of view of the archaeologist, the curse and the dragon can be seen as folk-beliefs that ensure that the goods taken out of circulation will remain unused. The goods must be formally declared *unnyt* (3168a) 'useless'" (163-64). Creed finds an incantation in the opening lines of the "Lay of the Last Survivor" (ll. 2247-49a) and discusses how ancient ideas can be preserved in oral verse.

1690 ——————. "A Student of Oral Tradition Looks at the Origins of Language." In *Studies in Language Origins, 1*. Ed. Jan Wind, Edward G. Pulleyblank, Eric De Grolier, and Bernard H. Bichakjian. Amsterdam and Philadelphia: John Benjamins Pub. Co., 1989. Pp. 43-52.

Theorizes that poems like *Beowulf* reinforce cultural memory, and that the meter of the poem provides the mnemonic means to accomplish that goal, primarily through two kinds of syllables: stressed, semantically weighty syllables and semantically light syllables which indicate relationships between the heavy syllables. With the aid of Norman Geschwind's work on aphasia, Creed postulates that these two different kinds of syllables are produced in different areas of the brain, the heavy syllables in Wernicke's area and the light ones in Broca's. Semantically heavy syllables, when linked together, sometimes form a memory capsule or "ideal structure" which can preserve a culturally important idea (see Creed [1173]) for centuries. Creed traces the alliterative collocation of *word* and *wield* from its Indo-European origins, through its place in *Beowulf* (ll. 30 and 79), to Shakespeare's use of it in *King Lear* and goes on to speculate about the evolution of human speech, pointing out that the syllable (a "bite" of sound) must have been more basic than the phone. The first human speakers probably spoke syllables of the Wernicke type, but learned to connect them and thus aided the development of Broca's area as well as affecting the development of the vocal tract.

1691   Eto, Yasuharu. "A Note on *Beowulf* l. 447a." *Medieval English Studies Newsletter* (Tokyo) 20 (1989): 16-18.

Believes that the adjective *fāh* always means 'bright, shining, decorated,' even when it is modified by a dative noun for blood and where others translate it as 'stained.' On the basis of this analysis, Eto reinterprets the phrase *d[r]ēore fāhne* in line 447a to mean 'shining, decorated with blood.' "[I]t may be inferred that the blood which occurs with *fah* has the symbolical meaning of bravery in action: in *Beowulf* the blood shed in action is not a stain, but a shining decoration" (17). Eto then paraphrases lines 445b-51: "If I die, you will not have to cover my head (even if Grendel leaves my head uneaten), because he will have me (gloriously) shining red with blood (and I wish my bravery to be seen). He will (surely) devour my body and (, therefore,) you will not have to worry about it" (17-18).

1692   Fajardo-Acosta, Fidel. *The Condemnation of Heroism in the Tragedy of 'Beowulf': A Study in the Characterization of the Epic.* Studies in Epic and Romance Literature, 2. Lewiston, NY: Edwin Mellen, 1989. Pp. viii + 215.

Argues that the poet condemns the flawed heroism of Beowulf and that this "anti-heroic vision belongs to an age-old Indo-European tradition in which the hero and the monsters he battles are essentially indistinguishable and equally condemnable from a moral point of view" (3). Fajardo-Acosta draws on a number of classical and medieval epics to solidify this point and endorses Huppé's belief [1437] in the Augustinian frame of reference for *Beowulf*. "The tragedy of Beowulf unfolds precisely around the transformation of Beowulf the man—essentially a mild and generous individual—into Beowulf the monster—the fierce and implacable warrior who will stop at nothing in his pursuit of fame and wealth. . . . Beowulf's tragic flaw is his weakness to resist the glittering allure of the heroic models and his failure to perceive the dark side of the hero-warrior. The monsters are embodiments of the temptations with which Beowulf is confronted—to all of which he succumbs—and also mirror-images of Beowulf, of what he slowly becomes as he moves up the ladder of heroic achievement" (2-3).

Chapter one, "The Name and Character of Beowulf," suggests that the hero's name may be derived from the elements *beorn* 'warrior or man' and *wulf* 'wolf,' indicating the paradox of Beowulf's character, with its human and bestial qualities. Fajardo-Acosta surveys Germanic and Indo-European lore about wolves and suggests that Beowulf's inglorious youth reveals his "gentle, peace-loving and even meditative disposition" (29), though his desire for heroic glory transforms him into an implacable beast. Beowulf may be the embodiment of the spirit of murder, greed, and violence first manifested in Beowulf I (Beow) as well as in the monsters and symbolized by Cain.

Chapters two and three, "Symbolic Kinship and Secret Identity" and "The Battles with Grendel's Mother and the Dragon," seek to show that the monsters (Grendel, Grendel's mother, and the dragon) "represent a series of temptations to which Beowulf succumbs and a series of mirror images of what Beowulf becomes as a consequence of his failure to resist those temptations" (36), also making a number of comparisons with Germanic and Indo-European epics. Chapter four, "Swords, Ships, Serpents, and Rings," attempts to link circular interlace patterns to webs of deceit and the coilings of venomous serpents. Swords bite like such serpents and are often decorated with serpentine patterns, indicating their demonic nature as does the association with infernal light. Ships also share "wavy, serpentine qualities," while classical traditions of sea-voyaging make it clear that "the sea-going journey is generally an impious, self-seeking undertaking" (145)—all of which reflect negatively on Beowulf's voyage to Denmark. The final chapter, "Point of View and the Puzzle of Fate," compares the concept of fate in *Beowulf* to that in the *Aeneid*, the *Odyssey*, the *Iliad*, and other classical works, emphasizing the self-destructive nature of heroic quests. To the blinded characters, fate seems inscrutable and powerful, but from the Augustinian point of view of the poet, fate is "an order which can be apprehended, understood and ultimately controlled" (176). Fajardo-Acosta concludes with a warning against modern manifestations of "the noxious ideologies of heroism" (180).

Reviews: R.P. Tripp, Jr., *In Geardagum* 11 (1990): 73-88; *OEN* 25.2 (1992): 48.

1692a Fujiwara, Hiroshi. "Parallel Expressions in Old English Verse." *Bulletin of the Language Institute of Gakushuin U* 12 (1989): 46-58. In Japanese.

Points out that in *Beowulf* parallel expressions are continually used, but in *The Battle of Maldon* they occur less frequently. This suggests that *Beowulf* was a product of a professional group of reciters, while *Maldon* was written by an individual poet in his cell. (HF)

1693 Fulk, R.D. "An Eddic Analogue to the Scyld Scefing Story." *RES* 40 (1989): 313-322.

Finds a previously unrecognized analogue to the Scyld Scefing story (ll. 4-19) in verses concerning Bergelmir (*Ber-* = 'barley') in the poetic *Edda*. This barley figure is placed in a *lúðr* 'flower bin' and may be connected to Estonian folk beliefs about Pekko (probably from proto-Germanic **beaww* 'barley'), a wax doll kept in a grain bin. Fulk finds the parallels between the Eddic story and the account of Scyld Scefing in *Beowulf* striking: "In both there is a child laid in a floating vessel associated with grain. The name of the castaway (or his son . . .) derives etymologically from a word for 'barley', and the name of the barley-figure's grandfather signifies a cereal plant" (318). Given the Estonian and Eddic analogues, the destitute boy in a ship in *Beowulf* must originally have been *Beow* 'barley', but was transferred to Scyld in the process of folkloric transmission. It seems more likely to Fulk that folk beliefs in heroic narrative shaped the written genealogies rather than written genealogies having influenced heroic narratives like *Beowulf.*

1694 Gerritsen, Johan. "Emending *Beowulf* 2253—Some Matters of Principle: With a Supplement on 389-90, 1372 & 240." *Neophil* 73 (1989): 448-453.

Proposes a new reconstruction of line 2253, arguing on paleographical and philological grounds that the word which Klaeber reconstructs as *feormie* 'polish' [S67] and Kiernan as *fægnige* 'welcome, receive with pleasure' [1564], should read *forð bere* 'bear away.' For lines 389-90 Gerritsen agrees that a lacuna has occurred but places the point of omission between *deniga* and *lēodum* (on evidence of a mark between them), suggesting that *lēodum* belongs to the on-verse of line 390 and that the missing half-line alliterating on *w* most probably would have been *Wedera lēodum*, accounting for the skip, though lines must be missing between the two. Finding a similar mark (indicating that the scribe paused to take ink) in line 1372, he supplies word *helan* 'to hide' which accounts for the scribe's mistake better than the other proposed restorations, *hydan* 'hide' and Klaeber's *beorgan* [S67]. Finally, a similar skip may account for line 240b, where the scribe mistook the *le* of *hwile* for an omitted *ic*; thus, the verse must originally have read *ic hwīle wæs* 'a long time I was. . . .'

1695 _____. "Have with You to Lexington! The *Beowulf* Manuscript and *Beowulf*." In *In Other Words: Transcultural Studies in Philology, Translation, and Lexicology Presented to Hans Heinrich Meier on the Occasion of His Sixty-Fifth Birthday*. Ed. J. Lachlan Mackenzie and Richard Todd. Dordrecht: Foris, 1989. Pp. 15-34.

Examines the codicology and paleography of the Nowell codex, opposing Kiernan's analysis of the *Beowulf* manuscript [1261] and speculating on the history of the codex through the time of Laurence Nowell. Gerritsen examines the various texts of the Nowell codex for variant word forms, their distribution of capitals, their relative percentage of scribal error, leading to the conclusion that the codex was conceived and executed as an integral whole and that it must have had a considerable textual history, stretching back to at least the ninth century. He believes that Laurence Nowell received the manuscript in a disbound state (explaining the pattern of worm holes and worn pages) and that Nowell himself may have attempted to restore manuscript readings on folios 182r (a palimpsest, according to Kiernan) and 201v. Also included is a brief survey of manuscript freshening in the age of Nowell.

1696 Glosecki, Stephen O. *Shamanism and Old English Poetry*. Garland Reference Library of the Humanities, 905. New York: Garland, 1989. Pp. xv + 257; ill.

A book-length study with two main purposes: "first, to define shamanism; second to show that a shamanic past underlies some Old English poems, particularly *Beowulf* and the metrical charms" (1). Throughout, Glosecki draws on evidence from a number of cultures and texts. Chapter one, "Defining the Dream Doctor," sees the shaman as a "[s]hape-shifting singer at the center of his tribe ... , exploring the dreamtime where gods and heroes are always present, continually reactivates the mythology of this race, keeping the gods and heroes alive in the midst of men. Moving between the worlds, he maintains tribal health, the tremulous balance of dreamtime and quotidian time. Arbiter of taboo, he keeps his people in touch with their moral code" (51).

Chapter two, "Vestiges of Animism," examines the boar image in *Beowulf* and finds it to act as a shamanic animal protector. "The spirit guardian of the seasoned warrior, Beowulf's boar retains notable reflexes of animism" (53). Here Glosecki examines boar images in the poem, most notably the *eoforlīc* 'boar image' or 'living boar body' (ll. 303b-306a) as well as archaeological evidence for the importance of boars on helmets. Weapons and gold, like the boar, are thought to be "alive" and possibly hostile. Chapter three, "Evidence of Ecstasy," examines the shamanistic ecstasy of Odin, the inspirer of visions and poetry (through the ecstasis of liquor), finding elements of the "ecstatic" traveler in the Old English elegies and Norse sagas in particular. Chapter four, "Shamanic Therapy," looks at charms which harm or heal: "shamanic therapy reflects pervasive concerns of the doctor's society as a whole: people with an animistic world view make healing and harming central to their culture because they blame all kinds of misfortune on malevolent spirits—*and* on those who control them, namely, hostile shamans" (103). Glosecki finds in the opening words of the Lay of the Last Survivor (ll. 2247-48a) evidence of a charm with its characteristic imperative. This charm of the last survivor, which commends the treasure to the earth, is powerful enough to cause the death of Beowulf and seal the doom of his tribe. It "coerced mother earth to curse her gold" (106). Glosecki finds parallels between the Old English metrical charms, which he sees in shamanistic terms, and a number of details in *Beowulf*.

Chapter five, "Patterns of Initiation," argues that Beowulf's descent into the mere parallels the "infernal descent of shamanic initiates" (152) but that issues of initiation can be seen in the larger structure of the poem. Beowulf is a slack youth (novice) who is initiated through a series of tests, in which Glosecki finds a number of shamanistic details, sometimes muted or transformed. "The overall pattern of the descent scene corresponds with the healing journey of a shamanic initiate, who reestablishes a wholesome equilibrium by entering the mana continuum, by moving between time frames to overcome evil spirits, to bring back knowledge, power, strong talismans to sustain the tribe" (17).

Chapter six, "Images of the Animal Guardians," associates Beowulf with a shamanic bear guardian, drawing on several Germanic sources to show the importance of bears in that culture. The reason that the bear is a central shamanic figure is that hibernation suggests how the initiated shaman falls into ecstasy and reawakens later. Though Beowulf's connection to the bear is not explicit, a number of indirect links make it clear: Beowulf's name 'bee wolf' may be a circumlocution for the tabooed word *bear*. Further, the story's origins are found in the bear's son folk tale, and Beowulf uses a "bear hug" to dispatch enemies like Dæghrefn. Also discusses other prominent animals and their shamanic qualities.

Glosecki concludes that if Beowulf stems "from a mythic warrior shaman with the bear as his *nigouimes*, this lost lineage would account for the overtones of shape-shifting implicit in Beowulf's name as well as in his habit of using the bear-hug in combat. The shamanic origin also helps to explain other obscure elements in the Old English epic, such as its hero's unpromising youth, his descent into the underworld, his 'cleansing' of the mere, his incremental initiation, his talismanic weaponry, his near dismemberment at the hands of infernal 'elsewhere-spirits'. . . . Gifted with size and strength and a quest to the underworld, Beowulf embodies the spirit of the bear, the huge strong hibernator who goes underground only to emerge again with the lengthening days" (207).

Reviews: R. Wehlau, *Scintilla* 7 (1990): 72-74; G. Russom, *Speculum* 66 (1991): 637-39.

1697 Gray, John. "The Finn Episode in *Beowulf*: Line 1085(b) *ac hig him gebingo budon*." In *Words and Wordsmiths: A Volume for H. L. Rogers*. Ed. Geraldine Barnes, John Gunn, Sonya Jensen, and Lee Jobling. Sydney: Department of English, U of Sydney, 1989. Pp. 32-39.

Argues that using the Finnsburh fragment to reconstruct the Finnsburh episode in *Beowulf* is misleading as well as methodologically unsound and proposes new readings based on the internal syntax of the passage. Gray points out that "One must particularly avoid the assumption that the Anglo-Saxons were fully familiar with, and eager to supply any needed background from, our modern reconstruction of a story" (33). Instead, the passage may be intentionally elusive, providing "delight in the narrative possibilities which remain tantalizingly open" (36). Following the internal syntax of the passage, Gray proposes that the *him* of line 1085b is a singular dative, referring to Finn and that the plural pronouns *hig* (*hie*) in lines 1085b, 1086a, and 1087b refer to the same group. Further, "two of the references to 'Eotenas' must refer to Finn's followers, and the other two may reasonably do so." That is, "they" (the Danes) offer terms to Finn and agree to clear a hall for him (Finn's having either been destroyed or occupied by Hengest's troop); in addition, Hildeburh's son and brother are slain by her husband Finn's retainers (the *Eotenas*). More broadly, "The problem of which group began hostilities does not arise in the Episode in *Beowulf*; rather, it is a problem which results only from the attempt to reconstruct in full 'the legend of Finn'. The narrative in the Episode leaves this question aside, insisting instead . . . that both Finn and Hengest's parties had put their trust in the firmness of treaties. In this, both parties are shown to be unwise" (39).

1698 Green, Brian. "*Lof*: Interlocking Denotations in *Beowulf*." *Unisa English Studies* 27 (1989): 21-25.

Argues that the word *lof* can mean not only 'earthly praise' and 'heavenly glory' but also 'protection' in an official, legal sense, and that these meanings intertwine to reconcile Christian and heroic themes. In his fight with Grendel's mother Beowulf seeks to achieve *longsumne lof* 'longlasting praise' (l. 1536a), but as Green points out, other occurrences of *lof* in the corpus of prose and poetry suggest that 'protection' is a possible meaning. The irony is that Beowulf achieves 'long-lasting praise' for himself but also 'long-lasting protection' for the Danes. The poet, through the interlocking connotations of the word *lof* unites pagan and Christian sensibilities. Beowulf follows "the pagan ethic of aggressively winning personal glory" but also follows "the Christian doctrine of sacrificially loving one's neighbour" (23). Green concludes: "at least four favourable connotations of *lof* emerge from the integrated themes of personal glory and public protection that I have outlined above: the achievement of personal ambition; the celebration of heroic strength; the fulfilment of social obligation; and the complexity of an uncompromisingly disruptive morality" (25).

1699 Hill, John M. "Revenge and Superego Mastery in *Beowulf.*" *Assays* 5 (1989): 3-36.

Undertakes an extensive reading of the poem as a battle of psychological forces unleashed in the Oedipal and pre-Oedipal stages of development. Hill sees exchange (gift-giving, reward, treasure) as central to the poem's meaning. Such rewards from a lord mirror the son's borrowing of power from the father for the repression of Oedipal and pre-Oedipal wishes by the superego, keeping the ego weak. The monsters reflect the barely repressed id, with its Oedipal desires for the mother and rage against the constraints of the father. The son internalizes a "punishing father-ideal" in the early stages, so that the superego becomes punitive and harsh. "Of course the poet states nothing like this; but he seems to intuit it given the close proximity of the monstrous and the good" (9). Hill traces these conflicts in the poem, seeing Beowulf and Wiglaf as representatives of the superego, while the monsters and monstrous humans represent the repressed id and its rage. The story of Cain itself "is one of fraternal rivals for the Father's favor" (13) and is the root of monstrousness as conceived in the poem. "Among men, in the best cases, Grendelian impulses are deeply repressed, their energies taken up somehow into superego mastery, into the generosity of a powerful king" (14). Grendel lives in the world of the mother—no father is known. "Perhaps, also, this orientation toward the mother accounts for the extraordinary difficulty of the fight with the dam" (23). Beowulf takes out superego revenge on the monsters, including the dragon, which reflects the most infantile stage of "Monstrous possessiveness and the death of all rivals—wishes never completely erased" (28). The curse on the treasure is the dead father's ancient curse and represents a more primal conflict. Hill also interprets the historical digressions as evidence of similar forces. Finally, in *Beowulf*, "Fathers are always good, although they may suffer tragic losses. This idealization of king and father suggests that Oedipal and pre-Oedipal conflicts are not completely resolved. Perhaps this is because the Oedipal crisis is fixed at a fairly early point in the heroic world" (31).

1700 Howe, Nicholas. *Migration and Mythmaking in Anglo-Saxon England.* New Haven: Yale UP, 1989. Pp. xiii + 198.

In a larger study of origin myths in Old English literature, devotes a chapter to the poem—"*Beowulf* and the Ancestral Homeland"—arguing that the poet reconstructs the pagan past using the geography of ancient Germania and then critiques that past: "In a Germania unsanctified by conversion, the Christian good of peace can be achieved only by the strong man and then only for a brief time" (174). The poem is a meditation on what the Anglo-Saxons might have become had they not undergone exodus and conversion, and in that sense it is a migration myth. But the critique of the past does not rise to a full rejection: "To condemn these pagans would be to betray the past of the English and also their historically imposed duty to lead other peoples into Christendom. Stories about the Danes and the Geats could serve as a powerful reminder of the Anglo-Saxons' origins, both geographically and religiously" (147). The digressions in particular map out the geography of the pagan north and dissect its structure. Howe undertakes a detailed analysis of several of the more central digressions (those concerning Sigemund, Heremod, the death of Hygelac, the Swedish wars) concluding that "The realpolitik of the north is brutally simple: Tribes without a famous warrior king are open to attack" (172). Beowulf himself learns this lesson about the north and tries to create an island of peace in Geatland by quelling all outside feuds. His peace cannot last, however, and the poem finally rejects individual heroism because it is not informed by any idea of ethical or political good. "Beowulf's tragedy is to apprehend the limits of individual heroism in a pagan world" (172).

Reviews: W.A. Chaney, *Albion* 22 (1990): 655-56; N. Jacobs, *N&Q* 37 (1990): 452-53; K.M. Schoening, *Comitatus* 21 (1990): 128-32; R.C. Stacey, *J of British Studies* 30 (1991): 83-99; R. Fleming, *American Historical Rev.* 96 (1991): 1529-30; S.A. Barney, *Envoi* 2 (1991 for 1990): 374-77; D.P. Kirby, *History* 76 (1991): 481-82; G. Russom, *Speculum* 66 (1991): 893-95; D. Wright, *Renaissance and Reformation* n.s., 15 (1991): 266-68.

1701 Huisman, Rosemary. "The Three Tellings of Beowulf's Fight with Grendel's Mother." *Leeds Studies in English* n.s., 20 (1989): 217-248.

Provides an extensive discussion of the three tellings of Beowulf's fight with Grendel's mother, from the point of view of M.A.K. Halliday's "social-semiotic" language theory, showing that each telling "is accommodated within the demands of the social structure within which it takes place" (231). Huisman proceeds by examining the systems of transitivity, mood, and theme on the clause level and how the different tellings choose different semantic resources from these language systems. Each telling (ll. 1492-1590, 1652-76, and 2131-51) constructs the relationship between one individual (the hero) and another (the lord) in terms of their social roles and also the relationship between Christian and heroic viewpoints. The relationship between hero and lord is "syntagmatic" (following a sequence) and "reciprocal" (involving an exchange of social recognition—the hero gives glory to his lord, and the lord returns favor). This reciprocal syntagmatic relationship constitutes the heroic view, which connects to the Christian view, which is directional and paradigmatic. "Essentially, each heroic action in the syntagm is sustained, paradigmatically, by the enabling 'giving' from God to the hero. In the telling of an heroic story, in the sequence of deeds and gifts, the Christian/heroic paradigm is textually invisible—until the sequence of heroic actions is blocked, and the hero cannot act. It is then that explicit divine intervention can enable the story to continue" (231). Includes an appendix on the linguistic-semiotic theory of M.A.K. Halliday.

1702 Irving, Edward B., Jr. *Rereading 'Beowulf'*. Philadelphia: U of Pennsylvania P, 1989. Pp. x + 183.

Modifies and broadens his earlier reading of *Beowulf* [S674] in light of recent theoretical work on oral-formulaic poetry. Chapter one, "The Approach to Heorot," reviews three recent critical approaches to the poem: the exegetical or neo-Augustinian approach, the New Critical approach, and the oral-formulaic approach. Both exegetical theory and New Criticism have their shortcomings. According to Irving, exegetical critics such as Lee [S841] often distort the text to accommodate their *a priori* assumptions about the Christian nature of the poem, assuming a covert, hidden meaning. New Critics, on the other hand, too often assume that *Beowulf* is a "literate" poem and focus on patterns of imagery which the original audience probably would not have detected and are further prone to find literate irony where it probably does not exist. Irving argues that the poem does not work by concealing its meaning: "Explicitness seems to be a constant feature of oral-delivered poetry" (10). Oral theory itself has developed from its narrow, more fanatical earlier forms (Magoun [S265]) into a more attractive theory. Irving then reviews nine characteristics of oral poetry proposed by Ong (*Orality and Literacy*, 1982) and applies them specifically to *Beowulf*.

Chapter two, "Characters and Kings," examines "some forms of characterization in oral-derived poetry" (36). In general, according to Irving, we are apt to misread oral-derived characterization if we expect "rounded" characters. Thus, many critics find subtle ironies of characterization which probably do not exist, though the poem "is capable of making characters interestingly complex ... in unfamiliar and oblique ways" (36). Irving then goes on to analyze several characters from the poem, at length: Unferth (as a personification of Danish interests and emotions, not an evil schemer), Hrothgar (as a type of the old king, but rounded in that his clear positive traits coexist with negative ones and the absence of positive ones), Beowulf (whose excellencies are thrown into relief by contrast to Hrothgar), Grendel's mother (as a stock female monster, deprived of separate identity, supposedly weak but with undeniable power), Thryth (a conventional figure who functions to show male superiority), Wealhtheow (as a strong woman, who yet succumbs to the conventional role of suffering victim) and Wiglaf (as an active representative of conventional communal values). Irving identifies three typical methods of characterization in *Beowulf*: contrast between characters, "zero-grade narration" (where an absence of an expected element contributes to characterization), and "embedding" (where characters are defined by a package of conventional social connections, so that finally such characters become "all matrix" [64]).

Chapter three, "Style and Story: Narrative Modes," examines the style and narrative structure of *Beowulf*, focusing mainly on the interlace of two great themes, *humanitas* (humanity) and *draconitas* ("dragonness") in part II of the poem. Irving accepts Leyerle's basic definition of interlace [S634] as a way of explaining oral narrative but rejects his "crypto-Christian" approach (81). On the stylistic level, variation can be seen as a type of interlace which returns to and emphasizes basic themes and motifs. The poet interweaves several sub-themes of *draconitas* in his description of the dragon's first attack (2270b-86). Other sorts of interlace include "the alternation of action with authorial comment" (86), "syntactic contrast between active and passive" verbs (90), "intricate interlacing of points of view, contrasts of inner with outer experience" (92), contrast between heroic action and severe constraints (in Beowulf's fight in the mere-hall), action and inaction in part II as a whole. Irving analyzes part II of the poem in detail, showing how the themes of *humanitas* (human warmth, "history, family, dynasty, continuity, and transitions," 100) contrast and interweave with *draconitas* (oblivion, death, stasis, "no names, no orderly successions, no dynasties, no society at all," 101). Irving defends Beowulf from the charge of greed, calling Beowulf's capture of the hoard and escape from its curse "a God-assisted defeat of a heathen power" (123). Though the social fabric is disintegrating in part II, Beowulf's funeral restores cohesion: the Geats are "now able to function communally with dignity and confidence.... [T]hey represent a reconstructed community and the final victory of *humanitas*" (129-30).

Chapter four, "The Hall as Image and Character," maintains that "the major controlling image throughout the poem from beginning to end is the hall" (133). "The hall is a fixed locus where the vital and affectionate interchanges of social solidarity, the giving and taking of rewards and service, responsibility and gratitude, all that constitutes heroic life, can be carried on over a long period of time" (137). Symbolically, Heorot hall dominates the first two-thirds of the poem. The creation and naming of the hall and what it represents first stirs up the enmity of Grendel, who is driven to destroy what it symbolizes. Throughout Grendel's attack, the poet adds touches of personification to the hall—its mouth is torn open and it suffers wounds, becoming the fellow-fighter with Beowulf. After the attack of Grendel's mother, the poem moves away from Heorot to the hall at the bottom of the mere—an anti-hall, to use Hume's terminology [S920]. In many ways, it is "a quite ordinary Germanic hall, described in the usual vocabulary" (150), opening the way to some open ironies about Beowulf's breach of etiquette. In the end, according to Irving, one hall conquers the other. Part II moves almost immediately away from the hall as a symbolic and emotional center: Beowulf's hall is destroyed by fire. The absence of the hall "forces major questions on us. What meaning can human life have without its center? Is life even possible outside the limits of the social world the hall stands for?" (154). By the end of the poem, Beowulf's barrow "resembles a hall or a model of a hall" which encourages the troop of Geats to re-form and become once again a functioning community.

Reviews: A.H. Olsen, *Envoi* 2.1 (1990): 101-08; P. Stafford, *Literature and History*, 2nd ser. 1.2 (1990): 85-86; R.P. Tripp, Jr., *In Geardagum* 11 (1990): 73-88; *OEN* 24.2 (1991): 32-33; M. Griffith, *MÆ* 60 (1991): 102-03; N. Howe, *MP* 89 (1991): 91-94.

1702a Karibe, Tsunenori. "*Beowulf* with its Japanese Translation Facing the Original (1)." *Bulletin of the College of General Education (Niigata U)* 20 (1989): 239-84.

Edits and translates (into Japanese) lines 1-1250 of *Beowulf*. Karibe's edition, whose collation is footnoted, is based on the facsimiles by Zupitza-Davis [SS14] and Malone [S499] as well as the texts of Dobbie [S256], Klaeber [S67], and Wrenn [S276]. (TK) See Karibe [1752] for a continuation.

1703 *Key-Word Studies in 'Beowulf' and Chaucer, 3*. Tokyo: Centre for Mediaeval English Studies, 1989. 207 pp.

Part of a continuing series of word studies. This installment contains the following entries: "Words for 'Heaven'" by Hiroshi Ogawa (pp. 1-10), "Man, Warrior and King (1): *Beorn, Cempa, Freca, Oretta, Wiga*, and *Wīgend*" by Shuji Sato (pp. 11-25), and "Words for 'Sea' in *Beowulf*" by William Schipper (pp. 27-39), along with various word studies relating to Chaucer. Each entry follows a similar format, usually listing the following items for each word: its etymology, frequency in *Beowulf*, definitions, collocations and variations, alliterative environment, and compounds.

Ogawa examines five words for 'heaven': *heofon, lyft, rodor, swegl,* and *wolcen,* observing that the five nouns are always used of the physical universe, not the "mythical heavens," and that they are synonymous and often interchangeable. The five, along with the compounds with *lyft-* and *swegl-*, always alliterate in *Beowulf,* implying that the choice of one or the other is less dependent on semantic content than on alliterative restrictions. Only three times does one of the five words occur as a subject: the rest of the time they occur as objects of the preposition or in genitive phrases. Further, they are never modified by adjectives.

Sato provides lists of the words for 'man,' 'warrior,' and 'king' mentioned above, with careful consideration of the forms recorded in the manuscript and the Thorkelin transcripts.

In "Words for 'Sea' in *Beowulf*," William Schipper provides grammatical information, frequency of occurrence, compounds, etymology, and definitions for the following *bæð, brim, faroð, ford, gārsecg, geofon, hæf, holm, hronrād, lagu, mere, sæ, sioloð, strēam, sund, swanrād, wæd, wæter, wylm,* and *ȳð*. Schipper's definitions consider meanings in their context in *Beowulf* and record the variety and range of the terms as evidence of the Anglo-Saxons' love-hate relationship with the sea, as well as "the linguistic and poetic inventiveness of the English" (27).

1703a Koike, Kazuo. "Descriptive Vocabulary concerning *Beowulf.*" *Obirin Studies in English Language and Literature* 29 (1989): 141-56. In Japanese.

Reviews the words and expressions characterizing Beowulf as a man, hero, and king, also noting that a physical description of the protagonist is lacking. (KK)

1704 Kolb, Eduard. "Schiff und Seefahrt im *Beowulf* und im *Andreas.*" [Ship and Sea Travel in *Beowulf* and *Andreas.*] In *Meaning and Beyond: Ernst Leisi zum 70. Geburtstag.* Ed. Udo Fries and Martin Heusser. Tübingen: Narr, 1989. Pp. 237-52.

Finds that the poem does not depict sea voyages realistically and that in general, Old English poetry and prose depict sea voyages in a sketchy, indistinct way, perhaps because the literary tradition prevents such realistic depiction or because Anglo-Saxon sea-craft eventually waned after the initial invasions. Kolb examines several scenes of sea journey in *Beowulf* and *Andreas* for accuracy and realism, finding them generally lacking in specificity or precision. Scenes involving the loading and unloading of ships (ll. 210-228, 1896-1924) are particularly inaccurate: the men load armor into the ship *before* pushing out, and vessels carrying horses are simply pulled on shore, whereas such ships were normally put on rollers. Further, the poet never mentions a rudder or oars. Kolb concludes that sea travel was somewhat alien to the poets ("die Seefahrt liegt den Dichtern ziemlich fern," 250). Also discusses words for ship (*scip, cēol, naca, flota, fær, bāt*), concluding that most are completely interchangeable, perhaps with the exception of *bāt*, and discussing a number of Old English terms applied to sea travel (*hringedstefna* 'ring-prowed ship,' *bront* 'steep,' *sægēap* 'sea-steep,' etc.).

1705 Lundberg, Patricia Lorimer. "The Elusive *Beowulf* Poet Self-Represented in the *I*-Narrator and the Scops." *Ball State U Forum* 30 (1989): 5-15.

Examines the poet's "self-representation . . . by studying the I-narrator and the scops of the poem itself" (6), suggesting that the poet "has written into the *Beowulf* poem an elegy not only for the death of the hero Beowulf and of the Germanic heroic age but also for the death of the scop upon the advent of written records in the vernacular." The narrator thus uses formulaic first-person references to "serve as reminders that this presentation is supposed to be oral" (7). Lundberg reviews the appearance of other scops within the poem and notes that as it becomes more elegiac, the scops disappear. Since the lament for a passing oral tradition would make more sense at a later date, Lundberg reviews the rationale for a late date for *Beowulf*.

1706 McGuiness, Daniel. "Beowulf's Byrnies." *ELN* 26 (1989): 1-3.

Notes that defensive armor receives more attention and praise than offensive weapons, particularly swords. McGuiness reviews a number of passages in which byrnies appear as important elements of the narrative. Byrnies are so prominent because they represent a nostalgia for better days and link the warrior to heroes of the past. They also symbolize the conquering of fear, which according to Carlyle (*On Heroes, Hero Worship, and the Heroic in History*) is the first duty of a hero: "a warrior may . . . put on a long dead hero's other skin to 'link' himself to ages absolved of fear and vulnerability and thus face terror defended by the past" (3).

1707 Meaney, Audrey L. "Scyld Scefing and the Dating of *Beowulf*—Again." *Bulletin of the John Rylands U Library of Manchester* 71 (1989): 7-40.

On the basis of genealogy, burial customs, and possible borrowings from hagiographical traditions in *Beowulf*, assigns a tenth-century date to the poem: "All in all, the reign of Athelstan (924-55) appears the most probable for the composition of the Scyld Scefing Prologue to *Beowulf*" (37). After comparing the Danish genealogy in Beowulf (ll. 4-19, 26-63) to the West Saxon genealogies, Meaney concludes that the genealogy in *Beowulf* must depend on that of Æthelwulf (translated by Æthelweard) which could not have been constructed before 858. Second, the prologue, with its account of Scyld's ship burial, may have been influenced by the account of Gildas's instructions for his ship funeral in the *Vita Gildae*, a text composed around 900 and most likely available in England after about 920. Finally, the ship burial of Scyld, though it resembles that of Sutton Hoo, also reflects details of Viking age ship burials, an argument which Meaney supplements with a review of archaeological evidence. Also discusses the relationship between *Beowulf* and the *Visio Pauli*, pointing out that since the *Visio Pauli* in some form may have influenced *Beowulf* before being incorporated into the Blickling Homiliary, the date of 971 (of the Blickling codex) is not firm "as a *terminus post quem*" for *Beowulf* (9).

1708 Mitchell, Bruce. "*Beowulf*: Six Notes, Mostly Syntactical." *Leeds Studies in English* n.s., 20 (1989): 311-317.

Makes the following observations on six syntactical cruces in *Beowulf*: 1) *hrysedon* (l. 226b) is probably transitive, as are most if not all of the other occurrences of the word in the corpus of Old English; if so, the phrase *syrcan hrysedon* would translate as "they shook their coats of mail," an operation described in *Exodus*, lines 172-78. 2) The antecedent of *hit* in line 779 is unclear; "The grammatical sequence *sē winsele* (l. 771), . . . *hē* (l. 772), . . . *hē* (l. 773), demands *hine*, and *hit* is quite clearly an aberrant anticipation of the situation in Modern English" (314). 3) Accepts the emendation of MS. *Sigemunde* to *Sigemundes* (l. 875a) because the MS. reading is syntactically awkward and because the separation of the dependent genitive *Sigemundes* from *ellendædum* 'deeds of valor,' the word on which it depends, is paralleled in *Beowulf*, lines 1180-81. 4) Takes issue with an editorial decision in Wrenn-Bolton [S276], which rejects the emendation of *egl* (l. 987a) to the adjectival form *eglu* because two adjectives in asyndetic parataxis in the same half-line supposedly make for odd syntax. Mitchell rejects this notion. 5) Endorses editors who retain the MS. reading *gesāwon* '(who) saw' (l. 2252a) and suggests that a colon or semi-colon follow *ofgeaf*. 6) Argues that *segn* is neuter in line 2958b and that it belongs to a class of nouns with fluctuating gender.

1709 Mizuno, Tomoaki. "Beowulf as a Terrible Stranger." *Journal of Indo-European Studies* 17 (1989): 1-46.

Suggests that Beowulf, as a dangerous stranger among the Geats, instigated the murder of Herebeald (as Loki instigated the murder of Baldr) and that Beowulf later feels guilt over this crime and believes that he has transgressed *ofer ealde riht* 'against the old law' (l. 2330a), that is, the law of "guest friendship." Mizuno draws on Japanese and Indo-

European concepts of the stranger, finding that to the Danes, Beowulf is a fortunate stranger, while to the Geats he becomes a terrible stranger. "Beowulf turns out to be an evil hero who is supposed to commit the apparently accidental murder of Herebeald" (1).

1710 Mizuno, Yoshiaki. "The Grandeur of *Beowulf*: A Statistical Survey." *Bulletin of Arts and Science* (Meiji Univ.) 216 (1989): 113-33. In Japanese.

Not seen.

1711 Momma, Haruko. "The 'Gnomic Formula' and Some Additions to Bliss's Old English Metrical System." *N&Q* 36 (1989): 423-426.

Argues that certain half-lines that constitute unclassified remainders in Bliss's metrical system [S353] form a gnomic formula and can be interpreted as variants of type B verse. Momma finds twenty-two examples of the formula in the corpus of Anglo-Saxon poetry, all possessing a distinct syntax: a main clause consisting of an interjection, a copula and pronoun, followed by a relative clause introduced by the particle *þe*. *Beowulf*, lines 183b *Wā bið þǣm ðe sceal* 'woe to him who shall . . .' and 186b *Wēl bið þǣm þe mōt* 'well is him who may . . .' show this structure. "If we follow Bliss's notation strictly, this type would be classified into the new Type B3" (425). The numeral three indicates the number of unstressed syllables "that constitute the dip between the stresses" (425).

1711a Nicolini, Mary B. "Is There a FOAF in Your Future? Urban Folk Legends in Room 112." *English Journal* 78 (1989): 81-84.

Uses modern urban legends to introduce students to folklore and oral narrative, drawing parallels between their structure and themes and those of *Beowulf*. *FOAF* stands for "friend of a friend," the usual source of urban legends.

1712 North, Richard J. "Kening Finn en it ferdrach fan Finnsboarch." [Understanding Finn and the Fire-dragon of Finnsburh]. *Us Wurk* 38 (1989): 1-11.

Provides the following summary in English: "To date the story embedded in the Finnsburh Fragment and Episode has defied any full elucidation. In this article I have raised two questions rarely if ever asked: how does the treaty between Finn and his 'Half-Dane' enemies operate? and why after killing Hnæf, the Danish leader, does Finn send his own Frisian warriors home and then safely spend the winter with these former enemies?" (1). The arguments made here appear in English in North [1758].

1713 Osborn, Marijane. "Beowulf's Landfall in *Finna Land.*" *NM* 90 (1989): 137-142.

Agrees with Robinson [S932] that the poet does not portray Beowulf as a character with superhuman strength and that "Beowulf and Breca do not come to shore at a supernatural distance apart or from where they started, and that the place name [*finna land*, l. 580b] may even reveal where the poet has located the land of the Wedergeats" (137). Osborn believes that Beowulf is washed up on his home shores, that he cleanses his own fjörd of water monsters, and that the land of the *Heaþo-Ræmas* [l. 519a] where Breca lands is close-by, thus eliminating the need for miraculous swimming strength on the part of Beowulf. Such an explanation takes *finna land*, where Beowulf ends up, as synonymous with Geatland or *Wedermearc* (l. 298b), his homeland, a connection which Osborn derives from certain etymological and textual clues. If these etymological connections are valid, "then Beowulf's *Wedermearc* almost has to be located in what is now Boshuslän, extending north of Göteborg to Oslo Fjörd" (142). She locates the land of the *Heaðo-Ræmas* "in the neighborhood of the outlet of Raum Älf, the river south of modern Oslo" (139).

1714 Parks, Ward. "Interperformativity and *Beowulf.*" *Narodna umjetnost* 26 (1989): 25-35.

Points out that the term "intertextuality"—often applied to *Beowulf*—is inappropriate for an oral-derived poem and proposes the term "interperformativity" to account for the analogous function in oral poetry. Parks defines interperformativity as the relationship a particular performance has with past performances, a relationship which relies much more on memory and the mnemonic devices of the oral tradition than does the materially verifiable nature of written texts (27). Texts are objects, but performances are events. Parks goes on to examine interperformativity in three contexts: in the narrator's statements about himself (using a first person pronoun), in gnomic commentary, and in narrative digressions. In the formulaic "I have heard" statements, the narrator places his poem into a network of songs, "as a performance in a succession of performances, not as a book cheek by jowl with other books in a library" (29). Gnomic statements (as shared wisdom) take place in a performative situation: they involve "not merely interrelations between gnomes, but interrelations between gnomes and people.... Throughout, discourse remains embedded in human life contexts" (31). Thus, modern interpreters who see irony in the gnomes may be applying literate sensibilities to oral discourse. Finally, the narrative digressions (hard to justify from a literate mentality) make sense in the context of interperformativity—through them the performer remembers and activates the memories of his hearers, often assigning praise or blame. Praise of Beowulf's exploit leads the poet to praise Sigemund and blame Heremod. Thus, the digressions arise through "immediate mnemonic juxtaposition" (32), which hearers would not find confusing since a flesh-and-blood performer (not a written page) accomplishes these interperformative acts.

1715 Peters, F.J.J. "The Wrestling in *Grettis Saga.*" *PLL* 25 (1989): 235-41.

In a study of wrestling in the *Grettis saga*, finds that the two distinct techniques are employed: "an older Nordic *hryggspenna* ['back breaking'] style against nonhuman adversaries, and a newer, exclusively Icelandic *glima* [sport 'wrestling'] against all human opponents" (235). Peters points out that Beowulf employs the *hryggspenna* technique against Dæghrefn (ll. 2507-08a). Since the *hryggspenna* could be used for both combat and sport, Peters suggests that Dæghrefn and Beowulf may engage in a "pre-battle contest to death between champions" (237). Analyzes in detail Grettir's use of wrestling against humans and monsters.

1716 Pintzuk, Susan, and Anthony S. Kroch. "The Rightward Movement of Complements and Adjuncts in the Old English of *Beowulf.*" *Language Variation and Change* 1 (1989): 115-143.

Provides the following abstract: "Although it has been generally recognized that Old English was a verb-final language with verb-seconding, the existence of clauses with main verb complements and adjuncts appearing after the otherwise clause-final verb seems to contradict the hypothesis that the language was strictly verb-final in underlying structure. There are three possible analyses to explain these clauses: variable word order in the base, leftward verb movement, and rightward movement of NPs and PPs. In this article, we demonstrate that only the third analysis adequately explains the data of the Early Old English poem *Beowulf*. Moreover, by investigating the mapping between syntactic structures and metrical units, we provide evidence for two types of rightward movement with two distinct structures: heavy NP shift, with a characteristic major intonational boundary between the main verb and the postponed NP, and PP extraposition, where the intonational boundary was much less common" (115). See also Pintzuk [1508].

1717 Raffel, Burton. "Translating Medieval European Poetry." In *The Craft of Translation*. Ed. John Biguenet and Rainer Schulte. Chicago: U of Chicago P, 1989. Pp. 28-53.

In a study of translation, compares the sensibility of the *Aeneid* to that of *Beowulf* to "get at what is distinctly medieval" about the latter (29). Unlike the *Aeneid*, *Beowulf* "aims to defend hard-won devices created in order to hold together a constantly splintering, often brutally militaristic society. The *Aeneid*'s audience needed to know how high above ordinary societies Rome soared. *Beowulf*'s audience, and particularly the princes and kings to whom it was in my judgment specifically directed, needed to know how to keep their world from collapsing" (31). Raffel concludes: "What the translator of *Beowulf* must do, it seems to me, is recognize and, as closely as he is able, transmit the poem's overwhelmingly protective, defensive, almost desperately guardianlike tone. The deliberate, exultant cadences of Virgil must give way to a poetic movement more halting, heavier, more circumscribed" (33). Also discusses the translation of *Sir Gawain and the Green Knight*, and Chrétien de Troyes' *Yvain*.

1718 Renoir, Alain. "The Hero on the Beach: Germanic Theme and Indo-European Origin." *NM* 90 (1989): 111-16.

Advances evidence that the hero-on-the-beach typescene, proposed by Crowne [S408], is not exclusively Germanic in origin but can be found in the Homeric poems and thus may possibly derive from Indo-European traditions. Contains a brief mention of *Beowulf*.

1719 Ross, Margaret Clunies. "Two of Þórr's Great Fights according to Hymiskviða." *Leeds Studies in English* n.s., 20 (1989): 7-27.

Though primarily an analysis of the *Hymiskviða*, mentions some points of comparison between *Beowulf* and the Old Norse poem: both bring together disparate mythic materials after an ideological shift (conversion to Christianity) and both contain elements of Proppian "wondertale" structure, though *Beowulf* is a purer example than the *Hymiskviða*, whose wondertale "syntagm" Ross diagrams.

1720 Stanley, Eric G. "A *Beowulf* Allusion, 1790." *N&Q* 36 (1989): 148.

Reports an overlooked reference to *Beowulf* in John Pinkerton's 1790 edition of John Barbour's *The Bruce*.

1721 ──────────. "Notes on Old English Poetry." *Leeds Studies in English* n.s., 20 (1989): 319-44.

Contains four notes on *Beowulf*. The first compares the opening formula of the poem to similar opening formulas in two Middle High German poems as well as in the Old English poems *Exodus*, *Juliana*, and *Andreas*, concluding that *Hwæt* since it does not alliterate, bears no metrical stress, that the words *wē* and *gefrūnon* are unusually far apart, and that first line contains a complex pattern of alliteration not present in other examples of the formula. The second note examines the "inceptive use of the non-alliterating initial position" (327), in particular the use of *cōm* 'came' as a function word, "a metrically unstressed pseudo-auxiliary" (329) in lines 702b, 710a, and 720a. Though it has been claimed that these three appearances of the word *cōm* contribute to the terror of the scene (Grendel's approach to the hall), Stanley points out that they occur in non-alliterating positions, and doubts that the poet had any notion of suspense here (see Renoir [S475]). The third note points out some cases in which alliteration gives exceptional stress to function words rather than to nouns. In line 563b, the alliteration foregrounds the pronoun *mē*, where Beowulf describes that it was *he* who was to be the feast of the water monsters in his youthful adventure. "Beowulf is the *me*, and that word is stressed and alliterates exceptionally.... In Beowulfs imagined account of what the monsters did not achieve, there is cruel irony, as he describes the feast they hoped for, a feast where they sit at a banquet near the bottom of the sea and Beowulf himself is food for them" (330). The fourth note discusses editorial punctuation and Old English syntax, arguing that in *Beowulf* in particular longer structures are "additive and annexive," using correlatives to build long paragraphs which stretch beyond the modern concept of the sentence (330). To give a sense of this sort of structure, Stanley takes an example passage (ll. 864-917a), repunctuates it (with fewer full stops), and offers a translation (relying on conjunctions and present participle constructions) to give a sense of the additive nature of the passage. Though long and complex, the sequence forms a single unit.

1722   Svec, Patricia Ward. "Water Words in *Beowulf*: Principles of Selection." *Ball State U Forum* 30 (1989): 5-13.

Examines words and compounds for water, concluding that the poet selected different words for water on the basis of alliteration, variation, and rhythm but also for "connotative value, exact expression and descriptive compounding" (13). Svec finds that *mere* refers exclusively to dark, foreboding water, discussing other words such as *sǣ* 'sea,' *hron-rād* 'whale road,' *swan-rād* 'swan road,' *gārsecg* 'spear man? spear sea,' compounds based on *-līðend* 'seafarer,' *strēam* 'stream,' and others.

1723   Tarzia, Wade. "The Hoarding Ritual in Germanic Epic Tradition." *Journal of Folklore Research* 26 (1989): 99-121.

Examines the role of treasure hoarding in *Beowulf* and the Sigurth legends in the light of recent theories about Bronze Age hoards, finding that *Beowulf* may preserve attitudes central to the ritual of hoarding. Following the archaeological work of Janet Levy, Tarzia believes that hoarding rituals eased tensions within a social group by enhancing the rank of the sacrificer, also taking valuable objects out of the hands of the powerful, thus easing the threat of social envy. Poems like *Beowulf* help to maintain the sanctity of the ritual long after the burial: "The primary message behind the poetry is this: *the deposition of the hoard must be maintained to prevent the recovery and circulation of the troublesome goods*" (107). Such is the function of the curse on the treasure (ll. 3051-57), which would have been a warning to would-be plunderers. The poem shows the disastrous consequences when the dragon's hoard is disturbed by a servant eager to regain his master's favor. Many critics have seen the uselessness of the treasure as an ironic conflict, since much stress is laid on the distribution of treasure as a proper kingly duty. Tarzia, however, explains that "a disturbed hoard must be returned to the place from which it came. The clash of the two themes . . . suggests that the poet is separated from the hoarding ritual by both time and religion" (111). Thus, Wiglaf appears as the ideal hoarding personality: he offers the disturbed hoard to public view and then buries it. Other characteristics of hoards in *Beowulf* and the Sigurth tale: a) hoards have a history of evil events, b) hoards have supernatural guardians, c) hoards must be returned to the place where they were originally found, d) if hoards are disturbed to increase social status, chaos breaks out. Includes a discussion of archaeological finds.

1724 Taylor, Paul Beekman. "Some Uses of Etymology in the Reading of Medieval Germanic Texts." In *Hermeneutics and Medieval Culture.* Ed. Patrick J. Gallacher and Helen Damico. Albany: SUNY Press, 1989. Pp. 109-120.

Postulates that in "traditional, or native, Germanic literatures, there is a recognizable style which draws attention to verbal polysemy, a style that is etymological in the sense that it isolates word elements so that they manifest latent meaning" (110) and traces such word play in *Beowulf* and other medieval Germanic texts. Taylor discusses a number of names in *Beowulf,* suggesting that the poet uses the technique of "refraction" ("breaking the name into its elements to point to its appropriate or inappropriate meaning" 112), to bring out their etymological meanings. Thus, in lines 2628b-29a, the poet uses the words *lāf* 'leaving, remnant' and *wīg* 'battle' to suggest meanings for the name *Wiglaf.* Similarly the poet repeats *-ferhþ* 'spirit, temper' close to the name *Hunferth* to cast doubt specifically on (H)unferth's cast of mind. Taylor finds a number of other etymological associations for these names in their contexts and also suggests that the poet employs refraction for Beowulf's name when he repeats the word *biorh* 'barrow' near it in lines 2806-07a: "it could appear that Beowulf is giving himself a new and final name—*Beorhwulf* ['barrow wulf']" (115). Finally, the poet plays with the words *untýdras* 'progeny' but also 'misbegotten progeny' (to qualify Grendel as a miscreated or unnatural enemy) and *gestrýnan* 'to win, obtain' but also 'to engender' (binding together the idea of treasure and genealogy). Contains brief notes on the names of Wealhtheow, Ongentheow, Ecgtheow (where the repetition of the root *-þēow* stresses etymological meaning).

1725   Teresawa, Jun. "Metrical Constraints on Old English Compounds." *Poetica* (Tokyo) 31 (1989): 1-16.

Explains the absence of possible compounds in *Beowulf* on the basis of two metrical constraints, accounting for many apparent exceptions with reference to epenthesis or syncopation. Though a number of synonyms could substitute for both elements in the compound *gūð-rinc* 'battle warrior,' Teresawa finds that many of the possible combinations do not appear and examines in detail compounds beginning with two synonyms for 'battle': *hild-* and *beado-*. He formulates the following rules: Metrical constraint I (which applies to *hilde-* type compounds) states that the poet avoids compounds with the combination _x-x. Metrical constraint II states that the sequence ~x-~x is avoided in poetic compounds (where ~ = short vowel), preventing *beado-* from forming a compound with the second element ~x or ~xx. Teresawa discusses exceptions to both constraints and looks at other compound systems (words for armor, hall, leader, etc.)

1726   Tripp, Raymond P., Jr. "Did Beowulf Have an 'Inglorious Youth'?" *SN* 61 (1989): 129-143.

Believes that Beowulf's reputation for an "inglorious youth" among the Geats arose "not from the hero's youthful shortcomings but from his later and altruistic refusal to accept Queen Hygd's offer of the throne after Hygelac's death" (130). After re-examining wording and syntax in lines 2177-89, Tripp proposes that the period of Beowulf's life referred to is not early youth but early maturity and also that the word *hēan*, usually glossed as 'lowly, mean, abject,' may carry literal, even legal connotations. Beowulf may be *hēan* [low], that is, *second* in command to Hygelac, Beowulf's *hēarra* [higher one, lord], and then to Heardred, in spite of Hygd's offer" (132). Beowulf's refusal of the throne reflects the fact that "He was gentle to the point of appearing slack" (134), a quality echoed in the last lines of the poem (ll. 3181-82).

Tripp finds a parallel to this situation in Alfred's translation of Boethius where the topic is the right exercise of power.

1727 Tristram, Hildegard L.C. "Der Insulare Alexander." [The Insular Alexander.] In *Kontinuität und Transformation der Antike im Mittelalter.* Ed. Willi Erzgräber. Sigmaringen: Jan Thorbecke Verlag, 1989. Pp. 129-55.

In a larger study of Alexander narratives in the Irish and Anglo-Saxon traditions, makes some observations about the Nowell codex, which contains *Beowulf* as well as *Alexander's Letter to Aristotle* and *Wonders of the East*, suggesting that the codex was not assembled arbitrarily and that it may owe something to the Anglo-Saxons' general conception of the East near the turn of the millennium (144). Tristram compares manuscript illustrations of the east in the *Mirabilia* (*Wonders of the East*) of the Nowell codex to those in later compilations (Cotton Tiberius B.v. and Bodley 614), finding evidence for a common tradition. She notes a number of similarities between the monsters of this pictorial tradition and the monsters in *Beowulf*. Such correspondences prompt the supposition that the illustrations of the Nowell codex as well as those of Cotton Tiberius B.v. reflect a common way of imagining the East about the year 1000.

1728 Weil, Susanne. "Grace under Pressure: 'Hand-Words,' *Wyrd*, and Free Will in *Beowulf*." *Pacific Coast Philology* 24 (1989): 94-104.

Noting the controversy over the concept of fate in the poem, Weil suggests a solution by seeing the power of the individual as the ultimate meaning of fate, a meaning reinforced by several gnomes and the strategic use of "hand" words. Weil points out that words for fate, like *gescipe*, come from roots meaning 'to shape,' as does the Old English word for the creator, *Scyppend* 'shaper.' The latter in particular must have had a pre-Christian meaning, but Germanic mythology provides no clue to the identity of this shaper. Weil suggests that it is the individual himself who shapes his destiny and that nine clusters of hand-words (including the name *Handscio*) appear in significant scenes to reinforce this idea, for the human hands shape and control. Gnomic statements (ll. 572b-73, 1534b-36, etc.) reinforce the idea that individual courage affects one's fate. Weil charts in detail the use of hand words in the battle between Beowulf and Grendel and suggests that this view of fate allows us to find "true compatibility between pagan and Christian ideas about the relationships of men to whatever force controlled the universe" (103). Finally, Beowulf himself "with that strength of thirty in his omnipresent hands, functions in the poem as a walking metaphor for the power of one's own will and courage to shape one's fate" (101).

1729 Ziegler, Heide. "Love's Labours Won: The Erotics of Contemporary Parody." In *Intertextuality and Contemporary American Fiction*. Ed. Patrick O'Donnell and Robert Con Davis. Baltimore: Johns Hopkins UP, 1989. Pp. 58-71.

Explores the intertextuality of John Gardner's *Grendel* [S793], including several remarks on Gardner's transformation of *Beowulf.*

1990

1729a Abbott, Joe. "Tolkien's Monsters: Concept and Function in *The Lord of the Rings (Part III): Sauron.*" *Mythlore* 16 (1990): 51-59.

Compares the monsters in Tolkien's *Lord of the Rings* to those in *Beowulf*.

1730 Bammesberger, Alfred. "The Conclusion of Wealhtheow's Speech (*Beowulf* 1231)." *NM* 91 (1990): 207-08.

Proposes a new analysis of the grammar of line 1231, *druncne dryhtguman dōð swā ic bidde*, taking *dryhtguman* as vocative (rather than nominative) and *dōð* as imperative (rather than indicative). Bammesberger provides the following translation: "oh retainers, having drunk [the royal mead], do as I ask!" (208). He accepts Robinson's contention [1513] that the phrase *druncne dryhtguman* refers to noblemen who have drunk royal mead in a drinking ritual, not to inebriated warriors.

1731 _____. "Die Lesart in *Beowulf* 1382a." [The Reading of *Beowulf* 1382a]. *Anglia* 108 (1990): 314-26.

Proposes that the form *wund-* followed by four minims in line 1382a should be construed as *wundnu*, most likely a Northumbrian form of the weak adjective *wundnan* or perhaps also a Northumbrian form of the instrumental with *-u* and that the form requires no emendation. Bammesberger rejects Wrenn's *wundini* [S276] and Kiernan's *wundun* [1261] on linguistic grounds, doubting that the form of this word sheds any light on the dating of *Beowulf*, since its occurrence is possible over a wide span of time.

1732 Clark, George. *Beowulf*. Twayne English Authors Series, 477. Boston: Twayne, 1990. Pp. xvi + 170.

A general introduction to the poem, with a selected bibliography (with brief annotations) as well as a chronology of major characters, events, and key points in the history of the transmission of the poem. Chapter one, "*Beowulf* to Our Time," reviews several strands of *Beowulf* scholarship, centering on the implications of Tolkien's British Academy lecture [S130] for a Christian reading of the poem, for structural and thematic interpretations. Chapter two,

"Traditions and the Poem," reviews the folktale-mythic backgrounds to the text as well as the relevance of proposed Germanic and Celtic influences. Chapter three, "The Heroic Age, Ideal, and Challenge," explores the importance of rightful kingship and heroic behavior, while chapters four ("The War against the Monsters—Past and Present in the Poem") and five ("The Old Kings—The Great Battles: Settings and Origins") provide a reading of major events and themes. In an afterword, Clark anticipates future trends in *Beowulf* studies, including the likely importance of archaeological research as well as new developments in lexicography and calls for more work on social backgrounds, predicting that post-structuralist readings may provide some new perspectives on narrative structure.

Reviews: R.D. Wissolik, *Choice* 28 (1990): 481; *OEN* 25.2 (1992): 45-46.

1733 Creed, Robert P. *Reconstructing the Rhythm of 'Beowulf'*. Columbia, MO: U of Missouri P, 1990. Pp. xiii + 216; ill.

Provides the following summary: "This study attempts to reconstruct the prosody of *Beowulf*.... Beginning with the manuscript text of *Beowulf*, I first show that it is possible to construct a working definition of the largest prosodic unit of the poem, the verse line, and to test that definition by eliciting verse lines systematically from the syllables as they are indicated in the text. Next, I show that each halfline consists of what I first refer to as *halfline constituents* . . . but later designate as *measures*, of which there are usually two but occasionally three in a halfline. Finally, I analyze every measure into two *Fine Parts*. The first Part contains a stressed syllable about 80 percent of the time; the second Part far more often than not contains an unstressed syllable or syllables. The disposition of the syllables into Fine Parts can be accounted for by a simple hypothesis: the two Fine Parts of the measure indicate *rhythm*. The first Part usually contains the syllable or syllables that mark the heavier downbeat; the second Part contains the syllable or syllables that mark the lighter upbeat. The relationship between the two Parts of the measure indicates the dynamic of the prosody: syllables are clustered together in each Part of the measure to mark the two phases of a rhythm. Two, sometimes three, measures repeat this rhythm in each halfline. The analysis of the measure into its constituents makes this study more than merely descriptive and static; it indicates at every level the relationships among hierarchically organized constituents" (5-6).

Creed provides an extensive analysis of lines 1-315 and 2946-3054, isolating their halfline constituents and measures and relineating them as outlined above. Includes appendices listing procedures for eliciting verse lines and half lines from manuscript lines, indicating how to scan verse of an edited text and explaining the encoding of syllables for computer analysis.

C.T. Berkhout, *Manuscripta* 35 (1991): 55-57; *OEN* 25.2 (1992): 42-43; C.B. Kendall, *Speculum* 67 (1992): 651-53.

1734 Cronan, Dennis. "Old English Water-Lands." *ELN* 27 (1990): 6-9.

Finds support for reading ēaland (l. 2333a) as 'coast' rather than 'island' from an interlinear gloss in the *Rushworth Gospels* containing the word ēaland (Psalms 6:23), though the supposed parallels in *Andreas*, *The Phoenix*, and *Solomon and Saturn* are shown to mean 'island.'

1734a Damico, Helen, and Alexandra Hennessey Olsen. "Introduction." In *New Readings*, pp. 1-26.

Introducing a volume of essays on women in Old English literature, makes some remarks on critical approaches to *Beowulf*, pointing out the often overlooked contributions of women scholars and critics and the male orientation of much of the criticism on the poem. Traditional analyses of the structure of *Beowulf* such as Tolkien's [S130] see the poem as a two-part structure revolving around male heroic characters but more or less ignoring the women in the center portion. Newer readings, including those of Rogers [S309], Hume [S962], and Chance [1536], however, opt for a tripartite structure which gives equal weight to the women characters (Grendel's mother in particular). Also discusses modern feminist literary criticism and surveys the extant criticism on women in Old English literature.

1735 Damon, John. "The Raven in *Beowulf* 1801: Bird of a Different Color." *Work in Progress (Dept. of English, U of Arizona)* 1 (1990): 60-70.

Argues that the raven which heralds the morning in lines 1801-02a may derive from an ancient literary tradition of the white raven (seen in Ovid's *Metamorphoses*, 2.534-41) while the ravens of slaughter and death in other parts of the poem belong to another, and that the adjective *blāca*, describing the raven, comes from OE *blāc* 'bright, shining, white' (related to ModE *bleach*) rather than *blæc* 'black,' as previously assumed. Damon surveys other uses of the word *blāc* in *Beowulf*, finding that they mean 'shining or white' and that the poet never uses *blæc* 'black.' In a number of Scandinavian sagas, which Damon surveys, the raven appears as a herald of dawn and announces and praises the hero. On the other hand, the tradition of the raven originally white but transformed into black (seen in Ovid's story of Phoebus' raven and retold by Aldhelm) revolves around the fact "that the state of the soul can be mirrored in the images of the black raven and its white counterpart" (67). Associating the young Beowulf with the white raven provides "a mirror for the state of Beowulf's soul, his purity of motive and deed" (68), while the crows of bloodshed and carnage which follow may imply the tainting quality of "a repeating cycle of bloodshed and fatality" (69).

1736 Duggan, Hoyt. "Scribal Self-Correction and Editorial Theory." *NM* 91 (1990): 215-227.

Argues against Kiernan's thesis [1261] that patterns of scribal correction show the text of *Beowulf* to be exceptionably reliable. Instead, Duggan shows that even manuscripts with a great number of self-corrections may contain many errors and misreadings, judged on the evidence of texts existing in multiple copies. Patterns of self-correction "cannot be used, as Kiernan proposed in the case of the *Beowulf* codex, to justify a conservative editorial policy. . . . The high rate of success in removing error that Kiernan claims for the *Beowulf* scribes . . . is not, lacking at least one other manuscript for comparison, capable of rational demonstration" (225). Much of the article concerns Mary Hamel's study of the self-corrections of the Middle English scribe Robert Thornton, who copied the *Morte Arthure* and other central Middle English texts.

1737 Foley, John Miles. *Traditional Oral Epic: 'The Odyssey,' 'Beowulf,' and the Serbo-Croatian Return Song*. Berkeley: U of California P, 1990. Pp. xi + 424.

Includes two chapters on *Beowulf* in a book-length study of oral epics in ancient Greek, Old English, and Serbo-Croatian, stressing differences in oral technique in the three traditions. Chapter six, "Traditional Phraseology in *Beowulf* and Old English Poetry," finds that the stress-based meter of Old English, as opposed to the colon-based or quantitative meters of the Homeric epics and the Serbo-Croatian songs, imposes a different set of constraints on formulaic composition. Further, the concept of formula or half-line is not sufficient to characterize the complex traditional patterns in *Beowulf* and Old English poetry: "alongside the classical half-line phrase stand single words, whole-line patterns, multi-line patterns, collocations, clusters, and themes. Likewise, even within these different categories not all members are equivalent; some formulaic systems are more variable than others" (235). To investigate this complexity, Foley analyzes in detail the traditional phraseology in Grendel's approach to Heorot (ll. 702b-30a), finding that a number of phrases that look like formulas cannot really be classified that way and pleads for a non-reductive approach to Old English meter and formulaics. This re-evaluation reveals that *word-type placement* forms the most far-reaching and pivotal set of rules (that is, rules which govern the placement of single words on the basis of their metrical and grammatical types). Foley lists nine interconnected rules for word-type placement found in *Beowulf* and goes on to describe briefly other rule systems, including those for collocations (alliterating pairs of words or roots), clusters (association of words outside of alliterative constraints), theme, and special rhetorical structures such as litotes.

Chapter nine, "Thematic Structure in *Beowulf* and Old English Poetry," argues that *Beowulf* and Old English poetry in general employ traditional narrative themes or type-scenes which have recognizable units and follow a particular traditional sequence as the Homeric and Serbo-Croatian epics do, but unlike themes in these two traditions, Old English narrative themes generally lack a high degree of verbal repetition, mainly due to the differing metrical conditions of Old English verse. After cataloguing twenty-four Old English themes or type-scenes identified by other scholars, Foley goes on to examine the theme of the "sea voyage" in *Beowulf*, finding three main occurrences: Beowulf's departure for Denmark (ll. 205-303a), Beowulf's return to Geatland (ll. 1880b-1919), and (in foreshortened form) Scyld's "departure" by funeral ship (ll. 26-52). From the first two, he derives the following basic structure: "A. Beowulf leads his men to the ship; B. The ship waits, moored; C. The men board the ship, carrying treasure; D. Departure, voyage on the sea, arrival; E. They moor the ship" (338). Various motifs concerning armor and meetings with a coast-warden are interspersed. Scyld's funeral follows this same pattern: the men are led to the ship, which is moored. They load treasure into it, and finally the ship departs. Instead of the final mooring, however, the poet claims that no one knows who received the cargo (ll. 50b-52). "the conspicuous absence of the traditional closure in the mooring of the ship powerfully evokes the cosmic overtones of this last and special journey" (343-44). Foley finds only limited patterns of verbal repetition between these scenes.

Reviews: E. Segal, *TLS* 12 July 1991: 3; *OEN* 25.2 (1992): 45; J.B. Hainsworth, *Slavonic and East European Rev.* 70 (1992): 311-12; J.L. Perkowski, *Slavic and East European J* 36 (1992): 266-67.

1738 Frantzen, Allen J. *Desire for Origins: New Language, Old English, and Teaching the Tradition.* New Brunswick, NJ: Rutgers UP, 1990. Pp. xviii + 260.

Includes a chapter on *Beowulf* entitled "Writing the Unreadable *Beowulf*," arguing that nineteenth-century editors and critics in particular have desired a complete, unified *Beowulf* and have produced it by re-reading and re-editing the poem, despite the fact that it has various unfillable gaps, both textual and narrative. Thus a knowledge of the history of textual editing (for example, the editorial reconstructions at ll. 389-90 and l. 2221) is essential to understanding the way "editors unavoidably rewrite and interpret the poems they publish" (172). Traditional readings seek to settle difficult questions (the pagan or Christian background or Beowulf's pride, for example) once and for all, though "the illusive and allusive nature of writing and reading in *Beowulf* discourages us from acts of closure, and indeed prevents those acts of interpretation ... sought by conventional criticism" (190). Instead, Frantzen suggests that teachers engage their students with the reception of the poem as a "vigorous alternative" (191) to such conventional approaches and proceeds to examine the political and institutional contexts of the work of Sharon Turner [S4], John Conybeare [S7], Benjamin Thorpe [S10], John Kemble [S8], Karl Müllenhoff [S13], N.F.S. Grundtvig [S6, S11], and other early editors and scholars. Students should also be encouraged to compare translations. Includes other suggestions for teaching the poem on the graduate and undergraduate levels and contains a critique of Bessinger and Yeager's *Approaches to Teaching 'Beowulf.'*

Reviews: A. Olsen, *In Geardagum* 12 (1991): 63-66; M. Griffith, *MÆ* 61 (1992): 118-19; *OEN* 25.2 (1992): 7-8.

1739   Galloway, Andrew. "*Beowulf* and the Varieties of Choice."
       PMLA 105 (1990): 197-208.

   Surveys expressions of choice, through uses of the verb
(ge)ceōsan 'to choose,' in order to "illuminate some issues and
terms that intersect and complicate the concept of fate and
doom in *Beowulf* and other Anglo-Saxon literature" (197).
Galloway surveys the use of *(ge)cēosan* in a number of Old
English texts, both heroic and Christian, concluding that
heroic poetry, including *Beowulf*, tends to see human
behavior in terms of fate, not choice, and the appearance of
the verb *(ge)cēosan* is often restricted to formulaic
expressions. Christian poetry on the other hand dwells on
moral choice at length. The *Beowulf* poet uses the verb eight
times, each time in a remarkable way. In line 1759b,
Hrothgar urges Beowulf to *ðæt selre gecēos* "choose the
better part," an injunction which "imbues the verb *(ge)cēosan*
with a force found nowhere else in the poetic corpus: the verb
describes an ability to choose with the efficacy and clarity of
theological choice, but within the social contexts of this
world" (202). In this and two other cases, Christian choice
proceeds from an earthly context. In deciding to fight the
dragon, Beowulf does not seem so much to choose as to react
inevitably to a threat only he can meet. Finally, Beowulf (as a
pagan) "is sealed off from Christian ideals," though the poet
explores "the middle ground of social and political choice,
common to Christians and pre-Christians" (206).

1740   Guidall, George. *Beowulf.* New York: Recorded Books,
       1990. 3 cassettes.

   An unabridged recording of the Gummere translation
[F720], read by George Guidall. Includes program notes.
   Reviews: J. Owen, *Library J* 116 (1991):124; *Publisher's
Weekly* 238.6 (1991): 45-46.

1741   Hanley, Wayne. "Grendel's Humanity Again." *In
       Geardagum* 11 (1990): 5-13.

   Surveys a number of studies on the humanity of Grendel,
including Baird [S572], Chapman [S315], Dragland [S1025],
Feldman [1244], O'Keefe [1271], Taylor [1516], Tripp
[1466], and others, also reviewing the epithets used of
Grendel, his position as an exile, and his human behavior.
Hanley concludes that "Grendel's actions, names, and

ancestry all point to a 'man,' not a 'monster,'" though his monstrous deeds cannot be denied (10).

1742 Harris, Anne Leslie. "The Vatic Mode in *Beowulf.*" *Neophil* 74 (1990): 591-600.

Identifies and discusses three types of prophecy in the poem: 1) references to events that will occur later in the poem itself, i.e., foreshadowing; 2) passages that affirm truths for the situation of the characters but also for the poet and his contemporary audience; and 3) passages that refer to events after the death of Beowulf but before the time of the audience. Harris denies that the original audience needed to possess a wide knowledge of Germanic lore and argues that the poem as an oral performance "appeals constantly to a listener and pulls him into the chronologically restrictive mode of hearing rather than the leisurely reflexivity of reading" (592). Given these conditions, prophecy depends on the reader's ability to verify, cross-reference, and judge character as the plot unfolds. "Prophecy in *Beowulf* is a mode of historical understanding.... The prophecies of the poem, narrative-bound, gnomic, and non-context-bound, all cue an audience to watch the characters who can draw conclusions, who share values expressed as still having value for the poet's contemporaries, and who promise no more than they can perform. Such figures give history meaning and direction, and thus are prophets" (598). Harris discusses Beowulf's prophecy about the feud between the Danes and the Heathobards, the Messenger's prophecy about the demise of the Geats after Beowulf's death, as well as prophecies about the destruction of Heorot in fire. In the last category of prophecy, she finds a Virgilian tone and notes parallels to prophecy in the Aeneid.

1743 Hasegawa, Hiroshi. *'Beowulf': The Fight with Grendel (Part 1)*. Tokyo: Seibido, 1990.

A partial student edition of *Beowulf* with facing Japanese translation. (HH)

1744 Hasenfratz, Robert. "The Theme of the 'Penitent Damned' and its Relation to *Beowulf* and *Christ and Satan*." *Leeds Studies in English* n.s., 21 (1990): 45-69.

Suggests that the depiction of Grendel as a sorrowful creature may have been influenced by a tradition that the damned undergo belated penitence in hell, a tradition available to the poet in various vernacular homilies as well as the *Visio Sancti Pauli*. Hasenfratz finds a number of verbal parallels between descriptions of hell in *Beowulf* and those in vernacular homilies and penitential poems. These include a gnome about the fate of the dead (ll. 183b-188), the epithets *wonsǣli wer* 'unhappy man' (l. 105a) and *earmlīc* 'miserable, pitiable' (l. 807a) as applied to Grendel, and a phrase describing Grendel's realization that his end has come (ll. 821b-22a)—for which Hasenfratz advances parallels from the vernacular homilies in the Blickling and Vercelli collections. Finds a similar pattern in the depiction of Satan in *Christ and Satan*.

1745 Hill, Joyce. "'Þæt Wæs Geōmuru Ides!': A Female Stereotype Examined." In *New Readings*, pp. 235-47.

Finds that the limited roles attributed to royal women in Old English poetry have a "fundamental historical reality" (239), but that when history transforms itself into heroic legend, the stereotype of the sorrowing woman dominates, finding both elements in the women of *Beowulf*. Hill first outlines the role of historical Germanic queens, describing their informal power as childbearers, counselors to the king, keepers of the dynastic line, and unofficial arbiters of succession. Their exercise of power is acceptable only if in a domestic and deferential manner, "contributing to dynastic stability, offering counsel, and upholding the dignity and status of the king through participation in the important practices of gift-exchange" (237). Wealhtheow and Hygd both participate in such public gift-giving. Wealhtheow counsels Hrothgar and uses her informal power to attempt to insure the succession of her sons. Hygd's delicate position in the Geatish dynastic struggles also seems realistically drawn as is Freawaru's role as political pawn between the Danes and Heathobards. However, the roles of these women are clearly subordinate to those of the men, with Freawaru in particular reduced to a "mere cipher" (239). Heroic legend transformed these limited historical roles of women into a single, predominate stereotype, that of the passive, sorrowing woman, thus emphasizing female helplessness. The *Beowulf*-poet uses this stereotype of the *geōmuru ides* 'sad lady' (l. 1075b) "to define the essentials of heroic tragedy," while the stereotyped male role of warrior embodies active heroic and social ideals (241). Hildeburh plays this part in the Finnsburh episode, as do the sorrowing women at Beowulf's funeral. The stereotype is also a factor in the characterization of women like Wealhtheow and Hygd, whose limited power and security will come to an end outside the frame of the story. Our reaction to these women is shaped by the dominant stereotype, "that the noble woman is, in the end, essentially helpless" (243).

1746 Hill, Thomas D. "'Wealhtheow' as a Foreign Slave: Some Continental Analogues." *PQ* 69 (1990): 106-12.

Speculates that the problematic meaning of Wealhtheow's name, 'foreign servant or slave,' might be explained by the practice of early Merovingian kings, some of whom married peasants, the most famous of whom was Bathild, a former Anglo-Saxon slave who married a Frankish king and produced heirs, a story described by Gregory of Tours. Such a hypothesis would shed a different light on Wealhtheow's concerns about the succession, especially since her sons would be defenseless after Hrothgar's death, having no powerful kinsmen on their mother's side.

1747 _____. "Beowulf as Seldguma: *Beowulf*, lines 247-51." *Neophil* 74 (1990): 637-39.

Believes that an Anglo-Saxon law code may shed light on the Coastguard's exclamation that Beowulf is no *seldguma* 'retainer' (ll. 247a-51a). Here, *seldguma* seems to designate "a man who was not an aristocrat, but who nonetheless served in a king's retinue" (638). Hill cites a law in the treatise "A Compilation on Status," edited by Dorothy Whitelock, which states that a *ceorl* 'freeman' may be elevated to noble status only by the acquisition of five hides of land. A *ceorl* who merely possesses a helmet, mailcoat, and sword (the weapons of an aristocrat) without the land is not considered noble. Since a foreigner like the Coastguard might mistake a *ceorl* for an aristocrat, he raises and then confidently dismisses this possibility: "Beowulf's aristocratic and heroic stature are so obvious that he must be what in fact he is—a man born to high status and the descendant of kings" (638). This reading highlights "the intensely aristocratic, royalist views of the *Beowulf*-poet" as well as his "almost obsessive concern with weapons and adornment" (638).

1748 Howard, Patricia J. "Irony of Fate in Cecelia Holland's *Two Ravens*: Echoes of *Beowulf* and Icelandic Saga." *The Comparatist* 14 (1990): 15-25.

Believes that *Beowulf* (as well as a number of Icelandic sagas) has influenced Cecelia Holland's novel *The Two Ravens*, set in twelfth-century Iceland.

1749 Hudson, Marc. *'Beowulf': A Translation and Commentary*. Lewisburg, PA: Bucknell UP, 1990. Pp. 178.

Translates the poem into modern English using a four-stress, non-alliterative line, attempting to "bring verse closer to the spoken language" (33) in the tradition of Yeats, Eliot, Williams, and Frost. Includes discussions of translation theory, diction, syntax as well as a critique of a number of *Beowulf* translations. Hudson analyzes in detail his translation of three passages: Unferth's challenge to Beowulf (ll. 506-15), the Finnsburh Episode (ll. 1069-1159), the Father's Lament (ll. 2455-61). Lines 4-11: "Time and again, Scyld Scefing dispossessed ravening bands of their mead benches,/ spread terror among men—he who, at first,/ was a mere foundling: for that he had recompense,/ he grew strong under the heavens, prospered in honors/ until his power reached to outlying princes/ beyond the whale's domain: they must kneel to him,/ yielding tribute. That was a good king!"
Reviews: R.P. Tripp, Jr. *In Geardagum* 12 (1991): 60-62; D.D. Evans, *Choice* 28 (1991): 1308; H.D. Chickering, *Speculum* 67 (1992): 689-94; M. Griffith, *MÆ* 61 (1992): 166-67; *OEN* 25.2 (1992): 52.

1750 Irving, Edward B., Jr. "*Beowulf*." *AN&Q* n.s., 3 (1990): 65-69.

Reviews several schools of criticism on the poem: historical-philological approaches, New Criticism, the patristic or neo-exegetical approach, oral-formulaic theory, feminist theory, and other newer approaches. Irving credits New Criticism for supplying an enduring critical vocabulary but warns that the exterior contexts demanded and proposed by more recent literary critics need to be viewed skeptically. With regard to dating the poem, it is important not to "confuse hunches with demonstrable truth" (66). He finds the oral-formulaic approach more promising than feminist readings or the patristic approach, which is "now certainly in decline if not in rout" (66). Finally, Irving makes a plea that future work on the poem respect "the physical text" (68).

1751 Jager, Eric. "Speech and Chest in Old English Poetry: Orality or Pectorality?" *Speculum* 65 (1990): 845-59.

Locates the chest rather than the mouth as the primary seat of speech, feeling, intellect, and vital functions in Homeric epic and Old English literature, concluding that in *Beowulf* such imagery "reflects an essentially pre-Christian notion of pectorality," overlaid with spiritual symbolism, but that *Genesis B* "reflects a heavily theologized notion of pectorality." In *Beowulf*, "Verbal prowess is collocated in the chest along with the vital powers and moral virtue, making the chest a 'center of action,' and a symbolic repository of heroic values" (849). Jager shows how the poet, through words such as *brēost-hord*, *word-hord*, *breōst-gehgyd*, *hreðer*, and *bearm* connects the idea of the chest with that of treasure hoards: "As the physical source of the individual's speech, and as the figurative repository of communal verbal resources, the *brēosthord* is part of a pervasive pectoral metaphorics in the poem" (852). He detects an explicit analogy between the dragon's barrow and Beowulf's chest (ll. 2542-58): both are hollow cavities, producing a kind of vocal utterance, fire from the barrow and a weapon-like word from Beowulf's chest, while Beowulf's barrow itself becomes a chest-hoard which speaks Beowulf's fame. Such chest/hoard images cluster in the dragon-fight section. Jager also analyzes images of pectorality in *Genesis B*.

1752 Karibe, Tsunenori. "*Beowulf* with its Japanese Translation Facing the Original (2)." *Bulletin of the Faculty of the Liberal Arts (Niigata Univ.)* 21 (1990): 187-227.

Edits and translates (into Japanese) lines 1251-2199 of *Beowulf*. See part one, Karibe [1702a], for a fuller description.

1753 Karkov, Catherine and Robert T. Farrell. "The Gnomic Passages in *Beowulf*." *NM* 91 (1990): 295-310.

Using the definition of a gnome formulated by Kenneth Jackson, classifies gnomic sayings into three categories and examines "the way in which major gnomic passages function within the poem, with particular attention given to elements of meter, punctuation and syntax" (295). Karkov and Farrell examine several individual gnomes of the following three types: gnomes dealing with the unknown (ll. 50b-52, 162b-63, and 3062b-65), specifically religious gnomes (ll. 440b-41,

456b, 572b-73, 930b-31, 1663b-64a, and 2291-93a), and instructional gnomes (making up two-thirds of the gnomic passages, four of the most important of which are in lines 20-25, 1057b-62, 2442-62a, and 3174b-77). Gnomes dealing with the unknown provide transitions between sections. Religious gnomes, on the other hand, are grouped in the middle of the poem, are spoken by Beowulf or Hrothgar five out of six times and are all clearly marked with punctuation in the manuscript, emphasizing their importance. Instructional gnomes are often connected to the historical "digressions," for "what the gnome establishes as an abstract principle, the historical episode backs up with concrete example" (303). Includes a discussion of several linguistic features of the gnome: the appearance of the modal auxiliary (*sceal* and *mæg*) and the verb *bið* as special gnomic markers, the repetition of key words, internal rhyme, and double alliteration within gnomes. Karkov and Farrell point out the speeches of Hrothgar (ll. 1724b-57) and Beowulf (ll. 2425-2509) are heavily gnomic. "The gnomic passages are highlighted by both theme and syntax, marked off from the narrative while simultaneously uniting the various parts of the poem" (307).

1754 Lucas, Peter J. "*Beowulf* 224: *Eolet æt Ende*." *N&Q* 37 (1990): 263-64.

After reviewing other *æt ende* constructions in Old English poetry, proposes that the difficult phrase *eoletes æt ende* (l. 224a) be emended to its metrically sounder equivalent *eolet wæs æt ende* and translated (in context) as "Then the sea was traversed, the water-stream at an end" (264), and *eolet* could mean "the water connecting (Geatland and Denmark)." For the word *eolet*, Lucas follows Holthausen, who takes the first element of the word to be *ēa*- 'water,' and Horgan [S495], who derives *-let* from *lǣtan* 'to pass.'

1755 _____. "The Place of Judith in the *Beowulf*-Manuscript." *RES* 41 (1990): 463-78.

Proposes a new ordering of the quires in the *Beowulf* manuscript, relocating quire 14 (containing Judith) to the beginning of the manuscript with a proposed lost quire *0 connecting old quire 14 with the present quire 1 (containing the *Life of St. Christopher*) and suggesting that "the *Beowulf*-manuscript is a compilation based on two collections, one containing *Judith* and *Christopher*, from which *io*-spellings have been eliminated, and one comprising *Marvels, Alexander's Letter*, and *Beowulf*, in which *io*-spellings were still relict" (474).

1756 Mitchell, Bruce. "*Beowulf*, line 1020b: *brand* or *bearn*?" In *Studi sulla cultura germanica*. Ed. M.A. D'Aronco. Romanobarbarica, 10. Rome: Herder, 1990. Pp. 283-92.

Rejects the customary emendation of MS. *brond* to *bearn* in line 1020b, arguing that the phrase *brond Healfdenes* is accusative and refers to Hrothgar's giving his grandfather's sword to Beowulf and that this sword is synonymous with the *mǣre māðþum-sweord* 'famous treasure-sword' of line 1203a and the sword described by Beowulf in ll. 2152-62. Without the emendation, the sentence has no expressed subject, a situation which Mitchell finds feasible, especially in light of Watanabe's analysis of subject-deletion in *Beowulf* and the *Heliand*. Mitchell further endorses a number of Watanabe's suggestions [1522, 1637a].

1756a ———. *A Critical Bibliography of Old English Syntax to the End of 1984 including Addenda and Corrigenda to 'Old English Syntax'*. Oxford: Basil Blackwell, 1990.

Provides an annotated bibliography of scholarship on Old English syntax to the end of 1984, with a section devoted to the syntax of individual poems, including *Beowulf*. Also contains addenda and corrigenda to Mitchell [1501].

1757 Morus, Iwan Rhys. "Uprooting the Golden Bough: J.R.R. Tolkien's Response to Nineteenth Century Folklore and Comparative Mythology." *Mallorn* 27 (1990): 5-9.

Contains a brief reference to Tolkien's famous British Academy lecture [S130] in an analysis of Tolkien's reaction to developments in nineteenth-century folklore and mythology studies. Essentially, Tolkien "was fighting two battles. Against Müller and the Comparative Mythologists he was fighting for the integrity and truth of mythological language whilst against the Folklorists he was fighting for the individual integrity of the authors of myth. The two battles coincided in his attempt as a Catholic to preserve the reality and singularity of the Christian myth and its author" (7).

1758 North, Richard J. "Tribal Loyalties in the *Finnsburh Fragment* and Episode." *Leeds Studies in English* n.s., 21 (1990): 13-43.

Undertakes a new reconstruction of the narrative underlying the allusive Finnsburh episode (ll. 1063-1159) and the *Finnsburh Fragment*, avoiding the unrestrained emendations and frequent recourse to the "heroic code" employed by previous scholars. North accepts only three emendations in the episode: *hē[o] ǣr mǣste hēold*, i[n]cge gold and *Finne [ea]l unhlitme* (ll. 1079b, 1107b, 1128b-29a) and offers the following reconstructed sequence, based on Germanic law and custom from a number of sources, including Old Norse materials. The reconstruction revolves around two proposals, first that there are Jutes on both sides and, second, that Finn requires Hengest to swear an oath of loyalty on the gold of the god Ing, ensuring that Hengest will not break his oath, since Ing is the patron of both Hengest and the Frisian royal house. Hengest stays in Frisia over the winter, though he was free to leave, because he secretly wishes to incite Finn's Jutes and Frisians to break the treaty. "For this reason he agrees to a Danish plan by which he makes over his command, and thereby his liability for the oath, to one of Hnæf's Scylding kinsmen" (15). Thus, when Hunlaf puts a sword in Hengest's lap he makes Hengest his vassal and takes over as leader of the Half-Danes. The Danes use Hengest to kill Finn, because Hengest is the only Dane whom Finn will allow close to his person (because of the oath to Ing). Hengest thus acts as an assassin, and the Danes loot Finn's home and take Hildeburh back to Denmark" (15). Also discusses the word *eoten* 'giants' or 'Jutes,' suggesting that the two proposed meanings are not irreconcilable: "in the Episode the poet may envisage 'Jutes' as a crowd of uncanny people grown out of an archaic race of 'giants'" (37). The reconstruction suggests new motivations for Hengest: "What is Hengest's dilemma, therefore, but the paralysis of an outmanoeuvred player? The Finnsburh Episode proceeds in this way more as a game of chess than a case study on heroic honour" (38).

1759 Oshitari, Kinshiro. *Beowulf*. Tokyo: Kenkyusha, 1990. In Japanese.

Translation of the poem into Japanese. Not seen.

1760 _____. "Reading Between the Lines of *Beowulf*." In *Studies in English Philology in Honour Shigeru Ono*. Ed. Koichi Jin. Tokyo: Nanundeo, 1990. Pp. 415-34. In Japanese with English summary.

Suggests that the literary sensibility of the *Beowulf*-poet is foreign enough to modern readers to force us to complete the poem by imagining and adding elements more congenial to modern tastes: "Since we have different literary taste and are little informed of what the audience of *Beowulf* must have known well, we are obliged to read the poem, supplying what is omitted, in order to appreciate it. At the same time, we cannot grasp the artistic effect of the poem just as it is without dismissing from our mind what we have supplied" (433). Oshitari discusses the poem's narrative technique, descriptions, characterization, pointing out that "there are parts left untold and portions only vaguely described. They are quite alien from those of more or less realistic works. As for persons, for example, character portrayal or psychological description is almost totally absent. The natural description is lacking in colour terms and what appeals to our eye is chiefly light and darkness, while kinesthetic imagery is dominant" (433). Instead of these things, the poet focuses on "human values and feelings" such as loyalty, hospitality, pride, glory, mutability, etc.

1761 Overing, Gillian R. *Language, Sign, and Gender in 'Beowulf'*. Carbondale: Southern Illinois UP, 1990. Pp. xxvi + 137; ill.

A book-length study which draws on insights from deconstruction, semiotics, and feminist theory, insisting that readings of *Beowulf* resist the urge to achieve interpretive closure but that the open-ended, dynamic nature of the text be recognized. Overing uses the central image of weaving and webs as well as Derrida's idea of *différance* to account for the text as an on-going process rather than a finished work.

Chapter one, "Language: An Overview in Process," argues that the poetics of Old English verse is more metonymic (with elements placed side by side) than metaphoric and that metonymy (in contrast to metaphor) suggests "flexibility of association and meaning; resistance to conclusion or decisive interpretation; avoidance of interpreting one thing in terms of another in favor of seeing those things for themselves; deferral, which can be indefinite, of resolving meaning into a static or fixed core; emphasis on the here-and-now of immediate perception, on the process and experience of meaning construction rather than on its end-product" (8). Metaphor, on the other hand, moves to resolve meaning by providing a fixed center for comparison. Overing sees metonymic qualities in Old English compounds, syntax, and narrative structure (digressions), distinguishing metonymy from Robinson's idea of apposition [1513] by its greater open-endedness. Overing examines lines 210-24 in detail.

Chapter two, "Swords and Signs: Dynamic Semeiosis in *Beowulf*," applies Charles Pierce's semiotic theories to sword imagery, finding that sword signs (as well as those for cups and rings) tend to form what Pierce calls an index rather than a symbol and that this "indexicality" resembles the interlace technique in Anglo-Saxon metalwork and manuscript illustration. In Pierce's three-fold system, an icon (an example of "firstness") foregrounds the physical attributes of a material object, while an index ("secondness") accrues meaning as a sign (a sword, cup, or ring) recurs throughout a text, indexing itself against the other occurrences and forging rich interconnections. Finally a symbol ("thirdness") suggests a kind of synthesis, though one which is unlike the closure of metaphor (see chapter one) in that thirdness is the result of a dynamic process between reader and text. "Secondness" dominates the poem, particularly in its use of signs like swords, which form "interwoven networks of association" and have an "indexical connective force" (43). However, critics have been too anxious to resolve oppositions and indexes into definitive hierarchies. Overing traces the indexicality of cup images which set up "a kind of chain reaction" (49) which she diagrams. Each time a new cup appears it reacts with and alters the index established by the other cups. The cup index points to attempts to establish unity or peace by a drinking ritual. The index built around references to the neckring given to Beowulf by Wealhtheow creates palpable irony, since the ring was worn by Hygelac on his last expedition, but it also connects past, future, and present. The sword index, in a similar way, "holds past, present, and future perspectives before us in a process of inevitable and dynamic coalition" (52). In Hrothgar's sermon (ll. 1700-84), the sword sign moves from index to symbol, it becomes a symbol of "change, or death, or transience, or mortality" (62). Finally, Overing asks "how or if we move from the dynamic indexicality of Secondness to the synthesizing symbolicity of Thirdness" or "To what extent is there resolution of meaning in the poem, or is the text infinite?" (57) Though "object signs are always expanding, cross-referencing, resonating, accruing, and continually translating meaning," she suggests that synthesis is possible: "We can choose to assign a definitive meaning, a Final interpretant to the sword sign.... The repetitions, convolutions, and wanderings of theme and structure might suggest that the entire poem is 'about' process—the nature of change, social, moral, and mortal—perhaps a form of continual questioning and examination of values, heroic and Christian" (64, 65). Includes diagrams of cup, ring, and sword "indexes."

Chapter three, "Gender and Interpretation in *Beowulf*," focuses on "the operation of desire within the narrative, on the ways in which desire is directed, redirected, and conflicted in *Beowulf*.... Marginal desire in *Beowulf*, whether this is monstrous, feminine, or even heroic, continually intrudes upon and deflects the progress of dominant desire, and this process offers an overarching context for the restless dynamic of the poem" (69). The dominant desire is male desire, one which seeks closure and death. Overing sees the women of *Beowulf* as hysterics (an idea derived from feminist theory), figures who lay bare cracks in the dominant system and who are essentially ambiguous as hero/victim. In the discussion that follows, Overing analyzes the positions of three women in *Beowulf*: the silent Hildeburh, the language-wielding Wealhtheow, and Modthryth. The silence of Hildeburh (and Freawaru) argues for "the utter nonsignification of women as peace-weaver" (85). But these figures are not merely passive sufferers: with her silence, Hildeburh lays bare and confronts the essential paradox of the masculine system. Wealhtheow, on the other hand, shatters the masculine connection between language and violence (a boast and its accompanying act of violence) by insisting that language prevail against its opposite, violence. Both Wealhtheow's speeches (ll. 1169-87 and 1216-31) contain irresolvable ambiguities and contradictions: as an hysteric she uses masculine language to create herself as a female subject, laying bare "the paradoxical core of the whole linguistic project" (100). Finally, Modthryth (ll. 1931-44) disturbs by rebelling against masculine objectification, refusing to be held in the masculine gaze. By killing those that look upon her, Modthryth "turns the masculine gaze back upon itself" (105) and becomes an autonomous sign, "something we that we know cannot exist in the world of the poem" (106).

In an afterword, Overing critiques her own approach and calls for further readings which include "an acknowledgment,

description, and analysis of the reader's desire in continual and collaborative conjunction with the text" (112).
Reviews: R.P. Tripp, Jr., *In Geardagum* 11 (1990): 73-88; D. Donoghue, *JEGP* 91 (1992): 419-21; *OEN* 25.2 (1992): 46-48.

1762 Parks, Ward. *Verbal Duelling in Heroic Narrative: The Homeric and Old English Traditions.* Princeton: Princeton UP, 1990. Pp. xi + 240.

In a general study of flyting or "verbal duelling" in Old English and Homeric poetry, uses material from *Beowulf* (the flyting between Beowulf and Unferth as well as that between Beowulf and the Coast-warden) to illustrate the main principles of such verbal contests. Parks stresses that verbal contests are essentially contractual, not just antagonistic (or "eristic"); that is, the contestants actually bind themselves to an outcome which will assign glory (*kleos*) to one or the other. In the case of the Beowulf-Unferth dispute, "Unferth predicts that Beowulf will lose his fight with Grendel . . . , while Beowulf boasts that he will prevail. Both positions presuppose that this particular heroic exploit will provide the definitive measure of Beowulf's heroic greatness and thus will determine which of the two flyters has won the quarrel. In short, Beowulf and Unferth are contracting for a fight between the Geat and Grendel" (44).

Parks finds four main stages in the archetypal flyting scene (and in the contest between Beowulf and Unferth): 1) *Engagement.* Two heroes meet at a typical contest site. 2) *Flyting.* The adversaries contend for glory (eristic function) and contract for a trial of arms or manly display to settle the issue (contractual function). 3) *Trial of Arms.* The contracted battle takes place with a clear winner or loser. 4) *Ritual Resolution.* The contest ends, sometimes with a speech reviewing the quarrel or with a symbolic action, often of reconciliation (as in Unferth's loan of Hrunting). There are two main variants to this pattern: the Guest-Host and Battlefield variants. The flyting with Unferth fits into the first, while Beowulf's verbal contest with the Coastguard begins as a battlefield contest but modulates into the guest-host pattern. Finally, Parks identifies several key linguistic features of stage two (the actual flyting)—features present in *Beowulf*: first, the flyter must identify himself by name (often the adversary asks for the identity of the opponent, as both the Coastguard and Unferth do). Next, the flyter refers to some past incident (Parks calls this "retrojection") to evaluate the mettle of the hero (in Beowulf, the controversy about Beowulf's swimming contest with Breca acts as a retrojection). Third, the adversaries project some future actions which have a bearing on worthiness for glory. Fourth, they assign evaluative qualities (of cowardice or bravery) to themselves and their adversaries. Finally, they indulge in a heroic comparison, to the adversary's disadvantage.

Reviews: R. North, *MÆ* 60 (1991): 300-1; A.H. Olsen, *In Geardagum* 12 (1991): 66-68; J.L. Boren, *JEGP* 91 (1992): 120-23; *OEN* 25.2 (1992): 31-32; J.D. Niles, *Speculum* 67 (1992): 465-67.

1763 Pigg, Daniel F. "Cultural Markers in *Beowulf*: a Re-evaluation of the Relationship between Beowulf and Christ." *Neophil* 74 (1990): 601-07.

Using Umberto Eco's idea of "cultural markers," argues "that several of the elements which exegetical critics have used to classify the poem as a Christian allegory might be evaluated more appropriately as biblical riddlings and symbolic touches which aid the poet in telling a story of ancient people to his audience" (601). The poet brings in Beowulf's similarity to Christ not to establish an allegory but to help explain a distant past to a Christian audience. Christ becomes a commentary, a cultural marker by which understanding of the Germanic past becomes possible. In distinction to McNamee [S423] and Donahue [S540], Pigg believes that Beowulf's descent into the mere or his conquering of the dragon, though they may invoke respectively the Harrowing of Hell and Christ's sacrificial triumph over evil, cannot be seen as full-fledged figurations of Christ's life, for Beowulf does not release anyone from the mere, nor does he die for anyone at the hands of the dragon. Allusions to Luke 1:42 (in ll. 942b-46a) and John 17:1 (in ll. 2794a-801b) function in the same way, as cultural markers.

1764 Pulsiano, Phillip, and Joseph McGowan. "*Fyrd*, *here* and the Dating of *Beowulf*." *Studia Anglica Posnaniensia* 23 (1990): 3-13.

Casts doubt on Kiernan's thesis [1261 and 1563] that the use of the words *here* and *fyrd* in *Beowulf* belies an eleventh-century date, arguing instead that the terms are roughly synonymous. Kiernan pointed out that in the *Anglo-Saxon Chronicle*, *here* 'army' is used to describe the invading Danish forces while *fyrd* 'army' describes the English forces, but that in *Beowulf,* *here* is used in positive contexts while Beowulf's cowardly companions are described as *fyrdgesteallan* 'companions in the *fyrd*.' Kiernan argued that such a state of affairs could only be possible after the rise of Cnut to the throne of England, and maintains that in this period *here* was increasingly used to describe English forces, while the word *fyrd* underwent pejoration. Pulsiano and McGowan, examining appearances of these words in the *Chronicle,* Ælfric's homilies, *Exodus,* and *Christ,* conclude that there is no clear distinction between the two terms after 1016 and that even in the pre-1016 Chronicle entries the terms could be interchanged. Further, *fyrd-* compounds in *Beowulf* (ll. 1641a and 2476a) bear clearly positive senses. The *Letter of Alexander to Aristotle,* despite Kiernan's claim, shows no "rigorously maintained" military terminology, using the terms *fyrd, here,* and *werod* 'company' interchangeably to translate Lat. *exercitus.* Thus, there is no "clear linguistic evidence" for Kiernan's claim, since the data fail to be "consistent and unambiguous under scrutiny" (12).

1765 Rowland, Jenny. "Old English *ealuscerwen/meoduscerwen* and the Concept of 'Paying for Mead'." *Leeds Studies in English* n.s., 21 (1990): 1-12.

Explains the difficult compounds *ealuscerwen* (l. 769a) and *meoduscerwen* (*Andreas,* l. 1526b) in light of drinking customs in Welsh poetry, particularly *The Gododdin.* Rowland puts forward a number of passages from Welsh poetry that speak of the bitterness of mead, a heroic paradox: "The taking of drink initially indicates the warrior's acceptance of the lord's service, and then, since this often led to death in battle, it is closely linked with death, bitterness, and sorrow" (2). She suggests that mead drinking in an Old English context may have developed the same symbolic overtones of death, bitterness, and destruction, helping to explain the development of *ealu-/meoduscerwen.* In *Beowulf,* the word refers to the terror of the Danes when they hear Beowulf and Grendel fighting in the hall. Since the Danes themselves are in no danger, however, the bitter drink may refer to a "common bitter outcome of the contract implicit in the dispensing of drink in the hall" (7), Beowulf having himself made a vow over drink. The Welsh materials shed more light on the passage in *Andreas,* suggesting that it is not a botched imitation of *Beowulf,* since the paradox of bitter mead (normally a sweet drink) occurs many times in Welsh poetry.

1766 Ryan, J.S. "Two Oxford Scholars' Perceptions of the Traditional Germanic Hall." *Minas Tirith Evening-Star* 19 (1990): 8-11.

Argues for a connection between Tolkien's depiction of Beorn's Hall (in *The Hobbit*) and his earlier work with E.V. Gordon on the structure of the Germanic hall, particularly relating to sketches appearing in Gordon's *An Introduction to Old Norse*. Contains a few passing references to the hall in *Beowulf* and the *Grettis Saga*.

1767 Smith, Roger. "Ships and the Dating of *Beowulf*." *AN&Q* 3 (1990): 99-103.

Dates *Beowulf* to the ninth or tenth century on the basis of ship construction mentioned in the poem. The Anglo-Saxons did not convert from oar to sail power until after 800, with the Scandinavians discovering the new method about a hundred years earlier. "In any case, Scandinavian ships, the sort an Anglo-Saxon poet might have thought of as northern, began arriving in numbers only late in the eighth century and early in the ninth, when Vikings began raiding the English coast" (99). Smith examines the poet's treatment of ships and finds that in all cases masts and sails are present or implied and that oars are never mentioned. "Since the ninth and tenth centuries were the heyday of the type of design the poem presents, the poet lived sometime in that period, rather than in the early eighth century" (101). Smith discusses ll. 36a, 47b, 217-18, 1898b, 1905a, and 1906a specifically and includes an analysis of the words *brentigas* 'tall-[masted] ships' (l. 2807b).

1768 Stanley, Eric G. "'Hengestes heap,' *Beowulf* 1091." In *Britain 400-600: Language and History*. Ed. Alfred Bammesberger and Alfred Wollmann. Anglistische Forschungen, Bd. 205. Heidelberg: Carl Winter, 1990. Pp. 51-63.

Explores the imaginative element in mythic history, particularly in the Finnsburh materials and Bede's account of Hengest and Horsa, the two possibly sharing a common origin. Stanley concludes that "Unlike the editors and commentators, I do not believe that a single factually self-consistent story can be got out of *The Finnesburg Fragment* and the Finnesburg Episode in Beowulf. The imagination of the *Beowulf* poet has been too brisk here, and his *inventio* . . . makes unhistorical use of the kind of material we know of from history" (58). He also discusses the possible relation between the Finnsburh materials and the story of Hengest and Horsa, with a discussion of the two names, commenting that "Whether or not Hengest and Horsa are wholly mythical, Hengest, as he appears in *Beowulf*, is myth, enriched by invention of detail to which historians can give no credence, not even to the names Hengest and Horsa" (63). Also reviews the appearance of Hengest in a number of medieval and renaissance texts.

1769 Swearer, Randolph, Raymond Oliver, Marijane Osborn, with Intro. by Fred C. Robinson. *Beowulf: A Likeness*. New Haven: Yale UP, 1990. Pp. 127; ill.

A retelling of *Beowulf* interwoven with photographs of artifacts, maps, and manuscript facsimiles, including an introduction by Fred C. Robinson, and an appendix, "Imagining the Real-World Setting of *Beowulf*," by Marijane Osborn. Robinson's introduction highlights the visual and poetic daring of the volume and includes a discussion of epithets for God (see Robinson [1513]). Osborn's essay provides a commentary on the visual images, some of them fanciful montages, others photographs of material objects from the ancient North, indicating how they connect with the world of the poem. Raymond Oliver does not so much translate as realize the story of *Beowulf*, using a variety of modern accentual-syllabic meters. The first six lines: "When Scyld the distant-father died of time,/ Old in winters, come to the end of deeds,/ His body being fresh as in his prime,/ Sweet as flowers newly mown in the meads,/ They wrapped it all in linen trimmed with gold,/ And otter-furs against the snowy cold."

Reviews: E.D. Warwick, *Wilson Library J* 65 (1991): 134; H.D. Chickering, *Speculum* 67 (1992): 689-94; S. Gutterman, *Print* 46 (1992): 126; *OEN* 25.2 (1992): 52-53; D.E. Stanford, *Sewanee Rev.* 100 (1992): 36-38.

1770 Taylor, Paul Beekman. "The Epithetical Style of *Beowulf*." *NM* 91 (1990): 195-206.

Argues that epithets in *Beowulf* reveal often complex meanings when viewed in context, dividing epithets into three categories: light (conventional, neutral identifications), heavy (affective, critical identifications, used by characters to imply a judgment of other characters), and mixed (epithets which seem light but are actually heavy because the context rules out a "light" reading). Taylor uses Lacan's concept of counter-transference to explain complexities in Wealhtheow's use of epithets (ll. 1169-73). The poet tends to use light or mixed epithets, while heavy ones appear most often in the direct speech of characters. In the latter case, the character "is inviting his hearer to measure the signification of the epithet to its particular context. Beowulf himself uses epithets for others to signal qualities of himself he would have them recognize" (195).

1770a _____. "The Old English Poetic Vocabulary of Beauty." In *New Readings*, pp. 211-21.

Surveys and analyzes a number of words for beauty in Old English poetry, including several words in *Beowulf*. Taylor divides them into four categories: beauty as brightness (in *Beowulf*: *deall* 'bright' l. 494a, *scīr* 'light' ll. 496a, 979a, and *wlite* 'fair aspect' l. 93a), beauty in an appealing physical form (in *Beowulf*: *ænlic* 'singular' ll. 251a, 1941b, *cȳmlīc* 'fair' l. 38a, *dōm* 'glory' l. 1645b, *geatolīc* 'adorned' ll. 215a, 308a, 1401a, and *wlanc* 'brave' l. 341a), quality recognizable in form or stance (in *Beowulf*: *frēolīc* 'comely' ll. 615a, 641a, *myne* 'desirable' l. 169b, and *sēl* 'better' ll. 860b, 1012b), and beauty by array (in *Beowulf*: *bēaghroden* 'ring-adorned' l. 623b, *bundenheord* 'with hair bound up' l. 3151b, and *goldhroden* 'gold-adorned' ll. 614a, 640b, 1948a, and 2025a).

1771 Tharaud, Barry. *Beowulf*. Illus. Rockwell Kent. Niwot, CO: UP of Colorado, 1990. Pp. 186; ill.

Translates *Beowulf* into modern English prose, providing a general introduction which covers such topics as the Germanic backgrounds to the poem, prosody, narrative structure, characterization, etc. Tharaud states that the translation "attempts to present the poem in a modern English idiom that is lucid and direct and conveys the moral forcefulness of the original poem.... In an attempt to make the poem more accessible and enjoyable to the nonspecialist, nonacademic reader, there are no footnotes, and pertinent historical, literary, or linguistic information is contained in the text or in the brief Introduction" (11). Lines 4-14: "Scyld Scefing often drove troops of foes from their mead hall benches; he put to flight the warriors of many tribes. In the beginning he was a foundling child; afterwards he found a

better life: He lived to find a recompense for his misfortunes, for he became a great leader under heaven and flourished in honor, until all his neighbors across the seas obeyed him and paid him tribute. That was a good king." Also includes genealogies, a map, pronunciation guide, an index of proper names, and an afterword on Rockwell Kent's illustrations, reprinted throughout the volume.
Reviews: R.P. Tripp, Jr., *In Geardagum* 12 (1991): 58-60; *OEN* 25.2 (1992): 52; E.G. Stanley, *N&Q* 39 (1992): 145-48.

1772 Vickman, Jeffrey. *A Metrical Concordance to 'Beowulf'*. Preface by R.D. Fulk. Old English Newsletter, Subsidia 16. Binghamton: CEMERS, 1990. Pp. xi + 46.

Provides a concordance of metrical types based on A.J. Bliss's system of metrical analysis [S353], correcting mistakes and tabulating new totals for each type. The preface, written by R.D. Fulk after the death of Vickman, is based on Vickman's original, unfinished preface. "For users of Bliss's system it should greatly simplify the process of locating and examining all instances of a particular verse type in *Beowulf*. This is a procedure that heretofore has required either a laborious search through Bliss's index or recourse to Pope's catalogue—the latter a particularly dissatisfactory alternative, since Pope's categories are sometimes more and sometimes less comprehensive than Bliss's, and often different altogether" (ii). Fulk goes on to warn that even Bliss's system, though widely accepted, is not entirely impartial and that the concordance should not further entrench Bliss's system. After listing Vickman's corrections, Fulk adds five more. The concordance itself devotes a section to each of forty-nine types, also listing remainders, defective, and hypermetric verses.
Reviews: *OEN* 25.2 (1992): 42.

AUTHOR INDEX

most references are to item numbers; an "r" or "(r)" indicates a review; item numbers for books are underlined; entries like "Vikings (r)" or "Donaldson (r)" refer to reviews of book collections (see pp. xiii-xviii)

Abbott, Joe: 1729a
Ackland, Michael: 1222
Adams, V.: 1501r
Albrecht, Roberta Adams: 1295
Alexander, Michael: 1302r, 1375
Allen, David G.: 1296
Amos, Ashley Crandell: 1223, 1232, 1297
Amsler, Mark E.: 1106
Anderson, Earl R.: 1163, 1224, 1298
Anderson, J. J.: 1376
Andersson, Theodore M.: 1164, 1420, 1475, 1675r
Dating of Beowulf (r)
Andrew, Malcolm: 1225
Arwidsson, G.: 1546r
Ashbee, Paul: 1063a
Atkinson, Stephen C. B.: 1421, 1527
Aubrey, James R.: 1219

Baker, Donald C.: 1317r, 1399r, 1401, *Beowulfian Scansion* (r)
Baker, Peter S.: 1273r, 1632r, 1639
Baker, Keith: 1401
Baker-Smith, D.: 1375r
Bammesberger, Alfred: 1165, 1166, 1299, 1481r, 1501r, 1528, 1730, 1731, *OEL in Context* (r), *Clemoes* (r)
Barksdale, E. C.: 1377
Barlow, F.: 1481r
Barney, Stephen A.: 1422, 1700r
Barquist, Claudia Russell: 1590
Bassett, Paul Merritt: 1273r
Bately, Janet: 1476
Bauschatz, Paul C.: 1300
Beard, D. J.: 1226
Berkhout, Carl T.: 1184r, 1372r, 1529, 1773r
Berlin, Gail Ivy: 1530
Berman, Myra: 1422
Bessinger, Jess B. Jr.: 1422
Bethel, Patricia: 1423
Bethune, Brian: 1424
Bhattacharya, Prodosh: 1531
Bitterling, K.: 1184r
Bjork, Robert E.: 1167, 1451r
Björnsson, Halldóra B.: 1378
Black, Vaughan: 1424
Blake, N.F.: 1261r, 1302r, 1375r, 1501r, *Greenfield* (r)
Bliss, Alan J.: 1107, 1184r, 1227, 1367
Blockley, Mary: 1684a
Bloom, Harold: 1591
Bloomfield, Morton W.: 1199, 1532
Boenig, Robert: 1592

Bohrer, Randall: 1301
Bologna, Corrado: 1022a
Bolton, Whitney F.: 1108, 1477, 1684
Boren, James L.: 1762r
Bosse, Roberta Bux: 1593
Boyle, Leonard E., O.P.: 1228
Bradley, S.A.J.: 1302, 1375r, 1396r, 1399r, 1685
Brady, Caroline: 1109, 1379
Braeger, Peter C.: 1533
Bragg, Lois: 1478
Bravo García, Antonio: 1479, *On Old English* (r)
Bremmer, Rolf H., Jr.: 1168, 1184r, 1414r, 1566r
Brennan, Malcolm M.: 1480
Brewer, C.: 1536
Bridges, Richard M.: 1110
Brinton, Laurel J.: 1594
Brook, G.L.: 1302r, 1367r
Brooks, N.P.: *Jones* (r)
Brown, Alan K.: 1169
Brown, George H.: *Hero and Exile*
Bruce-Mitford, Rupert: 1063a, 1546r
Brynteson, William E.: 1303
Budny, M.: *Clemoes* (r)
Burnley, J.D.: 1184r
Burrow, John A.: 1632r, 1640r
Busse, Wilhelm G.: 1229, 1513r, 1595
Butts, Richard: 1596

Cable, Thomas: 1223r, 1230, 1422
Caie, Graham D.: 1425
Calder, Daniel G.: 1201r, 1372r, 1399r, 1414r, 1427r, 1534, 1555, 1634a (r)
Caluwé-Dor, Juliette: 1240r
Camargo, Martin: 1231
Cameron, Angus: 1232
Campbell, Jackson J.: 1201r
Canitz, A.E.C.: 1535

Cassidy, Frederic G.: 1111, 1304
Cavill, Paul: 1380
Chance, Jane: 1169a, 1170, 1536
Chaney, William A.: 1273r, 1700r
Chase, Colin: 1112, 1233, 1234, 1481
Cherniss, Michael D.: 1422, 1686
Chickering, Howell D.: 1235, 1273r, 1399r, 1422, 1627r, 1687, 1769r
Christensen, Bonniejean: 1688
Christiansen, E.: *Vikings* (r)
Cilluffo, Gilda: 1223r
Clark, Francelia: 1236
Clark, George: 1422, 1732
Clement, Richard. W.: 1261r, 1426
Clemoes, Peter: 1113, 1237, 1537
Clover, Carol J.: 1171
Collier, L.W.: 1595r
Collins, Rowland L.: 1381
Conner, Patrick W.: 1482
Conquergood, Dwight: 1238
Corner, D.: *Clemoes* (r)
Corso, Louise: 1172
Cottle, Basil: *OEL in Context* (r)
Cox, Rosemary D.: 1538
Creed, Robert P.: 1064a, 1173, 1239, 1305, 1539, 1566r, 1597, 1602r, 1689, 1690, 1733
Crépin, André: 1114, 1115, 1183r, 1240, 1302r, 1382, 1418r, 1598
Cronan, Dennis: 1540, 1599, 1734
Cross, J.E.: 1184r, 1372r
Crossley-Holland, Kevin: 1600

Author Index

Dahlberg, Charles R.: 1483, 1640
Dahood, Roger: 1174
Daldorph, Brian: 1542
Damico, Helen: 1175, 1383, 1427, 1543, 1734a
Damon, John: 1735
Damon, Phillip: 1176
Dane, Joseph A.: 1306
D'Aronco, Maria Amalia: 1541
Davidson, Hilda R. Ellis: 1065a, 1116, 1183, 1273r
Davis, R. Evan: 1366
Davis, Victor: 1383a
Davis, R.H.C.: 1481r
de Gaiffier, B.: *Jones* (r)
de Looze, Laurence N.: 1428
De Roo, Harvey: 1117, 1307
DeLuca, Diana M.: 1422
Denton, Robert F.: 1641
Deratzian, David L.: 1484
Derolez, René: 1544, 1601
Dick, Ernst S.: 1300r, 1427r
Dieterich, Lana Stone: 1384
Diller, Hans-Jürgen: 1429
Doig, J. F.: 1241
Dolan, T.P.: 1634a (r)
Donoghue, Daniel: 1602, 1602a, 1544a, 1761r *On Old English* (r)
Dubois, M.-M.: 1555r
Duggan, Hoyt: 1736
Dumville, David N.: 1242, 1642
Duncan, Ian: 1603
Dunleavey, Gareth W.: 1148r
Earl, James W.: 1118, 1119, 1308, 1385, 1602a (r), 1604
Earnest, James David: 1177
Economou, George D.: 1331
Edwards, Paul: 1178, 1545
Edwards, A.S.G.: 1674r, 1602a (r)
Eliason, Norman E.: 1120, 1179

Ellis, Helen B.: 1309
Engberg, Norma J.: 1430
Enright, Michael J.: 1643
Erben, Johannes: 1121
Eto, Yasuharu: 1691
Evans, Angela Care: 1546
Evans, D.D.: 1749r
Evans, Jonathan D.: 1485

Fajardo-Acosta, Fidel: 1692
Farina, Peter: 1243
Farrell, Eleanor: 1547
Farrell, Robert T.: 1310, 1063a (r), 1753
Feldman, Thalia Phillies: 1122, 1244, 1605
Fenster, Valmai: 1184r
Finlay, Alison: *New Readings* (r)
Finnegan, Robert Emmett: 1148r
Fischer, A.: 1595r
Fleming, Robin: 1700r
Flóki, Alfreð: 1378
Florey, Kenneth: 1644
Foley, Joanne De Lavan: 1245
Foley, John Miles: 1064a, 1180, 1181, 1182, 1246, 1247, 1248, 1311, 1422, 1737
Frank, Roberta: 1184r, 1201r, 1249, 1312, 1313, 1513r, 1548, 1580r, 1602a (r), 1606, *Clemoes* (r)
Frantzen, Allen J.: 1536r, 1738, *OE Poetry* (r)
Frese, Dolores Warwick: 1314
Frey, Leonard: 1549
Fries, Udo: 1501
Fry, Donald K.: 1064a, 1184r, 1201r, 1250, 1261r, 1317r, 1422, 1555r, 1634a (r), *OE Poetry* (r)
Fujiwara, Hiroshi: 1441, 1550, 1551, 1645, 1646, 1692a, *Dating of Beowulf* (r)

Fulk, R.D.: 1261r, 1315, 1501r, 1607, 1693, 1772
Futhey, J.F.: 1481r

Gabbard, G.N.: 1552
Gahrn, Lars: 1553, 1608
Galloway, Andrew: 1739
Ganz, P.F.: 1674r
Garmonsway, George N.: <u>1183</u>
Gatch, Milton McC.: 1555r
Gates, Rosemary L.: 1632r
Georgianna, Linda: 1609
Gerritsen, Johan: 1647, 1694, 1695
Gillingham, John: 1302r
Gleissner, Reinhard: 1418r
Glosecki, Stephen O.: 1554, 1610, 1648, 1649, <u>1696</u>
Glover, Julian: 1621
Gneuss, Helmut: 1184r, 1555r, *OEL in Context* (r)
Godden, Malcolm: 1184r, 1223r, 1302r, 1367r, *Tolkien* (r), *Beowulfian Scansion, Jones* (r)
Godman, Peter: *Clemoes* (r), *Jones* (r)
Goffart, Walter: 1251
Goldman, Stephen H.: 1123
Goldsmith, Margaret E.: 1372r, 1399r
Gómez Lara, Manuel José: 1650
Gould, Kent: 1486
Graham-Campbell, J.: 1063a (r), 1546r
Gray, John: 1697
Green, Brian: 1698
Green, Eugene: 1487
Greene, Elizabeth: 1422
Greene, Jesse Laurence: 1316
Greenfield, Stanley B.: 1124, 1125, 1147r, <u>1184</u>, 1201r, <u>1317</u>, 1318, 1319, 1372r, 1399r, 1488, 1501r, <u>1555</u>
Griffin, Henry William: 1556

Griffith, Mark: 1566r, 1627r, 1632r, 1672r, 1674r, 1702r, 1738r, 1749r
Grinda, Klaus R.: 1350r
Guerrieri, Anna Maria: 1320
Guidall, George: 1740
Gutterman, Scott: 1769r

Haarder, Andreas: <u>1431</u>, 1651
Hall, J.R.: *Tolkien* (r)
Hallissy, Margaret: 1536r
Handelman, Anita F.: 1652
Hanley, Wayne: 1741
Hanning, Robert W.: 1386, 1432, 1640r
Hansen, Elaine Tuttle: 1321, 1422, <u>1653</u>
Harada, Yoshio: 1252, 1322
Hardy, Adelaide: 1126
Harris, Anne Leslie: 1323, 1324, 1654, 1742
Harris, Joseph: 1127, 1325, 1427r
Hart, Thomas Elwood: 1185, 1253
Haruta, Setsuko: 1557
Hasegawa, Hiroshi: 995b, 1186, 1254, <u>1743</u>
Hasenfratz, Robert: 1744
Hashimoto, Shuichi: 1326
Haudry, Jean: 1433, 1489, 1558
Haymes, E.R.: 1674r
Heinemann, Fredrik J.: 1387, 1611
Heinrichs, Heinrich Matthias: 1434
Helder, William: 1612
Hengen, Shannon: 1655
Henry, P. L.: 1255
Hermann, John P.: 1128
Hernández, Ann: 1219, 1327
Herzog, Petra: 1223r
Hieatt, Constance B.: <u>1328</u>, 1422, 1435, 1490
Hieatt, Kent A.: 1328

Author Index

Higley, Sarah Lynn: 1559
Hill, John M.: 1129, 1329, 1699
Hill, Joyce: 1437r, 1513r, 1745, *Greenfield* (r)
Hill, Thomas D.: 1130, 1330, 1399r, 1560, 1746, 1747
Hills, C.M.: 1063a (r), 1273r
Hines, J.: 1427r
Hinton, David A.: 1273r
Hirabayashi, Mikio: 1491
Hoad, T.F.: 1302r, 1660r
Hock, Hans Henrich: 1492
Hollis, Stephanie J.: 1388
Holloway, Betsy M.: 1131
Holtei, R.: 1229
Horowitz, Sylvia Huntley: 1256, 1436
Howard, Patricia J.: 1748
Howe, Nicholas: 1700, 1702r
Hudson, Marc: 1749
Huisman, Rosemary: 1701
Hume, Kathryn: 1187
Huppé, Bernard F.: 1331, 1437, 1613
Hutcheson, B.R.: 1632r

Ikegami, Yoshihiko: 1441
Ikegami, Tadahiro: 1201r
Ilsemann, Hartmut: *Beowulfian Scansion* (r)
Imaizumi, Youko: 1438
Irving, Edward B., Jr.: 1332, 1401r, 1437r, 1439, 1614, 1702, 1750
Jackson, W.T.H.: 1333
Jackson, Elizabeth: 1367r
Jacobs, Nicholas: 1148r, 1257, 1451r, 1700r, *Dating of Beowulf* (r)
Jager, Eric: 1751
Jiang, Zeiju: 1334
Jochens, Jenny: *New Readings* (r)
Johansen, J. G.: 1335
Jonk, J.: 1037a

Jorgensen, Peter A.: 1132, 1561
Joseph, Brian D.: 1336, 1389
Kabell, Aage: 1188
Kahrl, Stanley J.: 1422
Karibe, Tsunenori: 1223r, 1656, 1752, 1702a
Karkov, Catherine: 1753
Kasik, Jon C.: 1133
Kaske, Robert E.: 1440, 1493
Kavros, Harry E.: 1258
Keller, Thomas L.: 1259
Kellogg, R.: 1674r
Kelly, Birte: 1391, 1390
Kendall, Calvin B.: 1337, 1392, 1733r
Kent, Rockwell: 1771
Kerby-Fulton, Kathryn: 1640r
Kiernan, Kevin S.: 1261, 1262, 1393, 1442, 1494, 1563, 1564, 1565, 1566, *On Old English* (r)
Kindrick, Robert L.: 1263
Kinney, Clare: 1495
Kirby, D.P.: 1700r
Kjellmer, Göran: 1443
Klausner, David N.: 1148r
Klegraf, Josef: 1657
Klein, Thomas: 1658
Kliman, Bernice: 1422
Knapp, Fritz Peter: 1338
Knapp, Peggy A.: 1659
Köberl, Johann: 1616
Koch, Ludovica: 1617
Koerner, Konrad: 1501r
Koike, Kazuo: 1189, 1263a, 1339, 1394, 1617a, 1703a,
Kolb, Eduard: 1704
Koopman, Willem: 1501r
Krämer, Peter: 1444
Krishna, Valerie: 1340
Kroch, Anthony S.: 1508, 1716
Krol, Jelle: 1134, 1445
Kroll, Norma: 1567

Kubouchi, Tadao: 1441, 1615, 1501r
Kuhn, Sherman: 1135
Kumazawa, Sukeo: 1618
Kurylowicz, Jerzy: 1136

Landiss, Morris P.: 1341
Lapidge, Michael: 1342
Larrington, C.: 1653r
Larsen, Elizabeth: 1395
Lecouteux, Claude: 1137, 1350r
Lee, Alvin A.: 1148r, *Dating of Beowulf* (r)
Lehmann, Ruth P.M.: 1138, 1350r, 1660, 1661
Lehmann, Winfred P.: 1343, 1674r
Lehnert, Martin: 1152r
Leinbaugh, Theodore H.: 1353r
Lendinara, Patrizia: 1184r, 1302r, 1350r, 1375r, 1481r, 1501r, *Clemoes* (r)
Leslie, Roy F.: 1201r
Lester, G. A.: 1568
Liberman, Anatoly: 1076a, 1569
Liggins, Elizabeth: 1264
Lindström, Bengt: 1148r, 1566r
Locherbie-Cameron, Margaret A.L.: 1076b, *Greenfield* (r)
Lock, Richard: 1446
Logan, Darlene: 1344
Loganbill, Dean: 1139
Loikala, Paula: 1345
Lord, Albert B.: 1190
Loyn, H.R.: 1273r
Lucas, Peter J.: 1422r, 1619, 1632r, 1634a (r), 1754, 1755
Luecke, Jane-Marie: 1396
Lundberg, Patricia Lorimer: 1705

MacDonald, A.A.: 1602a (r)
Mackie, Sheila: 1621
Macrae-Gibson, O.D.: 1570
Maeth Ch., Russell: 1620
Magennis, Hugh: 1346, 1496
Magnusson, Magnus: 1621
Mann, Betty Tucker: 1078a
Mastrelli, Carlo Alberto: 1140, 1497
Matsui, Noriko: 1265
Mayr-Harting, H.: *Clemoes* (r)
Mazzuoli Porru, Giulia: 1498
Mc Hugh, Maire: 1622
McAlister, Caroline: 1499
McConchie, R. W.: 1183r, 1347
McCully, C.B.: 1632r
McGalliard, John C.: 1422
McGowan, Joseph: 1764
McGuiness, Daniel: 1706
McTurk, Rory: 1148 r, 1266
Meaney, Audrey L.: 1141, 1707
Medine, Renée: 1529
Meek, Mary Elizabeth: 1422
Meier, H.H.: 1501r
Mellinkoff, Ruth: 1142, 1267
Mertens-Fonck, Paule: 1079a
Mikami, Toshio: 807a, 881a
Mikawa, Kiyoshi: 1500
Miletich, John S.: 1662
Miller, William Ian: 1397
Miller, Miriam Youngerman: 1201r
Millett, B.: 1634a (r)
Milosh, Joseph E., Jr.: 1399r
Milward, Peter: 1292
Mirarchi, Giovanni: 1191
Mitchell, Bruce: 1184r, 1201r, 1348, 1398, 1501, 1602a (r), 1663, 1664, 1708, 1756, 1756a, *Clemoes* (r)
Miyazaki, Tadakatsu: 1040aa
Mizuno, Tomoaki: 1622a, 1709
Mizuno, Yoshiaki: 1710
Momma, Haruko: 1711

Monnin, Pierre E.: 1623
Mooney, Thomas J.: 1192
Moore, Bruce: 1193
Morris, B.: 1431r
Morrison, Stephen: 1194
Morus, Iwan Rhys: 1757
Müller, Wolfgang G.: 1665
Murphy, Michael: 1502
Murray, Alexander Callander: 1268
Myres, J.N.L.: 1063a (r)
Mytum, Harold: *Vikings* (r)

Nagler, Michael N.: 1195
Nagucka, Ruta: 1503
Nagy, Joseph F.: 1504
Nakagawa, Ryoichi: 1349
Navarro Errasti, Maria Pilar: 1666
Nelson, Marie: 1505
Nicholls, J.W.: 1536r
Nicholson, Lewis E.: 1196, 1447, 1571
Nickel, Gerhard: 1350
Nicolini, Mary B.: 1711a
Niles, John D.: 1143, 1197, 1261r, 1269, 1270, 1399, 1422, 1762r
Nishide, Kimiyuki: 1448
Nobumori, Hiromitsu: 1400
Noguchi, Shunichi: 1615, 1667
Nolan, Barbara: 1199
Nolcken, Christina von: 1634a (r)
North, Richard J.: 1712, 1758, 1762r
Nucciarelli, Franco Ivan: 1200

Ober, Warren U.: 1309
Obst, Wolfgang: 1401r, 1624, 1632r
O'Donoghue, H.: 1536r, *Vikings* (r), *Hero and Exile* (r)
Ogawa, Hiroshi: 1223r, 1615, 1703
Ogilvy, Jack D.A.: 1144, 1401
Ogura, M.: *On Old English* (r)
Ohba, Keizo: 1271
Oizumi, Akio: 1501r
O'Keefe, Katherine O'Brian: 1272
Oliver, Raymond: 1769
Olsen, Alexandra Hennessey: 1148r, 1201r, 1317r, 1351, 1422, 1449, 1625, 1702r, 1734a, 1738r, 1762r
Onega, Susana: 1506
Ono, Shigeru: 1441, 1501r, 1615
Opland, Jeff: 1201, 1202, 1203
Oresnik, Janez: 1450
Orton, P.R.: 1507
Osborn, Marijane: 1422, 1451, 1572, 1713, 1769
Oshitari, Kinshiro: 1441, 1452, 1668, 1759, 1760
Overing, Gillian R.: 1573, 1626, 1669, 1761
Owen, Gale R.: 1273, 1302r
Owen, John: 1740r
Ozeki, Yasuhiro: 1352

Page, R.I.: 1274, *Vikings* (r)
Parker, Mary A.: 1627
Parks, Ward: 1574, 1628, 1670, 1714, 1762
Pàroli, Teresa: 1353, 1402, 1629
Parry, Nicholas: 1672
Payne, F. Anne: 1145
Pearsall, Derek: *Donaldson* (r)
Peters, F.J.J.: 1715
Pezzini, Domenico: *Jones* (r)
Pfeiffer, John R.: 1146
Pheifer, J.D.: 1350r
Pigg, Daniel F.: 1763
Pilch, Herbert: 1147
Pintzuk, Susan: 1508, 1716
Pollock, John J.: 1219
Pope, John C.: 1275, 1354, 1555r, 1575, 1595r, 1671

Porsia, Franco: 1008a
Porter, John: 1672
Potter, Joyce Elizabeth: 1509, 1673
Pound, Ezra: 1355
Poussa, Patricia: 1276
Princi Braccini, Giovanna: 1453, 1454, *Dating of Beowulf* (r)
Psaki, Regina: 1640r
Puhvel, Martin: 1148, 1204, 1403
Pulsiano, Phillip: 1510, 1764
Purdy, Strother: 1576

Queval, Jean: 1277, 1278

Raffel, Burton: 1317r, 1717
Rausing, G.: 1511
Reddick, Robert J.: 1201r, 1501r
Redwine, Bruce: 1356
Reichl, Karl: 1201r, 1630, 1634a (r), 1674 (r)
Renoir, Alain: 1279, 1317, 1357, 1422, 1674, 1718
Reuter, Timothy: *Clemoes* (r)
Richardson, John: 1631
Riedinger, Anita: 1512
Rielly, Edward J.: 1422
Rigg, A.G.: 1358
Riley, Samuel M.: 1205, 1291, 1359, 1404
Rissanen, Matti: 1184r, 1223r
Rizzo, Carmela: 1317r
Roach, Bruce V.: 1291
Roberts, Gildas: 1455
Roberts, Jane: 1223r, 1375r, 1401r, 1602a (r), *OEL in Context* (r), *Greenfield* (r)
Robinson, Fred C.: 1149, 1184, 1422, 1451, 1501r, 1513, 1769
Robinson, L.S.: 1536r
Rogers, H.L.: 1456
Rollason, D.W.: 1273r

Romano, Timothy: 1360
Rosenberg, Bruce A.: 1064a, 1514
Ross, Margaret Clunies: 1427r, 1719
Rowland, Jenny: 1765
Rudanko, Martti Juhani: 1405
Russom, Geoffrey: 1632, 1633, 1634, 1696r, 1700r
Ruud, Jay: 1627r
Ryan, J.S.: 1766

Sakemi, Kisei: 1457, 1577
Salus, P.H.: 1365
Samuels, M.L.: 1184r
Sasabe, Hideo: 1150
Sato, Noboru: 1207, 1208, 1280, 1361, 1362, 1458, 1515
Sato, Shuji: 1261r, 1441, 1459, 1615, 1703
Sato, Suhi: 1578
Sauer, Hans: 1396r, 1555r, *Clemoes* (r), *Kaske* (r)
Schabram, Hans: 1151, 1281, 1414r
Schaefer, U.: 1595r
Schichler, Robert Lawrence: 1579
Schik, B.: 1399r
Schipper, William: 1703
Schmid-Cadalbert, Christian: 1460
Schmidt, Gary D.: 1461
Schneider, Karl: 1580
Schoening, K.M.: 1700r, *Greenfield* (r)
Schrader, Richard J.: 1209, 1406, 1407, 1462
Schubel, Friedrich: 1152
Schützeichel, R.: 1350r
Scragg, D.G.: 1653r, 1634a (r), *Greenfield* (r), *On Old English* (r)
Segal, Erich: 1737r
Seymour, M.C.: 1455r, 1513r

Author Index

Shaheen, Abdel-Rahman: 1282
Sheehy, Eugene P.: 1184r
Shimose, Michiro: 1092a
Shippey, T.A.: 1277r, 1401r, 1501r, 1566r, 1653r, *OEL in Context* (r)
Short, Douglas D.: 1210, 1211, 1422
Silber, Patricia: 1212, 1283
Simpson, Jacqueline: 1148r, 1183
Simpson, James: 1418r
Sisam, Celia: 1223r
Smilde, R.C.: 1134
Smirnickaja, O. A.: 1213
Smith, Roger: 1767
Smith, Sarah Stanbury: 1153
Smits, Kathryn: 1581
Solo, Harry Jay: 1422
Spamer, James B.: 1284
Spangehl, S.D.: 1632r
Stäblein, Patricia Harris: 1333r
Stacey, Robin Chapman: 1700r
Stafford, P.: 1702r
Stanford, Donald E.: 1769r
Stanley, Eric G.: 1154, 1155, 1214, 1261r, 1285, 1363, 1375r, 1399r, 1408, 1455r, 1501r, 1555r, 1566r, 1582, 1595r, 1602a (r), 1624r, 1634a (r), 1672r, 1720, 1721, 1768, 1771r, *Hero and Exile* (r)
Stephens, John: 1415
Stephenson, Edward A.: 1286
Stieg, Elizabeth: *Dating of Beowulf* (r)
Storm, Melvin: 1291
Strauss, Jürgen: 1350
Strite, Victor L.: 1422
Sullivan, C.W. III: 1463
Svec, Patricia Ward: 1722
Swanton, Michael J.: 1364, 1634a

Swearer, Randolph: 1769
Szarmach, Paul E.: 1555r

Tajima, Matsuji: 1215
Talbot, Annelise: 1409
Talentino, Arnold V.: 1156
Tandy, David W.: 1464
Tarzia, Wade: 1723
Taylor, Paul Beekman: 1201r, 1287, 1365, 1366, 1410, 1422, 1465, 1516, 1583, 1584, 1724, 1770, 1770a
Tejera, Dionisia: 1157, 1635
Temple, Mary Kay: 1585
Terasawa, Yoshio: 1441, 1615
Terasawa, Jun: 1725
Tharaud, Barry: 1771
Thompson, P.A.: *Greenfield* (r)
Thomson, R.L.: 1602a (r)
Thundy, Zacharias P.: 1411, 1412, 1586
Tilling, P. M.: 1288
Toda, Shizuo: 1216
Tolkien, J.R.R.: 1367
Toth, K.: 1223r
Trahern, Joseph B. Jr.: 1261, *Clemoes* (r), *Dating of Beowulf* (r)
Tripp, Raymond P., Jr.: 1158, 1217, 1218, 1289, 1368, 1413, 1414, 1451r, 1466, 1518, 1587, 1637, 1676, 1675, 1696r, 1726, 1749r, 1761r, 1771r
Tristram, Hildegard L.C.: 1147, 1674 (r), 1727
Trnka, Bohumil: 1290
Turville-Petre, Joan: 1201r
Tuso, Joseph F.: 1219, 1291, 1422, 1519

Ushigaki, Hiroto: 1369, 1414r, 1520, 1588

van der Zee, Popke: 1134, 1445

Vaught, Jacqueline: 1220
Verbraken, P.: *Clemoes* (r)
Verdonck, J.: 1370
Vickman, Jeffrey: <u>1772</u>
Vickrey, John F.: 1678, 1677
Vidal Tibbits, Mercedes: 1467
Vigil, Julián Josué: 1679
Viswanathan, S.: 1159
Volfing, Annette: 1674r

Wachsler, Arthur A.: 1521
Waite, Gregory: 1232
Warren, Lee A.: 1160
Warsh, Lewis: <u>1468</u>
Warwick, Ellen Donohue: 1769r
Watanabe, Hideki: 1522, 1536r, 1680, 1637a
Watanabe, Shoichi: 1292
Waterhouse, Ruth: 1415
Webber, Philip E.: 1416
Wehlau, Ruth: 1696r
Weil, Susanne: 1728
Weinstock, Horst: 1371
Weise, Judith: 1589
Weissman, H.: 1536r
Welch, M.G.: 1546r
Weldon, James: 1681
Wellman, Don: 1417
Wentersdorf, Karl P.: 1293
Wetzel, Claus-Dieter: 1223r, 1350r, 1455r, 1523
Whallon, William: <u>1418</u>
Whitman, F. H.: 1161
Wieland, Gernot: 1682
Wilcox, J.: 1566r
Williams, David: <u>1372</u>
Wilmont, Barry: 1419
Wilts, Ommo: 1162
Wissolik, R.D.: 1732r
Wolf, Alois: 1683
Wolff, Hope Nash: <u>1638</u>
Wood, I.N.: 1273r
Wrenn, Charles L.: <u>1684</u>
Wright, Louise E.: 1221
Wright, D.: 1700r

Wyatt, Jennifer Lee: 1593
Wylie, Betty Jane : 1383a

Yada, Hiroshi: 1294, 1373, 1524
Yamada, Jiro: 1469, 1525
Yamagata, Hiromitsu: 1615
Yamanouchi, Kazuyoshi: 1470, 1471
Yeager, Robert F.: <u>1422</u>
Yerkes, David: 1261r
Yoshida, Kiyoshi: 1472, 1526
Yoshimi, Akinori: 1473, 1474
Yoshino, Yoshihiro: 1615, *OE Poetry* (r)

Zellefrow, W. Ken: 1291
Ziegler, Heide: 1729
Ziolkowski, Jan M.: 1653r
Zyngier, Sonia: 1374

SUBJECT INDEX

references are to item numbers

accusative plus infinitive construction: 1503
adaptations of *Beowulf*: 1422, 1463, 1509, 1688, 1748, 1769, 1383a
adverbs: 1470, 1476, 1618
Ælfric: 1234, 1237, 1310, 1503, 1531, 1537
Aeneid: 1122, 1209, 1290, 1333, 1399, 1407, 1543, 1591, 1692, 1717, 1742
Æschere: 1125, 1190, 1360, 1376, 1442, 1487; name of: 1323
Æthelbald: 1364
Æthelred II, the Unready: 1229, 1642
Æthelstan, King of Wessex: 1268, 1399, 1586, 1707
Æthelwulf, genealogy of: 1707
Aethicus, *Cosmographia*: 1454
Álaflekks saga: 1561
Alcuin: 1209, 1312, 1382, 1510, 1513
Aldhelm: 1209, 1342, 1735
Alexander's Letter to Aristotle: 1114, 1228, 1303, 1426, 1727, 1755, 1764
Alfred the Great: 1124, 1144, 1234, 1268, 1276, 1303, 1312, 1727
allegorical readings: 1296, 1372, 1375, 1567, 1579, 1607, 1644

alliteration: 1136, 1181, 1200, 1248, 1280, 1290, 1337, 1366, 1392, 1418, 1470, 1471, 1506, 1507, 1539, 1540, 1597, 1624, 1632, 1655, 1721, 1722, 1737, 1753
Alliterative *Morte Arthure*: 1265, 1340, 1502
ambiguity in *Beowulf*: 1172, 1272, 1384, 1399, 1483, 1485, 1548, 1592
Ambrose: 1571
anacrusis: 1305, 1602, 1660, 1671
analogues: 1183, 1422; African: 1202, 1203; African American: 1127; Armenian: 1224; Biblical: 1142, 1593; Chinese: 1620; classical: 1298; Greek: 1195, 1224; Indian: 1176, 1195, 1243, 1411, 1433, 1497; Irish: 1148, 1255, 1732; Japanese: 1668; Latin: 1358, 1475; Old Norse: 1076a, 1127, 1132, 1148, 1164, 1171, 1187, 1226, 1249, 1255, 1259, 1266, 1300, 1325, 1347, 1383, 1414, 1420, 1433, 1465, 1514, 1521, 1543, 1561, 1584, 1606, 1649, 1658, 1681, 1693, 1696,

1732, 1735, 1758; Russian: 1377; Scottish: 1204
Andreas: 1117, 1230, 1232, 1237, 1281, 1387, 1534, 1602, 1611, 1704, 1721, 1765
Anglian elements in *Beowulf*: 1519
Anglo-Saxon Chronicle: 1764
Anglo-Saxons, conversion of: 1293, 1346, 1580, 1627, 1700
animals in *Beowulf*: 1331, 1579, 1648, 1696
Anskar, Saint: 1475
anthropological approaches: 1176, 1300, 1301, 1385, 1396, 1460
anthroponymy: 1628
aphasia: 1429, 1690
apocalyptic elements: 1308, 1433, 1673
apposition: 1507, 1513, 1544, 1661, 1684a, 1761
appositive style: 1513
Arator: 1209
archaeology: 1063a, 1065a, 1157, 1183, 1186, 1249, 1310, 1380, 1451, 1546, 1554, 1571, 1580, 1627, 1649, 1648, 1689, 1707, 1723, 1732, 1769
armor: 1063a, 1156, 1339, 1388, 1394, 1543, 1706, 1725
Asser, *Vita Alfredi*: 1234, 1342
assonance: 1362
Atilla: 1403, 1411
Atlakviða: 1076a, 1164, 1446
Atlamál: 1164
audience of *Beowulf*: 1147, 1169, 1202, 1229, 1371, 1640, 1663
Augustine: 1225, 1399, 1483, 1571, 1579; *De Civitate Dei*: 1119, 1256, 1372, 1437; Augustinian influence: 1296, 1437, 1640, 1692
authorship, theories of: 1209, 1261, 1262, 1342, 1371, 1404, 1429, 1476, 1580, 1586

Balder: 1273, 1433, 1709
Baldrs draumar: 1387
Bandamanna saga: 1171
baptismal imagery: 1078a, 1424
Battle of Brunanburh, The: 1250
Battle of Maldon, The: 1238, 1275, 1310, 1430, 1437, 1551, 1574, 1650, 1683, 692a
bear: 1521, 1649
Bear's Son Folktale: 1132, 1148, 1486, 1514, 1541, 1561, 1569, 1630, 1696
bears: 1255, 1554, 1648, 1696
beasts of battle: 1256, 1323, 1580, 1606
beauty, words for: 1770a
Bede: 1209, 1234, 1276, 1312, 1481, 1483, 1593, 1604, 1612, 1627, 1700, 1768
Bede's Deathsong: 1595
beer: 1178, 1418, 1513
Beow (Beowulf I): 1560, 1692, 1707; name of: 1622, 1693
Beowulf, and Moses: 1682; as Wiglaf's uncle: 1168; avarice of: 1107; barrow of: 1128, 1702; characterization of: 1197, 1231, 1330, 1372, 1430, 1435, 1467, 1529, 1541, 1655, 1735; Christ figure: 1353, 1424, 1763; death of: 1353, 1499, 1604, 1629, 1673; descent into Grendel's mere: 1118, 1319, 1674,

1696; **epithets for:** 1255, 1369, 1537, 1623, 1770, 1703a; **funeral of:** 1273, 1295, 1313, 1345, 1356, 1403, 1584, 1598, 1702, 1723; **hero:** 1158, 1207, 1220, 1259, 1296, 1332, 1333, 1359, 1374, 1375, 1382, 1428, 1461, 1504, 1505, 1547, 1611, 1620, 1638, 1665, 1692, 1700, 1634a; **inglorious youth of:** 1120, 1154, 1205, 1332, 1696, 1726; **king:** 1110, 1205, 1333, 1461, 1520, 1535, 1587, 1640; **monster characteristics of:** 1272, 1384, 1485, 1488, 1567, 1692; **murderer:** 1622a, 1709; **name of:** 1433, 1484, 1487, 1649, 1648, 1692, 1696, 1724; **old age of:** 1549; **petitioner in Hrothgar's court:** 1480; **pride of:** 1107, 1364, 1384, 1414, 1449, 1481, 1488, 1567, 1650, 1675; **salvation or damnation of:** 1107, 1169, 1176, 1348, 1439, 1663, 1667; **speeches of:** 1639; **superhuman strength of:** 1467, 1658; **surrogate for Hrothgar:** 1190; **swimming contest with Breca:** 1008a, 1118, 1171, 1220, 1290, 1319, 1436, 1489, 1548, 1606, 1628, 1631, 1713, 1762; **swimming feats of:** 1118, 1148, 1224, 1319; **youth of:** 1549
Beowulf-Unferth exchange: 1127, 1171, 1188, 1279, 1283, 1486, 1507, 1541, 1574, 1575, 1606, 1628, 1639, 1654, 1749, 1762

berserkers: 1148, 1226, 1648
Bible: 1130, 1194, 1331, 1372, 1571, 1579, 1667, 1682, 1763
bibliographies: 1152, 1184, 1211, 1247, 1327, 1386, 1401, 1408, 1615, 1732, 1756a
Bjarkamál: 1554
Blickling Homilies: 1194, 1381, 1531, 1563, 1707, 1744
boars: 1648
boasting: 1121, 1199, 1238, 1502, 1513, 1654
body politic: 1125
Boethius: 1108, 1144, 1275, 1312, 1633, 1726
Book of Kells: 1331
Böðvarr Bjarki: 1132, 1554, 1648
Breca: 1118, 1319, 1436, 1713
Brosinga mene: 1383, 1410, 1427
Byrhtferth: 1115
byrnies: 1706

Cædmon: 1627
Cædmon's Hymn: 1595
caesura: 1248, 1443
Cain: 1119, 1142, 1243, 1244, 1256, 1267, 1338, 1372, 1399, 1421, 1439, 1488, 1510, 1567, 1580, 1682, 1692, 1699; **name of:** 1106
Campbell, Joseph: 1220
Camus: 1160
Carlyle, Thomas: 1706
Cassian: 1510
Celtic elements: 1242
Celtic folklore: 1148, 1204, 1255, 1504
Ceolfrith: 1612
Chanson de Roland: 1176, 1291, 1331, 1333, 1446, 1547, 1683
chaos: 1193, 1245, 1377, 1604

characterization in *Beowulf*: 1113, 1152, 1435, 1580, 1614, 1623, 1658, 1702, 1745, 1760
charms: 1182, 1465, 1696
charters, allusions to *Beowulf* in: 1342, 1586
Chaucer, Geoffrey: 1325, 1415, 1502, 1675
choice in *Beowulf*: 1296, 1739
Chrétien de Troyes: 1432, 1446, 1717
Christ and Satan: 1744
Christ I: 1604
Christian allegory: 1296, 1372, 1375, 1579, 1763
Christian elements: 1106, 1123, 1126, 1129, 1133, 1144, 1145, 1153, 1157, 1194, 1243, 1263, 1293, 1308, 1338, 1353, 1359, 1364, 1399, 1401, 1404, 1422, 1424, 1437, 1439, 1475, 1486, 1488, 1490, 1513, 1531, 1539, 1567, 1579, 1580, 1591, 1593, 1604, 1605, 1612, 1627, 1640, 1645, 1663, 1685, 1698, 1700, 1701, 1728, 1732, 1751
Cicero: 1283, 1298
Cid, El—see *Poema de mio Cid*
classical literature, influence of: 1202, 1209, 1298, 1407, 1462
Claudian: 1462
clause structure: 1508, 1716
cliticness: 1450
closure in *Beowulf*: 1495, 1738, 1761
Cnut, King: 1261, 1262, 1476, 1642, 1764
Coastguard: 1318, 1440, 1480, 1574, 1628, 1639, 1747, 1762
Codex Theodosianus: 1298

codicology: 1228, 1261, 1426, 1647, 1695, 1755
color symbolism: 1558
color words: 1478, 1760
comitatus: 1125, 1126, 1205, 1229, 1296, 1372, 1425, 1481, 1487, 1549, 1643
comparative approaches: 1160, 1182, 1207, 1265, 1291, 1467, 1479, 1538
compounds: 1109, 1136, 1156, 1165, 1172, 1223, 1269, 1337, 1352, 1379, 1399, 1451, 1513, 1594, 1615, 1632, 1633, 1703, 1722, 1725
computer-assisted studies: 1112, 1305, 1314, 1477, 1590, 1597, 1733
concordances: 1350, 1679, 1772
conjunctions: 1161, 1320, 1524, 1684a
consolatio theme: 1153
Consolation of Philosophy, Alfred's translation of: 1108, 1144, 1312, 1726
contrast: 1108, 1152, 1176, 1193, 1205, 1214, 1264, 1332, 1435, 1437, 1461, 1483, 1506, 1513, 1555, 1557, 1611
conversion: 1402
coordination: 1684a
Corippus: 1209
Cotton Gnomic Poem: 1141
Cotton Vitellius A.xv: 1261, 1565, 1647
cowardly thanes: 1156
Cúchulainn: 1148, 1547, 1622
cultural markers in *Beowulf*: 1763
cups: 1761
Curtius, Ernst Robert: 1338
Cuthbert: 1234
Cynewulf: 1202, 1237, 1476, 1537, 1593

Dæghrefn: 1148, 1256, 1323, 1380, 1487, 1715
Danelaw: 1249, 1261, 1276, 1285, 1313
Danes, Anglo-Saxon relations with: 1268, 1274, 1276, 1399, 1764; characterization of: 1261, 1332, 1379, 1480, 1559, 1601, 1656; conversion of: 1475; paganism of: 1145, 1293, 1475, 1571, 1588, 1593, 1663
Daniel: 1230, 1533, 1593
date of composition: 1157, 1186, 1221, 1223, 1228, 1229, 1230, 1232, 1233, 1234, 1237, 1242, 1249, 1251, 1261, 1262, 1266, 1268, 1274, 1275, 1276, 1285, 1297, 1304, 1310, 1312, 1313, 1315, 1342, 1361, 1364, 1371, 1381, 1399, 1401, 1449, 1476, 1515, 1523, 1580, 1586, 1595, 1601, 1642, 1695, 1707, 1731, 1764, 1767
death, theme of: 1092a, 1117, 1160, 1472, 1526, 1547, 1617a
deconstruction: 1279, 1603, 1641, 1738
definite article: 1450
Deor: 1257, 1310, 1434
Derrida, Jacques: 1761
dialect: 1242, 1261, 1444, 1519
Dickey, James: 1538
diction: 1040aa, 1092a, 1109, 1152, 1155, 1156, 1172, 1189, 1232, 1244, 1260, 1269, 1282, 1288, 1322, 1339, 1352, 1356, 1394, 1399, 1418, 1464, 1478, 1506, 1513, 1519, 1540, 1550, 1562, 1584, 1606, 1615, 1623, 1627, 1633, 1645, 1704, 1725, 1770, 1770a, 1263a, 1617a
digressions: 1193, 1290, 1326, 1372, 1429, 1433, 1435, 1446, 1483, 1495, 1532, 1580, 1598, 1635, 1670, 1714, 1753
direct discourse: 1079a, 1483, 1650, 1652
dragon: 1151, 1218, 1289, 1331, 1437, 1533, 1571, 1576, 1620, 1689; anti-king: 1527; characterization of: 1505; fight with: 1107, 1137, 1164, 1300, 1399, 1414, 1428, 1436, 1485, 1504, 1603, 1674; hoard of: 1241, 1353, 1483, 1518, 1723; lair of: 1354, 1751; lore about: 1111, 1137, 1169, 1259, 1342, 1485; symbolism of: 1125, 1382, 1412, 1414, 1439, 1579, 1604, 1622, 1692, 1699, 1702
dreams: 1576
drink, words for: 1606
drinking customs: 1178, 1183, 1418, 1496, 1513, 1545, 1610, 1730, 1765

Ealhswith, Queen: 1268
Eanmund and Eadgils: 1168, 1397
Ecgtheow, name of: 1724
Ecgtheow's wife: 1487
editing of *Beowulf*: 1158, 1166, 1261, 1365, 1366, 1391, 1390, 1414, 1442, 1494, 1563, 1566, 1650, 1736, 1738, 1758
editions: 1235, 1442, 1651, 1684, 1685, 1687; partial editions: 1353, 1367, 1414, 1743, 1752, 1702a

editorial punctuation: 1166, 1201, 1437, 1507, 1518, 1667, 1677, 1721
Edward the Elder: 1586
Edwin, conversion of (flight of the sparrow): 1346, 1593, 1604
Egils saga: 1171, 1420, 1449, 1485, 1561, 1584
Eiríksmál: 1249, 1313, 1325
elegiac elements: 1076b, 1123, 1308, 1354, 1462, 1483, 1495, 1555, 1688, 1705
Elene: 1175, 1230, 1237, 1427, 1430, 1593
Eliade, Mircea: 1139
emblems: 1432
Enoch, Book of: 1142
Eofor, name of: 1323
Eomer: 1168
Eormenric: 1310, 1383, 1410
epic characteristics: 1122, 1202, 1252, 1333, 1399, 1434, 1547, 1630, 1638, 1658, 1683, 1544a
Epic of Gilgamesh: 1190, 1638
Er Tostuk: 1630
erfidrápa, memorial eulogies: 1249, 1313
etymologies: 1106, 1121, 1135, 1188, 1199, 1206, 1212, 1255, 1260, 1298, 1320, 1350, 1351, 1410, 1413, 1427, 1435, 1444, 1453, 1513, 1558, 1562, 1569, 1580, 1584, 1589, 1607, 1615, 1622, 1692, 1703, 1724, 1768
evil in *Beowulf*: 1119, 1160, 1172, 1193, 1493, 1506, 1567, 1603, 1605, 1644
exegetical approaches: 1106, 1112, 1130, 1210, 1225, 1267, 1296, 1372, 1437, 1493, 1510, 1579, 1612, 1702, 1750

exile: 1123, 1372, 1421, 1741
Exodus: 1230, 1606, 1633, 1682, 1721, 1764
Eyrbyggja saga: 1171, 1420

fabulous elements: 1118, 1224, 1319, 1372, 1399, 1658, 1660, 1713
Fáfnismál: 1167, 1259, 1584
fame: 1203, 1229, 1580
fate: 1129, 1133, 1144, 1404, 1461, 1547, 1580, 1627, 1692, 1728
Fates of the Apostles: 1230
Father's lament: 1076b, 1123, 1196, 1273, 1428, 1462, 1495, 1609, 1749
feast imagery: 1076a, 1115, 1117, 1245, 1258, 1300, 1346, 1360, 1721
Felix—*Life of Guthlac*: 1452
feminist approaches: 1750, 1761, 1734a
Fergus: 1504
feuds: 1397, 1442
Fight at Finnsburh: 1164, 1257, 1306, 1367, 1425, 1434, 1697, 1712, 1758, 1768
figurative language: 1534
Finn: 1367, 1678, 1697, 1712, 1758
Finn mac Cumaill: 1148
Finnsburh episode: 1076b, 1163, 1168, 1170, 1201, 1231, 1257, 1287, 1306, 1324, 1336, 1367, 1389, 1397, 1425, 1434, 1436, 1442, 1555, 1592, 1697, 1712, 1745, 1749, 1758, 1768
Fitela: 1168, 1249, 1325, 1487
fitt divisions: 1185, 1254, 1261, 1436, 1437, 1482
Flood, Noah's: 1267, 1682

flyting: 1127, 1163, 1171, 1188, 1238, 1279, 1283, 1574, 1628, 1762
folktale and folklore in *Beowulf*: 1065a, 1111, 1132, 1148, 1247, 1248, 1292, 1347, 1386, 1433, 1485, 1489, 1514, 1561, 1569, 1620, 1630, 1622a, 1681, 1696, 1732, 1757;
folktale morphology: 1210, 1485, 1486, 1514, 1542, 1711a, 1719
foreshadowing: 1147, 1530, 1611, 1742
formula studies: 1180, 1239, 1247, 1248, 1252, 1270, 1294, 1311, 1399, 1422, 1479, 1490, 1512, 1558, 1721, 1737; **individual formulas:** 1140, 1245, 1477
formulaic style: 1076a, 1279, 1340, 1401, 1418, 1489, 1537, 1662, 1674
***Fóstbroeðra saga*:** 1420
Franks: 1251
Franks Casket: 1310
fratricide: 1122, 1127, 1171, 1188, 1541
Freawaru: 1170, 1406, 1487, 1536, 1557, 1745, 1761
***Fredgar, Chronicle of*:** 1221
frequency analysis: 1540
Freudian readings: 1308, 1385, 1699
Freyja: 1383, 1427
Freyr: 1365
Frisians: 1162, 1367, 1445, 1712, 1758
funeral customs: 1065a, 1157, 1183, 1273, 1293, 1313, 1345, 1403, 1425, 1498, 1546, 1580, 1627, 1707, 1723

Gardner, John—*Grendel*: 1222, 1309, 1395, 1659, 1729
Geats: 1483, 1700; **characterization of:** 1139, 1156, 1332, 1379, 1396, 1424, 1518, 1702; **homeland of:** 1553, 1608, 1669, 1713; **identity of:** 1152, 1157, 1249, 1411, 1553
gender roles: 1141, 1170, 1175, 1169a, 1341, 1385, 1396, 1406, 1502, 1516, 1536, 1643, 1745, 1761
genealogies in *Beowulf*: 1173, 1268, 1291, 1325, 1342, 1463, 1560, 1580, 1693, 1707
general introductions: 1147, 1152, 1240, 1278, 1328, 1375, 1386, 1401, 1425, 1445, 1468, 1555, 1572, 1591, 1600, 1613, 1660, 1732, 1769, 1634a
***Genesis B*:** 1751
genesis of the poem: 1229, 1242, 1261, 1262, 1278, 1310, 1313, 1399, 1404, 1539, 1560, 1595
genitive, functions of: 1191, 1405, 1443, 1667
genres in *Beowulf*: 1147, 1164, 1182, 1313, 1321, 1325, 1495, 1603, 1683, 1544a
geography of *Beowulf*: 1608, 1669, 1713
Germanic character types: 1118, 1132, 1536
Germanic elements: 1123, 1127, 1148, 1188, 1202, 1226, 1243, 1263, 1269, 1273, 1290, 1300, 1308, 1329, 1338, 1343, 1359, 1364, 1383, 1386, 1387, 1396, 1397, 1399, 1401, 1406, 1410, 1420, 1425, 1427, 1465, 1496, 1540,

1541, 1554, 1560, 1569,
1580, 1607, 1643, 1648,
1658, 1758
Germanic history: 1116, 1157,
1296, 1310, 1330, 1371,
1409, 1411, 1412, 1428,
1531, 1700
giants: 1142, 1244, 1372, 1465,
1605; sword of: 1142, 1159,
1195, 1300, 1432, 1486,
1497, 1543, 1561, 1569,
1579, 1616
gift giving: 1132, 1329, 1388,
1406, 1535, 1745, 1756,
1637a
Gísla saga: 1175
glossaries: 1350, 1448
gnomic passages: 1141, 1172,
1173, 1215, 1264, 1318,
1321, 1440, 1488, 1495,
1653, 1711, 1714, 1728,
1742, 1753
Gododdin, The: 1242, 1765
Göngu-Hrólfs saga: 1561
Gordon, E.V.: 1766
Gower, John: 1415, 1625
Grágás: 1420
Gregorian chant: 1361
Gregory of Tours—*History of the Franks*: 1251, 1409, 1553, 1746
Gregory's *Pastoral Care*—Alfred's translation of: 1230
Gregory the Great: 1169, 1209, 1225, 1230, 1493
Grendel: 1106, 1111, 1139, 1142, 1172, 1193, 1196, 1225, 1255, 1258, 1437, 1493, 1516, 1527, 1567, 1576, 1596, 1610, 1658, 1665; arm of: 1148, 1216, 1335, 1376, 1424, 1543, 1668; as mock retainer: 1076b, 1117, 1421, 1611; Bigfoot?: 1192; characterization of: 1399, 1529, 1655, 1744; decapitation of: 1159; epithets for: 1244, 1272, 1449, 1466, 1741; fight with: 1125, 1179, 1190, 1204, 1220, 1384, 1399, 1436, 1460, 1504, 1521, 1561, 1569, 1665, 1668, 1686, 1728; glove of: 1148, 1298, 1465; his approach to Heorot: 1530, 1611, 1674, 1721, 1737; humanity of: 1272, 1692, 1741; instrument of God: 1119; invulnerability to weapons: 1226, 1301, 1456; magical powers of: 1465; mere of: 1196, 1319, 1331, 1358, 1381, 1399, 1407, 1414, 1548, 1559, 1569, 1596, 1682, 1696, 1763; name of: 1484, 1487, 1569; symbolism of: 1382, 1412, 1433, 1439, 1604, 1605, 1622, 1644, 1692, 1699
Grendel's mother: 1142, 1178, 1301, 1406, 1427, 1437, 1527, 1536, 1557, 1576, 1585, 1670; as avenger: 1421; attack on Heorot: 1686; characterization of: 1170, 1175, 1442, 1702; fight with: 1125, 1148, 1190, 1195, 1220, 1300, 1347, 1399, 1415, 1424, 1436, 1504, 1516, 1543, 1561, 1701; symbolism of: 1382, 1385, 1412, 1433, 1439, 1604, 1692, 1699
Grendel—John Gardner: 1222, 1309, 1395, 1659, 1729
Grettir: 1569, 1715
Grettis saga: 1132, 1188, 1226, 1347, 1420, 1489, 1497,

1521, 1542, 1561, 1569, 1584, 1715, 1766
Grimm, Jacob: 1408
Grimm, Wilhelm: 1408
Gríms saga loðinkinna: 1171
Grundtvig, N.F.S.: 1302, 1390, 1651, 1685
Gunnars saga: 1561
Gunnlaugs saga: 1171, 1226, 1446
Guthlac, St.: 1147, 1234, 1237, 1452
Guthlaf: 1487
Guthrúnarkviða: 1171

Hæthcyn: 1428, 1541, 1609
hagiography: 1234, 1452, 1481
Hákonarmál: 1249, 1313, 1325, 1387
Half-Danes: 1758
Hálfdanar saga: 1561
hall, concept of: 1385, 1413, 1425, 1604, 1683, 1702, 1766, 1634a
Halliday, M.A.K.: 1701
Ham: 1267, 1372, 1510
Hama: 1193, 1383, 1410
Hamðismál: 1164, 1410
Hand and the Child Folktale, the: 1148, 1204
hands: 1125, 1323, 1728
Handscio: 1076a, 1125, 1190, 1487, 1728; name of: 1323
harp: 1201
hart: 1183, 1358, 1559, 1571, 1579
haste: 1356
Háttatal: 1343
Hávamál: 1167, 1263, 1558
Healfdene's daughter: 1427, 1447, 1474, 1487
Healfdene's sword: 1522, 1756, 1637a
Heardred: 1168, 1436, 1487, 1560

Heathobard episode: 1163, 1372, 1432, 1436, 1742, 1745
Heiðarvíga saga: 1420
Helgi lays (*Helgakviður*): 1427
hell: 1111, 1225, 1744
helmets: 1063a, 1140, 1453, 1696, 1747
Hengest: 1231, 1287, 1367, 1397, 1592, 1678, 1697, 1758
Hengest, and Horsa: 1336, 1389, 1768
Heorogar: 1388; name of: 1433
Heorot: 1139, 1193, 1196, 1559, 1571, 1579, 1593, 1612, 1638, 1644, 1702; burning of: 1179, 1217, 1742; location of: 1669; name of: 1433
Heoroweard: 1388
Herebeald: 1196, 1428, 1609, 1709; name of: 1433
Heremod: 1154, 1193, 1201, 1249, 1272, 1325, 1414, 1435, 1437, 1527, 1558, 1603, 1616, 1700, 1714; name of: 1484
Hereric: 1168, 1487
heriot: 1397
hero on the beach: 1306, 1559, 1631, 1674, 1718
heroic values: 1076b, 1110, 1129, 1139, 1145, 1187, 1220, 1234, 1263, 1323, 1330, 1356, 1359, 1437, 1439, 1442, 1455, 1467, 1481, 1485, 1488, 1506, 1543, 1547, 1591, 1692, 1698, 1700, 1701, 1732, 1751, 1634a
Hetware: 1251
Hildebrandslied: 1121, 1164, 1279, 1658
Hildeburh: 1170, 1231, 1306, 1396, 1406, 1442, 1487,

1536, 1557, 1568, 1745, 1758, 1761; **name of:** 1165
historical allegory: 1412, 1586
historical elements: 1224, 1372, 1409, 1422, 1511, 1553, 1603, 1660, 1745
history, attitudes toward in *Beowulf*: 1126, 1129, 1293, 1312, 1372, 1412, 1433, 1658
Hlöðsviða: 1164
Hnæf: 1168, 1273, 1345, 1541, 1712, 1758
Hobbit, The: 1688, 1766
Holland, Cecelia: 1748
Homer: 1180, 1246, 1248, 1403, 1558, 1574, 1718
homilies: 1293, 1381, 1495, 1531, 1744
Hopkins, Gerard Manley: 1286
hospitality: 1170, 1197, 1581, 1585, 1709
Hrana saga: 1561
Hrethel: 1487, 1609
Hrethel's lament: 1120, 1123, 1609
Hrólfs saga kraka: 1132, 1255, 1427, 1648, 1678
Hrosvita of Gandersheim: 1312
Hrothgar: 1110, 1168, 1193, 1333, 1388, 1480, 1535, 1549, 1579; **characterization of:** 1119, 1132, 1262, 1364, 1441, 1461, 1581, 1614, 1623, 1702; **conversion of:** 1593; 1576; **epithets for:** 1369; **name of:** 1487; **sermon of:** 1076b, 1107, 1119, 1159, 1196, 1237, 1263, 1321, 1425, 1481, 1488, 1520, 1531, 1567, 1593, 1653, 1753, 1761; **weakness of:** 1190, 1601, 1614, 1656
Hrothulf: 1154, 1168, 1541, 1560

Hrunting: 1132, 1195, 1486, 1497, 1541, 1567, 1569, 1575, 1762
Hugas: 1251
humor in *Beowulf*: 1117, 1170, 1178, 1187, 1449, 1611
Hunlafing: 1109, 1336, 1367, 1397, 1758
Hygd: 1141, 1170, 1193, 1196, 1326, 1406, 1435, 1536, 1557, 1560, 1643, 1726, 1745; **name of:** 1484, 1589
Hygelac: 1008a, 1022a, 1120, 1168, 1193, 1205, 1332, 1342, 1369, 1535, 1623, 1700; **name of:** 1487, 1537, 1589; **raid of:** 1251, 1257, 1380, 1428, 1535
Hymiskviða: 1719
hyperbole: 1654
hypotaxis: 1340, 1665

Igor Tale: 1377
Iliad: 1122, 1176, 1180, 1190, 1306, 1333, 1543, 1558, 1574, 1692, 1718
imagery: 1237, 1331, 1540, 1702; **agricultural:** 1173, 1637; **animal:** 1331, 1559, 1579; **arrow:** 1196; **baptismal:** 1424; **bear:** 1554, 1649, 1648, 1696; **boar:** 1648, 1696; **chest:** 1125, 1751; **cups:** 1761; **feasts:** 1115, 1117, 1245, 1300, 1346, 1360; **fire:** 1149; **hall:** 1164, 1196, 1385, 1702; **hands:** 1323, 1728; **heads, hands, and feet:** 1125; **light and dark:** 1331, 1760; **ravens:** 1256, 1735; **sea:** 1295, 1331, 1352, 1437, 1452, 1596, 1633, 1673, 1703; **sexual:** 1170, 1382; **stag:** 1571;

weapons: 1109, 1573, 1626, 1692, 1761
immanence: 1113, 1604
Indo-European myth: 1336, 1389, 1433, 1489, 1497, 1504, 1558
Indra: 1433, 1497, 1504
information theory: 1597
Ing: 1580, 1758
Ingeld: 1163, 1434, 1487
initiation rites: 1402, 1542, 1696
interlace structure: 1114, 1196, 1331, 1532, 1554, 1692
interperformativity: 1714
intertextuality: 1714
Irish elements: 1135, 1148, 1504
irony in *Beowulf*: 1076b, 1117, 1152, 1156, 1172, 1187, 1212, 1258, 1264, 1530, 1536, 1559, 1585, 1631, 1676, 1702, 1761
Isidore of Seville: 1106, 1298, 1407, 1579
Iugurtha, King of the Numidians: 1154

Jakobson, Roman: 1429
Jerome: 1106, 1169, 1579
Job: 1119, 1169, 1493
Jordanes: 1403
***Judith*:** 1175, 1228, 1232, 1261, 1426, 1427, 1551, 1557, 1611, 1679, 1755
***Juliana*:** 1175, 1230, 1427, 1721
Jung, Carl G.: 1219
Jutes: 1157, 1367, 1411, 1553, 1758

kennings: 1092a, 1594, 1606
***Ketils saga hængs*:** 1171
kingship: 807a, 1110, 1125, 1154, 1193, 1296, 1329, 1333, 1364, 1369, 1388, 1421, 1461, 1481, 1483, 1487, 1504, 1527, 1535, 1560, 1614, 1638, 1640, 1732
kinship: 1168, 1330
Kuhn's Laws: 1227, 1392, 1619, 1646, 1544a

Lacan, Jacques: 1770
***Lagamon's Brut*:** 1610
last survivor: 1289
laws and legal traditions: 1155, 1293, 1298, 1351, 1364, 1397, 1420, 1709, 1747, 1758
***Laxdoela saga*:** 1420
Lay of the Last Survivor: 1076b, 1119, 1123, 1414, 1670, 1689, 1696
lays: 1164, 1325, 1399, 1427, 1495, 1569
Le Guin, Ursula: 1146
leadership: 1110
Leiden Riddle: 1595
Lévi-Strauss, Claude: 1176
Lewis, C.S.: 1344, 1556
***Liber Monstrorum*:** 1008a, 1022a, 1303, 1342, 1454
***Liedertheorie*:** 1246, 1261
linguistic approaches: 1136, 1223, 1232, 1242, 1275, 1285, 1356, 1429, 1476, 1590, 1595, 1716
literacy: 1202, 1460
literary history: 1209, 1281, 1292, 1304, 1381, 1537, 1595, 1597
literary influence of *Beowulf*: 1008a, 1281, 1304, 1381
literary theory: 1210, 1279, 1603, 1701, 1702, 1738, 1750, 1770
litotes: 1218, 1264, 1654, 1737
liturgical influence: 1424, 1598, 1612
***Lokasenna*:** 1171
Lord, Albert B.: 1236, 1247

Lord of the Rings, The: 1463, 1729a
Lucan: 1407
Ludwigslied: 1683

Madden, Sir Frederic: 1565
magic: 1140, 1141, 1273, 1410, 1465, 1486
manuscript illumination: 1137, 1331, 1422, 1727
manuscript punctuation: 1185, 1272, 1753
manuscript studies: 1197, 1228, 1254, 1261, 1262, 1297, 1303, 1315, 1386, 1426, 1482, 1494, 1563, 1641, 1647, 1657, 1694, 1695, 1755
matriarchy: 1301, 1385, 1396
Maxims I: 1427, 1604
memory: 1173, 1300, 1460, 1539, 1558, 1689, 1690
Mercian elements in *Beowulf*: 1261, 1268, 1580
Merovech: 1221
messenger: 1076b, 1436, 1520, 1742
metaphors: 1149, 1196, 1331, 1529, 1594, 1673
Meters of Boethius: 1230, 1275, 1633, 1544a
migration myth: 1700
Modthryth: 1170, 1175, 1193, 1296, 1301, 1332, 1406, 1427, 1435, 1536, 1557, 1567, 1580, 1702, 1745, 1761; name of: 1435, 1484
monsters: 1008a, 1139, 1142, 1160, 1187, 1196, 1219, 1267, 1272, 1273, 1303, 1319, 1351, 1372, 1375, 1382, 1412, 1421, 1454, 1527, 1554, 1576, 1587, 1604, 1623, 1644, 1699, 1727, 1732, 1729a, 1634a
morphology: 1232

Morris, William: 1288
music: 1355, 1361, 1515
mutability, theme of: 1076b, 1164, 1354, 1455, 1461, 1483
myth, elements of in *Beowulf*: 1176, 1195, 1243, 1374, 1389, 1433, 1538, 1603, 1622, 1631, 1638, 1719, 1757

Nægling: 1488
names: 1221, 1285, 1411, 1433, 1463, 1558, 1580; for God: 1439, 1513, 1580, 1769; personal: 1106, 1154, 1212, 1244, 1315, 1323, 1427, 1435, 1447, 1484, 1537, 1569, 1589, 1607, 1623, 1648, 1696, 1724, 1746, 1768; placenames: 1342, 1553, 1586, 1713; principles of naming: 1487, 1628
narrative technique: 1076b, 1113, 1115, 1129, 1164, 1176, 1205, 1214, 1246, 1258, 1290, 1300, 1320, 1324, 1415, 1428, 1451, 1483, 1495, 1530, 1532, 1603, 1609, 1614, 1644, 1742, 1760
narrator: 1205, 1428, 1609, 1705, 1714
nature in *Beowulf*: 1331, 1437
Nebuchadnezzar: 1533, 1593
neck-ring given to Beowulf by Wealh-theow: 1196, 1380, 1383, 1427, 1432, 1557, 1761
Neckham, Alexander —*De laudibus divinae sapientiae*: 1358
negation: 1206, 1287, 1398, 1506, 1654
Nennius, Pseudo-: 1358

Subject Index

New Criticism: 1750
Nibelungenlied: 1163, 1291, 1330, 1333, 1338, 1387, 1402, 1409
Njáls saga: 1171, 1226, 1420
Noachic tradition: 1142
Nowell, Laurence: 1695
Nowell codex: 1114, 1228, 1261, 1399, 1426, 1494, 1642, 1647, 1657, 1695, 1727, 1755
numerical structure: 1185, 1253, 1304, 1437

Odo of Cluny: 1312
Odyssey: 1122, 1190, 1195, 1245, 1246, 1248, 1279, 1333, 1543, 1574, 1638, 1692, 1718
Oedipus Tyrannus: 1207
Offa: 1157, 1175, 1193, 1285, 1296, 1310, 1326, 1434
Offa, King of Mercia: 1268, 1276, 1364
Ohtere and Wulfstan, voyage of: 1498
Ólafs saga Tryggvasonar: 1561
old age: 1532
Old Norse myth: 1175, 1273, 1300, 1313, 1365, 1465
Onela: 1168, 1397, 1436, 1473
Ongentheow, name of: 1724
oral composition: 1164, 1203, 1236, 1246, 1247, 1258, 1279, 1392, 1399, 1422, 1460, 1490, 1506, 1540, 1614, 1625, 1683, 1686, 1705, 1714, 1737
oral epics: 1190
orality and literacy: 1064a, 1112, 1114, 1127, 1143, 1163, 1173, 1180, 1182, 1190, 1195, 1201, 1202, 1210, 1239, 1247, 1248, 1270, 1279, 1338, 1340, 1399, 1401, 1460, 1464, 1537, 1539, 1554, 1558, 1574, 1597, 1628, 1631, 1633, 1662, 1670, 1683, 1689, 1690, 1702, 1714, 1718, 1750, 1751, 1692a
Orosius: 1238, 1312, 1498
orthography: 1232, 1447, 1476
Ortnit: 1151
Örvar-Odds saga: 1171
Oslaf: 1487
Oswald: 1234
Oswine: 1234
Oswine, St.: 1481
Oðinn: 1249, 1301, 1313, 1383, 1427, 1648, 1696
Ovid: 1735

paganism: 1076a, 1126, 1133, 1140, 1144, 1153, 1157, 1175, 1241, 1243, 1273, 1293, 1365, 1399, 1401, 1404, 1422, 1437, 1439, 1475, 1486, 1488, 1497, 1513, 1579, 1580, 1604, 1605, 1627, 1640, 1645, 1663, 1700, 1723, 1728, 1763
paleography: 1174, 1232, 1261, 1315, 1422, 1482, 1494, 1564, 1642, 1657, 1694, 1731, 1755
panegyric: 1325
parallelism: 1324, 1692a
parataxis: 1340, 1665
Paris Psalter: 1633, 1667
Parry, Milman: 1247, 1340
patriarchy: 1301, 1385, 1396
patristic lore: 1169, 1225, 1399, 1612
Peabody, Berkley: 1239
peace-weavers and peace-weaving: 1396, 1406, 1761
penance: 1744
Penda, King of Mercia: 1580
personal pronoun: 1516
Phoenix: 1252, 1306

phonological patterns: 1223, 1239, 1413, 1590
Physiologus: 1579
Pierce, Charles: 1761
Pinkerton, John, edition of Barbour's *The Bruce*: 1720
Pippin I: 1364
Pliny the Elder: 1169
poculum mortis: 1387
Poema de mio Cid: 1291, 1467, 1479
point of view: 1113
political concerns: 1125, 1263, 1296, 1329, 1388, 1412, 1480, 1567, 1675, 1726, 1746
power relationships: 1296, 1487, 1726, 1634a
prepositions: 1500
pronoun fronting: 1492
prophecy: 1742
Propp, Vladimir: 1486, 1542, 1719
prosody: 1136, 1138, 1161, 1181, 1200, 1223, 1227, 1230, 1239, 1248, 1285, 1286, 1290, 1305, 1311, 1314, 1327, 1337, 1343, 1349, 1355, 1357, 1366, 1392, 1399, 1401, 1416, 1422, 1423, 1470, 1471, 1507, 1512, 1539, 1540, 1570, 1597, 1602, 1619, 1624, 1632, 1634, 1646, 1650, 1671, 1690, 1711, 1721, 1725, 1733, 1737, 1753, 1772, 1602a
provenance: 1157, 1268, 1276, 1312, 1342, 1399
Prudentius: 1298
psychological approaches: 1079a, 1195, 1219, 1220, 1382, 1385, 1596, 1699

Rabanus Maurus: 1579
Ragnarök: 1308, 1433

Ragnarsdrápa: 1249
Raumer, Rudolf von: 1582
ravens: 1256, 1735
Ravenswood, battle at: 1256, 1257, 1324
realism: 1118, 1224, 1399, 1534, 1596, 1644, 1658
reception of *Beowulf*: 1209, 1229, 1304, 1381, 1720, 1738, 1760
recordings: 1064a, 1422, 1740, 1383a
relative and personal pronouns: 1664
relative clauses: 1161, 1551
Remigius of Auxerre: 1312
revenge: 1144, 1231, 1372, 1376, 1397, 1421, 1488, 1699
reversals in *Beowulf*: 1164
reviews of scholarship: 1112, 1152, 1210, 1233, 1247, 1278, 1297, 1391, 1390, 1401, 1523, 1651, 1685, 1702, 1732, 1738, 1750, 1734a
rhetoric: 1283, 1639
rhetorical patterns: 1115
rhetorical tradition: 1209, 1263, 1282
rhyme: 1362
Rimbert of Bremen: 1475
ring structure: 1143, 1506, 1670, 1686, 1692
Ruin, The: 1354
Rune Poem: 1484
runes, lore of: 1208, 1465, 1484, 1580
Ruotger—*Vita Brunonis*: 1312

saints' lives: 1147, 1169a, 1234, 1399, 1452, 1481, 1489, 1557, 1707
Sallust: 1154
salvation: 1763

sapientia et fortitudo: 1176, 1318, 1430, 1440, 1449
Saxo Grammaticus: 1116, 1127, 1132, 1171, 1188, 1226, 1259, 1678
Scandinavian elements: 1148, 1310, 1546
scholarship, history of: 1582; reviews of: 1408, 1569
scop: 1201, 1705; performance of: 1257
scribal editing of *Beowulf*: 1218, 1261, 1442, 1464, 1563, 1736
scribes of the Nowell Codex: 1228, 1261, 1262, 1315, 1458, 1482, 1533, 1642, 1657
Scyld Scefing: 1173, 1345, 1433, 1498, 1560, 1598, 1604, 1623, 1644, 1707, 1737; funeral ship of: 1065a, 1300; name of: 1560, 1622, 1693
sea imagery: 1295, 1352, 1437, 1452, 1596, 1673, 1703
sea voyages: 1180, 1193, 1250, 1331, 1669, 1704, 1737
Seafarer, The: 1123, 1354, 1604
secular allegory: 1372
semantics: 1665
semiotic approaches: 1485, 1573, 1626, 1701, 1761, 1763
senna: 1127
Serbo-Croatian epic poetry: 1180, 1236, 1248, 1662
sermons: 1744
setting: 1407
sexual imagery: 1170
Shakespeare, William: 1415, 1690
shamanism: 1649, 1648, 1681, 1696
ship burial: 1065a

ships: 1183, 1594, 1767; launching of: 1250, 1704
Sigemund: 1137, 1193, 1201, 1249, 1259, 1325, 1409, 1434, 1435, 1437, 1487, 1623, 1700, 1714
Sigrdrífumál: 1155
Sigurd: 1164, 1259, 1485, 1554, 1723
Sigurðar saga: 1485
Sir Gawain and the Green Knight: 1415, 1432, 1446, 1502, 1717
skaldic poetry: 1249, 1548, 1606
Snorri Sturluson: 1343
social institutions: 1187, 1364, 1377, 1385, 1422, 1504, 1537, 1567, 1605, 1701, 1702, 1723, 1634a
social norms: 1272, 1364, 1654, 1747
song-amalgams: 1180, 1246
Song of Bagdad: 1236
song of creation: 1331, 1490, 1580, 1612, 1670
Sörlaþáttr: 1383
Sörli: 1410
source studies: 1399, 1606; Biblical: 1130, 1142, 1194, 1372, 1612, 1682; classical: 1298, 1407, 1462; learned Latin: 1454; liturgical: 1424, 1598; patristic: 1106, 1169, 1225, 1372, 1510, 1571, 1612
Southwick codex: 1261, 1647
speech-act theory: 1127, 1238, 1650
sprung rhythm: 1286
St. Christopher, Life of: 1228, 1755
Statius: 1209, 1407, 1462
structuralist approaches: 1210, 1486

structure of *Beowulf*: 1076b, 1114, 1129, 1164, 1176, 1185, 1196, 1214, 1220, 1253, 1261, 1304, 1372, 1399, 1415, 1428, 1429, 1433, 1436, 1437, 1468, 1495, 1504, 1515, 1530, 1532, 1549, 1555, 1580, 1598, 1603, 1609, 1622, 1626, 1635, 1644, 1670, 1686, 1701, 1734a
style: 1147, 1149, 1223, 1237, 1265, 1269, 1282, 1283, 1320, 1362, 1386, 1399, 1476, 1479, 1506, 1513, 1540, 1582, 1590, 1594, 1614, 1623, 1639, 1654, 1655, 1721, 1770, 1602a
succession, questions of: 1364, 1388, 1560, 1643
Sutcliff, Rosemary: 1509
Sutton Hoo: 1063a, 1126, 1157, 1186, 1310, 1425, 1546, 1554, 1571, 1648
Swedish wars: 1372, 1425, 1436, 1483, 1609, 1700
Swerting: 1168, 1487
sword-hilt: 1159, 1195, 1300, 1432, 1497, 1569, 1616
swords: 1109, 1132, 1189, 1379, 1432, 1522, 1550, 1573, 1626, 1706, 1756, 1761, 1637a
symbolism: 1432, 1626
syntax: 881a, 1079a, 1108, 1161, 1191, 1227, 1232, 1284, 1300, 1316, 1320, 1324, 1340, 1349, 1384, 1392, 1398, 1405, 1443, 1450, 1464, 1476, 1477, 1491, 1492, 1501, 1503, 1507, 1508, 1524, 1551, 1570, 1582, 1583, 1592, 1618, 1632, 1646, 1654, 1664, 1665, 1667, 1677, 1684a, 1708, 1711, 1716, 1721, 1753, 1754, 1602a, 1756a, 1544a, 1692a
Tacitus: 1141, 1226, 1263, 1364, 1407, 1409
***Táin Bó Cúalnge*:** 1122, 1148, 1255, 1547, 1622
Taliesin: 1257
taunters: 1122, 1502
teaching *Beowulf*: 1110, 1160, 1219, 1291, 1422, 1556, 1666, 1738
Tertullian: 1510, 1513
textual emendations: 1166, 1174, 1179, 1197, 1212, 1217, 1218, 1271, 1287, 1307, 1360, 1365, 1366, 1391, 1390, 1398, 1447, 1457, 1510, 1522, 1528, 1533, 1563, 1564, 1568, 1571, 1575, 1577, 1580, 1587, 1605, 1650, 1652, 1671, 1676, 1678, 1694, 1708, 1731, 1736, 1754, 1756, 1758, 1637a
textual reconstructions: 1107, 1120, 1128, 1149, 1151, 1166, 1179, 1191, 1199, 1212, 1217, 1218, 1299, 1335, 1404, 1420, 1443, 1456, 1457, 1474, 1493, 1528, 1564, 1566, 1577, 1583, 1587, 1676, 1677, 1691, 1721, 1726, 1730, 1754
textual variants: 1563
themes in *Beowulf*: 1076b, 1152, 1164, 1210, 1245, 1272, 1386, 1412, 1425, 1437, 1468, 1513, 1555, 1635, 1761
thief: 1289, 1307, 1368, 1414, 1420, 1723
Thorkelin, Grímur Jónsson: 1393, 1565, 1566, 1651

Thorkelin transcripts: 1393, 1565, 1566, 1641
Thórodds þáttr Snorrasonar: 1561
Thrymskviða: 1543
time: 1129, 1139, 1214, 1300, 1424, 1446, 1472, 1483, 1495, 1526, 1532, 1622, 1732, 1742
time markers: 1592
Tolkien, J.R.R.: 1463, 1556, 1663, 1688, 1757, 1766, 1729a
tragedy: 1231, 1473, 1745
translations, Danish: 1419, 1431; Dutch: 1037a, 1370; English: 1183, 1235, 1302, 1317, 1328, 1437, 1451, 1455, 1600, 1613, 1621, 1660, 1672, 1687, 1740, 1749, 1771; English (partial): 1115, 1367, 1414, 1417, 1552; French: 1240, 1277; Frisian: 1134, 1445; Icelandic: 1378; Italian: 1617; Italian (partial): 1353; Japanese: 1743, 1752, 1759, 1702a; reviews of: 1131, 1177, 1288, 1363, 1422, 1431, 1661; theories of: 1114, 1124, 1131, 1138, 1177, 1370, 1413, 1717, 1749
treasure: 1300, 1329, 1353, 1483, 1584; curse on: 1107, 1241, 1518, 1667, 1689, 1723; uselessness of: 1576, 1689, 1723
treasure hoards: 1689, 1723
type-scenes: 1076a, 1115, 1127, 1163, 1164, 1180, 1190, 1236, 1239, 1245, 1258, 1279, 1306, 1399, 1489, 1490, 1558, 1559, 1581, 1611, 1625, 1631, 1674, 1718, 1735, 1737

typology: 1682
uncle-nephew relationships: 1168, 1396, 1487
Unferth: 1122, 1126, 1127, 1132, 1167, 1171, 1188, 1195, 1364, 1480, 1486, 1496, 1521, 1541, 1548, 1567, 1574, 1575, 1581, 1606, 1614, 1628, 1639, 1702, 1762; name of: 1122, 1188, 1206, 1212, 1366, 1447, 1541, 1607, 1724
unity of *Beowulf*: 1635
Valerius Flaccus: 1462
valkyries: 1140, 1175, 1427
variation: 1149, 1213, 1266, 1324, 1373, 1469, 1507, 1513, 1525, 1544, 1594
Vatnsdoela saga: 1420
Vedas: 1433
verb tense: 1300, 1495
verbs, auxiliaries: 1227, 1602a, 1544a; finite: 1113, 1471, 1492, 1507, 1618, 1544a
Vercelli Book, The: 1482
Vercelli Homilies: 1744
Verner's Law: 1290
verse grammar: 1619
Viking age: 1315, 1707
Virgil: 1209, 1403, 1407, 1591, 1742
Visio Pauli: 1381, 1407, 1707, 1744
Völsunga saga: 1259, 1330, 1409
voyages and voyaging: 1114

Waldere: 1434
Waltharius: 1164, 1549, 1683
Wanderer, The: 1123, 1238, 1354, 1430
Wanley, Humphrey: 1647
warriors: 1379
water, words for: 1722

Wealhtheow: 1115, 1141, 1170, 1329, 1341, 1388, 1406, 1427, 1480, 1502, 1536, 1557, 1579, 1581, 1643, 1702, 1745, 1761, 1770; name of: 1412, 1427, 1724, 1746
weapons: 1109, 1132, 1158, 1226, 1300, 1379, 1497, 1550, 1706, 1263a
weaving motif: 1196, 1761
Weland the Smith: 1310
Welsh elements: 1412, 1586
Welsh poetry: 1257, 1765
Weohstan: 1168, 1397, 1541; sword of: 1076b, 1397
wergild: 1372, 1397
West Saxon elements in *Beowulf:* 1261, 1268, 1342, 1707
***Widsith*:** 1257, 1310, 1434
Widukind: 1251, 1312
***Wife's Lament, The*:** 1341
Wiglaf: 1076b, 1125, 1168, 1259, 1296, 1333, 1461, 1487, 1520, 1549, 1586, 1623, 1638, 1675, 1723; name of: 1724
Wilfrid: 1234
wisdom: 1263
wisdom literature: 1321, 1653
Woden: 1126, 1273
wolves: 1692
woman mourning at Beowulf's funeral: 1170, 1406, 1520, 1557
women in *Beowulf:* 1141, 1170, 1175, 1169a, 1231, 1273, 1334, 1341, 1385, 1396, 1406, 1422, 1438, 1487, 1502, 1536, 1557, 1643, 1660, 1745, 1734a
***Wonders of the East*:** 1228, 1303, 1426, 1727, 1755
word studies: 807a, 995b, 1063a, 1076a, 1092a, 1107, 1109, 1114, 1117, 1119, 1121, 1122, 1125, 1128, 1130, 1132, 1133, 1135, 1137, 1140, 1141, 1144, 1149, 1150, 1151, 1155, 1156, 1158, 1159, 1165, 1166, 1167, 1172, 1173, 1188, 1189, 1194, 1199, 1221, 1239, 1241, 1244, 1245, 1249, 1255, 1260, 1272, 1275, 1285, 1287, 1293, 1295, 1299, 1300, 1313, 1320, 1330, 1335, 1339, 1348, 1351, 1356, 1359, 1360, 1364, 1365, 1369, 1372, 1379, 1387, 1394, 1400, 1410, 1413, 1418, 1427, 1430, 1432, 1440, 1441, 1444, 1447, 1449, 1453, 1456, 1458, 1459, 1465, 1476, 1478, 1493, 1496, 1497, 1498, 1500, 1513, 1524, 1529, 1533, 1541, 1544, 1548, 1550, 1562, 1568, 1569, 1578, 1583, 1584, 1585, 1587, 1592, 1597, 1599, 1603, 1605, 1606, 1610, 1615, 1616, 1627, 1637, 1640, 1661, 1663, 1667, 1673, 1678, 1677, 1680, 1691, 1696, 1697, 1698, 1703, 1704, 1708, 1722, 1724, 1725, 1728, 1731, 1734, 1735, 1739, 1744, 1747, 1751, 1758, 1764, 1765, 1767, 1770a, 1263a, 1617a
wordplay: 1154, 1158, 1295, 1323, 1413, 1435, 1447, 1584, 1637, 1698, 1724
wrestling: 1715
Wulf, name of: 1323
***Wulf and Eadwacer*:** 1396
Wulfgar: 1333, 1480
Wulfstan: 1237, 1310

Ynglinga saga: 1226, 1255, 1511, 1584
Ynglingatal: 1325, 1511
youth and old age: 1108, 1332, 1333, 1549
Yrse: 1427, 1487

Zhou Chu: 1620

WORD INDEX

references are to item numbers

ǣht: 1584
æl-mihtig: 1513
æ-lmihtiga, sē: 1615
ǣn-līc: 1770a
æppel-fealuwe: 1478, 1661
æsc: 1109
æsc-wiga: 1379
æt-: 1458
æþeling: 1239, 1544, 1615
āgend-frēa: 1379
āg-lǣca: 1135, 1155, 1272, 1351, 1603
aldor: 1578
aldor-ðegn: 1379
ā-lecgan: 1335
alf-walda: 1365, 1587
ā-limpan: 1413
al-walda: 1513, 1615
an-walda: 1615
ār: 1400, 1584

bæð: 1703
bald: 1615
bāt: 1704
bāt-weard: 1379
beado-lēoma: 1109
beado-rinc: 1379
beadu-grīma: 1109
bēag-hroden: 1427, 1770a
bēag-gyfa: 1379

be-gylpan: 1287
be-nemnan: 1107, 1241
bēod-genēat: 1379
bēor: 1418
beorht: 1109
beorn: 1703
bēor-scealc: 1379
bēot: 1121, 1199, 1300, 1379
bill: 1109
blāc: 1478
blaca: 1735
blæc: 1478
blǣd-āgand: 1379
blanca: 1478
blōd: 1478
blonden-: 1478
bolgen-mōd: 1255
bon-gār: 1109
bord: 1109
bord-rand: 1109
brentingas: 1767
brēost-gewǣdu: 1109
brēost-hord: 1751
brēost-net: 1109
brim: 1703
brōden: 1109
brond: 1109
bront: 1704
brūn: 1478
bunden-heord: 1770a
byrne: 1109

ceaster-būend: 1379
cempa: 1379, 1703
cēne: 1615
cēol: 1704
collen-ferhð: 1255, 1615
cuman: 1239
cumbles hyrde: 1379
cunnan: 1293
cwealm: 1615
cȳm-līc: 1770a
cyning: 807a, 1369, 1441, 1640

dǣd-fruma: 1379
deall: 1770a
dēað: 1597, 1615, 1617a
dēgan: 1444
dēmend: 1615
dēofl: 1605
dēor: 1615
dol: 1615
dol-līc: 1606
dōm: 1107, 1348, 1513, 1597, 1615, 1627, 1770a
draca: 1137
drēam: 1615
druncen: 1496
dryht-bearn: 1379
dryhten: 1364, 1459, 1513
dryht-guma: 1379

duguð: 1400
dyrne: 1141
dyrstig: 1615

ēacen: 1255
ēad: 1584
ēa-land: 1734
eald: 1550
ealde riht: 1709
ealdor: 1578
ealdor þegna: 1379
ealo: 1418
ealu-drincend: 1379
ealu-scerwen: 1117, 1387, 1610, 1661, 1765
earm-līc: 1744
earm-sceapen: 1533
ēaðo-līðend: 1379
eaxl: 1568
eaxl-gestealla: 1379
ellen: 1678
ende-sǣta: 1379
entisc helm: 1109
eofer-sprēot: 1109
eofor-līc: 1696
eorla hlēo: 1379
eorðe: 1441
eoten: 1155, 1244, 1372, 1447, 1616, 1697, 1758
ēst: 1107, 1584, 1627

fæder: 1615
fǣr: 1704
fāh: 1155, 1691
farod: 1703
fealu: 1478, 1661
feoh: 1584
fēond: 1244, 1605
feor: 1239
feorh-genīðla: 1379
feorran: 1128

fēðe-cempa: 1379
fēðe-gest: 1379
fīfel-cyn: 1244
flet-sittend: 1379
flet-werod: 1379
flota: 1704
flot-herge: 1379
folc-toga: 1379
ford: 1703
forht: 1615
for-swerian: 1456
for-sworen: 1465
fōt: 1125
frætwe: 1584
frēa: 1379, 1459
frēa-dryhten: 1379
frēa-wine: 1379
frec: 1615
freca: 1703
freca Scyldinga: 1379
frēcne: 1615
frēo-līc: 1770a
frōd: 1441
frōfor: 1615
frōfor ond fultum: 1194
from: 1615
fruma: 1578
frum-gār: 1615
fyll: 1615
fyrd: 1764

gafol: 1584
gamen: 1615
gamol-: 1478
gār: 1109
gār-berend: 1379
gār-holt: 1109, 1149, 1637
gār-secg: 1703, 1722
gār-wiga: 1379
gār-wīgend: 1379
ge- prefix: 1227
geato-līc: 1770a

geatwa: 1109, 1584
ge-cēosan: 1739
ge-hyld: 1615
ge-lād: 1599
geofon: 1703
geolo: 1109, 1478
gersum: 1584
ge-scād: 1440
ge-selda: 1379
ge-sīþ: 1114
ge-strēon: 1584
ge-strȳnan: 1724
ge-wǣde: 1109
ge-weorc: 1109, 1584
ge-wītan: 1092a
ge-wittig: 1441
gif: 1584
gif-stōl: 1404, 1493
gift: 1584
giftu: 1584
gifu: 1584
gīgantas: 1244
gilp: 1199
gilp-hlǣden: 1199
gleng: 1584
god: 1441, 1513, 1584, 1615
gold: 1478, 1584
gold-hroden: 1770a
gold-hwæt: 1107
gombe: 1584
grǣg: 1478
grǣg-mǣl: 1109
grīm-helm: 1109
grim(m): 1615
gum-fēða: 1379
gūð-beorn: 1379
Gūð-Scylfing: 1379
gūð-freca: 1379
gūð-fremmend: 1379
gūð-gewǣdo: 1109, 1156
gūð-helm: 1109
gūð-mōd: 1615

Word Index

gūð-rinc: 1379, 1725
gūð-sweord: 1109
gūð-wine: 1109, 1379

hæf: 1703
hæft-mēce: 1132, 1497, 1569
hæg-steald: 1379
hand / hond: 1125
hand-bana: 1379
hand-gesella: 1379
hand-gestealla: 1379
hand-scalu: 1379
hār: 1478
heal-ðegn: 1379
heard: 1615
heaðo-rinc: 1379
Heaðo-Scilfing: 1379
hel: 1605
helm: 1109, 1379, 1459
helm-berend: 1379
hel-rūne: 1465
heofon: 1703
heoro-hōcyhte: 1109
heorð-genēat: 1379
heoru: 1109
here: 1764
here-grīma: 1109
here-net: 1109
here-pād: 1109
here-wīsa: 1379
Het-ware: 1447
hild: 1165
hilde-bord: 1109
hilde-gicel: 1109
hilde-lēoma: 1109, 1149
hilde-mecg: 1379
hilde-rand: 1109
hild-freca: 1379

hild-lata: 1379
hlēo: 1379
holm: 1703
hond-locen: 1109
hord: 1584
hrægl: 1109
hrēoh: 1615
hrēð-mann: 1379
hringa þengel: 1379
hringed: 1109
hringed-stefna: 1704
hring-īren: 1109
hring-net: 1109
hron-rād: 1703, 1722
hrōðor: 1615
hryre: 1615
Hūn-lāfing: 1109
hūð: 1584
hwæt: 1615
hwæþer: 1360
hwīt: 1063a
hwyrft: 1130
hyldo: 1364
hyrde: 1459
hyrssan: 1708
hyrst: 1584
hyð-weard: 1379

icge, incge: 1758
ides: 1141, 1427, 1585
in-gesteald: 1584
īren-þrēat: 1379
īsig: 1498

kyning-wuldor: 1615

lāc: 1584
lǣne: 1166
lāf: 1109, 1158, 1432, 1584
lagu: 1703

land-weard: 1379
lēan: 1584
lenge: 1299
lēod: 1379, 1578
lēod Scyldinga: 1379
lid-manna helm: 1379
lind: 1109
lind-gestealla: 1379
lind-hæbbend: 1379
lind-wiga: 1379
līðend: 1722
locen: 1109
lof: 1698
lof-geornost: 1249, 1295, 1313, 1359, 1513, 1606, 1663, 1698
lyft: 1703

mǣg: 1379
mǣgen: 1400, 1430, 1513
mǣgen-wudu: 1109
mǣg-wine: 1379
mǣrðu: 1400
mago-dryht: 1379
mago-rinc: 1379
mago-ðegn: 1379
magu: 1379
māððum: 1109, 1584
māðþum-sweord: 1109
mēce / hæft-mēce: 1109
mēd: 1584
medu-drēam: 1150
meodo: 1418
meord: 1584
mere: 1548, 1703
mere-frēa: 1379
mere-wīoingas: 1221, 1285

metod: 1513, 1615
metod-sceaft: 1513
middan-geard: 1441
mōd: 1430
mōdig: 1615
morðor: 1615
mund-bora: 1615
myne: 1770a

naca: 1704
nīð: 1172, 1400, 1410
nȳd: 1119
nȳd-gestealla: 1379

ofer-sittan: 1199
ofost: 1356
ombiht: 1379
ombiht-þegn: 1379
on: 1500
ond: 1320, 1524, 1684a
orc-nēas: 1244
ord: 1379
ord-fruma: 1379
ōret-mecg: 1379
ōretta: 1121, 1379, 1703
or-wearde: 1166
oððe: 1320

rǣdend: 1615
rand: 1109
rand-hæbbend: 1379
rand-wiga: 1379
rēaf: 1109, 1584
regn-heard: 1109
ren-weardas: 1117, 1379, 1529
rīca: 1615
rinc: 1379
rodor: 1703
rōf: 1615
rūn-wita: 1379

sǣ: 1703, 1722
sǣ-gēap: 1704
sǣl: 1400
sǣ-mann: 1379
sceaft: 1109, 1119
scealc: 1379
sceat: 1584
sceaþan: 1173, 1583
scef: 1173
scip: 1704
scīr: 1770a
scop: 1188
scrīpan: 1130, 1441, 1680
scrūd: 1109
sculdor: 1568
scūr-heard: 1109
scyld: 1173, 1339
scyld-frēa: 1379
scyld-wiga: 1379
scyppend: 1615, 1728
searo: 1109, 1155, 1410, 1584
searo-hæbbend: 1379
searo-net: 1109
searo-nīð: 1330, 1410
seax: 1109
secg: 1109
sēl: 1770a
seld-guma: 1747
sele-rǣdend: 1379
sele-þegn: 1379
sele-weard: 1379
sendan: 1076a
seolfor: 1584
sib-æðeling: 1379
sibbe-gedryht: 1379
sīd: 1109
sinc: 1584
sioloð: 1703
sīþ: 1114
sīðian: 1092a

siððan: 1476
snell: 1615
snotor: 1441
sōð-fæst: 1348, 1667
sōð-fæstra dōm: 1107, 1667
stearc: 1615
stīð: 1615
stonc, stincan: 1151
strēam: 1703, 1722
sund: 1548, 1606, 1703
swā: 1107
swan-rād: 1703
sweart: 1478
swefan/swebban: 1092a, 1245
swegl: 1703
sweord: 1109, 1441, 1550
sweorda lāf: 1379
sweord-freca: 1379
swīð: 1615
swylt: 1615
symbel: 1245, 1300
synn: 1244, 1513, 1605
syrce: 1109

trēow: 1364
trēow-loga: 1379

þā: 1107, 1300
þæt: 1107, 1300
þē: 1677
þengel: 1379
þēod-cyning: 1249
þēoden: 1364, 1578
þēod-gestrēon: 1364
þrec-wudu: 1109
þrīst: 1615
þyle: 1122, 1167, 1188, 1379, 1541

Word Index 407

þyrs: 1244, 1449,
  1465

un- prefix: 1206,
  1337, 1458,
  1592
under: 1140
un-forht: 1615
un-glēaw: 1158
un-hlitme: 1592,
  1678
un-tȳdras: 1244,
  1724

wæd: 1703
wǣg-sweord: 1109
wǣl-rāpas: 1159
wǣll-seax: 1109
wǣl-steng: 1109
wǣter: 1703
wala: 1063a, 1453
waldend: 1513
wan: 1119, 1478
wealdend: 1615
wēa-lāf: 1379
weallan: 1673
weard Scyldinga:
  1379
wela: 1584
wēn: 1413
weorc: 1400
weorð: 1584
wiga: 1703
wīg-bord: 1109
wīgend: 1703
wīgendra hlēo:
  1379
wīg-freca: 1379
wīg-fruma: 1379
wīg-heafola: 1109
wīg-heap: 1379
wīn: 1418
wine: 1364, 1379,
  1578
wine Scyldinga:
  1379

wine-dryhten: 1379
wine-mǣg: 1379
wīs: 1441
wīsa: 1379, 1615
wist: 1584
wist-fyllo: 1413
witan: 1293
wītig: 1441
wlanc: 1770a
wlite: 1770a
wolcen: 1703
worold: 1441
wrǣt: 1584
wudu: 1109
wundini: 1275,
  1285, 1731
wundor: 1584
wylm: 1673, 1703
wynn: 1615
wyrd: 995b, 1133,
  1144, 1300,
  1513, 1627
wyrm: 1137

yrfe: 1584
yrfe-lāf: 1109
ȳð: 1703

LINE INDEX

*references after the colon are to item numbers;
a preceding "S" indicates an item in Short [1211]*

1-2: 1284, 1443, 1602a
1-3: 1513, 1544, 1721
1-6a: S946
1-9: 1447
1-19: S1
1-25: S265, S576, S1078
1-52: S202, S789, S1055
1-53: 1552
1-150: S806
1-458: S191
1-790: S506
1-2009: S364
1-2009a: S745
2a: 1632
4: 1173, 1501
4-6a: 1583
4-7a: S806
4-19: 1693, 1707
4-63: S821
5: S821
6a: 1632
9: 1152, 1632, 1671, S418, S821
11: 1464, 1640, S1079
12: S821
12-15: 1598
14: 1501, S246, S806
15: S418

16-18: S1079
18: 1501
19: S821
20-24: 1513
20-25: 1753, S378, S420, S945, S1079
24: 1501
26-27: S1082
26-31: S806
26-52: 1604, 1737, S627
26-63: 1707
28: 1501
29-52: S812
30: 1690
31: 1501
31-32: S319
32b-36: 1250
33: S389, S417, S779
33a: 1152, 1498
34: 1152
36a: 1767
36b-42: 1281
38: 1602a, S657
38a: 1770a
38-52: 1065a
44: 1632
47: 1767
49a: 1152
50-52: S1082
50b-52: 1544, 1753
51: S821
53-63: 1448

53-73: S1
56: S694
59-63: S268
61: 1684a
62: 1447, 1474, S228, S418, S952
62a: 1152, S94
64-101: S806
67: 1501
67b-69: S722
67b-70: S843, S1053
68-70: S602
69: 1501
70a: 1152
73a: S257
78: 1501
78a: S623
79: 1690
81: 1501
81a: 1245
81b-83a: S806
81b-85: 1179
82: S657
82-85: S202
83: 1299
84: 1179, 1217, S1048
86-183: S842
87-114: 1331
89b-90a: 1201
89-91: S1005
89b-92: S462
90: 1501

90a: 1632
90-98: 1490, S202, S829, S1079
90-100: S1079
90-101: S1082
90b-101: 1448
90-113: S22
92: 1513
93: 1602
93a: 1770a
98a: 1331
99-101: 1152, S781
99-105: S878
99-114: S839
100b-101: S722
101: 1225, 1245, 1331, 1605, S418, S610
102: 1501, 1602a
103: S677
103a: 1152
103b-104a: 1684a
104-114: S829
105a: 1744
106-110: S1079
106-114: S202
107: S956
107a: 1510
109-110: 1602a
111-113: S896
111-114: 1448, S204
112: S1008
118-119: 1602a
119: S806
119a: 1245
122: S806
125: S610
126: 1501
126-129a: S837
128: S806
128-140a: 1258
129b-149a: S1051
135-137: S839
138: 1501, S378
140b-142a: 1537

142a: S257
143-179: S795
153-158: S839
154: 1602a, S806
159a: 1135
159-163: 1495
159-193: 1448
160: S961
162: 1501
162-163: S798
162b-163: 1130, 1753
163: 1152, 1680, S1032
163a: 1465
164: S1048
166-169: S655
166b-169: 1493
168: S281
168-169: 1152, 1404, 1421, S257, S318, S461, S496, S722, S789, S842, S907
169: 1770a
170-188: 1293, 1663
175-183: 1593, S575, S1079
175-188: 1145, 1475, 1571, 1588, 1598, S22, S257, S645, S700, S789, S801, S829
178-183: S750
178-188: 1627
179a: 1152
182: S610, S997
183: 1632, 1711
183-188: S1079
183b-188: 1744, S420
186: 1632, 1711

189-370: 1457
194: 1501
194-195: S418
194-381: S399
196-197: 1513
198: S1001
198b-228: S432
200: 1602a, S293
202-204: 1592, S842
203: 1501
204: S610
205: 1501
205-303a: 1180, 1737
207b-215a: 1674
207b-216: 1152
207b-228: S581
208b-209: S319
210b-216: 1250
210-223a: S312
210-224: 1761
210-228: 1305, 1669
210b-228: 1704
210-233: S983
215: S997
215a: 1770a
215-228: S812
217-218: 1767
217-224: 1114
217-224a: S539, S915
218: S657
223: S568
223b-224a: S508, S561
224: S346, S436
224a: 1152, 1754, S214
224-225: S495, S685
224b-228: 1708
227: 1501
227a: 1156
227-228: 1513

Line Index 411

227b-228: S191
228: S378
229: S378
229-300: 1762
229-319: 1574, S323, S594
229-398: S703
232: 1501
234: 1602a
234-236: 1079a
235-236: S439
237-270: S1051
240: 1501, 1694
244: 1602a
247: S418
247b-251a: 1747, S602
248: 1501
249: 1152, S428, S476, S610
250: 1152, 1501, S205
251a: 1770a
253: S227
256: 1501
258: S333
258-259: 1079a
260-285: S1092
262: 1602a
262a: 1632
270-272: S836
272: 1501
274: 1501
276-277: 1513
277: S610
286: 1501
286-287a: 1079a
287-289: S1046
287b-289: 1318, 1440, 1558, 1639, S420
291-292: S574
296: 1501
300a: 1165
301-307: S408
303-305: 1513

303-306: S332
303b-306a: 1696, S280, S496
305: S246
305b-306a: 1152, S323
306: 1501
306b-311: S539, S915
308a: 1770a
314: S685
314b-315: 1079a
316a: 1632
320: S657, S721
320a: 1152
320-321: 1513
320-324: 1131
326: S483
330: S257, S732
330-331: S1079
331a: S257
331b-332: 1079a
332: 1366, 1447
333-335: S574
340: S333
340-342a: 1079a
341a: 1770a
342a: 1140
343-347: S1092
348: 1501
348-350a: 1079a
349: 1602a
354-402: 1356
356-359: S376
358: S378
358-360: 1079a
359: 1513
361: 1239, 1501
371: 1079a
371-558: 1577
373: 1602a
375a: S228
377: 1501
377-379a: S266
389-390: 1261, 1694, 1738

389b-390: 1079a
389b-390a: 1652
396a: 1140
397: 1602a
400: S378
402: 1501, 1671
402a: 1632
402-432: S751
403: 1261
404a: 1140
405: 1501
405-406: 1079a
406: S657
407: 1501
407-455: 1199, S1092
407b-455: 1238
413: S866
418: 1501
419-424: S202
419-424a: S259
419-426: 1124, 1155
423: 1501
425a: 1135
425b-426a: 1449
426a: 1465
426-432: S874
431: S717
431-432: 1197, S440
433: 1135
435: 1501
440: 1501, 1602a
440b-441: 1753
441: 1513
442-451: S527
445a: 1632, S418
445b-451: S227
446: S301
447a: 1691
448: 1602a
449-606: 1628
451: S527
454: 1366
455: S420

456: 1079a, 1753
457a: S717
459-462: 1602a
459-472: S202
461: 1261, 1366, 1501, S618, S692
461-469: 1602a
462: 1602a, S418
463: 1416
466-467: 1513
470: 1501
473: S223
478-479: S1046
478b-479: S257
480-481: 1513
480-488: 1076b, 1513
486: S721
489: 1152, 1501
489a: 1245
489-490: 1152, S440, S685
491-494: 1602a
491-661: 1115
493: 1602a
493-494: 1602a
494a: 1770a
495: 1632
496a: 1152, 1770a, S621
496-498: S1005
499: S1016
499a: 1152, 1261, 1447
499-505: 1079a
499-529: 1279
499-603: S202
499-606: 1171, 1283, 1762
499-610: 1574
501: 1632
502-505: S996
503-505: 1575, S782
505: S932

505a: 1575
506: 1501
506-515: 1749
506-528: 1606
506-548: 1236
506-581: 1118, 1507
506-581a: S417
506-588: S932
506-589: 1152
506-606: 1127
510: S472
510b-518a: 1639
510-1129: S472
511: 1632
512a: S647
512b: 1118
512-513: S378
513: S378
515a: 1152
518: 1501
518b-521a: S408
519a: 1713
529: 1079a
530: 1152, 1447, S378, S1016
530-606: S1092
531a: 1513
535: 1501
535-539: 1263
537: 1152
539: 1548, S932
539-548: 1639
539-567: 1331
540: 1152, S346, S788
542: S932
544-548: S179
549: 1602a
556a: 1135
559: 1436
562: S610
562-570a: 1631, S408
563: 1721
564a: 1245

565-567: S836
565-567a: 1008a
568a: 1152, S549
569-572: S179
569b-572a: S539
570a: 1632
572-573: 1602a, S1079
572b-573: 1144, 1728, 1753, S420
572-575: S836
574: 1152, S803
579-581: S179
580: 1713
580-606: 1236
581: S932
581a: 1118, S981
582a: 1410
586: 1152, 1261, S717
586a: 1152, S803
587: 1188, S488
588: 1152, 1501, S932
600: 1076a
600a: 1245
603: 1501
603-606: S592
606: S610
607-610: 1263
607-641: 1643
607-645: 1115
608a: 1632
610: S401
611-665a: 1427
614a: 1770a
615a: 1770a
617: 1501
619a: 1245
623: 1416, 1770a
628b-631: 1079a
632: S657
632-638: 1108, S1092
636-638: 1502

Line Index 413

640: 1770a
640-641: 1602a
641a: 1770a
643: 1602a
648: 1501, 1602a
649: 1501
650: 1680
652a: 1632
652-654: 1079a
658a: 1632
662-709: 1148
664: 1602a
665: 1152, S410
665-670: S1079
665b-670: S1052
665b-738: 1611
666: 1602
675-676: 1079a
677-687: S1092
679: 1245, 1501, 1602a
692: S410
692a: 1152
696: 1501
696-702: 1513
698a: 1194
700-702: S1079
700b-702a: S420
702: 1501
702a: 1721
702b-705a: S1086
702-727: 1674
702b-727: S475
702b-730a: 1737
702b-736: 1530
702b-736a: S626
702b-749: S1052
702b-836: 1272
703: 1152, 1245
703b-705a: S1052
703-709: S683
703b-828a: 1384
705: 1513
706: 1501
707a: 1272
710: 1501

710a: 1721
710-836: 1665, S510
712-713: 1602a, S625
714-716a: S539
716: S647
719: S610, S933
719a: 1152
720: 1602a
720a: 1721
720-724: S722
721a: S304
721b-722a: S657
721b-724a: S624
722-836: S506
723: 1255
723-727: 1579
724: 1632
724a: 1196
725: S483, S721
725a: 1152
726-727: 1513
728-734: S625
728-734a: 1258
729a: 1245
730: 1131, 1501
730a: 1680
733b-734a: 1413
736b-738: S1052
736b-739: S995
736b-823a: S155
738: S319
739: 1501
739a: 1135
739-767: 1686
740: S647
740-745: 1076a
742: S730
743: 1501, S772
743a: 1632
745b-7: S757
745b-749: S424
747: 1632
749: 1152, S155
750: 1501

750a: S647
750-751a: S264
753: 1501
753-757: 1602a
758a: 1632
759-765a: S257
762: 1501, S257, S677
762a: 1152
762-764: 1602a
765: S647
767-790: 1117
769: S246, S436, S476, S657, S802
769a: 1117, 1152, 1387, 1610, 1661, 1765, S156, S730
769-770: 1148
770a: 1117, 1529
770b-782a: 1708
771: 1501, S1079
778: 1501
780: 1366
780a: 1571
782: S685
783: 1416
784-805: 1424
785: 1501
786: S326
786a: S647
786-787: S585
787a: S647
788a: 1605
789-790: 1513
791: 1436
791-792: 1537, 1602a
794: 1501
796: 1602a
801-805: 1226
801b-805a: S646
803: 1602a
804: 1456, 1465, S68

804a: S938
807: S722
807a: 1744
809-812a: S264
810a: S938
811: S803, S938
814: S938
821a: 1632
821b-822a: 1744
825: 1239
826: S676
833b-852: 1181, 1182
834: 1335
837-856: 1407, S666
837-927: S564
839-840: 1602a
841b-843: 1664
845: 1548
847: 1501
847-852: 1331, S837
847b-877: S577
849: S714
850a: 1444
853-856a: S657
853-877: 1202
853-918a: S286
860: 1770a
863: 1464, 1640, S1079
864-886: S608
864-917a: 1721
867: S395
867a: S378
867b-875: S462
867-896: S491
867-915: S239
867b-915: 1460
868-870a: 1199
870: S223
871a: S239
871-872: S836
871-915: S202
874: S634

874a: S239
874-882: S839
874b-884a: 1708
874-897: S595
874-900: S750
874-915: S388
875-897: 1409
877-879: S836
879: 1501
881a: 1632
884b-897: 1137
889: S836
890a: S647
892-900: S836
893: 1602a
893a: 1135
895: S242
896: S836
898-904a: 1202
902: 1152, S631
902-904: 1616
902b-905a: S455
902b-906: 1152
905: 1501
908a: S647
917: 1501
917-920: 1602a
918: 1602a, S997
918-920: 1602a
922a: 1152
923b-924: 1427
924: S560
924-927: 1602a
926: S302, S560, S973
926a: S736
926-927: 1079a
926-987a: 1152
930b-931: 1753, S420
932-939: S276
933-934: 1602a
935: S895
936: S997
936a: 1501
939-940: 1602a

941a: 1632
942b-946a: 1763, S257
947a: 1632
948: 1501
949: 1398
954a: 1632
957: 1079a
957-979: S356
958-979: S1092
958-980: S510
960: 1501
960b-962: S382
963: 1501
963-992: S506
964: 1602a
965a: 1261
967: 1501
974-979: 1602a
976: 1366
977: 1602a
977-979: 1513
979a: 1770a
980: S1079
980-987: 1708
982: S223
982-984a: 1335
984b-987a: S513
985: S208
989: 1135
990a: S967
991: 1501, S685
991-992a: S292, S536
991-1009: 1495
991-1250: 1115
992a: S967
996: S378
997-1002: 1677
997-1010: S945
999: 1501
1000: 1135
1002-1008: S1079
1002b-1008a: S420
1003: 1501
1004-1008a: 1346

Line Index 415

1007-1008a: S326
1008a: 1245, 1346
1008b-1250: S674
1010: 1602a
1011: S643
1011-1012: S688
1012: 1770a
1015: 1632, S418
1017-1018: 1329
1017-1168a: S1051
1018b-1019: S846
1020: 1152, 1501, 1522, 1756, 1637a, S496
1020b-1022: S1039
1023a: 1756
1024b-1026: S439
1026a: 1632
1027a: 1632
1027-1029: 1329, S663
1030: S383
1030-1031: 1453, S257
1030-1033a: S280
1031: 1063a, S276, S383, S610
1033a: 1152
1035-1036: 1602a, S378
1042: S610
1045: 1329
1046: 1501
1046-1049: S439
1051: 1676
1053b-1: S945
1055: 1501
1056-1057: 1513
1056-1057a: S1098
1056-1062: S1079
1057b-1062: 1753, S420
1063-1068: S1005
1063-1159: 1306
1063-1159a: 1367, 1758

1063b-1160a: S911
1064: S851
1065: 1201, S417
1066a: S176
1068: 1501
1068a: S176
1068-1159a: S80
1069: S851
1069a: S79
1069-1159: 1749
1070: 1602a
1071-1159: 1163
1071-1159a: 1712
1072: 1152, S631
1073: 1261
1074: 1501
1079: 1758
1080: 1501
1080b-1087a: S780
1082-1085: S208
1084-1085a: 1152
1085: 1697
1085-1087: 1697
1088: S631
1088a: 1152
1091a: 1768
1096: 1501
1097: S605
1097a: 1152, 1678
1098: S694
1098-1106: S208
1099b-1100: S472
1104: 1501
1104-1108a: 1174
1107: 1152, 1758, S176, S405, S604, S1069
1107-1108: S827
1110-1113: 1513
1112: 1602a
1113: 1501, S610
1114-1118a: S280
1114-1159a: S836
1117: 1568
1117-1118: S638
1117b-1119a: S769

1117b-1120a: 1507
1118: 1152
1121: 1501
1125: 1436, 1602a
1125-1127: S208
1125-1129a: 1152, S393, S756
1125-1138a: S1057
1127-1134: 1592
1127-1137: S336
1127b-1141: S312
1128b-1129a: 1261
1129: 1501, S605
1129a: 1678, S1057
1129b-a: 1758
1129-1130: S910
1129b-1131a: 1287
1130a: 1287, S1057
1131-1137: S719
1131b-1137a: S1057
1132-1133: S326
1133: 1501
1134-1137: S1079
1138: 1501
1138b-1145: S173
1138b-1151a: S910
1138b-1159a: S1057
1141: 1501, S631, S680
1141a: 1152
1142: 1501
1142a: 1397
1142-1147: S282
1142-1159a: 1163
1143: 1149, 1367, 1501
1143a: S88, S157
1144-1145: S280
1145: S631
1145a: 1152
1148: S208
1151: 1447
1151-1152: S276
1154: 1501

1155: S604
1157b-1159: S722
1159-1161: S1005
1159b-1168: S837
1159b-1232a: 1427
1160a: 1201
1161: S772
1162b-1165a: S846
1162b-1168: 1079a
1163: 1632
1163a: 1632
1163-1168: 1261
1164a: 1632
1165: 1167, S1016
1165: 1152, 1447
1166a: 1632
1167a: 1632
1167b-1168a: S488
1169-1173: 1770
1169-1187: 1329, 1761
1170-1176: 1464
1172: 1602a
1173: 1501
1175-1187: 1557
1176: S224, S267
1179-1180: S906
1180: 1501, S906
1181: 1501
1182: 1501
1192: S607
1192-1201: 1410
1195: S623
1197-1201: 1383, S210
1197-1214: S202, S388, S676
1200: 1410
1201a: 1632
1202: 1152
1202-1207: S839
1202-1214: S254
1202-1214a: S284
1203: S647
1203a: 1168
1206-1207a: S790

1210: 1632
1210a: 1632
1215: 1079a, 1513
1216-1231: 1761
1219-1220: 1464, S676
1223: 1602
1228-1230: 1464
1228-1231: 1513, 1557
1229: 1152, S552
1230-1231: 1496
1231: 1730
1232-1237a: 1258
1232-1278: S577
1233: 1501
1239: S721
1242: S687
1247: S208
1248a: 1632
1250: S1079
1251: S822
1251-1590: 1442
1258-1266: 1585
1260: 1501
1260-1269: S829
1261: 1261, 1372, 1632, S803, S956
1261-1266: S22, S202
1263-1264: 1513
1267-1268: 1602a
1269: 1501
1270: 1501
1270-1271: 1513
1273: 1501
1273a: 1194
1274: S304
1274a: 1605
1275a: S304
1278: 1152
1278a: S647
1280a: 1245
1282: 1501
1282b-1284: S420

1282-1287: S725
1282b-1287: 1148
1286: 1442, S687
1290: S687
1290-1291: S378
1290b-1291: S496
1291: 1152
1292: S685
1296: 1501
1299b-1301: 1686
1302b-1306a: 1376
1303-1343: S506
1304: S1079
1306: 1464
1310: S666
1310-1315: 1587
1312: 1501, S685
1314a: 1365, 1587
1317: 1501, S721
1318: 1447
1319-1320: S378
1320: S607
1320a: 1152
1321: 1079a
1325-1328a: 1544
1327: S687
1328-1329: S1046
1331: 1360, S257, S995
1333: 1501, S610
1333a: 1528
1338b-1340: S839
1338-1417: 1320
1340: 1602a
1341-1344: S995
1343: 1501, S198
1343a: 1501
1345-1376: 1407, S666
1345-1379: 1596
1351: S304
1352: S304
1353: S205
1355: 1501
1355b-1357a: S257
1357b-1366a: 1381

Line Index

1357b-1376a: S365, S598, S931
1357-1378: 1627
1357-1379: 1138
1359a: 1599
1361: 1501
1361-1362: 1602a
1363: S230
1364: S687
1365: 1501
1366: 1501
1368: 1501
1368-1372: 1358, 1559, 1579, S230, S948
1372: 1694, S301, S687
1373: S685
1377b-1378a: S257
1379: 1501, S245
1379a: 1152, 1632
1379-1380: S803
1382: S223, S276
1382a: 1275, 1285, 1731
1383: 1079a
1384-1385: 1144
1384b-1385: 1231, S482, S995
1384-1389: S420
1384-1396: S1092
1386-1389: 1203
1390: 1602a
1392: 1516, S687
1392a: 1261
1394: 1516
1397: 1501
1399-1417: S511
1399-1590: 1148
1399-1650: S983
1401a: 1770a
1402b-1441a: 1331
1404: 1632
1408: 1152, 1501
1408-1417a: S915
1408-1423: S415

1408-1436: 1407, S666
1410: 1599
1411: 1381
1412-1413: 1602a
1414-1417a: 1381
1415: 1602a
1416b-1424: S312
1417b-1421: S574, S969
1420a: 1632
1421: S687
1422: 1501, S72
1423: S647
1423a: 1152
1423-1424: S326, S861
1424a: S647
1428: 1501
1429a: S647
1431-1432: 1602a
1432: 1501
1432a: S647
1435: 1501
1441b-1472: 1543
1443: 1501, 1602a
1448: S687, S902
1448a: 1063a
1448-1451: S134
1448-1454: S332
1448-1471: 1602a
1451: 1501
1451-1454: 1513
1453: S685
1455: 1152, 1501, 1602a
1456: 1167
1457: 1501
1457a: 1132, 1497, 1569
1459: S633
1459-1460a: S646
1463: S647
1465: 1501
1465-1471: S521
1467: 1501

1470: 1501
1473: 1079a
1473-1487: S416
1474: 1501
1474-1491: S1092
1481: 1501
1484: S418
1485a: 1632
1488: S1016
1488a: 1152, 1261, 1447
1490b-1491: 1108
1492b-1493: 1319
1492-1590: 1701
1492-1622: 1696
1495: 1152
1495b-1496: S932
1496a: 1632
1497a: S647
1497-1499: S264
1501-1569: 1170
1502: 1501
1503: 1501
1504: 1602
1506: 1501
1509: 1501
1513: S610
1516: S610
1516-1519: S948
1518-1569: S510
1519: 1501, S625, S801
1521: S647, S687
1521-1522: S326
1522: 1501, S647
1522a: S647
1522-1525: 1226
1523: 1149
1530: S276
1534: S1046, S1079
1534b-1536: S420
1534b-1537: 1728, S420
1536a: 1698
1537: 1501, S1014

1537-1546: 1300, S1021
1538a: 1632
1539: S625
1539-1540: 1148
1541: 1152, 1261, 1447, S535
1543: S625
1546: S250, S732
1546a: 1152
1547-1556: 1442
1550: 1501
1553-1556: S1079
1557: 1436
1557-1562: S332
1558: 1550
1559: 1501
1563: 1152, S625, S659, S852
1566: S625
1570-1572: S948
1571-1572: S849
1572-1590: S683
1573: S378, S488
1579: 1501
1584a: 1416, 1632
1584b-1590: 1501
1590: S687
1594: S378
1604a: 1320
1605b-1: S724
1605b-1608: 1454
1605-1617: S1058
1605b-1617: 1148
1607: 1501
1607b-1610a: S326
1607-1611: S336, S1079
1607b-1611: 1159, S646
1608-1611: S673, S719
1612: 1501
1614: 1501, S687
1614a: 1764
1620: 1602a

1620-1622: S948
1623: S687
1626-1628: S657
1627: 1501
1630-1631: S948
1632-1643: S286
1635: S687
1637: S687
1644: 1602a
1645: 1770a
1647: 1501
1649b-1: 1427
1651: 1079a
1651-2199: 1332
1652-1676: 1701, S1092
1655: 1501
1655-1666a: S510
1657: 1501
1663b-1664a: 1753
1666: 1501
1671: 1501
1672a: 1245
1677-1686: S624
1677-1698: 1616, S829
1677-1759: S674
1679a: S868
1687-1689: S332
1687-1691: 1602a
1687-1693: 1510
1687-1699: 1079a
1689-1690: S896
1694-1695: 1602a
1696a: 1632
1697b-1698: S696
1698: S607
1698a: 1152
1698-1784: S829
1699: 1501, S378
1700-1768: 1263, 1531
1700-1784: 1237, 1321, 1653, 1761, S789

1705-1706: 1430, S676
1706: 1602a
1708a: 1632
1709-1722: S202
1709b-1768: S998
1716: 1501
1717: 1602a
1718-1720: S939
1720b-1722a: S455
1724b-1727a: 1684a
1724b-1757: 1753
1724-1768: S1078
1724b-1768: S73
1727: S311
1728: 1602a
1735: 1501
1735-1739: S377
1735-1742a: 1258
1735-1745: S326
1739-1757: 1382
1741: 1245
1746: 1501
1748-1750: S939
1750b-1752: 1664
1756-1757: S939
1757: 1152
1759: 1739
1759a: 1632
1760a: 1483
1761b-1778a: 1119
1763-1768: S377
1764-1766: S1060
1766: 1152, S208
1766-1767: S903
1769: 1501
1769-1781: S430
1773: 1602
1775: 1501
1778: 1501
1780: S895
1782: 1245
1785: 1602a
1785-1793: 1115
1787-1793: 1258

Line Index 419

1791: 1602a
1792: 1501
1793: 1602a
1799-1803: S886
1800: 1245
1801-1802a: 1256, 1735
1802-1806: S408
1805-1806: 1239
1806a: 1255
1807: 1602a, 1501
1807-1809: 1602a
1812: S1079
1814b-1817: 1079a
1817-1835: 1637
1818: 1602a
1818-1839: S1092
1819-1820: 1602a
1822: 1602a, 1501
1822-1865: S254
1828: S320
1830: 1501
1834: 1149, 1501, 1637
1834-1838: 1513
1836-1839: 1388
1838-1839: 1513
1840: 1079a
1844: 1430
1844-1845: S676
1845: 1501
1845b-1853a: 1664, S498
1846: 1501
1853: 1501
1855: 1602a
1862: 1602a
1870-1880a: S654
1871: 1632
1873b-1876a: 1287, S654
1875: 1287
1875a: 1152
1877: 1602
1880b-1885a: S439

1880b-1919: 1180, 1737
1885: 1464, S685
1885-1886: S1079
1885b-1924: S1051
1887: 1501, S420
1888: 1602a
1888-1899: S408
1888-2199: S564
1889: S717
1889a: 1152
1890b-1903a: S594
1896: 1602a, 1501
1896-1924: 1704
1898: 1767
1900-1901: S378
1900-1903a: S439
1903: 1501
1903-1912: 1114
1903-1913: S812
1903b-1913: S539
1905a: 1767
1906a: 1767
1917: 1501
1917-1919: S601
1919: 1152
1921-1924: 1602a
1921b-1924: 1495
1925-1961: S607
1925-1962: 1193, S443, S542
1926: 1632
1927: 1501
1931: S607
1931-1944: 1761
1931-1962: S202
1931b-1962: 1332, 1557
1934-1935: S607
1935: 1501
1935a: 1152
1937: 1196
1938a: S116
1938b-1986: 1079a
1939: S420
1940b-1941: S420

1940-1943: S1079
1941: 1770a
1942: S776
1944: S506
1948a: 1770a
1949a: 1661
1950a: 1661
1952: S260
1957-1960: 1602a
1957-1978: 1602a
1960: 1261, 1366
1963-1966: S408
1965: 1602a
1967-1975: 1356
1968-2176: 1205
1970: 1602a
1973: 1602a
1975-2199: 1115
1977: 1501
1980b-1981: 1632
1981: 1261, 1366
1983: 1513
1987-1998: 1332, S844
1988-1989: 1602a
1996: 1602a
1999: 1079a
2000-2162: S1092
2001-2003a: 1191
2005: 1501
2005b-2007: 1287
2006a: 1287
2009b-2069a: 1115
2009b-2176: S364, S498, S745
2016a: 1150
2016b-2019: 1427
2020-2025: 1602a
2020-2031: 1163, S839
2024b-2031: S837
2024b-2069a: 1432, S836
2025: S990
2025a: 1770a
2029: 1501

2029-2031: S1046
2029b-2031: S420
2032: 1632
2034-2035: S607
2035: 1501, S680
2035a: 1152
2039: 1436
2041: S787
2041-2042: S418
2041-2046: 1079a
2042: 1152
2043: 1501
2049: S647
2049a: 1140
2053-2056: 1664
2057a: 1152
2060: 1245
2063-2064: 1602a
2065a: 1140
2068: S607
2069: 1501
2069b-2100: S510
2069b-2199: S611
2072-2099: S506
2073: 1602a, S610
2081: 1501
2081-2085: S837
2085: 1152
2085b-2088: 1298
2088: 1501, S651
2094: 1152, 1261, 1447, S535
2096: 1632
2101-2117a: 1115
2104a: 1245
2105a: S417
2105-2110: S483, S1005
2105-2114: S462, S608
2105-2117: 1201
2106a: 1501
2108: S417
2116: S607
2119a: S647
2122a: 1632

2124: 1501
2131-2151: 1701
2133: S311
2135: 1501
2135-2141: S510
2139: 1632
2140: 1632
2145-2149: 1602a
2147: S242
2148: 1602a
2150: 1501
2150a: 1632
2152: 1632
2152-2154: 1079a
2152-2162: 1756
2155-2159: S280
2155-2162: 1388
2160: 1501
2163-2199: S891
2164: 1501
2165a: 1478, 1661
2166: 1602a
2166-2169: S1079
2166b-2169: S420
2166b-2183a: 1205
2167a: 1196
2168a: 1141
2172: S528
2172-2176: 1427
2174a: 1152, S528
2177-2183: S676
2177-2189: 1120, 1726, S136
2177-2199: 1205, S1006
2179b-2180a: 1496
2183: 1726
2183-2188: S750
2183-2189: S202
2183b-2189: S234
2190: 1602a
2196: 1501
2196-2199: S636
2196b-2210a: S577
2199-2200: 1246
2200: 1437, 1501

2200-3182: S364, S498, S745
2206: 1168
2207-2252: 1261
2208-2214: S1060
2208-2239: 1315
2208b-3182: 1414
2209: 1464
2210b-2211: 1527
2210b-2220: 1289
2210b-2323: S840
2212: S472
2214-2226: 1383
2216: 1368
2216b-2217: 1152, S897
2217b-2218a: 1368
2219: S647
2221: 1368, 1738
2221-2225: 1289
2221-2226a: 1420
2223: 1307, 1420
2226: 1152, S238, S552, S264, S647
2226a: 1368
2228-2229: 1533
2231: S316
2231-2270: S58
2233-2270: S666
2238b-2241a: S1098
2244-2246: 1079a
2246: S1098
2247: 1501, 1602
2247a: 1632
2247-2248a: 1696
2247-2249: 1689, S177
2247-2266: 1354, S202
2247-2270a: 1123
2249b-2252a: 1708, S280
2253: 1694
2253a: 1564

Line Index

2255-2266: S496
2255-2266a: 1152
2256: 1245, 1602a
2262-2265: S1005
2263: S417
2265b-2266: S420
2267-2: 1673
2270-2271: 1602a
2270b-2275a: 1495
2272-2277: S420
2275: 1501
2278-2293a: 1289
2283-2284: 1149
2283-2290: S836
2286: S647
2287: S836
2287-2344: S880
2288a: 1151
2290a: 1141
2291: 1501
2291-2293a: 1753, S420, S1060
2294: S836
2295: S400
2297a: 1632
2297b-2298a: 1501
2297b-2299a: 1166, S927
2298: S472
2300: S647
2305: 1602a
2306: S836
2306a: 1150
2311-2312: S762
2312: S610
2312-2313: S836
2319b-2323: 1237
2321: 1602a
2327-2331: S216
2328: 1513
2330: S457, S637
2330a: S1098
2333: 1602a
2333a: 1734
2333-2335a: S257
2333-2336: 1237

2341: 1152, 1366, S552, S803
2349b-2399a: 1428, S493
2354: S254
2354-2368: S284
2354-2396: S202
2355-2372: S1051
2356: S223
2358: S417
2359b-2368: 1152, S820, S932
2360b-2368: S417
2361-2362: 1152
2362: S559
2363: 1501
2363a: 1251, 1447
2363-2368: S514
2365-2366: 1602a
2367a: 1319
2367-2400: S832
2368a: S304
2370-2376: 1602a
2372: S223
2373: 1501
2377-2379a: 1664
2389: 1602a
2390: S1079
2390: 1464, 1640
2391: 1436
2397: 1602a
2397-2400: 1602a
2401-2402: S683
2401-2424: 1289
2403-2413a: S1060
2409: 1368
2410-2411: 1513
2415-2416: S1079
2417: 1172
2419-2420: S544
2421: 1501
2423: 1501
2425: 1079a
2425-2437: 1609
2425-2443: 1428
2425-2471: 1123

2425-2509: 1753
2425-2515: S493
2426-2509: S202
2426-2512a: S1051
2426-2537: S1092
2428-2434: S234
2430: 1632
2431a: 1245
2435: 1632
2436: S326
2442-2462a: 1753
2444: 1501
2444-2446: 1462
2444-2449: S638
2444-2462: 1138, 1428, S372
2444-2471: S248
2447a: S647
2451b-2453a: 1120
2455-2459: 1196
2455-2461: 1749
2455-2462: 1462
2456-2459: S514
2457: S1083
2457-2459: S1005
2458: 1501
2460: S326, S647
2460-2461: S638
2461: 1501
2461a: 1152, S644
2462: 1501
2462-2471: 1428
2466: 1501, S224
2468: 1501
2468-2469: S514
2468-2470: 1664
2469: 1513, 1609, S642
2472-2508: 1428
2474: 1501
2476a: 1764
2478a: S839
2481: S208
2484-2486: 1495, 1602a
2488a: 1632

Line Index

2490-2499: S514
2490-2509: 1380
2491-2493: S1079
2496-2509: S254
2500-2508a: S284
2502: 1251
2503-2508: 1148
2507-2508a: 1715
2509a: 1632
2510-2511a: 1079a, S642
2511a: S647
2516-2518a: S642
2517: S647
2520a: 1135
2523: 1366, S72, S322
2523a: 1447, S342, S398
2526-2527: 1513
2526b-2527a: S400
2527: S655
2527b-2528: 1199
2528: S245
2532: 1501, S647
2534a: 1135
2535: S311
2535-2536: S676
2535-2537: 1513
2535b-2537: 1108
2538-2708a: 1137
2539a: 1140
2541: S647, S1079
2542: 1501
2542-2558: 1751
2542-2559: 1331
2550-2552: S683
2552-2553: 1602a
2557a: 1135
2562a: 1632
2563: 1158
2564: S436
2564a: 1152, 1158
2569: 1602a, 1680
2570-2575: S369

2570b-2575a: S338, S496
2575b-2578a: S827
2577: S405, S436, S604, S1069
2577a: 1152
2578: S250, S732
2578a: 1152
2586: S436, S647
2588a: 1632
2589: 1602a
2590: 1602a
2590-2591: S1046
2590b-2591a: S420
2592: 1602
2592a: 1135
2596-2597: 1513
2599b-2600a: S262
2599b-2602: S420
2599b-2627: S832
2600: 1501
2600-2601: S1046, S1079
2600b-2601: 1558, S262
2602: 1436
2602-2625: S202
2602-2626a: S262
2602-2891: S674
2603a: 1632
2604a: S852
2606: 1501
2609-2611: S836
2615: 1632, S250, S732
2615a: 1152
2616: 1397
2616-2618: S836
2617: 1156
2622: S311
2623: 1156
2625: S647
2628: 1501
2628b-2629a: 1724
2629: S647
2631-2632: 1079a

2633: 1501
2633-2638: S384
2642b-2646a: 1488
2645-2646a: S257
2646a: 1488, 1606
2646-2647: 1513
2646b-2650a: 1664
2648: 1602a
2650: 1632
2661-2662: 1079a
2663-2668: S262
2669: 1602a
2672: 1152, S276
2672b-2673a: S452
2673a: 1632
2677: S625
2682: S732
2684: 1501
2691: S625
2694: 1436
2695: 1537
2697: 1501, S369
2697-2699: S696
2697-2702a: S689
2699a: 1152
2705: 1537
2706: S223, S1079
2708-2709: S1046
2711-2820: 1353
2713: 1501, S647
2714: 1632
2715: 1501
2715-2719: 1602a
2717: 1501, 1507, 1602a, 1632
2719: 1501
2720: S895
2724-2728: 1079a
2724-2891: S805
2727: S868
2728: 1632
2729: 1602a, 1501
2729-2751: S1092
2730a: 1156
2732b-2743a: 1330
2734: S418

Line Index

2738a: 1410
2739-2743: 1602a
2743: 1602a
2746a: 1245
2747-2751: S676
2749: 1501
2752: 1501
2756-2762: 1602a
2764b-2: S1099
2764-2766: S177, S676
2764b-2766: 1354, S420
2770b-2786: 1702
2774: 1602a
2774a: S868
2776: S242
2777: 1501
2778a: 1501
2779: 1416, 1501
2781a: 1218
2785a: 1255
2788: 1650
2790b-2793: 1079a
2792: 1650
2792a: 1196
2794: 1501, S1092
2794-2798: 1584, S1060
2794-2801: 1763, S676
2796: 1513
2799: 1501
2802: 1602a, 1501
2802-2808: 1128
2804: 1501
2806-2807a: 1724
2807: 1767
2807a: 1632
2809-2812: 1079a
2810b-2812: 1684a
2813: S832
2819-2820: 1107, S216, S763, S906
2819b-2820: 1348

2820: 1152, 1667, S485, S906
2824b-2835: S624
2824b-2845a: 1505
2841-2842: 1602a
2844: 1602a
2844-2845a: 1166
2847: 1152
2848-2859: S420
2851a: 1156
2852: 1501
2853-2855: 1178
2858: 1602a
2858-2859: S1079
2860-2863: 1079a
2864-2872: S384
2867: 1501
2871: 1156
2880: 1501
2882: 1366, S584
2884: 1501
2890-2891: S1046
2890b-2891: S420
2891: 1632
2892: 1602a
2897b-2899: 1079a
2905a: 1135
2910-2913: S836
2910b-2921: S284
2910b-3000: S493
2910-3007: S202
2912: 1632
2913b-2921: S254
2914-2916: 1251
2916: 1447
2916a: 1447
2918-2919: 1513
2920b-2921: S90
2921a: 1221, 1285
2929: 1261, 1447
2932: 1320
2935: S889
2939-2941: 1513
2940: 1602a
2941-2981: 1324
2943: 1501

2945: S889
2946: 1436
2949: S889
2952: 1602a
2955-2956: 1513
2957b-2960: 1708
2963-2964a: S242
2972: 1261, 1447
2974-2975: 1513
2991-2995a: 1281
2995: 1602a, S657
2995a: 1632
2996a: 1632
2997: S228
2998: S226
2999-3007a: 1664
3001-3007: 1356
3002: 1501
3005: 1632, S334
3007: S311
3018: S304
3018a: S304
3019: S304
3020: S401
3020-3024: S1005
3020-3027: S328
3024b-3027: 1256
3027: S223
3027a: 1632
3030-3032: 1602a
3031: 1602a
3033-3034: 1602a
3038-3182: 1417
3040: 1501
3046: 1602a
3047-3053: 1518
3047-3075: S58
3048: 1320
3051-3075: 1107
3054b-3057: S420
3055: 1602a
3056: 1632, S208
3056a: 1501
3061: 1602a
3062-3065: S1079

3062b-3065: 1753, S420
3066-3073: 1348
3067a: 1410
3069: 1241, 1667, 1501
3069-3073: S369, S666
3069-3073a: 1241
3069-3075: S280, S1034
3074: 1501, S205, S208
3074-3075: 1107, 1348, S246, S369, S509
3076: 1079a
3076-3086: 1675
3077-3078: S275, S945, S1046
3077-3078a: S420
3077-3083: S844
3079-3081: 1513
3084a: 1632
3101: 1602a
3101-3102: 1632
3109: 1513
3110-3114a: 1079a
3114-3119: 1196
3114b-3119: S351
3115a: 1501
3116: S223
3117: S223
3123: 1152, S860
3124a: 1632
3126: S605
3126-3129a: 1166
3129: 1501
3131: S997
3137-3182: 1295, 1345
3143-3148a: S280
3146: S378, S512
3147b-3177: 1753
3150: S552
3150-3151: S307

3150-3153: S208
3150-3155: 1152, S650, S876
3150-3155a: S638
3151: 1770a, S245
3151a: S552
3152a: S647
3153: S722
3154: S552
3155: S512, S552, S722
3156-3182: S891
3159: 1501, S651
3159a: 1152
3163-3168: 1584
3166: 1602a, 1501
3166-3168: S177
3167: S369
3168: S866
3168a: 1152, 1689
3169-3182: S764, S1078
3171-3172: 1632
3173: S311
3174-3176: S1079
3174-3177: S1046
3174b-3177: S420, S945
3177: 1152, S552
3178-3182: 1598
3180: 1152
3180-3182: 1359, 1513, S888
3181a: 1682
3181-3182: 1726
3182: 1249, 1606, 1663, S501, S772